Paris ★ Lille Brussels

THE BRADT GUIDE TO EUROSTAR CITIES

Laurence Phillips

Bradt Travel Guides Ltd, UK
The Globe Pequot Press Inc, USA

This first edition published in 2002 by Bradt Travel Guides Ltd,
19 High Street, Chalfont St Peter, Bucks SL9 9QE, England
Published in the USA by The Globe Pequot Press Inc,
246 Goose Lane, PO Box 480, Guilford, Connecticut 06437-0480

Text copyright © 2002 Laurence Phillips
Maps copyright: London © Trialzoom Ltd 1996–2001
Paris/Brussels © Metropolis International/Carte Blanche 2001
Lille © Bradt Travel Guides Ltd
Métro maps © TCS

British Library Cataloguing in Publication Data
A catalogue record for this book is available from the British Library
ISBN 1 84162 045 9

Library of Congress Cataloging-in-Publication Data
Phillips, Laurence.
    Paris, Lille, Brussels : the Bradt guide to Eurostar destinations /
Laurence Phillips.
    p. cm.
    Includes bibliographical rferences and index.
    ISBN 1-84162-045-9
    1. Paris (France)—Guidebooks. 2. Brussels (Belgium)—
Guidebooks. 3. Lille (France)—Guidebooks. I. Title.

    DC708.P43 2001
    914.4'360484—dc21
                                                    2001053149

Cover design Concise Artisans
Cover photographs Train (Rail Europe); Eiffel Tower, Paris (Neil Setchfield);
Grand' Place, Lille (Yoann Matelski/Lille Tourist Office); Atomium, Brussels (Cees
van Leeuwan/Sylvia Cordaiy Photo Library)

Illustrations Carole Vincer
Cartography Steve Munns; TCS

Typeset from the author's disc by Wakewing, High Wycombe
Printed and bound in Italy by Legoprint SpA, Trento

Author/Acknowledgements

AUTHOR
Laurence Phillips has been escaping to Paris since boyhood and has written many and varied guides to France. His passion for the Eurostar cities has fuelled countless BBC radio broadcasts including Radio 4's *Allez Lille*. He combines wanderlust with a love for theatre and work as a critic, playwright and songwriter, and has written for the West End and Royal Shakespeare Company. His stage work has clocked up more travel miles than the author, being performed on four continents.

ACKNOWLEDGEMENTS
Special thanks to my friends and dining partners in the three cities for letting me reveal their secret tourist-free tables; to Judith, Isobel and Jerome for such fun in Lille; and most of all to my parents, Di and Ronald Phillips, for getting out the car and ferrying me from table to table, and wallowing in cholesterol when, as usual, the clock and the calendar said we'd never finish the infinite mealtime of summer.

DEDICATION

In loving memory and admiration of **Ann Passman**
who had the Talent to be there, the Wit to see it and the Wisdom of
discretion

Contents

How to Use this Book

Under each city listings fall into five categories:

Where to stay features hotels or alternative accommodation;

Where to go lists squares, parks, markets, bars, cafés and interesting sites or locations for watching the world go by or meeting the locals;

What to see contains details of museums, attractions and historical sites;

Where to eat entries generally feature restaurants that are worth a visit as an experience in their own right, a gastronomic treat or a special occasion, rather than as a mere refuelling stop. Otherwise, grab a bite at one of the bars or cafés listed in *Where to go*;

What to buy is our highly subjective shopping list.

M̲ Nowhere within the **Paris** Périphérique is more than a short stroll from a métro station. At the end of each listing address in the guide you will find the name of the nearest station. A large scale *plan du quartier*, showing clearly how to find every address in the neighbourhood, is displayed by the ticket office of every station. Hotels, stations and department stores offer free métro maps, and simplified street plans of the city can be picked up free from all hotel réception desks. In **Brussels** and **Lille**, where the métro network is less comprehensive, stations are listed only if within five minutes' walk. Bus and tram alternatives are given where more convenient.

E̲ This symbol suggests the most direct route from the Eurostar terminus.

Email addresses are published wherever possible. Where an establishment has a reliable website, we list the url in order that readers may view photographs, current prices, menus and last-minute information before mailing.

Hotel room rates apply for single or double occupancy.

Restaurant prices include all taxes and service charges. It is customary to leave a small tip (usually loose change) to reward good service. The price range indicates options from a basic set menu to indulgence à la carte. In France all restaurants are obliged to display their prices outside the front door, and most will offer a set-priced meal deal. Very expensive restaurants usually have a far cheaper *prix-fixe* menu at lunchtimes.

Prices in euros quoted in the text were correct at the time of going to press – however, they should be taken more as a comparative guide between entries. Although national currencies cease to exist after February 2002, we offer approximate comparative values in French and Belgian francs, since visitors from outside the Euro-zone may be more familiar with the old exchange rates.

Comparisons Hotel prices tend to be a little higher in Paris than in Lille, and Brussels rates are higher yet.

Opening hours Most restaurants tend to open for dinner from around 19.30 to 23.30, and lunch from 12.30 to 14.00. City-centre bars usually stay open until after midnight, generally closing between 01.00 and 02.00. Where establishments open or close later than usual, it will be mentioned in the text. With the exception of late-night brasseries, it is advisable to telephone in advance to make a reservation for dinner after 22.00 or for late lunches. Gastronomic restaurants tend to close for two to four weeks in summer.

In France, national museums close on Tuesdays, and city museums on Mondays, so do read the opening hours given in this guide carefully.

Credit cards Unless otherwise stated, most establishments accept payment by Mastercard or Visa. American Express and Diners may also be used at many hotels, restaurants and shops. Smaller museums and bars may refuse credit cards.

THE EURO

The euro, and its 100 cents, is the common currency of 12 European Union nations. Seven notes are valued at €500, €200, €100, €50, €20, €10 and €5; eight coins are worth €2 and €1, then 50, 20, 10, 5, 2 and 1 cents. States stamp national symbols on coins; French euros are easily distinguished by the traditional emblem of the French Republic. Belgian coins feature the king's profile. No matter the motif, all coins may be used anywhere inside the Euro zone. So a Spaniard may buy a *croque monsieur* in Montmartre with a euro featuring the Irish harp.

Exchange rate

€1 = 6.55957 French francs or 40.3399 Belgian francs.

The exchange rate between the euro and sterling or other currencies will fluctuate, but for UK travellers, fearing confusion after a generation of merely nudging the decimal point to work out out a rough exchange rate between the French franc and the pound, an easy-to-calculate formula for an approximate conversion is to regard every €10 as the (albeit loose) equivalent of around £6 sterling. So brush up your six-times-tables. At the time of going to press €10 was worth approximately US$9 or CanS13.50, or AU$17.

Travellers with old francs in their pockets may exchange them for euros free of charge at banks until June 30 2002. After this date, national banks will change coins until 2005 and notes until 2012. Details are on the website http://europa.eu.int/.

Introduction

A TALE OF THREE CITIES

No sight, no sound was ever more seductive. To an 18 year-old birthday boy, grabbing the key of the door to a city that was to call him back home ever since, the Gare du Nord was a veritable *Lorelei*: a noisy fanfare to Paris that greeted the bottle green boat train, a clattering, chattering station that sent a city to work, and me to play.

Two decades later, a blue and yellow wonder train links the city centres of London, Brussels, Lille and Paris in the popping of a champagne cork with a high-speed rail journey. Eurostar has rekindled the romance of travel, prematurely snuffed when the last Flèche d'Or boat train departed Victoria Station a generation ago. More than merely the fastest route, city centre to city centre, there is an unmistakable glamour and buzz around the journey, from effortless check-in at Waterloo's sleek modern terminal to the first Imelda-click of an *Elle*-turned heel on the platform of the Gare du Nord.

A welcoming on-board bar for socialising lends a sense of occasion to the cheapest bargain weekend return, and an upgrade to first class – which need not break the bank – fuels dinner parties, postcards and gossip before even leaving London. Kick-start the journey with freshly popped champagne, be pampered over dinner with courtesies, Belgian chocolates and constant coffee. Relax, settle back and gaze upon a star. There for the counting. On two recent trips I checked out a sitcom queen, two soap divas, a Hollywood remnant and – as I write – an elder statesman.

More than mere *paparazzi* pleasers, Eurostar travellers have a definite sense of occasion. The morning after *that* Galliano fashion show at the Opéra flew in the face of conscience and brought furs back into *Vogue*, the first-class carriage positively groaned under the weight of rediscovered wraps, not shouldered since the sixties – mothballs *à grande vitesse*.

As a veteran of every air service, train, coach, ferry and even hitching connection between London and Paris, I greeted the Channel Tunnel city link with wide open arms. When the same train brought two extra cities to my lap, I could not have been happier. And so, just when familiarity threatened to numb the tingle of wanderlust, I was able to open up another couple of chapters in my secret address book.

I fell utterly in love with Lille when I accidentally found myself in the city late one rainy night. The vitality and wealth of this modest town has long been ignored by the sophisticates of Paris and all points cosmopolitan. Countless visits later, I still find something to catch the breath every day. A genuine welcome, great choice of restaurants and a cultural heritage to rival many a capital city inspired the BBC Radio Four programme *Allez Lille* a couple of years ago.

Euroland and the brave new currency mean that national borders no longer define our playgrounds. Just half an hour from Lille, a two-hour excursion from Paris and 160 minutes from Waterloo, Brussels has both the comforting familiarity and quirky other-worldiness of a twilight zone. Although NATO and the Eurocracy anchor a certain reserve over huge tracts of the city, I have indulged myself in the central areas of Brussels where life is played out on the brink of a party and a song. Since Belgium's bickering twin cultures are tamed only by their capital's very internationalism, central Brussels takes free spirits to its heart and reaches out to make strangers ever welcome.

I make no apologies for the lion's share of this *carnet* of addresses and anecdotes belonging to Paris. Regular Eurostar travellers are already familiar with the well-worn sightseeing paths. To know Paris and to love Paris is to be comfortable in the streets and cafés of the city's 20 *arrondissements* – the local quarters where Parisians really live when the world is looking the other way. Some addresses are old favourites garnered over 20 years of serendipity (the hotel bedroom grafted on to a working church, with flying buttresses over the bed; the *bistrot* run by priests in a former sex shop; the flat where Edith Piaf's friends and admirers still gather to reminisce). The streets around the Gare du Nord have provided fresh treats: wonderful country cooking, timeless canals and a collection of crystal fit for an emperor all within a few minutes of the Eurostar. Inevitably, the international guides will eventually lasso several of our secrets. But at the time of writing, and hopefully on your next trip, we should find ourselves in more than one corner of the city where yours and mine should be the only non-local accents in the room!

In Lille, the charms of a region where hospitality comes as standard, stories of northern welcomes are legendary. I only regret that one off-beat gem has closed its doors, a B&B run by a former madame who after years of service to the garrison finally transfered her emphasis from the bed to the breakfast. Nevertheless we can still enjoy treats ranging from home baked *petit-déjeuner* brioche in a family home to a luxurious bedroom within a museum. And who could fail to fall for a town that erects a statue to a lullaby?

Brussels may be best known by its business-class visitors, but a forage through the city centre yielded many treats for the less formal traveller: the hotel which commissioned a different artist to design each bedroom, the geranium and bric-a-brac packed townhouse where all guests gather round the big dining-room table for breakfast, nightly screenings of silent movies with a piano accompanist, and a brace of museums that give back the simple joys of childhood.

Only an outsider could compile an insider's guide, so I make no apologies for being a Londoner who happens to call these cities 'home'. As long as they continue to provide the inspiration to fuel the imagination and the appetite, my cup will be in serious danger of running over on to my charger plate and each visit will always be as exciting as my first.

To anyone reading this book, and arriving in Paris, Lille or Brussels for the first time or the 100th, I bid you welcome, wish you a wonderful stay and *bon retour*.

Laurence Phillips
lolly@laurencephillips.com

Part One

General Information

The Eurostar User's Guide

THE SERVICE

With up to 35 departures each day, each 400m-long Eurostar train transports up to 560 standard-class and 206 first-class passengers from London to the great cities of mainland Europe. City centre to city centre at 300kph (186mph) in journey times to rival air travel: Paris in three hours, Brussels in 2h40 and Lille just two hours from Waterloo; an hour less from Ashford. From 2003, the introduction of the first section of high-speed line in the UK will cut a further 20 minutes from London times. When the British high-speed link is completed (some time after 2007), St Pancras will be the London terminus and journey times will be just two hours to Brussels, 2h20 to Paris and 1h20 to Lille.

A direct service from London to the gates of Disneyland Paris runs daily during the summer and school holidays, and weekly at all other times. Journey time three hours. Regular first-class facilities are replaced with the child friendly Castle Service. In winter, the twice-weekly Ski-Train leaves Waterloo for Moutiers and Bourg St-Maurice serving the alpine resorts in under eight hours. Future plans include direct Eurostar trains from London to popular French destinations including Avignon, Lyon and perhaps even Marseille.

THE TRAINS

The first major refurbishment of the trains begins in 2002. Each train has 18 air-conditioned carriages sporting their distinctive blue and yellow livery. Two train managers and their teams of uniformed stewards look after passengers, welcoming arrivals and reminding would-be smokers that the entire train is a no-smoking zone. Two bar-buffet carriages on each train are modelled on the TGV bars, with plenty of room to stand and chat over a drink. Baby-changing rooms at each end of the train, and toilets in each carriage. Red upholstered seats spaced three abreast, one single, one pair, in first-class carriages; two pairs of yellow and grey seats in second. Groups of four passengers should request seats around a table (more readily available in first class). First-class compartments have a number of business seating configurations, including a semi-private area for four or six passengers at the end of each carriage. Be warned, not all second-class tickets sold as 'window' seats are actually next to a window. Around four places are in fact against a solid wall. Regular passengers with a good book may not mind, but first timers and anyone who thrills to a view will be disappointed, so do insist when booking that your window seat actually has a window. For a first glimpse of the Sacré Coeur (see page 161) sit on the right side of the carriage when travelling to Paris, passengers on the opposite side of the carriage have a view of the Stade de France (see page 180). To see Big Ben on your return, sit by the left window.

TICKETS AND CLASS DISTINCTION

There are three classes of ticket and accommodation on Eurostar. Flexible fares are available in standard and first class, but best value are the 7- and 14-day advance-purchase Apex fares usually requiring a Saturday-night stay. Youth (under 26) fares usually offer greater flexibility. In the traditional tangle of ticket pricing, a first-class Apex fare is around half the price of a fully flexible standard ticket. First-class passengers enjoy complimentary newspapers, more spacious accommodation and a three-course meal served at their seat. According to the time of day, a welcome glass of champagne may be offered, and a choice of wines served with the meal. Food quality varies depending on the route (travellers from Brussels are often offered a Belgian chocolate after dinner). Vegetarian and other dietary requests should be made at least 48 hours in advance. Premium first-class passengers enjoy complimentary taxi transfers to and from the station and a four-course meal. For an inexpensive upgrade consider travelling with a tour operator (see page 5). Day-trip and weekend promotional rates are often advertised. One favourite deal has been the occasional £35 overnight ticket that offers evening outbound travel, returning first thing in the morning. A huge hit with nightclubbers who would leave London on Saturday evening and arrive on the continent in time for a fortifying meal before dancing until dawn, sleeping through the return trip and dozing on their own doorsteps by the time their friends and families awoke to the Sunday morning call of church and garden centre.

EUROSTAR PLUS

Rail Europe, the wing of SNCF French railways that also runs the former British Rail International operation, not only sells Eurostar tickets, but the Eurostar Plus products. These include onward travel by other European high speed rail services from Lille, Paris and Brussels to destinations as far away as Amsterdam, Cologne, Madrid and Rome. Rail Europe's offices in the UK and US also offer internal tickets on Belgium's Thalys and France's TGV high speed rail services between the principal Eurostar destinations, ideal if you are planning a twin-city break. Other options include Interail, Eurail and EuroDomino passes for unlimited rail travel across Europe, and from Scandinavia to north Africa. Travel on the Lille–Brussels route is by Eurostar or Thalys. Paris–Brussels services are operated by Thalys. TGV-Nord runs Lille– Paris services. New TGV services to the Mediterranean feature double-decker trains with extra legroom in all classes, laptop computer power points in first class, and dedicated compartments for mobile phone users.

BOOKING

Paris, Lille and Brussels tickets may be purchased directly from Eurostar, as well as at Rail Europe's counters and call centres. Rail Europe also offers

Eurostar Plus and internal European tickets for Thalys, TGV and regional trains. Many UK travel agents offer Eurostar tickets, although, at the time of writing, Thomas Cook, publishers of the *European Rail Timetable*, no longer sell continental train tickets.

Eurostar
Station ticket office Waterloo Station, SE1
Open Mon–Fri 04.15–21.30, Sat 05.00–21.30, Sun 07.00–21.30.
M̄ *Waterloo*.
Booking office 102-104 Victoria St, London SW1 5JL
Open Mon–Fri 09.00–17.00, Sat 09.00–15.00.
M̄ *Victoria*.
Call centre Tel: 08705 186 186; www.eurostar.co.uk
Open Mon–Fri 08.00–21.00, Sat 08.00–20.00, Sun 09.00–17.00.
France Tel: 08 36 35 35 39
Belgium Tel: 0900 10 177

Rail Europe
Shop 179 Piccadilly, W1
Open Mon–Fri 10.00–18.00, Sat 10.00–17.00.
M̄ *Piccadilly Circus or Green Park*.
Call centre Tel: 08705 848 848; www.raileurope.co.uk
Open Mon–Fri 08.00–20.00, Sat 09.00–17.00, Sun (Jun–Aug) 10.00–16.00.
USA Tel: 1 877 456 RAIL (09.00–21.00 EST)
Canada Tel: 1 800 361 RAIL (09.00–21.00 EST)

www.raileurope.com has contact details for all non-European countries.

Bargain deals, packages and cheap upgrades
A great way of avoiding the usual restrictions applying to so many tickets is to book travel and a hotel through one of the city break specialists. No rules about advance purchase nor Saturday night stays apply when you book a one-, two- or three-night stay with a major tour operator. They also often offer last- minute deals, 'early bird' discounts (for passengers willing to travel at around 06.30) and the prospect of an upgrade to first class for one or both legs of the journey from just £30. Late deals advertised in the London *Evening Standard*, free travel press or the operators' websites have included first class Eurostar travel and two nights hotel accommodation from well under £150 per person, a saving of over £50 on the published fare with the room thrown in for free! Check out hotel listings from the relevant brochures to find accommodation featured in this guide. If you discover a deal through an unfamiliar tour operator, check that it is listed with ABTA (the Association of British Travel Agents).

Travelscene Tel: 0870 777 4445; web: www.travelscene.co.uk
Cresta Tel: 0870 161 0920; web: www.crestaholidays.co.uk
European Life Tel: 0870 608 1385; web: www.europeanlife.co.uk
Eurostar Holidays Direct Tel: 0870 167 6767; web: www.eurostar.co.uk
(operated by Cresta)

Frequent travellers and business facilities

Premium First passengers and holders of Silver and Gold Eurostar Frequent Traveller cards may use the Clubhouse Lounges at London, Ashford, Paris and Brussels. Facilities vary but all include complimentary bar and café. In London and Ashford guests are offered complimentary newspapers, and may watch satellite news channels on TV. London's lounge also includes a modest library and has a computer workstation. Premium First, Business, Leisure Flexi First Class, Standard Flexi and Weekender tickets may earn Frequent Traveller points. Details on the scheme from 0990 104 105 (UK), 01 41 91 10 15 (France), 02 551 12 99 (Belgium). Mon–Fri 08.00–18.00, Sat 08.00–13.00.

Check fares and timetables

Current fares and offers, as well as timetables, updates and amendments may be accessed online at www.eurostar.com and www.eurostar.co.uk.

EATING ON BOARD

First-class and Premium First ticket holders have a full meal and refreshment service at their seats, although vegetarians should double check that their request has been recorded and should carry a sandwich in case the 'special meal' fails to materialise. In Standard class, the buffet bar offers a range of hot and cold snacks. An alternative to the trek to the buffet compartment for those encumbered with luggage, small children or delicious lethargy is an on-board picnic. In the UK, supermarkets such as Tesco Metro and Marks & Spencer offer a range of salads, snacks, sandwiches and sushi. A smaller selection is available from Boots the chemist at Waterloo Station. If sandwiches from the concourse do not appeal, check out the markets and delicatessen listed on page 339. In Paris, pick up a sandwich at the station or visit the various *traiteurs* listed in this guide. Best value is Flo Prestige for three-course plated meals with wine (see page 85). Lille's Carrefour hypermarket is located just across the parvis François Mitterand from the station. In Brussels trays of mezze are sold at the GB Supermarket at the Gare du Midi. Do make sure that food complies with international regulations. During the foot and mouth outbreak of 2001, meat products were banned.

PASSPORT CONTROL, CUSTOMS AND SECURITY

Eurostar terminals have passenger screening similar to airlines. The original plans for on-board passport inspections have been overtaken by more traditional checks by the appropriate authorities at arrivals as well as departures. Non-EU passengers should prepare to queue at their destination.

Check-in at all terminals is 20 minutes before departure. Those passengers with fully flexible tickets (first class or standard class), or who are members of Eurostar's Frequent Traveller Programme, are able to check in ten minutes before departure.

STATION GUIDE

All stations are fully equipped with facilities for special needs passengers. Avis has car rental desks at all six Eurostar stations and offers Frequent Traveller points to Eurostar travellers. Hertz, Europcar and other companies hire cars in Paris and Brussels. Local numbers are given here, should you have any problems. However, it is recommended that passengers make reservations through central booking bureaux.

Brussels Midi (Zuid)
Car hire
Major car hire desks can be found on the main concourse opposite entrance to Eurostar platforms 3 and 4.

Avis Tel: 02 527 1705
Europcar Tel: 02 522 9573
Hertz Tel: 02 524 31 00

Change
Bureaux de change, and a Western Union counter for money transfers, may be found on the main concourse opposite Eurostar check in (platforms 3 and 4).

Food
GB Supermarket opposite entrance to Eurostar check in (platforms 3 and 4). Sandwiches and prepared salad platters available to take on board. Food court at the other end of the station opposite platforms 17 and 18.

Left luggage
Enquire at Eurostar reception.

Public transport
After passport control, take the escalator from the platform to concourse level and follow signs to the main métro and underground tram platforms. Tickets may be purchased in the hall from the counter and machines. Buses and some street-level tram services may be found at the front of the station.

Shopping
A mini mall stretches the length of the station, selling clothes, CDs, books, food and flowers. Within the Eurostar departure lounge are a bar, news-stand and perfume and chocolate shops.

Taxis
After passport control, take the escalator from the platform to concourse level and follow signs to the underground taxi rank.

Tickets to other European destinations
Thalys information and reservation desks are just along the concourse from the Eurostar check in.

Tourist information and hotel reservations
On main ground-floor concourse.

Lille Europe
Car hire
An Avis car hire desk is situated at the centre of the concourse. Other car hire options are available in the town centre including electric car hire from Mobelec.

Avis Tel: 03 20 51 12 31
Mobelec Tel: 03 20 67 20 44

Change
Bureau de change desk on main concourse.

Food
A café bar and a sandwich counter may be found on the concourse. A Carrefour supermarket in Euralille (see page 236), across the parvis François Mitterand, stocks many local specialities from cheeses and patés to beers. The small Eurostar departure lounge has few facilities other than a vending machine.

Left luggage
Coin-operated lockers and a bureau des consignes are available on the main concourse.

Public transport
Take the escalator to the concourse and follow signs to the métro and tram station. For bus services, walk 400m along rue le Corbusier to place des Buisses alongside the Gare Lille Flandres.

Shopping
Just the Relay news kiosk on the station concourse. However the Euralille mall is just across the parvis François Mitterand from the station (see page 236).

Taxis
Take the lift or escalator from the concourse to street level and follow signs to kerbside taxi rank.

Tickets to other European destinations
Information and reservation counters midway along the concourse.

Tourist information and hotel reservations
On the main concourse. When closed take métro to Rihour (see page 17).

London Waterloo
Car hire
On the arrival level follow signs for the underground. The Avis desk alongside the ticket machines is generally manned 08.00–23.00. Tel: 020 7401 8164.

Change
Bureaux de change desks at departures and arrival levels of the Eurostar terminal, as well as Thomas Cook counters on the main station concourse.

Film rental
On-board movies may be rented (with a portable DVD player) from the Movies On The Move desk in the departure lounge. Choose the language or subtitles and your own screening time, and hand back both the disk and player at the collection point on the platform at Paris. At the time of going to press, rental charges were £10 or €15 and the service was only available on the London–Paris route. Credit card transactions only.

Food
On the main concourse are many sandwich, croissant and coffee shops. Sandwiches are also available from Boots the Chemists opposite the terminal entrance. Light meals are served at Bonaparte's Café & Wine Bar opposite the escalator to the Eurostar terminal, and within the departure lounge. The Reef (see page 339) and burger outlets offer alternative dining options. Within the Eurostar terminal are various cafés by the ticket hall, departure lounge and arrival areas.

Left luggage
By the entrance to the underground at Eurostar arrivals level.

Medical centre
From the main concourse take the lift for Waterloo East for the Waterloo Medicentre for private treatment by a doctor. Consultation fee £40. Vaccinations, tests and nursing treatments also offered. Tel: 020 7803 0732; web: www.medicentre.co.uk. Mon–Fri 08.00–18.00.

Mobile phone hire
From the tourist information counter at arrivals.

Passes
Buy métro passes for Paris, Lille and Brussels, plus sightseeing tours, La Carte museum pass (see page 27) and Disneyland passports (see page 179) before you leave London. Visit the Voyages Vacances counter in front of the Eurostar ticket office.

Voyages Vacances Tel: 020 7478 8213. Open: Mon–Thu 08.00–17.00, Fri 07.00–18.00, Sat 10.00–17.00.

Public transport
For underground services follow the signs at arrivals level. Buses depart from various points around the main station. See information posters on main concourse.

Shopping

A range of book and record shops is on the main concourse with small specialist outlets selling electrical goods, fashion accessories and stationery. In the departure area are two branches of WH Smith, a Eurostar Trading Co gift counter, chocolate shops, a mobile phone dealership and other retail outlets.

Showers

Shower facilities with soap and towels are provided at the main toilets at concourse level opposite the Eurostar Terminal. Price £4.

Taxis

A taxi rank is located at the arrivals point.

Tickets to other UK destinations

Information and reservation counters are situated along the main concourse.

Toilet alert

A word of warning. Although food and drink are available, there are no public toilets at the arrivals level.

Tourist information and hotel reservations

Opposite arrivals.

Paris Gard du Nord

Car hire

On arrival take the steps down opposite the platform to the underground car park level for car hire desks.

Avis Tel: 01 53 32 79 10
Europcar Tel: 01 53 20 66 70
Hertz Tel: 01 55 31 93 21

Change

On arrival, the principal bureau de change is to the right of the main station entrance. Other facilities are available in the Eurostar departures area.

Film rental

On-board movies may be rented (with a portable DVD player) from the Movies On The Move desk in the departure lounge. Return both the disk and player at the collection point on the platform at Waterloo. Rental €15. Credit card transactions only.

Food

On the main concourse are many sandwich stands, bars and coffee shops, and a brasserie. For a first or last meal try the Terminus Nord opposite the station or the excellent restaurants at the rue Belzunce (see pages 173–4). Within the Eurostar departure area are cafés and sandwich counters.

Left luggage

Take the steps opposite arrival platforms down to the underground car park level for left-luggage facilities (signposted *Consignes*).

Public transport

For métro line 4, use the steps next to the welcome kiosk opposite the arrival platforms. For métro lines 2 and 5 and RER B, D and E follow signs to the eastern end of the station. Buses depart from various points around the station. See posters at bus stops or ask at the RATP information desk at the métro station.

Shopping

Relay kiosks on the main concourse and in the Eurostar waiting room sell books, magazines and snacks. Food and wine as gifts may be purchased in the Eurostar departure lounge.

Showers

Walk down the steps (signposted *Métro*) opposite the arrival platforms and next to the welcome kiosk to the shower facilities. Price €6.

Taxis

On arrival take the steps opposite arrival platforms down to the underground car park level for taxi rank.

Tickets to other European destinations

At the side of the station (by platform 1) cross the Cour des Départs to the Espace Grands Voyageurs. The international ticket office is on the first floor.

Tourist information and hotel reservations

Opposite arrival platforms.

Ashford International

Currency exchange and ATM facilities, a frequent traveller lounge and free parking for Premium First ticket holders are available at the Kent terminal which also connects with local domestic rail services. Avis car hire tel: 01233 639 196.

Calais-Fréthun

At the French entrance to the tunnel, around 12km out of town, this is very much a pick-up and set-down point, with few facilities. Taxis meet each train and a free shuttle bus service to and from Calais town centre is timed to connect with each stopping service. Avis car hire tel: 03 21 85 94 85

Practical Matters

BANKS AND MONEY MATTERS
The Euro
See inside back cover for information on local exchange rates.

Banks
France
Open 10.00–17.00 Mon–Fri (some closed 13.00–15.00), sometimes 10.00–13.00 Sat. Some Lille banks may close Mon. Banks close earlier than usual on eve of holidays.

Belgium
Open 09.00–15.30 Mon–Fri. Some may open Sat morning. Outside the centre, some branches may shut for an hour at lunchtime.

Currency exchange
Available at most banks and post offices. Bureaux de change counters may also be found in department stores, railway stations, airports and near tourist sites. Caution: even though exchange rates are fixed, commission rates are flexible. They must therefore be clearly indicated.

Credit cards
Visa and Mastercard are widely accepted, and American Express and Diners may also be used in many tourist and business areas. There is often a minimum purchase requirement of around ∈ 12. Depending on the type of card, you may withdraw up to ∈ 450 at automatic teller machines and banks. French credit cards contain a computer chip (*puce*), and users may be asked to key in a private PIN number during transactions. The magnetic strips on old-style credit cards from other countries sometimes fail to be read by the local swipe machines. Should this be the case, ask for your card number to be typed in manually.

Should you lose your card, you must notify the issuing bank as soon as possible to block fraudulent charges. Keep a note of your credit card number. Please call the appropriate customer service number:

France
American Express Tel: 01 47 77 72 00
Diner's Club Tel: 01 47 62 75 75

Eurocard-Mastercard Tel: 01 45 67 84 84
Visa Tel: 01 42 77 11 90

Belgium
American Express Tel: 02 676 21 11
Diner's Club Tel: 02 206 98 00
Eurocard-Mastercard Tel: 070 34 43 55
Visa Tel: 070 34 43 55

Travellers' cheques
Whether in local or international currencies, these may be converted in banks, exchange outlets and selected post offices. You are insured in case of loss or theft.

EMBASSIES AND CONSULATES
Paris
American Embassy 2 av Gabriel, 75008; tel: 01 43 12 22 22
American Consulate 2 rue St-Florentin, 75001; tel: 01 43 12 22 22
Australian Embassy 4 rue Jean-Rey, 75015; tel: 01 40 59 33 00
British Consulate 16 rue d'Anjou, 75008; tel: 01 44 51 33 01
British Embassy 35 rue du Fbg-St-Honoré, 75008; tel: 01 44 51 31 00
Canadian Embassy 35 av Montaigne, 75008; tel: 01 44 43 29 00
Irish Consulate 4 rue Rude, 75016; tel: 01 44 17 67 00
New Zealand Embassy 7ter rue Léonard de Vinci, 75016; tel: 01 45 01 43 43

Lille
British Consulate 11 sq Dutilleul, 59800; tel: 03 20 12 82 72
Canadian Consulate 30 av Emile Zola, 59000; tel: 03 20 14 05 78

Other nationals should contact their embassy in Paris.

Brussels
American Embassy 27 bd du Régent, 1000; tel: 02 508 21 11
Australian Embassy 6 rue Guimard, 1040; tel: 02 231 05 00
British Embassy 85 rue Arlon, 1040; tel: 02 287 62 11
Canadian Embassy 2 av de Tervuren, 1040; tel: 02 741 06 11
Irish Embassy 89 rue Froissart, 1040; tel: 02 230 53 37
New Zealand Embassy 47–48 bd du Régent, 1000; tel: 02 512 10 40

HEALTH
No inoculations are required to visit France. Citizens of EU countries should carry an E111 form, available from post offices. This enables the traveller to claim reimbursement of medical and pharmaceutical expenses in the event of illness or accident. Nationals of other countries should arrange necessary private insurance cover before travelling. Insurance is recommended for all travellers to cover additional costs such as repatriation or extra nursing care.

France
Ambulance Tel: 15
Emergency doctor (Paris) Tel: 01 47 07 77 77

Emergency pharmacist (Paris) Tel: 01 45 00 35 00
Emergency dentist (Paris) Tel: 01 43 37 51 00
Hospital and medical emergencies (Lille) Tel: 03 20 44 59 62
Franco-British Hospital 3 rue Barbès, 92300 Levallois Perret; tel: 01 46 39 22 22
American Hospital 63 bd Victor Hugo, 92200 Neuilly sur Seine; tel: 01 46 41 25 25

Brussels
Ambulance Tel: 100
Emergency doctor Tel: 02 479 18 18
Emergency dentist Tel: 02 426 10 26

Pharmacies

Pharmacies are easily identified by the green cross sign and are open usual shopping hours. Out of hours, condoms may be purchased from supermarkets and vending machines. Details of out-of-hours opening are posted in pharmacy windows. In Paris, a 24-hour emergency pharmacy delivery service is available for prescription and non-prescription drugs. **Pharma Presto** (Tel: 01 42 42 42 50). Delivery charges ∈ 53.50 (18.00-08.00) and ∈ 38 at other times.

English-speaking pharmacists in Paris
6 rue Castiglione, 75001; tel: 01 42 60 72 96
62 av des Champs Elysées, 75008; tel: 01 43 59 29 52
1 rue Auber, 75009; tel: 01 47 42 49 40
37 av Marceau, 75016; tel: 01 47 20 57 37
98 bd Rochechouart, 75018; tel: 01 53 28 06 08

Pharmacies open 24 hours in Paris
6 pl Clichy, 75009; tel: 01 48 74 65 18
84 av des Champs-Elysées, 75008; tel: 01 45 62 02 41

Emergency pharmacy in Brussels
02 479 18 18 for up-to-date information and addresses.

LANGUAGE
France
English is spoken in most central areas of Paris, although efforts to speak French are always appreciated. Most museums and attractions in France offer bilingual (English/French) information. Lille's own patois *Chti* may also be used in neighbourhood bars and cabarets. In some parts of Vieux Lille, Flemish may also be spoken. Basic English may well be spoken in shops, but you will probably have to rely on your schoolroom French in markets! Department stores provide free interpretation services.

Belgium
English, as well as French and Flemish, is widely spoken in Brussels. French may be used anywhere, although in Flemish-run establishments it is advisable to use English. Trilingual information is generally available.

POST OFFICES

At the post office you may buy stamps, post letters and parcels, make phone calls, send faxes and receive your mail poste restante. In France you may use the Minitel (a trailblazing forerunner to the internet, now a quaint old-fashioned box of tricks that gives free access to directory enquiry services), and buy pre-franked envelopes. Many post offices accept payment by Visa and Mastercard. Stamps may also be purchased from tobacconists, kiosks and bars displaying the red cigar *tabac* symbol. Letterboxes are painted yellow in France and red in Belgium.

France

Post offices are generally open from 08.00 to 18.30 on weekdays and from 08.00 to 12.00 on Saturdays. The Paris post office at 52 rue du Louvre, 75001 (01 40 28 20 00) is the only counter in Europe open 365 days a year, 24 hours a day. In the small hours this post office is the unofficial rendezvous for penniless gap-year backpackers trading lifts, accommodation and travel tips. Lille's post office in the Euralille centre is open until 19.00 Monday to Saturday.

Belgium

Post offices are usually open on working days from 09.00–16.00. However, some post offices close for lunch. The post office at the Centre Monnaie in Brussels opens later on Friday evenings and Saturday mornings. Late-night counter service available at 1E–F av Fonsny, 1000; tel: 02 538 33 98.

PUBLIC HOLIDAYS

France	Belgium
Jan 1	Jan 1
Easter Mon	Easter Mon
May 1, 8	May 1
Pentecost Mon	Ascension Thu
July 14 (national day)	Whit Mon
August 15	July 21 (national day)
Nov 1, 11	Aug 15
Dec 25	Nov 1, 11 (15 banks only)
	Dec 25

SHOPPING HOURS

France

Most stores open 10.00–19.00 Monday–Saturday. Department stores open late Thursday until at least 21.00. Supermarkets and hypermarkets remain open until 21.00 or 22.00. Some smaller shops in Lille may close Monday and lunchtimes 12.00–14.00. Food shops usually open at 08.00 even on Sunday. Bakeries open mornings even on public holidays.

Belgium

Shops are open Monday–Saturday 10.00–18.00 or 19.00. Some independent shops may close for lunch. Large stores are usually open later; some even stay open until 21.00 Friday.

TELEPHONES

*When calling **France** from outside the country, use the country code (33) and ignore the first 0 of the listed number. When calling **Belgium** from outside the country, use the country code (32) and ignore the first 0 of the listed number.*

Not all public phones are the same. According to where they're located, they will accept different forms of payment. Phones on board Eurostar and other trains require Mastercard or Visa. Call boxes on the Brussels métro and in French restaurants may accept coins, whilst most public telephones require a phone card (*télécarte*) available from post offices, railways stations, tobacconists and news kiosks. Calls from hotels are invariably more expensive. Ask at reception for their rates per unit, and length of each unit: some hotels charge in units of 15 seconds! Post offices (in France) and call bureaux (in Belgium) offer fax services. Some internet cafés may offer web phone services.

Dialling

To call overseas, dial 00 then the country code and number (omitting the first 0). To call within France, dial the ten-digit telephone number. To call within Belgium, dial the full domestic number including area code (02 for Brussels, 03 for Antwerp). For operator-assisted dialling from France, dial 00+33+ country code. For operator-assisted dialling from Belgium, dial 1324.

Country codes

Australia	61	Ireland	353
Belgium	32	New Zealand	64
Canada	1	United Kingdom	44
France	33	USA	1

Discounted rates

In **France** discounts of 20–50% apply to domestic and European calls made 19.00–08.00 weekdays, Saturday 12.00–24.00 and all day Sunday. Discounts on calls to the US and Canada apply 19.00–13.00 weekdays and all day weekends.

Smaller discounts are offered on calls made in **Belgium** between 20.00 and 08.00, and all day Sunday.

Useful numbers

France
Operator 12
Police 17
Fire 18
Ambulance 15
SOS (English-language crisis line) 01 47 23 80 80
Info (national) 12
Info (international) 00+32+(country code)
Public transport (in English) 08 36 68 41 14
Weather (France) 08 36 68 02 75
Weather (Paris) 08 36 68 01 01
Lost property 01 55 76 20 00 (Paris); 01 40 30 52 00 (on métro and buses)

Belgium
Operator 1324
Police 101
Fire and ambulance 100
Info (national) 1307
Info (international) 1204
Public transport 02 515 20 00
Weather 09 00 27 00 3
Lost property 02 517 96 11; 02 515 23 94 (on métro or buses)

TIME
From the end of March through to the end of October, Continental European time changes from GMT+1 to GMT+2.

TIPS AND SERVICE
Restaurant bills in **France** are obliged to include service charges (15%). However it is traditional to round up the total in restaurants and bars, leaving small change behind. Hotel porters should be tipped a small denomination note, and chambermaids left an appropriate gratuity. Tip taxi drivers 10–15% of the fare. Hairdressers should be left 15%. Cloakroom attendants should be given ∈1. Public toilet attendants usually expect around 50 cents. In cinemas and theatres tip the usherette 50 cents.

Restaurant prices in **Belgium** include 16% service charge and 21% tax. Leave loose change for exceptional service only. In hotels, porters may be tipped a small denomination note, and chambermaids left an equivalent gratuity. Taxi fares include service charge, although 5–10% tips are acceptable. Tip hairdressers 20%. Cloakroom attendants should be given ∈1. Public toilets usually display charges. If not, leave small change for the attendant. In cinemas and theatres tip the usherette 50 cents.

TOURIST OFFICES
Paris 127 av des Champs-Elysées, 75008; tel: 08 92 68 31 12 (premium rate); email: info@paris-touristoffice.com; web: www.paris-touristoffice.com [3 F5]
Open 09.00–20.00 (Sun in low season 11.00–18.00). Closed May 1.
M̄ *George V;* Ē *RER to Châtelet-les-Halles then RER A to Charles-de-Gaulle-Etoile. Walk down the Champs Elysées (south side).*
As well as traditional information and reservation services, a CCF currency exchange office is open daily 09.00–19.30. Additional offices may be found at Gare de Lyon, 20 bd Diderot, 75012, open Mon–Sat: 08.00–20.00, and the Eiffel Tower (see page 114) May–Sep, open daily 11.00–18.00

Lille Palais Rihour, place Rihour 59002; tel; 03 20 21 94 21; email: info@lilletourism.com; web: www.lilletourism.com [14 E4]
Open Mon–Sat 09.30–18.30, Sun and holidays 10.00–12.00, 14.00–17.00
M̄ *Rihour;* Ē *Métro 2 to Gare-Lille-Flandres then line 1 to Rihour*
Excellent information and reservation service. Many free publications include street maps and suggested cycle routes. Tourist information is also available at Lille Europe station, and town centre assistance available from the yellow-coated stewards on duty in shopping streets.

Brussels Hôtel de Ville, Grand' Place, 1000; tel: 02 513 89 40; email:
tourism.brussels@tib.be; web: www.tib.be [12 E2]
Open Mon–Sat 09.00–18.00, Sun 10.00–14.00 (winter), 09.00–18.00 (summer).
Closed Jan 1, Dec 25, some winter Sundays
M̄ *Bourse or Gare Centrale;* Ē *Underground tram to Bourse then follow signs or take the rue
au Beurre behind the Bourse building.*
See page 256 for more on this oft eccentric service.

London Southwark Tourist Information Centre, London Bridge (see page 330);
tel: 020 7403 8299; web: southwark-information.co.uk [16 G3]
Open (summer) Mon–Sat 10.00–18.00, Sun 11.00–18.00; (winter) Mon–Sat
10.00–16.00, Sun 11.00–16.00.

From the UK
French Travel Centre 178 Piccadilly, London W1. An excellent one-stop shop
for buying guidebooks, booking tickets for events, and picking up the free
Traveller in France reference guides, as well as plenty of advice. Or call the
premium-rate France Information service, 09068 244 123, web:
www.franceguide.com, for free brochures and maps.

Brussels has two tourist offices in the UK:

Ardennes 225 Marsh Wall, London E14 9FW, free brochure service on 0800
9545 245; premium-rate information service on 0906 3020 245, web:
www.belgium-tourism.net
Flanders 31 Pepper St, London E14 9RW; premium-rate information line 0891
887 799; web: www.visitflanders.com

VISAS, PASSPORTS AND CUSTOMS
European Union nationals need carry only a valid identity card or passport.
For nationals of non-European Union countries, passports are required.
Nationals of some countries require visas. Check with the local embassy or
consulate while planning your trip (taking into account the time it may take
for visas to be issued).

Travelling within the EU there is officially no limitation for purchases
destined for personal consumption by EU citizens, although the
recommended limit are cigarettes (800 pieces) and alcohol (90 litres of wine
and 10 litres of spirits). Travellers from countries outside the EU must take
heed of duty-free regulations and make a customs declaration and pay duty on
items of a value over €220. However, they may also claim approximately 13%
tax discount on their purchases. (Information from department stores see
pages 66–7.) Narcotics, some pornographic material, illegal drugs, weapons,
live plants and ivory may not be carried across borders.

For customs advice in France tel: 01 53 24 68 24; in Belgium tel: 02 210 30
11; in the UK tel: 0845 010 9000.

Part Two

Paris

Introduction

The young come to Paris to grow up, and the old return to rediscover their youth. For Paris is a canny mirror, ever reflecting all our other selves. If Paris can teach the frivolous to appreciate beauty and truth, this is also the place where the studious learn to laugh. Here millionaires may break bread on a riverbank, and paupers walk through palaces.

Parisians try to change their city, and like almost no other capital, Paris is constantly being rebuilt; yet it never loses its former identities. Street signs, as ever in France, are constantly changed to honour heroes and events. The quaint names of Victor Hugo's era have all but disappeared. Still the streets and their spirits remain.

In my teens, I would rush over the road to the station brasserie for the first coffee of the stay, and take the métro a few stops to my simple no-star hotel. Today's Gare du Nord may have its Salon Eurostar, but the brasserie remains (see page 176), as does the old hotel (see page 156). Yet since that first welcome, the city has shown me her other guises.

Over the years I have learned to love each of the many faces of this city. Each district, each *arrondissement*, each quarter is a Paris quite apart. The well-to-do socialite of the avenue Kléber knows nothing of the villager in Belleville. Can the students sharing red wine with existentialists in St-Michel live in the same city as the scrum lurching into the bargain baskets in the discount clothes stores at the foot of Montmartre?

Unlike many cities, Paris fits comfortably into any budget. The flair of the St-Honoré or Champs Elysées is revealed in the wit of a Chanel creation, the sparkle of a purchase from the place Vendôme, and the crisp crack of wealth on marble. Yet in the poorest alley on the Left Bank, the sudden view of Notre Dame, the sound of a fiddler in a late-night café or the smell of a street market offers something simply priceless.

Some attribute the city's many faces to its shifting focal points. Each major reign gave Paris a new centre. From a cathedral city on an island to a Left Bank seat of learning. From the Palace of the Louvre to Napoléon's sweeping boulevards and Arc de Triomphe. In the eras of great exhibitions, first the Eiffel Tower then the Trocadéro claimed centre stage. De Gaulle's La Défense, Pompidou's Beaubourg, Mitterand's Bastille and Bercy, the Fifth Republic has continued an imperial tradition of reinvention.

In other countries this incessant *agrandissement* might destroy a city's identity. But bigger than the towers and palaces is the French spirit of

21

disrespect for authority. France has a culture of menfolk doing a great deal of gathering. Farmers traditionally protest in city centres, and taxi drivers believe in blockading roads. If there are no trains running today, or your bus stop has been taken out of service, you know that somewhere, nearby, menfolk will be gathering. This may be a gesture of spontaneous anger regarding mad cows or a deep-rooted concern over a threatened national paperclip shortage. Who knows, who cares? In the 18th century, the young stormed the Bastille, in the 19th they barricaded the streets, in the 20th they ripped the cobbles from the very streets. The men who gather in the 21st century do not have the anger of youth. They belong to a non-political movement that scratches its upper trouser area and believes in letting the wife do the heavy stuff.

As long as the people of Paris are happy to run their own lives, and leave the politicians to build their monuments, the spirit of Paris will flourish. It was, after all, a transport strike that led to the greatest social event of recent times.

With métros and streets paralysed by industrial action in 1995, Parisians discovered roller skates. Bankers, office workers, shop assistants and civil servants swapped their briefcases and totebags for backpacks, and their Gucci loafers for in-line skates. Around four million Parisians would glide into work, weaving through traffic jams, gliding along the banks of the Seine and spinning, leaping and generally showing off on the broad squares of Hôtel de Ville and République.

Suddenly the hippest club in town became the Main Jaune, a skating rink designed by Philippe Stark, and the phenomenon of the Friday Night Fever was born. This is a 30km rollerblading tour of the city every Friday that still pulls around 20,000 skaters to the place d'Italie each week, and closes the Champs Elysées to motor vehicles (see page 89).

Plus ça change, plus ça reste Paris!

ORIENTATION

Within the Périphérique, the city is divided into 20 *arrondissements* or quarters, spiralling out from the Louvre (1st *arrondissement*). The number of the *arrondissement* is incorporated in the five-figure postcode for addresses in the Paris area.

01	Elysées–Louvre
02	Grands Boulevards, Elysées–Louvre
03	Marais
04	Marais, The East
05	Left Bank, The East
06	Left Bank, Montparnasse–Eiffel
07	Left Bank, Montparnasse–Eiffel
08	Elysées–Louvre, Grands Boulevards, The West
09	Grands Boulevards, Montmartre–Clichy
10	Gare du Nord, Boulevards, The East
11	The East
12	The East
13	The East
14	Montparnasse–Eiffel
15	Montparnasse–Eiffel
16	The West

17	The West
18	Montmartre–Clichy
19	Gare du Nord, The East
20	The East

Free maps are available from hotel receptions and the Paris tourist office (see page 17).

GETTING AROUND
Public transport
Roller skates are all very well, but most of us rely on the RATP métro, bus and our own two feet for exploring the city.

Métro and RER
Paris is justifiably proud of its métro system, the most efficient way to travel round the city, with 14 city lines and a station within 300 yards of almost any address in town. Interchanges are clearly marked on maps, and each route is known by the name of its terminus. So to travel south on line 4 from Gare du Nord to Strasbourg-St-Denis find the platform marked Porte d'Orléans. To use the métro, pass your ticket through the turnstile and follow signs for your platform or arrows marked *Accès aux Quais*. When you leave a métro train, either follow the blue and white signs marked *Sortie* for the exit, or look for an orange and white notice indicating *Correspondances* (interchanges) and head for the connecting service. The métro connects with the high-speed RER underground-overground expressway to the suburbs, Disneyland, airports and surrounding towns. The RER is usually the quickest route across town, cutting journey times by half. Métro and RER services run 05.30–00.30.

Some connections are more tortuous than others. At Châtelet-Les-Halles Montparnasse-Bienvenue, Auber and Bastille, platforms may be five minutes apart. Entertainers and hawkers set up stalls along the corridors, and RER interchange halls have cafés, shops and bars for breaking the journey. Many stations are worth a visit in their own right. Read the declaration of the Rights of Man on the platforms at Concorde, see replicas of museum exhibits at Louvre-Rivoli, and admire the stunning new architecture of the newest stations on Line 14 and RER E.

Buses
Buses are often ignored by tourists, yet they provide an inexpensive sightseeing tour. Route 24 runs along the banks of the Seine and crosses the river twice. A few of the old-style buses are still in service, with their open galleries at the rear where passengers may smoke or flirt with motorists. All bus stops have a name, and clear routes and timetables are displayed at bus stops. Unless you have a transport pass, bus journeys are often more expensive than the métro. Services run 06.30–20.30, with key routes operating until 00.30. On Sundays and summer holidays a special Balabus service links most key sights. Look for stops marked Bb. Nightbuses (Noctambus) cover the city from the place Châtelet when the métro is closed.

ANNEXES: THE LITTLE TABLES OF THE GRANDS CHEFS

The *Tour d'Argent* is arguably one of the world's greatest restaurants: the view across the Seine is unrivalled, the duck divine, and the wine cellar legendary. For most mortals, the bill at this silver tower is also of mythological proportions. At well over €150 (1,000FF) for dinner, and lunch around half that price, this restaurant appears on more wish-lists than itineraries.

With Claude Terrail's Tour and the dining rooms of Guy Savoy, Michel Rostang and Alain Ducasse keeping the class system in business, Paris has long separated the expense-account men from the bistro-budget boys. But mealtimes they are a-changing.

The phenomenon of the *annexe* has taken Paris by storm. *Les Bookinistes* on the Left Bank is a perfect example of this culture, in which the respected grand chefs return to their roots, creating unpretentious menus at affordable prices. For many of the top names, the fun had simply disappeared from the game: in order to keep their Michelin ratings, they now have to meet the most exacting standards from the right labels on their napkins to cutting-edge cutlery designs. Consequently, many great restaurateurs have discreetly established second homes, where formality is off the menu and where the maestros themselves (and their carefully nurtured protégées) are rediscovering the simple joys of cooking for ordinary people, rather than dancing attendance on critics and corporate spenders.

For around €35 (240ff) any of us may savour the flavours of genius. You will find several annexes in the main listings pages, but here is my choice of the best 15 outposts of the *Grands* that I am sure you will enjoy. *A vos fourchettes mes braves*, the storming of the Silver Tower *est arrivé!*

Alain Ducasse
Main restaurant: **Plaza Athénée** 23-27 av Montaigne, 75008; tel: 01 53 67 65 00
Annexes:
Spoon (see page 49)
Le 59 Poincaré 59, av Raymond Poincaré, 75116; tel: 01 47 27 59 59

Tickets

Tickets and maps for bus, RER and métro are available from métro stations (where free maps may be obtained). One ticket costs €1.25 (8FF), whilst a carnet (10 tickets) costs €9 (58FF).

Tourist tickets *Paris-Visite* are valid for one, two, three or five days. These may be obtained for the central zones (1–3) or a wider area. Zone 1–5 includes Disneyland, Versailles and the airports. Costs: one-day €8.50–17 (55–110FF); two-day €14–27 (90–175FF); three-day €18.50–37.50 (120–245FF); five-day €27–46 (175–300FF). Always validate and keep your ticket with you, as you may be fined for travelling without a valid ticket. For English-language information tel: 08 36 68 41 14; web: www.ratp.fr.

Claude Terrail
Main restaurant: **La Tour d'Argent** 15 q de la Tournelle, 75005; tel: 01 43 54 23 31
Annexe: **La Rôtisserie du Beaujolais** (see page 135)

Guy Savoy
Main restaurant: 18 rue Troyon, 75017; tel: 01 43 80 40 61
Annexes:
Les Bookinistes (see page 132)
Le Bistrot de l'Etoile 19 rue Lauriston, 75016; tel: 01 40 67 11 16
Le Cap Vernet 82 av Marceau, 75008; tel: 01 47 20 20 40
La Butte Chaillot 112 av Kleber, 75016; tel: 01 47 27 88 88

Michel Rostang
Main restaurant: 20 rue Rennequin, 75017; tel: 01 47 63 40 77
Annexes:
Coté Mer Bistrot (see page 133)
Bistrot d'à Côté (see page 150)

Alain Dutournier
Main restaurant: **Carré de Feuillants** (see page 45)
Annexe: **Au Trou Gascon** (see page 107)

Jacques Cagna
Main restaurant: 14 rue des Grands-Augustins, 75006; tel: 01 43 26 49 39
Annexes:
Rôtisserie Monsigny (see page 65)
l'Espadon Bleu 25 rue des Grands-Augustins, 75006; tel: 01 46 33 00 85

Albert Corre
Main restaurant: **Pergolèse**, 40 rue Pergolèse, 75016; tel: 01 45 00 21 40
Annexe: **L'Ampère** (see page 149)

Bernard Loiseau
Main restaurant: **La Côte d'Or** in Burgundy
Annexes:
Tante Marguerite (see page 136)
Tante Louise (see page 50)

Taxis

Taxi ranks can be found near métro and main-line stations. There is often an extra charge for pick-ups from ranks, or for ordering a cab by telephone. Hail a taxi in the street when the white light on the roof is switched on.

Officially, most taxis are licensed to carry up to three passengers, so if you are travelling in a foursome you may find yourselves rejected by the first half dozen cabs you flag down, or charged a supplement. At night, all three of you may have to squeeze in the back seat, as it is not unusual for the driver's dog to sit in front. The best value white-knuckle ride in town is to be had in the back of a Paris taxi. Do not expect a sedate ride, each gear-change is a testament to testosterone.

Taxis Bleus tel: 01 49 36 10 10
G7 Taxis tel: 01 47 39 47 39

Sightseeing tours

Plenty of conventional guided coach trips take in the must-see sights and sites with the usual English-language commentary. Of course, as in any city, these may be as frustrating as they are informative, since the most interesting subject of the tour is always the one that whizzes past the window denying the sensation seeker the chance of further exploration. Free spirits therefore prefer **L'Open Tour**, an open-top bus which meanders from the Eiffel Tower to Notre Dame, with connecting satellite routes up to Montmartre and across to Bercy. Tickets are available for one or two days unlimited use and passengers may hop on or off at will. Buses depart at 25-minute intervals for the full 2 hour 15 minute circuit. Tickets at €22.50–24.50 (145–160FF) may be purchased on board, at principal métro stations and tourist offices.

More traditional guided tours with cassette commentary are offered on distinctive buses marked **Cityrama** and **Paris Vision**.

Cityrama 4 pl des Pyramides, 75001; tel: 01 44 55 60 00
L'Open Tour 13 rue Auber, 75009; tel: 01 42 66 56 56; web: www.paris-opentour.com
Paris Vision 214 rue de Rivoli, 75001; tel: 01 42 60 30 01; web: www.parisvision.com

Riverboats

Riverboats offer spectacular views of Paris from the Seine. Unless your holiday package offers a free ticket for the more modest sightseeing boat trips, go for the corny, pricier, much-mocked, but nonetheless thrilling evening dinner cruise on the Bâteaux Mouches, which illuminate monuments as you pass. At lunchtime travel in the company of the best voices in the land. 'Secrets of the Seine' is the title of a midday journey through time. The riverboat *Crystal II* departs from the Eiffel Tower to sail along the Left Bank to Bercy and return along the right bank to the Statue of Liberty, as a four-course lunch is served. Actors Annie Duperey, Patrick Préjean and Gérald Rinaldi provide voices to a specially commissioned sound show in music and drama telling the tale of the city and its river, its laughter and tears, scandals and pride. Party frocks welcomed, jeans and trainers turned away. Boarding every day at 12.15, *Crystal II* returns to the quayside at 14.30. Price, including coffee and wine, tax and service, from €46 (300FF). Details and menus on the web: www.bateauxparisiens.com; reservations tel: 01 44 11 33 55.

Alternatively use the summer river shuttles between the sights. From May to September, Batobus (01 44 11 33 44) operates a hop-on-hop-off riverbus serving key points between Eiffel Tower and Notre Dame from 10.00 to 19.00. Combined passes are available with the OpenTour bus service. Don't forget the canals (page 170).

Cycling

If you would rather travel under your own steam, but are not quite ready for roller skates, hire a bike. Bicycles, like blades, made their comeback on the city streets during the great strikes of the 1990s. A network of compulsory cycle lanes (*pistes cyclables*) is being introduced. The main north–south route runs along the boulevard Sébastapol and boulevard St-Germain, and the east–west route is the Champs Elysées – rue de Rivoli. On Sundays, the banks of the Seine and Canal St-Martin are closed to cars for several hours and can be an exhilarating alternative to street-level traffic. You may even take your bike underground. On Sundays, bikes may be taken on Line 1 only, until 16.30, (except for Louvre-Rivoli and La Défense stations). RER lines A and B welcome cyclists to specially marked front and rear carriages, except during peak hours (06.30–09.00, 16.30–19.00). Pick up the cyclist map of Paris from tourist offices.

The RATP public transport authority runs the **Maison Roue Libre** at Les Halles. Weekday bike hire from €4.50 (30FF). They also organise regular sightseeing cycle tours of the city. Alternatively visit the long-established **Paris Vélo** on the Left Bank which hires bicycles and scooters.

Maison Roue Libre 95bis rue Rambuteau, 75001; tel: 01 53 46 43 77. Mon–Fri 09.00–19.00. M̄ Les-Halles; Ē RER to Châtelet-Les-Halles (exit Forum des Halles). Take the escalator to rue Rambuteau, then walk east towards rue Pierre Lescot.
Paris Vélo 2 rue du Fer à Moulin, 75005; tel: 01 43 37 59 22. 10.00–12.30 14.00–18.00; M̄ St-Marcel; Ē Métro 5 to St-Marcel.

Walking

I always advise friends to wear their most comfortable shoes in Paris. Although one is rarely out of sight of a station entrance, be it the modern yellow M sign or the traditional Guimard art nouveau ironwork, sights are so close together, and streets so full of tempting diversions, that most people end up walking far more than they anticipated. Free street maps are available from hotel reception desks, major department stores and the Paris tourist office (see page 17). These show only main roads however, so nip into the nearest métro booking hall to consult the *plan du quartier* large-scale wall map of local streets. Regular visitors should invest €6 (40FF) in the pocket-sized *Paris Pratique* map guide published by *Editions Indispensible* and available from news kiosks.

GET THE CARD

La Carte Museum Pass saves time and money, with automatic queue jumping, direct admission to the popular collections and unlimited access to around 70 museums and monuments in Paris. Priced at €12.50 (80FF) for one day, €24.50 (160FF) three days and €37 (240FF) five days, the pass may be obtained from métro stations, museums and tourist offices (see page 17). It may also be collected in advance in the UK from **Voyages Vacances** (French Travel Centre, 178 Piccadilly, London W1V OAL or from their desk at Waterloo station).

Elysées–Louvre

The bandages are off – and the most famous facelift in France has emerged blinking in the summer sunlight. Scarred by the ravages of too many years of fast food and fast cars, the **avenue des Champs Elysées** has now been re-landscaped according to Le Nôtre's original design, with twin rows of trees on each wide pavement, and the off-street parking consigned to new underground car parks. Even the polyurethane burger joints were ordered to tone down their act.

The street is always packed, even at 3am, with sightseers and high-spirited Parisians tooting their horns. Trailing streamers, flags or confetti, according to the celebration, it is here that the results of everything from elections to the World Cup to the Tour de France to a successful wedding are proclaimed through car windows and sunroofs in the small hours. Some landmarks change: Le Fouquets (we pronounce the 't'), the Renault Pub and the hotel George V, around the corner, have all seemingly defied their Gibraltar-status by disappearing for a season, but they return grander than ever. *Plus ça change*: the Lido still kicks a mean chorus line, the Queen nightclub still sets the party standard and the statue of President Clemenceau still stands guard over the fountains.

From the Rond Point, and below the avenue Montaigne, gardens still line the avenue, shading the Grand and Petit Palais and the memorial to Jean Moulin, hero of the French Resistance. In July, women stroll barefoot on the cool pavement, their elegantly uncomfortable high-heeled shoes strung by their straps over one finger and hung nonchalantly over one shoulder, after the agonising catwalk parade of the shopping strip. In September, Englishmen on their best behaviour look at the carpet of conkers on the grass. If only we were at home and eight years old, here is any number of potential 36-ers. But the Parisians don't play conkers, and anyway where would we find the string? These are the real *champs*, or fields, and provide five minutes gentle reflection before the avenue opens out to the magnificent 18th-century place de la Concorde, the start of the colonnades of rue de Rivoli, and straight ahead the majestic Tuileries Gardens of the Louvre. At the time of writing, the square was the home of the Millennium Ferris Wheel, saved from post-celebration dismantling by popular demand. The wheel is set to be moved to a new permanent site from 2002.

Look ahead through the gardens to see the Louvre's miniature Arc du Carousel, then turn back to gaze up the avenue to the great Arc du Triomphe at place de l'Etoile. Behind the gatehouses to the place de la Concorde is the Palais de l'Elysée, residence of the president.

The palace gives on to the rue du Faubourg St-Honoré, an address found on the letterhead of the top boutiques and the most distinguished embassies. Once one of Paris' main streets, the Faubourg St-Honoré, and its successor the rue St-Honoré, is today a clogged artery with traffic holding in its breath in order to squeeze between improperly parked cars. The narrow pavements have reassuringly prohibitively priced boutiques and furriers, expense-account restaurants and the occasional convivial café. The dull grey car park that once stood on the place du Marché St-Honoré, and loomed over the gastronomic Renaissance of the district, has at last been replaced by something more suited to a corner of a charmed quarter. Now young chefs may flex their mussels, langoustines and *confit de canard* in order to compete with the established stars of the restaurant scene.

The place de la Madeleine has its classical church at the centre but is actually a temple to the goddess Gluttony: Fauchon on one side of the square, with its queues of the fashionably dressed passing through the glass doors of the choicest grocers in France; the great Lucas Carton restaurant on the further corner. Mid-morning sees the young *commis de cuisine* and kitchen porters sneaking a cigarette break on the pavement's double-sided bench. In the middle of the square, the market wafts tantalising aromas of ripe cheese and fresh fruits across the line of theatre-goers at the half-price ticket kiosk.

The rues Royale and de la Paix are streets where the concept of price tags is considered vulgar. Maxims, setting of Lehar's *Merry Widow*, gained notoriety as the only restaurant in the city not to display its menu and prices outside the front door. Place Vendôme is where Lorelei Lee famously turned her back on the central Napoleonic monument in order to set her sights on the Coty sign. The great jewellery counters are discreetly set in this charming ring on the cheque-signing finger of the Ritz. This side of town has long been home to those plastic-slapping, platinum-card-carrying gentlemen who prefer blondes who prefer nothing so much as a spree. Primed with travellers' cheques, boundless credit-limits, even ready money, serious shoppers know no other Paris.

From here one can see the park railings of the Tuileries, and step out of the sun along the colonnades of the Rivoli thoroughfare that entertains the purse from Concorde to Bastille, passing shops, department stores and the Italianate frontages of grand hotels. The Palais Royal and Louvre take up many city blocks. This vast museum and its garden is so large that there are four métro stations along its walls. You can take the train from one end to the other. The ride is worthwhile, if only to see the imaginative décor of the Louvre-Rivoli station, once the main entrance to the Louvre, with its platform reproductions of the museum's treasures.

Eventually the museum surrenders its visitors' attention to Les Halles, the former market place that now acts as a *bourse* of shopping and dining. Heading north, baser appetites are served on the *trottoirs* of rue St-Denis. Unlike many of the city's red-light districts, the St-Denis has an improbably stagey feel, although the well-polished Hollywood sheen of the bright costumes and carefully applied face paint of the street girls seem incongruous against the new neon grafitti of shuttered doorways. No furtive back street, rue St-Denis has learnt the rules of retail and the lessons of service. I recall reading the notice outside Club 88, as a PA system from within the sex store announced the launch of a customer loyalty card: 'We apologise to patrons for any inconvenience during the installation of a new escalator to our second and third floors'.

Although the main department stores are clustered around the Opéra and Grands Boulevards, this is the part of town where spending is never something of which to be ashamed. Shopping on the Champs Elysées itself may no longer be exclusive. The fashion houses stand on more sedate streets. On the avenue, people spend their money at Virgin's Megastore or the late-night supermarket. Addresses featuring the magic words Montaigne, St-Honoré, Rivoli and Vendôme are the centre of *haute couture*, deluxe hotels and expansive entertainment. Style comes as standard. I know of a British couple in the quarter for their silver wedding, seeking that special dress. They stepped over an elegant threshold on the rue St-Honoré. Just a handful of original designer gowns hung on a rail against the simple white-tiled walls. The wife's eyes lit up as she saw the very outfit. 'Could we? Should we? May I?'. Twenty-five years of a better life than any of us deserve inspired the tender kiss of devoted acquiescence that answered her question, and together they lifted the polythene-wrapped beaded creation and carried it in awe-struck silence to the Louis XV desk at which sat the exquisitely painted *vendeuse*. The husband opened his wallet and selected a platinum card. The saleswoman raised a geometrically perfect eyebrow and lifted an immaculately manicured hand in protest. '*Mais non, Monsieur*. Your dry cleaning ticket, if you please.'

WHERE TO STAY

Agora 7 rue de la Cossonnerie, 75001; tel: 01 42 33 46 02; email: hotel.agora.f@wanadoo.fr [4B7]
M̄ *Châtelet-Les-Halles;* Ē *RER to Châtelet-Les-Halles. Use the Forum des Halles/Pierre Lescot exit.*
Straight up the escalator from the métro's most central interchange, *et voilà!* Ideally located for the visitor afraid of missing a second's bustle, a light's twinkle of the big city buzz. The eclectic first-floor reception is cluttered with paintings, caged birds and bric-a-brac ranging in style from the charming, through kitsch, to downright naff. Staff are friendly and helpful, and the rooms vary from the bright and balconied on the second floor to the sixth-floor garrets with skylight views of the rooftops of Les Halles and the bustling streets. Not for those seeking complete bed rest, as the noisy quarter has restaurants and clubs open until 05.00. Prices around ∈ 87 (570FF).

Britannique 20 av Victoria, 75001; tel: 01 42 33 74 59; web: www.hotel-britannique.fr [4B8]
M̄ *Châtelet-Les-Halles;* Ē *RER to Châtelet-Les-Halles. Use the Avenue Victoria exit.*
The Britannique was a Quaker mission during World War I. Today it is an inoffensively decorated, peaceful base, with helpful staff. Some rooms are rather

compact for € 137 (900FF), but all are clean and well fitted, and off-season
bargain rates are often available. The avenue Victoria from Châtelet to the Hôtel
de Ville is arguably the centre of Paris. All the city's nightbuses leave and return
from the avenue, and the charms of the Marais, Les Halles, Ile de la Cité, Left
Bank and Louvre fan out from here. The hotel is tucked away at the quiet end of
the street just opposite the Théâtre du Châtelet. Informative website.

Costes 239 rue St-Honoré, 75001; tel: 01 42 44 50 00 [3 J6–7]
M̄ *Tuileries;* Ē *RER to Châtelet-Les-Halles then métro 1 to Tuileries. West along the rue de
Rivoli, turn right into rue de Castiglione and left on to rue St-Honoré.*
The king was dead – so long live the spirit of Napoléon III. When the legendary
Hôtel George V was boarded up for the duration of its rebirth as a Four Seasons
Hôtel, not too many people noticed its absence – because the fickle crowd-du-
moment had flocked to the ultra-now Hôtel Costes where a cocktail of 19th-
century imperial elegance, Mediterranean excess and North African promise
made it the perfectly designed address for travellers with an image to maintain.
The brothers Costes have always been the names to follow in Paris; their
erstwhile café in Les Halles was the only place to see and be seen in the 1980s.
Now today's recording stars and rich romantics have adopted the hotel. They
love networking in the bar-restaurant and adore the fitness centre for people with
mobile phones attached to their bronzed shoulders. A bit too lifestyle-magazine
for my tastes, but since people are bound to ask, I'll tell you: double rooms € 350
(2,300FF) upwards, private garage parking extra, and sunglasses *de rigueur* at the
€ 23 (150FF) breakfast during fashion week.

Cygne 3 rue de Cygne, 75001; tel: 01 42 60 14 16; email:
hotel.cygne@freesurf.fr [4 B7]
M̄ *Etienne-Marcel;* Ē *Métro 4 to Etienne-Marcel. From rue Pierre Lescot turn left into rue
de Cygne.*
Use the oft-ignored métro station of Etienne Marcel, rather than the complicated
underground maze at Les Halles, to reach this simple € 76 (500FF) a night hotel.
Located in the heart of what the establishment would like to promote as the
restaurant and shopping district, but which a 10-yard stroll round the corner
reveals to be the central sex-shop and red-light area. Do not be put off by the
bawdy neon promises of the neighbours. This tiny street is ideally located for
walking and travelling absolutely anywhere, and there are plenty of cheap eats
nearby. The family-run hotel has been charmingly refurbished, with 17th-
century rooms upgraded to en-suite standard. Some bedrooms are on the titchy
side, but have TV, safe and even a houseplant or two. The reception lounge is
nicely furnished and the staff always eager to please.

Florence 26 rue des Mathurins, 75009; tel: 01 47 42 63 47 [5 J5]
M̄ *Havre-Caumartin;* Ē *RER E to Haussmann-St-Lazare, then walk down rue
Caumartin to rue des Mathurins.*
Madame Fabre runs the Florence, but it was her spaniel that provided my first
welcome as he rushed to greet a travel-weary newcomer to this 20-room hotel,
conveniently situated by the food hall temples of the Opéra district – Galleries
Lafayettes for the British, and the late Marks & Spencer for the French. She may
just serve breakfast these days, but once upon a time there was always a chicken
in the pot. Before Haussmann altered the shape of the streets, this was the home
of Napoléon's cook who, according to Mme Fabre, was obliged permanently to
have a *poulet* prepared to rush round to the imperial table day or night. In
1822–26 Georges Sand lived here. Not that you could tell from the style of the

rooms – bland, simple, clean and (those facing the road) double-glazed. I can vouch for the soundproofing, having sat up all night watching the British election results on cable TV, and the morning clarion of traffic did not penetrate my eventual doze. Rooms around € 100 (650FF).

Le Lion d'Or 5 rue de la Sourdière, 75001; tel: 01 42 60 79 04; web: www.hotelduliondor.com [3 K7]
M̄ *Tuileries;* Ē *RER to Châtelet-Les-Halles then métro 1 to Tuileries. Rue de 29 Juillet towards the place du Marché St-Honoré, turning right on rue St-Hyacinthe to rue de la Sourdière.*
I first stumbled across Monsieur Ammour's remarkable bargain accommodation in the heart of the pricey tourist-trap district years ago when tramping the streets in the week that sterling plummeted by over 20% against European currencies. No lift, but a warm welcome behind the St-Honoré feeding frenzy, with a well-furrowed pile of English and French magazines and paperbacks in the reception area. The most welcome improvement over recent years has been the end to midnight corridor expeditions to find the loo. These days you'll find workaday, clean bathrooms en suite. The room rate remains decent value at € 57–88 (380—580FF). Regulars love the place so much that they return in cyberspace, thanks to the hotel's on-line chat-room.

Meurice 228 rue de Rivoli, 75001; tel: 01 44 58 10 10; web: www.meuricehotel.com [3 J7]
M̄ *Tuileries;* Ē *RER to Châtelet-Les-Halles then métro 1 to Tuileries.*
In 1817, Augustin Meurice, the Calais Postmaster, decided that British VIPs required a luxury hotel in Paris after travelling 36 hours in his post chaises from the coast. Popular with the young Napoléon III, Queen Victoria, Edward and Mrs Simpson, and most of the crowned heads of Europe, the hotel has unashamedly based its style on the Palace of Versailles. Even today, little compares to the right royal thrill of flinging open a tall bedroom window and looking across the gardens of the Tuileries to the Musée d'Orsay clock window opposite. The Louis XV-style tea room, hosted by an enormous portrait of Madame de Pompadour, is an experience for the eyes, ears and tastebuds. A true Palace Hôtel, offering luxurious silence behind the Rivoli clamour, the hotel recently reopened, pampered, polished, furnished and ever refurbished to glorious effect. All accommodation now features fax and internet connections and marble bathrooms. The famous art nouveau glass roof over the winter garden has been lovingly restored, a lovely oasis of potted palms and baguettes; room rates from around € 485 (3,200FF). The hotel has its celebrated *Espace de Bien-Etre*, a renowned health spa for upmarket pampering, and is famous for its weekend packages offering best seats at the Opéra.

Molière 21 rue Molière, 75001; tel: 01 42 96 22 01; email: moliere@worldnet.fr [3 K7]
M̄ *Palais-Royal-Musée-du-Louvre;* Ē *RER to Châtelet-Les-Halles then métro 1 or 7 to Palais-Royal-Musée-du-Louvre. Rue de Rohan to place Colette. Past the Comédie Française, turn right into rue Molière.*
A graceful oval staircase betrays the building's history as a private house and home of one of France's great writers. But not the eponymous rompeur – this was once *chez* Voltaire, who first gave private performances of his work in this very building. Just a dramatic gesture away from the Comédie Française, this popular Opéra district hotel is almost opposite the Molière fountain and filled with pictures of the great playwright, born Jean-Baptiste Poquelin. A good base

for the classic museums and sights, being a brief stroll to the Louvre, barely ten minutes from the Orsay and on the most central métro line, which strings the Pompidou Centre, Les Halles, Bastille and the Champs Elysées. If it is somewhat top heavy with English-speaking guests, that may be excused because so many of them work with the fashion houses or the couture catwalks of the Carrousel du Louvre, so the gossip and scandal at breakfast is an eavesdropper's delight. The ground-floor breakfast room regularly presents exhibitions by rising young artists, though the garish oeuvres displayed during my stay seemed inclined to bring on indigestion. With rates in the region of € 129 (850FF), one expects, and receives, the usual extras: minibar, bathroom goodies, hairdryer and so on. You draw the short straw if your room number ends in a three or a four, but the ones and twos are charming, with quaint en-suite bathrooms, and the fives have bathrooms big enough for a modest dinner party! Service is never less than smiling and helpful.

Newton Opera 11 bis rue de l'Arcade, 75008; tel: 01 42 65 32 13; web: www.hotel-newton-opera.com [3 J5–6]
M̄ *Madeleine;* Ē *RER E to Haussmann-St-Lazare then métro 12 to Madeleine. The rue de l'Arcade begins on the west west side of the square.*
Napoléon's favourite tipple, mandarin liqueur (see *Domaine Mandarin Napoléon* in Lille page 242) awaits new arrivals at this welcoming hotel situated at the crossroads of all the new transport routes in the city. The brand new cross-town métro line is a few steps away, and there's serious shopping on either side of the Madeleine. Although the official room rate is around € 145 (950FF), the hotel has developed some excellent weekend deals for couples, with dinner in a local restaurant, champagne and a moonlight boat trip thrown in – so do telephone, or check the website, before booking.

Queen Mary 9 rue de Greffulhe, 75008; tel: 01 42 66 40 50; web: www.hotelqueenmary.com [3 J5]
M̄ *Havre-Caumartin;* Ē *RER E to Haussmann-St-Lazare, then walk down rue Caumartin to turn right to rue des Mathurins and left to rue de Greffulhe.*
A rather neat little hideaway nearer the Grands Magasins than the traffic-go-round of the Etoile, it has a civilised welcome as you step past the striped awnings and into the reception. A welcome decanter of sherry on a side table in the € 145 (950FF) bedroom, or an apéritif in the blue and yellow bar downstairs – all in all a pleasant retreat between the hurly-burly of bare knuckle consumerism and the glitter of an evening on the town. Popular with dedicated followers of chic shopping, breakfast even includes a slimmers' special for those size tens who have just spent a small fortune on a size eight original.

Relais Carré d'Or 46 av George V, 75008; tel: 01 40 70 05 05; toll free: 0800 964 470 (UK), 800 525 4800 (USA); email: carre-dor@calva.net [3 F6]
M̄ *George-V;* Ē *RER to Châtelet-Les-Halles then métro 1 to George V. The Relais is a few steps along from Fouquets.*
The former home of royal courtiers, the Polignac family, is now an all-suite residence with spacious reception rooms, balconies overlooking the avenue, well equipped bathrooms and separate bedrooms with a second TV. Grander suites have flamboyant wall hangings and curved staircases leading to mezzanines. Kitchens have dishwashers, fridges and freezers as standard (great to be able to pour drinks from full-sized bottles and make a late-night snack). Unlike the Suites St-Honoré, where everything is fully stocked as standard, all crockery and cutlery must be requested from room service or by prior reservation. Breakfast is

MONTORGUEIL – THE OTHER LES HALLES

When Les Halles was saved from oblivion by big bucks and big business, its spirit moved a couple of streets to the north. Quietly and with no fanfare, the Montorgueil area across the rues Etienne Marcel and Turbigo has become a food lover's delight. Plenty of little restaurants, fabulous cheese counters and inexpensive florists. Everything in fact that Les Halles used to be.

Halfway along rue Montorgueil is the **Stohler Pâtisserie**, an unexpected royal wedding present to the quarter. Perhaps Marie Leczynska had a premonition that she would spend the next ten years in a state of near-permanent pregnancy and thus laid plans for the cravings that lay ahead. We shall never know. Nonetheless, when Marie arrived in Paris to marry the teenage Louis XV in 1725, she brought along her favourite Polish pastry-chef. Five years later Monsieur Stohler opened his shop, which is still one of the best addresses in town for feel-good treats. In 1864, Paul Baudry, who painted the foyer of the Paris Opéra Garnier, redecorated the pâtisserie in his opulent style. If you have a sweet tooth you will be tempted by the chocolate masks, gâteaux and tarts in the left-hand window. Savoury buds will tingle at the delicious flans, salads and *terrines* in the other vitrine, perfect picnic fare for the journey home.

In the morning the pavements of the rue Montorgueil are packed with chefs and housewives picking out the best vegetables from shop-front trestle tables and the most succulent guinea fowl and *poussin* from the butchers.

The rue Tiquetonne wakes up at around midday. During the morning, the only visitors will be greengrocers and bakers making their deliveries to shuttered restaurants. Between the restaurants are some vibrant new boutiques. The most talked about designers of the moment sell one-off outfits through **Kokon to Zai**, where media starlets choose that special ensemble to guarantee catching the eyes and lenses of the paparazzi. A mix of new and 'recycled' clubwear is stocked at **Kiliwatch**.

My favourite hideaway for a few minutes' rest and recuperation is **Le Denicheur**, a gem of a junk shop that doubles as a coffee shop every afternoon, except Monday. Sit down for a coffee or a quiche and ten minutes with the paper. And should you like the lampshade, the coffee cup or even your chair, the laid-back staff will slap it on the bill and hand it over – for everything on the table, floor, shelves and exposed beam walls is for sale.

Evenings see the lights glowing from the windows of a dozen or so tiny Tiquetonne restaurants. Appropriately opposite the Loup Blanc is the out-and-proud **Aux Trois Petits Cochons**, where Frédéric and Thierry decide on the menu according to what they find in the street market of

served in suites or in a first-floor club-lounge. A hidden courtyard garden just yards from the bustle and deaf to the traffic on the Champs Elysées is an option for cocktail hour. It makes for a useful base for city living, in walking distance of the better dining areas. Budget around € 686 (4,500FF).

Montorgueil. Spring may bring warm pig's trotter *carpaccio* with truffle oil and shredded white asparagus, whilst the arrival of summer might presage free-range Barbary duckling with peaches. Autumnal dishes could include oven grilled figs in a *zabaglione* mousse cream, and a popular winter starter is grilled beef marrow on toast accompanied by a mixed salad with truffle vinaigrette. The daily menu at € 22 (145FF) and € 26 (169FF) is posted on the restaurant's website www.auxtroispetitscochons.com.

Across the road are three smart addresses with *Lyonais*-style shop fronts of bright red woodwork and engraved glass. **Le Tir Bouchon** is a traditional *bouchon* (wine bar of Lyon) serving market fresh food. The **Bar au Grappillon** serves traditional French dinners. A *traiteur* along the road, **Terre et Soleil**, sells many of the delicious restaurant dishes to enjoy at home or as a picnic.

Stohler Pâtisserie 51 rue Montorgueil, 75002; tel: 01 42 33 38 20 [4 B7]
M̲ *Etienne-Marcel;* E̲ *Métro 4 to Etienne-Marcel. Walk west on rue Etienne Marcel, turn right onto rue Montorgueil.*

Kokon to Zai 48 rue Tiquetonne, 75002; tel: 01 42 36 92 41 [4 B7]
Open Mon–Sat 11.00–20.00.
E̲ *Métro 4 to Etienne-Marcel. Walk west on rue Etienne Marcel, turn right into rue Française, then left on rue Tiquetonne.*

Kiliwatch 64, rue Tiquetonne 75002; tel: 01 42 21 17 37 [4 B7]
Open Mon–Sat 11.00–20.00.
E̲ *Métro 4 to Etienne-Marcel. Walk west on rue Etienne Marcel to junction with rue Tiquetonne.*

Le Denicheur 4 rue Tiquetonne, 75002; tel: 01 42 21 31 01 [4 B7]
M̲ *Etienne-Marcel. Walk east on rue de Turbigo, turn left into rue St-Denis and sharp left to rue Tiquetonne.*

Aux Trois Petits Cochons 31 rue Tiquetonne, 75002; tel: 01 42 33 39 69 [4 B7]
E̲ *Métro 4 to Etienne-Marcel. Walk west on rue Etienne Marcel, turn right into rue Française, then left on rue Tiquetonne.*

Le Tir Bouchon 22 rue Tiquetonne, 75002; tel: 01 42 21 95 51 [4 B7]
E̲ *Métro 4 to Etienne-Marcel. Walk east on rue de Turbigo, turn left into rue St-Denis and sharp left to rue Tiquetonne.*

Bar au Grappillon 32 rue Tiquetonne, 75002; tel: 01 40 28 96 04 [4 B7]
E̲ *Métro 4 to Etienne-Marcel. Walk west on rue Etienne Marcel, turn right into rue Française, then right on rue Tiquetonne.*

Terre et Soleil 20 rue Tiquetonne, 75002; tel: 01 42 33 64 22 [4 B7]
E̲ *Métro 4 to Etienne-Marcel. Walk east on rue de Turbigo, turn left into rue St-Denis and sharp left to rue Tiquetonne.*

Les Suites St-Honoré 13 rue d'Aguesseau, 75008; tel: 01 44 51 16 35 [3 H6]
M̲ *Madeleine or Concorde;* E̲ *RER E to Haussmann-St-Lazare, then line 12 or 8 to Madeleine. From rue de Surene, rue d'Aguesseau is the third street on the left. Hotel is on your right.*

Isn't it always the way? Sipping champagne on the Eurostar, you fall into conversation with your favourite Hollywood star, you share a cab with the American ambassador, and the first person you meet at Fouquets is that charming Contessa who lent you her villa in Tuscany last summer. You really should repay the hospitality but the notice at your hostel expressly forbids guests in your room after 8pm. Had you decided on the upmarket self-catering option, then you might have been spared the embarrassment of smuggling Julia Roberts and Harrison Ford up the fire escape or serving drinks to a diplomat from plastic toothbrush tumblers. Almost opposite the British Embassy and just around the corner from the Elysée Palace, this excellently refurbished building has just 13 superb private apartments. The Suites St-Honoré, now ten years old, are all different sizes and different styles. You may go for the contemporary sharp look of the top storey duplexes, with their roof terraces, but I prefer the classic apartments on the lower floors. Under the guidance of the original director Betty Bougeaud, none of the accommodation has that glass and space art gallery sterility of other short-let apartments in Paris. Decorated to an excellent standard, even the smallest suite is bigger than the average Parisian home. A comfortable bedroom with picture frames at the bedside for your own snaps of loved ones (a homely touch), not only a marbled bathroom, with porcelain bowls of cotton buds and cotton wool as well as the usual soaps and shampoos, but a second luxury shower room, and yet another cloakroom by the front door. When I first visited, I rejected a second bedroom in favour of an office with fax, telephone, stylish furniture and guest sofa bed, as my retreat when cloistered against a publisher's deadline. The main living room was huge, expensively and expansively furnished with TV, video and hi-fi, even a CD player. Dining tables may be set with fine place settings for a meal prepared in the lavishly kitted-out kitchen, with its fridge-freezer, cooker, coffee-maker and microwave, as well as all the utensils. Although there is a dishwasher, you don't even have to switch it on since discreet staff pop in to clean up whenever you nip out to the shops. Shopping is St-Honoré-Vendôme wonderful. If you are budgeting for a Palace Hôtel stay, then the suites offer an irresistible challenge to the anonymity of a hotel. Rates, irrespective of the number of occupants, from just €243–973 (1,600–6,400FF) per night. Prices are substantially lower for stays of more than six nights. Suites may double as conference meeting rooms, whilst allowing the family freedom to enjoy half the apartment without butting in on business.

There is no restaurant on site, but the super-efficient staff can summon outside caterers to your apartment in the blinking of an eye. Nonetheless, for me, the joy of the suites is that I can actually take advantage of the good food shopping around the Madeleine and create a dinner party for two or 20 in the comfort of my own home. So far I've just entertained old friends, but next time I share a cab with Dame Judi, a passport queue with Messrs Brosnan, Kissinger or Malkovich, or even find myself stuck in a lift with Tony and Cherie, I'll be prepared.

Vendôme 1 pl Vendôme, 75001; tel: 01 55 04 55 00; toll free reservations through Small Luxury Hotels 0800 964 470 (UK), 800 525 4800 (USA); email: reservations@hotelvendome.com [3 J6]
M̄ *Tuileries;* Ē *RER to Châtelet-Les-Halles then métro 1 to Tuileries. West along the rue de Rivoli, turn right into rue de Castiglione towards place Vendôme.*
There are more branches of Cartier on and around the place Vendôme than you can shake a diamond-encrusted stick at, and the most celebrated name around the Napoleonic column is the Ritz, nemesis of cabinet ministers and mecca for cookery students at the Escoffier school. Recently, however, those in the know have discovered the discreet Hôtel Vendôme, just a precious stone's throw from its more famous neighbour and completely refurbished since taking on its new identity in 1998. A pretty curved and lacquered lift takes the guest to the 30 stylish bedrooms, which, with their wood panels and gentle fabrics, elegant fittings and cool air conditioning, are a haven from the St-Honoré crush outside the window. A brass-framed console next to the bed allows instant touch control of curtains, air conditioning, music and much more – standard perhaps for NASA, but a genuine novelty off the rue de Rivoli. They haven't yet found a way of electronically bringing the museums, galleries and shops into the bedroom, so you still have to get out of bed occasionally. Perhaps to investigate the **Café Vendôme** downstairs, a classy new brasserie whose *caviares* and *côtes d'agneau* with cumin had been freely praised to me by a taxi driver as we passed the place a few weeks earlier. Menus under ∈ 38 (250FF) provide an affordable opportunity to discover the talents of Gérard Salle, previously of the Plaza Athénée. Hotel breakfast is a staggering ∈ 25 (165FF) though – room rates closer to ∈ 456 (3,000FF). Lovely little extras are hidden in the rooms, to be discovered by accident. I loved the map on a string to be worn around the neck of the fit or the *embonpoint*-aware, with its suggested route from the hotel and through the Tuileries gardens across the road. Not forgetting the little bottle of mineral water with the label 'Take me with you when you go jogging – I cost ∈ 3 (20FF)'. A big deep bath and well-equipped

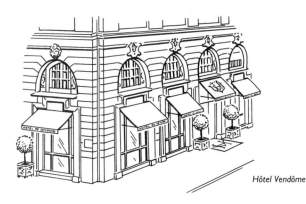

Hôtel Vendôme

bathroom with fresh flowers, snuggly robes and huge towels. Very helpful staff and a genuine small-hotel welcome, with château-hotel class.

WHERE TO GO

Arc du Triomphe pl du Général de Gaulle, 75008; tel: 01 55 37 73 77 [2 E5] Open Oct–Mar 10.00–22.30, Apr–Sep 09.30–23.00. Closed Jan 1, May 1, Dec 25. Open after ceremonies on other holidays ∈ 6.60 (42FF). Under 18s free. Free for all 1st Sun each month.
M̄ *Charles-de-Gaulle-Etoile;* Ē *RER to Châtelet-Les-Halles then RER A to Charles-de-Gaulle-Etoile.*
Napoléon's triumphs immortalised for all time. Prices are for access to the roof with its views across the city from the centre of the Etoile. From the roof, the Arc du Carrousel and the Grand Arche de la Défense seem to be the same size. A trick of perspective: La Défense is twice the height and twice the distance from the Etoile. On July 14 and Armistice days the president leads the ceremonies at the tomb of the unknown soldier.

l'Atelier Renault 53 av des Champs Elysées, 75008; tel: 01 49 53 70 00 [3 G6] Open 08.00–02.00.
M̄ *Franklin-D-Roosevelt;* Ē *RER to Châtelet-Les-Halles then line 1 to Franklin-D-Roosevelt.*
This was always the most fun of the car showrooms on the Champs Elysées. A museum of racing cars and saloons, and its restaurant, with booths designed to resemble vintage racing cars. No wonder this was the place for divorced fathers to take the kids on a Sunday afternoon. Now, under its *'créateur d'aumotobiles'* slogan, the Renault Pub has reinvented itself as l'Atelier Renault, and blatantly rejected its sideshow image in favour of a more sophisticated studio look. So out go the ice-cream-bingeing ten-year-old boys and in comes the launch party dry-white-wine-and-media-kit crowd. The comprehensive collection of veteran vehicles has been replaced by installation art focusing on prototype vehicles of the future. Light snacks or the full serious restaurant menu are served in the glass-encased dining room, suspended above the gallery, and a long sweeping cocktail bar is the place for looking smart and swivelling on a bar stool with a tall slim summer cooler.

Café Marly Cour Napoléon, 93 rue de Rivoli, 75001; tel: 01 49 26 06 60 [3 K7] M̄ *Palais-Royal-Musée-du-Louvre;* Ē *RER to Châtelet-Les-Halles then métro 1 to Palais-Royal-Musée-du-Louvre. From the street level exit, the café entrance is through the arch and to the left.*
Straddling the razor edge of sophistication between a welcome and arrogance, the service is sharp, the crowd even sharper, for the Marly is housed within the Louvre itself. Café patrons regard themselves as the equal of any exhibit housed in the great museum, and, in good weather, competition for a terrace table is fierce as the Absolutely Fabulous set try to upstage the pyramid itself. Even those of us who long ago gave up the march of *haute couture* flop gratefully into the embrace of a sofa after a half day trooping the world's greatest art treasures, before ordering our life-saving caffeine fix with a mineral water chaser. Ladies who lunch light need to spend ∈ 23 (150FF) at least.

Carrousel du Louvre 99 rue de Rivoli, 75001; tel: 01 43 16 47 15 [3 K7] Open Tue–Sun 11.00–20.00.
M̄ *Palais-Royal-Musée-du-Louvre;* Ē *RER to Châtelet-Les-Halles then métro 1 to Palais-Royal-Musée-du-Louvre.*
The grand entrance to the Louvre museum is a modern-day temple – a temple to

the goddess Lifestyle. Here in this sleek underground shopping mall are to be found shops and chain stores, the famous catwalk for Paris Fashion Week, a studio theatre annexe to the Comédie Française and an auditorium for the Louvre itself where film shows and concerts are programmed for lunchtimes and evenings. The main dining rooms of the museum may be accessed through the Carrousel. The most useful of these, for families or groups, is the international food court with a dozen or so counters serving specialist meals from Tex-Mex to vegetarian, and plenty of tables.

Le Fouquets 99 av des Champs Elysées, 75008; tel: 01 47 23 50 00 [3 F6]
M̲ *George-V;* E̲ *RER to Châtelet-Les-Halles then métro 1 to George-V. Head for the southern corner of the Champs Elysees and av George V.*
Lloyd George knew my Croque Monsieur and Churchill sat just yards from where you are sitting right now. The awestruck whispers at Le Fouquets have everything to do with the legend, and little to do with the menu. For Fouquets is the highest uncommon denominator that links anyone who was anyone in the past century with no degrees of separation. Frank Sinatra, the Duchess of Windsor and Johnny Hallyday have all been regulars at the legendary restaurant on the corner of the av George V. The Comte de Paris, pretender to the throne, could be seen hobnobbing with Jean-Paul Sartre or film-maker François Truffaut in the only restaurant ever successfully to blend the worlds of the Left and Right Banks. Renovated for its centenary celebration by new owners Groupe Lucienne Barrière, since opening on November 8 1899 Le Fouquets has passed many milestones, including hosting the Champs' first cinema in 1928, and being declared a national monument in 1988. For years the management frowned at unaccompanied women drinking at the bar, and the old-fashioned attitude pervades within. However, the pavement terrace is the best spot on the avenue for watching stylish Paris shimmer, glitter and glide in front of your very eyes. Worth paying the 'think of a number and double it' cost of an overpriced coffee.

Les Halles 75001 [4 B7]
M̲ *Châtelet-Les-Halles;* E̲ *RER direct to Châtelet-Les-Halles.*
For consumerist troglodytes, the Forum des Halles, on the site of the former wholesale meat and vegetable market, was in the 1970s and 1980s a peerless shopping mall: a glass cascade of underground streets, most with ample natural sunlight, home to boutiques, cinemas and a massive swimming pool. Emile Zola once described the old market area as '*Le ventre de Paris*' (the stomach of Paris). However, as the development snaked underground, from the massive métro hall towards the Louvre, it was to earn a new reputation. Recession hit the site which became known as the *trou* (the politest translation is 'pit', but the hole in the ground was referred to with almost anatomical contempt). Shops closed and the tourists stayed on street level. The whirligig of time has given the place a new life now, with those empty shops below the streets taken over by the young fashion designers of tomorrow, and the area breathes again. Touch-screen computer terminals on each level offer shopping and tourist information in both English and French, and the cinemas and swimming pool are as popular as ever.

Above ground, skateboarders and buskers show off around the Fontaine des Innocents, and cafés and restaurants animate on each street corner. The Pizza Pino is something of a late-night institution. Open until 05.00, its year-round heated terrace is an international melting pot. Showgirls turn heads when they turn up to share gargantuan pizzas at 3 in the morning, sparrows are so tame that they sit next to your plate casting covetous glances at your bread roll, and you can watch the people parade all night long.

Banana Café and l'Amazonial are among the fashionable bars and restaurants on rue Ste-Opportune and rue de la Ferronerie. Comfortable restaurants line the rue Pierre Lescot, and there are quieter corners at the foot of rue Montorgueil. All these and the takeaway counters between the red-light lures of rue St-Denis, make the area a prime refuelling stop between self-indulgences, at any hour. Even though each year brings the closure of another *bistrot* legend of the old days, the old market tradition of onion soup and snails at sunrise has not quite disappeared. As long as the giant snail hangs outside the Escargot Montorgueil, Les Halles will remain the place to end a night on the town. Since the 12th century this has been the city's main marketplace. The famous iron and glass market houses which were built in the second half of the 19th century have, alas, all disappeared to be replaced by box hedges and urban gardens. Yet something of the romance of the market remains. Where pretty, rich girls once flirted with *Gîtane*-puffing porters, you may still find those late-night *bistrots* where Parisians, rather than tourists, are happy to confuse dawn with dusk.

Jardins du Palais Royal pl du Palais-Royal, 75001 [3 K7]
Open dawn–dusk.
M̄ *Palais-Royal-Musée-du-Louvre;* Ē *RER to Châtelet-Les-Halles then métro 1 to Palais-Royal-Musée-du-Louvre.*
Recollect your emotions in the tranquillity of this living chessboard of a courtyard. Designed by Daniel Buren, the strange black and white columns are surreally soothing. Even the street entertainers are quiet here, as the place seems to attract an extraordinary number of mimes and living statues. The Palace, now the ministry of culture, acquired its royal title by accident, when the widow of Louis XIII decided that her apartment in the Louvre was too draughty, and took over Cardinal Richelieu's *pied à terre*.

Lido de Paris
116bis av des Champs Elysées, 78008; tel: 01 40 76 56 10; web: www.lido.fr [3 F6]
M̄ *George-V;* Ē *RER to Châtelet-Les-Halles the RER A to Charles-de-Gaulle-Etoile and walk down the avenue.*
See *Entertainment* (page 184) for more on the factored to the max, amplified parade of plumes, tiaras and powdered flesh.

Place de la Concorde [3 J6–7]
M̄ *Concorde;* Ē *RER to Châtelet-Les-Halles then métro 1 to Concorde.*
This is the largest square in Paris. Grandeur guaranteed at every turn. West is the Arc du Triomphe along the Champs Elysées; north the classical temple of La Madeleine at the head of the rue Royale; the Louvre and its gardens to the east; and south, across the Seine, the Assemblée Nationale. The sense of classical calm has not always pervaded. In 1792, revolutionaries not only removed the statue of Louis XV from the square but, with the aid of a guillotine, removed the heads of his successors, Louis XVI and Marie-Antoinette. The Luxor obelisk now stands in the centre, and all around the square is adorned with extravagant fountains and lamp posts. The best view belongs to a privileged few wealthy enough to take a suite at the **Crillon** hotel. The rest of us climb the steps of the Tuileries gardens and take our snapshots from the Orangerie and Jeu de Paume terraces.

Place de la Madeleine [3 J6]
M̄ *Madeleine;* Ē *RER E to Haussmann-St-Lazare, then line 12 or 8 to Madeleine.*
The Church of La Madeleine, with its 52 Corinthian columns, dominates the square like a classical Greek temple. Climb the steps if only to take in the fantastic view down rue Royale, home of Maxims and pricey shopping, across

place de la Concorde and over to the parliament building. Pass through the bronze doors, adorned with images of the Ten Commandments, to the cool and shadowy nave of the church where Camille Saint-Saëns composed some of his greatest works. Outside, a market selling flowers, cheeses and fresh fruit surrounds the half-price ticket kiosk, where theatre seats for today's shows are sold at 50% discount. Remember Paris theatres close on Monday, but have late matinee performances on Sunday afternoons.

Place Vendôme [3 J6]
M̲ *Opéra;* E̲ *RER to Châtelet-Les-Halles then RER A to Auber. Follow rue de la Paix to pl Vendôme.*
A masterpiece of regal splendour that defies the encroachments that time has imposed upon the rest of pre-Revolutionary Paris, the octagonal place Vendôme is an architectural jewel box designed by Jules Hardouin Mansart, who gave his name to the distinctive roofline windows. Originally conceived as a circle of buildings surrounding the mandatory equestrian statue of Louis XIV, the original place was built on the sites of a convent and the Duke of Vendôme's mansion, with the intention of bringing together the national library, academy, royal mint and embassies. Such was the plan. It never quite panned out. The place des Conquêtes became known as the place Louis de Grand. At the Revolution it was dubbed place des Picques and the royal statue was destroyed. The Austerlitz column at the centre of today's place Vendôme was commissioned by Napoléon and cast from recycled cannons captured on the battlefield. The present statue of the emperor is the fifth figure to stand atop the monument since its inauguration in 1810. The string of arches that line the square are home to the most celebrated jewellers in Paris. Here you will find Alesandre Réza, Van Cleef & Arpels, Boucheron and Chaumet, with Cartier and many others on the rue de la Paix.

Pont des Arts [4 A8]
M̲ *Pont-Neuf;* E̲ *RER to Châtelet-Les-Halles then métro 7 to Pont-Neuf. Walk along the quai du Louvre to the bridge.*
If you have come to Paris to hold hands, kiss or go down on one knee, choose your day, choose your hour, but choose this bridge. Paris fell in love with its first iron footbridge from the very day that it opened in 1803. Simplicity can be beautiful, and this pathway from the Louvre to the Left Bank is adorned with nothing but a chain of lamp-posts. Vistas of both banks are charming, but the views of the river itself are simply breathtaking. Important memories deserve the Pont des Arts. So come here to kiss goodnight by moonlight, or say yes without words. Never say goodbye, but promise to meet here in 25 years time. Better yet, don't say anything as the sun rises behind the spire and towers of Notre Dame, spilling honeyed light over the arches of Pont Neuf, bathing the tip of the Ile de la Cité in heavenly morning glory and turning the waters of the Seine into golden champagne. This is the moment when Paris achieves absolute perfection.

Samaritaine Building 2, 19 rue de la Monnaie, 75001; tel: 01 40 41 20 20 [4 A8]
Open Mon–Wed and Fri–Sat 09.30–19.00, Thu 09.30–22.00.
M̲ *Châtelet or Pont-Neuf;* E̲ *RER to Châtelet-Les-Halles then either cross rue de Rivoli at street level or take métro 7 to Pont Neuf for direct access to the store.*
The best free view in Paris is to found on the top floor of this department store (see page 53). The roof-terrace bar offers a 360-degree panorama, looking northwards towards Montmartre, across the river to Notre Dame and westwards to the Louvre. A marvellous opportunity to see so much statuary not always visible from street level. A mosaic viewing-table marks out monuments for easy identification.

Tuileries [3 J–K7]

M̄ *Tuileries or Concorde;* Ē *RER to Châtelet-Les-Halles then métro 1 to Tuileries or Concorde.*

This extravagant stretch of luxurious landscaping continues the grandest stroll in town, from the top of the Champs Elysées to the embrace of the Louvre. At the place de la Concorde entrance are two raised pavilions. The Orangerie is due to reopen in 2002 as the permanent home of Monet's Water Lilies. The Jeu de Paume tennis court, opposite, stages modern art shows. The shaded river-wing of the gardens has long been a noted station on the flirtation circuit. The main gardens were restored to a close approximation of their original 17th-century design to complement the expansion of the Louvre. Now statuary is scattered amongst the avenues of trees and ponds. From late June until August a funfair is held on the rue de Rivoli side of the Tuileries and in winter a skating rink offers a seasonal diversion.

WHAT TO SEE

Chapelle Expiatoire 29, rue Pasquier – square Louis XVI, 75008; tel: 01 42 65 35 80 [3 J5]

Open Wed only Apr–Sep 09.30–13.00, 14.00–18.00; Oct, Feb, Mar 10.00–13.00, 14.00–17.00; Nov–Jan 10.00–13.00, 14.00–16.00; closed holidays. Free.

M̄ *St-Augustin;* Ē *RER to Châtelet-Les-Halles then RER A to Auber. Walk west on bd Haussmann to rue Pasquier. Ignore street numbers, since the chapel is in the centre of the square.*

Essentially visited as a trump card for dinner-party boasting. Everybody knows from whence Marie-Antoinette departed for the guillotine (see *Conciergerie*, page 77), but who can tell you what happened to the leftovers? This discreet residential square in the shadow of St-Lazare was the cemetery for the 1,343 unfortunates who met the plunging blade on nearby place de la Concorde. By the steps leading to the little chapel you will see the tomb of Charlotte Corday, who famously stabbed Marat in his bath (a scene bloodily recreated at the Musée Grevin waxworks, see page 60). When the king's younger brother returned to Paris in 1815 and took the throne as Louis XVIII, he found the bodies of Marie-Antoinette and Louis XVI in the crypt (where the altar now stands) and had them removed to the royal family's tomb at St-Denis (see page 180). Fabulous allegorical marble monuments to the royal couple show them safely in the care of the angels.

Musée de Jacquemart-André 158 bd Haussmann, 75008; tel: 01 42 89 04 91 [3 G5]

Open 10.00–18.00.

M̄ *Saint-Philippe-du-Roule;* Ē *RER to Haussmann-St-Lazare then métro 9 to St-Philippe-du-Roslu. From av Herrick bear left on Rue de Courcault to bd Haussmann.*

Many museums have wonderful art collections, but few manage to convey the effect that the great works must have had when originally displayed in the homes of wealthy patrons of the arts. So do try to make time for this out of the way treat. A private collection behind the high walls of an elegant 19th-century home on the Boulevard Haussmann, the Musée Jacquemart André displays the many works acquired by banker Edouard André and his wife Nélie Jacquemart. Take advantage of the offer of an English-language audio guide in order to appreciate fully the house and its treasures. In the library, admire some splendid 17th-century Dutch masters, and enjoy the couple's fine selection of 18th-century French art from Boucher to Watteau. The Renaissance is equally well represented by Donatello and Botticelli. The artworks by no means eclipse the house itself. Many rooms are furnished as in the family's heyday, and the main staircase is quite splendid. Visit the tea room, if only to admire the genteel ladies in gloves and hats who take tea with their friends between appointments with dressmakers and hairdressers. Proof that the lifestyle you have just glimpsed has not yet quite disappeared.

Musée du Louvre cour Napoléon, 75001; tel: 01 40 20 51 51; web: www.louvre.fr [3 K7]
Open Thu–Sun 09.00–18.00, Mon 09.00–21.45 (some galleries closed after 18.00), Wed 09.00–21.45; closed Tue and holidays. ∈7 (46FF) reduced prices after 15.00 and Sundays. Free for under 18s.
M̲ *Palais-Royal-Musée-du-Louvre;* E̲ *RER to Châtelet-Les-Halles then métro 1 to Palais-Royal-Musée-du-Louvre.*
The past is not enough for the new Louvre. Ieoh Ming Pei's famous glass pyramid is but the tip of a volcano. When President Mitterand launched Grand Louvre, his imperial plan to revive a building that was museum, royal palace, government offices and landmark, he ignited an explosive combination of culture, consumerism and life itself that celebrates every passion in the city with enthusiasm and flair. From the métro, visitors pass through the malls and auditoria of the Carrousel du Louvre (see page 39) into the pyramid. From here they are thrust into daylight and the Cour Napoléon on a balletic sweep of staircases or the magnificent wheelchair lift. The main pyramid appears to float on a shimmering sheet of water, a huge prism reflecting its illustrious setting in a kaleidoscope of enduring architecture and inconstant skies.

Outside the Pyramid, within the open arms of the main wings of the museum, look ahead through the arc du Carrousel to the Tuileries gardens and the Champs Elysées beyond. Behind you is the clock tower of the Renaissance Cour Carrée, and to your right the terrace of Café Marly (see page 38).

It makes sense to take a moment in the open air in order to help you plan which part of the museum you wish to visit. Since the Louvre is in fact several world-class museums in one vast palace, do not even attempt to walk the full five miles of corridors and salons now open to the public, since the staterooms once occupied by government have been added to the public galleries.

From the ticket hall under the Pyramid you may enter via the Sully, Denon or Richelieu wings. Richelieu takes you, via two splendid sculpture galleries, past some truly wonderful Dutch masters. Vermeer, Jordaens, Van Dyck, Rubens and Breughel are amongst the vivid glories of the Low Countries. This alone would be worth the price of admission, but the first and second storeys also boast a comprehensive tour of French painting from the 14th century to the age of Ingres' classicism and heroic Delacroix.

For the Louvre as museum, rather than art gallery, choose to start your visit through the Sully entrance. The first treat here is the greatest architectural discovery made during the excavations of 1989, when the original 12th-century fortress, over which the present palace was built, was revealed. True romantics may walk, within touching distance, all the way round a true storybook *Boys Own* fantasy of a castle. On upper storeys the Egyptian collections not only present a comprehensive chronological view of the dynasties of the Pharaohs, but show scenes of daily life from baking bread to mummification. On Tuesdays, when the museum is officially closed, blind visitors are encouraged to touch these exhibits.

The most famous treasures of the Louvre are housed in the Denon wing. If time is of the essence, do not be daunted by the sheer size of the collection. If you have half an hour to spare, you may still see everything you need in order to hold your own at dinner parties, and do not need to queue for tickets. Simply take the lift to the first floor, turn into room 6 to see the *Mona Lisa*, safely behind bullet-proof glass, smaller and disconcertingly like the lid of a jigsaw box. Walk back, past the lift to the Drau staircase, at the top of which stands the dynamic statue representing the *Winged Victory of Samothrace*, and down to room 12 which is dominated by the ethereally beautiful *Venus de Milo*. Follow the exit signs for the métro.

Musée de la Publicité 107 rue de Rivoli, 75001; tel: 01 44 55 57 50; web: www.ucad.fr/pub [3 K7]
Open Tue, Thu, Fri, 11.00–18.00, Wed 11.00–21.00, Sat–Sun 10.00–18.00. ∈ 5.50 (35FF). Under 18s free.
M̄ *Palais-Royal-Musée-du-Louvre;* Ē *RER to Châtelet-Les-Halles then métro 1 to Palais-Royal-Musée-du-Louvre. Leave the station at street level. Museum entrance is on rue de Rivoli, just west of rue de Rohan.*
French advertising posters now rival the *Mona Lisa* and Robert Doisneau's *Kiss* as the essential décor for the world's *bistrots* and wine bars. At this museum, a branch of the *Union Centrale des Arts Décoratifs,* discover more about the artists, the products and the advertising campaigns that led to all those champagne, biscuit and cocoa advertisements reproduced as tins, wall-plaques, framed prints and postcards. Lautrec's *Moulin Rouge* ads may be seen here as well as Cassandre's legendary images of the 1920s and 1930s. Who could forget that imposing image of the bow of the *Normandie*? He was also responsible for so many striking railway and Pernod images of the period. A fascinating collection is augmented by a multimedia library of classic radio, TV and cinema commercials. Tickets are also valid for the *Musée de la Mode et du Textile* and the *Musée des Arts Décoratifs* at the same address.

Tour Jean-Sans-Peur 20 rue Etienne Marcel, 75002; tel: 01 40 26 20 28 [4 B7]
Open school holidays Tue–Sun 13.30–18.00; otherwise Wed, Sat, Sun 13.30–18.00. ∈ 4.50 (30FF).
M̄ *Etienne-Marcel;* Ē *Métro 4 to Etienne-Marcel. The tower is almost opposite the station.*
Just when you thought Paris had shown off all its great and noble buildings, the city opens the doors of another celebrated residence. Ignored for years, and tucked away in a school playground, this tower is all that remains of the townhouse of Jean Sans Peur, Duc de Bourgogne. Most of the house was demolished with the city walls, but this extravagant tower survived, and visitors can see some fascinating glimpses into the style and power of the Burgundian Empire. As you climb the steps, notice the ornate horticultural carvings on the vaulting, symbols of the wealth and might of Jean 'the fearless', whose notoriety was assured as much by the assassination of Louis, Duc d'Orléans, cousin of King Charles VI, as his own prowess in battle.

WHERE TO EAT
Café Mosaic 46 av George V, 75008; tel: 01 47 20 18 09 [3 F6]
M̄ *George-V;* Ē *RER to Châtelet-les-Halles then métro 1 to George-V. The Mosaic is just a few steps along from Fouquets.*
'Cabillaud à la fish and chips' for ∈ 19 (125FF) is on the *carte* for this discreet, stylish and ever so *8ème* restaurant at the Champs Elysées end of the av George V. The restaurant came into its own when both Fouquets and the George V closed for renovation at the same time. It was up to the newcomers to set the pace, and fish and chips was probably the ultimate symbol of turn-of-the-Millennium food fadiness. The dish had already arrived in Posh Paris thanks to

the best British restaurant in town, **Berties** (1 rue Délibes, 75016; tel: 01 44 34 54 34), and is served without newspaper. Mosaic takes its inspiration from the world cuisine available in the district, so Japanese references abound on the menu, and even traditional dishes are given a mouth-watering Asian spin: pigeon with peanut and kumquat, for instance. Chef Paul Pairet's globetrotting does not allow him to neglect his native cooking, so consider trying such homage to French regional cuisine as snails in marrow-bone. Pay ∈ 38 (250FF) à la carte and ∈ 31 (200FF) for the menu. The restaurant is housed in the former home of the Polignac family – favourites at court from Louis XIV to Charles X. Upstairs is the somewhat unassuming **Relais Carré d'Or** (see page 33)

Carré des Feuillants 14 rue Castiglione, 75001; tel: 01 42 86 82 82 [3 J6]
Closed Sat lunch, Sun.
M̄ *Tuileries;* Ē *RER to Châtelet-Les-Halles then métro 1 to Tuileries. West along the rue de Rivoli, turn right into rue de Castiglione towards place Vendôme.*
What happens to great country cooking when it grows up and enters the rarified world of riches and beauty? Come here and witness the alchemy for yourself. The simple flavours of Gascony that Alain Dutournier first served the city from his cosy *bistrot* in the Deaumesnil district (see **Le Trou Gascon**, page 107), are transformed into a subtle gastronomic sensation. Those farmyard traditions that won the *Landais* chef such acclaim are refined into sophisticated ideals in this former convent. The striking glass-enclosed cloister of the Castiglione arcade, off the place Vendôme, is the perfect setting for food that has given Dutournier a brace of Michelin stars. If the prospect of *barigoule de poivrades et d'escargots (petits gris escargots* presented with violet artichokes), *daube de taureau aux premiers cèpes*, and *figues fraîches à la crème de noix et glace à la fourme d'Ambert* set your heart racing in anticipation, then prepare to pay nearly ∈ 140 (900FF) for the multi-course experience. Lunch at ∈ 54 (360FF) is a more affordable entrée into the glittering other world of fine dining. If, however, your mouth waters but your wallet shudders, take the métro or taxi across town to the 12th *arrondissement*, where Mme Dutournier keeps the spirit of the family's original southwest country dining room alive for the rest of us.

Les Cartes Postales 7 rue Gomboust, 75001; tel: 01 42 61 23 40 [3 K6]
Closed Sat lunch, Sun.
M̄ *Pyramides;* Ē *RER to Châtelet-Les-Halles then métro 14 to Pyramides. Walk north on av de l'Opéra. At the junction with rue St-Roch turn left into rue Gombost.*
The vogue for Japanese cuisine in the early 1990s gave Paris a much-needed shock and woke the city to the truth that there is more to cuisine than *confit de canard*. Many established chefs took lessons from the newcomers. Of the rising sons of the era, one of the few remaining in the Marché St-Honoré area is M Watanabe, whose establishment has hardly changed from my first visit nearly a decade ago. Décor is kept to the absolute minimum, just a few framed art postcards on the wall. The original rules apply in the kitchen: only the freshest, and only the best. Whether langoustine or red meat, the food will be light, subtle and elegant. Use the same adjectives for the service. A lunch menu of ∈ 22 (135FF) is worth considering; otherwise budget around ∈ 60 (400FF). Serviceable wine list, excellent *carte*.

Chez Denise – la Tour de Montlhery 5 rue des Prouvaires, 75001; tel: 01 42 36 21 42 [4 A7]
Closed Sat, Sun, 14 July–15 Aug.
M̄ *Châtelet;* Ē *RER to Châtelet-Les-Halles. Leave the station at rue Berger. Follow the road westwards to turn left on to rue des Prouvaires.*

Tourists are unimpressed by the ordinary-seeming *bistrot* behind Les Halles. They head off to focus-group-inspired eateries and miss out on the basic country *pâté*, *steak-frites* and chocolate mousse meals at any time of the night. *Chez* Denise Benariac, and husband Jacques, the welcome is low-key working-class Parisian *bistrot* – jugs full of table wine, noisy chatter, and swift-moving waiters negotiating the shortest route between the tables and the kitchen.

Chez la Vieille Adrienne 37 rue de l'Arbre-Sec, 75001; tel: 01 42 60 15 78 [4 A7] Closed Sat, Sun, Aug.
M̄ *Louvre-Rivoli;* Ē *RER to Châtelet-Les-Halles then métro 1 to Louvre-Rivoli. Follow rue de Rivoli eastwards and turn left on to the rue de l'Arbre-Sec.*
Adrienne herself is not as *vieille* as all that, but her cuisine comes from a venerable lineage of *Lyonnais* meats, family recipes and classic winter warmers. We are talking rural comfort foods, from plates of *maman's* stews to chunks of hearty *terrine*. Of note, the spicy glazed *jarret du porc* and little known country wines. Fixed price meals at €23 (150FF), otherwise budget double. Be warned, the chairs get stacked on the tables from 21.30, so come early or save this one for lunch.

l'Ecluse 15 place de la Madeleine, 75008; tel: 01 42 65 34 69 [3 J6]
M̄ *Madeleine;* Ē *RER E to Haussmann-St-Lazare then métro 12 to Madeleine.*
Fight the temptations of Fauchon, resist the olfactory overdose of the cheese market, and defer the €185 (1,200FF) bill from neighbour Alain Senderens, purveyor of perfect *foie gras* at **Lucas Carton**. A lesser-known treat on place de la Madeleine is l'Ecluse. The wine bar is a living tribute to the *crus* of Bordeaux, listing fine wines by the bottle, half bottle, big glass and little glass. The menu helpfully suggests the perfect tipple for every dish. If you choose the tarragon-laced *Onglet de Veau* with its silky smooth buttered spinach accompaniment you will be counselled towards '*un St-Emilion ou un Pommerol, mais un château de la Rive Droit surement'*. There is even a different recommendation for each cheese, Maroilles requiring nothing less than a Margaux. I was introduced to the place by a colleague with an incurably sweet tooth. For her, the wine list is just a front for pigging out on the *gâteau de chocolat 'comme au début'*. Other branches include the **Quai des Grands Augustins** near St-Michel in the 6eme. Budget €30 (200FF) plus drinks.

L'Entrecôte de Paris 29 rue Marignan, 75008; tel: 01 42 25 28 60 [3 G6]
M̄ *Franklin D Roosevelt;* Ē *RER to Châtelet-Les-Halles then métro 1 to Franklin D Roosevelt. At the Pizza Pino restaurant turn into rue Marignan.*
A modest institution for a quarter of a century, l'Entrecôte has done the unthinkable. It now offers a choice of main courses. In its heyday, the Entrecote's unique attraction was its legendary menu, a culinary Hobson's choice of just one starter and a single main course. The first course a light green salad, the main course the famous *entrecôte* steak prepared at the table in its delicious sauce – the exact recipe for which is the restaurant's closely guarded secret. Part of the fun of the meal is analysing the aromatic speciality and guessing at its constituents. The steak is served with *pommes allumettes à volonté* to mop up the delicious sauce. There are now four other items on the menu – but the €13 (88FF) classic meal still has pride of place. Wines are still around the €15 (100FF) mark and desserts under €6 (40FF). Last orders after midnight. Loss of nerve in augmenting the menu is balanced by reliability and value.

La Fermette Marboeuf 5 rue Marboeuf, 75008; tel: 01 53 23 08 00 [3 F6]
M̄ *Alma-Marceau;* Ē *RER E to Haussmann-St-Lazare then métro 12 to Alma-Marceau. On av George V take second right to rue Marboeuf.*
Bienvenue to the *Belle Epoque* winter garden – a sleeping beauty that lay dormant

and unknown for most of the century until, in 1978, builders accidentally knocked through the formica walls of a naff caff to discover a treasure trove of art nouveau ceramics, columns and stained glass. In 1982 the owners painstakingly transferred 5,000 stained-glass panes one by one from a country home in the Parisian suburbs into what is now the exquisite back room, and the following year the place was classified as a national monument, whose exotic panels of pastoral scenes are pretty well unique. Happily chef Gilbert Isaac is more than equal to the setting and his brasserie menu of simple stalwarts is well presented, and served with grace and flair by a staff unusually friendly for such a touristic quarter. Whether *fruits de mer* or today's twist in a barnyard tail, the market fresh menu is always good value at € 25 (170FF), and à la carte should set you back not much more than € 46 (300FF) including wine from the well-chosen and fairly priced cellar.

Le Grand Vefour 17 rue du Beaujolais, 75001; tel: 01 42 96 56 27 [4 A6] Closed Aug, Sat lunch, and Sun.
M̄ *Palais-Royal-Musée-du-Louvre;* Ē *RER to Châtelet-Les-Halles then métro 1 to Palais-Royal-Musée-du-Louvre. From pl du Palais Royal take rue de Valois, turning left into rue du Beaujolais.*
At around € 105 (700FF) a head this is not a place for a casual snack, but a unique dining experience *quand même*. Until 1820 it was known as the Café de Chartres. Established in the heart of the establishment, practically within the Palais Royal itself, it has always been a haunt of the greats. You may ask to be seated at the favourite table of Napoléon, Colette or Victor Hugo. Décor is sumptuous, opulent and officially classified as a national treasure. The wine cellar is amongst the greatest in the world and Guy Martin's cuisine faultless. Book a generation in advance and you might be able to enjoy lunch for € 53 (350FF) (otherwise budget ever so much more including wine.)

A la Grille St-Honoré 15 pl du Marché St-Honoré, 75001; tel: 01 42 61 00 93 [3 K6]
Closed Sun, Mon, Aug.
M̄ *Tuileries;* Ē *RER to Châtelet-Les-Halles then métro 1 to Tuileries. Rue de 29 Juillet towards the place du Marché St-Honoré.*
La Grille has been an institution since the days before the square became foodie cool. The place du Marché St-Honoré was conceived as posh Paris' response to the newly fashionable Les Halles, way back when the central shopping complex was first opened. An ugly concrete multi-storey car park dominated the square between the rue St-Honoré and place Vendôme. Now, at long last, the promised revamp has happened and the blockhouse has been replaced by a magnificent 21st-century response to the boulevard quarter's 19th-century glazed arcades. A glass-walled, glass-roofed triumph from Barcelona architect Ricardo Bofill, it magnifies the night sky and reflects the twinkling lights of the latest restaurants and pavement terraces. There has always been a sense of *cuisine du moment* about the square, so many restaurants change with the fashions. I mourn the small-town genius of Serge Granger who served St-Malo's finest catch and took a nightly lap of honour around the tables. Not to mention the long-gone ultra-cool brasserie where we dined next to a swarthy *Gauloise*-puffing priest who looked like a mariner from the mind of Genet (we strongly suspected tattoos under the cloth). One survivor of the old days is the Grille. So I raise my glass to Monsieur and Madame Speyer for their staying power. Sometimes tables are scattered on the pavement outside the eponymous barred windows; always the dining room is packed. Some come back for the wood-pigeon with wild mushrooms, others for crustacean inventiveness – a crab *bavarois* is the house speciality – but all return time and again for the warm

welcome from hostess Nicole with husband Jean in the kitchen. This is a winning team: French rather than Parisian! Good wine selection and a menu from under ∈ 31 (200FF); à la carte around ∈ 15 (100FF) more.

Gros Minet 1 rue des Prouvaires, 75001; tel: 01 42 33 02 62 [4 A7]
Closed Sun, Sat lunch, Mon lunch.
M̄ *Châtelet-Les-Halles;* Ē *RER to Châtelet-Les-Halles. Leave the station at rue Berger. Follow the road westwards to turn left on to rue des Prouvaires.*
You know, I almost forgot to include this fat kitten in the guide. It has been part of my Paris furniture for so long now, I've rather taken it for granted. It was only when mourning the passing of the old market café, Les Deux Saules (where generations had savoured onion soup and sausages) under the juggernaut of fast food, that I recalled that Gros Minet was still defiantly un-foodie, un-chic and under-priced on the other side of the forum. A couple of doors from *Chez Denise*, and the epitome of cheap eats in Les Halles, this dotty old market porters' bar is still churning out good basic meals for under ∈ 15 (100FF). Kitsch spare-bedroom décor with whiskey terriers, Hallmark card kittens and political cartoons covering any wall space that has not been taken by the owner's collection of rugby souvenirs and a selection of caps that must surely be trophies (gendarme caps and matelot berets amongst the scalps). A hearty welcome to all diving into the ∈ 12 (78FF) lunch and ∈ 14 (95FF) menus of *magret, foie* and *volaille* and hefty great big salads.

Meurice 228 rue de Rivoli, 75001; tel: 01 44 58 10 10; web: www.meuricehotel.com [3 J7]
M̄ *Tuileries;* Ē *RER to Châtelet-Les-Halles then métro 1 to Tuileries.*
At the restaurant of the recently restored hotel of the same name, Burgundian chef Marc Marchand reigns supreme. His talent, recognised by the coveted Michelin star, has developed with the restaurant and long-time diners have been delighted to watch his maturity from salad days of overworked truffles and flour-and-water *sorbets* to cutting edge creativity. The Marchand style blends new ideas, from the young talent with which he likes to surround himself, with the influences of his Colette-country grandmothers. Lobster dishes now packed with wild vegetables, herbs and chanterelles, and the simpler desserts include such treats as autumn fruits roasted in salted butter and nuts. The Meurice style is reassuringly classy: a sparkle of crystal and silverware; a generosity of cut flowers; young, keen staff darting from table to table; and music from a pianist whose hands are the feet of Fred Astaire, yet whose face has the discretion of a deputy chairman of a modest insurance company. Menus from ∈ 54 (360FF) at lunch, and ∈ 92-145 (600—950FF) at all times. À la carte around ∈ 92 (600FF).

Au Pied de Cochon 6 rue Coquillière, 75001; tel: 01 40 13 77 00 [4 A–B7]
M̄ *Les-Halles;* Ē *RER to Châtelet-Les-Halles (exit rue Rambuteau). Walk left on rue Rambuteau to rue Coquillière.*
The first and last of the great Les Halles dawn-farewell favourites from the days of the old market, this is where Cinderellas go when they've pumpkin stains on their dresses. Most Parisians, at some stage in their lives, will build their own memory of starting or finishing their day Au Pied de Cochon. Having danced the night away, and unwilling to return home to the smell of fresh-baked croissants, this is where they will gorge on some of the best onion soup in town and a plateful of the title dish: grilled pig's trotter in *bearnaise* sauce. In truth, the place has become a victim of its own success. All the major guidebooks classify it as 'typically Parisian'- which is true enough, but only when all the tourists have

returned to their hotels, making way for the genuine locals. If you do decide to go before three in the morning you will have to book. Be warned. It is noisy and chaotic until the 02.30 night buses have left nearby avenue Victoria. Even if you have not been dancing, the place has a certain magic in summer when you step outside the door to the unique harmonies of the dawn chorus and knife-grinders. Allow € 46 (300FF) à la carte, € 28 (180FF) for the menu. Open 24 hours a day, even on Christmas Day!

Spoon 14 rue de Marignan, 75008; tel: 01 40 76 34 44; web: www.spoon.tm.fr [3 G6]
Closed Sat, Sun, Aug.
M̲ *Franklin-D-Roosevelt;* E̲ *RER to Châtelet-Les-Halles then métro 1 to Franknli-D-Roosevelt. At the Pizza Pino restaurant turn into rue Marignan.*
Welcome to the brave new world of food. Alain Ducasse has invented *cuisine du moment,* where every single diner has a unique experience. The spoon concept has been exported to London's Sanderson Hotel, but this is where it started. The room is so hip it's pelvic, and the contemporary décor mid-way between maritime and dentistry – for this is a spoon with a cutting edge. Ducasse is the only man alive with six – count 'em, six – Michelin rosettes, so no one would have expected him to take the easy option joining the annexe circuit. Therefore, when he redefined the concept of the restaurant menu, Paris stopped, looked and listened. Whether tucked away in a wooden booth or exposed amid the pastel shades of the main dining area, diners spend the first 15 minutes of their visit studying hard. For the Spoon menu takes to heart the Ducasse reputation for trusting the quality of his ingredients. Choose your fish or poultry, choose your cooking style (steam, spit roast, wok or grill perhaps), select your sauce, consider the ideal vegetable accompaniment and then watch the kitchen prepare your bespoke luncheon in minutes. Obviously there are suggested house classics: perhaps candied pumpkin in pumpkin soup or lobster with mango chutney. I admit to being seduced by the *morue mantecato* topped with soft boiled egg, and a friend who is severely vegan raved for ages over a dish of wheat kernels and pulses prepared with sea salt, wine vinegar and olive oil. The favourite with the many bright young Parisians working in the fashion houses of the area appears to be the house take on a BLT. The varied tableware particularly struck us both, different styles at each place, and the choice of conventional cutlery or chopsticks. Solitary lunchers were offered international magazines, and very few diners, solo or otherwise, could resist using the jotters and notebooks on the table for doodling and note making. All these extras, including the free coffee refill, might have been a sign of style way over and above substance. The joy of Spoon is that the substance of the cuisine is so much more than merely stylish. Though Ducasse himself is more likely to be found in his new flagship at the plaza Athénée, where diners happily pay € 220 (1,450FF) for the most expensive menu, here, just off the Champs Elysées, his disciples offer his ideals on a plate for around € 46 (300FF).

Tante Louise 41 rue Boissy d'Anglas, 75008; tel: 01 42 65 06 85; web: www.bernard-loiseau.com [3 J6]
Closed Sat lunch, Sun, Aug, Christmas.
M̲ *Madeleine;* E̲ *RER E to Haussmann-St-Lazare then métro 12 to Madeleine. Cross the square and walk a few yards along the rue Boissy d'Anglas towards place de la Concorde.*
For all the media darlings of the capital, hard-core foodies are only too well aware that the truly great chefs are to be found miles and miles away from the big city.

The very best has now joined the annexe culture, installing his protegés in the better quarters of the capital. Bernard Loiseau, one of the fathers of great modern French cuisine, draws the good and the greedy to Saulieu in Burgundy where his **Côte d'Or** restaurant is chuffed with three Michelin stars and 19 G&M toques at the last count. A short while ago Loiseau worked his magic on the bourgeois lunchery on the Boissy d'Anglas between the Crillon and Lucas Carton, and brought a little bit of Burgundy to Paris. The 1930s décor is a welcome in itself, with stained-glass scenes of rural life on the mezzanine and the portrait of the aunt herself by the door. A well-chosen front of house team of all ages has experience ranging from the parent restaurant to the Frères Roux in the UK. Classic dishes include the *oeufs en meurette à la bourgignonne* – poached eggs in wine with bacon – and the celebrated house sole presented on a *lit* of *duxelles* mushrooms with a secret seafood sauce. A *ragoût* of *escargots* and fungi sends shivers through the cheeks and a piquant chilled tomato soup, sprinkled with filings of onion, cucumber and pepper, is served with croutons of goat's cheese and chives. Vegetables are an object lesson in texture and flavour and the dessert surprise for me is the fabulous *sorbet* duo of *fromage blanc* with lemon-laced chocolate, lighter than spring-water. The wine list is an *hommage* to the greats of Burgundy and the distinctive sharp Chardonnay flavour complements the regional flavours on the plate. The dining room of choice for lean and thrusting captains of industry, tailored St-Honoré types and inveterate portly lunchers with their nipped, tucked and liposucked wives in town for meetings and shopping, all of whom may be found established in the comfortable carvers. You might easily pay upwards of € 50–70 (325–450FF), but a € 30 (195FF)) menu can keep the occasion within budget. Loiseau has now opened two more auntie outposts in Paris (**Margueritte** and **Jeanne**).

Aux Trois Petits Cochons 31 rue Tiquetonne, 75002; tel: 01 42 33 39 69 [4 B7] M̲ *Etienne-Marcel;* E̲ *Métro 4 to Etienne-Marcel. Walk west on rue Etienne Marcel, turn right into rue Française, then left on rue Tiquetonne.*
Small, flamboyant, and often inventive little restaurant in the newly fashionable Montorgueil district. (See page 34.)

Yvan 1 bis rue Jean-Mermoz, 75008; tel: 01 43 59 18 40 [3 G6]
Closed Sat lunch, Sun.
M̲ *Franklin-D-Roosevelt;* E̲ *RER to Châtelet-Les-Halles then métro 1 to Franklin-D-Roosevelt. Rue Jean-Mermoz is just north of the Rond Point.*
With his sun-bleached blond looks, Yvan Zaplatilek could be the darling of the gossip columns and nightclub circuit on a teeth-and-tan basis alone. However, the restaurateur with a taste for glamour and parties runs a clutch of fab eateries that just seem to get better. His new *bistrot* in Paris and his essential see-and-be-seen address in St-Tropez may be the current media favourites, but this, his original Champs Elysées dining room, with its extravagant floral displays and bucket chairs, is one of the best gastro-bargains of the quarter. Yvan, who couldn't rest on his laurels if you tied him to a bay tree, is one of the best chefs to come out of Belgium for many a *moule* and his inventiveness graces five set-price menus ranging from a great value € 28 (180FF) to the *dégustation* at around € 48 (320FF). The Belgian influence and his own imagination may be tasted in the *strudel de jeune cochon* with green cabbage laced with beer. Even potentially basic dishes are given a special twist from the herb garden and spice jar. Service is confident and professional. Value for money comes as standard. Wit and originality, matched with the deftest of light touches, forces the world of good food to take this party boy very seriously indeed.

WHAT TO BUY

Carrousel du Louvre 99 rue de Rivoli, 75001; tel: 01 43 16 47 15 [3 K7]
Open Tue–Sun 11.00–20.00.
M̄ *Palais-Royal-Musée du Louvre;* Ē *RER to Châtelet-Les-Halles then métro 1 to Palais-Royal-Musée du Louvre.*
Shopping mall linking the Louvre with its métro station (see page 39).

Le Denicheur see page 34.

Drugstore Publicis 131 av des Champs Elysées, 75008; tel: 01 44 43 79 00 [3 F5]
Open 10.00–02.00.
M̄ *Charles-de-Gaulle-Etoile;* Ē *RER to Châtelet-Les-Halles then RER A to Charles-de-Gaulle-Etoile.*
Almost the last of what was once a Paris institution, the Drugstore on the Etoile tip of the Champs Elysées is a strange place. To sit here in the small hours is rather like whiling away a flight delay at some far-flung duty free shop. This drugstore, like its distant cousin at St-Germain, is part café-bar, part mini-mall. Here you can pick up a newspaper, toothbrush, Walkman and sounds-of-the-70s-style cassette at half-past one in the morning, when even the late stores on the Champs Elysées have long shut up shop.

Fauchon 30 pl de la Madeleine, 75008 [3 J6]
M̄ *Madeleine;* Ē *RER E to Haussmann-St-Lazare then métro 12 to Madeleine.*
If Fauchon is a grocer's shop, then Harrods Food Hall is a convenience store. For food as souvenirs you could hardly do better than lose yourself amongst the teas and coffees, jars of preserved fruits and trays of wonderfully expensive chocolates.

FNAC 74 av des Champs Elysées, 75008; tel: 01 53 53 64 64 [3 F6]
Open Mon–Sat 10.00–24.00.
M̄ *Georges V;* Ē *RER to Châtelet-Les-Halles then métro 1 to Georges V and walk down the left side of the street.*
The main branch may be in Les Halles, and the newest at Montparnasse, but FNAC Champs Elysées belongs to the shopping-all-hours brigade of the avenue. As usual, there are the gently lit disc racks for music lovers, books and mags for the homesick traveller and the full range of hi-fi, photographic and techno gadgets. Book tickets for concerts and events on site.

Galignani 224 rue de Rivoli, 75001; tel: 01 42 60 76 07 [3 J7]
Open 10.00–19.00.
M̄ *Tuileries;* Ē *RER to Châteler-Les-Halles then métro 1 to Tuileries.*
Old-style international bookshop which retains all the courtesies of the greater days of 'travelling through'. Art books, guidebooks, and good literature in English and French.

Harpo 19 rue de Turbigo, 75002; tel: 01 40 26 10 03; web: www.harpo-paris.com [4 B7]
Open Mon–Sat 10.00–18.30.
M̄ *Etienne Marcel;* Ē *Métro 4 to Etienne Marcel.*
Ethnic jewellery, paintings and artefacts by Native American tribes are sold in this stylish boutique. Navajo pots from €300 (2,000FF) and beautiful Zuni necklaces for around €750 (5,000FF). Over the road, **Cowboy Dream** sells 'authentic' Western gear should you wish to take the theme any further.

Louvre des Antiquaires 2 pl du Palais Royale, 75001; tel: 01 42 97 27 00 [3 K7]
Open Tue–Sun 11.00–19.00. Closed Sun in Jul and Aug.
M̄ *Palais-Royal-Musée-du-Louvre.*

Fine art and antiques-dealing complex. Top price tags for top of the range furniture and *objets d'art*. In an environment designed to inhibit bartering, only hardened traders manage to hammer down prices.

Madelios 23 bd de la Madeleine, 75001; tel: 01 53 45 00 00 [3 J6]
M̄ *Madeleine;* Ē *RER E to Haussmann-St-Lazare then métro 12 to Madeleine.*
Breaking through the last great gender stereotype, *bienvenue* to Paris' only shopping mall for men. 'For men' is usually a euphemism, rather as 'adult content' often translates as 'adolescent fantasy'. Here, however, Madelios is precisely what it declares itself to be, a shopping mall with dozens of stores selling clothes, accessories and toiletries for men only. Serious spenders may be invited to the VIP lounge. The centre even provides personal shoppers for men like me who wouldn't know a clashing tie if it strangled them and who should not be allowed anywhere near an item of clothing that has not been vetted by a woman-who-knows. Male beauty salons and spas are also available for soothing aftercare to the culture shock.

Métro & Bus Paris RER interchange hall [4 B7]
Open Mon–Fri 10.30–19.30.
M̄ *Châtelet-Les-Halles;* Ē *RER to Châtelet-Les-Halles.*
Among the perfume counters, bookshops and coffee stands in the main interchange hall of the station, this shop for transport buffs sells souvenirs of the métro. Buy badges, mugs and boxer-shorts with maps on, or begin some serious research with the studious tomes on transport and social history.

Monoprix 52 av des Champs Elysées, 75008; tel: 01 53 77 65 65 [3 G6]
Open Mon–Sat 10.00–24.00.
M̄ *Franklin-D-Roosevelt;* Ē *RER to Châtelet-Les-Halles then métro 1 to Franklin-D-Roosevelt. The shop is on the ground floor of the Virgin Megastore building.*
Monoprix and Prisunic supermarkets are to be found across the city, but this branch stays open until midnight. For everyday shopping at sensible prices, come here for toiletries, tights, hairbrushes and other essentials. Downstairs is a modest-sized food hall ideal for picking up a large bottle of mineral water for just a few cents rather than paying hotel minibar prices.

Paris Musées Forum des Halles, 1 rue Pierre Lescot, 75001; tel: 01 40 26 56 65 [4 B7]
Open 11.00–19.00.
M̄ *Les-Halles;* Ē *RER to Châtelet-Les-Halles (exit Forum des Halles). Take the escalator to rue Pierre Lescot, the shop is on your left.*
Why pay to visit a museum if you only want to visit the shop? All the best gifts from the city collections (not the national ones) are sold here, from the catalogues, postcards and headscarves to copies of classic exhibits. Mock Roman remains are best left on the shelf, but the reproduction wine glasses, as seen at George Sand's salon (see page 161), and some stylish jewellery from the Modern Art Museum are genuinely classy souvenirs.

Rue de Rivoli [3 J7–4 C8]
M̄ *Louvre-Rivoli, Palais-Royale-Musée-du-Louvre, Tuileries or Concorde;* Ē *RER to Châtelet-Les-Halles then use line 1 between Louvre-Rivoli and Concorde.*
In the noonday sun, the Napoleonic arcades of the rue de Rivoli alongside the Louvre offer the chance of shaded window shopping. Ninety per cent of shops sell overpriced day-glo tee-shirts and horrid Eiffel Tower paperweights, but a few discreet tailors and lace merchants may be found here. Galignani was the first

English-language bookshop on the Continent, and has old-fashioned charm and courteous service. WH Smith along the road is also useful for stocking up on extra paperbacks and magazines. I once criss-crossed the country chasing summer festivals and found Smith's the perfect staging post for literary refuelling between trains. Both these bookstores also sell US editions of titles not stocked in the UK (and vice versa). If you recall the lovely tea-room at Smith's, the bad news is that it has closed down, but do try Angelina and the Hôtel Meurice for afternoon tea as an art form. The further end of the rue de Rivoli is a more bustling high street, with department stores and international chain stores packing the pavements.

Samaritaine rue de Rivoli or quai du Louvre, 75001; tel: 01 40 41 20 20 [4 A8] Open Mon–Wed and Fri–Sat 09.30–19.00, Thu 09.30–22.00.
M̄ *Châtelet or Pont-Neuf;* Ē *RER to Châtelet-Les-Halles then either cross rue de Rivoli at street level or take métro 7 to Pont-Neuf for direct access to the store.*
With Printemps and Galeries Lafayette holding a virtual monopoly of tourist spending on the Grands Boulevards, most visitors ignore this sprawling department store between the rue de Rivoli and the river. The lack of marketing savvy actually contributes to the charm of the place. Great art nouveau staircases, metalwork and glass, which elsewhere might have been restored to the point of artificiality, are almost hidden behind the piles of stock in this charmingly disorganised emporium. Founded by Ernest Cognacq, whose art museum is one of the hidden treats of the Marais (see page 79), the shop is named after the Samaritaine pump under the Pont Neuf which used to supply the Louvre with water from the Seine. The trading floors are spread through a number of buildings. Visit shop 2 for its amazing rooftop views (see page 41).

Virgin Mégastore 52–60 av des Champs Elysées, 75008; tel: 01 49 53 50 00 [3 G6] Open Mon–Sat 10.00–24.00.
M̄ *Franklin-D-Roosevelt;* Ē *RER to Châtelet-Les-Halles then métro 1 to Franklin-D-Roosevelt.*
FNAC (see above) is such an institution amongst the image-conscious lifestyle quality controllers, that it was something of a gamble for Virgin to threaten its supremacy on the hallowed avenue itself. However, the Branson concept was an instant success. Virgin is now the best-known corner site on the strip, and is the barometer of the Champs Elysées, positively bustling until midnight. One of the most comprehensive music ranges in the city.

Grands Boulevards

Each of us has our own private Paris, and all our cities of the Right Bank meet at the Grands Boulevards. Here the hedonists and Bohemians of Clichy find respectability, and the brokers and bankers of the Bourse may let their hair down. The opera house gives the boulevards a raffish air, the art and antiques dealers above the Palais Royal woo potential clients with another bottle of wine over lunch, and the prospect or memory of the theatres provide a delicious *frisson* of anticipation or recollection.

What today we know as the Grands Boulevards were the original city walls. Two old city gates remain from the fortifications. The Porte St-Denis and Porte St-Martin were given a new century wash and brush up and now gleam proprietarily over their eponymous streets and *faubourgs* (those once suburban extensions of the lanes beyond the walls). In the tide of Napoleonic exuberance, Baron Haussmann orchestrated the transformation of the walls into wide thoroughfares, where Parisians would take the air, strolling, sitting, and scanning their neighbours.

In time, theatres opened along the boulevards and, even today, they remain the southern strip of orthodox theatreland. This is where boulevard comedy found its name and its staunchest audiences. Those farces, drawing-room comedies and star vehicles still pull in the crowds every night, and Sunday afternoon. Side streets around the ostentatious church of Trinité are home to big-budget Broadway musicals, and at the less fashionable east end (by place République) were once the circuses. The western boulevards lead to the Opéra Garnier.

The 20th century brought even bigger stars to the boulevards, when Hollywood landed on the widest sidewalks. Dozens of billboards above plate-glass doorways announce the blockbuster *du jour* and the heartthrob *du moment*. Biggest and best of all, the dome of the Grand Rex cinema still attracts flocks of celebrities whenever the searchlights illuminate the sky for a major première. Bonne Nouvelle métro station is undergoing a tinsel town makeover with images from the movies inspiring the platform décor. Showbusiness exists in the very street signs. The boulevard des Italiens gets its name not from an early desire to promote a united Europe (France's first plan for a non-federal Europe was a unilateral decision by Napoléon), but from an incessant stream of popular Italian operetta flowing from the Opéra Comique.

Where music played, dandies were made: flamboyant fashions were constantly paraded along the boulevards, as Haussmann's dramatic sweep through the city, from the place de l'Opéra to the place de la République, became the place to be seen. To be honest, today's true dandies play elsewhere. They would find little inspiration in the conventional brasseries, American chain restaurants and a few modest shirt shops that line the streets. In the evenings, tables fill with theatregoers, and nightclubs and fashionable discothèques prepare to open their doors at midnight. Then the Grands Boulevards once more bring a touch of excitement to a district whose daywear is the sober suit appropriate to the Banque de France and the stock exchange.

The true character of the district is to be found behind the boulevards. The delightful covered arcades are worth an afternoon's indulgence in their own right (see page 58). In the streets to the south are simple *bistrots* of a type your grandparents would remember, and several contemporary annexe-kitchens from the big name chefs of the posher districts. Much of the cultural heritage of the hinterland has been preserved, even if the small hotel converted from Toulouse Lautrec's former home has now been hammered through to its neighbour's and redeveloped as standard three-star accommodation.

Take the lively streets north past bazaars and butchers to climb the hill towards the fleshpots of Pigalle, or find your delights closer to the boulevards near the junction with the faubourg Montmartre. This is, after all, a district dedicated to pleasure, however simple. By Grands Boulevards métro station, the city's only 24-hour news kiosk is crucial for solitary diners who, like me, cannot endure a late-night snack without a magazine propped against the cruet.

Shopping is more sensible here than in the pricey St-Honoré and Champs Elysées districts, and the flighty boutiques of Les Halles and the Marais. Boulevard Haussmann, with Galeries Lafayette and Printemps spread through multiple buildings and along pavement traders, shared it glories with Marks & Spencer, until the notorious night of the short emails, when all staff in continental branches of the British company were dismissed by electronic memo. This led to the April revolution when Prime Minister Lionel Jospin spoke for the nation and condemned perfidious Albion for stealing the very scones and Stilton from the mouths of the masses. Crowds lined the boulevards to sign books of condolence in memory of lost lingerie and *salmon en croute perdu*.

Not as louche as Montmartre, nor as elegant as the west; not as trendy as the east, nor as philosophical as the Left Bank, the Grands Boulevards have showbiz and shopping. But nobody said that sensible people are not allowed to have fun…

WHERE TO STAY

Des Arts 7 Cité Bergère, 75009; tel: 01 42 46 73 30 [4 A6]
<u>M</u> *Grands Boulevards;* <u>E</u> *Métro 4 to Strasbourg-St-Denis, then lines 8 or 9 to Grands Boulevards.*
La Cité Bergère is a particular novelty of the quarter. A charming little street off the rues Bergère and fbg Montmartre, with narrow archways leading to rows of two- and three-star hotels. All have grand frontages and most are nicely dated – rather than knowingly period – in style, carpets sometimes a little thin, light

bulbs with that low wattage exclusive to French hotels. All in all, exactly what one remembers from early first visits to France. The bonus of a night or two in this street is the tranquillity. No traffic in the district of nightclubs and all-night news-stands. My personal choice of the parade is the **Hôtel des Arts**, a simple, family-run two-star with a cheery welcome, brighter lighting, a liberal display of museum and theatre posters and a tumble of flowers and plants at the entrance. Room rates have hardly risen since my first visit in 1992, €53–51 (360–400FF). Great value. And surely it couldn't have been the same parrot jabbering away with the flow of visitors through the bustling reception? Rooms are surprisingly spacious and top floor garrets have charm. The neighbouring three-star hotels are more tourist class despite their room rates topping €76 (500FF): the **Victoria** at number 2bis (tel: 01 47 70 20 01) and the **Mondial** at number 5 (tel: 01 47 70 55 56), where Chopin is said to have taken rooms in 1833.

Chopin 46 passage Jouffroy, 75009; tel: 01 47 70 58 10 [4 A6]
M̲ *Grands-Boulevards;* E̲ *Métro 4 to Strasbourg-St-Denis, then lines 8 or 9 to Grands-Boulevards, walk west to passage Jouffroy.*
At the centre of this arcade (see page 58) is the charming Hôtel Chopin. Small well-maintained rooms look out over interior courtyards rather than the constant traffic of the boulevards. A family piano and stacks of children's books of yesteryear in the foyer, parquet and houseplants in the breakfast room, yet still a budget hotel at €68 (450FF) for a double room. The welcome is genuine, witness the number of returning guests who continue to recommend the place to their friends and regard guidebook entries with trepidation, fearing that this modest *hôtel du charme* will succumb to popularity and

fame. Have no fear – the people behind this place are canny decent folk who understand just what makes the hotel work, and continue to keep up the standards and *rapport qualité-prix.*

Millennium Opéra Paris 12 bd Haussmann, 75009; tel: 01 49 49 16 00 [4 A5]
M̲ *Richelieu-Drouot;* E̲ *Métro 4 to Strasbourg-St-Denis, then lines 8 or 9 to Richelieu-Drouot.*
The welcome is genuine. A recently revived incarnation of the former Hôtel Commodore is 50 yards and a full world away from the sniffy old Hôtel Ambassador at number 16. This refurbished *déco* discovery is brimming with good ideas, but not at the expense of the original atmosphere, and everyone involved is justifiably proud of it. The lobby lounge has its obligatory Grands Boulevards glass dome and a library packed with antiquarian editions of Voltaire and Corneille. Rooms sport a masculine country-house class, softly tempered with flowers and fruits in the suites. Original furnishings blend well with commissioned pieces, such as the comfortable reading chair with brass lantern. All have classic parquet, rich carpets and fabulously tiled bathrooms with

chrome, marble and beech washstands. Room rates €290 (1,900FF). A €30 (200FF) upgrade to Club Class features bathrobes and refreshing Hermès orange-scented colognes as well. Ironing boards, trouser presses and the usual gadgetry too. Do not be afraid to ask about the pretty fair weekend room rate available most of the year. One to watch as it finds its feet. The **Brasserie Haussmann** next door also shows promise (see page 63). Should a guest prefer a quiet chat to the brasserie bustle. And lunch may be served at the library fireside.

Scribe 1 rue Scribe, 75009; tel: 01 44 71 24 24 [3 K6]
M̄ *Opera*; Ē *RER E to Haussmann-St-Lazare, then walk down rue Caumartin, turn left on bd Haussmann and right at the Opéra to rue Scribe.*
Joséphine Baker loved this place so much that she legally adopted the bell-boy. Hidden in the Opéra quarter of plush luxury hotels is the discerning VIP traveller's hideaway. Deceptively spacious – the discreet entrance dates back to its days as the home of the Paris Jockey Club – the hotel offers service and quality of the old school. Nothing stuffy, though: there is an unmistakable sense of coming home – even on a first visit – that makes me wish I had attended one of the hotel's legendary New Year's Eve parties. Apparently the entire place, staff to management, décor to cuisine, gets caught up in the theme of the season, be it the heyday of jazz cabaret or 19th-century Egyptomania! Rooms range from the Hermès-perfumed, hi-fi equipped duplex suites, in gaudy oriental kitsch or English racing green, that have the air of a pad of a ne'er-do-well black sheep in exile (perhaps a legacy of the hotel's long association with Sir James Goldsmith), to the understated comfort and charm of a conventional double overlooking the Grands Boulevards. Baccarat chandeliers and décor of the golden age of travel dictate the sumptuous style of the salons where the Lumière brothers screened the first cinema show in Paris, yet service is comfortably understated. Savour Lapsang Souchong tea with toast on a damask-draped tea-tray in your room for around €12 (80FF), or elect to dine in luxury in one of the two gastronomic restaurants. **Les Muses** showcases the subtle and deft cuisine of Philippe Pleuen, whose spicy caramelised *jarret de veau* and indulgent desserts have won an audience all their own. Budget around €60 (400FF) for dinner. Room rates begin at €335 (2,200FF) per night for a double room including breakfast and a diary of the Paris Social Season.

WHERE TO GO

Arcades (see feature pages 58–9)

Le Gramont 15 bd des Italiens,75002; tel: 01 42 97 59 50 [4 A6]
M̄ *Richelieu-Drouot*; Ē *Métro 4 to Strasbourg-St-Denis, then lines 8 or 9 to Richelieu-Drouot. Follow bd des Italiens to the corner of rue Gramont.*
A typical pavement café on the Grands Boulevards, the Gramont is a great place to slump after walking the boulevards. From the pavement tables you have sneak preview of the Sacré Coeur atop the Butte Montmartre, reassuring proof that no matter how hard your shoes are pinching, Paris is pretty compact after all. Late at night, it is worth going inside for a brasserie supper at around €23 (150FF).

Grands Magasins (see *What to buy*, pages 66–7)

Le Grand Rex 1 bd Poissonnière, 75002; Les Etoiles du Rex; tel: 08 36 68 05 96 (premium rate); web: www.legrandrex.com [4 B6]
Etoiles du Rex open 10.00–19.00 Wed–Sun term time (every day in school holidays). €7 (45FF), €11.50 (75FF) inc film at the Rex.
M̄ *Bonne-Nouvelle*; Ē *Métro 4 to Strasbourg-St-Denis, then lines 8 or 9 to Bonne-Nouvelle. When the station is closed, continue to Grands Boulevards, 200m along the street.*

ARCADES – MINI MALLS FROM AN AGE OF ELEGANCE

The **Passage Jouffroy** at 10 bd Montmartre is among my favourites of the glass-roofed arcades in the city. Here you will find not only the Grevin waxworks museum, but a bijou little theatre and surely the world's most enchanting toy shop with dolls' house furniture, tuppence-coloured, penny-plain theatres and teddy bears that look as though they've already been tested by seasoned thumb-suckers. La Boutique des Tuniques has been selling blouses here for nigh on a century, and Ségas has offered walking sticks to the gout-struck gentry for donkeys years. With a café, a restaurant and even a hotel (see Hôtel Chopin, page 56), you might spend an entire rainy weekend here without stepping into the outside world. Many of these *passages couverts* date back to the 18th century, when royalty built arcades to raise rent money from upwardly mobile families keen to have an address close to the Court. It was during the rise of the upper-middle-class boulevard set in the mid 19th century that the arcades became popular with the wealthy and elegant crowds, delighted to parade in their finery away from the risk of splashes from passing carriages. In these sleepy galleries are to be found second-hand booksellers, art dealers and stamp markets. Alongside the national library, the gorgeous **Galeries Colbert** and **Vivienne**, set around a glass rotunda, are famous for antiquarian books and prints. Come here for the smartest of window-shopping and an elegant *fin du siècle* café. Along the mosaic paths, with their indoor avenues of bay trees, you may even come across a specialist store selling theatrical costumes of the past. No wonder that Jean-Paul Gaultier's main boutique is situated next to the entrance to the arcades. The **Passage des Panoramas** on the Grands Boulevards, almost opposite the *Jouffroy*, is something of a stage-door canteen. Restaurants serving the Théâtre des Variétés, and centuries-old engravers and print shops, line a mini-network

If ever a screen was bigger than the stars it has showcased, then Le Rex, the last and greatest of the great movie palaces of the world, is that cinema. A listed monument, this 1932 art deco legend has to be visited at least once in a lifetime, if only to taste the wonder and glamour that was Hollywood. The Grand Rex is the original three-tiered auditorium with its neon-arched sweep of a stage and breathtaking panoramic Mediterranean night sky under the dome. In the Rex's heyday, 150 people would be involved in the lavish floor show that preceded each screening, and the stage can still call on its outrageously camp dancing waters for special occasions. Marilyn Monroe, Alfred Hitchcock, Liz Taylor have trodden the boulevard Poissonnière red carpet past popping flashbulbs. Jackie Cooper inaugurated Europe's first ever cinema escalator, and Jean-Luc Besson spent the night before the première of *The Big Blue* slaving in the projection booth in preparation for its debut on the biggest screen in the country. During the war the Nazis commandeered the cinema for their troops, but the Rex soon returned to the heart of a nation still passionately in love with Tinsel Town. Each year sees a dozen big star concerts on the stage, and *La Nuit des Publivores,* an all-night screening of the

of smaller passageways, without the elegance of the Colbert, but an atmosphere no modern mall could ever recreate.

Passage des Pavillons (1784) 6 rue du Beaujolas, 75001. [4 A6] M̄ *Pyramides.*

Passage Des Panoramas (1800) 11 bd Montmartre or 10 rue St-Marc, 75002. [4 A6] M̄ *Grands-Boulevards.*

Galerie Vivienne (1823) 4 pl des Petits Champs. [4 A6] M̄ *Bourse.*

Galerie Colbert (1826) 6 rue des Petits-Champs, 75002. [4 A6] M̄ *Bourse.*

Galerie Véro-Dodat (1826) 19 rue Jean-Jacques Rousseau, 75001. [4 A6] M̄ *Palais-Royal-Musée-du-Louvre.*

Galerie Vivienne

Passage Choiseul (1827) 44 rue des Petits-Champs, 75002. [4 A6] M̄ *4-Septembre.*

Passage Jouffroy (1845) 10 bd Montmartre, 75009. [4 A6] M̄ *Grands-Boulevards.*

Passage Verdeau (1847) 31 bis rue du fbg Montmartre, 75009. [4 A6] M̄ *Le-Pelletier.*

Ē *Métro 4 to Strasbourg-St-Denis, then lines 8 or 9 to Grands Boulevards. Or métro 4 to Réaumur-Sébestopol, then line 3 to Bourse. The rue Vivienne leads up to the boulevards and down to the rue des Petits Champs from which most passages may be reached.*

world's greatest cult TV commercials, with party food and drink, is the essential youth culture event of the year. If you have not yet witnessed a thousand French kids joining in Maureen Lipman's BT punchline, then shrieking with joy as a Perrier bottle experiences what Meg Ryan could only fake on screen, then frankly you are nurturing a void in your life. The Rex's nightclub remains hot stuff. The nation's youth was introduced to Garage, House and Jungle sounds within these very walls. London's top DJs, and their fans, take the Eurostar to the Rex one-nighters. Behind the Grand Rex are half a dozen newer screens and plans are in hand for a multiplex annexe with restaurants and bars. The story of the cinema and film-making is told in a thrilling special-effects-packed attraction, **Les Etoiles du Rex**, taking visitors on a backstage tour through the very building and time itself. Riding a glass elevator behind the big screen of Grand Rex, taking part in action movies and walking through the night sky, we meet the stars of yesteryear. Since the 50-minute tour begins every five minutes, you may choose the English- or French-language version to best appreciate the experience. Fabulous and worth every sou.

WHAT TO SEE

Bibliothèque National 58 rue de Richelieu, 75002; tel: 01 47 03 82 26; web: www.bnf.fr [4 A6]
Open Mon–Sat 09.00–18.00. Closed holidays. Free.
$\overline{M}$ *Bourse;* $\overline{E}$ *Métro 4 to Réaumur-Sébastopol, then line 3 to Bourse. Rue des Filles leads to rue Richelieu.*
Palais Mazarin, named for the cardinal who amassed an impressive collection of art and literature, is usually known by the name of another cleric. The **François Mitterand National Library** on the banks of the Seine officially supplanted the Bibliothèque Richelieu and its sister libraries in Versailles. But whilst the great glass warehouse on the water stores the bulk of the state-owned hardbacks, this splendid building behind the Palais Royal displays the treasures that only a Philistine would shove into a skyscraper. There have been national libraries on this street since the days of the Sun King, and the name Colbert, immortalised in the neighbouring arcade, refers to the statesman charged with developing the Bibliothèque du Roi. In 1858, a commission chaired by Prosper Mérimée, author of *Carmen*, oversaw the construction of a Bibliothèque Impériale on the present site. Temporary exhibitions are held in the Galerie Mansart and Mazarin's former library, where fabulous Romanelli ceiling frescos outshine the most illustrious displays. A fine collection of maps and a reference library devoted to the arts may be consulted on site, and the Palais Mazarin is also home to the Cabinet des Médailles et des Antiques.

Fragonard – Musée de la Parfumerie 9 rue Scribe, 75009; tel: 01 47 42 04 56 [3 K6]
Open Mon–Sat 09.30–17.30, Sun (Apr–Sep) 09.30–16.30. Free.
$\overline{M}$ *Opéra, Auber;* $\overline{E}$ *RER to Châtelet-Les-Halles then RER A to Auber.*
The story of 3,000 years of perfume told in a slick guided tour of many of the artefacts accumulated by the famous Provence perfume house, with plenty of unusual bottles and travelling cases to admire. Should you hunger for more scent-inspired objets d'art, visit Fragonard's second free gallery at 39 rue des Capucines, 75002.

Musée Grevin 10 bd Montparnasse, 75009; tel: 01 47 70 85 05; web: www.musee-grevin.com [4 A6]
Open 10.00–19.00 (last entry 18.00). ∈12 (78FF).
$\overline{M}$ *Grands-Boulevards;* $\overline{E}$ *Métro 4 to Strasbourg-St-Denis, then lines 8 or 9 to Grands-Boulevards; walk west towards passage Jouffroy.*
The Madame Tussaud's of Paris still somehow manages to convey the image of a 19th-century sideshow. Overhauled in 2001, the splendid dome, marble staircase and luxuriant ornate colonnades set off the wax effigies of the good and the great to fine effect. Whilst London's Tussaud's came into being as a direct result of the French Revolution, the origins of the Paris attraction are much more edifying. It was journalist Arthur Meyer, founder of the newspaper *Le Gaulois*, who had the idea of creating a 3D virtual newspaper for the masses, so that the great unwashed could see images of the sporting, cultural and political figures of the day. Alfred Grévin sculpted the figures, and the museum opened in 1882. Eiffel Tower impressario Gabriel Thomas joined the company and suggested the addition of historical tableaux and other fairground attractions to woo sensation seekers from the boulevards. Best of these is the Mirage room, first seen at the Universal Exhibition of 1900, and still using mirrors to create special effects unsurpassed by computers. Among the artifice look out for some true historical curiosities, among them Marat's bathtub. A 320-seat Italian theatre, designed by

Antoine Bourdelle, saw, in 1892, the world's first ever screening of an animated cartoon. Every year, a dozen new waxworks arrive at the Musée Grevin. Where else in town could you see the Marquis de Sade, Alfred Hitchcock, Lara Croft and soccer stars Barthez and Zidane under the same roof?

Opéra Garnier pl de l'Opéra, 75009; tel: 01 40 01 25 14 [3 K6]
Open 10.00–16.30; closed Jan 1, May 1 and during rehearsals and matinees. €9 (60FF).
M̄ *Opéra, Auber;* Ē *RER to Châtelet-Les-Halles then RER A to Auber.*
Nothing less than the divinity of Mozart could outshine the splendour of the Palais Garnier, the magnificent opera house in the heart of the city. This, the 13th home of the opera company, was commissioned as a centrepiece to the Haussmann boulevards. Charles Garnier was an unknown 35-year-old architect when he won the contract, but his name will live for ever through this one project which was completed in 1875 after a 15-year labour of love. The great marble staircase is a masterpiece: nobody should leave Paris without seeing it. The twists, turns, galleries, balconies, alcoves and sweeps of the staircase turns every audience into a stage show. As you climb to the various levels, the theatre itself appears to come to life, and as you descend towards the twin bronze *torchières*, you feel ever taller and grander. Upstairs, the main foyer almost out-Versailles Versailles, with mirrors and windows looking down towards the Louvre and Palais Royal. The eight-ton crystal chandelier, immortalised forever by Gaston Laroux's *Phantom of the Opera*, hangs from a ceiling painted by Marc Chagall in 1964. The Opéra also holds a branch of the national library and an interesting collection of paintings and photographs. The unaccompanied visit is good fun, and at 13.00 daily groups of ten or more can enjoy an escorted tour of the house.

Paristoric 11 bis rue Scribe, 75009; tel: 01 42 66 62 06
Open Apr–Oct 09.00–08.00, Nov–Mar 09.00–18.00. €8 (50FF).
M̄ *Opéra, Auber;* Ē *RER to Châtelet-Les-Halles then RER A to Auber.*
A 45-minute audio-visual tour of Paris past and present. Victor Hugo presents everything you always wanted to know about the city on the Seine from the Roman colonisation of Ile de la Cité to the *grands travaux* of the 1990s. Tourists are hustled through the doors happy to do all their sightseeing in under an hour and so spend more time and money in the nearby stores.

WHERE TO EAT

Chartier 7 rue de Faubourg, Montmartre, 75009; tel: 01 47 70 86 29 [4 A6]
M̄ *Grands-Boulevards;* Ē *Métro 4 to Strasbourg-St-Denis, then lines 8 or 9 to Grands-Boulevards. A few paces up the faubourg Montmartre then turn left at the sign of the arrow.*
They come down the little passageway off the faubourg Montmartre in search of cuisine that is hot rather than *haute*, and little has changed since this *bouillon* (soup kitchen) first appeared in the *Guide Bleu* 100 years ago. Still the stucco and gilt walls, still the brass coat rack and the polished wood. And still the stroppy waiters who scrawl your order on the tablecloth and who could avoid eye contact even in a headlock. But there are items on the menu priced at less than €3 (20FF) and a full meal for €11.50 (75FF). Choose from soup, *pot au feu*, or crispy roast chicken with *frites*. If you are a stickler for service then give the place a miss, since inconvenience is an institution at Chartier. You can't book, you can't sit where you want, they shut the doors at 21.00 sharp, and the waiter gets cross if you spend too long mulling over the menu.

Chez Clémentine 5 rue St-Marc, 75002; tel: 01 40 41 05 05 [4 A6]
Closed Sat, Sun.
M̲ *Bourse;* E̲ *Métro 4 to Réamur-Sébastopol, then line 3 to Bourse. Walk north on rue Vivienne and turn right on to rue St-Marc.*
Like **Gavroche**, this is yet another improbable gem in this seemingly ordinary street. Closing at 22.30, a good couple of hours before its neighbour, it remains a midday favourite, invariably booked up at lunchtimes by the expense account diners from the banks on the boulevards. So you might have better luck in the evening at this fabulously down to earth traditional *bistrot* with its capricious, ever-changing menu *selon du marché et du saison* but always classic regional French cuisine. The bonus here is the rich Bordeaux wine list at more reasonable prices than the better known addresses of the quarter. Menu is ∈21 (135FF).

Chez Georges l rue du Mail, 75002; tel: 01 42 60 07 11 [4 A6]
Closed Sun, Aug.
M̲ *Bourse;* E̲ *Métro 4 to Réamur-Sébastopol, then line 3 to Bourse. From pl de la Bourse, take rue Notre Dame de la Victoire south to the corner with rue du Mail.*
Lunch-hour secrets find their way from the Bourse to the city pages via hefty chunks of turbot in a *sauce béarnaise* and good fillet steaks. Eavesdropping is the speciality of this favourite bistro, for the journalists, bankers and brokers of the 2nd *arrondissement* dine elbow to elbow in front of a row of imposing arched mirrors. Wines are reasonably priced and a good old-fashioned meal should set you back ∈38 (250FF).

Les Coulisses 19 Passage des Panoramas, 75002; tel: 01 44 82 09 52 [4 A6]
Closed Sun.
M̲ *Grands-Boulevards;* E̲ *Métro 4 to Réamur-Sébastopol, then line 3 to Bourse and walk north on rue Vivienne and turn right on to rue St-Marc. Or métro 4 to Strasbourg-St-Denis, then lines 8 or 9 to Grands-Boulevards to the passage des Panoramas.*
Lunch costs ∈12 (79FF) in a bright and airy dining room opposite the Variétés stage door; unhurried service, and space between the tables – rare in this quarter. A little more roomy than its neighbours, but usually a little less busy. If you are into healthier eating, then come here for a summer salad; if you and your arteries are up for some fun however, dive into the more crowded old-fashioned *bistrots* on rue St-Marc.

Flo 7 Cour des Petites-Ecuries, 75010; tel: 01 47 70 13 59 [4 B–C5]
M̲ *Château-d'Eau;* E̲ *Métro 4 to Château-d'Eau. Walk west on rue du Château-d'Eau then left on to the fbg St-Denis and right into the Cour des Petites-Ecuries. Look for the seafood stand.*
One of the oldest brasseries in Paris now heads a chain of classic addresses. Don't be put off by this, since the parent company has restored each site to its original style and personality without suffocation by corporate identity. By far the best of the bunch, it is known for its traditional menus at less than ∈20 (130FF) and efficient chaos on a Saturday night. Eat early to miss the crowds. Arrive late for an hour's wait for a table in a true party atmosphere. Waiters slice through the crowds carrying huge trays of seafood and ice, cheese and bamboo. Enjoy the clatter of platters and yells of barmen insulting the serving lads. You might be poured a complimentary *coupe* at the bar to compensate for losing your place in the queue to a foppish fedora-sporting actor with his entourage of chorus girls. You may even be asked to share a table. The atmosphere of this unexpected backstreet tavern with its Alsatian charm will seduce you. One of the cheaper menus, served after 22.00, offers main course and dessert with a

quarter of wine. Oysters a must and the *granité* of icy calvados clears the way for the richer desserts.

Le Gavroche 19 rue St-Marc, 75002; 01 42 96 89 70 [4 A6]
M̲ *Bourse;* E̲ *Métro 4 to Réamur-Sébastopol, then line 3 to Bourse. Walk north on rue Vivienne and turn left on to rue St-Marc.*
This unassuming neighbourhood bar is so often ignored by visitors taking the short cut from the sightseeing to shopping districts – after all, who but a local would know that it was once voted the best *bistrot* in Paris? Neither a place for private conversation nor a romantic idyll, there is certainly no chance of falling into a reverie and forgetting where you are. Sit cheek by jowl with your neighbours and be prepared to stay at the table for the entire lunch hour. The minuscule dining room beside an *estaminet* bar has vacuum-packed as many tables in a limited space as possible. The place absolutely heaves from noon onwards with good wives and men-with-souls in suits-with-ties scoffing classic French heartland fare such as *fromage de tête persillé*, and *terrine de lapin* on a remarkably good value €11 (75FF) menu. Open until well past midnight. This is precisely that which we expect a Parisian restaurant to be, yet rarely find in real life.

Haussmann 12 bd Haussmann, 75009; tel: 01 49 49 16 09 [4 A5]
M̲ *Richelieu-Drouot;* E̲ *Métro 4 to Strasbourg-St-Denis, then lines 8 or 9 to Richelieu-Drouot.*
On the shady side of the boulevard, in that tranquil hinterland of cool finance between the heat of the cinemas and the department stores, is a smart reinterpretation of the brasserie. Clean contemporary feel with stained glass, wicker seats and Parisian globes in evidence, but everything in its place and no suggestion of clutter. Does the modern approach suit the food? Well, it is early days, but I think it's getting there. Nice ideas include the Sunday brunch buffet, and an afternoon snack menu with such options as crab *gazpacho* and the ubiquitous crumble. There is also slightly more than a nod towards the lighter appetite and cholesterol-conscious diner. The chef is still finding his own style. He is less successful when unwisely venturing into the fashionable New World. Piquant baby olives and a blatantly balsamic vinaigrette rendered unto a Caesar salad that which, though Italian, was most certainly not Caesar's. However on home ground the place shows real promise. *Sandre* on a bed of chicory and fresh green apples proved to be an idea well worth stealing for home entertaining use, and a soup of orange served with blood orange *sorbet* was a very satisfying pretence at virtue in the face of many choc and pastry alternatives. A nice spot for people-watching (would-be honeymooners angling for proposals on the corner of rue Lafitte and young bankers whizzing homeward on their roller skates at close of business). Pay upwards of €26 (170FF). And in answer to the original question: does the modern approach suit the food? Yes!

Julien 16 rue de Faubourg-St-Denis, 75010; tel: 01 47 70 12 06 [4 B6]
M̲ *Strasbourg-St-Denis;* E̲ *Métro 4 to Strasbourg-St-Denis. Walk behind the archway along rue de Faubourg-St-Denis. The restaurant is on your right.*
Yet another of the great **Flo** resuscitations, Julien is probably better known for its stunning blend of art nouveau glassware and mahogany fittings with starched white napkins and rows of white globe lighting than for its *cassoulet* and seafood menu. A classic post-theatre hangout, if it all looks terribly familiar, the *déjà vu* is due to its role as the inspiration for the BBC's soccer World Cup studio. Prices as for Flo (see page 62).

Mavrommatis 106 rue de Richelieu, 75002; tel: 01 53 29 00 71 [4 A6]
M̲ *Richelieu-Drouot;* E̲ *Métro 4 to Strasbourg-St-Denis, then lines 8 or 9 to Richelieu-Drouot.*
As the rue Richelieu gets a long overdue clean-up for the Millennium, a new, smart and understated Greek restaurant is a world away from the Little Athens hustlaria of the Left Bank. Menus at €8 (70FF) and €14 (90FF) feature beef-filled aubergines and oregano vinaigrettes.

Les Muses 1 rue Scribe, 75009; tel: 01 44 71 24 24 [3 K6]
M̲ *Opera;* E̲ *RER E to Haussmann-St-Lazare, then walk down rue Caumartin, turn left on bd Haussmann and right at the Opéra to rue Scribe.* (See *Hôtel Scribe,* page 57.)

Les Noces de Jeanette 14 rue Favart, 75002; tel: 01 42 96 36 89 [4 A6]
M̲ *Richelieu-Drouot;* E̲ *Métro 4 to Strasbourg-St-Denis, then lines 8 or 9 to Richelieu-Drouot. Rue Favart is just off the bd des Italiens.*
Les Noces, named after a 19th-century operetta by Victor Massé, graces a corner site opposite the *Opéra Comique,* and the restaurant, with its retro dining rooms and lovely old mirrored staircase, is itself a setting straight out of an operetta.

Created by the proprietors of Montmartre's successful **Crémaillère** (see page 163), it has the same atmosphere of a shared joke: we the diners, as well as the waiters, are in on the *Belle Epoque schtick.* A couple of rooms are dressed up in imperial style, another in the style of a Latin-Quarter *bistrot,* still more dining rooms tarted up as cocktail lounges. Good-natured service and a €25 (165FF) menu offering such reliable fare as *blanquette de veau à l'ancienne* and an *andouillette* sausage rated AAAAA (that's *Association Amicale des Amateurs des Andouillette Authentique*). Sharing the pretty pretence of days gone by are a good mix of local business lunchers and hicks from the sticks in town for the day.

Au Petit Riche 25 rue le Peletier, 75009; tel: 01 47 70 68 68 [4 A5]
Closed Sun.
M̲ *Richelieu-Drouot;* E̲ *Métro 4 to Strasbourg-St-Denis, then lines 8 or 9 to Richelieu-Drouot. On bd Haussmann turn right into rue le Peletier.*
The name comes from the local term for the bourgeoisie who flaunted themselves along the boulevards showing off headgear, carriages and the latest fashions before and after retiring to some elegant dining room. Mistingett was one of those who joined the tail end of the procession and held court in this very room. Though service, décor and style have strong echoes of old style formality, a young and dynamic restaurant manager is inspiring a much-needed wind of change through what was in danger of becoming a stuffy museum piece. Pay €25 (165FF) at midday and around €38 (250FF) in the evening for three courses. *Canard au verjus, lapin en gelée* and a succulent *tarte aux pommes* share the Loire influence that dominates the wine list.

Pierre à la Fontaine Gaillon pl Gaillon, 75002; tel: 01 47 42 63 22 [3 A6]
Closed Sat lunch and Sun.
M̲ *4 Septembre;* E̲ *Métro 4 to Réamur-Sébastopol, then line 3 to 4 Septembre. Walk west on rue 4 Septembre, turning left on rue de la Michodière past the theatre to place Gaillon.*
Actors and bankers, aunts and nieces have been indulging themselves here since the 19th century. I was a little tardy in stumbling across the surprising welcome around the fountain in the Duc de Richelieu's Mansart-built home behind the Grands Boulevards. Better late than never. Now, my idea of a perfect sunny lunchtime would begin with the intensely refreshing, mother-love-packed *vichyssoise* (thick as summer ice-cream, bracing as the sea, and with sharp, just-picked chives that detonate between the teeth). The meal should end with the fruit salad drenched in warm *zabaglione* and topped with melon *sorbet,* caramelised orange and the ubiquitous red fruit *coulis.* In between I'd happily dither around the *marmite* of the best of Brittany's catch of the day, or advise a best friend to dig into the *escalope de foie de canard* with its quince *compôte.* I could be lazier still and let the waiter choose for me from the *plats du jour.* The waiters are attentive without being oppressive, and intent on ensuring diners get the best from the meal. A textbook classic wine list is available for special occasions, but when I asked just for a glass of house white with my lunch I was poured a generous measure of a 1996 Chablis *1ᵉʳ cru.* The set menu is under €27 (180FF) for three courses, and an additional €9 (60FF) indulgence brings out a small but judicious selection of ripe cheeses. A humming *cantal* and unctuous *fourme d'ambert* with crusty bread is pretty unbeatable stuff. The terrace is literally wrapped around the eponymous fountain, with its trident-wielding cherub supervising the comforting trickle of cool water. Diners inside may enjoy the splendid light and bright dining rooms with their panels, crystal chandeliers and sundry regalia, with certificates of gastronomic *confréries* liberally sprinkled around the rooms. Eavesdropping ranges from frankly boring business deals to the animated gossip overspilling from the *Théâtre Michodière* opposite. Budget around €45 (300FF) or so.

La Rôtisserie Monsigny 1 rue Monsigny, 75002; tel: 01 42 96 16 61 [3 A6]
Closed Sat lunch.
M̲ *4-Septembre;* E̲ *Métro 4 to Réamur-Sébastopol, then line 3 to 4-Septembre. Follow rue Monsigny to the Théâtre des Bouffes Parisiens. The restaurant is opposite.*
Jacques Cagna has embraced the cult of the annexe with three rôtisseries and an up-and-coming fish restaurant serving his distinctive smart food to diners with avenue tastes on a boulevard budget. The perfect example of one of his new populist establishments is this smart venue facing the red and gold thousand-and-one lights of Offenbach's original Paris playhouse, the Bouffes Parisiens. Of course the restaurant is open before and after the show, but more than just a post-footlights crowd come here. *Aficionados* of Cagna's elegant style arrive for the food and the ambience. A piano plays boulevard themes from Offenbach to Michel Legrand on Friday and Saturday nights, as diners nibble at the celebrated home-baked six-grain bread, with *beurre d'Isigny* (naturally) in anticipation of the meal. *Terrines* come straight from the pages of a fine-dining glossy magazine, colour, texture and flavour all just so, steaks are precisely prepared to exacting requirements and served with succulent vegetables. House specials such as rôtisserie fowl and Cagna's mother's family recipe for *joues de cochon au carrottes et pommes fondants* are main-course favourites and the legendary *Paris-Brest* the dessert of choice. The smart dining rooms (one smoking, one non) are anything but stuffy. A notice on the tables describes the current exhibition on the

restaurant walls and encourages diners to wander around and look at the pictures. The rôtisserie also serves its house champagne by the carafe for €27 (180FF) – now there's stylish informality for you. The formula is carte-menu with mix-and-match choices at €20 (130FF) for two courses and €27 (180FF) for three. (See pages 24–5 for details of the other Cagna restaurants in Paris.)

Les Variétés 12 passage des Panoramas, 75002; tel: 01 42 36 98 09 [4 A6] Closed Sat, Sun.
M̄ *Grands-Boulevards;* Ē *Métro 4 to Strasbourg-St-Denis, then lines 8 or 9 to Grands-Boulevards. Walk through the passage des Panoramas.*
Like **Gavroche** around the corner, this is the place where local workers come to lunch. A €8 (50FF) *plat du jour* – perhaps a *coq au vin* or basic *gigot d'agneau* – brings businessmen and actresses together in this old-fashioned *bar-resto* around the corner from the stage door of the Théâtre des Variétés, in this charming arcade of stamp dealers, *salons de thé* and refugees from summer showers (see *Arcades*, page 56). The lace and bric-à-brac packed bar is so bijou that the restaurant has claimed a pocket-handkerchief stretch of the indoor pavement to squeeze in four tiny tables.

Le Vaudeville 29 rue Vivienne, 75002; tel: 01 42 33 39 31 [4 A6]
M̄ *Bourse;* Ē *Métro 4 to Réamur-Sébastopol, then line 3 to Bourse.*
The Vaudeville was in its heyday a staging post for *boulevardiers*, lotharios and merrymakers en route to a rollicking comedy at the Théâtre des Variétés. These days one is as likely to be sitting alongside hacks and financiers from the AFP news agency and the stock exchange along the road, as a genuine *bon vivant* and his entourage. But who cares? This is another of the celebrated **Flo** rescue missions (see page 62), and the potted plants, polished brass and art deco *faux marbre* columns set just the right tone for the meal. Menus around €21–27 (135–190FF) may feature an *escalope de saumon*, that is salmon in flavour as well as colour (no mean achievement in a boulevard brasserie these days) or a platter of the group's famous oysters. To round off a summer meal you might even be lucky enough to find a *soupe des fraises* that is a veritable trove of the tiniest, sharpest little wild woodland strawberries ever to be tamed by a sensible *sorbet*.

WHAT TO BUY
Arcades (see box page 58)

Brentano's 37 av de l'Opéra, 75002; tel: 01 42 61 52 50 [3 K6]
Open Mon–Sat 10.00–19.30.
M̄ *Opéra;* Ē *Métro 4 to Gare de l'Est then line 7 to Opéra. Use av de l'Opéra exit.*
Practically twinned with Hogwarts, this is where clued-up French kids come to buy Harry Potter in English (major playground status symbol) or dumbed-down American (serious *faux pas*). The rest of us come to the bookshop in order to stock up on those titles we can never get our hands on at home. Walking distance to the rue de Rivoli bookshops (see page 53). Pick up the English-language free-sheets here for news of the ex-pat American and Irish communities.

Galeries Lafayette 40 bd Haussmann, 75009; tel: 01 42 82 34 56; web: www.galerieslafayette.com [3 K5]
Open Mon–Wed, Fri, Sat 09.30–18.45, Thu 09.30–21.00.
M̄ *Chaussée d'Antin or Auber;* Ē *RER to Châtelet-Les-Halles then RER A to Auber.*
Like its neighbour, Printemps, Galeries Lafayette is not one but several department stores, all in a row. All the key *pret à porter* collections in Paris may be found under one domed roof, and the weekly free fashion show is a must. Just

reserve your seat in advance on 01 42 82 30 25, take the rue Mogador escalator in the main building to the 7th floor and show your passport to enjoy the spectacle of posh frocks and clever lighting. Catwalk strutting at 11.00 every Tuesday and 14.00 on Friday afternoons in summer (April to September). If you would rather browse for yourself, give yourself enough time, since lingerie alone takes over an entire floor. The store is famous for its publicity stunts. Within months of the end of World War I a pilot landed on the roof, signalling nearly a century of one-upmanship between the *grands magasins* of the Grands Boulevards. Although famous for fashion, the store has one building devoted to household goods, and the pavement is lined with stalls manned by gadget demonstrators showing you ever more labour-saving ways to iron your shirt and slice your onion. If you suffer guilt-pangs from too much time spent at the shops, head for the sixth floor of the main building and call it sightseeing, There are fabulous views to be enjoyed from the restaurants. To convince yourself that you are actually saving money, ask at your hotel reception for 10% discount passes for Galeries Lafayette or Printemps. Show the card and your passport at the cash desk before you buy for 10% off most items in store except books, music and food.

Printemps 64 bd Haussmann, 75009; tel: 01 42 82 50 00; web: www.printemps.com [3 J5]
Open Mon–Wed, Fri, Sat 09.35–19.00, Thu 09.30–22.00.
M̄ *Havre-Caumartin, Auber or Haussmann-St-Lazare;* Ē *RER E to Haussmann-St-Lazare.*
The rivalry between Printemps and Galeries Lafayette keeps both stores on their toes, and Printemps' latest gimmick is a team of roller-skating staff equipped with webcams. You can now play 'hunt the thong' or choose your new handbag from the comfort of your own cyberspace, whilst giving directions to shopping's answer to Lara Croft as she whizzes and skims through the aisles. This generally hip young image is reflected throughout the store, with more mix-and-match designer accessories than anywhere else in town. The fifth-floor Miss Code department is geared towards the teenage market. Even the menswear building looks sharp and stylish. As with the Galeries, there are designer-wear fashion shows every Tuesday morning at 10.00, with additional parades on Friday mornings from April to October. Both stores produce street maps of Paris distributed to all the capital's hotels and tourist offices.

Marais and the Islands

A Parisian paradox: in a land that is practically overrun with palaces and fairy-tale châteaux, the most popular building is the Pompidou Centre. What is more, that eternally controversial architectural intestinal structure is also the gatehouse to the oldest quarter of the Right Bank.

Go straight to the nearest bar, order a drink and raise your glass on high, for the toast is 'To Neglect!'. Had not this district been dismissed as utterly beyond salvation by those brave planners who reinvented the rest of the city during the 19th and 20th centuries, we might never have kept this window into the past. Happily the Marais is one corner of Paris that remains faithful to its past identity from the age of kings and storytellers. Those quaint dark narrow streets, heaving with grand *hôtels particuliers* and rickety 16th- and 17th- century townhouses, never fell victim to the sweeping boulevards and Babel towers of political *agrandissement*. When Revolution brought the bloodiest spring cleaning to the homes of the great families, the mansions on the marshlands were left to fester in their own shadows until the 1960s. Then, like a Sleeping Beauty pushing aside the tendrils of dereliction, Paris awoke to its vanishing heritage and slapped a preservation order on the entire district from the Grands Boulevards to the Seine, from République and Bastille almost as far west as Les Halles.

Left to its modest immigrant population, life had shuffled on as usual in a village forgotten by the city. The first gay bars opened in the streets behind the rue Ste Croix de la Bretonnerie, away from the gaze of mainstream society. Of course, it was only a matter of time before this led to renovation and reclamation of the garrets, shops and streets by a fashionable element whose penthouse apartments overlook the old byways. Now, shop windows are more likely to display Buick hub-cap-clocks and designer cufflinks than meat and vegetables. In any other district that might have killed community spirit. Yet here, despite the fact that a shopkeeper is unlikely to be roused in the small hours with the cry, 'Open up, Monsieur. 'Tis *Maman*. She has urgent need of a *rétro* lava lamp, a chrome toaster and a Warhol print', a true sense remains of people and place. *Café-théâtre* flourishes in the Blancs Manteaux, Point Virgule and Dépardieu's cradle, the Théâtre de la Gare, and smaller galleries take the risk of promoting unknown artists to potential patrons from the moneyed classes.

This trendy Marais rests remarkably comfortably alongside ghettos even older than the now dispersed gay scene. The Jewish district around the rue des Rosiers has hardly changed in decades. Many a *mikvah* (ritual bathhouse), kosher butchery and tiny synagogue are to be found within a mobile's ringtone of the sophisticated wines bars. Across the quarter, a comprehensive museum of Jewish life and art can be appreciated in a mansion on rue de Temple.

Across the rues de Rivoli and St-Antoine, the *quartier* St-Paul is window shoppers' paradise, where antique and art-inspired covetousness is nurtured with taste. The greatest treat in the Marais is glimpsing the secret grandeur and elegance that hide behind the huge doors of those stately private residences, the *hôtels particuliers*, whose buildings are floodlit at certain times of the year. When these tall street gates swing open they reveal stunning courtyards. Visit the Hôtels Carnavalet, Rohan, Salé and Soubise, homes to many of the area's fine museums, the most famous of which is devoted to Picasso.

Hard to imagine that this area was once merely a slushy bog to the north of the island that was Paris. Uninhabitable until the 13th century, when monks converted the swamps around the rue St-Antoine to farmland, gradually the Marais became a fashionable alternative to the city centre. In the late 14th century it even became a royal retreat for Charles VI. Place des Vosges, the oldest square in Paris, is one of very few remaining pre-Revolution *places* in France.

For the more animated caller, a spirited nightlife spills over from the borders with both Bastille and Les Halles. The studious visitor has the Conservatoire des Arts et Métiers and the national archives. Hard-core clothes horses discover a playground filled with accessories shops and the *pret à porter* merchants of the wholesale clothing district. No wonder that visitors to the quarter have been known to ignore the rest of the city.

Fortunately the place Hôtel de Ville, scene of the famous kiss photographed by Robert Doisneau, is the perfect wide-open space to tempt one away from the narrow byways of the Marais. From Christmas, and through January, the square in front of the ornate town hall is transformed into a fabulous ice rink, where couples skate glove in glove after dark, and office workers forgo lunch in favour of a sandwich and the thrill of a triple salchow.

Here one is but half a river's-breadth away fron the original city of Paris. The fishermen of ancient Gaul founded Lutetia around 250BC, building a settlement on the largest island in the Seine. It remained a modest settlement until Julius Caesar conferred power and status to the Ile de la Cité in 52BC. In the 9th century the island became capital of France. The growth of the universities and churches on the left bank of the river began the expansion of Paris, but for centuries the *Cité* remained the seat of government and justice.

Of course the most famous building on the island is the cathedral of Notre Dame. The place du Parvis provides the classic view of the cathedral, as seen on good tea towels and bad travelogues. To the left of the coaches disgorging their passengers and the souvenir hawkers on the Parvis is the **Hôtel-Dieu**, my personal sanctuary from the hustling, bustling pilgrimage. The hospice, founded in the 7th century, was rebuilt in the late 19th century. Still a working hospital, the cloisters are a haven of tranquillity for a hassled visitor to Paris.

The island furnishes a full itinerary of sightseeing, The Palais de Justice, the wonderful Gothic Sainte-Chapelle and Marie-Antoinette's prison cell at the Conciergerie are within minutes of each other. In the morning, true romantics, with hearts bigger than their budgets, come to place Lepine's marketplace to buy armloads of fresh flowers to transform the simplest and cheapest hotel room into a bower.

Across a little bridge is the Ile St-Louis, too often trimmed from the tour programme. In the 17th century the king gave permission for architects to create a new fashionable district on the river. They joined together two undistinguished islands, the Ile aux Vaches and the Ile Notre Dame, and created the Ile St-Louis, with peaceful streets, expensive shops and a select few high-priced, secluded hotels for the discerning.

WHERE TO STAY

Axial Beaubourg ll rue du Temple, 75004; tel: 01 42 72 72 22; web: www.axialbeaubourg.com [8 C1]

$\overline{M}$ *Hôtel-de-Ville;* $\overline{E}$ *RER to Châtelet-Les-Halles then métro 1 to Hôtel-de-Ville. Take the street down the side of BHV department store and take rue de Temple to junction with rue de la Verrerie.*

If you've been away from Paris for a while and have fond memories of this street dividing the Beaubourg and Marais quarters, do not expect to return to the run-down little one-star hotel, with its steep climb to the upstairs reception, tiny little rooms and rickety *La Bohème* shutters that let in the stars. One day, when we were all looking the other way, the legendary Unic closed its doors and reopened as the three-star Axial Beaubourg, complete with en-suite bathrooms, modem connections and a stylish new ground-floor reception. The new welcome is smartly efficient and the respectable hotel, though comfortable and up to date, is less Marais Bohemian and more Beaubourg tourist. Room rates €99 (650FF).

Caron de Beaumarchais 12 rue Vieille du Temple, 75004; tel: 01 42 72 34 12; web: www.carondebeaumarchais.com [8 B1]

$\overline{M}$ *Hôtel-de-Ville;* $\overline{E}$ *RER to Châtelet-Les-Halles then métro 1 to Hôtel-de-Ville. Walk east along rue de Rivoli and turn left into rue Vieille du Temple.*

As you enter this hotel, named for the author of the subversive comedy *The Marriage of Figaro*, you might have stepped on to the stage of an 18th-century comedy, the cast having popped out for a moment. The reception is not so much a foyer as a prettily dressed *tableau vivant*. Family-run hotels and classy hotels usually belong in two separate Parisian categories. But the deep blue façade, rich old oak beams within and welcome throughout make this a rather special exception to the rule. Gold-leaf flecked mirrors and 18th-century adornments make each of the, admittedly small, 19 bedrooms a pretty retreat from the Rivoli traffic and Marais rat runs. I always feel a distinct pang when I look at the pictures on the wall: framed pages removed from early editions of the greatest hit of the eponymous playwright and one-time neighbour. Yet, with *bouquinistes* selling torn pages from first editions along the river banks a few hundred yards away, I suppose I should accept it as the custom of the country. Rooms around €120 (800FF).

Chevaliers 38 rue du Turenne, 75003; tel: 01 42 72 73 47 [8 C1–2]

$\overline{M}$ *Chemin-Vert;* $\overline{E}$ *Métro 5 to République then line 8 to Chemin-Vert. Rue St-Gilles and left to rue du Turenne.*

My warmest memories of Ghislaine Truffaut's cosy Marais hotel are of an oasis of welcome during times of chaos. One of France's periodic transport strikes had abandoned me by the English Channel, shown me more motorway service areas than I ever knew existed, dumped me on the dodgiest fringes of town and imprisoned me in a Paris taxi for the best part of an hour and 200-franc note. So I was in no mood for roughing it any further. Cue two tiny Yorkshire terriers who defined me as something between a long lost friend and the doggie Messiah. Ego massaged and heart melted, I detached my shoelaces from the canine doormen and checked into this one-time private house of the 16th century - just around the corner from the place des Vosges. Discreetly modern décor with valet stand, hairdryer, cable TV and mini-bars. As I came through the door, Ghislaine's father rushed out. He was operating a one-man rescue service, collecting stranded guests from all points gridlocked. The welcome continued throughout the stay and, I learned from other guests, was typical of the Truffauts.

The hotel has just 24 rooms at around €100 (650FF) and many look into the tiny trellised well of a courtyard. British guests prefer the top two floors with their rooms under the eaves. But it is the charm of the hosts even more than the décor that makes the Chevaliers special. At bedtime one might find a *bijou* box of sweets on the pillow, or a little fruit basket at the bedside. Do not rush to give your gold card a workout before chatting with Ghislaine. Before opening the hotel, she spent years in the rag trade, and will steer guests towards truly Parisian boutiques and shops rather than the conventional department stores promoted by every other reception desk in town. Her enthusiasm for her hotel, guests and neighbours is infectious; over the years clients have become penpals. Occasionally she organises a wine tasting or art show in the breakfast cellar, once the site of an auberge in the days of the royal tournaments.

Deux Iles 59 rue St-Louis en l'Ile, 75004; tel: 01 43 26 13 35 [8 C2]
M̄ *Pont-Marie;* Ē *RER to Châtelet-Les-Halles then métro 1 to Pont-Marie. Cross the bridge to rue St-Louis en l'Ile.*
A charming and cosy old-style hotel set around a glass enclosed courtyard. Comfortable country-style rooms have attractive blue-and-white-tiled bathrooms, and a welcoming reception lounge and homely cellar prove chill-out sanctuary after a hard day's shopping. Rooms cost €137 (900FF). If it's full, try the neighbouring **Hôtel Lutèce**, at number 65, a slightly higher priced annexe under the same management.

Grand Hôtel de Loiret 8 rue des Mauvais-Garçons, 75009; tel: 01 48 87 77 00 [8 C1]
M̄ *Hôtel-de-Ville;* Ē *RER to Châtelet-Les-Halles then métro 1 to Hôtel-de-Ville. Rue des Mauvais-Garçons is a tiny side street north of rue de Rivoli.*
Not to put too fine a point on it, when I first knew this place it was a total dump with hot and cold running wallpaper, and guests were advised to take their soap to the public baths by the river. So when it closed down and reopened, I was inclined to raise an eyebrow, suppress a smug smile and pass by on the other side. But what a pleasant surprise: completely renovated, invariably *complet*, some rooms even have en-suite facilities, and genuine bargain room rates hovering around the €53 (350FF) mark. There is even a lift (I recall agonizing climbs to the top-floor rooms back in the days when they cost 80 francs a night!). Helpful and pleasant staff, and clean and inoffensive bedrooms.

Jeu de Paume 54 rue St-Louis en l'Ile, 75004; tel: 01 43 26 14 18; web: www.hoteljeudepaume.com [8 C2]

M̲ *Pont-Marie;* E̲ *RER to Châtelet-Les-Halles then métro 1 to Pont-Marie. Cross the bridge to rue St-Louis en l'Ile.*

An archway leads to the 17th-century courtyard of the former royal *jeu de paume*, or real tennis court, an ideal retreat for the visitor jaded by too much whitewash and chrome. The glass lift affords a superb view of the court and its galleries, which are cleverly fitted as comfortable breakfast and lounge areas, centuries-old beams grandly supporting this airy central well. Each of the rooms has its own individual style, with mod cons and bathrooms *comme il faut*. Ten lucky guests are able to sleep under the eaves, reaching their beds via private spiral staircases. No danger of traffic noise since the rue St-Louis, although the main throroughfare of the tiny island, leads absolutely nowhere. Guests may use the hotel's sauna, jacuzzi and mini-gym. Rooms cost in the region of €199 (1,300FF), breakfast is a somewhat steep €12 (80FF).

Pavillon de la Reine 28 pl des Vosges, 75003; tel: 01 40 29 19 19; web: www.pavillon-de-la-Reine.com [8 D2]
M̲ *St-Paul or Bastille;* E̲ *Métro 5 to Bastille. Follow rue St-Antoine and turn right on rue de Birague into the square.*

Before the Revolution, the place des Vosges was known as the place Royale, and the square had lodges dedicated to the king and queen. The queen's pavilion is the only truly château-style hotel in the quarter. It may not actually be a real château, but gracious living comes as standard. The exterior positively drips with age-old ivies and creepers, and the public rooms luxuriate in rich tapestry and sumptuous textiles. A surprisingly young team runs the hotel with efficiency and discretion. There is no barman, however, since there is no bar in which to entertain friends nor anywhere for non-residents to drop in for a glass or two. Guests may 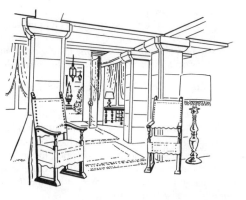 serve themselves a drink in the imposing main salon, where an 'honesty' system of trust prevails, or unscrew a bottle in the bedrooms. These bedrooms, reached by a quaint trompe l'oeil lift, are charmingly understated: a row of scatter-cushions on a yellow quilted bedspread against exposed wall timbers, or an undraped bare iron bedstead amongst warm terracotta tints. The air-conditioned grandeur serves the well-heeled who can afford €252-457 (1,650-3,000FF) per night. The tiny courtyard garden is a sweet bonus but the true delight is a base on the lovely pre-Revolution square where English nannies push prams on a summer's morning, and some superb restaurants and *salons de thé* are just a stroll along the arcades. Private parking within the hotel.

Place des Vosges 12 rue de Birague, 75004; tel: 01 42 72 60 46; email: globermar@easynet.fr [8 D2]
M̲ *Bastille;* E̲ *Métro 5 to Bastille. On rue St-Antoine, rue de Birague is on the right.*
Just off the southern arcade, not quite on the square itself, is this €84 (550FF) a night mid-range hotel with most comforts, and simple bathrooms. A new wave

of modern marble-tiled suites is currently sweeping through the building. A courteous welcome in the spacious reception leads to the adventure of the lift, designed for one small person with half a small suitcase.

St-Merry 78 rue de la Verrerie, 75004; tel: 01 42 78 14 15 [4 B8]
M̲ *Hôtel de Ville;* E̲ *RER to Châtelet-Les-Halles then métro 1 to Hôtel de Ville. Walk up rue du Renard and turn left on to rue de la Verrerie. The hotel is on your right.*
A room with a view is all very well, but I love a room with a 16th-century church en suite. The most fab, groovy, rocking, cracking, super, spiffing and splendid hotel bed in the city is to be found in Room 9 of the Hôtel St-Merry. Forget your four-posters and your Sanderson drapes, this bed is quite o'ercanopied by the flying buttresses of the church next door. Raid your bar budget and raise a glass to Monsieur Crabbe, whose idea it was to create this Gothic bolthole, where the interior of the hotel is the exterior of the church next door. The church of St-Merri stands shoulder to waist alongside the Pompidou Centre. Around 300 years ago a presbytery was grafted on to its side, using the buttresses, windows and statuary of the original church as one wall. Forty years ago the building had become a run-down bordello, and M Crabbe decided to convert it into a hotel. No lift, no TV, it may not be to everybody's taste, but those who share the Crabbe passion for glorious 19th-century Gothic furniture and ex-ecclesiastical fittings will love the place. Rein in your natural impulse to swing from wooden and iron chandeliers or fight dastardly villains around the spiral staircase in the style of Errol Flynn, and relish the atmosphere created by furniture recycled from long closed churches. Choir-stall panelling, confessionals as phone booths: M Crabbe has been known to close a bedroom for six months until just the right furniture can be found. Some rooms have tiny windows high in the walls, ideal for peeking into the church during the weekend concerts of baroque or world music. Others, like room 12, have fine views of the spooky Tour St-Jacques. Each double room, at €130–275 (850–1,800FF), is priced according to its Gothic splendour. Thankfully the bathrooms are definitely of the present century and fully fitted with all mod cons and hairdryers. Advance reservation is essential, as I have found to my cost. Since first writing about the place, it has been nigh on impossible for me to turn up unannounced and get a room!

Septième Art 20 rue St-Paul, 75004; tel: 01 44 54 85 00 [8 D2]
M̲ *St-Paul;* E̲ *RER to Châtelet-Les-Halles then métro 1 to St-Paul. Walk east on rue St-Antoine and turn right into rue St-Paul. The hotel is on your left.*
Lights, camera, action! Paris is the city of cinema. Some 300 films, from Katherine Hepburn classics to the latest releases, are screened each week. Movie buffs should aim to spend a night in this very stylish two-star Right Bank hotel. The spirit of Hollywood is everywhere – with golden age posters over the beds and black-and-white-tiled bathrooms, framed star photographs from the reception to the bar and proof if any were needed that the glamour of the movies began in the 20s and ended in the 1960s. Comfort-wise, the hotel comes up trumps too, with soundproofed bedrooms, safes, hairdryers, and even a laundry service available to guests at an additional charge. Pay from around €53–105 (350–700FF) – rooms from singles to mini-suites. Book early, as guests quickly become regulars and rooms tend to be snapped up in season, especially my favourite which is dedicated to Rita Hayworth. The reception has a dinky movie memorabilia shop well suited to its location in a street of antique and collectors' markets of the village St-Paul.

Vieux Marais 8 rue de Plâtre, 75004; tel: 01 42 78 47 22 [8 C1]
M̲ *Hôtel-de-Ville;* E̲ *RER to Châtelet-Les-Halles then métro 1 to Hôtel-de-Ville. On rue des Archives, rue de Plâtre is third street on the left.*

Once a favourite with many of us who'd known the quarter since before gentrification, here are neat rooms within walking distance of the Pompidou Centre. These days the warm friendly welcome of old is less evident, although some regulars still like to keep the place to themselves, so book early. The €100 (660FF) price now reflects the area's popularity.

WHERE TO GO

Beaubourg (see *Centre National d'Art Contemporain Georges Pompidou*, page 77) [8 B1]

Berthillon 31 rue St-Louis-en-l'Ile, 75004; tel: 01 43 54 31 61 [8 C2]
Open Wed–Sun 10.00–20.00 (eat in 14.00,20.00); closed Jul, Aug.
M̄ *Pont-Marie;* Ē *RER to Châtelet-Les-Halles then métro 7 to Pont-Marie, cross the Ile de la Cité on Pont Marie, taking rue de Deux Ponts to rue St-Louis-en-l'Ile.*
Define Parisian: Parisian is an ice-cream shop that closes in the summer because the locals will be on holiday and only several million tourists will be in town. The Chauvin family, descendents of Monsieur Berthillon, create the greatest *glaces* and *sorbets*. There is always a queue of expensively dressed people of taste waiting to be served. Staff are polite and take their time scooping the ice-cream into tubs and cornets. If the Chauvins were ruthless and businesslike, they could knock Ben & Jerry's and Haagen Dazs into oblivion, but in Parisian society, the profit motive is considered vulgar, therefore Berthillon sticks to one shop, only lets customers eat inside after lunch, and takes a two-month summer holiday. So there.

Café Beaubourg 100 rue St-Martin, 75004; tel: 01 48 87 89 98 [8 B1]
M̄ *Hôtel-de-Ville;* Ē *RER to Châtelet-Les-Halles (exit Forum des Halles). Take the escalator to rue Pierre Lescot, turn right then left to rue Berger. Cross the boulevard and head towards the Pompidou Centre. The café is on your right.*
Of all the cafés, bars and restaurants created by the Costes team, this is the least pretentious and most comfortable. At any time of day you can sit on the terrace and chill out as you watch the swarm of humanity buzzing around the hive of the Pompidou Centre. In early afternoon the effect is of being mellow and in control of a fast forward and pause button. Since I am not a great fan of hotel breakfasts, I usually prefer to wake myself up as the Parisians do – in street-corner bars and cafés. The street-corner bar next to my hotel satisfies me. With espresso machines gurgling and windows steaming, Café Beaubourg does a more extensive breakfast than most – fresh orange juice, eggs however you like them and a selection of breads and croissants, with access to the morning papers and a stack of paperbacks, all for €10 (70FF). Tables are cannily positioned to benefit from summer breezes.

Gallerie 88 88 quai de l'Hôtel de Ville, 75004; tel: 01 42 72 17 58 [8 C2]
M̄ *Hôtel-de-Ville;* Ē *RER to Châtelet-Les-Halles then métro 1 Hôtel-de-Ville. Walk around the Hôtel de Ville itself to the row of shops facing the riverbank.*
If the buzz and zest of fashionable cafés and bars seems too much to take and you would rather slob and slouch like a real Parisian across the water on the Left Bank, then this is the very place to hang out with friends. After a heavy night in midwinter, turn up at lunchtime to nurse a hot toddy of honey, lemon juice and ginger. Trust me, it works wonders. It is a great place for meeting up with vegetarian friends as the meatless salads and snacks are straight from the Med, with delicious *tapenades* and fruits for healthy eating.

Hôtel Dieu (Cloister) pl du Parvis Notre-Dame, 75004; tel: $ free [8 B2]
M̄ *Cité or St-Michel;* Ē *RER B to St-Michel-Notre-Dame. From quai St-Michel cross the Petit pont to parvis Notre Dame (see page 69).*

Passage Molière rues Quincampoix and St-Martin, 75003 [8 B1]
M̄ *Rambuteau, Les-Halles;* Ē *RER to Châtelet-Les-Halles. From Pierre Lescot exit, turn left, then right into rue Rambuteau, cross the boulevard and take first left into rue Quincampoix, then first right.*
My, how this place has smartened itself up over the years. It is now an unlikely treat just yards from the Pompidou Centre. You could spend ages musing among the mews galleries. Molière's own muse is served by the bookshop at number 16 and the theatre. Regular poetry recitals are programmed here as well as literary and drama festivals. Next door, at number 12, **Au Vieux Molière** (tel: 01 42 78 37 87) is a stylish restaurant for sophisticated dining amongst the photographs, autographs, soft lights and softer seats of a restaurant offering a gentle welcome, good wines and a classic fish and farmyard dinner for around €46 (300FF). Across the passage is the intriguing shop window of artist **Brigitte Massoutier**. If you would like to see your feet, fingers or lips transformed into works of art, Brigitte will immortalise a pose in plaster. The window display features scores of casts of hands and feet in elegant poses. She is hardly ever in so call her on 06 61 97 47 99. Charges from €152 (1,000FF) for children and €228 (1,500FF) for adults. For €30 (200FF) extra she will visit you at your hotel.

Place Dauphine [8 A1–2]
M̄ *Pont-Neuf;* Ē *RER to Châtelet-Les-Halles then métro 7 to Pont-Neuf. Cross the bridge to Ile de la Cité and turn left.*
I am always amazed that this pretty triangle of peace at the true crossroads of Paris, where the Left and Right banks exchange their tourists, remains so tranquil. Once a royal botanical garden, now an enclave of some charming brick and stone buildings, the place is an ideal location for picturing Paris past. From here, climb down the steps behind the statue of Henri IV to the last part of the original Ile de la Cité, before cathedral builders and kings raised it high above the waterlevel. The square du Vert Gallant is a great place to picnic by the river's edge, below street level and below the arches of the Pont Neuf.

Place des Vosges [8 D2]
Open Tue–Sat 10.00–17.40. Admission €3.50 (22FF) but free on Sunday 10.00–13.00.
M̄ *St-Paul or Bastille;* Ē *Métro 5 to Bastille. Follow rue St-Antoine and turn right on rue de Birague into the square.*
Here are the gardens where families take the air with their perambulators on Sunday mornings, and lone bookworms relax with a well-thumbed paperback. But this is also the last glimpse we have of what Paris would have looked like before the Revolution, Napoléon and the era of great urban planners redefined the city. The former place Royale, built in the reign of Henri IV, comprises 36 houses forming a symmetrical pattern of arcades. Good food is served here, and antiques are sold on the pavements of the colonnades. The Pavillon du Roi, on the south side, was once a royal residence. It faces the Pavillon de la Reine, now a hotel, to the north. From 1832 to 1848, Victor Hugo lived in the **Hôtel de Rohan-Guéménée** at number 6 (tel: 01 42 72 10 16). For the past century it has been preserved as a museum devoted to the life of the great man.

Rue Vieille du Temple [8 C2–D1]
M̄ *Hôtel-de-Ville or Rambuteau;* Ē *RER to Châtelet-Les-Halles then métro 1 to Hôtel-de-Ville. Walk east along rue de Rivoli and turn left into rue Vieille du Temple.*
The Vieille du Temple is the Meridian Line of the northern Marais. To the west is the hip trip of rendezvous with fleeting acquaintances, café theatre and

designer portions on designer dinner plates, eastwards is the rue des Rosiers and the self proclaimed ghetto with kosher chicken soup and Yiddish story-telling. During the day you may walk north from the rue de Rivoli and choose between the archives to your left and the Picassos on your right. But come here after dark and pick the bar for an evening of chat, music, flirtation or debate. At number 31, **La Belle Hortense** (tel: 01 48 04 71 60) is a wine merchant's shop, a wine bar and a bookshop, sparking with lively conversation around midnight. For discussions that simply refuse to die down continue over a generous glass of St-Emilion, post theatre or post dinner party, Hortense offers the ideal way to end a night out. The crowd across the way at number 34, the **Etoile Manquante** (tel: 01 42 72 48 34), may have spent a little longer dressing for the evening. Painfully trendy, this place has had so many incarnations and is always so sharp that it impales itself on its own cutting edge. The truly laid-back crowd hangs out next door at **Le Petit Fer à Cheval** (see pages 86–7), where lycra cycle shorts are not a fashion statement, merely proof of ownership of the bike chained up outside. On the corner of rue Ste-Croix de la Bretonnerie, 33 rue Vieille du Temple, is the **Hôtel Central** (tel: 01 48 87 99 33), one of the oldest gay bars in the district. Known for its muscular bronze torso on the stone wall, it is nonetheless very much a neighbourhood bar. Even more casual is the **Amnesia Café** (tel: 01 42 72 16 94) at number 42, on the corner with rue de Rosiers, where gay meets straight and Jew meets Gentile, and friends plot the evening together over tall glasses of *menthe à l'eau* as they lounge in wicker chairs. Through the potted palms of the Amnesia, they peer across at the mellow crowd chilling out to Motown sounds in the candlelit corners of **Chez Richard** at number 37 (tel: 01 42 74 31 65) under the archway. The perfect halfway house, midway down the street in the middle of the Marais, to weigh up the evening's prospects on a pavement where the very last goodbyes are air-kissed at two in the morning.

WHAT TO SEE

Archives Nationales 60 rue des Francs Bourgeois, 75003; tel: 01 40 27 60 96 [8 C1]
Open Mon, Wed–Fri 10.00–17.45, Sat–Sun 13.45–17.45; closed holidays. ∈3 (20FF).
M̱ *Rambuteau or Hôtel-de-Ville;* Ē *RER to Châtelet-Les-Halles then métro 11 to Rambuteau. Follow rue Rambuteau eastwards and cross over the junction with rue des Archives.*
Shakespeare dismissed her as La Pucelle, the people called her the Maid of Orleans and Shaw and the Church remember her as St-Joan. Ask nicely at the national archives and someone will show you the original transcript of the trial of Joan of Arc. You might prefer to read the wills of the famous, or perhaps rummage amongst the private papers of Marie-Antoinette. Even if wading through dusty manuscripts does not appeal, walking behind the unimpressive outer walls of the Hôtel de Guise will bring history most vividly to life. This was the magnificent family home of the influential Rohan-Soubise dynasties until the *Ancien Régime* was overtaken by the Terror. The interior splendour is well worth the detour and you will find fewer distracting groups of sightseers than at the better known Hôtels Carnavalet and Salé.

Centre National d'Art Contemporain Georges Pompidou (Pompidou Centre) pl Beaubourg 75004; tel: 01 44 78 12 23; web: www.cnac-gp.fr [8 B1]
Open Wed–Mon 11.00–21.00; closed May 1. ∈4.5 (30FF) free one Sunday every month.

View from the Pompidou Centre

M̲ *Rambuteau;* E̲ *RER to Châtelet-Les-Halles then either take walk from rue Pierre Lescot left along rue Berger, across the boulevard to the centre, or choose to take métro 11 directly to Rambuteau behind the building.*

More people come to gawp at the outside than to peek at what lies within the Pompidou Centre, better known to the locals as Beaubourg. But whatever the lure, it attracts more visitors than anything else in town. With almost 1,500 permanent exhibits that date from 1905, where the Musée d'Orsay leaves off, and plenty of great temporary shows, there is always a good reason to revisit the centre. Travel on the external glass-tube-encased escalators. Most famous stopping points for cultural quick fixes are level 4 for Andy Warhol and all who sailed on his shirttails from the 1960s and beyond; level 5 for Miro, Matisse, Picasso and chums; and the top floor for the view. The Costes team recently took over the in-house catering, but their Café Beaubourg next door still manages to out-perform the restaurant and café inside the building. Although more conventional buildings usually cope with a hundred years of visitors before beginning to creak, Rodgers' and Piano's controversial inside-out design required a complete physical overhaul at the end of the 20th century. However you look at it, it provides a great backdrop to the sunken piazza where hundreds of visitors gather to picnic on the cobbles, enjoy street entertainers and be unashamedly touristy. The atmosphere remains that of Les Halles across the way. Just to one side of the building a deliciously silly collection of fountains flaps and spits as the water cools the crowds in a year-round holiday mood.

Conciergerie Palais de la Cité, 1 quai de l'Horloge, 75001; tel: 01 53 73 78 50 [8 A–B2]
Open summer 09.30–18.30, winter 10.00–17.00; closed holidays. €5.50 (36FF).
M̲ *Cité;* E̲ *Métro 4 to Cité. From pl Lepine walk to the quai de la Course and turn left.*
This neat building on the island is nice and clean, as befits a royal palace, but close your eyes to the present and imagine it during the reign of Terror, when the palace became a prison. Visit the very cell where Marie-Antoinette spent her final days and nights before being carted across the bridge to her final rendezvous with Madame la Guillotine. Check out the doorway, since the lintel was deliberately lowered for her arrival, in order that the queen be obliged to bow her head as she entered the cell. Hapsburgs are made of stronger stuff, and instead she bent her knees and held her head high. As far from her life at Versailles (see page 183) as anyone might fear. For a gruesome footnote to her story visit the **Chapelle Expiatoire** by St-Lazare (page 42). Other Very Important Prisoners included Danton, Madame du Barry, Robespierre and the poet André Chenier.

Above the cells, visit the splendid, Gothic vaulted great hall and the kitchens of the 14th-century fortress.

Hôtel Carnavalet 23 rue de Sévigné, 75003; tel: 01 42 72 21 13 [8 D1]
Open Tue–Sun 10.00–17.40; closed holidays. €4.50 (30FF).
M̄ *Chemin-Vert;* Ē *Métro 5 to République, then line 8 to Chemin-Vert. Walking south on bd Beaumarchais, turn right on rue du Pas de la Mule to rue des Francs Bourgeois and right into rue Sévigné.*

Once upon a time there was a city called Paris and it all lived happily ever after in this mansion and the Hôtel Peletier de St-Fargeau next door. Everything you have forgotten about the story of Paris is remembered in the museum of the city's history. Souvenirs of times of wealth, of prosperity, of poverty, of tranquillity, of wartime and revolution are on display, as are recreations of the very elegant 16th- and 17th-century domestic settings for which the *hôtels particuliers* of the Marais were originally conceived.

Hôtel de Sens 1 rue du Figuier, 75004; tel: 01 42 78 14 60 [8 C2]
Open Tue–Fri 13.30–20.00, Sat 10.00–20.30. Free.
M̄ *Pont-Marie or St-Paul;* Ē *RER to Châtelet-Les-Halles then métro 1 to St-Paul. Behind the station take the narrow rue du Prévôt to rue du Figuier.*

If you have hammered the budget too hard at the other museums, here is a treat for free. Just beyond the riverbank, the oldest medieval house in the Marais makes quite a contrast to the splendour of the Renaissance residences in the northern Marais. If you make arrangements in advance, you may be able to visit the Forney library of great volumes dedicated to the arts.

Memorial de la Déportation sq Ile de France, 75004
Open summer 10.00–12.00, 14.00–19.00, winter 10.00–12.00, 14.00–17.00; closed last Sun in April. Free.
M̄ *Cité or St-Michel-Notre-Dame;* Ē *RER B to St-Michel-Notre-Dame. From quai St-Michel cross the Pont de l'Archevêché to sq Ile de France.*

Behind the cathedral, beneath the gardens of the square Ile de France, where Napoléon once built a public morgue, may be found the low-key monument to Parisians rounded up during the Nazi occupation. Underground, at the very tip of the island, is the cellar from whence victims of the Nazis were deported to death camps. With just a simple metallic sculpture by Desserprit and the tomb of the Unknown Deportee, there is little to see here, but a great deal to feel. If you cross the footbridge to the Ile St-Louis and follow signs to Pont Marie métro, you will pass a wall plaque telling of how entire families were taken from a house on the rue des Deux Ponts.

Musée d'Art et Histoire du Judaisme (Jewish Art and History Museum), Hôtel de Saint-Aignan, 71 rue du Temple, 75003; tel: 01 53 01 86 60 [8 C1]
Open Mon–Fri 11.00–18.00, Sun 10.00–18.00; closed Sat and Jewish holidays. €6 (40FF).
M̄ *Rambuteau;* Ē *RER to Châtelet-Les-Halles then métro 11 to Rambuteau. Follow rue Rambuteau eastwards then left on to rue du Temple.*

After the Spanish Inquisition, European Jews scattered across the continent. United in the splendid Hôtel de Saint-Aignan, the worlds of many of these Jewish communities are brought together. This remarkable collection is superbly displayed with an excellent audio commentary that may be adjusted to the visitor's own pace and interests. I was fascinated by the variety of everyday artefacts, such as the *menorah* and *chanukiah* candelabra from as far away as the Ottoman Empire, and a complete painted *succah* (harvest festival house) from central Europe. A fabulous art collection includes paintings by Chagall, festive scenes from the Venice Ghetto and a picture of the cemetery at Krakow. The last was the first picture I have ever seen of the town from which my grandmother's family fled to England after the pogroms of the late 19th century. Other refugees built models of the synagogues and *shtetls* (villages) that they had left behind them, and these miniatures are beautifully displayed.

Social history and explanations of the *Sephardi* and *Ashkenazi* cultures are well illustrated, and an archive of anti-semitism from Zola and Dreyfus to recent years is a reminder that life in the ghettos has always been fragile. A glaring omission to the story of Jews in France and Europe is the lack of any substantial reference to the Holocaust. There is merely an obscure exhibit following the fate of the building's wartime inhabitants. However, a ten-minute walk across the Marais leads to the archive records of every family deported from Paris, housed in the **Memorial du Martyr Juif Inconnu**, 17 rue Geoffroy l'Aisnier, 75004; tel: 01 42 77 44 42. M̄ Pont-Marie (Sun–Thu 10.00–13.00, 14.00–18.00, Fri 14.00–17.00; closed Sun. ∈3 20FF). The Jewish Museum has an excellent shop, but even better is the art gallery next door that specialises in contemporary Judaica.

Musée Cognacq-Jay Hôtel Donon, 8 rue Elzévir, 75003; tel: 01 40 27 07 21 [8 B1]
Open Tue–Sun 10.00–17.40; closed holidays. ∈2.50 (15FF). Free to under 26s and over 60s (except exhibitions).
M̄ *St-Paul* Ē *RER Châtelet-Les-Halles then métro 1 to St-Paul. Follow rue Pevée, turn left on to rue Franco Borgoises, then right to rue Elzévir.*
This Marais *hôtel particulier* is home to the art collection of the founding family of Samaritaine department store. Whilst their emporium on the banks of the Seine was hailed for its contemporary art nouveau style, when it came to decorating their home, Ernest Cognacq and his wife Louise Jay preferred the old-style romantic approach to art and furnishing. So, with the obvious domestic favourites Watteau and Fragonard, delight in their selection of canvases by Sir Joshua Reynolds, Rembrandt, Rubens and good old Canaletto.

Musée de la Curiosité 11 rue St-Paul, 75004; tel: 01 42 72 13 26 [8 C2]
Open Wed, Sat, Sun 14.00–19.00 (also daily during half-term holidays in winter). ∈7 (45FF).
M̄ *St-Paul;* Ē *RER to Châtelet-Les-Halles then métro 1 to St-Paul. Walk eastwards towards Bastille on the rue St-Antoine and turn right on to rue St-Paul.*
When I was a little boy, I had an uncle who would produce ceramic eggs from an empty velvet bag. I was enchanted. Of course in those days no one had even heard of PlayStation. My faith in the pulling power of magic was bolstered when my own nephews announced that they too would rather see something appear out of thin air than something nuked in cyberspace. In Sam's case, all birthday money is now spent on silk handkerchiefs that vanish at will and wooden boxes that defy the laws of physics. So I cannot wait to take the boys to the Museum of Curiosity, this little cellar of prestidigitation, *léger du main* and illusion. Magicians escort visitors into a world where nothing is as it seems. The exhibition boasts fairground automata and the original tricks, mirrors and cabinets of such 18th- and 19th-century giants of the art as Robert Houdin, inspiration of Houdini. Live conjuring shows are always staged here and careers may be started at the little magic shop. Should the muse strike when the *musée* is closed, check out the magic shop across the river at 8 rue des Carmes (M̄ *Maubert-Mutualité* [8 B3]).

Musée Picasso Hôtel Salé, 5 rue de Thorigny, 75003; tel: 01 42 71 25 21 [8 D1]
Open Wed–Sun winter 09.30–17.30, summer 09.30–18.00; closed Dec 25 and
Jan 1. €4.50 (30FF), Sun €3 (20FF).
M̄ *Rambuteau;* Ē *RER to Châtelet-Les-Halles then métro 11 to Rambuteau. Follow rue
Rambuteau eastwards then left on to rue du Temple and right on rue de la Perle to pl de
Thorigny.*
The ornate staircase and beautifully renovated rooms of the elegant 17th-century
Hôtel Salé are home to a comprehensive collection of Picasso's work. Walk
through the famous periods, from blue to pink to cubist, with 200 paintings,
scores of sculptures and countless sketches. When the artist's family donated the
art collection to the state, in lieu of death duties, they also included many
canvases by other painters that Picasso had accumulated during his lifetime. You
may not be surprised to see works by Braque hanging here, as his paintings are
often displayed alongside Picassos in many major galleries. The unexpected treat
is stumbling across Renoir and Cézanne in this most unlikely of settings.

Musée de la Poupée Impasse Berthaud, 75003; tel: 01 42 72 73 11 [8 C1]
Open Tue–Sun 10.00–18.00. €5.50 (35FF).
M̄ *Rambuteau;* Ē *RER to Châtelet-Les-Halles then métro 11 to Rambuteau. Just north of
the junction with rue Rambuteau, walk to the end of this alleyway and enter the pretty
garden forecourt of the museum.*
A very Victorian childhood is cherished for all time in this dark old house at the
end of the alleyway. In glass display cabinets are staged little tableaux from the
lives of much-loved dolls. Porcelain and biscuit faces smile from under flowing
blonde locks and dainty bonnets in tea party and garden scenes. The father and
son curators care for 300 dolls, and also act as doll-doctors to damaged toys
brought to their door by tearful little girls or heartbroken grandmothers. The
collection dates from 1850 to the present day, and is augmented by some
splendid temporary exhibitions. Never mind Karl Lagerfeld at the Carousel du
Louvre, *le tout Paris* flocked to the amazing beach party scenes that featured every
skimpy outfit worn to the seaside by Barbie and Ken since the 1950s.

Notre Dame 6 pl du Parvis Notre Dame, 75004; tel: 01 42 34 56 10 [8 B2]
Open Mon–Fri 08.00–18.45, Sat–Sun 08.00–19.45; closed to tourists on Holy Days.
M̄ *Cité or St-Michel-Notre-Dame;* Ē *RER B to St-Michel-Notre-Dame. From quai St-
Michel cross the Petit Pont to parvis Notre Dame.*
All road distances in France are calculated to and from the great doors of the
cathedral. Look for the kilometre zero mark on the square outside. The rose
window and Sunday afternoon organ recitals lure the camcorder-wielding masses
from all points north, south, east and west to one of the most magnificent Gothic
cathedrals in the world. The first pagan settlers in Paris worshipped on this very
site and their altar still lies beneath today's church. The present building took 200
years to build, finally completed in 1345, and carefully restored through the years,
most recently in 1999. To climb the 387 steps to the top of the towers and re-
enact your Quasimodo fantasies pay €5.50 (35FF). Once you regain sensation in
your calves, experience the view over flying buttresses and out across the river,
before coming face to face with *Emmanuel*, the 13-tonne bell. Open most days
from morning until just before dusk (call 01 44 32 16 72 for current hours). From
Tuesday to Sunday visit the crypt under the parvis Notre Dame to view
archaeological treasures dating back as far as the Roman era, and learn the story of
the island. Tickets €4 (26FF) or €6 (40FF) for a joint pass with *Musée Carnavalet*
(see page 78), open 10.00–18.00. A simpler museum of the cathedral's history
opens Wednesday, Saturday and Sunday 14.30–18.00 and costs €2.50 (15FF).

WHERE TO EAT

Amadéo 19 rue François Miron, 75004; tel: 01 48 87 01 02 [8 B2]
Closed Sun.
M̄ *Hôtel-de-Ville;* Ē *RER to Châtelet-Les-Halles then métro 1 to Hôtel-de-Ville. Walk down rue de Loubeau towards the river. The pl St-Gervais on your left leads to rue François Miron.*
In this tiny corner of the quarter, Mozart made his Parisian debut, and in this blue-and-ochre-hued dining room his spirit continues to provide the musical backdrop to *confit* and *chèvre plats du jour.* Live performances twice each month provide delightful diversions, ideal for a romantic anniversary. A little precious, perhaps, but worth considering. Budget €38 (250FF).

Ambassade d'Auvergne 22 rue du Grenier-St-Lazare, 75003; tel: 01 42 72 31 22 [8 C1]
Closed end July.
M̄ *Rambuteau;* Ē *RER to Châtelet-Les-Halles then métro 11 to Rambuteau. Walking north on rue Beaubourg, and turn left on rue du Grenier-St-Lazare.*
The volcanic Auvergne region of central France is famous for its fables and fairy-tales. Good little boys and girls go to sleep with the story of the shepherd boy who, chasing his true love, left a cheese sandwich in a rock by a stream and inadvertently invented Roquefort cheese. Naughty children are nudged towards their nightmares with tales of the *Bête du Gévaudan,* said to have stolen and devoured 100 women and children in the distant past. Happy ever afters are pretty much guaranteed in the fairy-tale quaint embassy of the region's cuisine. Once upon a time, long before the area became fashionable, the Petrucci family opened their Auvergnat restaurant. Three generations on, they are still preparing rich, wholesome, full-flavoured dishes you'd be hard to find anywhere else in the capital. The old tables positively creak under the weight of dishes such as duck *daube* and puy lentil *cassoulets* you could stand a spoon in. The Ambassade serves the best ham in the district, according to far wiser counsel than me, but my personal weakness is the *aligot,* a knockout potato dish with garlic and heady cantal cheese of a quality rarely seen outside wayside inns deep in the heart of the Auvergne. A set menu of €25 (170FF) is good value; otherwise anticipate a bill of around €38 (250FF) per head. The reasonably priced cellar includes many local wines, mostly unknown outside the region, so do ask your waiter for guidance.

Bistrot Beaubourg 25 rue Quincampoix, 75004; tel: 01 42 77 48 02 [8 B1]
M̄ *Les-Halles;* Ē *RER to Châtelet-Les-Halles (exit Forum des Halles). Take the escalator to rue Pierre Lescot, turn right then left to rue Berger. Cross the boulevard heading towards the Pompidou Centre. Turn right into rue de la Reynie.*
Really on the rue de la Reynie, that odd little square off the bd Sébastopol, between Les Halles and Beaubourg, it is something of an oddity, this old-fashioned budget restaurant surrounded by so many more expensive fashionable dining rooms and terraces. Pay more at the *rétro*-looking establishment to the right and to the sometimes g-stringed serving staff at Krokodil on the other side. At the *Bistrot Beaubourg,* simple wooden tables, wicker chairs and gingham-draped lamp shades are the order of the day. The dish of the day costs just €6 (40FF) and may be a *pâté,* steak or *boudin blanc* served with a green vegetable and potatoes, sautéed or *à la vapeur* in the old-fashioned way. Specials of *tripe à la mode* or *escargots* will still only set you back around €8 (50FF). Pay €11 (75FF) for the meal. Eat inside in the *bistrot* itself, papered with posters of cabarets and shows current and past, or sit outdoors and enjoy the buskers playing for the more expensive neighbours.

Bofinger 5-7 rue de la Bastille, 75004; tel: 01 42 72 87 82 [8 D2]
M̄ *Bastille;* Ē *Métro 5 to Bastille. Rue de la Bastille is a small side street on the northwest corner of the place Bastille.*
Sit under the dome in one of Paris' oldest brasseries, a national institution since opening its doors in 1864. Or perhaps play the Victorian *roué* in a little side room designed for indiscretion. First timers come to this bustling brasserie with its sumptuous period décor for the ambience rather than the food. Regulars return for oysters and simple cooking in a district packed with pricey lures to the followers of politics, media, fashion, entertainment and opera. A good €26 (169FF) menu often includes *foie gras, choucroute,* and a spectacular *vacherin* of strawberries and blackcurrants. Except in the private rooms, this is generally not the place for an intimate meal *à deux* – tables are close together and it's difficult not to catch a large part of your neighbour's conversation.

Chez Jenny 39 bd du Temple, 75003; tel: 01 42 74 75 75 [4 D7]
M̄ *République;* Ē *Métro 5 to République. The restaurant is on the southern corner of the square, a few yards along bd du Temple.*
Perched on her high pavement at the corner of place République, Jenny from Alsace is the self-styled Queen of *Choucrouteries.* For those unfamiliar with the national dish of her region, this is the ideal place to try your first *choucroute.* Alsatian sauerkraut is more than cabbage; it is a winter-warming stew of meats and surprises piled high on a plate. Try not to stray too far from the traditional version; Jenny's variations on the theme are less than ideal. However, the fish variety is an acceptable option for non-meat eaters in your party. Portions are colossal, defeating most newcomers, whose dishes rarely return to the kitchen scraped clean. The *Vosgienne* meringue isn't too heavy, unlike the delectable house speciality, *gâteau de fromage blanc,* as rich and wicked as it sounds. Prices are reasonable with €22 (149FF) and €30 (179FF) menus, guaranteeing a full stomach. Alsatian wines make good companions to the sturdy food – a pitcher of Gewürztraminer washes everything down nicely. But Alsace is as much a country of beers as of wine, so feel free to order a pitcher of ale. Even the *apéritif maison* is made with beer and *sirop de citron.* On winter nights the lights twinkle in the window, creating an irresistible welcome. The typically Alsatian interior makes much of lace, polished wood and ornate lights, and there is some splendid marquetry in the upstairs dining room. Service is brasserie-style and brisk, but staff are mostly friendly and willing to take time to help newcomers with the menu. The place gets absolutely packed at weekends.

Le Hangar 12 impasse Berthaud, 75003; tel: 01 42 74 55 44 [8 C1]
Closed Sat lunch, Sun.
M̄ *Rambuteau;* Ē *RER to Châtelet-Les-Halles then métro 11 to Rambuteau. At the station exit, impasse Berthaud is off rue Beaubourg, just north of the junction with rue Rambuteau.*
The impasse Berthaud, on the wrong side of the Pompidou Centre, is one of my favourite dead-end streets in all Paris. Not only because, above the long-bricked-up shopfronts facing the barbed-wire-trussed lot opposite, a lone eruption of vibrant and stunning blooms sprouts from just one window; nor because of the secret garden of childhood safely behind the big iron gates of the Musée de la Poupée (see page 80); nor even yet for the fabulous dolls' museum itself; but also for Le Hangar. Plain yet clean inside with reading material for solo diners, the terrace, heated in winter, is the place to be. It is open from breakfast time and the welcome is warm. Even lighter eaters (I opted for just a couple of starters and the bill) are served with a smile by a waitress with the poise of an off-duty Bluebell Girl. No set menu, just à la carte that should set you back around €24 (160FF)

plus drinks. A refreshing green-olive tapenade is offered as an appetiser; starters include a fluffy *bavarois* of asparagus and good soups; acceptable main courses feature steaks and pan-fried *foie gras*. Best value of all, and the reason I come back, is the wine list of family favourites. They serve wine by the glass also, but with a half-bottle of a 1996 Crozes-Hermitage for around €8 (50FF), why be churlish? A popular, yet understated, venue around the corner for those evenings when you cannot quite face trekking into the bustle of the city centre, despite – or perhaps because of – the grotty location. This is after all what the back streets of Paris were like before the city became internationally self-conscious. Be prepared – no credit cards accepted.

Jo Goldenberg 7 rue des Rosiers, 75004; tel: 01 48 87 20 16 [8 C1–2]
M̲ *St-Paul;* E̲ *RER to Châtelet-Les-Halles then métro 1 to St-Paul. Go north on rue Pavé and take second left to rue des Rosiers.*
Neither trends nor terrorists have been able to put a halt to one of the great Sunday lunchtime traditions of the Marais. The only place where the new Marais actually sits down with the old, Jo Goldenberg has survived the gentrification of so much of the area, and a sobering plaque on the site remembers the tragic victims of a terrorist attack in 1983. A typical Jewish restaurant, if not *glatt-kosher* (certified kosher), it attracts diners as much for the unintentional cabaret of the service as for the *haimishe* (homely) *Ashkenazi* (eastern European) cooking. Orders are taken and dishes flourished with that same ironic insolence that transcends language barriers and is the hallmark of great kosher deli-restaurants the world over, from Wolfes in New York to the late lamented Blooms of Whitechapel. Sit in the packed back room for portions a mother would serve of steaming goulash, or perch at the bar to eavesdrop as locals pop in to collect pastrami, *gefilte* fish and falafel to go. Pay in the region of €38 (250FF).

Pain, Vin, Fromage 3 rue Geoffroy-l'Angevin, 75004; tel: 01 42 74 07 52 [8 C1]
M̲ *Rambuteau;* E̲ *RER to Châtelet-Les-Halles then métro 11 to Rambuteau. At the station exit, rue Geoffroy-l'Angevin is just off rue Beaubourg.*
Bread, wine and cheese. Why else do we come to France? This old-fashioned restaurant, just behind the Pompidou Centre, has served nothing but these three pillars of gastronomy for donkeys' years. Whilst the name may provoke visions of a ploughman's lunch with a glass of Chardonnay, you will be amazed at the choice on the menu. On my first visit, patient waiting-staff steered me through delicious indecision, proof of Charles de Gaulle's famous lament that it was impossible to govern a country that produces 370 varieties of cheese. Mix and match regional platters with good strong wines, or opt for a winter fondue. There is no *prix-fixe* option, so budget €38 (250FF) for an evening meal, or have just a main course at about €15 (100FF).

Picolo Teatro 6 rue des Ecouffes, 75004; tel: 01 42 72 17 19 [8 C2]
Closed Mon and Aug.
M̲ *St-Paul;* E̲ *RER to Châtelet-Les-Halles then métro 1 to St-Paul. Walk west on rue de Rivoli and turn right into rue des Ecouffes.*
There are vegetarian restaurants on the trendier streets of the Marais, but they cannot hold a candle to this seemingly traditional *bistrot* in the slightly less fashionable kosher district. Old stone walls and packed wooden tables are not what you expect of a meat-free eaterie in Paris. But scrumptious cheesy *tartiflettes* served in their oven dishes are heartier fare than the cholesterol-free lentil and celery concoctions of the health-food circuit. Good selection of menus from €9 (60FF) upwards, and plenty of red wine to go with the meal.

Le P'tit Gavroche 15 rue Ste Croix de la Bretonnerie, 75004; tel: 01 48 87 74 26 [8 C1]
Closed Sat lunch, Sun lunch, summer lunch.
M̄ *Hôtel-de-Ville;* Ē̄ *RER to Châtelet-Les-Halles then métro 1 to Hôtel-de-Ville. From rue des Archives, take the second street on the right. The restaurant is on your right.*
The very last of the old Marais bars not to have been made over for the moneyed classes. For as long as I can remember, this tiny backstreet bar, with its restaurant tables on all floors, has provided three-course lunch for under ∈8 (50FF), and dinner for not much more. The basic menu is chalked up on a tiny blackboard hanging outside the front door, and invariably offers a choice of three or five main dishes of the *coq au vin* and simple casserole variety, sandwiched between a *pâté* and the *tarte maison*. Even à la carte won't set you back much more than ∈15 (100FF) for the food. Spend your small change on a beer or *pichet* of wine or knock back a *calva* or cognac with the locals at the bar – a good old-fashioned Paris *zinc*.

Au Tibourg 29 rue du Bourg-Tibourg, 75004; tel: 01 42 74 45 25 [8 C1]
M̄ *Hôtel-de-Ville;* Ē̄ *RER to Châtelet-Les-Halles then métro 1 to Hôtel-de-Ville. Rue de Bourg Tibour is a few yards on your left walking east of BHV.*
Au Tibourg is so traditional that its *cassoulet Grandpère Jean* might have danced off the pages of Elizabeth David, yet its *familiale* welcome is boyishly youthful, kind and gentle. The *foie-gras maison* is genuine, as is the distressed plaster and exposed beam look in this true find in the old Bourg-Tibourg. As befits the home cooking, the place manages to stay out of the style trap without becoming stale. Outside is a street that is in danger of becoming so commercially aware that the cobbles could develop barcodes. Inside, however, the old values reign supreme: the *brandade de morue* is rich and savoury, the *marrons glacés* spiked with whisky. This is not a place to watch the pennies nor waistline. Let it go and let it be. Ardèche wines by the glass, bottle or jug. A menu at around ∈18 (120FF), à la carte for double that (including wine). Love it for its simplicity and style and the hospitality of both the chef and the host, Frédéric and Gérard.

WHAT TO BUY
Albion 13 rue Charles V, 75004, tel: 01 42 72 50 71 [8 D2]
Open Tue–Sat 09.30–19.00.
M̄ *St-Paul;* Ē̄ *RER to Châtelet-Les-Halles then métro 1 to St-Paul. Walk east and turn right into rue St-Paul then left to rue Charles V.*
Between the worlds of the Marais and the Seine, pick up something to read and escape fashionable Paris to thumb through the pages on the quietest riverbanks of the Ile St-Louis a short stroll away.

Berthillon 31 rue St-Louis-en-l'Ile, 75004; tel: 01 43 54 31 61 [8 C2]
Open Wed–Sun 10.00–20.00 (eat in 14.00–20.00); closed Jul, Aug.
M̄ *Pont-Marie.*
(See page 74.)

BHV 52–64 rue de Rivoli, 75001; tel: 01 42 74 90 00; web: www.bhv.fr [8 B1]
Open Mon–Wed, Fri 09.30–19.00, Thu 10.00–21.00, Sat 09.30–20.00.
M̄ *Hôtel-de-Ville;* Ē̄ *RER to Châtelet-Les-Halles then métro 1 to Hôtel-de-Ville. The store has its own private métro entrance.*
Cool or what? For boys, at any rate, this is the least chic and most fun of all the Paris department stores. Bazar de Hôtel de Ville has intriguing specialist counters: on the 5th floor is a vast area selling nothing but self-assembly mezzanines to double the floor space of your Paris apartment; in the basement

find a range of wine presses for your inner city vineyard. All this plus the usual pens and perfumes, handbags and clothes. Behind the main building are equally fascinating specialist annexes where you might pick up hospital beds, dentist's chairs and useful surgical appliances for coping with the aftermath of over-enthusiastic DIY.

Idem 4 rue de Rivoli, 75004; tel: 01 40 29 08 64 [8 C2]
Open 10.00–19.00
M̄ *St-Paul;* Ē *RER to Châtelet-Les-Halles then métro 1 to St-Paul. The shop is opposite the station.*
Just when the window shopping begins to hurt (how on earth do real people afford all those beautiful things that fill every other shop in the Marais?), a cheery little place selling budget kitchenware and household items that have genuine style. Imaginative lamps, fun tableware and grown-up gifts at pocket-money prices.

Flo Prestige 10 rue St-Antoine, 75004; tel: 01 53 01 91 91; web: www.floprestige.fr [8 D2]
Open 08.00–23.00.
M̄ *Bastille;* Ē *Métro 5 to Bastille (exit rue St-Antoine). A few yards from place Bastille along rue St-Antoine.*
When the Parisian returns home after a long day at the office and a long evening sharing a *verre* or two with chums, does he take a Findus box out of the freezer? No. He brings the restaurant meal home with him. If you are self catering – or travelling second class on Eurostar – you would do well to enjoy the handiwork of a Parisian chef. Fabulous prepared poultry dishes or plates of lobster, perhaps the scrumptious *artichaut norvégien* to start with (artichoke wrapped in creamed and grated celeriac, topped with a poached egg and draped in smoked salmon) for €7 (45FF). Telephone in advance for a *coffret de chef,* box dinner trays at €16–31 (107–210FF). €22 (149FF) buys a meal of *compôte de laperau aux pommes et pruneaux, faux filet* with *haricots verts,* cheese, walnut bread and dessert. A suggested Médoc costs €9 (59FF). A €22 (145FF) *coffret* features a starter of *poêlée* of prawns in soy and coriander, *gigot d'agneau* with ratatouille, a cheese and a dessert. €7 (46FF) buys a Côtes du Rhône to go with it. As in the Brasseries Flo, daily specials are available and a superb-value lunch menu for collection only suggests six varieties of main course, dessert and drink for just €8 (50FF). Perhaps *jambon à l'os* with *chèvre*-stuffed potato, a *julienne* of white cabbage in sweet mustard and a roll, followed by *oeufs à la neige,* and a bottle of beer. Chilled wines from €4.50 (30FF) a full bottle. Ideal for the three-hour train journey home. Flo also sells beautifully prepared food and drink gifts – a lifesaver for presents when most shops are shut on a Sunday afternoon. There are 15 branches all over town. For local branches call 01 45 63 03 03 or check the website. Branches close at 22.00 or 23.00. Meals can also be delivered to your hotel for a supplement of €20 (130FF) or €27 (180FF) after 18.00.
    Branches include: **St-Honoré** 42 place du Marché Saint-Honoré, 75001; tel: 01 42 61 45 46; M̄ Pyramides or Tuileries. **St-Germain** 69 rue de Rennes, 75006; tel: 01 53 63 40 20; M̄ St-Sulpice. **Ecole militaire** 36 av de la Motte Picquet, 75007; tel: 01 45 55 71 25; M̄ Ecole-Militaire (closes 22.00).

Le Mouton à Cinque Pattes 15 rue Vieille du Temple, 75004; tel: 01 42 71 86 30 [8 C2]
Open Mon–Sat 10.30–19.30.
M̄ *Hôtel de Ville;* Ē *RER to Châtelet-Les-Halles then métro 1 to Hôtel de Ville. Walk east along rue de Rivoli and turn left into rue Vieille du Temple. The shop is on your left.*

CAFÉ SOCIETY

The greatest landmark in Paris is neither a tower nor a pyramid; the hub of French culture is no opera house nor gallery; the heart of the city lies on every street corner: for Paris is undoubtedly the kingdom of the café.

The Pavement Café, where visitors ogle the city parade; the Student Café, where intellectuals argue politics and philosophy from late morning to early evening; the Chic Café, where the well-to-do sport dark glasses, Hermès scarves and chiselled cheekbones after a day at the shops or a night at the opera. These are the indelible images of Café Society.

Dyed-in-the-wool Parisians know another *demi-monde* of the *demi tasse*: the disappearing world of *Les Zincs*, once street-homes to the likes of Yves Montand and Edith Piaf. Immortalised in 1940s' cinema and Brassai photographs, these bars were named for their polished-metal bar tops, and, in their heyday, were as integral a part of working-class Paris as market pubs were to the East End of London.

As Parisian as the sound of the accordion itself, *Zincs* were the birthplace of that most indigenous of sounds, *'La Java'*. Fréhel and other such street songstresses made the swinging rhythm of the *Java* ballad famous. The *Java* got its name thanks to the rich *Auvergnat* accents of the bartenders habitual *'Ça va?'* greeting to their customers. *Rétro-chic* may have revived the desirability of a traditional metal counter, yet barely a dozen original *Zincs* still remain.

Over these bars Paris developed its own *patois*, France's answer to cockney rhyming slang: one would never merely drink, *'on s'arrose le couloir'* ('sprays the corridor'); wine was known as *'jus'*; red wine, in wartime tribute to Uncle Joe, was a *'Staline'*; an empty bottle darkly referred to as a *'cadavre'*; and nobody ever admitted to frequenting a bar or café. Instead one visited *'chez le notaire du coin'* ('the notary on the corner').

A lively *zinc* (real not retro) that has never lost its popularity with locals is the tiny **Petit Fer à Cheval**, with its horseshoe counter on the edge of the Marais. Also still thriving are the Rive Gauche haunts of the great thinkers and writers. The **Café Flôre** and **Les Deux Magots** next door, on the corner of the square of St-Germain, bustle late into the night. The *déco* décor of the Flôre reflects the style of its heyday, though today's crowds are more likely to wield a camcorder than a pen, the genuine Latin Quarter crowd have moved away and into the back streets. They may still be found, those spiritual successors to Hemingway and Sartre, tucked away at the pavement cafés behind the Mouffetard and Bucci street markets.

To be truly Bohemian, a café must act as a magnet to the sort of young man every mother dreads her daughter meeting (and whom every well-bred daughter dreams of finding). The free-thinking youth of Montmartre hangs out at **Le Sancerre**: the Paris of first love and last chances that Hollywood myth nurtured from the age of *absinthe* to our days.

Charmed lives require more public a podium. Those who insist on an extra chair on which to display their Chanel, Dior or Fauchon carrier bags should consider the **Café de La Paix**, which spills on to the pavements outside the Opéra and is reassuringly expensive. Not to mention staggering distance from the rue St-Honoré and place Vendôme.

Better haircuts and sharper dressing up and dressing down are to be seen at the cooler stylish hangouts. One venue to weather the whims of fashion is **Café Marly** (see page 38). It is, after all, housed within the Louvre itself. The Marly crowd shares its favours with a longer-established favourite, **Café Beaubourg** (see page 74) by the Pompidou Centre. Wicker chairs, healthy food, and the place to see and be seen in the heart of town.

At both of these addresses it is considered stylish to be either Cool Britannian or East Coast American. *The Sunday Times* (New York or London) is the ultimate accessory, and the drink of choice is not coffee but tea, taken black. For those in the know who prefer to skip the posing, take to the quiet streets behind the Musée d'Orsay.

At **Tea and Tattered Pages** (see pages 127–8), tea is taken between the bookshelves of a bibliophile Aladdin's cave.

For tea with lemon, milk or simply Parisian *je ne sais quoi*, an elegant *salon de thé*, such as the gentlewomen's favourite **Angélina**, is an unforgettable experience of a bygone age. Gentility and finesse come as standard. But for those whose taste in leaf-tea borders on the passionate try **Mariage Frères**, gentlemen of the tea trade since a time when the waters of Boston Harbour were tannin-free. Choose from nearly 400 blends served by smart waiters in white aprons. Timeless elegance; only the prices belong to the present day.

Tea tends to be taken indoors; coffee is enjoyed in public view, so choose your drink as you choose your table, even as you choose your Paris.

Angélina 226 rue de Rivoli, 75001; tel: 01 42 60 82 00 [B J6]
M̄ *Tuileries;* Ē *RER to Châtelet-Les-Halles then métro 1 to Tuileries.*
Au Petit Fer à Cheval 30 rue Vieille-du-Temple, 75004; tel: 01 42 72 47 47 [8 C1]
M̄ *St-Paul;* Ē *RER to Châtelet-Les-Halles then métro 1 to Hôtel-de-Ville. Walk east along rue de Rivoli and turn left into rue Vieille du Temple.*
Le Sancerre 35 rue des Abbesses, 75018; tel: 01 42 58 08 20 [4 A3–4]
M̄ *Abbesses;* Ē *Métro 4 to Marcadet-Poissonniers, then line 12 to Abbesses. Walk west on rue des Abbesses.*
Café de la Paix 12 bd des Capucines, 75009; tel: 01 40 07 30 20 [3 K6]
M̄ *Opéra;* Ē *RER to Châtelet-Les-Halles then RER A to Auber. Exit place de l'Opéra.*
Mariage Frères 30 rue du Bourg-Tibourg, 75004; tel: 01 42 72 28 11 [8 C1] Closed Mon.
M̄ *Hôtel-de-Ville;* Ē *RER to Châtelet-Les-Halles then métro 1 to Hôtel-de-Ville. Rue de Bourg Tibourg is a few yards on your left walking east of BHV.*

A French dictionary of the *bistrot* slang, *L'Argot du Bistrot* by Robert Girault, is published by Editions Marval, Paris.

The sheep may have five feet, but the trousers have two legs and the tops have two sleeves, even if not everything comes with a label sewn in the back. This is where those in the know come to buy designer *prêt à porter* wear at the end of the season at a fraction of the price demanded at the official outlets. If you have an eye for fashion you will be able to sort out some *pukkah schmutter*. Other branches are on the Left Bank at 19 rue Grégoire de Tours, 138 bd St-Germain and several stores along rue St-Placide.

Olivier Desforges 94 rue St-Antoine, 74004; tel: 01 42 72 11 03; email: contact@desforges.fr [8 C2]
Open Mon 14.00–19.00, Tue–Sat 10.00–19.00.
M̄ *St-Paul;* Ē *RER to Châtelet-Les-Halles then métro 1 to St-Paul. The shop is opposite the station.*
Practically by appointment to the sandman, this is the place for pyjamas, pillowcases, snuggly bathrobes and soft, toe-caressing slippers. Pay well for a good night's sleep happy ever after.

Village St-Paul [8 D2]
M̄ *St-Paul;* Ē *RER to Châtelet-Les-Halles then métro 1 to St-Paul. Walk eastwards towards on the rue St-Antoine and turn right on to rue St-Paul.*
With seemingly impromptu antique markets set up in every nook and cranny of the charming courtyards behind every other doorway, the Village St-Paul is a treat for browsers and collectors alike. Plenty of quaint *bistrots* for lunch, the magic museum and a witty little hotel mark this southernmost street of the Marais as essential for anyone whose wallet needs to shed some weight. Always enchanting in the weeks before Christmas.

The East – Bastille, Belleville and Bercy

It is Friday night and the place d'Italie is absolutely fizzing with anticipation. From every corner and métro entrance come ever more guests to the ultimate party on wheels. Officially the meeting place is in front of 40 avenue d'Italie, about 50 yards from the Gaumont cinema, but the crowd has long overflowed any definable boundaries, 'Around 10–15,000 people, I should guess,' says Jean-Paul, an engineer from the southern suburbs, 'But it is still early. Usually maybe 20,000 people,' he adds as he rummages in his backpack for elbow and kneepads. As promised, the gathering gets bigger and bigger: from the boulevard Blanqui comes a family group of parents and teens unashamed to be seen in public together and three women of an age past such parental responsibility. On the *place* itself are six or seven office mates in competitive mood. Behind them, a nervous-looking Canadian tourist sporting a maple-leaf sweatshirt swaps his trainers for in-line skates. A clutch of students whose cigarettes suggest a decidedly organic provenance arrive from Tolbiac station further down the avenue, and, skirting the group, the stewards are issuing constant reminders of the rules: 'Has every one eaten something tonight? Keep to the right, overtake on the left, don't overtake the leaders, and don't try to hitch a ride on passing cars!'

Now come the motorcycle cops to hold back the traffic, and the cacophony of excited chat is punctuated by the ringing of mobile phones as first-timers desperately try to find their friends in the melée.

At last it is ten o'clock. And, as if by magic, a chaotic scrum becomes a parade as the first roller-bladers take to the tarmac. On the route there is not a seat to be had at café tables as the unofficial opening ceremony of the Parisian weekend gets under way. Every Friday night is the same. The grand roller-skating marathon that tours the entire city with a police escort. 'I'm King of the World!' cries an American student at the tail of the swaying crocodile as it makes its way on to the avenue des Gobelins. Each week the tour takes a different route and Parisians of all classes get to know their city as never before. At least once a month, the Champs Elysées is closed to vehicles around midnight as the shrieking swarm gets its second wind hurtling down towards the place de la Concorde on the way home. The group, somewhat depleted, returns in a state of exhilarated exhaustion to the starting point at around one in the morning, to merge with the midnight matinée cinema crowds at the place d'Italie.

Should anyone demand proof that the eastern side of Paris has truly come of age, they need only make their way to the rendezvous for Friday's great skate. Or join the smaller gathering outside the Nomades store on place Bastille at 14.30 on a Sunday, when inexperienced skaters have their beginners' introduction to the marathon.

It is hard to believe that an unkind city used to suggest that the best the east had to offer were the Gare de Lyon and Gare d'Austerlitz – the fastest route out of the area. It was never true. Even before the great revival (one might even say resuscitation) of the eastern quarters, Bastille was known as a playground. Edith Piaf used to trawl the clubs of the rue de Lappe, *à la recherche du* rough *trouvé*. Then and now, the working-class shopkeepers of the area had their *bals publics* and tea dances. I've spent many a Monday afternoon watching the middle-aged half-day-closing crowd step-two-threeing to an accordion under a glitterball.

These days, the nudge of gentrification has thoroughly elbowed across from the neighbouring Marais, and bold poster-paint colours are gradually replacing the reassuringly drab beiges and browns of shopfronts. The inevitable ochres, yellows and terracotta heat-hues and blues of southern France are appearing in cafés, bars and restaurants whose only previous provincial inspiration had been the northern skies of Belgium and the eastern winters of Alsace. The *sans culottes* destroyed the old prison two centuries ago, and the *sans soucis* (without-a-care yuppies of the 80s and 90s) were responsible for the cultural revolution. Artists ousted artisans in a bloodless *coup d'éclat*. But whilst the landscape and entertainment has redefined so much of the area, much of the charm still comes from local heritage and tradition. The solid, stolid local character is made of stern enough stuff, and just as long as there is still a junk shop behind an old-fashioned shop sign somewhere in the quarter, the Bastille will never really fall.

The glittering modern opera house dominates Bastille, even outshining the stunning statue of the Genius of Liberty, star of the last ever ten-franc coin. The Arsenal basin, a pleasure port, may be seen from the square and one platform of the tortuous Bastille métro interchange, but soon disappears under the pavements before reinventing itself as the Canal St-Martin by Gare de l'Est. At night, the square echoes to the sound of motorbikes revving up, and dodgems whirring and crashing. Poets, musicians and a new generation of lotos eaters hang out along rue Oberkampf (see page 190).

At the eastern edge of Paris is the other Bois. Parisians know that spring has arrived when the funfair sets up camp in the Bois des Vincennes. The Foire du Trône opens each spring at Pelouse de Reuilly (tel: 01 46 27 52 29). The Bois de Boulogne in the west may have its celebrated restaurants and social season, but Vincennes is parkland and woodland complete with the only genuine royal château to be served by the urban métro. Better than public transport is the leisurely walk towards the Bois on the amazing Promenade Plantée, a remarkable overhead garden landscaped above the traffic.

Warehouses in Bercy, once the river-rail freight district, have given way to some of the most adventurous new architecture in town. The Palais Omnisports with its sloping lawn roofs, and the futuristic bridge-like steel-and-glass Ministry of Finance building are symbols of national pride. From

Bercy to the Bois, the avenue Daumesnil is lined with some excellent restaurants.

Over the water, where once only Chinatown tempted visitors away from the conventional sights, the Bibliothèque Nationale carries cult status into the once beyond-the-pale Austerlitz bank of the Seine. Brave new artists were quick to colonise the semi-demolished concrete refrigeration depots of the railway's past, and now this is an essential stop on the art-shopping route.

The main artists' colony in Paris is centred on Belleville, north of République. For four days in May, the artists of the quarter throw open the doors and skylights of their studios and workshops. Potters, painters, sculptors – the Rodins, Degas, Lautrecs *de nos jours*, who make up the city's new Bohemia – allow uninvited guests to enter their private spaces. Visitors are welcome between 15.00 and 21.00. Lists of studios and addresses may be picked up at the information points at the place des Fêtes and at 2 boulevard de la Villette (tel: 01 46 36 44 09).

If you are not in town for the open days, you may always pay a visit to the artists and writers of the past. Père-Lachaise cemetery is home to almost a million Parisians and is unexpectedly welcoming, a celebration of great lives rather than a *memento mori*. The perfect illustration of the paradox of eastern Paris, where the past and the future create an energetic, invigorating and effervescent present.

WHERE TO STAY

Beaumarchais 3 rue Oberkampf, 75011; tel: 01 53 36 86 86; web: www.hotelbeaumarchais.com [4 D7]
M̄ *Filles-de-Calvaire;* Ē *Métro 5 to République, then line 8 to Filles-de-Calvaire. The hotel is at the side of the Cirque d'Hiver.*
Bright contemporary colours, sharp modern furnishings but reassuringly old-fashioned room rates. Double rooms at €90 (590FF) have been designed and decorated by the new owners. Salmon pinks, sunflower yellows, terracottas and spring green shades refelect the trendified nature of the streets around the Cirque d'Hiver and République. Breakfast is served on a morning-after friendly patio deck with nature kept safely at bay by trellis and Versailles tubs.

Claret 44 bd du Bercy, 75012; tel: 01 46 28 41 31 [9 F4]
M̄ *Bercy;* Ē *RER to Châtelet-Les-Halles then métro 14 to Bercy.*
Memories of Bercy's past life as the wine cellar of Paris. Long before the warehouses were pulled down to make way for the brave new world of civil servants and sportsmen, the district's post office was reborn as a hotel dedicated to the area's vintage past. Your room key is attached to an enormous cork, the lift is papered with labels from countless bottles of Bordeaux, and the path to your €100 (650FF) bedroom is a veritable *route des vins*. The corridor is reminiscent of a maze of wine cellars, with each of the 52 bedrooms named for a different great wine. Bland furnishings, yet décor is raised above the mid-range hotel norm by the framed oversized wine label on the wall and an actual bottle of the wine itself on a shelf. I have spent the night in the shadow of a *Château de la Petit Thouars*. Bathroom tiles continue the wine motif. The *coup de grâce* of the theming is that every one of the wines named on a bedroom door may be tasted in the hotel's cellar wine bar. Some rooms overlook the railway lines that still criss-cross the

PARIS, JE NE REGRETTE RIEN
In the footsteps of Edith Piaf

'Allez, venez, Milord' came the invitation. I was only 18 years old. Is it any wonder that three bars of a ballad, sung in a voice that dripped life, could seduce a boy alone in the city?

The love songs of Edith Piaf are the fuel of any Parisian romance, and my first 20-franc cassette of *The Best Of...* has coloured my every moment here ever since. I cannot peer from a hotel window in November without humming *Autumn Leaves*, nor walk down the street on the cusp of a summer Saturday night and forget *Padam, Padam*, nor could I pass young lovers counting centimes and not consider *Les Amants d'un Jour*. The rue St-Denis at 2am in the rain with lycra-lashed working girls evokes *l'Accordéoniste*, and the rue de Mont Cenis at sunrise reminds me of my *Vie en Rose*.

Let's face it, 'La Mome' Edith Piaf is the true and unmistakable voice of Paris. That cry from the gutters to the stars, singing such classics as *Je Ne Regrette Rien* and *Les Trois Cloches*, and battering her soul into our hearts with *Mon Dieu*, is Paris for so many people, surviving the ravages of club remixes and Elaine Paige. The image of that tiny frail figure in the simple black dress, those eloquent arthritic hands and pleading arched eyebrows, will be forever etched behind our eyes, whenever we hear her sing. Her life story, with its shadows of drugs, unsuitable men, tragic romance and finally a strong young lover in her last years, has made her something of an icon for divorcees, dreamers, gay men and aspiring victims. The French Judy Garland if you like. Her appeal crosses generations in a way that her contemporaries could never attain. Can you see hip clubbers chilling out with Doris Day or Alma Cogan? Not on your life. Piaf could always appeal to both young and old without resorting to kitsch.

To call **Les Amis d'Edith Piaf** a fan club would be crude and crass. More than an Elvis-cult, since Piaf has never left the building, these genuine friends run a private museum in a Belleville apartment dedicated to her memory and life. The flat is open to visitors by prior arrangement with the curator Bernard Marchois. Here the friends have amassed hundreds of documents, clothes, shoes, albums and personal photographs. There is no official entrance fee. Donations are left to the discretion and generosity of each visitor. Many of those who knew and worked with her drop by and

quarter between Gare de Lyon, the Bercy motorail depot and the Périphérique. So if you would prefer a quieter outlook, mention it when booking.

Devillas 4 bd St-Marcel, 75005; tel: 01 43 31 37 50; web: www.hoteldevillas.com [8 C–D4]
M̄ *St-Marcel;* Ē *Métro 5 to St-Marcel. Hotel is at the junction of bds St-Marcel and de l'Hôpital.*
The welcome may not be overpowering, but it is genuine. Regulars tend to regard the inoffensively modern and basic Devillas as a home from home in the

her spirit fills the place. My good friend Marc, who has played her songs on his own accordion since boyhood, spends many an afternoon reminiscing with Piaf's back-up singers, *Les Compagnons de la Chanson*, in the flat, and commiserated with fellow aficionados when the funeral cortège of Piaf's old friend Yves Montand wound through the quarter towards his final resting place at Père-Lachaise.

There are but three other addresses for private pilgrimages. I don't count the famous Olympia music hall, since it moved a couple of doors down the street, and the lady don't sing there no more. But the **Balajo**, in Bastille, is a truly happening club by night and a charming tea dance by day. Genuinely late-40s–early-50s rather than knowingly retro, this place is not merely camp, it's a movie buff's overdose, where jungle sounds may be interrupted by barmen in striped *matelot* jerseys recalling Sinatra and Kelly in a well-choreographed 'knife' fight over a girl. The eclectic music policy, which cheerfully blends contemporary club tracks with *Songs For Swinging Lovers*, well suits a dance hall that is as comfortable with an accordion as a DJ's decks. You wouldn't be surprised to see Peggy Lee wearily climbing the spiral staircase to join the band singing *Pete Kelly's Blues*, or Marlene demanding a 'ciga-wette', or Astaire clearing the floor in search of silk stockings. Here it was that Piaf used to trawl for rough and parade on the arm of Marcel Cerdan – her married prize-fighter lover doomed to die tragically young in a plane crash and for whom she wrote her chilling anthem, *Hymne à l'Amour*.

A couple of doorways to ponder: 67 bd Lannes, 75016 (M̲ *Porte-Dauphine*) way across the cultural divide on the wealthy side of town, where she lived until her death at 47 in 1963. And 72 rue de Belleville, 75019 (M̲ *Belleville*). A plaque marks the steps where Edith Piaf was born. That is to say, where she was found as a baby, wrapped in the folds of a policeman's cape. The inscription, unveiled by Maurice Chevalier, reads 'On the steps of this house was born, 19th December 1915, in the greatest destitution, EDITH PIAF, whose voice, later, would overthrow the world.'

Les Amis d'Edith Piaf 5 rue Crespin-du-Gast, 75011; tel: 01 43 55 52 72 [F6–7]
M̲ *Menilmontant*.
Open Mon–Thu afternoons by appointment.

capital. Guests are given a personalised email address for the duration of their stay so that family and friends may keep in touch. With bedrooms at €61 (400FF), and no floral vinyl wallpaper in sight, the plain but clean décor gets my vote. Considering that I paid twice that at a very disappointing three-star visitor-processing plant at the Opéra the previous week, I found the plain blue carpet and sunshine yellow walls a modest price to pay for inexpensive city centre accommodation. Truthfully, it is more than slightly off-centre, across the water from the Gare de Lyon and up-and-coming Bastille district, walking distance from nightlife, and the wrong part of the Left Bank for the coach parties. It is actually quite convenient for the Mouffetard feeding troughs and the Monde Arabe and Tour d'Argent peaks, not to mention the Jardin des Plantes, the Bibliothèque Nationale and the new riverside developments of Austerlitz.

Palma 77 av Gambetta, 75020; tel: 01 46 36 13 65; web: www.hotelpalma.com [5 G7]
M̄ *Gambetta;* Ē *Bus 26 to place Gambetta.*
A night at the modernised but bland Palma did not inspire me to rush home with an urge to give the spare bedroom a makeover in memory of my stay. Despite this, I found it a clean and reasonably priced option in an area not exactly brimming with choice. Who would complain about polite, efficient staff, hairdryers in the bathroom and cable TV in a two-star hotel, and convenient garage parking within yards of the front door, even if the compact baths bring you closer to your knees than ever before. Pay around €60 (390FF).

Le Pavillon Bastille 65 rue de Lyon, 75012, tel: 01 43 43 65 65; email: hotel-pavillon@akamail.com [8 E2–3]
M̄ *Bastille;* Ē *Métro 5 to Bastille.*
Opposite the strident modernity of the opera house this seemingly traditional old townhouse seems somewhat incongruous. But do not expect dusty 17th-century furnishings and gloomy corridors. Refurbished as a smart contemporary hotel with blue and yellow drapes setting the tone, the mood is that of a private house in summer. Very much at the heart of a lively quarter of restaurants, culture and nightlife, the Pavillon offers a tranquil base to which to return. A smart-card opens the front door and staffing is discreetly low-key. The rather small rooms at around €137 (900FF) are well equipped. Large robes and a fluffy bale of towels make bathtime a leisurely treat. A useful information pack gives the low-down on local shopping, eating and hairdressing.

La Porte Dorée 273 av Daumesnil, 75012; tel: 01 43 07 56 97 [9 J5]
M̄ *Porte-Dorée;* Ē *Métro 5 to Bastille, then line 8 to Porte-Dorée.*
This is where anxious parents would send their daughters, secure in the knowledge that the kind lady at reception would not let anything untoward happen to her. One of those nice old-fashioned two-star hotels tucked safely away from harm, the half-panelled corridors with their painted mirrors lead to surprisingly spacious rooms equipped with well-tiled, good-quality shower and bathrooms. Nothing is too much trouble for the helpful staff. When I asked if I might return to collect my suitcase at half past midnight, nobody batted an eyelid. The €5.50 (30FF) breakfast is taken either in the bedroom or in one of the two bright morning rooms. With room rates which begin well under €50 (330FF), the Hôtel de la Porte Dorée, a 20-minute bus ride to the Opéra district, or longer and lazier walk to Bastille along the Promenade Planté (see page 98), is a bargain.

Résidence des Gobelins 9 rue des Gobelins, 75013; tel: 01 47 07 26 90 [8 B5]
M̄ *Les-Gobelins;* Ē *RER to Châtelet-Les-Halles then métro 7 to Les-Gobelins. Rue des Gobelins is on the west side of av des Gobelins.*
Philippe and Jennifer Poirier offer a genuine welcome to their modest, yet comfortable hotel by the Gobelins workshops (see page 102). Around €68 (450FF) buys you a spanking clean and efficiently fitted double room. One of those places we all know in rural France, but rarely find in the cities, where *acceuil* means more than merely handing over a room key and minibar checklist. Chatty, family-style concern for comfort, plenty of good advice on tap and a decent €6 (40FF) breakfast in the garden during summer months, or in the dining room during the grey season.

WHERE TO GO

Balajo 9 rue de Lappe, 75012 [8 E2]
Open Mon, Thu–Sat 23.00–05.00.
M̲ *Bastille;* E̲ *Métro 5 to Bastille. From rue de la Roquette turn right on to rue de Lappe.*
Classic night club. Monday and Thursday evenings have their unique blend of contemporary and retro entertainment. (See page 93.)

Bastille [8 D2]
E̲ *Métro 5 to Bastille.*
The musical world of the *bastoche* is well and truly back in business. It is amazing what just one simple world-class opera house can do for the fortunes of a neighbourhood. Until Carlos Ott's glistening new Opéra rose from the place Bastille, the only outsiders to visit the area were the biker gangs that would rev up above the Arsenal basin. Entertainment was strictly working-class local. The singer Fréhel, on whom Piaf modelled her act, would sing *La Java Bleu* in the bars run by families who had left the depressed rural areas of Auvergne, and shop workers would head off to the city limits to drink and dance in waterside *guinguettes.*

Now, brasseries like Bofinger live again and clubland thrives along the rue de Lappe. Rue Keller and rue de la Roquette have become the ultimate in chic, virtually eclipsing the neighbouring Marais. The defining characteristic of the area is music. Tickets for the Opéra Bastille are hard to come by, but you can take the backstage tour for ∈9 (60FF), call 01 40 01 19 70. At the **Café de la Plage**, 59 rue de Charonne, 75012, jazz lovers nurse their Jack Daniels during late-night jam sessions in the basement.

Best of all is the métro, since the buskers in this warren of passageways are breathtakingly good. Follow the music along a tiled passage, up some steps and into the interchange hall beneath the open-air platforms of Line 1 that overlooks the pleasure port in the Arsenal basin. Some 40 or 50 may be gathered, held in thrall by a Voice with a capital 'V'. At the end of each song, the applause and cheers can turn an encounter into an occasion. Those in the know visit the Bonne Journée snack bar counter a few yards away and indulge in good coffee and very pleasant croissants, cakes and quiches to legitimise their loitering. Others stand open-mouthed, enthralled, frozen in mid-step on a staircase, or leaning against the posters on the wall, and prepare to be entertained.

One afternoon, I had settled and nestled by a photo-booth, listening to bluesy *chanteuse* Christiane Maillard, when a smartly dressed *Parisienne* in teetering heels all but scampered across from the rue fbg St-Antoine entrance and squeezed to the front. 'Have I missed much?' she panted, 'I was late today, couldn't get away from the office. Is this your first time?' A good half-hour and countless shelved train-connections later, Christiane performed her final song. It was half past seven. 'Tomorrow night's concert will be here at the same time', promised the singer, 'And I will be performing at the **Bar Phonograph** in rue Roquette from 10 o'clock tonight'. And with that she scooped up handfuls of coins from her open case and blended into the early evening commuter blur.

Bercy [9 F4]
M̲ *Bercy, Cour-St-Emilion;* E̲ *RER to Châtelet-Les-Halles then métro 14 to Bercy or Cour-St-Emilion.*
Welcome to a brave new world, where orchestras fly through the air, lawnmowers climb up the walls and fairground attractions of the past live again in the palace playground of a thousand tax collectors. This is not a new wing of a putative museum of surrealist installation art, but an unofficial shrine to the

greatest of all French institutions, *des Fonctionnaires* – civil servants. Some 123 acres of land on the Right Bank of the Seine has been transformed into a futuristic landscape. At its heart is the outrageously up-front Ministry of Finance building that launches itself like an indecisive bridge a quarter of the way across the river. An architectural curiosity, it seems to have taken one look at the new library on the other bank, then determined not to take one step further for fear of being overturned. The building has its own pier from which the Finance Minister may be whisked at high speed along the Seine to the Parliament building. Personally, I reckon the building was constructed over the water for far more practical reasons. The French are fond of insurrection and I imagine that, come the next Revolution, Bercy will be the Bastille of the 21st century and civil servants will require an easy escape route. Known to the locals at the 'Tax Palace', the ministry was moved here when its previous home in the Louvre was handed over to the museum for extra galleries. Four restaurants and a post office may be found within the walls of a building erected over the very boundary wall where once taxes were levied on wines and spirits coming into the capital.

The wine warehouses that stood on the site have mostly disappeared. More than three dozen brick *chais* have been restored and relaunched as Bercy Village, a café-bar complex along the Cour St-Emilion. Biggest of these wine bars is the phenomenal Club Med World (see page 97) for a year-round bank holiday mood. Smartly dressed types hang out, meet up and have one last drink at the Vinéa Café before heading off to a party across town. With all this *al fresco* drinking along the tree-lined cobbled paths between the *entrepôts*, the area has taken off with the young good-time crowd. Fresh air is to be enjoyed at the Parc Bercy, with its memorial garden to Yitzhak Rabin and museum of funfair art (limited opening, 01 43 40 16 22). If the finance building looms large in the quarter, the 17,000 seat Palais Omnisports stadium blends modestly and literally into the landscape. Where other cities might hide their tax-men in a bunker and put their heroes in a palace, Paris has opted to keep its sports and entertainment centre underground. The 45° walls of the complex are laid to lawn. Inside the stadium can stage anything from opera to windsurfing events, and on one occasion even flew an entire orchestra on wires above a production of *La Vie Parisienne*. If you happen to be in the quarter, or have tickets to a concert, show or event at the stadium, come and wander around this strange new land. I would not suggest spending the entire weekend here.

Butte Aux Cailles [8 B6]

E̲ *Métro 5 to Place-d'Italie. From bd Blanqui take rue des Diamants. Alternatively, from rue Bobillot, follow rue de la Butte aux Cailles.*

If you come here looking for the legendary landscape of watermills and windmills, landing site of the first ever hot air balloon flight in 1783, then you will be disappointed. But forget the story of Pilâtre de Rozier's adventures in physics and flight, do not even try to find the last bastion of the Paris Commune that held on to the Butte aux Cailles in 1871, simply take the Butte as you find it. Twenty years ago, nobody gave the area a second thought. It was but a working class dormitory gently lapped by the overspill of Chinatown. Then Paris rediscovered the place d'Italie. Kenzo Tange designed the **Centre du Septième Art** with the biggest cinema screen in the land and the multiplex set defined the area around the *place* as nineties cool. The Butte itself, a 63m-high hill, rises between the bd Blanqui, rue du Moulin des Prés, rue Vergniaud and rue de Tolbiac, and makes a fabulous setting for a stroll around neat squares and charming streets. If you remember the Marais when it was just finding its fashionable feet and had not priced itself beyond the reach of ordinary visitors, you will welcome the stylish new galleries and shops that are staking their claims on the Butte.

Club Med World [9 F5]
39 cour St-Emilion, 75012; tel: 01 44 68 70 00; web: www.clubmedworld.fr
Open Mon, Wed–Sat 12.00 until late, Sun 11.00 until late.
M̲ *Cour-St-Emilion;* E̲ *RER to Châtelet-Les-Halles then métro 14 to Cour-St-Emilion.*
Club Med, the brand, is practically shorthand for beach holidays in the company of the fit, the bronzed and the comfortably off. The name conjures images of barbecues on brilliant white sands, dancing until sunrise with jugs of fruit-packed punch under bamboo parasols. Now a new destination has been added to the impressive roll call that already includes Mauritius and Martinique and the Med itself. Welcome to the goods yard by the Paris ring road. Here, in a converted wine warehouse in Bercy-Village, the famed upmarket package-holiday people recreate the mood of their resort parties for the after-work crowd. Office workers come to relive last year's beach-bop and dream of next year's tropical location. And so, with juggling barmen, copious quantities of alcohol and tans from jars and sunbeds, Bercy serves as a makeshift paradise. Britney Spears and Robbie Williams are among the international stars whose names are liberally dropped and photos flourished as *habitués*– even if their appearances were most probably at private media parties. Despite the possible shortage of chart-toppers at the next table, young swinging Paris has taken this place to its heart. A café, sushi bar, **Oliveraie** restaurant and travel agency on the ground floor, not to mention the shops; go underground to hear Latin bands play live, hit the dance floor or meet up with chums at the *tapas* bar.

Flèche d'Or 102 bis rue de Bagnolet, 75020; tel: 01 43 72 04 23 [5 H7–8]
M̲ *Alexandre-Dumas;* E̲ *Take bus 26 to Pyrénées-Bagnolet. From the bus stop return to the junction with rue de Bagnolet and turn right on rue de Bagnolet.*
Imagine what would happen if you gave an abandoned local railway station to a group of students. Turn up at the front door of this converted station on the *Ceinture* ring, where trains trundle around the edge of the city, and see for yourself. This neighbourhood bar has a student union feel. Posters, murals and railway sleepers pay lip service to interior décor. Mornings and lunchtimes are for the quiet communion of tobacco and newspapers. As the afternoon wears on music segues from mellow to funky, and by the evening, noise levels bubble to that point midway between conversation and a party. The afternoon 'Café Psycho' offers group analysis *à la* Oprah or Jerry Springer. On dance club nights a modest door charge may be levied. If you intend to travel by métro, prepare for a ten-minute walk along a busy street past ethnic groceries and improbably gentrified alleyways before you find the place.

Au Folies 8 rue de Belleville, 75020
M̲ *Belleville;* E̲ *Métro 5 to République, then line 11 to Belleville.*
Stop, look and listen. Don't even try to blend in. The particular charm of this essentially local hang out is that nobody blends, they just mix. The earnest young man in turtle-neck sweater, pebbles glasses and great coat, deep in conversation with his dreadlocked flatmate eking out a last roll up. They have little in common with the rouge-embalmed woman with the broadcast laugh who has modelled for 101-too-many promising artists, none of whom ever turned out to be the next great discovery. The codger in a flat cap, cursing a racehorse, nods to the stylish young Vietnamese waiter from the restaurant at the corner who tonight sports an off-duty Nehru jacket for an evening with a willowy blonde

girlfriend. By the door stands a young middle-class couple recently moved into the area, aglow with the thrill of belonging to such a dazzling cosmopolitan community. If you are passing, drop in.

Piscine Butte-aux-Cailles 5 pl Paul-Verlaine, 75013; tel: 01 45 89 60 05 [8 B6] Open Tue–Sun 07.00–18.00 (hours may vary). €2.5 (16FF).
M̱ *Place-d'Italie;* E̱ *Métro 5 to Place-d'Italie. Follow rue Bobillot, walk to pl Paul-Verlaine.*
A national treasure only belatedly remembered by the nation. In September 2000, Louis Bonnier's art nouveau brick swimming baths were added to the list of historic monuments celebrated on national heritage day. For the people of the quarter, listed status matters little; after all they have been taking the waters of the indoor and outdoor pools since 1924. The waters of an artesian well beneath the hill feed the baths.

Promenade Planté – Viaduc des Arts 9-129 av Daumesnil, 75012; tel: 01 44 75 8066 (galleries) [8 E3–F4]
M̱ *Bastille, Ledru-Rollin, Gare-de-Lyon, and other stations along av Daumesnil to Vincennes;* E̱ *RER to Châtelet-Les-Halles, then RER C to Gare-de-Lyon. In front of the station, rue de Chasles leads to av Daumesnil and the Viaduc des Arts.*
Who said that town planners lack a soul? Climb the stairs above the bumper-to-bumper traffic behind the Bastille opera house and Gare de Lyon to breathe in the fresh air of enlightened progress. Before the RER created a high-speed underground link to the suburbs, old-fashioned trains creaked and rattled their way to the Bastille atop brick railway arches and viaducts above the crowded streets. Now the sleepers and coal have been swept away and the railway lines replaced with leafy arbours, shady trees, shrubs, lawns and flower beds. Welcome to Paris' most unlikely park, a slender strip of green at bedroom-window height that runs from the Opéra Bastille to the Bois de Vincennes. Townies

may at last take a long walk in the countryside without moving out of earshot of the sounds of city life, and children can run ahead of their parents with no danger from traffic on this 16-acre strip of nature. The route to the Bois continues at ground level via Jardins de Reuilly and Charles Péguy. There are many entrances and exits along the route, but my tip is to climb up to the Promenade Planté by way of the Viaduc des Arts, a grand row of 60 red-brick and white-stone railway arches newly refurbished as home to artists and craftsmen. Before visiting the garden, have a look around the vaulted studios and showrooms. See wrought-ironwork, furniture and cabinet making, visit silversmiths in their workshops and stone masons restoring antique sculptures. Browse and marvel at long-forgotten skills, then hang out at the VIA design centre and the Viaduc Café.

Roller-skate tour of Paris 40 av d'Italie, 75013; tel: 01 43 36 89 81 [8 C6]
Fri 22.00 returning at 01.00.
M̄ *Place-d'Italie;* Ē *Métro 5 to Place-d'Italie. Pass Gaumont Grand Ecran and walk 50m along av d'Italie.*
See the begining of this chapter for details of the Friday night skate-athon that launches every weekend in the capital. The event is strictly limited to experienced skaters, as the course demands skill and stamina. Information from the organisers, Pari-roller, 3 rue Lachelier, 75013. If you have left your skates behind, you may buy or hire from Nomades (see below).

Beginners' version:
Nomades, 37 bd Bourdon, 75004; tel: 01 42 72 08 08; web: www.rollernet.com/nomades [8 D2]
Sun 14.30 returning at 17.30.
M̄ *Bastille;* Ē *Métro 5 to Bastille, walk along bd Bourdon at the west side of the Arsenal.*
Lower-key Sunday afternoon roller-skate excursion for beginners and anyone apprehensive about taking part in the Friday Night Fever. Participants meet outside the Nomades skate-hire shop. In wet weather the event is cancelled. Organised by Rollers et Coquillages.

Scene-Est rue Louise Weiss, 75013 [8 D–E5]
Open Tue 14.00–19.00 (hours and days may vary for individual galleries, but all are usually open at these times).
M̄ *Chevaleret;* Ē *Métro 5 to Place-d'Italie, then line 6 to Chevaleret. Follow bd Vincent Auriol towards the river and turn right into rue Louise Weiss.*
The reclaimed land above and around the railway tracks of Austerlitz has been colonised by the new art generation of Paris since long before the old buildings were demolished. Where artists once set up studios in abandoned refrigerated warehouses, now rows of contemporary galleries line the flourishing rue Louise-Weiss. These gallery owners are the arbiters of the new cultural scene, and what hangs on their walls this year will be seen next year in the smart lofts of New York and the boardrooms of Canary Wharf. To see the best of the young Japanese artists try the two galleries of **Emmanuel Perrotin** at numbers 5 and 30. Otherwise catch sharp new photographic images at **Galerie Almine Rech** at number 24, *rétro* furniture at **Jousse Projects**, number 34, and the latest discoveries exhibiting at **Air de Paris,** number 32, or perhaps **Galerie Jennifer Flay,** at number 20. This is by no means an exhaustive list, but since the road reflects the changing face of the art world, every season brings a new star to the circuit.

Vincennes
Château de Vincennes; tel: 01 48 08 31 20
Open 10.00–18.00 summer, 10.00–17.00 winter. €4–5(25–32FF) depending on length of visit.
M̄ *Château-de-Vincennes;* Ē *RER to Châtelet-Les-Halles then line 1 to Château-de-Vincennes.*

Bois de Vincennes
M̄ *Porte-Dorée, Liberté, Porte-de-Charenton, Berault, Château-de-Vincennes RER Vincennes, Fontenay-sous-Bois, Joinville-le-Pont;* Ē *For the funfair, Lac de Daumesnil and temple take RER to Châtelet-Les-Halles then line 1 to Porte-Dorée. For the Ferme de Paris take RER to Châtelet-Les-Halles then RER A to Joinville-le-Pont, then follow route de la Pyramide to turn left on route de la Ferme.*

GUINGUETTES AND BARGES – THE WATERSIDE DANCE HALLS

Today's brightest young things who, like all bright young things, invented pleasure, would hate to think that their idea of a good night out hardly differs to that of their grandparents. Paris entertainment has come full circle, with the re-emergence of a new generation of music by the river. The original *guinguettes* were waterside dance halls and bars on the edge of eastern Paris where the working classes would spend their Friday and Saturday nights.

Contemporary Paris has adopted as its playground *du moment* the riverbanks alongside the National Library. Here the clubs and bars are to be found in a variety of boats moored along the Left Bank of the Seine. Fireboats, barges and houseboats called into service as music venues, bars and nightclubs. Best known are the **Guinguette Pirate**, a Chinese junk, and the *Batofar* light boat (see pages 190–1). Along the quayside mellower sounds can be heard from the **Péniche Blues Café**, a barge popular with a slightly riper crowd content to sit around nodding contentedly to late-night jazz and reggae. *Time Out* listings and pages in *Pariscope* magazine feature details of programmes and events.

For the true spirit of the old-time riverbank dance halls, rummage in the attic for your old Utility party frock and take the RER to the river just

France's last remaining medieval royal fortress can be reached with a central métro ticket. Whilst Versailles, Fontainebleau and the rest of the regal residences are a day trip away, the **Château of Vincennes** is to be found at the end of line 1. Since Louis XIV and his ilk abandoned the place, it has been used as a state prison, Napoleonic arsenal, porcelain factory and military base. This is a castle that looks like the sort of castles little boys dream of playing with. No fancy Renaissance frills, just crenellations and turrets. Visit the restored towers, royal pavilions, chapel, courtyard and Charles V's bedchamber. A museum of army insignia on site is open twice a week.

The last king to hold court here was Shakespeare's Henry V over the Millennium season, when the famous play received its long overdue Paris première at the exciting **Cartoucherie** theatre complex. How many of the enraptured theatregoers, thrilling to the oratory of this recreated Agincourt, knew that they were sitting within yards of the very room in which the real Henry V died of dysentery in 1422? Audiences take a free shuttle bus from the station.

The estate provides the city with its largest park, the Bois de Vincennes. Sunday is the day that good little boys and girls are taken to the Paris Zoo. From Palm Sunday to Easter everyone comes to the Lac de Daumesnil where, since 957, the Foire du Trône has been the essential funfair. Once a monastic bake sale, now it is thrills, spills and *barbapapa* candyfloss. Just south of the lake is the temple with its 10m gilded Buddha. Commune with nature at the Parc Floral and Jardin Tropical. The Paris City Farm is on the route de Pesage, and is a working mixed farm. Adults pay €3.50 (22FF). If you want to spend the day exploring the Bois, follow the clearly marked Red Trail to see everything. Alternative Blue and Yellow routes offer limited highlights.

beyond the Bois de Vincennes where the River Seine meets the River Marne. *Joinville-le-Pont* was once a popular dance tune and, from the station of the same name, hurry down to the waterside to find **Chez Gégène**. This is just one of the few remaining *guinguettes* that once thrived outside the city walls. Here you can dine for around €33 (220FF), have an *apéro* or a beer and take to the floor when the band strikes up a foxtrot, tango or jive. Live music on Friday and Saturday nights from April to October. Arrive after 21.00 and be prepared to kiss goodnight well past the witching hour. On Sundays dancing is to recorded music only. If the Gégène crowd is not quite your scene, wander along the banks of the Marne and check out rival dance halls. Punters ranges in age from young courting couples to those of generation that might still use that term.

Barges Port de la Gare, Port de Tolbiac (see *Entertainment*, page 190) [8 E5]
Ē *RER to Châtelet-Les-Halles then métro 14 to Bibliothèque-François-Mitterand. Walk to the riverbank.*

Chez Gégène 162bis quai de Polangis, 94340 Joinville-le-Pont; tel: 01 48 83 29 43 [9 F6]
€14 (90FF) includes first drink.
M̄ *Joinville-le-Pont;* Ē *RER to Châtelet-Les-Halles then Joinville-le-Pont. Cross the bridge over the Marne via the rue Mermoz to quai de Polangis.*

WHAT TO SEE

Bibliothèque Nationale François Mitterand quai François Mauriac, 75013; tel: 01 53 79 53 79; web: www.bnf.fr [8 E5]
Open Tue–Sat 10.00–20.00, Sun 12.00–19.00. €3 (20FF) (pre-booked guided tours free).
M̄ *Bibliothèque-François-Mitterand;* Ē *RER to Châtelet-Les-Halles then métro 14 to Bibliothèque-François-Mitterand. From rue Neuve Tolbiac turn left on rue Jean Anouilh to rue Emile Durkheim. Follow signs to the east and west entrances.*
Although the original national library, by the Palais Royal, still displays the notable antique collections in splendidly ornate galleries, the rest of France's books were shipped downriver to this final chapter of the *grands travaux*. The lofty glass library building, with its 1,600 reading-room seats, had to install moving wooden shutters to turn away the sun from the millions of books stored here. Nearly 200,000 volumes are available on demand to anyone over the age of 16. Designed by Dominique Perrault, the library comprises four skyscrapers around a central area planted with mature trees from the former royal forests. This of course was the last of the great self-monuments commissioned by France's larger than life uncle 'Tonton', President Mitterand. The architect explained to the great man that the four pillars of the library represent open books. Whenever I, a traveller in this antique land, pass by those vast and trunkless legs, I find myself wondering whether the library contains a slim volume by Shelley, and I look on this mighty work, and despair.

Les Gobelins (National Tapestry Workshop) Manufacture Nationale des Gobelins de Beauvais et de la Savonnerie, 42 av des Gobelins, 75013; tel: 01 44 08 52 00; email: isabelle.gobin@culture.fr [8 B5]

Open Tue, Wed, Thu 14.00 and 14.45; closed holidays. €8 (50FF).
M̄ *Les-Gobelins;* Ē *RER to Châtelet-Les-Halles, then métro 7 to Les-Gobelins.*
The building may date from 1914, but the work of the factory itself is over 300 years old. But for a revolution, this place would be known as the Royal Tapestry Factory. Even today, the weavers working over the looms of these carpet and tapestry workshops use the same techniques that once met the exacting standards of Louis XIV, the Sun King. It is thanks to the scarlet dyes made on this site along the banks of the River Bièvre that the threads of this village workshop caught the eye of the kings of France. The Gobelins workshops had already served several reigns by the time they were called in to work on Louis XIV's many châteaux and palaces, and help define that opulent style that was eventually named after the king.

A plaque in the rue Berbier du Mets recalls the original dyeworks founded in 1440. Over the years, the carpet and tapestry workshops of Beauvais and La Savonnerie were relocated to the site, but still the original Gobelins tradition continues; even now, all threading of the looms and selection of threads has to be done under natural light. More than 5,000 tapestries have been produced and the distinctive motifs of Gobelins tapestries can always be recognised: gold and scarlet interwoven with motifs of hunting and the seasons. Despite the 17th-century methods, Les Gobelins is a working factory. In the 20th century it produced wall hangings to designs by Picasso, and nowadays creates tapestries for state occasions and historic buildings. Guided tours of all three workshops are held on three afternoons every week.

Musée National des Arts d'Afrique et d'Océanie 293 av Daumesnil, 75012; tel: 01 44 74 84 80 [9 J5]
Open Wed–Mon 10.00–17.30; closed May 1. €4.50 (30FF) discounts on Sun, under-18s free.
M̄ *Porte-Dorée;* Ē *Métro 5 to Bastille, then line 8 to Porte-Dorée. Cross the sq des Combattants d'Indochinie. The museum is alongside the Périphérique opposite the Bois de Boulogne.*
No dusty old imperial collection of tribal masks and spears, the stunning museum of the art and cultures of Africa and the Pacific islands conjures a truly tropical mood. In the basement an aquarium and live crocodiles perk up the interest of anyone facing cultural burn-out. Fabulous textiles from Maghreb, inventive tribal jewellery and exciting aboriginal art displayed upstairs. The rooms themselves are as interesting as the exhibits, with some inspirational 1930s' art deco touches.

Père Lachaise Cemetery Bd du Menilmontant 75020; tel: 01 55 25 82 10 [5 G7–H8]
Open Mon–Fri 08.00–18.00, Sat 08.30–18.00, Sun 09.00–18.00; Nov–Mar closes 30 minutes earlier.
M̄ *Philippe-Auguste or Père-Lachaise;* Ē *Bus 56 to Gymnase Japy, walk along bd Menimontant to the main gate, or take rue du Repos for the side entrance.*
If the majority of residents of Belleville may no longer speak to us, their words have already spoken volumes. For these are the residents of the world's premier A-list necropolis, Père Lachaise cemetery. Molière and Proust lie here, Balzac and Rossini are remembered with flowers. Oscar Wilde courted controversy beyond his grave. Epstein's Sphynx memorial outraged a certain prudish element, which hacked off the genitalia of the statue – these private parts now serve as a paperweight in the manager's office. Other incomplete occupants include Chopin (his heart is in Warsaw).

The roll of honour is seemingly endless: Les Girls – Sarah Bernhardt, Colette and Isadora Duncan – are all remembered within these walls. Their followers pass through the various entrances of this surprisingly welcoming and attractive city of the departed. Graffiti, with helpful arrows, is the reminder of the highest profile in town, as rock fans carry guitars and their own music to the over-inscribed memorial to Jim Morrison. Come here for dramatic masonry and wry epitaphs, which sometimes reveal much more than any 500-page biography. Gertrude Stein and Alice B Toklas, for example, share a single headstone. Guess whose name is the only one immediately visible, and whose appears in small print on the reverse side of the stone? Put that in your brownies and bake it. Sometimes, as you sit peacefully, paying respects to divine talent, it seems incongruous to even imagine the pomp and pageantry of funerals taking place amid this tranquil dignity. Yet it felt as though half of Paris came to pay its final respects on the day the great Yves Montand was carried through the streets to lie in the memorial grounds that protect his close friend, the legendary first lady of the quarter and Paris' little sparrow, Edith Piaf (see pages 92–3).

Amid this homage to talent, take time to consider Père Lachaise's other face. It is testament to the victims of bigotry and hatred. Those who weep over star-crossed lovers pause by the tomb of Abelard and Héloïse where, legend tells us, Abelard reached out from his grave to embrace in death the love that he had been denied in life. Refugees and expatriates bring flowers to the cenotaphs of the nations. Political pilgrims lay tributes at the Mur des Fédérés cemetery wall, against which were massacred the last 147 martyrs of the Paris Commune, shot with the final bullets of 1871.

Officially this is still the municipal cemetery for eastern Paris. Should you wish to put your own name down for burial at Père Lachaise, plots cost around €7,000 (45,000FF). However, to be considered for a place here, you will need either to die in Paris, having made some contribution to national life, or to be officially resident in the city at the time of your death.

WHERE TO EAT

Astier 44 rue Jean-Pierre Timbaud, 75011; tel: 01 43 57 16 35 [4 E6]
Closed Sat Sun, Aug, late Dec.
M̲ *Parmentier; Go west on av de la République, turning right on rue de Nemours and right again on to rue Jean-Pierre Timbaud.*
You will not get a table without booking, since, despite the seedy décor, the good folk of République know a bargain when they eat one. Noisy, unpretentious, and with service just this side of elsewhere, they come to eat hearty food with hearty friends. The meal costs €21 (140FF), and is packed with French comfort food. Start with the obligatory *escargots*, warm leeks in vinaigrette or marinated anchovies, then dive into the main courses, perhaps the famous *lapin à la moutarde* or the popular *magret au cidre*. Huge cheeseboards and generous appetite-defeating desserts included in the price. With the money you save on food, go a little crazy with the wine list. If you are really lucky, you will get a table in the front room. If you are merely lucky, you will get a table.

A la Biche au Bois 45 av Ledru Rollin, 75012; tel: 01 43 43 34 38 [8 E3]
Closed Sat, Sun mid–July to mid-Aug.
M̲ *Gare-de-Lyon;* E̲ *RER to Châtelet-Les-Halles then RER A to Gare-de-Lyon. Rue de Lyon to junction with av Ledru Rollin.*
'The cuisine here is first class, first class cuisine attracts first class clients, so everyone is happy.' So reads the notice in the window. A set four-course menu at less than €20 (130FF) these days provides a budget alternative to the blue train if

you are in the area between rail journeys. To be honest, if food takes precedence over setting, then this ordinary good-value *bistrot* has a good deal going for it. Good grub, interesting and unadulterated: over the years we've enjoyed *terrines* of wild boar, venison and other game in season. Summer pavement dining is an option if your mood can rise above car fumes and screeching brakes. Excellent-value wine list sees stalwart southern standards at well under €15 (100FF) a bottle.

Les Fernandises rue de la Fontaine-au-Roi, 75011; tel: 01 43 57 46 25 [4 D–E6] Closed Sun, Mon.
M̲ *Goncourt;* Ē *Métro 5 to République, exit fbg du Temple. Walk along the rue fbg du Temple. Just past the canal turn right on the rue de la Fontaine-au-Roi.*
The Seine is the river of Paris; the Seine is the river of Normandy. Ergo Paris is Normandy. The logic may be rusty, but have lunch chez Fernand and I defy you to prove me wrong. *Tripes à la mode de Caen, beurre d'Issigny,* Pont l'Evèque cheese, these are the simple foods from the pages of Elizabeth David and an age far removed from cutting edge Parisian cuisine. Fernand Asseline scorns the markets of the capital, and relies on trusted suppliers from his native Normandy. Even the special cider (reserved for friends) is made by his nephew back home. Sea trout is prepared with mussels and *crème fraîche.* My weakness is for the surprisingly fat-free mackerel *rillettes,* and the simple cream and garlic sauce of the *cassoulette* of salt cod. An impressive array of home-cured camembert with nuts, redcurrants, even cumin, is almost a meal on its own, especially with the home-made bread and home-made butter that Fernand's regulars have cherished for years. Apple tart and crêpes round off any meal. When he saw me, a mere foreigner, ignoring the wine list and ordering the cider with my main course, Fernand came over and chatted. Chat led to reminiscences of Normandy, and memories led to our spending the afternoon working through his impressive Calvados collection, from a green blow-your-socks-off version, poured straight from the freezer, to a smooth and eyeball-warming 1933 vintage. No wonder locals call this place the Normandy Embassy. Even without the benefit of Fernand's company, service is homely. The bill should come to around €38 (250FF) per head, unless you go for the set menus at €21 (140FF) or the even cheaper bistro lunch menu.

La Fontaine aux Roses 27 av Gambetta, 75020; tel: 01 46 36 74 75 [5 G7] Closed Sun lunch, Mon.
M̲ *Gambetta;* Ē *Métro 5 to République, then line 3 to Gambetta. Walk along the avenue; the restaurant is at the junction with rue des Muriers.*
A comfortable choice of reliable fare at this unpretentious and relentlessly floral little corner restaurant opposite the high walls of Père Lachaise. The set menu offers traditional steaks, fricassée of quail, an imaginative range of fish dishes and house classics such as the *sanglier* prepared with mango. Lunch is around €19 (125FF), but dinner at €27 (180FF) is still excellent value, including a *kir royale,* house wine and coffee and no hidden extras. Appetising appetisers, a creditable *feuilleté* of asparagus and some rich and warming baked smoked salmon crêpes in generous portions. Ignore the bland brie and choose one of the homely desserts, nice fruit tart or enormous profiteroles. Cheery service and a good mix of genuinely local customers. As my father said to me, 'This is just the sort of place you imagine when you talk about having a bite to eat in France'. All the tables are packed, everyone is talking and everybody is enjoying the food.

La Gourmandise 271 av Daumesnil, 75012; tel: 01 43 43 94 41 [9 J5] Closed Sun, Mon, Aug.
M̲ *Porte-Dorée;* Ē *Métro 5 to Bastille, then line 8 to Porte-Dorée.*

From a restaurateur with Maxims and the Tour d'Argent on his CV comes a keen eye for flavour and quality and budget! Alain Denoual's witty cuisine comes at cheeky prices. Just €27 (180FF) for lunch so that ordinary folks with good taste can share the dining room with €61 (400FF) à la carte expense-account customers. A marriage of lamb and artichokes is excellent and the *magret de canard aux poivres* won praises from our table. The wine list is honestly priced, with a good daily selection on the menu at well under €23 (150FF). Sensibly, half bottles are younger vintages than the full bottle as they mature much more quickly. You can walk off the meal in the Bois de Vincennes, just a couple of hundred yards away.

Le Mange Tout 24 bd de la Bastille, 75012; tel: 01 43 43 95 15 [8 D2–3] Closed Sun, Aug.
M̲ *Bastille;* E̲ *Métro 5 to Bastille. Take exit to bd de la Bastille , and follow the boulevard above the port to the bridge.*
It may look casual Bastille trendy, but have no fear: under the smart art colours of contemporary chic, there beats the heart of a Left Bank restaurateur with the soul of authentic rural France. Michel Simon, for years a stalwart of the Rive Gauche scene, manages to strike the right balance between fashion and simplicity. He brings the riches of southwest France to those who have no wish to leave the table heavy and bloated. More than a decade ago, Monsieur Simon moved his operation to this choice site overlooking the Arsenal Port of the Seine. Unpretentious staff provide laid-back and helpful hospitality, and raise no eyebrows should light-lunchers decide to forgo the delicious-sounding main courses and opt for a starter and salad instead. My poached eggs in *bleu de causses* were an object lesson in the meaning of the word *tiède*. At neighbouring tables, sturdier diners got stuck in to vibrant and colourful (and, I was assured, equally well flavoured) *confits* and fish dishes. The wine list leans towards the robust Cahors and the subtler Bordelais, and the house wine is precisely what it should be, a good personal choice of the restaurant rather than dregs from a job lot past its sell by date. A recommended crispy and refreshing young white from the Tarn suited me perfectly. À la carte will come to around €38 (250FF), but the menu, available evenings and lunchtimes, is less than half that price.

Le Pas'Sage 18 passage de la Bonne Graine, 75011; tel: 01 47 00 73 30 [8 E2] Closed Sat lunch, Sun.
M̲ *Ledru-Rollin;* E̲ *Métro 5 to Bastille, then line 8 to Ledru-Rollin. A few steps east along the rue du fbg St-Antoine, turn left into the passage de la Bonne Graine.*
Only three things matter in the passage de la Bonne Graine: the wine list at Le Pas'Sage, the *andouillette* sausage at Le Pas'Sage and the customers at Le Pas'Sage. Accurately describing itself as a *Restaurant à Vins*, this is the only place I know where one chooses the food after reading the wine list. And what a wine list! No exaggeration, but it is genuinely heavier than the Paris *Yellow Pages*. A good 350 wines ready for drinking and countless more yet untouchable, but catalogued with pride, passion, and sheer obsession. Fascinating articles from wine journals have been inserted between the pages so be prepared to take your time. If a few thousand francs on a Bordeaux legend is beyond your budget then try a glass of a vintage Crozes Hermitage perhaps. A dozen or so bottles of fine wines are always open behind the bar, for drinking by the glass. Even the house choice is likely to be something for the memoires. When you finish with the cellar bible then scan the blackboards for details of wines at their peak this month. The proprietors, Soizik de Lorgeril and Gerard Pantanacce, and chef Frédéric Boyer, have another

particular indulgence: half the menu is devoted to one sausage: the *AAAAA* reigns supreme. One may spend a happy five minutes discussing the relative merits of the *andouillettes* of Messieurs Duval of Drancy, Gast of Lyon, Lemelle of Troyes, Soulie of Chablis, or Madame Frère of Formerie. Each *charcutier* has his or her individual recipe, and your eventual selection will be served with puréed split pea and lentil and *haricot verts*. Pay €12–21 (80–135FF) for the course. Late-night diners should try the **Café de Passage** wine bar around the corner at 12 rue de Charonne, until 02.00. Most Saturday afternoons see spectacular wine tastings at the café. For an invitation or programme telephone 01 49 29 97 64 or leave your number at the restaurant.

Au Pressoir 257 av Daumesnil, 75012; tel: 01 43 44 38 21 [9 J5]
Closed Sat, Sun, Aug.
M̄ *Porte-Dorée;* Ē *Métro 5 to Bastille, then line 8 to Porte-Dorée.*
One of so many golden doorways at the Porte Dorée end of the avenue Daumesnil, Henri Seguin's dining room has seen many a waistcoat strained to its limits and more than its fair share of button loosening by contented diners. Do not expect a light lunch, but come prepared to do justice to the legendary *pot au feu d'homard* or *lièvre à la royale*, depending on the season. Tradition comes with a twist, so do not be shocked to see peanut ice-cream listed with the desserts. Dining amongst the honeyed wood panels should set you back around €91 (600FF), set menu at €64 (420FF).

Un Saumon à Paris 32 rue de Charonne, 75011; tel: 01 49 29 07 15 [8 E2]
Closed Aug.
M̄ *Ledru-Rollin;* Ē *Métro 5 to République, then line 8 to Ledru-Rollin. Walk north on av Ledru Rollin, turn left to passage l'Homme and second sharp right to passage St-Antoine and left on rue de Charonne.*
See *What to Buy* for details of this grocery that doubles as a restaurant. Three-course meals for €10 (69FF) at lunchtime, or €12 (79FF) in the evening, attract well-heeled local shoppers during the day, and the *jeunesse dorée* of rue de Lappe clubland later on. Try the *oeuf coccotte* with salmon roe. The restaurant usually closes mid-afternoon and opens again for service from around 18.00.

Le Train Bleu Gare de Lyon, 1st floor, 20 bd Diderot, 75012; tel: 01 43 43 09 06 [8 E3]
M̄ *Gare-de-Lyon;* Ē *RER to Châtelet-Les-Halles then RER A to Gare-de-Lyon.*
The look on Margaret Thatcher's face must have been one to cherish when she learnt that President Mitterand had decided to host a summit luncheon for world leaders at the station buffet of Gare de Lyon. Perched high above the platforms where rows of bright orange TGV locomotives head off to Provence and the Med, this is as much a historic as a gastronomic monument. Forget images of curly sandwiches on formica tables. Prepare instead to meet all your romantic *Belle Epoque* dreams of the golden age of travel and adventure rolled into one. Lovingly refurbished, it looks even more glorious than when it starred with Maggie Smith in the film *Travels With My Aunt*. Much of Le Train Bleu's sumptuous architecture and paintings remain from its days as a station buffet at the beginning of the century when train travel was a luxury: luxuriant red drapes, extravagant gilts and mirrors, solemn moustached waiters in ankle length starched aprons. Today's restaurant is good by station standards, but do not go expecting a quick ten-minute snack; service is notoriously slow and trains don't wait. Stick to simple dishes with simple names. Likewise, try not to stray from the €39 (255FF) menu – drinks included.

Au Trou Gascon 40 rue Taine, 75012; tel: 01 43 44 34 26 [9 G4]
Closed Sat lunch, Sun.
M̲ *Daumesnil;* Ē *Métro 5 to République, then line 8 to Daumesnil. Rue Taine is on the southwest corner of pl Félix Eboué.*
Serious food lovers know Alain Dutournier for his famous restaurant, *Le Carré des Feuillants* by the Ritz, where his culinary flair easily persuades the appreciative to part with very large denomination notes for every course (see page 45). The restaurant where Dutournier first won the hearts and stomachs of the big city with gastronomic memories of his childhood in Gascony is far from the quartier Cartier. On a street corner of the Daumesnil dinner trail is the original kitchen from which Dutournier recreated the recipes of his Landais home. Today the restaurant is run by his wife Nicole, and Madame Dutournier's skills as a hostess in the *fin de siècle* dining room are well matched by the kitchen talents of Alain's protegé Jacques Faussat who recreates the flavours of the southwest. Eating à la carte, one might savour the *velouté de châtaignes* with pheasant and the legendary *cassoulet aux haricots tarbais.* Or you could, like me, relish the ∈30 (200FF) lunch menu. Perhaps a fresh and flavoursome *oeuf au pipérade froid*, before feasting on *saumon aux primeurs* – a picture-perfect example (in this age of food as a photo-opportunity) of the virtue of never regarding vegetables as mere garnish. Great cheeseboard and dessert selections, but little can touch the house speciality, *tourtière landaise*, served with delicious prune ice-cream, wafer thin, thrilling, and proof that the humble *pruneau* can hold its own with the world's great fruits. From the shrewd and varied winelist a regional southwestern accompaniment to the meal would cost ∈30–53 (200–350FF), though the evening menu at ∈56 (370FF) includes wines. The Dutournier welcome and service is a practised and relaxed combination of the professional and friendly.

WHAT TO BUY

Friperie La Lumière 21 av de la République, 75011; tel: 01 43 57 51 26 [4 E6–7]
Open Mon–Sat 10.00–19.30, Sun 13.30–19.30.
M̲ *Oberkampf;* Ē *Métro 5 to Oberkampf. Go east on rue Timbeaud. The shop is on the opposite side of av de la République.*
Seriously cheap good-quality second-hand wear, at refreshingly realistic prices for a city that has taken retro as its latest creed. You would be hard pressed to find anything over ∈22 (150FF).

Galerie Gaultier 30 rue du fbg-St-Antoine, 75012; tel: 01 44 68 84 84 [8 E2]
Open Mon–Sat 11.00–19.30.
M̲ *Bastille;* Ē *Métro 5 to Bastille.*
The most visible designer in Paris has come a long way since upgrading Madonna's bustline from uplift to outreach. Whilst his Boutique Jean-Paul Gaultier by the Grands Boulevards is designed to shock the middle classes, at this trendy Galerie eyebrows are about the only body parts unlikely to be raised. Find the JPG ready-to-wear collection here, kinder on the wallet than the *couture* range.

Les Puces de la Porte de Montreuil av du Prof André Lemière, 75020 [9 K2]
Open Sat, Sun, Mon 07.00–20.00.
M̲ *Porte-de-Montreuil;* Ē *Métro 4 to Strasbourg-St-Denis, then line 9 to Porte-de-Montreuil. Cross place de la Porte de Montreuil to the other side of the Périphérique for the market.*
Not on the same gargantuan scale as the fleamarket at Clignancourt, and hardly a mecca for collectors, this neighbourhood rummage sale has fun pickings for junk junkies. Crockery, household goods and cheap second-hand clothes.

Un Saumon à Paris 32 rue de Charonne, 75011; tel: 01 49 29 07 15 [8 E2]
Open Mon–Fri 10.30–02.00, Sat 17.30–02.00; closed Aug.
M̲ *Ledru-Rollin;* E̲ *Métro 5 to République, then line 8 to Ledru-Rollin. Walk north on av Ledru Rollin, turn left to passage l'Homme and second sharp right to passage St-Antoine and left on rue de Charonne.*
A charming little grocers' shop specialising in smoked and preserved fish has a double life as a restaurant serving caviar, salmon and delicately smoked trout. If the sight of all those jars and platters is too much for you, succumb to temptation, pull up a chair and go for it!

Montparnasse-Eiffel

This is the hinterland of the Left Bank. Let the river-hugging cafés attract the dreamers and sensation seekers; real life south of the Seine is lived in the shadow of the two great towers. As to Gustave Eiffel's masterwork, we have radio to thank for its continued appearance in posters, postcards and Ealing comedies. The controversial structure, erected in 1889, was built as a rather natty flagpole for the centenary of the Revolution. It certainly was not expected to last another hundred years. Then Marconi and his cronies made their contributions to the field of communications and a large mast was required. Thus the luxuriously latticed ironwork in the Champ de Mars was spared to the bicentennial, the Millennium and beyond.

Further from the water's edge is the Tour Montparnasse. In a district named after the home of Apollo's muses, the tower pierces the heavens to guide all navigation *rive gauche*. With a nightclub and TGV station at its foot, and buses shuttling out to Orly Airport, this is the southern equivalent of the Gare du Nord district north of the river.

Here all is cosmopolitan and Parisian, with a touch of good manners thrown in. Walking back to a hotel late one night, a friend and I walked towards a heavily tattooed chapter of bikers adorned with enough body piercing to inspire insurance exclusion clauses regarding fridge-magnets. As we passed them, they chorused politely *'Bonsoir Monsieur-Dame'*. Not only was this a reminder that we were getting older, but proof we had discovered a place where people have no qualms over talking to strangers.

If the *Quartier Latin* may appear just too much of a visitor attraction, here at La Coupole, night-people gossip the small hours away with total strangers over a coffee or late-night blow-out. This brasserie was among the handful of other venues that created Paris café society in the first half of the 20th century. Those pioneering intellectuals who once packed these tables now rest in peace at the Montparnasse cemetery where Baudelaire, Sartre and de Beauvoir are amongst the famous denizens. Less illustrious former residents are filed, with disturbing efficiency, in the caves and crannies of the catacombs.

This is a side of the city where present-day Parisians work, rest and play. One of the secrets they keep to themselves is the rue du Cherche-Midi. At midday the road is chock-a-block with Renaults desperately *cherche*-ing a parking place before playing 'hunt the table'. The choice of restaurants is enviable, and a short break in Paris could be gastronomically fulfilled without ever leaving the street. Beyond the tower, less distinguished, if no less authentic, local restaurants feed local people too tired to cook after a hard day at the office. This sleepy quarter boasts at least two gastronomic giants amongst its chefs.

To live here is not necessarily proof of a contented stay-at-home nature: before 1917, Lenin lived at 4 rue Marie-Rose. His lively chats with houseguest Trotsky may not have raised eyebrows at the local bars and cafés, but they raised a few red flags further afield. These days the local proletariat is rarely seen in chains, but instead sports cut-price designer wear, since around Alésia are small outlet stores where fashionable labels are sold at end-of-season prices far below the charges levied in the city centre.

There is plenty of scope for taking a good bracing walk this far away from the heart of the metropolis. Close to the city limits is the Parc Montsouris, where an hour watching the swans makes for good battery re-charging. At the Parc Georges Brassens, a highly scented garden has been designed for the blind. Contemporary twists on landscaping at Parc André Citroën include a hot-air balloon and computerised fountains. There is even a tropical beach out here: Aquaboulevard, the tidal swimming-pool theme-park, with tennis and golf among the less watery attractions.

All this may have been designed for the natives, but a good lunch far from the gadding crowd, followed by some quality time under the trees, is the perfect gulp of fresh air before hopping on a bus or métro to plunge back into the irresistible whirlpool of central Paris.

WHERE TO STAY

Lecourbe 28 rue Lecourbe, 75015; tel: 01 47 34 49 06; email: hotel.lecourbe@easynet.fr [7 G4]
M̄ *Sèvres-Lecourbe;* Ē *RER B to Denfert-Rochereau, then métro 6 to Sèvres-Lecourbe. Take pass des Charbonniers then turn right on to rue Lecourbe.*
Family-run and friendly, clean, comfortable and cheap for its location just ten minutes from Montparnasse. Worthwhile forking out a little more for one of the suites at the end of the courtyard where rooms are not only larger, but lack the constant noise of traffic on the busy rue Lecourbe which plagues the front rooms. The welcome is professional and sober; likewise the décor with pastel shades the norm. Substantial buffet breakfasts are served in the central patio in summer. Rooms around €78 (575FF).

La Loire 39 bis rue du Moulin Vert, 75014; tel: 01 45 40 66 88 [7 J6]
M̄ *Alésia;* Ē *Métro 4 to Alésia. From av de Maine turn left on to rue du Moulin Vert, the hotel is just after the junction of rue des Plantes.*
Ask Madame Noel for one of the small ground-floor rooms facing the sweet little garden near the appropriately named rue des Plantes. Otherwise settle into a first-floor bedroom overlooking the trees, shrubs and clay tiles. Like the bedrooms, bathrooms are clean and basic. Meet the other guests over coffee and baguettes at breakfast time when everyone gathers around the large family dining table. This simple but heartfelt hospitality is more typical of a small French town than the capital city, but then the Alésia district is not the Paris of dollar bills and *haute couture*. Real people live here and pay far less for their shopping than fellow

Parisians closer to the centre of town. Budget around €60 (400FF) per night.

Lutétia 42 bd Raspail, 75006; tel: 01 49 54 46 46; web: www.lutetia-paris.com
M̲ *Sèvres-Babylone;* E̲ *RER E to Haussmann-St-Lazare, métro 12 to Sèvres-Babylone.*
The secret of the Lutétia's success is that, despite its much needed facelifts, this place has always managed to remain more Left Bank than grand hotel. The only high-profile hotel of the Rive Gauche was take over by the Tatinger Group at a point when, to be honest, it had become draughty, dowdy and neglected, with radiators rattling through the night. A dynamic young management team spent years restoring the place. The reception and main salons grew splendid in their red plush glory and, one by one, the bedrooms were refitted and redesigned. Styles varied: one room might be decked out with authentic furniture from 1910, another more practically fitted for the laptop classes. Best of all is the honeymoon suite, straight out of those stylised *American in Paris* dance routines, where the bed is found atop a wooden staircase in an eyrie nook high above the hotel's famous neon sign, thrust into the Paris skyline itself. The view from the stone cave of a balcony is perfect, the hills of the martyrs and the muses – Montmartre to Montparnasse – and, straight ahead, the Eiffel Tower itself. For the locals the Lutétia, like the **Bon Marché** department store across the road, is the essential heart of the quarter. The red drapes of the salon and bar are expansive enough a background for the hotel's neighbour and most celebrated *habituée,* Cathérine Deneuve, often seen holding court with scribes and photographers, scribblers from *Madame Figaro* and *Elle.* The gastronomique restaurant, **Le Paris**, and the bustling **Brasserie** are both essential meeting-places for business breakfasts or intimate celebrations. Hotel guests' breakfast in the Salon Borghese, serenaded over Sunday brunch by musicians in the minstrels' gallery. Rooms onwards and upwards from €290 (1,900FF).

WHERE TO GO

Aquaboulevard de Paris 4 rue Louis-Armand, 75015; tel: 01 40 60 15 15 [6 C6]
Open Mon–Fri 09.00–23.00, Sat–Sun 08.00–23.00. €18.50 (120FF).
M̲ *Balard;* E̲ *Métro 4 to Strasbourg-St-Denis, then line 8 to Balard. Av Porte de Sevres to the roundabout and turn left to rue Louis-Armand.*
This *Forest Hills* water-park is the city's premiere wave-making beach resort. Swimming as a family outing may be great for the kids, but adults on the *rive gauche* may prefer the simpler pleasures of taking the waters in the 1920s' setting of the **Butte aux Cailles** pools (see page 98) or the late-night dips at the classic 1930s' municipal baths of **Pontoise** (see page 127).

Le Bar à Huîtres 112 bd du Montparnasse, 75014; tel: 01 43 20 71 01 [7 J–K4]
M̲ *Vavin;* E̲ *Métro 4 to Vavin. The restaurant is just across the place Picasso.*
If you remember the movie *Cover Girl,* when Gene Kelly, Phil Silvers and Rita Hayworth spent their midnight hours sitting at a New York bar cracking 'ersters' in search of the trophy that would make their fortune, you can do the same here with the late-night Montparnasse crowd. Stay at the oyster bar until two in the morning and choose from as fine a range of Bréton beauties as ever hid a pearl. If you are looking to eat, the dining room has an excellent maritime *carte* including traditional salt cod dishes and the inevitable *fruits de mer.* €19 (128FF) menu but you could spend around €38–46 (250–300FF) including wine for the full sit-down meal.

Carrefour Vavin pl Picasso, 75014 [7 J–K4]
M̲ *Vavin;* E̲ *Métro 4 to Vavin.*
This crossroads of the boulevards Montparnasse and Raspail was once the summit of the hill from which the district gets its name. For the past 100 years it has been the magnetic pole of the area, the starting and finishing point for many

an evening's carousing. Traditionally this part of Montparnasse has been the haunt of foreign writers and artists, including James Joyce, Samuel Beckett and Ernest Hemingway, Eisenstein, Picasso and Man Ray. The Babel babble is always a high-decibel cacophony of French and American-English with a liberal sprinkling of Spanish. Even the ubiquitous text-message has not quite subverted the traditional communication network of the quarter. Gossip is passed, and dates are made by the age-old method of table hopping at the café brasseries **La Coupole** (see below), **Le Dôme**, **La Rotonde** and **Le Sélect**. Rodin sculpted the statue of Honoré de Balzac at the centre of the roundabout.

La Coupole 102 bd du Montparnasse, 75014; tel: 01 43 20 14 20 [7 J–K5]
M̄ *Vavin;* Ē *Métro 4 to Vavin.*
The Montparnasse spirit of Terpsichore lives on. La Coupole has been the brasserie rendezvous of bright young things on their way to parties and nightclubs since the days when Picasso still believed in anatomy. The upstairs dance hall is as popular as it ever was. Trends come and go, but the trendy still flock to this legend for late breakfast, gossipy lunches, afternoon teas and seafood suppers. Meal menus €12–30 (89–200FF).

Rue de la Gaité [7 J4]
M̄ *Gaité or Edgar-Quinet;* Ē *Métro 4 to Montparnasse-Bienvenue then either line 13 to Gaité or 6 to Edgar-Quinet. Rue de la Gaité links the two stations.*
This little Montparnasse street has six theatres, an academy of Commedia del'Arte and the Bobino music hall, where sang Piaf and George Brassens among others. Most famously Joséphine Baker gave her final performances at Bobino, making a glamorous comeback at the age of 69, wooing the critics and dying peacefully at the moment of her greatest triumph. As befits a former country lane that has promised cabaret glamour and dance halls since the 18th century, it also has its cafés, brasseries, burlesque revues and sex shops and is every bit as naughty as
Paris is supposed to be. Happily, all attempts to clean up the area along the lines of Giuliano's New York and turn it into the respectable 'West End' of the 14th have so far failed, and the *Gaité* retains its raffish charm. The beautiful Théâtre Montparnasse, on a street corner, is a 19th-century gem. Great stars still come down here, and artistes join theatregoers and locals squeezing into the little street café in a corner of the foyer, a real old-style bar with a rack of hard-boiled eggs on the counter. During rehearsals you might spot a

fading movie legend chomping on *navarin d'agneau* in the brasserie at the dress-circle level of the theatre.

WHAT TO SEE
Catacombes de Paris 1 pl Denfert Rochereau, 75014; tel: 01 43 22 47 63 [7 K5]
Open Tue–Fri 14.00–16.00, Sat–Sun 09.00–11.00, 14.00–16.00; closed holidays.
€5 (33FF).
M̄ *Denfert-Rochereau;* Ē *RER B to Denfert-Rochereau.*

Post-Revolutionary administrative zeal led to this subterranean network of Roman passageways being called into service as an ordered ossuary. The putrid cemeteries of the city were emptied and re-landscaped, and the thighs and skulls of the departed removed to the catacombs. The wartime Underground lived up to its name, using these very passageways as a secret HQ during the war. Today this short route through the bones and stones is open to visitors for a few hours each day. Intriguingly, remains are neither categorised by name, nor by era. Filing is strictly according to limb size. Irony is not intentionally included in this bizarre exhibition of *memento mori*. I cherish an Eastmancolor postcard showing a 1960s' model in twin-set displaying a thighbone in the unconsciously kitsch manner of an Ideal Home Exhibition demonstrator.

Lion de Belfort pl Denfert-Rochereau, 75014
M̄ *Denfert-Rochereau;* Ē *RER B to Denfert-Rochereau*
The most famous lion in town has had a facelift, thanks to the craftsmen of the town of Argenteuil. The original statue of the Lion of Belfort is carved 22m wide and 11m high into the fortifications of the Franche Comté city of Belfort. Architect Auguste Bartholdi, best known for his Statues of Liberty Enlightening the World in Paris' Pont de Grenelle (see page 142) and Jardins de Luxembourg (see page 126), as well as in New York, created the lion as a tribute to Colonel Pierre-Philippe Denfert-Rochereau, who as governor of Belfort during the 102-day siege of 1870, allowed the territory to remain French when neighbouring Alsace was taken by the Germans. This smaller copper version of the lion, as built by Gustave Eiffel, has long grazed on the square named for the hero. As the rest of the city caroused into the new Millennium, the lion was removed from his plinth, since time, damp and the attentions of the pigeon population had corroded much of the original steel frame and copper coating. But at the end of 2001, gleaming and stronger than ever, the king of the urban jungle returned to retake its rightful place just a roar away from the Paris meridian line.

Memorial Maréchal Leclerc et Musée Jean Moulin 23 allée de la 2e DB, Jardin Atlantique, 75015 [7 H4]
Open Tue–Sun 10.00–17.40; closed holidays.
M̄ *Montparnasse-Bienvenue;* Ē *Métro 4 to Montparnasse-Bienvenue, leave the mainline station at bd Vaugirard. In front of the Air France office take a lift to an overhead walkway. Cross to and through an office building to the Jardin Atlantique.*
It is awkwardly signposted, but do hunt out the museum in these gardens planted above the railway station. Well worth the trouble to discover two museums dedicated to great heroes of World War II. The nation has never stinted on the laurels heaped upon its allies. The names of Churchill and other great military men from the US and the UK are marked on road signs throughout the land. But on every street map in the nation you will also find the names of the remarkable Frenchmen remembered here. Maréchal Leclerc, who died in 1947, was actually only posthumously accorded the rank of Marshal in 1952. A 270-degree panoramic cinema relives the tension and joys of the Liberation, when Général Leclerc regained Paris for France. Jean Moulin is here recalled as an artist, martyr and freedom fighter. This is the bescarved leader of the French Resistance who cut his own throat so as not to betray his comrades when he was first interrogated by the Nazis. Excellent temporary exhibitions have included Vichy propaganda comics portraying Churchill as a figure of fun, a buffoon and a child killer, and recordings of de Gaulle's famous *Free France* broadcasts from London.

Musée Bourdelle 18 rue Antoine-Bourdelle, 75015; tel: 01 49 54 73 73; web: www.paris.france.org [7 H4]
Open Tue–Sun 10.00–17.40; closed holidays. €3.50 (22FF).
M̄ *Montparnasse-Bienvenue;* Ē *Métro 4 to Montparnasse-Bienvenue. From pl Bienvenue exit, turn left into rue Antoine-Bourdelle.*
The lofty, airy spaces of the artist's studio and home display the works of Antoine Bourdelle, Rodin's most celebrated student. With drawings and paintings as well as the monumental sculptures and friezes, the collection traces the artist's progress from his early naturalistic figures, created in the late 19th century, to grand interpretations of virtues and concepts unveiled in the 1920s.

Tour Eiffel Champ de Mars 75007; tel: 01 44 11 23 23; 01 45 55 20 04 (Altitude 95 restaurant); 01 45 55 61 44 (Jules Verne restaurant); web: www.tour-eiffel.fr [6 E1]
Open Sep–Jun 09.30–23.00, mid Jun–Aug 09.00–24.00. €3.50–7 (24–45FF).
M̄ *Bir-Hakeim; RER Champ-de-Mars-Tour-Eiffel;* Ē *RER B to St-Michel-Notre-Dame, then RER C to Champ-de-Mars-Tour-Eiffel. Quai Branly to the tower.*
1,063ft of ironwork, Gustave Eiffel's greatest work, is France's tallest story. 7,000 tons of prime anecdote that upstages even its own views, the Eiffel Tower attracted around 186 million visitors in its first century, and its popularity shows no sign of waning. There are four ways to visit the tower. The penitent can climb all 1,710 steps; the hurried may use the network of lifts to the observation platform at the top level; the hungry might lunch at the **Altitude 95** restaurant on the first floor, styled as an airship moored above the city; and the gourmet should reserve a table at the gastronomic **Jules Verne** restaurant on the second. Although dinner at this Michelin-starred dining room is priced higher than the tower itself, a lunch menu is around €45 (300FF), but you will have to book in advance.

To encourage the weary climber, annoy fellow passengers in the lift, or make small talk over dinner, it is always useful to memorise fascinating trivia about the tower. Do not mention the fact that it was originally built as a temporary structure for the 1889 World Exhibition. Everybody knows that. Instead, try these ten conversational gambits.

- In January 2001 the tower grew more than 5m taller, with the introduction of new radio masts. The official tip of the building is now 324m above street level.
- The original radio masts intercepted the signals that trapped Mata Hari.
- The sparkling diamond effect of the illuminations is created by 20,000 lightbulbs screwed on to the structure. For the Millennium celebrations each bulb was covered with a sapphire-blue filter for one week.
- During the Nazi occupation, resistance fighters hid vital elevator parts so propagandists could not photograph Hitler atop the symbol of France.
- Mail posted from the first floor is franked with an image of the tower. But Eiffel himself had the tower address on his business letterhead.
- The tower is painted every seven years.
- The Altitude 95 restaurant was originally a theatre.
- Arnold Palmer played golf on the third floor.
- Eiffel's memorial is not at the top of the tower, but stands modestly alongside the north pillar.
- Many famous people disliked the tower. Gounod, Maupassant, Dumas (the younger) and Garnier hated it so much that they signed a petition condemning it as an eyesore.
- Although, on a clear day, you may see 42 miles from the top of the tower, the most impressive view is from ground level, looking up through an overwhelming mesh of iron latticework.

Tour Montparnasse 33 av du Maine, 75015; tel: 01 45 38 52 56; web:
www.tourmontparnasse56.com
Open Sep–Jun 09.30–22.30, Jul–Aug 09.30–23.30. ∈8 (50FF).
M̲ *Montparnasse-Bienvenue;* E̲ *Métro 4 to Montparnasse-Bienvenue. Cross pl Dautry from
the station to the tower.*
It says something about a district when the most popular attractions are
opportunities to look as far away as possible. The Montparnasse Tower has views
as far as the woods and even Orly Airport. A 40-second lift ride takes visitors to the
56th-floor viewing platform, with its bar and restaurant, 209m above ground level.
In the basement is the super trendy nightclub, L'Enfer (see pages 190–2).

WHERE TO EAT
La Cagouille 10 pl Brancusi, 75014; tel: 01 43 22 09 02 [7 H5]
Closed Sun, Aug.
M̲ *Gaité;* E̲ *RER E to Haussmann-St-Lazare then métro 13 to Gaité. South on av du
Maine, turn right into rue de l'Ouest, entrance by number 23.*
In the unlikeliest of up-and-coming areas, in the very shadow of Paris' innovative
public housing projects, the cheery Cagouille attracts an intriguing mix of foodies,
business types and government ministers with their mistresses. So what if the
seashell and chandlery décor might be naff even on the coast; trust me, this
remains one of the finest fish restaurants in the city. The menus are scribbled on
large boards erected at your table, and first courses are advised for the hungry,
because the service is so slow that even the generous bowl of seafood served as an
appetiser might not last until the main course. Menus, at around ∈30 (200FF) for
two courses and ∈37 (250FF) for three, allow you to have your pick of the à la
carte selection. A winter warmer of grilled sea bream with cumin is delicious.
Salmon, trout and tuna are accorded the same respect due to *charolais* beef, so be
prepared to order *à l'unilatérale* – lightly flamed on one side, and raw at its heart.
Reservations are essential, and even then may not guarantee a coveted seat by the
window in summer. A breath of the port in the landlocked 14th arrondissement.
If you are travelling by taxi, ask the driver for 23 rue de l'Ouest.

Chez Germaine 30 rue Pierre Leroux, 75007; tel: 01 42 73 28 34 [7 H3]
M̲ *Vanneau;* E̲ *RER B to St-Michel-Notre Dame. Follow signs to Cluny-La-Sorbonne for
métro 10 to Vanneau. Walk west on rue de Sèvres to turn right into rue Pierre Leroux.*
So what if they don't take credit cards here; loose change buys lunch in this gem
first discovered by resourceful students. They queue early to pay ∈12 (80FF) for
three courses with wine. The chef's *batterie* doubtless includes a can opener for
entrées and desserts, because all energies are concentrated on producing decent
home-made main courses. Summer doorstep wedges of cold roast beef and
potato salad, or a winter-warming stew, we are talking about hearty meals as
raided from a mother's fridge. Informality is the order of the day, tables and
water jugs are shared and the wine list reflects the budgets of the regulars.

La Coupole 102 bd du Montparnasse, 75014; tel: 01 43 20 14 20 [7 J–K4]
M̲ *Vavin;* E̲ *Métro 4 to Vavin.*
See *Where to go*, page 112.

La Croque au Sel 131 rue St-Dominique, 75007; tel: 01 47 05 23 53 [7 F4]
M̲ *Ecole-Militaire;* E̲ *RER B to St-Michel-Notre-Dame, then RER C to Invalides and
métro 8 to Ecole-Militaire. On av Bosquet, third left on rue St-Dominique.*
Seeking the basics? Slap bang next door to the illustrious Fontaine de Mars (see
page 116), and hidden behind the very fountain itself, it is rough, ready and

inexpensive. The cuisine is not as refined as that of its celebrated neighbour. In fact it is extremely basic home cooking. Where a team of black-tied waiters hovers around the linen tables of the better known *bistrot*, here one lone host does the rounds of his own tables with a pair or two of helping hands when required. Don't expect gastro-novelty nor the refinement of next door's *plats*, and don't select the most unusual item on the specials board. Stick with standards for a pleasant evening either inside the cosy dining room or the other side of the pretty painted windows on the tiny square itself. Starters (of the chicken liver salad and *terrine* variety) and desserts are more successful than main courses – even on a very quiet Tuesday evening, the *plat de jour* was 'off' by 19.30 – but with a two-course menu at €8 (60FF) (until 20.00) and the full meal at €15 (100FF), enjoy the budget, enjoy the location and, in summer, enjoy the sunshine.

La Fontaine de Mars 129 rue St-Dominique, 75007; tel: 01 47 05 46 44 [7 F4] M̲ *Ecole-Militaire;* Ē *RER B to St-Michel-Notre-Dame, then RER C to Invalides and métro 8 to Ecole-Militaire. On av Bosquet, third left on rue St-Dominique.*
To the sharp-suited lunch set, this is just the canteen on the corner. To passing visitors, it is the gingham-draped *bistrot* of everyone's Maigret-monochrome memory. These days plenty of restaurateurs know how to arrange a row of copper pans on a wall, but at the Fontaine de Mars, the chef knows how to use them in the kitchen. The house showpiece is a *fricassée de canard*, and a lobster salad with a tart hazelnut dressing to tickle behind the teeth is a summer special. Daily specials are worth considering, such as the mouthwatering *oeufs en meurette*. The wine list has some workaday reliable stalwarts around the €15 (100FF) mark. Unless you have chosen the midday €14 (95FF) menu, by the time that you fold up your red linen napkin you should have parted with at least €33 (220FF).

Joséphine 'Chez Dumonet' 117 rue du Cherche-Midi, 75006; tel: 01 45 48 52 40 [7 H3]
Closed Sat, Sun, July.
M̲ *Sèvres-Babylone;* Ē *RER E to Haussmann-St-Lazare, métro 12 to Sèvres-Babylone. South along bd Raspail, take the first right on to rue du Cherche Midi.*
Walk to Joséphine's on a Wednesday. Years before the serious critics tumbled to the truth, any local could have told why you won't find a parking space on the rue du Cherche-Midi on a Wednesday lunchtime. The restaurant serves lamb every weekday, but on Wednesday, and only on Wednesday, the world grabs its forks and licks its lips in anticipation of the legendary *gigot d'agneau*, served with its Vendéan dish of beans. You will happily pay €46 (300FF) for the experience, but even a glance at the wonderful wine list tells you that this is no run-of-the-mill *bistrot* but the restaurant that sets the pulse of all its neighbours on the Cherche-Midi. When Chez Dumonet is closed, try the *rôtisserie* next door – it shares the same kitchen!

La Marlotte 55 rue du Cherche-Midi, 75006; tel: 01 45 48 86 79 [7 J3]
Closed Sun, Sat lunch, Aug.
M̲ *Sèvres-Babylone;* Ē *RER E to Haussmann-St-Lazare, métro 12 to Sèvres-Babylone. South along bd Raspail, then first right on to rue du Cherche-Midi.*
Rack of lamb, rich chocolate desserts, all those dishes that make one choose a plain *bistrot* over a posh restaurant. One speciality alone, liver served in a raspberry vinegar, has been luring one resident through the door ever since she moved to the quarter a decade ago. When a friend first introduced me to Lucie Agaud and Michel Bouvier's modest establishment, the décor was naff and plastic. Since then, the guinea fowl *pastilla* and turbot specialities have wooed and won writers, politicos and publishers, and the place has had a facelift to reflect its new clientele. But the food and value remain the same. Pay under €30 (200FF) for lunch or dinner.

Natacha 17 bis rue Campagne-Première, 75014; tel: 01 43 20 79 27 [7 K4]
Closed Sun, Aug.
M̲ *Vavin;* E̲ *Métro 4 to Vavin. East on bd Montparnasse to turn right into rue Campagne-Première.*
The food is good enough – trendy pastas, *hachis parmentier* and light fried rabbit
– but be honest, we really come here to be fawned over by Natacha herself and
play 'spot the movie star'. The famed hostess's well-trained voice helps novices
identify Mick Jagger at 30 paces. Meanwhile, the constant flow of hot and cold
running supermodels, Hollywood hunks and Polanski child-brides is better
than a floorshow. You can also tell which of the celebs is working or who is
resting by checking out who declines the creamy desserts. Pay in the region of
€30 (200FF).

Pavillon Montsouris 20 rue Gazan, 75014; tel: 01 45 88 38 52 [8 A7]
RER Cité-Universitaire; E̲ *RER B to Cité-Universitaire. Walk round the park from rue Jourdan to rue Gazan.*
In the pretty park with a pretty lake is a pretty pavilion, just like the restaurants in
France's turn-of-the-century spa towns. A view to pander to the pensive, it has
welcomed starry-eyed lovers whose Paris was painted in shades of monochrome
by *RKO Radio Pictures*, and it has hosted prandial thinkers from Lenin to Sartre. In
recent years, the view has almost been eclipsed by the plate, thanks to chef Jerôme
Mazur providing inspiration for the romantic gesture: monkfish *carpaccio* or a *foie
gras au pain brioché aux raisins*, and top-notch service under the eye of the patron
Yves Courault, formerly of the Grand Vefour (see page 47). Budget €40 (270FF).

La Régalade 49 av Jean Moulin, 75014; tel: 01 45 45 68 58 [7 H7]
Closed Sat lunch, Sun, Mon, midsummer.
M̲ *Alésia;* E̲ *Métro 4 to Alésia. Walk along av Jean Moulin. The restaurant is on your left just pass the sq de Châtillon.*
Long before the superstar-chefs decided to open up their annexes, this room was
where the first of the high flyers went native, turned his back on a charmed career
and decided to cook the food that he loved for hard-working Parisians. A decade
ago, when I first found myself in this dormitory district of Alésia, the Régalade
was virtually unknown outside the 14th arrondissement. Now one has to beg for a
table. Yves Camdeborde, formerly number two at the Hôtel Crillon, created a
little gem, serving imaginative dishes to please both the palate and the wallet. The
menu is €27 (175FF) for three courses, although a seasonal *dégustation* may be
prepared to suit specific parties. The shrewd, predominantly young wine list
includes at least a dozen creditable offerings for local budgets. Eschewing the
foppish fancies offered elsewhere as *amuse-gueules*, Régalade punters are presented
with a large earthenware pot of the house *terrine du porc* with an Excalibur blade at
its heart. Be warned, let it not lead you unto temptation. The brunch-like
appetiser belies the finesse of the cuisine that follows, so keep the taste buds on
hold. A *terrine de poireaux et queues de boeuf au vin rouge* is something quite different.
And as for the *pisaladière de thon mi-cuit aux olives noires,* just imagine the wafers of
subtly heated tuna on the crispest fine pastry base, topped with a nest of fresh
herbs. A revelation. The *hachis parmentier* of *boudin noir béarnaise* and *dos de carralet*
presented to my lunch-chum were masterly improvements on the traditional
servings, the latter bearing no relation to the bland offering of many Paris
restaurants, served here on a bed of warm and crispy white cabbage and chives.
The triumphant *soufflé* finale was a masterpiece of flavour and imagination. Since
the place has been discovered by the food world, I am delighted to report that
success has not spoilt this unexpected treasure.

La Route du Château 36 rue Raymond Losserand, 75014; tel: 01 43 20 09 59
[7 H–J5]
Closed Sun.
M̄ *Pernety;* Ē *RER E to Haussmann-St-Lazare then métro 13 to Pernety. The restaurant is two blocks along the rue Raymond Losserand.*
On the wrong side of the Tour Montparnasse, a time-warp of a 1930s provincial dining room in one of those out-of-the-way corner restaurants for neighbourhood appetites. The dark walls bear dark pictures of darker 19th-century aunts in darker yet frames. West of France grandmotherly specialities include rabbit in cider, and home-made flans, and comfortingly fussy old-fashioned service. €15 (100FF) is within most modest budgets.

WHAT TO BUY
Rue d'Alésia [7 H–K6]
M̄ *Alésia;* Ē *Métro 4 to Alésia.*
The rue d'Alesia is an unofficial factory outlet in a modest residential quarter. Blanc Bleu, Cacherel and countless other designer labels may be picked up for a fraction of the city-centre price. Look for the keyword 'Stock' in shop windows. This indicates end-of-line fashion bargains.

Les Cousines d'Alice 36 rue Daguerre, 75014; tel: 01 43 20 24 86 [7 J5]
Open Mon 15.00–19,00, Tue–Sat 10.00–19.00, Sun 11.00–13.00.
M̄ *Denfert-Rochereau.*
A proper old-fashioned toyshop, with wooden tops, cuddly toys and lots of dolls. Batteries not required.

Maine-Montparnasse Centre Commercial Pl du 18 Juin 1940, 75015 [7 J4]
M̄ *Montparnasse-Bienvenue;* Ē *Métro 4 to Montparnasse-Bienvenue.*
A dark and anonymous shopping mall in the shadow of the tower, with Habitat, C&A and a branch of Galeries Lafayette. Before the area was redeveloped, and the new TGV station built 500m further south, the place 18 Juin 1940 was the site of the original Gare Montparnasse, where Leclerc installed his headquarters on the liberation of Paris (see *Memorial Maréchal Leclerc*, page 113). A plaque, disgracefully tucked away at the entrance to the mall, reveals that this was where the German military governor signed his surrender.

Marché Grenelle bd de Grenelle, 75015 [6–7 E–F3]
Open Wed, Sun 07.00–13.00.
M̄ *La Motte-Picquet-Grenelle or Duplex;* Ē *RER B to St-Michel-Notre Dame. Follow signs to Cluny-La Sorbonne for métro 10 to La Motte-Picquet-Grenelle.*
A good cook's market. Best to come here on your last day in Paris for jars of olive oil from Provence, strings of pink garlic and plenty of herbs and spices.

Marché du Saxe-Breteuil av de Saxe, 75007 [7 G3]
Open Thu, Sat 07.00–14.00.
M̄ *Ségur;* Ē *RER B to St-Michel-Notre Dame. Follow signs to Cluny-La Sorbonne for métro 10 to Segur. Rue Perignon leads to av de Saxe.*
On a sunny day, bring your camera with you to the place Breteuil for snapshots of neat piles of fruits and home-made preserves with the Eiffel Tower and the dome of Les Invalides obligingly providing background colour. Not as lively as the markets in poorer districts, but a good source of bottles and jars of gift food as souvenirs.

Left Bank

There is so much more to the Left Bank than the Latin Quarter. Between Napoléon's tomb at Les Invalides and the Institut du Monde Arabe, the wisest counsel deliberates weighty decisions: from the everyday housekeeping of politicians at the Assemblée Nationale to the crucial choices of chefs and housewives selecting vegetables at the street markets.

The riverbanks themselves have a life of their own. The *bouquinistes* selling antiquarian editions to the discerning, 1950s' movie magazines to the smitten and cheeky postcards to the majority, open their lock-up stalls on the *quais*. Further away from such ready money, the city's fire department gives us a magical and impossible bridge of rainbows on sunny Sunday mornings, as young *pompier* cadets are given lessons on directing their power hoses on the riverbank below the quai Voltaire.

An institution poised for revival across the water from the Tuileries, the Piscine Deligny was more than a swimming pool; it was a shrine to the body beautiful. Men and women with unbelievable tans and even less probable waistlines would sunbathe on the top decks of the floating freshwater pool. Nary a child's shout was ever heard here. People comported themselves with the utmost decorum, since splashing might have left traces of marbling on the delicately applied Ambre Solaire. In the evening, society hairdressers would mingle with the darlings of the nightclub circuit, sipping long cool drinks as the sun set over the Seine. Until one night in 1993 when the Piscine Deligny slipped its moorings and sunk beneath the waters of the river, and a legend disappeared from the social scene. Thankfully no one was aboard at the time. Paris never quite got over its loss, and plans are afoot to raise the Deligny and re-open one of the pleasures of summer in the city.

Such hedonism is a far cry from the spirit that first colonised the Left Bank. The Latin Quarter itself was created by the Romans, yet it was the birth and development of the universities in the Middle Ages that gave the area its name and character, and remains the beating heart of the scholastic district, the 13th-century Sorbonne and the medieval charms of Cluny. The narrowest streets of the student quarter largely escaped the grand town planning designs that pass within a whiff of the cafés where students debate the hours, and where midnight is no excuse to say goodnight.

Close to the cheap bookshops are plenty of diversions. Any Frenchman too important to be buried at Père Lachaise, Montmartre or Montparnasse may be visited at the Panthéon high on the restaurant-dotted hill of St-Geneviève. Overlooked by the gargoyles of Notre Dame, the small 13th-century church of St-Julien-le-Pauvre once hosted student councils until tempers flew too high in the 16th century and the church reluctantly returned to its religious rather than political obligations. As in the Cluny ruins, the calm of St-Julien is underscored by a regular programme of midweek afternoon concerts.

The rue Mouffetard, with its markets, old-world twists and turns and New World eateries, is popular with visitors who believe they've found the true flavour of the Left Bank. They haven't. Hunt for restaurants in the quieter backstreets of the quarter. You might stumble across the remains of a 2nd-century Roman arena. The Arènes de Lutèce were discovered just over a century ago and today form a simple park. Here veterans play *boules* where once sport was played for higher stakes.

Most of us discover the quarter from the place St-Michel. Noisy, boisterous with a hint of celebration about it, this is the first step on the great boulevards of the Left Bank. The 'Boul' Mich', as the boulevard St-Michel is universally known, along with the boulevard St-Germain, threads past most of the sites of the south, and almost all roads will lead to one or other of them. So instead take the old and winding rue St-André des Arts with its even smaller tributaries such as the passage de l'Hirondelle and the rue Gît-le-Coeur. Restaurants, cafés, hotels and galleries line the narrow street. Here stood the first guillotines, here lodged musketeers, here is the Paris that the cinema promised us.

Cinema matters on this side of the Seine. And for 'cinema' read 'Golden Age'. If the lines outside the picture palaces of the Grands Boulevards and Champs Elysées lead to the worlds of Stallone, Willis and Eddie Murphy, queues form here for Marilyn Monroe and the Marx Brothers. The sound of a modern teenage audience convulsed by the monochrome antics of Cary Grant and Katherine Hepburn is a heady and intoxicating delight.

Hugging the boulevard St-Germain are streets of 'typical Left Bank hotels' that have filled the honeymoon scrapbooks of Boston and Wisconsin, Guildford and Edinburgh. Unfortunately many of the boulevard shops have fallen into the hands of the international chains, purveyors of Vuitton and Dior to the lovestruck. Shoppers in search of something extravagant and browsers with a taste for the extraordinary will adore the antiques and art dealers of the Carré Rive Gauche, or the galleries near rue Bonaparte and rue de Seine.

Despite its overt tourist-consciousness, the Left Bank somehow manages to retain its identity. Eccentrics flourish here, from George Whitman at Shakespeare and Co to the clairvoyant florist on the rue Monge who intuitively reveals the taste of whoever you intend to compliment with flowers. The local community manages to appear completely unaware of the outsiders ever pointing, snapping and passing through. On Sundays, when tour buses disgorge their human cargo at St-Michel, Les Invalides and the Musées d'Orsay and Rodin, anyone who actually lives here simply retires to the Luxembourg Gardens, where the 20th century simply never happened.

WHERE TO STAY

Duc de St-Simon 14 rue St-Simon, 75007; tel: 01 44 39 20 20; email:
duc.de.saint.simon@wanadoo.fr [7 J2]

M̲ *Rue-du-Bac;* E̲ *RER E to Haussmann-St-Lazare, then métro 12 to Rue-du-Bac. From
rue Courier turn left into rue St-Simon.*

This was once a humble family pension, but you'd never believe it. This is the
sort of rustic simplicity that comes with a price tag. Even as you step into the
200-year-old courtyard with its climbing wisteria and geranium pots, you are
transported to another world of tranquillity and quality. This is where those with
the taste to back up their wealth would choose to stay when they could afford to
have opted for a grand international palace hotel. No glitz, no designer chic, just
an obvious appreciation for the genuinely good things in life. Here is the *grande
luxe* of a country manor house, in the city. Bedrooms practically creaking with
the weight of the antiques have a very particular charm, one that is carried
through into the *trompe l'oeil* public areas, especially the lovely bar and lounge
converted from the old stone cellars. Many rooms look out on to the lush
gardens which are, alas, closed to guests. Others have rooftop terraces. Rooms do
not come cheap at around €229 (1,500FF), but they are the nearest thing to
perfection that you'll find at the price. After years of resistance, the hotel now
takes credit cards. Breakfast is €11 (75FF).

Esméralda 4 rue St-Julien le Pauvre, 75005; tel: 01 43 54 19 20 [8 B2]

M̲ *St-Michel;* E̲ *RER B to St-Michel-Notre Dame.*

Next door to the improbably romantic bookshop, sanctuary and otherworld
known as Shakespeare and Co, the eccentric (some say, delightful) Hôtel
Esméralda may not be everyone's cup of tea. In fact, in high season, attitudes may
seem a little brusque. Happily, in recent months the welcome seems to have
returned, and the view of the newly renovated towers of Notre Dame, the eclectic
décor and sheer 15th-century ricketiness of the house continue to delight. The
gypsy spirit of the place's namesake lives on in the feisty independence of the
hotel cat and the Bohemian décor. Be aware that some rooms are vulnerable to
early morning street noise, and some have no bathrooms, but some have
wonderful views of Notre Dame. So do make sure that you are specific in your
booking requests. Rooms from under €30 (200FF) for a basic single to €91
(450FF) for a double with facilities, and €91 (600FF) for a room for four.

Grand Hôtel Lévêque 29 rue Cler, 75007; tel: 01 47 05 49 15; web:
www.hotel-leveque.com [7 G1–2]

M̲ *Ecole-Militaire;* E̲ *RER B to St-Michel-Notre-Dame, then RER C to Invalides and
métro 8 to Ecole-Militaire. From av de la Motte Piquet, rue Cler is first on the left.*

Tucked away between a café and a cheese shop in a pedestrianised side street is this
small, modest hotel. A pretty glass lift, green and yellow double rooms with en-
suite bathrooms at €62 (415FF) and none of the pretentions often associated with
hotels in the shadow of the Eiffel Tower. Value-for-money accommodation with
no-smoking options, and rooms equipped for the disabled available on request.

Grandes Ecoles 75 rue du Cardinal Lemoine, 75005; tel: 01 43 26 79 23 [8 B3]

M̲ *Cardinal-Lemoine;* E̲ *Métro 5 to Austerlitz, then line 10 to Cardinal-Lemoine. Walk
along rue du Cardinal Lemoine to the junction with rue de Rollin.*

Take breakfast on the lawn taking in the scent of summer flowers under the shade
of old plane trees. Surely the height of self indulgence on the always overcrowded
Left Bank. The garden of the hotel, hidden down an unlikely little alleyway, is its
greatest charm, yet the endearingly old-fashioned rooms, both in the main house

and its annexes, are fussily grandmotherly in style. Lots of lace and dark wooden furniture. Spend a weekend in the country from around €91 (600FF)

L'Hôtel 13 rue des Beaux Arts, 75006; tel: 01 44 41 99 00; web: www.l-hotel.com [7 K2]
M̲ *St-Germain-des-Prés;* E̲ *Métro 4 to St-Germain-des-Prés. Rue Bonaparte to rue des Beaux Arts.*
The grand luxuries and imposing décor give no hint that this was the hotel in which England's most famous Irishman declared 'Either that wallpaper goes, or I do'. For this was once the Hôtel d'Alsace where Oscar Wilde 'died beyond his means'. Today's visitors might follow in his wake if unaware of the room rates. Almost €600 (4,000FF) for the very room itself, or perhaps the oval boudoir fitted with nightclub queen Mistinguett's exotic bedroom furnishings. Once a *pavillon d'amour*, the building evolved into a six-storey hotel. The street has always attracted the great and the good. Mérimée, Pradier and Corot were amongst the former residents. In 1968 the hotel was reconstructed so that guests, these days paying €274 (1,800FF) per night, may enjoy a fine restaurant, comfortable salons, and imposing luxury. As I was tying up loose ends for this book, I heard that the new owner, Jean-Paul Besard, has commissioned leading stylist Jacques Garcia to freshen up the hotel's style, without losing its distinctive feel.

Nevers 83 rue du Bac, 75007; tel: 01 45 44 61 30 [7 J2]
M̲ *Rue-du-Bac;* E̲ *RER E to Haussmann-St-Lazare, then métro 12 to Rue-du-Bac. Walk south on the rue du Bac, the hotel is on your left.*
Rejoice! Although Nevers is under new management, the spell cast by its long-time owner, the delightful Mme Ireland, continues undimmed. Once an annexe to an adjacent convent, the Nevers is known for its flowers. Rooms have flourishing window-boxes and each of the 11 bedrooms is named after a different bloom. On the first three floors there are only two rooms to a landing. The hotel has no lift, so only the very fit will benefit from the ever-popular top floor. Room 11 is the cherished secret of many regulars who adore its tiny, yet completely secluded, roof-top terrace for private sunbathing or romantic breakfasts. Rooms are well fitted, with good bathrooms, minibar, but no TV. The nightly rate is a good value €76 (500FF) with bath.

d'Orsay 91 rue de Lille, 75007; tel: 01 47 05 85 54 [7 J1]
M̲ *Assemblée-Nationale;* E̲ *RER E to Haussmann-St-Lazare, then métro 12 to Assemblée-Nationale.*
In this hotel just behind the Musée d'Orsay, take the lift to the fourth floor, then climb the extra flight of stairs to the servants' quarters. Here weekend Bohemians can find their sanitised Parisian garret romance in the top-floor bedrooms under the eaves. Sweet, prettily decorated bedrooms with tiny bathrooms hidden in cupboards. Room rates around the €115 (750FF) mark include the cost of breakfast which may be served in the rooms, but should really be taken in the very attractive little morning room decorated with a collection of plates and porcelain. A very nice little hotel that retains its charm despite its popularity. Advance booking advisable.

Parc St-Severin 22 rue de la Parcheminerie, 75005; tel: 01 43 54 32 17; email: hotel.parc.severin@wanadoo.fr [8 B2]
M̲ *Cluny-La-Sorbonne;* E̲ *RER B to St-Michel-Notre-Dame. From place St-Michel follow rue de la Harpe, turning left into rue de la Parcheminerie.*
A rather nice surprise. The paperback and pitta kebab casbah of St-Michel, with its lamb-brochette hustler alleyways and quayside *bouquinistes*, gives way to a tranquil churchyard. On a corner site, by the Canadian-run Abbey Bookshop, is

an unexpectedly classy hotel. Pretty, understated bedrooms, some with an antique occasional table or a 19th-century easy chair, look out over the cloisters of the eponymous church. Rooms on the top floor have roof terraces for sunrise breakfasts amongst the spires and chestnut treetops of the Left Bank. Top-of-the-range comfort for a three-star hotel. Double-room rates start at €97 (635FF) and rise to around €230 (1,500FF) for the light and spacious terrace suites.

Prince de Condé 39 rue de Seine, 75006; tel: 01 43 26 71 56 [7 K2]
M̲ *Odéon;* E̲ *Métro 4 to St-Germain-des-Prés. From rue Bonaparte, turn right on rue Visconti to rue de Seine.*
So it costs €152 (1,000FF) a room, but I had the best night's sleep I ever enjoyed on the Left Bank when first I stumbled into this modest little 12-room hotel in a road of antiquarian booksellers and double-parked Renaults, between the haunt of brasserie and Kodak crowds and the riverbank itself. Walls are plush with warm red fabric, a little booklet at the bedside gives helpful hints for a peaceful slumbers, staff are discretion incarnate and all fittings pamper-perfect. The same management as the more modern Hôtel Quartier Latin around the corner in the 5ème.

Quartier Latin 9 rue des Ecoles, 75005; tel: 01 44 27 06 45; email: H2782-GM@accor-hotels.com [8 B3]
M̲ *Cardinal-Lemoine;* E̲ *Métro 5 to Austerlitz, then line 10 to Cardinal-Lemoine. Walk to the foot of rue du Cardinal Lemoine and turn left on to rue des Ecoles.*
A bibliophile's delight, this contemporary, calm, witty and charming little hotel, designed by Didier Gomez. Décor is understated, and all is a tribute to the great writers of the past 1,000 years. On a picture rail above the bed will be perhaps a small framed photograph of Colette or Prévert. Public rooms double as modern libraries with neat paperbacks that scream out 'read me' as you pass. The frieze on the breakfast-room walls offers you the wisdom of Baudelaire with your croissants, eggs and fresh fruit. Furnishings are stark modern, linens are starched white, staff completely on the ball and bookshelves filled with both English- and French-language editions. Part of the Libertel Grande Tradition network, with rooms at €187 (1,225FF).

Relais Christine 3 rue Christine, 75006; tel: 01 40 51 60 80; web: www.relais-christine.com [8 A2]
M̲ *Odéon;* E̲ *RER B to St-Michel-Notre-Dame. From quai des Augustins, take rue des Grands Augustins. Rue Christine is second on the right.*
From a convent to a sanctuary: this former religious retreat is now a haven of measured sanity in a hectic quarter. Since coming under new ownership it is better than ever. Rooms may vary in size and décor, but share an elegance, from the pretty printed fabrics of the duplex rooms under the eaves (numbers 50 and 56) to the pink Portuguese marble bathrooms, and the splendid vaulted breakfast room which could put many a restaurant to shame. The honesty bar (one serves oneself from bottles and decanters), chessboards in public rooms, private garage parking and plenty of heavy trunks in corners contrive to play the game of a weekend retreat. Favourite rooms look out on to the courtyard – but there is a price to pay, €343 (2,250FF).

Résidence des Arts 14 rue Git-Le Coeur, 75006; tel: 01 55 42 71 11; web: www.residence-des-arts.com [8 A2]
M̲ *St-Michel;* E̲ *RER B to St-Michel-Notre Dame. From the riverbank, rue Git-le-Coeur is the first side street after place St-Michel.*
You could hardly find a better location for living out your Left Bank garret fantasy than this 16th-century house at the livelier end of the Git-le-Coeur.

Charmingly decorated studios, suites and full-on apartments in the heart of the Left Bank, yet the merest stroll from the Rive Droit. Rooms are well appointed and studio rates start at under €122 (800FF) – though they rise liberally thereafter! Fax and modem connections, housekeeping and even parking provided. The residence's rather touristic **Café Latin** restaurant provides sustenance on tap. When the entrance to the residence is locked, the barman at the café keeps a weather eye on the keys and the residents.

Le Rives de Notre Dame 15 quai St-Michel, 75005; tel: 01 43 54 81 16; email: hotel@rivesdenotredame.com [8 B2]
M̄ *St-Michel;* Ē *RER B to St-Michel-Notre Dame.*
Bright summery fabrics, dried and fresh flowers, and gentle attentive service, a four-star hotel with a difference, along the busiest of Left Bank highways. Philippe-Guillaume Degravi has turned this 16th-century private house into a genuine sanctuary, a mere gargoyle's yawn from Notre Dame itself. From the moment you enter the lobby to be greeted by a receptionist, sitting not at an austere desk, but an antique table laden with fresh cut roses, the hustle of tourist-trap corner quickly evaporates. A central, stone-walled, wooden-beamed conservatory has caged songbirds and some highly inviting and thoroughly 'sinkable' sofas. Room-rates start at €168 (1,100FF) and, if the €381 (2,500FF) suite feels a little extravagant, then €236 (1,550FF) would find a room with a private lounge area. Quality is assured, and you don't have to step an inch away from the heart of the Left Bank in order to find it. A little treasure, priced accordingly.

St-André des Arts 66 rue St André des Arts, 75006; tel: 01 43 26 96 16; email: hstand@minitel.net [8 A2]
M̄ *Odéon;* Ē *RER B to St-Michel-Notre-Dame. From place St-Michel, take rue St-André-des-Arts.*
If you were introduced to Paris through costume drama, but balk at the cost of reliving the elegance of a château lifestyle, go for 'downstairs' authenticity in this former residence of the royal musketeers. Eccentricities of décor and furnishings throw back to the days of fiction and romance: pew seats, little low doors, and the quaint toilet between the first and second floors. Rooms at €81 (480FF) are pleasingly furnished, but nothing is in the luxury class. Nonetheless, the atmosphere of the place and the informal and helpful staff keep a loyal clientele, even amongst the beautiful people who could afford something far more sleek and chic. Sunday morning's breakfast is a muted cavalcade of bright young things coping with the effects of Saturday night.

St-Germain 88 rue du Bac, 75007; tel: 01 49 54 70 00; web: www.hotel-saint-germain.fr [7 J2]
M̄ *Rue-du-Bac;* Ē *RER E to Haussmann-St-Lazare, then métro 12 to Rue-du-Bac. Walk south on the rue du Bac, the hotel is on your right.*
Well-stocked bookcases, Murano glass and exposed oak beams: this hotel is at home in the discreet wing of the Left Bank. Rooms overlooking the garden or terrace never let you forget that this was once a 16th-century private home. Doubles with shower at €129 (850FF). An ideal base for trekking on foot to the Orsay, Rodin, Louvre and Légion d'Honneur collections, and yet not too far from the designer-label haunts.

St-Michel 17 rue Git-le-Coeur, 75006; tel: 01 43 26 98 70 [8 A2]
M̄ *St-Michel;* Ē *RER B to St-Michel-Notre-Dame. From the riverbank, rue Git-le-Coeur is the first side street after place St-Michel.*

Modest budget accommodation in the most sought after part of town brings the romance of the Left Bank within anyone's reach. So three cheers for the Mécelle family for providing a friendly welcome in their spotlessly clean one-star hotel. Tucked away behind the métro and thronging pavements of the bustling place St-Michel, the quaintly named rue Git-le-Coeur (a bastardised version of *Gilles le queux* or cook) is an improbable haven of tranquillity as convenient for the Right Bank as the Left. Halfway down the road, between the scramble and the Seine, guests follow the scent of pot pourri to find the place. In the tiny reception area is a modest bookcase with Agatha Christie and Enid Blyton paperbacks in both French and English: useful in a hotel that has no televisions in the rooms and shuts its front door at 1am sharp. Accommodation ranges from the modest single room 22, at €35 (228FF), to the mini-suite number 14 at just over €84 (554FF) for an entire family. Breakfast, included in the room rate, is taken in an excavated cave at the foot of the pretty, centuries-old spiral staircase. The hotel has no lift and takes no plastic.

St-Paul 43 rue Monsieur le Prince, 75006; tel: 01 43 26 98 64; email: hotel.saint.paul@wanadoo.fr [8 A2–3]
M̄ *Odéon;* Ē *Métro 4 to Odéon. Hotel is on the left side of rue Monsieur le Prince.*
The Sureté may have its Maigret, but the rue Monsieur le Prince has Detective Sergeant Hawkins, late of Scotland Yard. Three decades ago, when DS Hawkins was seconded to Interpol, he fell hopelessly in love with the Left Bank. So rather than return to the Met, he stayed and bought the hotel next door to the Polidor restaurant. The Hawkins' attention to detail nudged the place upmarket; from its humble budget-basic origins it now rates three stars. The French adore the place – perhaps for the charming décor, the pocket handkerchief garden that lures a bright variety of butterflies and birds into the funnel of a courtyard, or Mr Hawkins's eccentric hobby of cultivating tomatoes in the bedroom window boxes. English management continues to nurture the original charm of this 18th-century house. Bedrooms on lower floors are tall and stately with wonderful wooden beds. Room rates begin at €125 (820FF). Breakfast is served in the old cellar which boasts its original old stone well.

Sully St-Germain 31 rue des Ecoles, 75005; tel: 01 43 26 56 02; web: www.sequanahotels.com [8 B2]
M̄ *Maubert-Mutualité;* Ē *RER B to St-Michel-Notre-Dame. Follow signs to Cluny-La-Sorbonne for métro 10 to Maubert-Mutualité. Take rue des Carmes then right on rue des Ecoles.*
Good news. There are new faces at the front desk and a fresh attitude at large – and about time too! Those who may have shared my experience of the hotel in the 1990s should now be persuaded to return. The sullen and unwelcoming weekend receptionist did not get my first visit off to a good start. In fact at these prices, I was furious. Happily I can now report that staff are charming and efficient, service is ever at hand, the place has grown into its charges, and the promised improvements are now in place. The once confusing warren of basement rooms that originally led to my accidentally having breakfast in the hotel next door has been opened out, no such mix-ups these days. Décor is mix and match airport-medieval, with stone walls, fabric hangings, tapestries and gleaming suits of armour. A bonus is the fitness centre with its fully equipped gym, jacuzzi, sauna and steam baths. Rooms are attractively furnished, some laid out as duplexes. Do insist on a large bathroom, as some of the smaller ones have toilets designed to be ridden sidesaddle. All usual mod cons and freebies, hairdryer and cable TV. Rates around €168 (1,100FF).

WHERE TO GO

Café de Flôre 172 bd St-Germain, 75006; tel: 01 45 48 55 26 [7 K2]
M̄ *St-Germain-des-Prés;* Ē *Métro 4 to St-Germain-des-Prés.*
The Left Bank café where tourists watch other tourists and street
entertainers. Monday nights in winter promise English-language play readings.
On the first Wednesday of each month, English-speaking philosophers meet to
talk late into the night.

Cluny-La-Sorbonne métro station [8 A2]
Ē *RER B to St-Michel-Notre-Dame. Follow signs to Cluny-La-Sorbonne.*
Platforms are decorated with famous quotations, as befits the local station for
France's oldest university.

Les Deux Magots 6 pl St-Germain-des-Prés; tel: 01 45 48 55 25 [7 K2]
M̄ *St-Germain-des-Prés;* Ē *Métro 4 to St-Germain-des-Prés.*
For café society read camcorder society. This is the spot where those who come
in search of Hemingway and Sartre find others who have come in search of
Hemingway and Sartre. Homage is paid with a click and a whirr and a coffee at
the 'very tables ...' Tourists flock here all year – as well as to the Café de Flôre
next door. But its location, right on place St-Germain-des-Prés, warrants a visit.
Food is standard café snacks. Outside, jugglers and street performers entertain all
those who never found the great existentialists and philosophers. I'm skint,
therefore I ham.

Rue de la Huchette [8 B2]
M̄ *St-Michel;* Ē *RER B to St-Michel-Notre-Dame. With your back to the river, rue de la
Huchette is on your left from place St-Michel.*
Run the gauntlet of the *hoummus* hustlers as you move from the commercial
place St-Michel to the studious simplicity of the Latin Quarter with second-hand
bookshops at each end. This is the food equivalent of a red-light area, with
sharp-dressed men in doorways sidling up to likely punters and extolling the
virtues of a voluptuous *moussaka*. Some *pitta*-pimps flourish photographs of
dolmades, taramasalata and olives, as though they were limited-edition photographs
for the discerning gentleman-collector. Should your baser appetites break your
will, and you find yourself lured through one of these doorways marked
'Minotaur', 'Parthenon', 'Aphrodite' or 'Zeuss', be prepared for either the fastest
or slowest meal of your stay. In the first case the ready-plated meal may be
slapped on the table within seconds of your arrival. In the second, your waiter
might be so busy touting for trade on the pavement that you could wait a good
20 minutes before seeing a menu. There is an absurd sense of theatre about this
narrow street, and fortunately a playhouse to reflect the surrealism of the
moment. The Théâtre de la Huchette presents a varied bill featuring the longest-
running play in Paris, Ionesco's *La Cantatrice Chauve (The Bald Prima Donna),* the
only production in the world to come close to the longevity of *The Mousetrap.*

Jardin du Luxembourg [7 K3–8 A3]
M̄ *Luxembourg;* Ē *RER B to Luxembourg*
Discover the simple pleasures of life in a park that espouses the values of another
age. Children, who elsewhere would be sitting on a bench, eyes focused on a
Gameboy, or composing text-messages for schoolchums, here may choose from
more traditional activities. Raise your ice-cream cone in tribute to Napoléon, for it
was the emperor himself who decreed that the principal function of these
seemingly grown-up formal gardens should be the entertainment and indulgence
of the children of Paris. Thus 21st-century *enfants* discover the pleasures of past

generations, whether pedalling cars on a mini race track or enjoying donkey rides, screaming approval at the Guignol puppet theatre or sailing model boats on the lake. You do not have to be 11 years old to appreciate the gardens. Students have been coming to the 'Luco', as they call it, since Marius met Cosette in *Les Misérables*. Adults taking the air in these gardens behind the Senate building admire the monumental Medici fountain and the Delacroix memorial. Always a favourite with young women, here old-fashioned romantics perfect the art of the strategically dropped handkerchief along the paths, whilst feminists have long taken inspiration from the many statues of French heroines that populate the terraces.

La Mosquée de Paris pl du Puits de l'Ermite, 75005; tel: 01 43 31 18 14 (baths); 01 45 35 97 33 (tea room) [8 C4]
Tea room open 10.00–24.00; baths (women) Mon, Wed–Sat 10.00–21.00, (men) Tue 14.00–21.00, Sun 10.00–21.00. Tea room free, baths ∈13 (85FF).
M̄ *Censier-Daubenton or Monge;* Ē *RER to Châtelet-Les-Halles then métro 7 to Monge. Walk south on rue Monge, turn left to rue du Puits de l'Ermite.*
In season, when the Left Bank becomes the 51st state of the USA and the Latin Quarter seems just too small to contain the never-ending flow of overseas visitors, follow me to a quiet haven in quite another continent behind the Jardin des Plantes. Come to the Paris Mosque, where Rita Hayworth was married, for a cup of that wonderful green mint tea that might have been designed to calm the stressed refugee from the world of 'Ici on parle Kodak'. For a more thorough de-stressing, consider the mosque's Turkish baths.

Piscine Pontoise Quartier Latin 19 rue Pontoise, 75005; tel: 01 55 42 77 88 [8 B3]
Open Mon–Fri 07.00–08.30, 12.15–13.30, 16.00–20.45, 21.00–23.45, Sat 10.00–19.00, Sun 08.00–19.00. ∈4 (25FF) before 20.45, ∈7 (45FF) after 21.00.
M̄ *Maubert-Mutualité;* Ē *RER B to St-Michel-Notre-Dame. From quai de la Tournelle turn right into rue Pontoise.*
Since the Piscine Deligny sunk under the waters of the Seine (see page 119), this 1930s' municipal pool, surrounded by two tiers of changing cubicles, has been the place to enjoy a midnight dip. Late-night swims are hugely popular as an energy boost for students who have worked well into the evening and need an invigorating spot of exercise before hitting the bars and cafés. Squash, gym and other exercise possibilities on site. If you are struck by a sense of *déjà vu*, blame it on *Bleu*, Kristof Kieslowski's movie, starring Juliette Binoche, which was filmed here.

Tea & Tattered Pages 24 rue Mayet, 75006; tel: 01 40 65 94 35 [7 H3]
Open 11.00–19.00, Aug 12.00–18.00; closed Sun in Aug.
M̄ *Duroc;* Ē *RER B to St-Michel-Notre-Dame. Follow signs to Cluny-La-Sorbonne for métro 10 to Duroc. Walk east on rue de Sèvres to turn right into rue Mayet.*
The noble Earl Grey and Dame Agatha Christie welcome you to this absolute gem of a bolthole. A cluttered second-hand English and American bookshop (novels on the ground floor, thrillers in the basement) hides a dinky little café tucked away behind a stack of yellow *National Geographics* and blue *Pelicans*. Transatlantic and cross-Channel snacks such as a bagel filled with *chèvre* and *herbes de Provence* to go with your Fitzgerald, or a huge bowl of apple and peach crumble with your Richmal Crompton. No credit cards accepted.

Le Village Ronsard 47 Terrasse bd St-Germain, 75005; tel: 01 43 25 07 95 [8 B3]
M̄ *Maubert-Mutualité;* Ē *RER B to St-Michel-Notre-Dame. Follow signs to Cluny-La-Sorbonne for métro 10 to Maubert-Mutualité.*

As you leave the métro, enter a world of food, with rows of fresh endive and artichoke, baskets of organic herbs, buckets of sea urchins, clusters of guinea-fowl, and lush piles of greenery speckled with flashes of carrot and radish. This is the market and this is where the market café gets its fresh produce. Sip a coffee in the morning to watch the widows, housekeepers, chefs and otherwise-pennywise of the quarter as they calculate their menus. At mealtimes have a sandwich (a negligible supplement brings proper *pain de campagne* instead of the usual *baguette)*. Later in the day, long after the traders have gone home, you might opt for the dish of the day with a cup of mulled wine, or pay €12.50 (80FF) for the express menu, if an evening's entertainment beckons you elsewhere.

WHAT TO SEE

Les Egouts de Paris (The Paris Sewers) Opposite 93 quai d'Orsay, 75007; tel: 01 53 68 27 82 [7 F1]
Open Sat–Wed (summer) 11.00–17.00 (winter) 11.00–16.00; closed two weeks in Jan. €4 (25FF).
RER Pont-l'Alma; E̲ *RER B to St-Michel-Notre-Dame, then RER C to Pont-l'Alma. Walk a few yards east of the bridge.*
The sewers of Paris are now so much a part of popular culture, blending urban myths of subterranean tribes with the movie *Subway* and great moments in literature, that most visitors never even worry about the possibility of any stench until a few moments before they arrive at the Pont l'Alma. One tour company even teases its passengers by handing out scented handkerchiefs as they step off the bus. Have no fear; whether or not the place lives up to your fantasies, the tour is spotless and odour free. Essentially a museum of public hygiene and water supplies, the attraction offers a glimpse at the incredible underground network of vaulted streets and squares that mirror exactly the ground-level map of Paris. Using gravity and giant Indiana-Jones-scale rolling balls, each of the smaller tunnels is regularly cleaned, just as water is shot into the gutters and kerbs of the main roads to rinse streets on dusty summer afternoons. The sheer scale of some of the chambers underneath the major squares is breathtaking, and you can easily imagine the dramatic impact of the illegal raves held under the city during the 1970s and 1980s. Visitors are warned against trying to explore the sewer system, with cautionary tales of flooding and rats. Cuddly rats are among the souvenirs sold in the on-site shop, as are dinky little watches filled with simulated purified sewage.

Hôtel des Invalides Esplanade des Invalides, 75007; tel: 01 44 42 37 72; www.invalides.org [7 G–H2]
Open summer 10.00–18.00, winter 10.00–17.00; closed holidays. €6 (38FF).
M̲ *Invalides or Tour-Maubourg;* E̲ *RER B to St-Michel-Notre-Dame, then RER C to Invalides.*
Mansart designed the stunning Eglise du Dôme, most famous for the ornate, multi-layered tomb of Napoléon, but there is another church to be visited in this grand military compound. At the Soldiers' Church of St-Louis-des-Invalides, flags and pennants from 300 years of glorious campaigns remind you that this complex was originally constructed as a home for army pensioners. Today, 100 veterans of 20th-century campaigns live here, and their presence gives an immediacy to the exhibitions of the nation's warfaring past. Strategy and weaponry are remembered at the Musée de l'Armée, and newer displays are devoted to World War II, Charles de Gaulle and testimonies of resistance and

freedom fighters. On the fourth floor, a Musée des Plans Relief contains models made by the military architect Vauban of all the fortified towns in Louis XIV's kingdom. The models of the fortresses of northern France and Flanders are housed at the Palais des Beaux Arts in Lille (see page 230).

Musée Maillol 59 rue de Grenelle, 75007; tel: 01 42 22 59 58 [7 J2]
Open Wed–Mon 11.00–18.00; closed holidays. €6 (40FF).
M̱ *Rue-du-Bac;* Ḙ *RER E to Haussmann-St-Lazare, then métro 12 to Rue-du-Bac. Rue du Bac south to rue de Grenelle.*
Dina Vierny should be hailed as the original supermodel. Not only was she Maillol's muse, but she became an art collector in her own right. Here are drawings and sculptures by Maillol himself, as well as Madame Vierny's enviable collection of works by Matisse, Cézanne, Dufy, Degas, Picasso, and some of those Rodins not to be seen in the Hôtel Biron.

Musée de l'Institut du Monde Arabe 1 rue des Fossés-St-Bernard, 75005; tel: 01 40 51 38 38; web: www.imarabe.org [8 C3]
Open Tue–Sun 10.00–18.00. €4 (25FF).
M̱ *Jussieu;* Ḙ *RER B to St-Michel-Notre-Dame. Follow signs to Cluny-La-Sorbonne for métro 10 to Jussieu. From rue Jussieu turn right on rue des Fossés-St-Bernard.*
Jean Nouvel's splendid glass tower on the banks of the Seine is home to a comprehensive museum of Arab and Islamic art from around the world. Illuminated editions of the Koran, exquisite miniatures and religious artefacts in the permanent collection, but the associated programme of temporary exhibitions and performances is never less than surprising. A successful series of displays and events recently looked at the world of flamenco and the Arab influences on the culture of Andalucia. Always worth checking at the tourist office for details of current events.

Musée National Eugène Delacroix 6 rue de Furstenberg, 75006; tel: 01 44 41 86 50; web: www.musee.delacroix.fr [7 K2]
Open Wed–Mon 09.30–17.00. €3.50 (22FF); free on 1st Sun each month and for under 18s.
M̱ *St-Germain-des-Prés;* Ḙ *Métro 4 to St-Germain-des-Prés, then at the bottom of the square turn right into rue de l'Abbaye and left into rue Furstenberg.*
In this unexpectedly quiet ghetto of art dealers, just yards from noisy cafés, the artist's home and studio is the perfect place to appreciate his life and work. Alongside sketches and studies for well-known works are oil-paintings, pastels and watercolours. Photographs and letters of friends and family are also displayed in his apartment. Visit early in the day to appreciate the full effect without the distraction of school groups.

Musée National du Moyen Age – Thermes de Cluny 6 pl Paul Painlevé, 75005; tel: 01 53 73 78 16; web: www.musee-moyenage.fr [8 A3]
Open Wed–Mon 09.15–17.45. €4.50 (30FF). Free 1st Sun and under 18s.
M̱ *Cluny-La-Sorbonne, St-Michel;* Ḙ *RER B to St-Michel-Notre-Dame. The museum is along the bd St-Michel at the junction with bd St-Germain.*
Remains of the 2nd-century Roman baths, splendid medieval remains and newly restored medicinal herb garden. All good stuff, but sometimes horrendously full of 21st-century glassy-eyed tourists being processed through two millennia. I arrive just as the place opens to enjoy the sensations of the past free from the sound of shuffling trainers and whine of tour guides battering history back into its box. The tapestries are superb, among them the world renowned *La Dame à la Licorne*.

Musée d'Orsay l rue de la Légion d'Honneur, 75007; tel: 01 45 44 41 85 [7 J1]
Open summer Tue, Wed, Fri–Sun 09.00–18.00, Thu 09.00–21.45, winter Tue,
Wed, Fri, Sat 10.00–18.00, Thu 10.00–21.45, Sun 09.00–18.00; closed Jan 1, May
1, Dec 25. €6 (40FF). Under 18s free. Sun €4.50 (30FF).
RER Solférino; E̅ RER B to St-Michel-Notre-Dame, then RER C to Musée-d'Orsay.
Built in just two years, more palace than railway station, with a metallic structure
heavier than the Eiffel Tower's and a nave larger than that of Notre Dame, the
Gare d'Orsay opened to a fanfare on Bastille Day 1900, bringing to southwest
France the railways of the 20th century. Within four decades it had closed, and
from 1939 this magnificent building languished by the river, serving as
temporary auction house, prisoner reception centre and occasional film location
(Orson Welles filmed *The Trial* here). In 1977, President Giscard d'Estaing
announced that the *gare* should live again, decreeing that it would become a
museum of 19th-century art. Six years later, his successor, François Mitterand,
declared the Musée d'Orsay the link between the art treasures of the Louvre and
the modern works of the Pompidou Centre. The magnificent building alone is
worth a visit – quite apart from the priceless art collection housed within. The
absolute essentials are the Impressionists on the upper level. Van Gogh's *Church
at Auvers-sur-Oise*, Renoir's *Bathers* and Degas' *Blue Dancers* must not be missed.
Among the Monets are his interpretations of *The Houses of Parliament* and *Rouen
Cathedral*. Arrive early to beat the crowds gazing at a remarkable parade of the
works of Cézanne, Gauguin, Matisse and Sisley, in shafts of natural sunlight.
You'll need a good day to do justice to the many treasures (all enhanced by
natural light). If you have the time, take in art nouveau and realism on the first
two floors. Admiring the arts needn't stop at lunchtime. The restaurant here is a
far cry from the standard dark and dingy basement museum canteen. Elaborate
belle époque dominates: gold, gilts, mirrors, marble cherubs, chandeliers
throughout. The privilege of dining here doesn't even break the bank. Pay under
€15 (100FF) for a buffet of interesting salads and *terrines*, a pitcher of wine and
dessert. On late-night openings do try to experience the unforgettable glory of a
sunset dancing with the huge hands of the great clock window.

Musée de la Préfecture de Police 1b rue des Carmes, 75005; tel: 01 44 41 52
54 [8 B3]
Open Mon–Fri 09.00–17.00, Sat 10.00–17.00; closed holidays. Free.
M̅ *Maubert-Mutualité; E̅ RER B to St-Michel-Notre-Dame. Follow signs to Cluny-La-
Sorbonne for métro 10 to Maubert-Mutualité. From the marketplace, cross to the police
sentry box at the foot of rue de la Montaigne Ste Généviève. Climb stairs to police station.
Take lift to second floor.*
These galleries in a local police station provide much more than the usual black
museum. Paris is a city where insurrection has punctuated almost every page of
its history book, from the Revolution to the student uprisings of almost every
generation between the days of Victor Hugo and the 1960s. More chilling than
the guillotine blade and execution swords, closer to home than the early cameras
and the uniforms straight out of *Les Misérables*, are the papers, the handwriting
and the curtly typed notes. I left shaken and stirred after reading documents of
Zola's Dreyfus affair and a memo from the police chief in occupied Paris
refusing to grant the right to work to 41 Jewish lawyers interned at Drancy.

Musée Rodin 77 rue de Varenne 75007; tel: 01 44 18 61 10; [7 H2]
Open Tue–Sun summer 09.30–17.45, winter 09.30–16.45; closed Jan 1, May 1,
Dec 25. €4 (28FF).
M̅ *Varenne or Invalides; E̅ RER E to Haussmann-St-Lazare then métro 13 to Varenne.*

On sunny days the best room in the museum is the garden. Find *The Thinker* and *Burghers of Calais* amongst the rosebushes, lawns and paths in the grounds of the Hôtel Biron. The building itself was home to the great sculptor Auguste Rodin in his later years, and its salons now display his best-known works, most notably *The Kiss*. Other residents of the house in its prime included Isadora Duncan, Jean Cocteau and Matisse. The museum often presents temporary exhibitions by other artists and maintains a permanent display of the works of Camille Claudel.

Panthéon pl du Panthéon, 75005; tel: 01 44 32 18 00 [8 B3]
Open summer 10.00–18.30, winter 10.00–18.15; closed Jan 1, May 1, Dec 25.
∈6.50 (42FF). Free first Sun, and under 18s.
M̄ *Maubert Mutualité or Luxembourg;* Ē *RER B to Luxembourg. From bd St-Michel follow rue Soufflot to the Panthéon.*
Construction on this great domed church began during the last days of the monarchy. When it opened, religion had gone out of fashion and it was re-designated as a temple of reason. Here are entombed the nation's greatest figures, from Voltaire to Pierre and Marie Curie. In the crypt, Victor Hugo, Jean-Jaurès and Emile Zola receive a steady flow of pilgrims.

WHERE TO EAT

Alcazar 62 rue Mazarine, 75006; tel: 01 53 10 19 99 [8 A2]
M̄ *Odéon;* Ē *Métro 4 to Odéon. From carrefour de l'Odéon go north along rue de l'Ancienne Comédie which becomes the rue Mazarine.*
Savaged by the foodies, favoured by fashion victims, London's *grandpère terrible* of big-scale eating launched himself in Paris with all the image of the London Conran restaurants but unfortunately fewer of the flavours. Had he only shown Paris just what young British chefs are capable of producing. Alas, this place is neither a patch on Terence Conran's riverside restaurants in London (see pages 336–7), nor neighbouring brasseries on the Rive Gauche. Chomp on acceptable *pissaladière tartelette, pot au feu,* and boring *brie*-loaded cheeseboard, but you could eat better elsewhere in the quarter for far less than the ∈27 (180FF) set menu or ∈38 (250FF) free-range forage. Décor, it seems, is all. Massive metal bar upstairs; mirrored ceilings and glass wall to spy on the chefs downstairs. From the skylight to a twee seafood counter the place is trendily Eurostyle and rather sterile for a former cabaret spot. Marvel at the vast floral display, the size of most local restaurants, gasp at an entrance gallery featuring loads of Conran's merchandising, and gaze upon a dining room packed with Brits and would-be-Brits. A mezzanine bar now boasts top DJs for pre-club sessions (see page 191).

Atelier de Maître Albert 1 rue Maitre Albert, 75005; tel: 01 46 33 13 78 [8 B2–3]
Closed Mon lunch, Sun.
M̄ *St-Michel;* Ē *RER B to St-Michel-Notre-Dame. Follow the quai de Montebello to the third street on your right after the pont au Double.*
When first introduced to this place I was told to expect a classic Parisian *auberge* where Cyrano de Bergerac would have felt at home. True enough I was greeted by old oak beams, vast open fireplaces and roaring log fires, and subtly augmented candlelight. Yet the textile-draped stone walls are hung with modern art and the neat tables have modern linens and simple clear glassware. It is unashamedly geared at the tourist trade, but food more than lives up to the timeless surroundings. ∈20–27 (130–180FF) menus are excellent, and ∈36 (240FF) brings the cream of the kitchen to your table with wines to accompany the succulent fish *quenelles, magret de canard* and a delectable *crème brulée*. Spit-

roasted meats are the speciality of the house, and chef Vincent Demelier's trademark apple tart is pretty much as good as it gets.

Les Bookinistes 53 quai des Grands-Augustins, 75006; tel: 01 43 25 45 94 [8 A2] Closed Sat lunch and Sun lunch.
M̄ St-Michel; Ē RER B to St-Michel-Notre-Dame. Walk along the quai des Grands Augustins.
No prizes for finding Guy Savoy's lively modern *bistrot* on the banks of the Seine, on the corner with the rue des Grands-Augustins opposite the *bouquiniste* antiquarian and souvenir book-and-print-sellers that give the restaurant its name: just look for the cluster of would-be diners gathered on the narrow strip of pavement, patiently awaiting their table whilst sipping glasses of the house white. For the proof of success in this town is customer loyalty, and who would begrudge half an hour's happy loitering, quizzing departing diners about their choice of main course from the *carte-menu?* Les Bookinistes is a perfect example of the new annexe culture, where the respected grand chefs of Paris relax with unpretentious menus at affordable prices, and where the public flock to sample imagination normally reserved for those least imaginative diners – expense-account suits. Away from the constant regimented competition to achieve, maintain and augment their coveted Michelin *macerons*, it is in the 'annexes' such as these that the chefs get the chance to let their hair down. They may take risks and generally have the fun in the kitchen that lured them into their chosen careers, way back when.

Inside, Daniel Humair's post-war multi-tinted décor is understated without being cold or minimalist. Yellow nappery, lightly painted plaster walls, a few bright sconces and several signed playing cards on the ceiling (ask the waiter – the story is better told than printed). A hive of smart young men in amusing ties spin cheerily around the room, taking orders, dispensing wine and flourishing plates. Small tables are packed close together, which is useful because the food is good enough to break the ice, so that neighbours at the end of a meal lose no time in counselling wavering newcomers faced with the mouth-watering menu. 'Oh, the tuna was wonderful, the veal was wonderful and the chicken was wonderful,' a departing matron called across to a young couple holding hands across a crowded napkin. 'You should try the fish,' suggested her husband, as he pocketed his gold card 'Uh, it was wonderful.' I found other adjectives, and I am not afraid to use them. The *carte-menus* of €21 (140FF) and €24 (160FF) (with a three-course veggie option – a rare concession even these days) are excellent value, with renowned combinations of the raw and the cooked, the sweet and the sour. Sunday night's 180FF version is augmented by some last-minute market inspirations which are always well worth a detour.

Of Guy Savoy's four major satellites, this is the one where his talented right-hand man William Ledeuil gets to play in the kitchen. Sometimes the menu-speak teases so much you simply have to order to satisfy your curiosity. Take our choice of starters: *raviolis des concombres* revealed themselves to be less raviolis than tiny sandwiches of tomato, haddock *compôte* and surely that was basil amongst the herbs, presented between two crisp, chilled and juicy slices of cucumber. Zing went the buds in my mouth! Lacquered brochette of chicken wings proved to be lightly caramelised and served with an unctuous and heavenly purée of avocado topped with a bush of dandelion leaves. And we never even tried the anchovy and coriander gazpacho, with its floating salad of asparagus and butter beans. Still, we managed to inhale some from the next table! Roast saddle of rabbit for the main course was packed with savoury time bombs of pine kernels, shallot and garlic cloves and especially the coating of fine slices of spicy Spanish *chorizo* sausage. A trio of tiny baby sole fillets, pan-fried with dill, capers, *cornichons* and chives, melted and slid off the bone – so subtle, so light, so Sunday night.

Since it was that time of year, and the city was buzzing with its final thrill of July (the Tour de France had ended just hours earlier), I decided to celebrate the season with strawberries, served, our waiter announced, *comme un cappuccino*. The fruit had been barely blended, retaining shape and texture within the purée, poured into a glass and topped, instead of the usual frothy milk and chocolate, with a thin layer of *mascarpone* cheese and flecks of vanilla. I would swear on a stack of Elizabeth Davids that I tasted hints of raspberry and hazelnut in the final confection. A small yet appropriate wine list includes wine by the glass, and drinks are not exorbitant. Budget around €30–38 (200–250FF) for the evening of wit, originality, flavour and verve.

Coté Mer Bistrot 16 bd St-Germain, 75005; tel: 01 43 54 59 10; web: www.michelrostang.com
M̲ *Maubert-Mutualité;* E̲ *RER B to St-Michel-Notre-Dame. Follow signs to Cluny-La-Sorbonne for métro 10 to Maubert-Mutualité. Walk east along bd St Germain.*
Michel Rostang's *bistrots* may lack the finesse of Loiseau or Cagna, and they may be short on the panache and verve of Ducasses Spoon and Savoys Bookinistes, but they are generally reliable and well-judged pavement pleasers – even if the Paris annexes are not always in the same league as his excellent prodigal over the water in London (The Terrace at Le Méridien, Piccadilly). When I last visited this particular offspring at the far end of the boulevard St-Germain, it was known as Chez Raffatin & Honorine and followed the *bistrot da coté* formula (see page 150). This *bistrot* had some of the impetuosity of youth to recommend the menu, offering bolder and spicier combinations of flavours than its siblings. Then pretentious menu-speak rather got in the way of the facts: an enticingly dubbed *boudin* of *morue fraîche* and green cabbage was in old money a somewhat leaden roulade of fish and greens on a warm nest of leeks in a rich sauce not as compatible as it sounds. Now, under a fresh alias, its new resident chef Olivier Fontaine has created a menu straight from the port, and reinvented the restaurant as a seafood and fish *bistrot*. Plenty of tall food, fashionably constructed, and many scrummy, chocolate-packed desserts in the Rostang tradition. In the evening, eat inside, sitting against the stone walls and mirrors that evoke St-Germain past. At lunchtimes, choose to watch the dog walking and daily life of the 5th from the pavement terrace. Entrées around €8 (50FF), main courses €16 (100FF).

Le Coup Chou 9–11 rue de Lanneau, 75005; tel: 01 46 33 68 69 [8 B3] Closed Sun lunch.
M̲ *Maubert-Mutualité;* E̲ *RER B to St-Michel-Notre-Dame. Follow signs to Cluny-La-Sorbonne for métro 10 to Maubert-Mutualité. Take rue des Carmes, continue across, rue des Ecoles then turn right into rue de Lanneau.*
For years I'd heard stories of this gloriously dotty and ivy-covered auberge-style restaurant, named after the favoured tool of Paris' own demon barber and tucked away in a timeless, tourist-free corner of the quarter. It takes some finding, as there appears to be no entrance to the restaurant. Eventually you will find your way in through a side door off the passageway of a private house in a nearby street (the impasse Charretière). Messieurs Nani, Lemonnier and Azzopardi create a delightful menu that is no more straightforward than the entrance. Even the canny and loyal regulars have to ask for elucidation of the mouthwatering suggestions, such as *magret de canard* cooked with peaches, or the famous coddled eggs. The welcome is of the warmest, and the table appointments refreshingly simple: brass candlesticks and functional cruet on plain white linen. Set menus never dull at €23 (150FF) and €30 (200FF).

Le Divellec 107 rue de l'Université, 75007; tel: 01 46 51 91 96 [7 G1]
Closed Sun, Christmas, New Year.
M̄ *Invalides;* Ē *RER B to St-Michel-Notre-Dame, then RER C to Invalides. Walk west along quai d'Orsay and turn left on rue Fabert to rue de l'Université.*
Whenever there's a pearl in the month the good, the great and the nostalgic mariners head to the quartier des Invalides. For Brittany's own sea captain turned chef, Jacques le Divellec, knows oysters. Europe's destiny has been shaped over many a seafood supper in this very room, as leaders of France have mellowed over a range of oysters, prepared to impress the most demanding diner, matched by an audacity that never fails to intrigue. Divellec has braved the deep as a trawlerman, and his instinct for quality rarely fails him. Today's treats might be a tartare of lobster and tuna, or the unforgettable tournedos of prime mackerel with Riesling. Divellec was, naturally enough, the first to serve *foie gras* with St-Jacques, when contemporaries still regarded such combinations as little more than surf'n'turf. Friends, on tasting the experiment, and knowing how wary I am of dubbing a two-star Michelin establishment a bargain, sat me down in front of the menu and ordered me to order. A usually flat sole levitated to glory via a hollandaise that wafted the heady scent of Pouilly Fuissé. And, on dry land, desserts are equally heroic. Fixed-price menus start around the €46 (300FF) mark, and à la carte will cost in the region of €91 (600FF). Just close your eyes and open wide.

La Méditerranée 2 pl de l'Odéon, 75006; tel: 01 43 26 02 30 [8 A2]
M̄ *Odéon;* Ē *Métro 4 to Odéon. Rue l'Odéon to place de l'Odéon.*
The actors, directors and audience of the National Theatre have been loyal to this restaurant as it has slipped in and out of fashion over the years. The winds of change are blowing in the right direction at the time of writing, and the kitchen is producing sharp contemporary cuisine on menus well under €30 (200FF). Eat well, from the *bouillabaisse*, through the catch of the day, to the *amaretto charlotte*. 'Thanks to La Méditerranée, the sea has arrived at the Place de l'Odéon,' wrote Jean Cocteau in 1960 and his penmanship and sketching adorns the menus and plates. The refurbished décor throughout the restaurant is the original work of artists and stage designers of the 20th century. The Belloni ceiling of the inner room is well worth a peek.

Perroudin 157 rue St-Jacques, 75005; tel: 01 46 33 15 75 [8 A3]
Closed Sat lunch, Sun, Aug.
RER Luxembourg; Ē *RER B to Luxembourg (exit rue Gay Lussac). From rue Royer Collard turn left on rue St-Jacques.*
A good, old-fashioned family restaurant serving good, old-fashioned French cooking to the good, old-fashioned university crowd. And at good, old-fashioned prices to boot. Leave the Visa card for another day; just bring your change and your appetite. Thick French onion soup, *boeuf bourguignon*, *escargots* in butter, *crème caramel* – home cooking *à la française*. The unofficial student and staff canteen of the Sorbonne, with a wine list of modest choices served by the pitcher or glassful, Perroudin's legend lies in its prices. In the past seven years, my usual lunch bill has risen by just three francs. Pay €9 (63FF) at midday – otherwise bank on €15 (100FF) a head.

Le Petit Prince 12 rue de Lanneau, 75005; tel: 01 43 54 77 26 [8 B3]
M̄ *Maubert-Mutualité;* Ē *RER B to St-Michel-Notre-Dame. Follow signs to Cluny-La-Sorbonne for métro 10 to Maubert-Mutualité. Take rue des Carmes, continue across rue des Ecoles then turn right into rue de Lanneau.*

Menus under €15 (100FF) for two courses and around €23 (150FF) for three
are served and enjoyed at leisure with no fear of being hustled out into the streets
as soon as the credit card has been swiped. For donkeys years Gilles Gobe and
Armand Floux's place has been a reliable late-night standby for reliable late-night
standards cooked by the book. Duck, veal and quenelles with no surprises nor
any nasty shocks.

Polidor 41 rue Monsieur le Prince, 75006; tel: 01 43 26 95 34 [8 A3]
M̄ *Odéon;* Ē *Métro 4 to Odéon. Restaurant is on the left side of rue Monsieur le Prince.*
People who can afford to eat elsewhere come here for the uncomplicated pleasure
of dining with their hair down. Business types, backpackers and bookworms all
rub shoulders and pass the bread basket on shared tables designed for six or 16. If
you want privacy, ask to be seated in the pretty back room. Two people can eat
well for under €30 (200FF), including half a jug of wine. Evening menus may
cost slightly more than lunch, but usually offer an extra course. Food is variable,
but waitresses tend to steer clients away from the kitchen's dodgier efforts, so be
prepared to be guided. We judged our *truite meunière* fine, *poulet basque* bland, *sorbet*
over-sugary, but chocolate tart scrummy. Details of daily specials are scrawled
around the room across mirrors and blackboards. A triumph of genuine
atmosphere over gastronomy, the Polidor is a deep brown memory of lunchtime.

Le Procope 13 rue de l'Ancienne Comédie, 75006; tel: 01 40 46 79 00 [8 A2]
M̄ *Odéon;* Ē *Métro 4 to Odéon. From carrefour de l'Odéon go north along rue de
l'Ancienne Comédie.*
Yet another Left Bank pilgrimage. Three-centuries worth of celebrities have
flocked to Le Procope. Of course, the original Comédie Française was based over
the road, but still Rousseau, Hugo, Balzac, Robespierre et al are definitely A-List.
Voltaire even left his desk behind for all to admire. Over dinner, so it is said,
Benjamin Franklin read the draft of the American constitution to local
philosophers. Today's Americans are more concerned with their own
constitutions as they refuel on brasserie standards. To be honest, these big names
from the past, rather than the food from the present, prove the real lure. So
weigh the €19 (123FF) menu with these ghostly superstars against the merits of
a meal with lesser starlets chez Conran down the road.

La Rôtisserie du Beaujolais 19 quai de la Tournelle, 75005; tel: 01 43 54 17
47 [8 B–C3]
Closed Mon.
M̄ *Maubert-Mutualité;* Ē *RER B to St-Michel-Notre-Dame. Follow the quai de
Montebello to quai de la Tournelle.*
They say that if you can't see it from the window of the legendary Tour
d'Argent restaurant it is not in Paris. So the next time you are dining at Claude
Terrail's €152 (1,000FF)-a-head flagship, risk vertigo and look straight down. At
the foot of La Tour, and on the opposite corner, is La Rôtisserie du Beaujolais.
Terrail's baby annexe is less a *bistrot*, more of an *auberge du terroir*, offering real
country food – including of course hints of those arterial challenges that are a
gastronomic rite of passage, with much animal fat in evidence for those who
wish it. Otherwise snuffle and choose around classic dishes from *terrine du
laperau en gelée* and poultry from Challans, to *daube de boeuf* and other country
kitchen stables. Of course this is not a simple country kitchen; far from it. Food
arrives piled high, with contemporary layered presentation on big white plates.
The walls are garlanded with official testimonials to the chefs, and scores of
framed, autographed compliments from the nation's most celebrated diners.

The atmosphere is informal: a strong selection of Beaujolais wines from Georges Duboeuf, the restaurant cat curving its cautious way around chair legs, and diners sporting 'Major Thomson goes to Clochemerle' moustaches. If it wasn't for the excellent decorative order one could be in 1950s regional France. The dining room is perfumed with the mouth-watering smell of steaks and fish sizzling on the grill and chicken turning on the rôtisserie itself, as the kitchen is open to the restaurant. The staff understand the joys of first-rate ingredients, simply cooked. I know this because I arrived for lunch a few minutes before the place was open for business and enjoyed the sight of the full *équipe* sitting down to massive portions of *steak frites à son ketchup d'Heinz*! There is no set menu, but one might eat until replete from €30–46 (200—300FF) per person. From the saucer of crisp radishes, in place of the fancy appetisers, to the plonking down of the wooden sabot containing the bill, an enjoyable experience in the little room where the gourmet entertains the gourmands.

Tante Marguerite 5 rue de Bourgogne, 75007; tel: 01 45 51 79 42; web: www.bernard-loiseau.com [7 H1]
Closed Sat, Sun.
M̲ *Assemblée-Nationale;* E̲ *RER B to St-Michel-Notre-Dame, then RER C to Invalides. Walk down rue Esnault Pelterie, turning left on to rue de l'Université to place du Palais Bourbon. The restaurant is at the beginning of rue de Bourgogne.*
Just days after Bernard Loiseau discreetly opened his second capital home in midsummer, I watched Paris restaurant word-of-mouth happen. Lunching at the Burgundy masterchef's **Tante Louise** (see 50), I heard talk of the new project, so a few hours later, at around 19.30, I turned up at the restaurant behind the Assemblée Nationale. Barely a handful of diners were outnumbered by the smart army of front-of-house staff, led by a discreet poaching from the Crillon across the Pont de la Concorde and Loiseau's right-hand man from the Michelin three-star Côte d'Or in Saulieu on a fortnight's secondment.

The light-wood and full-mirrored décor reflected the sunflowers on the cream and yellow linens, and the sparkle of glassware. Painted champagne flutes are a sign that the *apéritif coupe* will be Perrier-Jouet, and as I sipped through the menu, at ten to eight came the entrance of a casually dressed presence with a majestic girth, pouch wallet and loyal acolyte – all signs of either a gourmet, a member of the *Académie Française* or a taxi driver – if not all three. By eight, a couple on the far horizon of late middle age, very much in love and with a youthful spark of menu-lust in their eyes, greeted the *maître d'hôtel* as an old friend. They huddled and giggled over the *carte* and clinked affectionate toasts as they interrogated staff on unfamiliar dishes, Their order taken, the lady boomed out passages of a letter from a loved one, regaling her companion, and the rest of us, with accounts of holiday meals in far off places.

Three smart suits with bushy eyebrows, amber cufflinks and a dog that bore a disturbing resemblance to George Bernard Shaw arrived to take a corner table, followed at 20.15 by a society party: a hostess with killer coiffure and coutured to the *neufs*, a West Highland terrier and two nattily dressed men in their forties who reeked showbusiness *à la française* (remember Michel Serault in *La Cage aux Folles* and you'll appreciate the skilled projection that carried the wicked aside when the head waiter was mischievously complimented on his nice *estaminet* – a working class café-bar in a front room). Next came gilded youth with floppy hair, Gap khakis and *bon chic, bon genre* companion to pick up the tab; then a stunning vision in a waterfall of jewellery, escorted by besotted squire, and the first of the understated well-to-do couples of the quarter.

All this people-watching might distract from a meal, unless the meal is as good as this. Despite *croussillant de tête de veau*, poached egg *en gelée* and *jambon persillé*, the menu *chez* this aunt is geared more towards fish than *chez Tante Louise*. I dithered between two red mullet dishes, with either a *fondue de fenouil* or grilled vegetables. I chose the latter, slices of aubergine, courgette and mushrooms with a coriander and tomato compôte – the dish pulled off the double for crispness and moist juiciness! Simple, light and packed with flavour. As was the soup of *melon au porto*, not too chilled so as not to bruise the gentle subtlety. And the apricot *tatin* was tart in all senses of the word. Budget ∈68 (450FF) à la carte with wine, or ease the strain in the wallet by dining from the three-course ∈35 (230FF) evening menu, or lunch at ∈30 (200FF).

The restaurant's location – the site of the former Chez Marius – augurs well for its success amongst the nation's elite. I should imagine more than a few senior politicians will adopt this particular aunt for lunch dates before very long. Considering Monsieur Loiseau named the restaurant after the 13th-century Marguerite de Bourgogne, who married political royalty and became a great civic benefactress in her own right, what could be more appropriate? Meanwhile, before the great French gastro-guides discover her address, make sure that you pay auntie a visit.

Thoumieux 79 rue St-Dominique, 75007; tel: 01 47 05 49 75 [7 G1]
M̄ *Tour-Maubourg;* Ē *RER B to St-Miche-Notre-Dame, then RER C to Invalides and métro 8 to La-Tour-Maubourg. Walk up bd de la Tour Maubourg, left on to rue de Grenelle and right on rue de la Comète, then left on rue St-Dominique.*
Fashionable couples squeeze past cash-crisis students as the two identities of the district merge in one enormous bistro where cheap is actually chic. The 1930s' soup kitchen atmosphere is bolstered by the bonhomie of our *Corèzien* hosts, M et Mme Bassalert. If the prices have skipped slightly ahead of inflation in recent years, perhaps this is because the house now accepts credit cards. Even so you would be stretched to pull two notes out of your wallet to pay the bill here. A good reliable menu at ∈13 (85FF), wines from ∈9 (60FF) and even pushing out the à la carte boat will probably keep you on the safe side of ∈30 (200FF). Best of all, according to the two regulars who introduced me to the place, is to have nothing more than a hefty portion of *tête de veau*. Others disagree (albeit usually through a mouthful of duck, or *boudin* with chestnuts, or simple *truite aux amandes*). They insist on working their way through the full ∈24 (160FF) menu, *vins compris*.

WHAT TO BUY
Abbey Bookshop 29 rue Parcheminerie 75005; tel: 01 46 33 16 24 [8 B2]
Open Mon–Sat 10.00–19.00.
M̄ *Cluny-La-Sorbonne;* Ē *RER B to St-Michel-Notre-Dame. From place St-Michel follow rue de la Harpe, turning left into rue de la Parcheminerie.*
The maple leaf flutters proudly in this Canadian corner of the Latin Quarter. Come here for good books in English and French, free papers and news of literary events on the Left Bank.

Au Bon Marché 22 rue de Sèvres, 76007; tel: 01 44 39 80 00 [7 J3]
Open Mon–Wed, Fri 09.30–19.00, Thu 10.00–21.00, Sat 09.30–20.00.
M̄ *Sèvres-Babylone.*
The essential department store for Parisians (rather than the Galeries Lafayette and Printemps which essentially market themselves to visitors) was designed by Gustave Eiffel, and favoured by French movie stars.

Carré Rive Gauche web: www.carrerivegauche.com [7 H1–K2]
RER Musée-d'Orsay; Ē RER B to St-Michel-Notre-Dame, then RER C to Musée-d'Orsay.
The Carré Rive Gauche is the association of around 120 art and antique dealers in the streets behind the Musée d'Orsay, on the rues Allent, du Bac, de Beaune, de Lille, des Saint-Pères, de l'Université and de Verneuil, and the quai Voltaire. Five days each summer, these most discreet addresses on the Left Bank clear their throats as an invitation to view their most treasured possessions, for the *Cinq Jours de l'Objet Extraordinaire*. Each member selects one special item to show the world. Perhaps an exquisite pair of 18th-century *Suzanne biscuit de Sèvres* statuettes of gardeners at Galerie Verneuil-Bac; or maybe a 16th-century figure of St-Vincent, the patron saint of wine *chez* Jacqueline Boccador; or six Louis XV armchairs, signed by Blanchard, and covered with Beauvais tapestries of La Fontaine's fables, at the Galerie André Métrot. Well in advance of the event, and to help plan your fantasy window-shopping afternoon, many of the extraordinary objects may be previewed on the website.

Librairie Pinault 36 rue Bonaparte, 75006; tel: 01 43 54 89 99 [7 K2]
Open Tue–Sat 10.00–12.00, 14.00–19.00.
M̄ *St-Germain-des-Prés; Ē Métro 4 to St-Germain-des-Prés, walk through the square to rue Bonaparte.*
This is a shop window designed for prying eyes, for this is a bookshop that sells the most delicious of ephemera, epistels, notes and diaries of literary and historic figures. The last time I passed, I had glanced at the scrawl of Flaubert and George Sand, and was trying to decipher the family gossip noted by Louis XV, in a letter to a friend, when I overheard two formidable ladies discussing a few lines by Colette. 'She must have been very young when she wrote that. I could barely recognise her handwriting.' The shops along this street and the rues Jacob and Seine are sheer serendipity. Every other window provides an unexpected delight. There are more respected art dealers in this unassuming corner of the quarter than anywhere else in Paris. The Right Bank, Eastern and Marais galleries may have more glamorous PR and celebrity-packed launch parties, but these poky streets have the real McCoy, and the more discerning punters.

Marché St-Germain bd St-Germain, 75005 [8 B3]
M̄ *Maubert-Mutualité; Ē RER B to St-Michel-Notre-Dame. Follow signs to Cluny-La-Sorbonne for métro 10 to Maubert-Mutualité.*
Just at the top of the métro station, a predominantly fruit and veg market, with one or two stalls selling handbags and leather goods.

Rue Mouffetard [8 B4]
M̄ *Monge or Censier-Daubenton; Ē RER to Châtelet-Les-Halles, then line 7 to Censier-Daubenton. Rue Daubenton to rue Mouffetard.*
Market-type cafés for coffee breaks during food shopping, and loads of tempting specialist stores for mouth-watering snacks for picnics in the nearby Jardin des Plantes.

Tea & Tattered Pages 24 rue Mayet, 75006; tel: 01 40 65 94 35 [7 H3]
Open 11.00–19.00, Aug 12.00–18.00; closed Sun in Aug.
M̄ *Duroc; Ē RER B to St-Michel-Notre-Dame. Follow signs to Cluny-La-Sorbonne for métro 10 to Duroc. Walk east on rue de Sèvres to turn right into rue Mayet.* (See *Where to go*, page 127.)

Shakespeare and Co 37 rue de la Bucherie, 75005 [8 B2]
Open 12.00–24.00.
M̲ *St-Michel;* E̲ *RER B to St-Michel-Notre-Dame. Along the riverbank, the street is set back from the waterside, opposite Notre Dame.*
Eccentric and courteous and always surprising, this is such stuff as bibliophiles' dreams are made of. The notice-board by the door advertises the most improbable second-hand goods, from spy-planes to dolls' houses. No credit cards are accepted, but no one in need is ever ignored. Here George Whitman, venerable patron saint of the young and inspired, presides over the world's most wonderful bookshop and sanctuary. This is Sylvia Beach's shop that published James Joyce when the literary establishment scorned his work.

Upstairs and down, new, second-hand and antiquarian books, all English-language editions, are piled higgledy-piggledy in nooks and crannies. Between shelves, a rucksack may be stowed here, a blanket spread there, for penniless students and bibliophiles to sleep when the shop is closed. When, some years ago, a fire ravaged part of the tumbledown shop and destroyed much of the stock, it could not touch the place's heart. For here, Whitman's indomitable spirit still burns as truly as it has for the past several decades, a spirit encapsulated in the text above the door that reminds us not to be inhospitable to strangers, lest they be angels in disguise.

Village Voice 6 rue Princesse, 65006; tel: 01 46 33 36 47; email: voice.village@wanadoo.fr [7 K2]
Open Mon 14.00–20.00, Tue–Sat 11.00–20.00.
M̲ *Mabillon;* E̲ *Métro 4 to St-Germain des Pres. Walking east on bd St-Germain, turn right into rue des Cisseaux then left to rue du Four and right to rue Princesse.*
The ex-pat rendezvous of the quarter. Transatlantic students come here in search of familiar paperbacks for the homesick and a friendly face in a foreign land.

Fireman cadets on the Left Bank

SUMMER IN THE CITY
Sunshine in the Twilight Zone

Hooray for the *Rentrée*! The reassuring plink-plink-fizz of September after the hedonism of the July-August holidays is at once sobering and refreshing and incredibly reassuring. The French are so very good at summer. Enough to know when they have had too much of a good thing. So, as the city returns to business as usual and French accents return to the boulevards, shop windows sing out the virtues of sobriety.

The antidote to too much pleasure *à la française* is, naturally enough, a healthy dose of reticence *à l'anglaise*: thus store promotions embrace the shorter evenings and greyer skies with images of all things British. Burberry-wrapped families with a Range Rover in the drive, labrador by the hearth and plenty of chunky knitwear within reach. The shelves of gastronomic grocers also present what Paris considers (with a healthy disregard for the auld alliance) 'English': Scottish smoked salmon, Heinz beans and Marmite.

So what brings about this *faux* puritanism every September? To understand you need to take six weeks of industrial strength French holiday: every July the entire city decamps to all points north, south, east and west the morning after the Bastille Night before. To replace the straying natives, a constant stream of holidaymakers is siphoned in. By August 1, the common language of Paris is American. Should you hear a genuine French accent, you tip it.

I confess to sharing the capricious native pride that the very best ice-cream parlour in town always closes in July and re-opens in September (see page 74). However, one summer, not so very long ago, I found myself in Paris in August – not only that, but I was to spend my time in my least favourite part of town. The reason – this book.

If you have read this far you will understand why I left researching the posh areas to the West until last. There is an unwritten rule that informality and welcome diminishes in an inverse ratio to proximity to the Champs Elysées. Posh Paris = Snooty Paris.

But hey, the taxi driver laughed and joked about the traffic snarl (the *Tour de France* was in town) without cursing, and the few remaining locals actually stopped and offered assistance to tourists blinking myopically at city maps.

I found myself walking the Champs Elysées at a civilised pace with my eyes raised above shoe level. I spent five minutes at the statue of Clemenceau, taking in for the first time how the artist had presented not merely a statesman, but a man one could really enjoy talking with and listening to.

Over in Les Halles, where it is tourist season all year round, bonhomie was nudging towards fever point. I passed the party-time restaurant *l'Amazonial*, where the resident terrier Nougat welcomes guests. I did not even blink to find Nougat's place taken by a large and docile camel, lying patiently alongside a table. A sign in the window promoting a Middle Eastern food event urged diners to dress and accessorise as North African. Someone had evidently responded with enthusiasm. Had to be a local.

So who remains behind in summer? Many theatres close for the duration, key chefs return to their châteaux and hometowns, even restaurant critics fold their napkins and put away their pens. Catching the final meal at the good tables before they shut up shop is a skill. I heard gossip that Burgundy's masterchef Bernard Loiseau had opened a new restaurant in Paris. Deliberately doing so when the foodie establishment was safely out of town. Thus I watched Paris gastro-word-of-mouth perform its unique alchemy (see pages 137–8).

Any such fix of real Parisians determines me to venture beyond wealthy Paris to see who else from the real world might have dropped a house on a witch and landed in this Technicolor version of the city. Inevitably I head North. My favourite cheap and cheerful corners of Paris are the areas below Gare de l'Est and beyond Gare du Nord. The place hums, even up by the canal and La Villette. So what if the overhead métro line may be closed for urgent structural repairs; we can all melt in furnace-like buses. Tati – that endless string of cheap, cheap, cheap clothes stores, where one might pick up jeans for €4.50 (30FF) and an entire holiday wardrobe for the price of a coffee on the Champs Elysées, will be as hectic as ever – and the back-street shoe shops stack trestles with €8 (50FF) footwear.

After days of finding friendly faces in usually high places, playing hunt-the-open-restaurant and forgetting that French is one of the official languages of Paris, seeing life continuing as normal in streets without tourist traps always gives me a few pangs of nostalgia for the overcrowded, hurrying city of cabbies that bang their horns as nature and George Gershwin intended. Just as soon as I glimpse the first billboard poster showing a roaring fire and digestive biscuits, I remember what makes the September *Rentrée* quite so special. I enjoy Paris with its hair down, but feel so much safer when the city returns to normal, and re-adjusts its nose to a more arrogant position.

Don't get me wrong, summer in Paris was a wonderful place, and you were there, and you were there, and you, and you – but the prodigals have returned, and there's no place like home.

The West, Batignolles to the Bois

The west of Paris has the most famous forecourt in the city: the avenue des Champs Elysées. At its head, the Arc de Triomphe stands at the centre of the place de l'Etoile, that celebrated, choreographed chaos of traffic that has never seen a single car crash. Since no French insurance company pays out on collisions on the Etoile, police have developed a convenient strain of myopia that prevents them from noticing pranged Peugeots and wrecked Renaults being pushed on to any of the dozen avenues that radiate from the star.

Each of these roads leads to another incarnation. Northern avenues from the Etoile stretch out as far as the railway sidings and goods yards of Clichy and Batignolles that span the hinterland between the Arc de Triomphe and Montmartre. Fortunately, it has been discovered by talented young chefs and club promoters happy to experiment away from the unforgiving gaze of the seriously moneyed. This means realistic prices for a good night out, and a chance to sniff out today the lifestyle that you will not be able to afford tomorrow.

Avenue Foch and several of its neighbours take sensation seekers to the **Bois de Boulogne**, a region in its own right, with the excellent restaurants, racecourses and the night-time no-go areas. Follow the avenue de la Grande Armée beyond Porte Maillot and the conference centres to **La Défense** and its famous arch. Avenue Kléber is the fastest route to the imposing, if fire-damaged, **Palais de Chaillot** at **Trocadéro**, where roller-bladers skate around the world's outside broadcasters who present the view from here against an unrivalled view of the **Champ de Mars** and the **Eiffel Tower**. Neither booksellers nor starving young artists nor writers mark out this stretch of the Seine. Around the **Radio France** building, moneyed young media types air-kiss and Motorola-mobile-flip at lunch and dusk. Lovers' rendezvous might be made on the **Allée des Cygnes**, a strip of an island on the river, but all eyes in this district are set westward, like those of Bertholdi's miniature **Statue of Liberty** on the tip of the Pont de Grenelle, towards the land of opportunity.

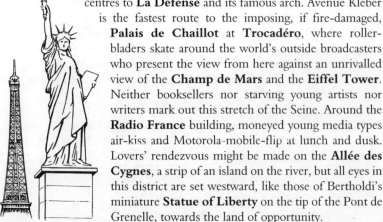

There is serious money southwest of the Etoile, but no showy glamour. Great restaurants where €150 (1,000FF) a head fits comfortably on a charge card, and valet parking is the norm. Not much in the way of simple counter lunches, but for the expense-account diner, an education in the ways of the table. Just about the only part of Paris that can make the **St-Honoré** district look common, this is the shopless village of ordinary senior diplomats, five-star celebrities, tycoons and old families. Here apartments have rooms so big that no doorway has less than two doors, and society is split between those who tip and those who are tipped.

To non-residents, unable to afford the higher restaurant prices, the postcode Paris 75016 can seem cold and unwelcoming. The icy personality cracks slightly at year's end, when France's great touring circuses pitch their tents near the **Périphérique**. Nonetheless, in the main, this is but a wealthy dormitory with little to do in the evenings. A mild diversion is to date the *Marianne* busts carved above the doorways of expensive apartment houses. Depending on the era, this symbolic face of the Republic might have been modelled on Cathérine Deneuve or Brigitte Bardot. You won't find too many representations of the latest face of France. *L'Oréal* model Laetitia Casta blotted her copybook when she decided to live in London, and commute to her modelling duties in Paris on the *Eurostar*. Call me biased, but I would say that a combination of frequent travel points, looks and sheer chutzpah make her the ideal candidate for the face of *Europa*.

WHERE TO STAY

Du Bois 11 rue du Dôme, 75016; tel: 01 45 00 31 96; email: hoteldubois@wanadoo.fr [2 E6]
M̄ *Charles-de-Gaulle-Etoile;* Ē *RER to Châtelet-Les-Halles then RER A to Charles-de-Gaulle-Etoile. Av Victor Hugo then left to rue du Dôme.*
Close by the fashion houses and posh frocks of the Victor Hugo district, you can lose the extra inches required for that Balmain or Dior original by climbing the stairs to bed – since there is no lift. Cheery welcome, clean redecorated bedrooms and an average room rate of around €107 (700FF), make this a popular choice for Brits who need to be at the centre of things by the Etoile, but have no intention of paying Champs Elysées prices.

Pergolèse 3 rue Pergolèse, 75016; tel: 01 53 64 04 04; web: www.hotelpergolese.com [2 E5]
M̄ *Argentine;* Ē *RER to Châtelet-Les-Halles then métro 1 to Argentine.*
Cutting-edge designers had their sous-worth in the design of this sharply styled hotel, with interesting furnishings, from the *très*-loft styled

bedside workstations to remarkable washbasins in the bathrooms. Spend an enjoyable five minutes coming to terms with the lighting options and discovering precisely what in fact the furniture does! Very contemporary, very €185(1,200FF)-plus.

Regents Garden 6 rue Pierre Demours, 75017; tel: 01 45 74 07 30; email: hotel.regents.garden@wanadoo.fr [3 F5]
M̄ *Ternes;* Ē *Métro 4 to Barbès-Rochechouart, then line 2 to Ternes. Go west along av des Ternes to pl Tristan Bernard. Rue Pierre Demours is on your right.*
The European temple to road rage, aka place de l'Etoile, is just a brake's screech away, but this floral sanctuary erases all thoughts of traffic stress and the pressures of modern life. A pretty garden brings summer butterflies and the only sound from the bedroom window is the dawn chorus; most fitting for a house built by Napoléon III for his doctor. More recently the light and airy high-ceiling rooms have been decorated and fitted to a standard appropriate to the building's dignity. Most rooms overlook the garden where breakfast is taken from spring until late summer. The two ground-floor rooms are the most spacious. Double rooms from €130 (850FF). Seventy of Paris' top restaurants are but a brisk walk from the front door.

St-James Paris 43 av Bugeaud, 75016; tel: 01 44 05 81 81; toll free (0800 964 470 (UK); 800 525 4800 (USA); email: stjames@club-internet.fr [2 C–D6]
M̄ *Porte-Dauphine;* Ē *Métro 4 to Barbès-Rochechouart, then line 2 to Porte-Dauphine. Av Bugeaud leads to pl Adenaur and the hotel gates.*
Through the stone gateway along the imposing sweep of the drive to the steps – you have arrived in the only walled château in the heart of Paris. Just the classy side of informal, this private mansion, built by the widow of President Thiers, is the perfect discreet sanctuary by the Porte Dauphine. Cher, Sophia Loren, Monica Seles and the Dalai Lama choose this address when in town, and it is easy to see why. Larger suites may have conservatory terraces, or wonderful high ceilings with dual aspect views. Gatehouse lodges offer greater privacy at a price. In summer dine for €38 (250FF) in the garden of the restaurant. Exclusive to hotel guests and dining-club members, the restaurant is almost unique in not serving passing trade. A first-rate gymnasium, sauna and jacuzzi in the basement, chess and backgammon in the lounge, and a library of early editions in the bar, provide physical and spiritual stimulation. Extra buzz comes from the lounge pianist and occasional jazz band. Should the champagne of vitality still course through your veins then a jogging map for the area – into the woods of the Bois – is available. If shopping has drained all dregs of spirit, hotel staff are happy to walk your dog for you – simply call room service! Delighted to report that the traditionally warm welcome has improved with the years, and the place is as enjoyable a retreat as ever. Double rooms from €345 (2,100FF).

Square 2 rue Boulainvilliers, 75016; tel: 01 44 14 91 90; toll free 0800 964 470 (UK); 800 525 4800 (USA) [6 C2]
M̄ *Av-Président-Kennedy;* Ē *RER to St-Michel-Notre-Dame then RER C to Kennedy-Radio-France (check destination board on the platform). Walk along av Président Kennedy to pl Adler.*
There is nothing square about the Square. One of the refreshing new breed of 'designer' hotels springing up in the west of the city (see *Pergolèse*), this is a response to a new generation of visitors: those who come to Paris seeking challenging and imaginative art and design, and who see no reason to spend

their nights in a less stimulating environment. Thus Patrick Derdérian's hotel, with its in-house art gallery promoting the work of fashionable fresh talents, its permanent art collection in the atrium, lobby and guest rooms, and its courteous, efficient and welcoming staff, sporting outfits of absolute-catwalk black, has proved a hit. A perfect example of how the style-setters of the new century will define a 'small luxury hotel'. Nor is there anything square in the geometric sense in the shape of the hotel, nor its rooms: the name is almost an ironic challenge to its striking, curved, sweeping response to the famous circular Radio France building opposite. Rooms defy right angles wherever possible, though the hotel's hallmark stripes appear in terracotta and burnt orange (in my room), greys, blues and golds as hangings, fabrics and wooden furniture. Big bold bathrooms have basins hewn of solid marble slabs and the little luxuries for a modern visitor are everywhere. Separate fax-lines, a stereo radio in the bathroom, a state-of-the-art CD and mini disc player (with a selection of Ray Charles, Ella, Saragh Vaughan, Serge Gainsbourg and Ravel laid out for my listening), potted plants on the desk and proper full-sized bottles of water in the minibar. The next day's weather forecast is placed on the pillow before bed. If TV does not appeal, there are plenty of current glossies and a couple of books at hand for late-night reading – although the French translation of *Titus Andronicus* next to the room service menu gave me pause for thought, considering the notorious offspring-ivorous nature of the Bard's *plat de* that particular *jour*. In the morning the **Zebra Square** restaurant (see page 152) provides continental breakfast for hotel guests. Secure parking available. Room rates way, way upwards of €228 (1500FF).

Villa Maillot 143 av de Malakoff, 75016; tel: 01 53 64 52 52 [2 D5]
M̲ *Porte-Maillot;* E̲ *RER to Châtelet-Les-Halles then métro 1 to Porte-Maillot.*
Restored art déco at its expensively comfortable best in the former Embassy of Sierra Leone. Pink marble bathrooms, comfortable bedrooms and very stylish lounges make it a choice of those who cheerfully part with €244 (1,600FF) a night for a pampered respite from meetings in the Porte Maillot conference district.

WHERE TO GO
Bois de Boulogne [2 A4–C8, 6 A1–B2]
M̲ *Porte-d'Auteuil (for Hippodrome d'Auteuil), Avenue-Henri-Martin, Avenue-Foch, Porte-Dauphine or Porte-Maillot;* E̲ *RER to Châtelet-Les-Halles then métro 1 to Porte-Maillot.*
'I know a bank whereon the wild thyme blows, where oxlips and the nodding violet grows, quite over-canopied with luscious woodbine, with sweet musk roses and with eglantine.' Not a forest near Athens, but a wood on the edge of Paris. There's rosemary, that's for remembrance, and all the herbs strewn by poor Ophelia, not to mention all those roses that by any name still smell as sweet. All the flowers mentioned by the Bard of Avon may be found in the Shakespeare Garden of the Pré Catalan park within the Bois de Boulogne, where the plays are often performed in English and French. The arts are equally cherished in the Bagatelle, where each summer sees a season of Chopin recitals in the Orangerie. Sport reigns supreme in this former royal hunting ground which is home to the nation's two major racecourses, Longchamps and Auteuil, the Roland Garros tennis courts, and the Parc des Princes, the former national soccer stadium.

With lakes, islands, waterfalls and woodlands for nature lovers, and gloriously expensive restaurants for the wealthy epicure, the Bois de Boulogne is not so much a park as a catalogue of contrasts. During the day, children play safely in the magical Jardin d'Acclimatation, where they may ride miniature trains, play with animals and birds, experiment in the museum at the Musée en l'Herbe, see fairytales come to life on stage, and discover an enchanted river. By night the Bois is transformed into the city's most notorious red-light area, where transsexual prostitutes await their verdure-crawling clientele in a state of virtual undress. The Wallace Collection, now in London, was originally acquired by the Hertford family and housed here in the Bagatelle estate. The Wallis collection on the other hand is shrouded in mystery, the legends surrounding the Duke and Duchess of Windsor remaining safely locked behind the high walls of their former home in the Bois.

La Défense Grande Arche, 92044, Paris la Défense; tel: 01 49 07 27 27
Open 10.00–19.00. €7 (46FF).

Musée de l'Automobile pl du Dôme, 92044, Paris la Défense; tel: 08 36 67 06 06
Open 10.00–19.00. €5.50 (35FF).
M̄ *La-Défense-Grande-Arche;* Ē *RER to Châtelet-Les-Halles, then RER A to La-Défense-Grande-Arche.*
Bienvenue à Boystown-sur-Seine: despite great shopping, good restaurants and equal opportunity employers around the parvis de La Défense, the quarter feels coldly masculine. High-tech attractions and a classic car museum, the **Colline de l'Automobile**, hint at the unspoken shout that bigger is better at this business district on the outskirts of town. Never mind, you can get here and back into town within minutes thanks to the RER, and the main attraction is the view. The **Grande Arche de la Défense** is less a modern reinterpretation of the **Arc de Triomphe** along the av de la Grande Armée than a huge hollow marble-and-glass cube. The vista from the top and the panoramic lift ride to get there are both thrilling. The ticket price includes entrance to a museum with models and films about Otto von Spreckelsen's monumental construction created for the 1989 bicentennial of the French Revolution. Beneath the arch on the stark modern *parvis* are even more modern statues and an Imax cinema. Incidentally, although President Mitterand took the bows when La Défense opened for business, this city of the future was actually conceived by Charles de Gaulle.

Fondation le Corbusier Villas Jeanneret and La Roche, 8–10 square du Dr Blanche, 75016; tel: 01 42 88 41 53 [6 B2]
Open Mon, Thu 10.00–12.30, 13.30–18.00, Fri 10.00–12.30, 13.30–17.00; closed Aug, holidays and Dec 25–Jan 1. €2.50 (15FF).
M̄ *Jasmin;* Ē *RER E to Haussmann-St-Lazare then métro 9 to Jasmin. From rue Jasmin turn right into rue Henri Heine them left on rue Dr Blanche to the square.*
These are the houses that Le Corbusier built in 1923. Casual visitors would be happy to gasp their reaction from outside, but admirers of the pioneering master of concrete will want to step over the threshold. The *Villa Jeanneret* is closed to the general pubic, although the foundation may allow serious students to see archives in the private library which houses most of Le Corbusier's drawings, studies and plans. The *Villa La Roche*, next door, welcomes visitors to an exhibition of paintings, sculpture and furnishings.

Place de l'Alma [3 F7]
M̄ *Alma-Marceau;* Ē *RER E to Haussmann-St-Lazare then métro 9 to Alma-Marceau.*
There is a chilly coincidence in the name of the square behind the notorious Alma tunnel by the Seine. The place de la Reine Astrid brings memories of the

*The unofficial
Diana Memorial*

Belgian beauty who died so tragically young in a car accident. Of course, the tunnel was where Diana, Princess of Wales, was killed, and as diplomats dithered over an official memorial, the statue of the Liberty Flame in the street above the crash site has become her unofficial shrine. During the last weekend in August, on the anniversary of her death, it is all but obliterated by hundreds of flowers and tributes. The glamour with which Diana was associated in life lives on in the nearby avenue Montaigne, home to the great couture houses, and the **Théâtre des Champs Elysées**, where Joséphine Baker made her European debut. The Palais de Tokyo, on the other side of the place de l'Alma, is the home of the city's **Modern Art Museum** (see below), built on the site of the former **La Savonnerie tapestry workshop** (see *Les Gobelins*, page 102).

Palais de Chaillot pl du Trocadéro, 75116 [2 E7]
M̄ *Trocadéro;* Ē *RER E to Haussmann-St-Lazare then métro 9 to Trocadéro.*
This final gesture of grandeur, before the chill of war reduced the city to monochrome, was created for the Universal Exhibition of 1937. A wonderful sweep of white stone, with its guard of golden statues, this palace of culture replaced the original Trocadéro buildings, and remains the best place in Paris to see the showpiece of the previous great exhibition, the Eiffel Tower. Alas, fire damaged many of the museums and the theatre that had called the palace home for so long, so for most visitors the attraction is the photo opportunity afforded by terrace and tiered gardens. Although the cinema collection is being moved to a new home, the **Musée de la Marine** remains open for business (see page 148).

WHAT TO SEE
Musée d'Art Moderne de la Ville de Paris (Modern Art Museum) Palais de Tokyo, 11 av du Président Wilson, 75016; tel: 01 53 67 40 00 [3 F7]
Open Tue–Fri 10.00–17.45, Sat, Sun 10.00–18.45; closed holidays. €4.50 (30FF). Free for under 26s, free Sun 10.00–13.00.
M̄ *Alma Marceau;* Ē *RER E to Haussmann St-Lazare then métro 9 to Alma Marceau.*
Unofficially known to tour leaders as 'the other one', this is the modern art museum that most people forget to visit. Every major city in France has its modern art museum, and Paris is no exception. Since the national modern art

collection is housed in the Pompidou Centre, its fame tends to eclipse this municipal museum at the Palais de Tokyo. The building itself is a splendid example of 1930s visionary architecture and has light airy rooms to showcase its trophies, most notably Raoul Dufy's *La Fée Electricité*, created for the space as part of the 1937 exhibition. Excellent tapestries and furniture are well worth a look and the walls offer a good range of canvases by Braque, Matisse, Picasso and Utrillo.

Musée de la Contrafaçon 16 rue de la Faisanderie, 75116; tel: 01 56 26 14 00; web: www.unifab.com [2 C6]
Open Tue–Sun 14.00–17.30; closed holidays and weekends in Aug. €2.50 (15FF).
M̄ *Porte-Dauphine or Avenue-Foch; Métro 4 to Barbès-Rochechouart, then line 2 to Porte-Dauphine. From av Foch walk down rue de la Faisanderie.*
Psst! Wanna see a dodgy Barbie, or an iffy pair of trainers? How about some Louis Vuitton that falls apart the minute you open the clasp? Play spot the fake at this national rip-off collection. Counterfeit designer-wear, imitation kitchen appliances and some dubious bottles of perfume. The cheap copies are displayed alongside the real thing in a fascinating exposé of commercial piracy.

Musée Guimet 6 place d'Iéna, 75016; tel: 01 56 52 53 00 [2 E7]
Open Wed–Mon 10.00–18.00. €5.50 (35FF). Free to under 18s, free to all first Sun.
M̄ *Iéna;* Ē *RER E to Haussmann-St-Lazare then métro 9 to Iéna.*
One of the world's finest collections of Asian art reopened its doors in 2001, with stunning new exhibits from Cambodia and Afghanistan. True to the spirit of the collection's founder, Emile Guimet, who wanted to share with the world the joy he discovered in his travels through Egypt and the Far East, this celebration of the world's oldest civilisations is now excellently displayed in new and spacious galleries. The redesigned museum uses as much natural light as the architects Henri and Bruno Gaudin could create. A subtle shift in emphasis for the new century highlights the differences between the various cultures represented rather than their similarities. Tickets, valid all day, also allow access to temporary exhibitions as well as the **Buddhist Panthéon** (next door at number 16 avenue d'Iéna). This celebration of Buddhism contains Chinese and Japanese religious art from the 4th to the 19th centuries as well as some splendid Buddhas. Do take time for a few contemplative moments alone in the Panthéon's Japanese garden.

Musée de la Marine (Navy Museum) Palais de Chaillot, 17 place du Trocadéro, 75116; tel: 01 53 65 69 69 [2 E7]
Open Wed–Mon 10.00–18.00; closed Jan 1, May 1 and Dec 25. €6 (40FF).
M̄ *Trocadéro;* Ē *RER E to Haussmann-St-Lazare, then métro 9 to Trocadéro.*
Imposing figureheads and model ships from the 17th to 20th centuries are the main attractions for younger visitors, whilst studious adults take time over displays recounting tales of France's seafaring history. Unlike in Britain and Spain, the French naval heritage leans more towards commercial trawling than pivotal battles. One of the largest maritime museums in the world, it also houses a surprisingly comprehensive art collection.

Musée Marmottan-Claude Monet 2 rue Louis Boilly, 75016; tel: 01 42 24 07 02 [2 B8]
Open Tue–Sun 10.00–17.30; closed May 1, Dec 25. €5 (35FF).
M̄ *Ranelagh;* Ē *RER E to Haussmann-St-Lazare, then métro 9 to Ranelagh.*
If you cannot face the holiday crowds at the Musée d'Orsay, come to the city's lesser-known collection of 100 masterpieces by Claude Monet. The familiar

views of London, Rouen and the Giverny gardens are here in the family home of
the 19th-century industrialist Jules Marmottan, on the edge of the Bois de
Boulogne. For years, the cognoscenti came here to view the Monet *Waterlilies*,
until the opening of a dedicated museum in the Tuileries gardens' Orangerie.
The artist's youngest son, Michel, set up the Monet exhibition, which features
Impression Sunrise, the work that gave its name to the entire movement. Other
riches to be found here include canvases by Degas, Gauguin, Sisley, Renoir and
Pissarro. The museum welcomes children and organises monthly painting
competitions inspired by the classics in its collections. The winning work is
posted on the museum's website.

Museé Nissim de Camondo 63 rue de Monceau, 75008, tel: 01 53 89 06 50;
web: www.ucad.fr [3 G–H4]
Open Wed–Sun 10.00–17.00. €4.50 (30FF).
M̄ *Villiers or Monceau;* Ē *Métro 4 to Barbès-Rochechouart, then line 2 to Villiers. On rue
de Miromesnil take first right to rue de Monceau.*
Count Moise de Camondo gave his home to the nation in memory of his son
Nissim, who was killed in action in 1917. The count and countess had inherited
a house backing on to the Parc Monceau, and they decided to build this
reconstruction of an 18th-century residence on the site. Modelled closely on the
Petit Trianon of Versailles, and with architectural trophies from other great
houses, this opulent mansion, with its main carpet from the Louvre, is the ideal
setting for priceless artworks, furnishings and much silver and gold. The Huet
Salon on the ground floor is a delightful period piece, with walls covered in the
gloriously slushy and romantic pastoral idylls of Jean-Baptiste Huet whose
canvases chronicle the loves of a shepherd and his shepherdess. The effect is that
of a *Hello* magazine feature on the lives of Bo Peep and Little Boy Blue.

Musée du Vin rue des Eaux; 5 sq Dickens, 75016; tel: 01 45 25 63 26; web:
www.museeduvinparis.com [2 D8]
Open 10.00–18.00; closed holidays, Dec 24–Jan 1. €4.50 (30FF).
M̄ *Passy;* Ē *RER B to Denfert-Rochereau, then métro 6 to Passy. From rue d'Alboni turn
right into rue des Eaux.*
This place reminds me of a school trip: identical waxworks disguised with the
occasional beret, medal or moustache representing 'The Miracle of Champagne
Bubbles', 'The Art of the Cooper', or 'Napoléon, Mighty Emperor and Social
Drinker'! Tableaux and maps in the cellars of a former 14th-century abbey tell
the story of French wine-growing and the regions. It is all quite jolly, and there is
a chance of a tasting at the end of the trip. Nowhere near as comprehensive as
London's **Vinopolis** (see page 336), it nonetheless provides a suggestion of real
France in a district that is more Parisian than French. More interesting is the
programme of special events, lectures and Saturday tutored *dégustations*.
Telephone for details.

WHERE TO EAT
L'Ampère 1 rue Ampère, 75017; tel: 01 47 63 72 05 [3 G3]
Closed Sat lunch, Sun.
M̄ *Wagram;* Ē *RER E to Haussmann-St-Lazare, then métro 3 to Malesherbes. Rue
Jeoffroy d'Abbans to the junction with rue Ampère.*
Junior suits in the know and on a budget have sussed that there is a little more than
meets the eye to a smart corner *bistrot*. Smart young couples of all ages may also be
found sitting on the narrow summer terrace or ensconced inside amid the claret
and mustard décor. For the Ampère is yet another annexe of a Michelin man. In

this case it is the up and coming Albert Corre who has been starred for his Pergolèse by the Bois de Boulogne. Undemanding simple menus are chalked up on a huge wooden-framed blackboard that is hauled from table to table by the waitresses. The food is a step up from standard street-corner fare, entrées piled high in true tall-food manner – *céleri rémoulade* bolstering a tower of *foie gras*, salmon tartare is stacked with home-made lattice chips and drizzled with a *ravigotte* sauce. Main courses tend to spread more liberally across the plate: a generous *magret* that oozes blossom honey, a fan of *rouget fillets* on a bed of pesto ratatouille embraced by light and creamy olive-oiled *pomme purée*. Pay €35 (230FF) à la carte or go for the lunch menu at €14 (99FF) (great value, but no choice of dishes). Informal, cheerful service epitomised by the brace of lollipops that accompanies the bill.

Epicure 108 108 rue Cardinet, 75017; tel: 01 47 63 50 91 [3 G3]
Closed Sat lunch, Sun.
M̲ *Malesherbes;* Ē̲ *RER E to Haussmann-St-Lazare, then métro 3 to Malesherbes. From place de Gl Catroux, go north on bd Malesherbes to turn right on rue Cardinet.*
Tetsu Goya is the Japanese ambassador of Alsace in this no-man's-land between the Etoile and Montmartre. The hearty brasserie fare of eastern France, all sausages and sauerkraut, is given the kiss of sophistication by one of the capital's most imaginative Japanese chefs. The area may be less than picturesque, but, in choosing to open so far from the wealthier side of the quarter, Tetsu Goya is able to keep prices low without compromising quality. So we can enjoy market-fresh ingredients and a smart dining room, without the obligation of dressing up for the occasion. I saw grown men whimper over a *boudin blanc de poissons et grenouilles et lentilles vertes*, when I had ordered just a simple plate of vegetables as my starter. For 'simple', read gossamer tower of fine slices, suffused with a dill and tomato aromatic vinaigrette. Main courses are equally imaginative. Game is a seasonal speciality, but at other times discover the magic combination of fried ginger, smoked salmon steak and crème fraiche. A dessert of *croqignoles de chocolat à la marmalade de poires* is in a platter of pretty pastry parcels of chocolates that explode gently in the mouth to release a delicate pear purée. Menus from €23 (150FF).

Bistrot d'à Coté Villiers 16 ave de Villiers 75017; tel: 01 47 63 25 61; www.michelrostang.com [3 G–H4]
Closed Sat lunch, Sun.
M̲ *Villiers;* Ē̲ *Métro 4 to Barbès-Rochechouart, then line 2 to Villiers.*
The pavement tables, a piano by the door and those 19th-century drinks posters on the walls tell you this is a typical neighbourhood bistro. The daily specials on the blackboard offer no surprises. It is only when you check the name above the door that you realise that the kitchen staff has been trained by a living legend, Michel Rostang. Disappointingly, there are few of the scaled-down classic fireworks that Rostang has transferred to the British annexe at Le Méridien Piccadilly. Nonetheless a chilled soup of melon and anise tickled with vervaine olive oil is an interesting starter and main courses such as pan-fried calves liver with potato fritters, and the herbed haricots with the dish of the day provide occasional flashes of inspiration. Trawl the menu for those Rostang shock combinations that work oh so well and you could choose a *filet mignon à la fourme d'ambert* with the creamiest polenta ever. Desserts include the house variants on *pot au chocolat*. Mix and match from the *carte* menu from €31 (189FF) or go for the three-course lunch at €20 (129FF). The wine list offers exceptional value with many bottles at €15 (99FF) (half bottles for €8 (55FF) and some bargain basement classics such as the 1992 Chambolle Musigny for just €37 (240FF). A

handful of sibling *bistrots* dotted around Paris include the fine Dessirier (see *Annexe* feature, page 24) and Chez Raffatin in the fifth (see page 133). Worth a visit for the wine list and a canny combing of the menu to find the value gems.

Caves Pétrissans 30 av Niel, 75017; tel: 01 42 27 52 03 [3 F4] Closed Sat, Sun.
M̄ *Ternes;* Ē *Métro 4 to Barbès-Rochechouart, then line 2 to Ternes. Go north on av Wagram and turn left on rue Laugier to av Niel.*
Jean-Marie Allemoz runs the restaurant attached to his wife Marie Christine's family business – a wine shop in a prime upmarket street. Naturally Monsieur Allemoz is not blind to the en-suite cellar. Diners at his hip *bistrot* nestle in moleskin seats as they prepare to raid the wine list, secure in the knowledge that a lively Côtes du Rhône at under €17 (100FF) with lunch may be bought on the way out to share with friends at home in the evening! Food is simple but fab. The house *terrine* is pampered with *confiture d'oignons,* and prime cuts of beef glide off the knife. One of the places where food is more than good enough to lubricate conversation, rather than so fine that it stifles banter. From the big, bold, informal charger plates to the final clatter of spoon on scraped clean dessert plate, the €37 (240FF) lunch or dinner is money well spent.

Faugeron 52 rue de Longchamp, 75016; tel: 01 47 04 24 53 [2 F7] Closed Sat lunch, Sun.
M̄ *Trocadéro;* Ē *RER E to Haussmann-St-Lazare then métro 9 to Trocadéro, av Kléber exit. Follow the avenue to turn left on to rue de Longchamp.*
Madame Faugeron is the perfect hostess, as skilled in the art of the unobtrusive welcome as is her chef husband in the cutting of black diamonds. Truffles have their place on the menu year round, with Henri Faugeron's trademark soft-boiled and creamy *oeufs coque à la purée de truffes,* and feature in ever more inventive dishes on the new year's menu from January until March. Winter is the season for game, so from mid October start dreaming of hare, guinea-fowl and venison. One of the best wine lists in the area and a selection of fine desserts give plenty of reasons to linger in the light oak dining room. Probably the most endearing quality of the place, apart from the food, is the fact that the stranger opting for the €53 (350FF) lunch menu is accorded the same attention and respect as the VIP spending €115 (750FF) and above à la carte. In a quarter known for its snooty attitude, this is very refreshing.

La Grande Cascade allée de Longchamp, Bois de Boulogne, 75016; tel: 01 45 27 33 51; email: contact@lagrandecascade.fr
M̄ *Porte Maillot;* Ē *RER to Châtelet-Les-Halles then métro 1 to Porte Maillot. It is a very long walk along the allée de Longchamp, so take a cab.*
The great Alain Ducasse himself suggested Jean-Louis Nomicos as chef for this legendary restaurant in the beautiful Bois de Boulogne, where seductions and proposals take place in the movies. Macaroni pumped with *foie gras* or calamari risotto in ink nudge couples into the holiday mood. If you've cash left at the end of your trip, hang the budget and fall in love: the *belle époque* style of the Grande Cascade is the place for intimate evenings *à deux* – no one else is here on business! Immortalised in countless love stories, that theatrical façade has been the gateway to romance since this most exciting of the park's restaurants served its first dinner at the 1900 World Fair. Outdoors terrace dining in summer surrounded by flowers and birds, at the very spot where Napoléon III and Empress Eugénie once gazed at their own private waterfall. Service is attentive and discreet. Budget €55 (355FF) if you stick to the cheapest menu. But be prepared to triple it if you are planning a foray into the endless wine cellar, and an excursion à la carte.

Zebra Square 2 rue Boulainvillers, 75016; tel: 01 44 14 91 90 [6 C2]
M̲ *Avenue-Président-Kennedy;* E̅ *RER B to St-Michel-Notre-Dame then RER C to Kennedy-Radio-France (check destination board on the platform). Walk along av Président Kennedy to pl Adler.*
The Zebra Square brasserie in front of the Hôtel Square (see page 145) is bold, modern and warm. On the terrace the personalised ringtones of Nokia-chattering classes provide the cicada-chorus soundtrack to the watering hole by the Pont de la Grenelle. Inside, trademark zebra stripes on mosaic and lamps complement the bronzes and browns of a dining room packed with *grands crus* and serving *tartares* well past midnight to a hip 30-something crowd of media *dorée*, paying their own way. Lunch is ∈18 (115FF), and evening meals cost closer to ∈40 (280FF). After last orders, the terrace and lounge can buzz until four in the morning.

WHAT TO BUY

Dépôt Vente du 17e 109 rue de Courcelles, 75017; tel: 01 40 53 80 82 [3 F4]
Open Mon 13.00–19.30, Tue–Sat 10.30–19.30.
M̲ *Pereire;* E̅ *RER E to Haussmann-St-Lazare then métro 3 to Pereire. Walk south on rue de Courcelles, the store is on your right.*
Prada for next to nada? Not quite, but up to 50% discount on the official *prêt à porter* price. This is the outlet for Gucci, Chanel, Hermès and Christian Dior ready-to-wear outfits and accessories at a fraction of the official rates on the av Montaigne.

Ely Fleur 82 av de Wagram, 75017; tel: 01 47 66 87 19 [3 F4]
M̲ *Courcelles;* E̅ *Métro 4 to Barbès-Rochechouart, then line 2 to Courcelles. Take rue de Courcelles to av de Wagram.*
24-hour florist serves your most romantic gestures at any time, day or night.

Franck et Fils 80 rue de Passy, 75016; tel: 01 44 14 38 80 [2 C8]
Open Mon–Sat 10.00–19.00.
M̲ *La-Muette;* E̅ *RER E to Haussmann-St-Lazare, then métro 9 to La-Muette.*
If you must go department-store shopping, at least come home with a bag that only a select few will recognise. An old-style emporium, Franck et Fils spent much of the 20th century as the soul of discretion, catering to the sartorial whims of the incurably rich. Now it is admitting new money into its cash registers with a fully revamped fashion floor featuring the likes of Jérôme l'Huillier, Alexander McQueen and bootmaker to the catwalks Bruno Frisoni, as well as more traditional names in couture.

Réciproque 88, 89, 92, 95, 97, 101 and 123 rue de la Pompe, 76016; tel: 01 47 04 82 24 [2 C7–D6]
Open Tue–Sat 11.00–19.00; closed Aug.
M̲ *Rue-de-la-Pompe.*
Don't expect an elegant *vendeuse*, nor a gilded salon. If you just want the Versace frock, the Chanel little black dress or the Lacroix ensemble, spend the morning rushing up and down rue de la Pompe, picking up handbags in one store, gloves in the next and that Moschino number across the road. Massive discounts on showroom prices. It is possible to kit yourself out top to tail in Chanel, and still have change from £300. There is even a menswear department, so no excuses for travelling home in the same old clothes you wore for the journey out.

Montmartre and Clichy

Was squalor and sleaze ever this romantic? Simply raise your eyes from the naughty neon promises of the boulevard Clichy and seek inspiration in the heavens. A skyline from the Arabian nights, the silhouette of the Sacré Coeur atop the butte is proof, if any were needed, that, from the flash of Pigalle to the trash of the flea market, Montmartre is a world apart.

It was ever a village apart. Originally outside the city limits, it was beyond the city's jurisdiction. So when the cancan was banned from the theatres of Paris, the *bals publics* of Montmartre welcomed clients to their dance floors, where the shameless gavotte was performed *sans dessous* by the prostitutes of the hill. Sanitised by respectability, and the efforts of one Monsieur Durocher who, each night, sat in the wings to verify that the dancers were wearing their knickers (with a pocket full of safety pins for running repairs to any entrepreneurial tears in the undergarments), the dance was the making of the Moulin Rouge. From Edward VII to Cole Porter, the good and the nearly-good came to see the high kicks and hear the squeals at the finale of the floor show at the night club, named for the windmills that once dotted the hill. Renoir's picturesque *Moulin de la Galette* may still be glimpsed on the slopes of the butte.

The floor show is still one of the great draws of Pigalle, but the bd Clichy is also home to much of the contemporary clubbing scene, and the Folies Pigalle hosts a marvellous multiracial Sunday tea dance. However, the streets leading down towards the Grands Boulevards district hide oases of tranquillity for cooling the blushes of the faint-hearted. *La Vie Romantique* of George Sand and Chopin is relived in a quiet courtyard. Quaint little streets, such as the tiny circus around St-Georges métro station, are reminders of a simpler life. Further towards Trinité are the Mogador and Casino de Paris theatres where big Broadway musicals are performed in French.

Refreshed by the culture fix, climb back up to the main thoroughfare of bargains and pleasures. The bargains come from scores of bazaars selling discount everything, from hairbrushes to wedding dresses, slippers to suitcases. This is the heart of the Goutte d'Or district, where Arab and African shops lure visitors past the graffiti into a true community quarter – an antidote to the sanitised chrome and glass smugness of the city centre.

The exciting shopping scrum of one of the poorest corners of Paris is ever a carnival. The triumphant shouts of joy around the bargain buckets of Barbès

Rochechouart, the aroma of strong coffee and cheap tobacco and the tantalising scent of sandwiches of baguettes stuffed with chips, chicken and spicy *merguez* sausages.

High above all this, Montmartre's past poverty is today's *nostalgie*, for woven into the world's consciousness are the legends of poor laundresses carrying baskets up steep stepped streets, Toulouse Lautrec recording the morning-afters of the ladies of the night before, and the many Mimis and Rudolphos of a thousand *La Bohèmes*.

Is it any wonder that the hill is amongst France's most tourist-packed attractions? Despite the overpowering place du Tertre, with its permanent rush hour of holidaymakers, artists, waiters and souvenir hustlers, the constant bleep-bleep of coaches reversing by the meringue domes of the basilica and the wall-to-wall oils and watercolours of a Paris so idealised they could make a postcard blush, Montmartre somehow manages to remain true to its past.

This is the home of a tiny Parisian vineyard, an exclusive cemetery and more than one alleyway or face that might have been painted by Lautrec himself. High locked gates protect secluded private mansions on streets so steep that they have banisters.

We visitors climb the slopes from Anvers station, or perhaps indulge our calf muscles and take the funicular train up the harshest gradient. The *Montmartrois* themselves are in less of a hurry. They have seen it all before so loiter in the rue Lepic, with its twists, turns, markets and little food shops. At the top of the hill, the wittier explorer discovers the outrageously surreal melting wristwatch at the gift shop of the Swiss-run museum devoted to the creations and sounds of Salvador Dalí, where the fantastically wealthy may even buy an exhibit or two. The Europe-in-14-days crowd buys *naif* pictures of impossibly empty squares and colourful churches.

Backpackers strum guitars and drink cheap wine in front of the Sacré Coeur. Here all are allowed music wherever they go, from the early morning violinist playing Mendelssohn to *crêpes* and modern jazz at midnight in the cramped basement of Le Tire-Bouchon, to waiters dancing with their *patronnes* and *caissières* at 3am when the last stranger has left the square. La Butte Montmartre may well be the *cliché* of Clichy, but that does not mean that the magic does not exist. No need to ask the poorest of couples counting the final sous of an enchanted weekend and sharing a carton of *frites* and mustard under a 19th-century street lamp. With the entire sparkling city spread out at their feet, you see in their eyes the joy of untold wealth.

WHERE TO STAY
L'Ermitage 24 rue Lamarck, 75018; tel: 01 42 64 79 22 [4 A3]
M̄ *Lamarck-Caulaincourt;* Ē *Métro 4 to Marcadet-Poissonniers, then line 12 to Lamarck-Caulaincourt. Walk east along rue Lamarck.*
Breakfast *chez* the Capinel family in the garden under the age-old vines of Montmartre, a rare opportunity to see inside a typical Napoléon III residence. The Capinels had far too much respect for the house to turn it into a conventional hotel, with rooms of uniform standard and size. In order to

retain the style of the original home, accommodation can vary from rooms 11 and 12 with their own private terraces, to rooms 6 and 10 opening out over the rooftops of Paris. A regular guest at the hotel advised me to ask for a bedroom on the second floor if I wanted to look out on the garden, but (and this with nose-tapping conspiratorial wisdom) not to book room 8. He did not explain why, just nodded sagely and changed the subject. Considering that everyone in the world wants to stay in this overcrowded quarter, prices are pretty fair at €75 (480FF), including breakfast, for a double, and advance booking is recommended.

Lille 2 rue Montholon, 75009; tel: 01 47 70 38 [4 B5]
M *Poissonnière; Bus 48 to Paradis.*
Rooms with en-suite facilities at €30 (200FF) are a bargain in this basic, clean hotel which recently double-glazed all front windows. No extras, but flowers in windows facing the rue Montholon on the first and second floors. Fifth-floor rooms have tiny balconies with planted shrubs as a consolation for the long walk upstairs – there's no lift. Credit cards not accepted.

Pavia 29 rue de la Bruyère, 75009; tel: 01 48 74 50 60 [3 K4]
M *St-Georges;* E *Métro 4 to Marcadet-Poissonniers then line 12 to St-Georges. Uphill, turn left into rue de la Bruyère.*
Budget clean and tidy hotel with some surprisingly spacious rooms from around €65 (430FF). Situated midway between the Boulevards and Pigalle, a convenient base for theatres and nightlife.

Prima Lepic 29 rue Lepic, 75018; tel: 01 46 06 44 64 [3 K3]
M *Blanche;* E *Métro 4 to Barbès-Rochechouart, then line 2 to Blanche.*
At a twist in the tortuous corkscrew hillside street market of rue Lepic, that climbs from boulevard Clichy to Montmartre itself, is a promise of no-nonsense hospitality. A typical Montmartre hotel, packed with backpackers, paperback readers and penny-counting young couples, this is a narrow six-storey cluster of 40 small rooms. For under €60 (400FF), rooms are furnished with good second-hand tables and chairs and have stark old-fashioned bathrooms, appreciated by those who eschew marbling and heated towel rails in favour of traditional Parisian style. Three family 'apartments' at around €90 (600FF) are among the bargains of Montmartre, packing four people in the budget of one guest elsewhere. The lobby is decorated as a typical Montmartre street scene, and breakfast served in the packed *trompe l'oeil* garden salon. Everything comes under the eye, thumb and wing of Madame Reloug, who scours the flea markets for bedside tables and chairs for the never-ending furnishing and refurbishment programme. Thanks to the Reloug philosophy that guests on a budget should never be short-changed in the hospitality department, discover the nicely fitted washroom off the main lobby, where late-departing guests returning for their bags may have a final wash and brush up before catching the evening flight home. You would not find that elsewhere at twice the price.

Timhotel Montmartre 11 pl Emile-Goudeau, 75018; tel: 01 42 55 74 79; email: montmartre@timhotel.fr [4 A3]
M *Abbesses;* E *Métro 4 to Marcadet-Poissonniers, then line 12 to Abbesses. Take any turning north to rue Gareau and place Emile-Goudeau. The hotel is on the rue Ravignon side of the square.*
Stay a walk away from the Moulin Rouge and the Sacré Coeur for €103 (680FF). An undistinguished chain hotel is redeemed by the stunning panoramic views

from bedrooms on the fourth and fifth floors. Other windows open on to the virtual bird sanctuary of pretty place Emile Goudeau. Light, sleeping night-owls should beware the dawn chorus after the midnight chorus line.

Titania 70 bis bd Ornano, 75018; tel: 01 46 06 43 22 [4 B2]
M̄ *Porte-de-Clignancourt;* Ē *Métro 4 to Porte-de-Clignancourt.*
St-Exupéry, author of *Le Petit Prince,* lived here for two years, and at the age of 18 I first discovered Paris from these large and simply furnished rooms. For years the long-time proprietress, Madame Sautour, was the *châtelaine* of my memories and since the days, nearly two decades since, when I graduated to more luxurious lodgings, how I've missed her eccentric ways. She always kept her reception *salon* in pristine condition. Antique furniture, a million vases and plastic covers on the seats. People should keep off the furniture; cats could, and did, wander freely, knocking over pots of plants in the courtyard and glaring at visitors in the window. I remember the dawn chorus of *Madame* shrieking admonition at the unfortunate chambermaids protesting their innocence in the matter of disappearing hand towels. I remember the wide smile of welcome whenever I arrived at the heavy old front door, and the slap should I leave without hanging up my room key on its allotted hook. And how I recall the darned candlewick bedspreads, the cold floors on the moonlit pad to the bathroom, the low wattage bulbs. On my later visits she had departed from her sentry post, and I mourned the end of an era. When, a few years ago, I popped into the Titania for nostalgia's sake, there, with her hair as black, and smile as firmly fixed, as ever, *Madame* presided over the reception desk. A couple of weeks later I booked a room and found everything as before. I read aloud to her a translation of the story I had written of my early stays at the Titania (she understood no English), and we shared a tear when she told of her family's insisting on her retirement the next month. Madame Sautour has left the Titania, but her spirit lives on. Rooms are still only ∈23 (150FF) for a double – around ∈38 (250FF) with shower. No breakfast, but plenty of bakeries and sandwich bars nearby. Forget the shabby lift and the dimly lit passages and embrace a typical Paris hotel where impoverished writers and daydreaming pilots should live out their days. The flea market is just 100m away and it was outside the window that Paris' last great gangland shoot-out took place. Whenever film companies require an unfashionable unmodernised hotel for location filming, a world away from the touristy Montmartre side of the 18th, the phone on the big desk at reception is certain to ring.

Utrillo 7 rue Aristide Bruant, 75018; tel: 01 42 58 13 44; email: adel.utrillo@wanadoo.fr [3 K3]
M̄ *Abbesses;* Ē *Métro 4 to Marcadet-Poissonniers, then line 12 to Abbesses. West along rue des Abbesses, then fourth left.*
Pay around ∈60 (400FF) for a room and step out on to the rooftops as Paris' answer to Mary Poppins – the chimney pots around the sixth-floor windows are very evocative of old songs and other times. Warm welcome and clean rooms.

WHERE TO GO
Café Carmen 20 rue de Douai, 75009; tel: 01 45 26 50 00 [3 K4]
Open from 20.00.
M̄ *Blanche;* Ē *Walk down rue Fontaine and turn left on to rue de Douai.*
On Tuesday evenings the world of operetta and music hall is evoked by the lyric soprano Véronique Forcaud-Hélène, a distant cousin of Toulouse Lautrec

himself. Her repertoire conjures images of the era in a house which was no stranger to the arts. As the name suggests, this was once the home of Georges Bizet. Dinner and entertainment from around €38 (250FF).

Cimetière de Montmartre; 20 av Rachel, 75018; tel: 01 43 87 64 24 [3 J–K3]
Open Mon–Sat 08.00–18.00, Sun 09.00–18.00 (closed 30 minutess earlier Oct–Apr). Free.
M̲ *Place-de-Clichy, Blanche;* E̲ *Métro 4 to Barbès-Rochechouart, then line 2 to Place-de-Clichy. Follow bd Clichy to turn left on rue Caulaincourt and take the staircase to the cemetery.*
Anyone touched by *La Traviata* will wish to lay a camellia on the tomb of Alphonsine Plessis, for here lies the true *Dame aux Camélias*, inspiration of Dumas and Verdi. This place may not have quite the *cachet* of Père Lachaise (see pages 102–3), but so many of the *habitués* of the quarter in its heyday were laid to rest here. Dumas the younger, Degas, Offenbach, Berlioz and Stendhal are among the illustrious named on the headstones. In legend, Terpsichore lived on Mount Parnassus, but her spirit is cherished here on another hill by those who visit the graves of Nijinsky and Lautrec's muse, La Goulue. More recently, François Truffaut entered this salon of the departed.

Folies Bergères 32 rue Richer, 75009; tel: 01 44 79 98 98 [4 B5]
M̲ *Cadet;* E̲ *From Magenta station or Gare de l'Est take line 7 to Cadet. Follow rue Saulnier to turn left at rue Richer.*
How many generations of sensation seekers have crossed over the art déco threshold to see the legends of French cabaret step out on the most famous revue stage in France? Maurice Chevalier played here, Mistinguett virtually took up residence, and Joséphine Baker most notoriously wore that skirt of bananas when the Folies Bergères poached her from *La Revue Nègre* in which she had first taken Paris by storm at the Théâtre des Champs Elysées. Don't come here in search of the successors to the stars of yesteryear. The Folies saw out the century with a rock and roll tribute show, and launched itself into 2001 with *Les Boy'z Dance Lovers*, a male strip show in which the stars divest themselves of kilts, dinner jackets, rugger shirts, firemen's uniforms and surfers boardies. Whether the names of Greg, Brandon and Shawn eventually join those of Yvette Guilbert and Charles Trenet in the pantheon of the Greats of the rue Richer, only time will tell. However, in the scheme of things, I have no doubt that this Monty *monté* will be comfortably eclipsed by the plumes and sequins of the past. Check listings magazines in the hope that, by the time you visit, traditional Revue will have once again taken its rightful place at the Folies Bergères.

La Fourmi 74 rue des Martyrs, 75018; tel: 01 42 64 70 35 [4 A4]
M̲ *Pigalle;* E̲ *Métro 4 to Barbès-Rochechouart, then line 2 to Pigalle, walk east along the boulevard and turn right to rue des Martyrs.*
This is Pigalle's community bar where locals outnumber visitors. Genuinely mixed, vibrant and lively, where the toothless old lady in a heavy winter coat on a heavier summer afternoon chain smokes through her gums. Here, the impressionable American gap-year student, in a dress her mother might have worn in the '70s, hangs on every word spoken by the shaggy-haired, bearded and misunderstood young artist, thrilling as much at the prospect of her father's disapproval as to the philosophies spouted by her new best friend. Come here to read *Libération* in the morning, or *Pariscope's* listings in the evening. Take your coffee black and strong with a glass of tap water at the side, and make it last an hour.

Au Lapin Agile 22 rue des Saules, 75018; tel: 01 46 06 85 87 [4 A3]
Open Tue–Sun 21.00. €20 (130FF).
M̅ *Lamarck-Caulaincourt;* E̅ *Métro 4 to Marcadet-Poissonniers, then line 12 to Lamarck-Caulaincourt. Walk east on rue Lamarck and turn right on to rue des Saules.*
Of all the Montmartre cabarets on the hill, this ivy-smothered house with the green shutters, just along the road from Berlioz's home, is the last of the original haunts of the penniless artists of the beginning of the 20th century. Picasso and his circle would spend their evenings here listening to music and good conversation, and the accordion is taken up each night for today's audiences thirsty for any hint of the cabaret's past life. In the 19th century the house was known as the Cabaret des Assassins, redefining itself several times before being settling on the name Le Lapin Agile. Despite the concessions to international audiences, this is a far closer approximation to the cabarets of the period than the slick petticoat parade of the Moulin Rouge. Admission prices include a first drink. Other traditionally Montmartois entertainments include **Madame Arthur** (named for an Yvette Guilbert song) and the decidedly dated **Chez Michou**, a drag revue where celebrities would come to watch themselves being parodied by the artistes. The reception area is plastered with snapshots of Marlene, Liza, Mireille *et al* applauding their grotesque *doppelgangers*.

Marches aux Puces av de la Porte de Clignancourt, 75018; web: www.antikita.com [4 A1]
Open Sat, Sun, Mon 07.00–19.30.
M̅ *Porte-de-Clignancourt;* E̅ *Métro 4 to Porte-de-Clignancourt. Cross the bd Ney to the start of the market.*
For decades this sprawling area between Porte de Clignancourt and Porte St-Ouen has been a bargain lover's Sunday treat. Not so much a market as a maze of shops and specialist dealers, cafés and snack bars, it is a wonderful place for people-watching and a delightful antidote to an overdose of elegance and sophistication. A little-known sideline of the market is the inexpensive tailoring service offered by many of the immigrant gents' outfitters dealers. They can often run up a suit over a weekend. Be measured on Saturday, fitted on Sunday and suited on Monday. For details of the second-hand and antique markets see page 164–5.

Montmartre Vineyard rue des Saules, 75018; tel: 01 42 62 21 21 (harvest festival information) [4 A3]
Open first Sat in Oct.
M̅ *Lamarck-Caulaincourt;* E̅ *Métro 4 to Marcadet-Poissonniers, then line 12 to Lamarck-Caulaincourt. Walk east on rue Lamarck and turn right on to rue des Saules. The vineyard is at the junction with rue St-Vincent.*
If you are in Paris on the first weekend in October, climb the steep steps of the hill to the junction of rue St-Vincent and rue des Saules. In the tiniest of vineyards the Saturday grape harvest is cause for celebration. The pocket-handkerchief sized vineyard was planted in the 1930s as a reminder that, long before the artists colonised the hill, Montmartre was a wine-growing area outside the city. On Saturday night, once all the grapes are gathered in, the party continues in the bars and clubs of the butte. Jazz, toasts and dancing are the order of the day well into the night. The carefully tended vines in the well-nurtured soil of the butte are not the only stock to be found in the quarter. Look above you as you walk the streets of the quarter. Flat-dwellers tend vines in tubs on their apartment balconies and take their grapes to the winemakers' co-operative in order to make their own table wines.

Bal du Moulin Rouge Moulin Rouge, 82 bd de Clichy, 75018; tel: 01 53 09 82 82 [3 K4]
Dinner 19.00, show 21.00, 23.00. Show €57 (370FF), dinner €118–150 (560–770FF).
M̄ *Blanche;* Ē *Métro 4 to Barbès-Rochechouart, then line 2 to Blanche.*
The famous cancan. See page 189.

Le Mur des Je t'Aime 5 sq Jean Rictus, pl des Abbesses, 75018; web: www.lesjetaime.com [4 A3]
M̄ *Abbesses;* Ē *Métro 4 to Marcadet-Poissonniers, then line 12 to Abbesses.*
Everyone Says I Love You according to the title of Woody Allen's movie filmed on the banks of the Seine, and here in this garden on the hill are enough *Je t'aimes* to give Jane Birkin laryngitis. Frédéric Baron wanted to learn how to say those three little words in 80 languages. Every time he met a foreigner he asked them how to write and pronounce the simple declaration. Calligrapher Claire Kito transcribed the billet doux and Daniel Boulogne converted over 1,000 'I Love You's into a mural of 511 enamelled lava tiles, liberally sprinkled with broken hearts. On the website visitors can even listen to pronunciations of the more obscure translations, and in the garden itself, you can make your feelings known to the strange and silent stranger who stole your heart away by pointing to your innermost thoughts in Cantonese or Catalan, Occitan or Yiddish, Esperanto, Bambara, Navajo or Basque.

Place du Tertre [4 A3]
M̄ *Anvers;* Ē *Métro 4 to Barbès-Rochechouart, then line 2 to Anvers. Rue de Steinkerque leads to the funicular train to rue St-Eleuthère to pl du Tertre.*
The 'artist's' square where postcards, 'I Love Paris' baseball caps and such gems as 'My Mum Went To Paris And All I Got Was…' lousy T-shirts are sold, portraits are painted full face and coffee costs the earth. Come here very early in the morning to see why the place was once so special. A coffee on the square before 10.00, and the shady place du Tertre is very nearly beautiful. See page 154.

WHAT TO SEE

Espace Montmartre 11 rue Poulbot, 75018; tel: 01 42 64 40 10 [4 A3]
Open 10.00–18.30 (Jul, Aug 10.00–21.00). €6 (40FF).
M̄ *Abbesses or Anvers;* Ē *Métro 4 to Barbès-Rochechouart, then line 2 to Anvers. Follow rue Steinkerque and take the funicular railway. At the top double back down a few steps of rue Chappe then turn right on rue Gabrielle and right again up rue de Calvaire to rue Poulbot.*
A far cry from the neat snapshot paintings being churned out on the cobbles of the place du Tertre at the corner of the road, this private museum holds France's

largest collection of original works by Salvador Dalí. Soft watches, surreal tableaux, even installation pieces; this museum in unique in offering its exhibits for sale. After seeing a hundred or so identical interpretations of the Sacré Coeur, Dalí's oblique view of the world is invigorating.

Musée de l'Erotisme 72 bd de Clichy, 75018; tel: 01 42 58 28 73; web: www.eroticmuseum.net [3 K4]
Open 10.00–02.00. ∈6 (40FF).
M̲ *Blanche;* E̲ *Métro 4 to Barbès-Rochechouart, then line 2 to Blanche.*
The latest refit at the Louvre may win more column inches, but, as we learn here, inches may be over-rated. In any case, the Musée de l'Erotisme more than makes up for in body parts what the Venus de Milo lacks in limbs. Two millennia of turn-ons from five continents over seven storeys so close to the strip-strip of Clichy might encourage a clientele not usually associated with the beaux arts. Even so, this fascinating, and often witty, overview of the Urge as Inspiration blends 19th-century domestic *objets de pénétrage* with the work of serious artists. Items are regimented neither geographically nor chronologically, but displayed (you will excuse the expression) willy nilly, with English-language descriptions.

Allegorical apples and bananas apart, admire a manly 2,200 year old Roman *tintanabulum* wind chime. The museum also illustrates the relationship between sex and religion. A Tibetan oil lamp with a reservoir resolutely intra-uterine, and seemingly proper Buddha with remarkable relief carvings that put the probe into probity. Should such Eastern promise promote smugness among Europeans, monastic accessories from sources closer to home lean more towards the vaginal than virginal. One saintly temptation in particular would, but for a vowel in the verb, beggar belief. A Talmudic quotation reassures visitors that three things are essentially indefinable and indefinite: the Sun, the Sabbath and the Act. Secular sensation includes furniture designed to interact with the sitter in an anatomically representative if proportionately optimistic fashion.

The walls make fascinating viewing with prints and posters by Beardsley, Picasso, Klimt and Dalí. A public notice warns bar owners not to allow their female employees to 'sit' with male customers. A political cartoon by Reisser declares that 'Racists have Small Penises'. Largely hardcore Victorian postcards lay, among other things, the pretty fiction that all the butler saw were frilly petticoats and pert buttocks. There is also more than a nod and shake towards those activities hitherto assumed to be the province of the smallest room. Vulgar wine labels for *Côte du Rhône Cuvée Orgasme* are displayed above some predictably anatomical corkscrews. By the time one sees the Lautrec at the exit, Pigalle's former artist in residence seems more like Mabel Lucy Atwell.

Musée de Montmartre 12 rue de Cortot, 75018; tel: 01 46 06 61 11 [4 A3]
Open Tue–Sun 11.00–17.30. ∈3.75 (25FF).
M̲ *Lamarck-Caulaincourt;* E̲ *Métro 4 to Marcadet-Poissonniers, then line 12 to Lamarck-Caulaincourt. Walk east on rue Lamarck and turn right on to rue des Saules. Rue Cortot is third on the left.*
This sweet little museum is a delightful souvenir of the romantic story of Montmartre. Regular exhibitions offer glimpses into the lives of the artistic community that once made its home in these old streets. As you would expect there are plenty of posters and trinkets from la vie Bohème, Lautrec's nightlife, and even a reconstruction of the Café de l'Abreuvoir, where once locals chose absinthe over abstinence. Visitors are always surprised to stumble across tributes to figures whose lives were very far removed from those of the artists and prostitutes of the hill. Georges Clemenceau is commemorated here, but not

through any hitherto undisclosed scandalous intrigue. The great statesman is remembered as mayor of the district, in 1870.

Musée de la Vie Romantique (George Sand's salon) 9 rue Chaptal, 75009; tel: 01 48 74 95 38; email: musee.vieromantique@free.fr [3 K4]
Open Tue–Sun 10.00–17.40; closed holidays. €4.50 (30FF).
M̄ *Blanche, St-Georges;* Ē *Métro 4 to Barbès-Rochechouart, then line 2 to Blanche. Walk down rue Blanche. Rue Chaptal is third on the left.*
The playground squeals from the primary school next door might prompt you to hurry past the narrow driveway halfway along rue Chaptal. But do follow the path to a little courtyard to enter the world of Little Athens. Nothing to do with the dolmades and moussaka merchants of the Left Bank, the reference is to a literary and cultural clique, the free-thinking artistic symposium of the 19th century headed by a remarkable baroness. Amandine-Aurore Lucille Dupin, Baronne Dudevant, who lived at the Château de Nohant in Berry, had a secret life. 'My profession is to be free,' she wrote, and in the salons of Paris she achieved immortality as the novelist, playwright and feminist George Sand. Look up at the pretty leaded windows with their green slatted shutters, and the tiny garden and conservatory to your right, then follow the steps leading up into the house, where George Sand held court when she came to town. In the principal salon you may find a gathering of today's young students and literary dreamers at their own symposium, sprawled on the carpets and sitting on the staircase, rapt young faces resting on palms as an eloquent guide chats about life in the so-called Athenian circles. We hear how George played society twice as skilfully as any suffragette in order to put women's rights on the social and political, as well as the intellectual, agendas. We imagine her conversations with Liszt and her trysts with her lover Chopin. And take time in this place out of time to wander through the rooms, pause by the art works and appreciate her trinkets and jewellery.

Sacré Coeur parvis du Sacré Coeur, 75018; tel: 01 53 41 89 00 [4 A3]
Open 06.00–23.00 (dome & crypt 09.00–18.00). €2.50 (15FF).
M̄ *Anvers;* Ē *Métro 4 to Barbès-Rochechouart, then line 2 to Anvers. Follow rue Steinkerque and take the funicular railway to the rue du Card and steps of the basilica.*
The first of the Paris landmarks to be seen from the windows of the Eurostar is as much a part of the skyline as the Eiffel Tower. It always comes as a great surprise to visitors when they learn that the basilica was not consecrated until after World War I. The monument was commissioned from architect Abadie after money was raised following the nation's defeat in the Franco-Prussian War. The view from the parvis and steps in front of the Sacré Coeur is fantastic, but should you need an extra thrill, climb up the dome.

WHERE TO EAT
Beauvilliers 52 rue Lamarck, 75018; tel: 01 42 54 54 42 [4 A3]
Closed Sun, Mon lunch
M̄ *Lamarck-Caulaincourt;* Ē *Métro 4 to Marcadet-Poissonniers, then line 12 to Lamarck-Caulaincourt. Walk east along rue Lamarck.*
The lunch menu brings this gaudy, flower-filled, stage-door-bordello-styled dining legend within the reach of mortals with a credit limit. Just the sort of restaurant one might imagine Lautrec's fashionable floozies choosing for post cancan tête-à-tête with a wealthy married man, the domain of Monsieur Carlier actually boasts some of the finest cuisine at this altitude, a hips' swivel from the rue St-Vincent. Fabulous combinations such as artichoke, crab and pistachio – and (newly reclaimed by fashion) sweetbreads in many guises. If the décor of the

salon is just a bit too much, opt for the breezy, leafy terrace. Either way pay ∈28 (185FF) for lunch as opposed to a good ∈76 (500FF) à la carte.

Le Bistrot du Curé 21 bd de Clichy, 75009; tel: 01 48 74 65 84 [3 K4] Closed Sun and religious holidays.

M̲ *Pigalle;* Ē *Métro 4 to Barbès-Rochechouart, then line 2 to Pigalle. Restaurant is on the left of the bd, west of place Pigalle.*

Heard the one about the curate and the sex shop? Nestling in the heart of Pigalle's naughty nightlife, sandwiched between the Sexodrome peep show and a leather and latex emporium, is the unlikely success story of the quarter. In an area where ladies of the night walk the streets, even during the day, a young curate at the church of Trinité decided that missionary work should begin at home. So he persuaded the parish to buy the lease of a sex shop in the neon twilight zone of Montmartre and Pigalle. Volunteers rallied round to convert the shop into a modest *bistrot*, and within weeks the church was providing a good square meal for anyone who cared to drop in. Run by a team of parishioners, with two full-time staff, the restaurant attracts surely Paris' most varied clientele. Prostitutes and transvestites and the alumni of sex clubs and strip shows mix with showgirls, students and passing tourists. The staff often includes at least one plain-clothed priest, but there is no tableside proselytising. The church wants only to show the local community that it accepts all its members. However, the duty cleric is available for quiet confession away from the dining room. For working girls and conventional punters alike, the attraction has always been nourishing food at incredibly low prices. Reliable fare includes *pot au feu, coq au vin* and steaks. Ten years on, the *bistrot* can still provide a main course and dessert for ∈7 (45FF). A wider choice is to be had on the ∈14 (95FF) menu. For locals, the most politically incorrect fun is in watching out-of-towners on Moulin Rouge package tours as they realise that the glamorous lady at the next table has an adam's apple. The bar serves no alcohol, and closes on Sundays, when the management returns to the day job.

Le Bistrot des Deux Théâtres 18 rue Blanche, 75009; tel: 01 45 26 41 43 [3 K4–5]

M̲ *Trinité;* Ē *RER E to Haussmann-St-Lazare then métro 12 to Trinité. Restaurant is on the right-hand side as you climb rue Blanche.*

If you like musicals, you'll probably end up dining here by default since, as its name implies, it's the closest restaurant to the theatres that host home-grown and Broadway shows. The Casino de Paris and the Théâtre Mogador are just along the road. It has served me well after successive productions of *Cats, Les Misérables* and *Starmania*: reliable, efficient, good value – no surprises from the kitchen, just classic French cooking. My fresh salmon served with *beurre nantais* sauce was cooked to perfection. The three-course ∈25 (169FF) menu includes *apéritif* and a very drinkable Côtes du Rhône.

Charlot Roi des Coquillages 81 bd de Clichy, 75009; tel: 01 48 74 49 64 [3 J4] M̲ *Place-de-Clichy;* Ē *Métro 4 to Barbès-Rochechouart, then line 2 to Place-de-Clichy. Follow the boulevard.*

The rivalry is not worth the story-telling. Simply take my word for it. This place is not to be confused with **Charlot I**er across the road. Something of an institution, this seafood brasserie where Hooray Henris opt for one of the many lobster dishes, and peak-capped locals go for a platter of seafood and natter over the shells late at night. The real reason for a trip to Charlot is the legendary *bouillabaisse*, that somehow brings the sleazy Clichy district that much closer to Marseille. Since the place joined the empire of the Frères Blanc, a fashionable after-theatre crowd has joined the post-Moulin Rouge parties. Pay ∈50 (330FF).

La Crémaillère 1900 15 pl du Tertre, 75018; tel: 01 46 06 58 59 [4 A3]
M̄ Anvers; Ē Métro 4 to Barbès-Rochechouart, then line 2 to Anvers. Rue de Steinkerque leads to the funicular train to rue St-Eleuthère to place du Tertre.
With walls painted like a circus side show and garden tables in the kitschest *faux* village setting, with a dinky windmill, I don't think we're in Kansas anymore. OK, it is rather like dining in a postcard, but if you've decided to eat on the most tourist-packed square in all France you may as well enter into the spirit of things. There are as many tables on the square as artists peddling views of the Moulin Rouge, silhouettes and caricatures. At least the Crémaillère offers the best choice of simple food – if you stick to good onion soup, big salads or acceptable grills. Menus begin at €20 (130FF) for lunch. With wine, à la carte comes to around €49 (320FF).

Marie-Louise 52 rue Championnet, 75018; tel: 01 46 06 86 55 [4 B2]
Closed Sun, Mon, Aug.
M̄ Porte-de-Clignancourt; Ē Métro 4 to Porte-de-Clignancourt. Bd Ornano to place Kahn, left on rue Championnet.
If you tire of the budget couscous, pizza, Vietnamese and Portuguese food served among the sweat-shops and laundries behind the bd Ornano, do like the locals. When they pine for old-fashioned French food they return to Jean Coillot's traditional little formica, copper and lamp-shade-style dining room. At Marie-Louise they find the simple veal dishes they remember from childhood: *tête de veau*, *rognons* in Madeira and *côte de veau grand-mère*. Set lunch for under €23 (150FF).

Rendezvous des Chauffeurs 11 rue des Portes-Blanches, 75018; tel: 01 42 64 04 17 [4 B2]
Closed Wed, Aug.
M̄ Marcadet-Poissonniers; Ē Métro 4 to Marcadet-Poissoniers then walk north on bds Barbès and Ornano and turn right to rue des Portes-Blanches.
Steak or steak or steak, with maybe a sausage or some *rognons* as an alternative, in this basic local restaurant that has been serving the same meal to very much the same faces – straight out of a Montmartre sketchbook – since before the Great War. The prices have hardly risen either. Menu – with house wine included – for less than €10 (65FF). Good honest value for money.

Le Restaurant 32 rue Véran, 75018; tel: 01 42 23 06 22 [3 K3]
Closed Sat lunch, Sun.
M̄ Abbesses; Ē Métro 4 to Marcadet-Poissonniers, then line 12 to Abbesses. Go west on rue des Abbesses, take third left rue Audran to the restaurant.
If you lose the map, follow your nose to this light and bright corner restaurant a discreet pace behind the better-known streets of Lepic and Abbesses. The aroma of spices from the kitchen pervades everywhere, circulated by the breeze through the trellised windows. The spices and scents continue through the menu. Even vegetable dishes have a spice to match each texture on the plate: a light and smooth asparagus mousse with sweetcorn vinaigrette is given a piquant twist. Chef owner Yves Peladeau, formerly of Lucas Carton, also finds his flavours away from the spice rack. A recent visit dressed up veal in an anchovy sauce, and offered a bone-marrow tart with wine, stewed onions and oyster omelettes. I usually forsake the desserts, despite the lure of pears poached in liquorice and spiced *crème brulée*, because here are some of my favourite *sorbets* in all Paris: from the sharpest of apricot to the smoothest of *charentais* melon. The bill of fare changes regularly, even on a €11 (70FF) lunch menu and the €18 (120FF) menu

served at all times. À la carte works out at around €38 (250FF) per head. A relatively young but well-considered wine list complements the brief *carte* with a good selection at the €30 (200FF) mark. Service from the glamorous Nora and her team is never less than professional in a cheerful dining room where single diners seem to be appreciated as much as couples and groups, and not shunted into a corner for daring to read at table.

La Table d'Anvers 2 pl d'Anvers, 75009; tel: 01 48 78 35 21 [4 A4]
Closed Sat lunch, Sun, Aug.
M̲ *Anvers;* E̲ *Métro 4 to Barbès-Rochechouart, then line 2 to Anvers.*
The times, they may be changing. The unthinkable has happened. The Conticini brothers reigned supreme here for years, Christian is a master of the main course and always at the forefront of contemporary innovations and regular recipient of Michelin stars. But brother Philippe has finally flown the coop. Widely regarded as the best pastry-chef in Paris, Philippe's Dacquise confections of meringue and almonds were always as much a part of any meal as Christian's brilliance with veal, lamb and pigeon. I've not had a chance to sample the desserts of Philippe's successor, but can vouch for the fabulous flavours of the main courses, even if portions are designed for a less than robust appetite. A four-course menu costs €53 (350FF), lunch is €25 (170FF) and à la carte a hefty €107 (700FF).

WHAT TO BUY
Têtes en l'Air 65 rue des Abbesses, 75018; tel: 01 46 06 71 19 [3 K3]
Open Tue–Sat 10.30–19.30, closed Aug.
M̲ *Abbesses;* E̲ *Métro 4 to Marcadet-Poissonniers, then line 12 to Abbesses. Walk west along the rue des Abbesses.*
Outrageous milliners with creations so over the top that by comparison your average drag queen would look like Princess Grace. Hats for headliners made to measure or off the shelf. Don't be surprised to walk out the front door with a miniature park on your head, or sporting neon advertisements. You will have to pay cash since any credit cards flourished within these walls will be snatched for conversion into trimmings.

Marchés aux Puces av de la Porte de Clignancourt, 75018; web: www.antikita.com [3 A1]
Open Sat, Sun, Mon 07.00–19.30.
M̲ *Porte-de-Clignancourt;* E̲ *Métro 4 to Porte-de-Clignancourt. Cross the bd Ney to the start of the market.*
To find a true bargain, collectors turn up well before the official opening hours in order to catch the stall-holders and shopkeepers before the day's treasures ever make it to the display tables. This is the biggest and most distinguished fleamarket in Europe. So large in fact that it is always referred to in the plural. There are now ten major *Marchés aux Puces*, and countless smaller official markets in this sprawl of free enterprise in the shadow of the Périphérique between the Clignanourt and St-Ouen entrances to the city: the **Marché Biron** (85 rue des Rosiers) is the place for Louis XV *escritoires* and rare works of art; browse for general bric-à-brac on the crates outside stalls and doorways of the **Marché Combo** (75 rue des Rosiers); lithographs, religious trinkets and ecclesiastical ephemera are sold at the **Marché Dauphine** (140 rue des Rosiers). If your concept of Parisian chic is rooted in the images of *Les Années Folles*, and 1920s' deco table lamps and pre-war clocks are your passion, go straight to the **Marché Jules-Vallés** (7 rue Jules-Vallées). Specialist dealers in rare items, from specific schools and periods, tend to cluster around the **Marché Malassis** (142 rue des

Rosiers). Greatcoats and tutus, bridesmaids' dresses and hiking boots, army surplus uniforms and hats for a summer wedding may all be found in the second-hand clothes stalls of the **Marché Malik** (53 rue Jules-Vallées). Fashion students and even one or two well-known designers forgo their weekend lie-in to forage around the **Marché Michelet** (av Michelet) which specialises in textiles and accessories. Come here for beautiful shoes and handbags, and fantastic original 1920s beading. Exotic items from around the world, African masks, oriental stick puppets and fine silks are to be seen at both the **Marché Serpette** (110 rue des Rosiers) and **Paul Bert** (18 rue Paul-Bert). The **Marché Vernaison** (99 rue des Rosiers) specialises in books, toys, bronze and silver. If you come on a specific quest, hunch your shoulders and charge into the fray. Armed with a cheap map of the markets, available from any of the stores on the outskirts of the *Puces*, head directly to the specialist ghetto. Alternatively you can visit the fleamarkets on line. The website is a useful shoppers' search engine that homes in on the most likely tradesman for any item. Tourist offices, bookshops and local tobacconists sell specialist guidebooks and directories to the daunting warren of tradesmen, very useful for the timid shopper wishing to distinguish between the antique dealer, the junk merchant and the conman.

Rue Lepic [3 K3–4]
M̱ *Blanche;* Ē *Métro 4 to Barbès-Rochechouart, then line 2 to Blanche.*
This winding street that meanders up the slopes of Montmartre from place Blanche has countless small food shops and stalls and is a fine hunting ground for planning a picnic to be taken on the steps of the Sacré Coeur or on the Eurostar journey home.

Tati 4 bd de Rochechouart, 75018; tel: 01 55 29 50 00; web: www.tati.fr [4 B4] Open Mon–Sat 10.00–19.00.
M̱ *Barbès-Rochechouart;* Ē *Métro 4 to Barbès-Rochechouart.*
Mikhail Gorbachev was once late for a meeting of world leaders, because his wife Raisa, she of the cover-girl style, had fallen for the charms of Tati. At the bustling crossroads of Barbès Rochechouart, Tati is France's bargain basement. Security guards try their best to keep at bay hordes of local shoppers determined to secure a pair of trousers for the price of a coffee, a skirt for the cost of a sandwich or an entire wedding trousseau for less than €76 (500FF). Tati is an institution. Here the carnival spirit of the January sales pervades all year round, and it is not just the locals who come. Since Kylie Minogue wore an outfit inspired by Tati's own-label pink gingham, and Hockney painted the pattern, even the well-to-do habitués of the St-Honoré hide behind shades and Hermès scarves to join in the scrum. So what if 90% of the stuff is ghastly, and the wedding dress is so polyester-rich it could raise enough static electricity to discipline the naughtiest pageboy at a single touch. Who cares? Cotton T-shirts are cotton T-shirts, and the kids will grow out of the €3 (20FF) denims long before the seams surrender. Anyone who has found angora and cashmere hidden behind the naffest cardies is hooked for life. Tati has branches all over town (the best of the rest are at 63–90 av du Maine, Montparnasse and 13 pl Republique) and around the country, but this is the most remarkable collection. Around two dozen stores span several blocks of the boulevard, some linked by internal stairways, other demanding you pay up in one shop and start queuing all over again elsewhere. The Tati empire just keeps expanding. They sell jewellery and holidays now, too, not to mention gingham condoms, disposable cameras, kitchenware and sweets.

Gare du Nord and the Canals

When the first Eurostar arrived at Gare du Nord, northeastern Paris came of age. The Golden Arrow boat trains had always chugged towards these platforms and, for passengers from Roissy Airport, this was ever the first RER subway port of call in the city. Since indicator boards began trumpeting the arrival of high-speed trains from London, Lille and Brussels, the city's most exciting cultural melting pot has provided the liveliest and most honest of welcomes.

Gare du Nord and its neighbour, the Gare de l'Est, may be surrounded by gaudy pizza parlours, sandwich bars and burger emporia. Cross a couple of main roads and soon enough this sometimes noisy, always cheerful quarter will reveal its true colours. The eastern side of the district is a bargain hunter's delight. Afro hairdressers, wig boutiques, rag-trade outlets, even a religious iconographer make for fabulous window shopping. Honest unpretentious *bistrots* on street corners serve the locals, but will always find a chair for a like-minded stranger.

Across the wide boulevards from the Eurostar terminus is a covered food market and an impossible quiet quarter of fabulous restaurants where you can dine within five minutes of stepping off the train.

The bd Magenta itself leads north towards the Périphérique. To the left, pass the great Barbès-Rochechouart soukh below Montmartre. Here African psychics hand out business cards, and hawkers sell battery-operated back-flipping puppies around the pillars of the overhead métro line. Right of the boulevard are the railway sidings and Peter Brook's legendary run down Bouffes du Nord theatre, where once I queued all day for a ticket to see the world's most thrilling dancer Zizi Jeanmaire (equal parts ballerina, showgirl and embodiment of Carmen) do her one-woman show. One woman singing and dancing alone for the entire evening until her encore, when she stepped out with seemingly dozens of muscular chorus boys sporting ostrich feathers and chanting '*Mon truc en plumes*'.

Keep on walking up the boulevard, passing countless discount shoe shops. Here, as we waited for her train to London after a farewell lunch, I persuaded one of my best friends to treat herself to a pair of those cream and blood-red bad-girl shoes that should never be worn in public by anyone below the rank of Joan Crawford.

This is the same Paris I fell in love with at 18. Cheap, cheerful and never quite what it seems. From the butte Montmartre, the rue de Mont Cenis was always my way home after a night in the music cellars. At the end of bd Ornano is the famous Clignancourt-St-Ouen fleamarket (see *Montmartre*, page 164), and it was here, early one morning, that France's master criminal Mesrine finally met his maker. Having escaped from every prison cell that had never managed to hold him, the folk hero of 1970s crime was gunned down by police in a Hollywood-style trap, with undercover cops disguised as market traders and nuns.

Such dramatic events are rare, and the true charms of the northern quarters lie in their very tranquillity. Behind the stations, a great sweep of Périphérique and railway track might leave you under the impression that there's little to bother with between the ring road and the boulevards. You could not be more wrong. Let the T-shirt-buying masses pack out the Seine riverboats. We have no need for the river. The Canals St-Martin, St-Denis and de l'Ourq can be discovered behind the Gare de l'Est, as they head out of the city. Take time away from the concept of time and take the boat trip that climbs the canals, lock by lock. These waterways that once transported coal through France, and water to the capital's fountains, still flow through the newly created quarter of La Villette; strolls at the waterside are a way of life here. Once a self-contained village, a miniature town, hence Ville-ette, until the 19th century, it was an area of dance halls that gave their name to a local white wine, *guinget*. Napoléon announced his canal-building scheme in 1812, and the area's future as a service district for the capital was inevitable. Standing proud in what was once a stinking abattoir district, the modern Cité des Sciences, with its exhibitions, concert hall, gardens, planetarium and spherical cinema screen, is the Epcot that Disneyland forgot. The nearby music museum is as interactive as its neighbours.

I have no need for interactive entertainment. The combination of fresh air and water is heady enough for me. Let me spend an afternoon by the canal, leaning over the lock bridges at the locks, or just whiling away an hour on the banks, flicking at bees, a bottle of Badoit by my side and a favourite paperback to shield me from the sun. I might stroll along the quaysides, each one named after a great river. On a late summer weekend I can walk the Loire, the Seine, the Charente and Gironde to earn my coffee in a local bar where meat workers (yes, the butchery business has not quite disappeared) wipe bloody hands on grubby work clothes and read the sporting papers.

La Villette may have its techno park, its jazz festival and its open-air movie shows, but it is never allowed to stray too far from real life. Most magical of all, I can escape deep into the French countryside, without stepping across the parish boundaries. I will be crossing dramatic gorges, and climbing mountains. For here is Paris' greatest treasure of them all – the Parc des Buttes Chaumont.

WHERE TO STAY

Apollo 11 rue Dunkerque, 75010; tel: 01 48 78 04 98 [4 C4]
M̲ *Gare-du-Nord;* E̲ *Opposite the station.*
A find, this one. If your budget will not quite run to the Terminus Nord, then almost as convenient, a hundred yards away, is the Apollo. Two-star hotels are

rarely the *dernier cru* regarding luxury, but here the modest bedrooms are at least soundproofed – and for a hotel opposite one of the busiest railway stations in France with a pretty permanent building and redevelopment programme, that is essential. The single rooms, though cheap, are not for the claustrophobic, but pay around €65 (420FF) for comfortable accommodation, a strong shower and modern WC, satellite TV and the convenience of avoiding the strain and taxi expense of ferrying luggage across town. Breakfast is served in the bedrooms or in a rather noisy salon opposite the station. The true attraction of this old-fashioned establishment, with its Persian rugs on the stairwell walls and its pretty lift studded with miniature prints of British Guards Regiments, is the warm and cheery service, from the front desk to the chambermaids. Everyone treats guests as, well, as guests!

Laumière 4 rue Petit, 75019; tel: 01 42 06 10 77 [5 F3]
M̄ *Laumière;* Ē *Métro 5 to Laumière. Rue Petit is second left on av Laumière.*
This hotel will never find itself in a catalogue of the quaint and picturesque treasures of Paris, but at least it tries its best to offer a warm welcome in a quarter that still tends to react with surprise that visitors want to stay here. A decade ago the Laumière was the only establishment in the 19th arrondissement to squeeze grudging acknowledgement from the Michelin guide. Gradually the efforts of its hard-working staff and management have made the most of the place, from the bright modern first-floor reception to the bedrooms. If you recall the threadbare towels and faded bedspreads of the past, you will be pleasantly surprised by the improvements. Good value at €58 (380FF) for a double room.

Nord-Est Hôtel 12 rue des Petits Hôtels, 75010; tel: 01 47 70 07 18 [4 C5]
M̄ *Poissonière, Gare-du-Nord;* Ē *From the Eurostar terminus walk along bd de Denain, turn left on to bd Magenta then right to rue des Petits Hôtels.*
There is a secret village just across the way from the raucous bazaar that surrounds the Gare du Nord – see restaurant listings below for the culinary secrets of the rues de Belzunce and Petits Hôtels – and that joy lies in the blessed ignorance of those package punters being pumped through the station all day every day. The little streets off the rue Lafayette are well worth discovering. They are sandwiched between two saints – the Marché St-Quentin, one of the last local covered food markets of Paris, where the good housewives of the 10ème buy their *quenelles de brochet* and fresh chicken, and the imposing church of St-Vincent de Paul whose pretty, tiered, city churchyard garden descends into the place Franz Liszt. The Nord-Est Hôtel has pleasant, if standard, bedrooms, a double rate of €65 (430FF) including breakfast, and is hidden behind a well-matured and nurtured front garden of its own. A quiet haven from the taxi horns and bustle you would normally expect from the quarter.

Parc des Buttes Chaumont l pl Armand Carrel, 75019; tel: 01 42 08 08 37; web: www.hotel-du-parc-bc-paris.com [5 F4]
M̲ *Laumière;* E̲ *Métro 5 to Laumière. Walk along av Laumière towards the park. The hotel is on your right.*
The business-class hotels around La Villette, a few hundred metres away, nudged the rather complacent traditional accommodation into tarting up their image, brightening their rooms and smartening up their service. Regulars at the Hôtel du Parc are more than happy with the improvements here. However, it's not the décor but the view that calls us back, time and again. Insist on a top-floor bedroom overlooking the park. My windows opened out over the enchanting lake and gorge of the hilly wonderland (see page 170) that, no matter how often one sees it, is always a magical oasis in the heart of such a residential quarter. Start the day with a breath of fresh air, and a stroll, wander or jog, to work up an appetite for the slightly better than average breakfast. Inexpensive garaging available on site. Polite staff will book tickets for local fringe theatres for you – there is a good music-hall tradition of rough and ready song-shows. Occasionally open-air theatre in the parks can brighten even a November evening. Local charm comes at a slight price, and I don't mean the €84 (550FF) room rate. Be prepared to suffer the toots and hoots of Parisian traffic sounds well into the night.

Paris Liège 36 rue de St-Quentin, 75010; tel: 01 42 81 13 18 [4 C4]
M̲ *Gare-du-Nord;* E̲ *rue de St-Quentin is opposite the main entrance of the station.*
Another of that rare breed – a budget station hotel just yards from the Eurostar terminus, yet free from the blight of budgetitis. Rooms are clean and comfortable, and individually styled, with romantic names (Victoria, Aurora etc) and floor-to-ceiling drapes to shut out the world. A convenient budget option for those whose principal requirement of a Paris hotel is somewhere to sleep between shopping, supping and sipping. Staff are reasonably polite and efficient, and accommodation with en-suite facilities costs €53 (350FF).

Terminus Nord 12 bd de Denain, 75010; tel: 01 42 80 20 00; email: H2761@accor-hotels.com [4 C4]
M̲ *Gare du Nord;* E̲ *Opposite the station.*
I blush to recall my original review of this hotel – in the early 1990s. 'Negotiating the maze of corridors to the bedroom could well qualify guests for the Duke of Edinburgh Bronze Award in orienteering.' This I wrote back in 1993, when I swore that 'no amount of refurbishment could disguise this warren'. Happy – oh so happy – is the critic who is proved so wrong: just imagine my delight when revisiting the hotel after its acceptance into the Libertel stable to discover a true haven of charm, practically inches from the Eurostar platform. The public areas have been opened up to reveal art nouveau stained-glass windows, a splendid lobby atrium dispelling the gloom of the bad old days. It is frightfully British Country House now with a few transcontinental touches, such as the smart bellboy and valet parking lads in their neat uniforms hovering around next door's seafood stall. The place has been *faux-marbréd* to the nines and huge canvases and statuary are liberally scattered around the place. Breakfast is served in a pretty first-floor salon, directly above the famous brasserie facing the bustling station. (see separate listing, page 176). More than 200 rooms are swished out in regency stripes and floral drapes, some rooms have concave curved walls. The place is soundproofed and sunny, and who would have believed that? And the bathrooms are pretty, as one would expect from such a hotel, with none of the stolid old-fashioned upright utilitarian washbasins of yore. Double rooms cost around €176 (1,160FF) these days, suites €260 (1,735FF). I managed to check in within four

minutes of my train pulling into the station! Because nothing else in its class may be found so conveniently located for Channel Tunnel and airport passengers arriving in the city, I have no hesitation in recommending the new and wonderfully improved Terminus Nord as the ideal base for the Eurostar traveller.

I have just learnt that Libertel plan to renovate the Terminus Est around the corner opposite the Gare de l'Est. Comments welcomed.

WHERE TO GO

Canals

Canauxrama Basin de la Villette, 13 quai de la Loire, 75019; tel: 01 42 39 15 00; web: www.canauxrama.com [4 F4]
09.45 and 14.45. ∈12.50 (80FF).
M̄ *Jaurès;* Ē *Métro 5 to Jaurès, exit quai de la Seine.*
(See feature page 167.) A three-hour trip aboard the Arletty or Marcel Carné travelling through the locks of the Canal St-Martin and the beautifully vaulted Bastille tunnel to the port de Paris-Arsenal. Services from the Arsenal to La Villette depart 15 minutes earlier. Ferry services across the Villette Basin are also available at ∈2.50 (15FF).

Paris Canal Basin de la Villette, 19–21 quai de la Loire, 75019; tel: 01 42 40 96 97; web: www.pariscanal.com [4 E4]
14.30. ∈15.50 (100FF)
M̄ *Jaurès;* Ē *Métro 5 to Jaurès, exit quai de la Seine.*
Afternoon excursions leave from outside the Grande Halle de La Villette, and follow the canals and the Seine to the Musée d'Orsay. Morning trips depart from Musée d'Orsay at 09.30.

Parc des Buttes Chaumont [5 F4–5]

M̄ *Laumière, Botzaris or Buttes-Chaumont;* Ē *Métro 5 to Laumière. Walk along av Laumière towards the pl Armand Carrel and the main gates of the park.*
If you seek a monument to Baron Haussmann, ignore his famous boulevards and follow me to a miracle of open countryside within the city limits. From outside, this park might be a modest-sized garden surrounded by traffic. But inside it is a vast region in its own right, with dramatic rocky cliffs, waterside strolls, woodland paths and a complete escape from the city. When the Grands Boulevards were built, the twin hill to Montmartre was looted to provide the stone for the project. The quarry soon became the city tip, and the remaining hillocks and basin were a putrid mass of muck and trash. Then, with the blessing of Napoléon III, Haussmann created what, to my mind, was his St-Paul's. This multi-tiered park is a celebration of the natural environment and outrageous artifice. Art and nature thus allied flooded the quarries into a winding lake, then raised the bald hills even higher, piling rocky peaks to be crossed by suspension bridges and crowned with a Temple of Love. Within three years, fast track stalactites and stalagmites were installed in a cave, and a waterfall created in the eastern corner, and the first public park in the north of Paris opened in 1867.

To appreciate the entire park fully would take some time, and though it may not have the vast expanses of the Bois de Boulogne it can still boast at least one excellent restaurant (see *Pavillon Puebla*, page 174). Here are treats for all the ages of man: mewling infants and whining schoolboys have traditional *guignol* puppet theatres at the Bolivar and Armand Carrel entrances, whilst lovers have the footbridge over the ravine. The justice, slapping his capon-lined belly, has a choice of dining tables, and the lean and slippered pantaloon may be seen playing *boules* on a summer's afternoon. On Sunday mornings the park is the rendezvous for the jogging club whose members negotiate rocks and spaniels with enviable skill as they bound around the mounds in garish tracksuits, *sans* taste, *sans* everything.

Le Pavillon du Lac parc des Buttes Chaumont, 75009; tel: 01 42 02 08 97 [5 F4] M̄ *Laumière;* Ē *Métro 5 to Laumière. Walk along av Laumière towards the pl Armand Carrel and the main gates of the park. Turn right to climb the hill. The Pavillon is on your right just past the bridge.*
The other side of the park to the Puebla (See *Where to eat*) this has the benefit of a view across the remarkable lake to the hilltop lookout. The mealtime menu is rather too expensive for the quarter, and not in the class of the Puebla, but during the day the restaurant doubles as a good old-fashioned *salon de thé*. Old ladies muffled in moth-eaten furs squint myopically at dog walkers and honeymoon meanderers taking the hidden footpaths to the Temple of Love. Families enjoy the promised ice-cream and, at around €6 (40FF) for a *glace*, it won't break the bank.

WHAT TO SEE
Cité de la Musique 21 av Jean Jaurès, 75019; tel: 01 44 84 45 45 [5 G3]
Music Museum open Tue–Sat 12.00–18.00, Sun 10.00–18.00.
M̄ *Porte-de-Pantin;* Ē *Métro 5 to Porte-de-Pantin.*
The canal de l'Ourcq is the dividing line between the arts and sciences. Across the water from the Cité des Sciences is the Zenith concert hall, a huge hangar-like space for pop concerts. On the far side of Bernard Tschumi's *avant garde* gardens, the Grande Halle de La Villette is home to classical music and jazz festivals, open-air cinema in summer and major exhibitions. Beyond the hall is a modern piazza, architectural declaration that this side of the water is yet another themed 'city'. Welcome to the Paris of musicians. Everyone, busker, maestro, singer or academic, is catered for, whether they play a Stradivarius or a Fender. The Paris Conservatoire now stands alongside specialist libraries and research centres, not to mention various purpose-built concert halls, boasting a near-permanent programme of entertainment. Mere music lovers should visit the museum with its collection of instruments from the Renaissance to the present day and art works. Guided tours are available, but best of all are the family-friendly workshop tours (14.30 Wed), story tours (11.00 Sun) and play tours (15.00 Sun).

Cité des Sciences 30 av Corentin-Cariou, 75930; tel: 01 40 05 12 12; web: www.cite-science.fr [5 F–G2]
Open Tue–Sat 10.00–18.00, Sun 10.00–19.00. €8 (50FF), Sat €5.50 (35FF).
M̄ *Porte-de-La-Villette;* Ē *Métro 4 to Gare de l'Est then line 7 to Porte-de-La-Villette.*
The symbol of the entire La Villette park is the huge hemisphere of the Géode cinema, a landmark for traffic roaring by on the Périphérique ring road. Not only Omnimax and Cinaxe special effects cinemas; here too is the city's planetarium and interactive science museum, opened for the advent of Halley's Comet in 1986. Exhibits are housed in separate halls designed for various age groups. Young and old alike approve of the *Argonaute*, a real submarine that can be explored in the park, and everyone enjoys the aquarium. The modern gardens and customised waterways provide a futuristic contrast to the Buttes Chamont, half a mile away.

Musée Baccarat 30bis rue de Paradis, 75010; tel: 01 40 22 11 67; web: www.paris.org/musees/baccarat [4 B5]
Open Mon–Sat 10.00–18.00; closed holidays. €2 (10FF).
M̄ *Poissonière or Château-d'Eau;* Ē *Bus 26 direct to pl Franz Liszt stops outside the museum.*

Rue de Paradis (see *What to buy*, page 176), in a district of cheap hardware stores, where every other shop sells vinyl aprons and plastic kitchenware, is the unlikely centre of the fine china and glassware trade. Glass does not come finer than the legendary crystal produced by Baccarat. One hundred and fifty years of craftsmanship that might usually be viewed in the world's great palaces may be seen in this 19th-century *dépôt*, Baccarat's Paris home since 1832. Whether the grandeur of a chandelier or the simplicity of a perfume bottle, the Baccarat style is unmistakable. See the glasses especially created for Napoléon and the Shah of Iran. Best of all, determine the household style of your loved ones. The on-site gift shop, perfect for those last-minute wedding presents, is just ten minutes' walk from Gare du Nord.

WHERE TO EAT

Au Boeuf Couronne 188 av Jean-Jaurès, 75019; tel: 01 42 39 44 44 [5 G3]
M̄ *Porte-de-Pantin;* Ē *Métro 5 to Porte-de-Pantin, exit av Jean-Jaurès. The restaurant is on the opposite side of the road.*
Beef and pork are on the menu and near-perfect steaks have kept this end-of-the-street restaurant bustling practically every night these past 70 years. Of course when the kitchens first started grilling, pan-frying and casseroling, the clientele did not arrive in limousines. It is only in recent years that this stretch of the avenue Jean-Jaurès attracted a row of peak-capped commissionaires to assist guests to and from their cars. For at the beginning of the last century this was the quarter of the abattoirs, and the butchers – who knew their meat – would not have settled for a cheese sandwich and green salad. Just as Les Halles encouraged some legendary tables in its market days, so the meat markets nurtured their own. Today, with the business and executive trade at La Villette, the welcome is smarter but the quality remains the same, with my Parisian friends declaring this the *royaume* of the finest *filet mignon* and the best *tête de veau* in the east of the city. This particular *belle époque* steakhouse carves half-kilo *châteaubriand* to the gentle flow of Médoc into polished glass for the most traditional of tastes. Menus from €24 (160FF), indulgence for around €61 (400FF). Plenty of neighbouring beef palaces, should the place be full.

Chalet Maya 5 rue des Petits Hotels, 75010; tel: 01 47 70 52 78 [4 C5]
M̄ *Gare-du-Nord;* Ē *From the Eurostar terminus walk along bd de Denain, turn left on to bd Magenta then right to rue des Petits Hotels.*
On the seedy side of the Marché St-Quentin is this unexpectedly glamorous flourish of gastronomy. A sharply modern kitchen hides behind a temple of nostalgia. When Jean Cocteau was invited to decorate the marriage salon at Menton, on the Riviera, he immortalised his companion Jean Marais in the official portrait of Marianne, the goddess symbol of France. At the end of a distinguished film and stage career, Marais decided to return the compliment with this restaurant devoted to the cinema that both men shared. Huge portraits of Marais' screen triumphs fill the walls and the house cocktails are named after the great *oeuvres* of Cocteau himself. Most evenings Jean Marais would make his grand entrance and tour the tables escorted by whisper-waisted pretty-boy waiters.

When Marais died in 1999 I wondered if the restaurant could survive on the strength of its all-inclusive €15 (100FF) menu. So we arrived at around midnight one Monday in May, and even on that notoriously quiet night, the conversational hum proved that the magic still lingered. The menu cards with their famous 13 starters and 13 main courses were flourished as ever by the golden boys. My guest enthused with a mouthful of a *tartelette* of *boudin noir* and caramelised apple, as I chomped slender white fingers of asparagus hollandaise. Then came a *fricassé* of rabbit with *anise* and cinnamon served with polenta causing further grunts of satisfaction and *paupiette* of salmon with savoury *pomme purée*. Any lingering doubts that we had been cheated of the *tournedo d'agneau* or the seafood *timbale*, which had been crossed off the menu by the time we ordered, were banished by the smacking of our lips. Spices are everything here: a splash of paprika with the *pâté*, a dessert pear poached in saffron. Palate revival comes as standard in a laid-back dining room where the fashion-conscious go to forget about fashion. A courtyard garden for quieter conversation is available in the summer months.

Chez Casimir 6 rue de Belzunce, 75010; tel: 01 48 78 28 80 [4 B4]
Closed Sat, Sun, Aug.
M̄ *Gare-du-Nord;* Ē *From the station take rue de Compiègne, cross the boulevard to rue de Belzunce.*
Transformed from its original identity as a cheerily unfashionable family-style dining room, Casimir is now the 'annexe' of Thierry Breton's main dining room (see *Chez Michel* below). Newer, trendier, light and bright open design gives the place the air of a city wine bar: plenty of tables for twosomes, chalked-up menus of fishermen's soups, stews, veal and sweetmeat favourites, and a smart informal buzz at lunchtimes and early evenings. Pay ∈15–22 (100–150FF).

Chez Michel 10 rue de Belzunce, 75010; tel: 01 44 53 06 20 [4 B4]
Closed Sun, Mon, Aug.
M̄ *Gare-du-Nord;* Ē *From the station take rue de Compiègne, cross the boulevard to rue de Belzunce.*
A la recherche des chomps *perdus* in the gastronomic minefield surrounding the Gare du Nord, a meeting place of the cultures of fast food and the faster buck, many people give up the chase and dive into the métro in search of a first or last taste of France. Ten years ago I stumbled across the tranquil oasis just across the boulevard Magenta. The rue de Belzunce, behind the church of St-Vincent de Paul, was even then home to Chez Michel, where serious food was served in the timbered and draped dining room. Today, Thierry Breton's ∈27 (180FF) *carte-menu* is famous for bringing the best of Brittany to the capital. Check the specials board for the morning catch from St-Malo, and begin salivating over the prospect of *bistrot* delights that include goose eggs with wild mushrooms, roast pigeon and jugged hare all washed down with good-quality country cider. Book early to guarantee one final aromatic memory of eating *à la française* before catching the afternoon Eurostar.

Chez Papa 206 rue Lafayette, 75010; tel: 01 42 09 53 87 [4 D4]
M̄ *Louis-Blanc;* Ē *Métro 5 to Stalingrad, then line 7 to Louis-Blanc. Restaurant is just past the junction with the fbg St-Martin.*
Bargain meal of the district here, where huge plates and bottomless bowls are filled with the strong flavours of southwestern France. For *cassoulet* and *magret* the hungry come to take their fill of basic popular fare until late into the night. *Escargots* are served in a number of ways, including with a leek *confit*, and the traditional version drenched in garlic. A salad of *frisée au lardons* comes in a bowl big enough to feed a small village for a month. Although eating à la carte would scarcely break the bank, the absolute must is the three-course menu for ∈9 (60FF), served until 22.00 midweek, and lunchtime on Saturdays. Last orders are taken at 01.00 every day of the week, and the place is always packed with impoverished youngsters and raucous old timers from the mean streets between the canal and the railway tracks.

Dagorno 192 av Jean-Jaurès, 75019; tel: 01 40 40 09 39 [5 G3]
M̄ *Porte-de-Pantin;* Ē *Métro 5 to Porte-de-Pantin, exit av Jean-Jaurès. The restaurant is on the opposite side of the road.*
A neighbour of Au Boeuf Couronne along the 'Who's afraid of BSE' route, Thierry Atlan flourishes his *tournedos* and *entrecôtes* with the best of them, but is equally attuned to the future so offers contemporary seafood dishes, *volaille* and lighter fare to the non-red-meat fraternity. Open until after midnight, which makes it a popular choice for the trendy types heading to, or from, the Zenith rock venue.

L'Echo de Chinon 12 rue de Belzunce, 75010; tel: 01 48 78 40 03
Closed Sat, Sun.
M̄ *Gare-du-Nord;* Ē *From the station take rue de Compiègne, cross the boulevard to rue de Belzunce.*
Regional cuisine in Paris usually refers to the rich flavours of the southwest or the Riviera colours of the Med. So a lighter, and quite refreshing alternative is to be welcomed. The northwest comes to town in the rue de Belzunce where Thierry Breton (see *Chez Michel*) has so successfully made his mark. Now, on the opposite corner of the road, the echo of Chinon rings loud and clear. All menus, the ∈15 (100FF) lunch and the ∈16 (110FF) and ∈26 (170FF) alternatives, are designed to bring out the best in the wine list. Dominating the wine list are some 13 Chinons, so expect Loire favourites on the menu – freshwater fish and farmyard preparations – with the odd nod towards the Med, as it seems that no restaurant in Paris can afford to ignore olive oil and balsamic vinegar these days!

Le Jaurès 1 av Jean Jaurès, 75019; tel: 01 42 08 76 12 [4 E4]
M̄ *Jaurès;* Ē *Métro 5 to Jaurès.*
A bar really, and a regular corner site at the junction of the quai de la Loire and the av Jean Jaurès, but listed for a pretty good value *menu belge. Moules-frites* and a *bière blanche* for ∈8 (55FF). Good-natured service with a smile, whether you are eating or merely taking the weight off your feet with a coffee after a stroll along the canal. Less than 100m from the Rendezvous de la Marine, and opposite the métro station.

Pavillon Puebla Parc des Buttes-Chaumont, 75019; tel: 01 42 08 92 62 [5 F5]
Closed: Sun, Mon, Aug.
M̄ *Buttes-Chaumont;* Ē *Métro 5 to République, then line 7bis to Buttes-Chaumont. Walk along rue Bozartis to the gate by the junction with av Simon Bolivar. Follow signposts along the winding paths in the park.*
In the most spectacular rural setting, discover Paris style with class and not a snob in sight. What more could you ask for? To the rich and judgemental, this part of town is simply not on the social map. When we invited Parisian friends from the more fashionable west of the city to dine here, they came because it would have been rude to refuse, but we sensed the rhetorical question in their fixed smiles: 'Could there possibly be anywhere decent to eat in such a quarter?' At the park gates, in the shadow of the hilltop temple and facing the prospect of nature red in tooth and claw, you could smell their regret at having accepted our invitation. Five minutes later, as we stepped through the doors of the Second Empire hunting lodge, we pretended not to hear the welcome sound of dropping jaws and and racing heartbeats that accompany the discovery of hidden treasure.

Christian Vergès' Pavillon has the twin merits of being one of the city's gastronomic high spots and a superbly run restaurant. Just as elegant as her surroundings, Madame supervises the service of her husband's imaginative creations. The cuisine is Catalan tradition bathed in southwestern gastronomy, and spectacular sauces are the house speciality. From the autumn fruit accompaniment to the *quenelles* of warm rabbit pâté, through the vinaigrette with the roquefort to the triumphant finale, a soup of marinated fruits and *sorbet*. Steaks are prepared just so and a *niçoise* of fish is delicately perfumed with basil. A wisely compiled wine list complements the meal. À la carte could cost €68 (450FF) but the menu of the day provides a set five-course lunch for around €30 (200FF). Arrive early. You might not think that you could get lost in such a small urban garden, but you could find yourself working up a bigger appetite than you had planned for if you try to take a hurried short cut in this remarkable park. So rather than venturing unaided over hill and dale, stick to the signposted path or ask a local the way to the Pavillon Puebla.

Rendezvous de la Marine 14 quai de la Loire, 75019; tel: 01 42 49 33 40 [4 E4] Closed Sun, Mon.
M̲ *Jaurès;* Ē *Métro 5 to Jaurès, exit quai de la Seine.*
In a district which has swiftly become fashion victim to the makeover culture, this is a real *bistrot du port* and to my mind the best reason in the world for visiting the 19th. Whilst the young *technomecs* and cool cats of of the Cité des Sciences and loft apartments have their designer brasseries that skirt La Villette, and the expense-account *conférenciers* in shirtsleeves order beef on avenue Jean-Jaurès, still the Rendezvous remains an unspoilt treasure on the canalside. The well-to-do may throng at the Rendezvous des Quais on the opposite bank, and pleasure craft and sports types may take to the waters by the lock, but this side of the waterway has kept its local character. As many tables as possible are squeezed into a room whose walls are covered with pictures of the famous from the days when Liz meant Taylor and not Hurley. You will have to book because every table is always taken. Although (or perhaps because) the place is always packed, there is always a convivial and hearty welcome from the staff – never too busy to be friendly to regulars. And those regulars are families with their children, retired couples arguing past disputes, and workers on their meal break. The kitchen is of the school that believes that the white of a plate should never be uncovered in public, so portions are enormous. A starter salad is bigger than a main course anywhere else. Rare meats melt into hearty sauces, salt cod is flaky and chewy, haricot beans and other vegetables are market fresh. The style of food ranges from Normandy specialities to the house favourite paella (24 hours notice required). For dessert, apple tart *flambéed* in Calvados is tempting but I am weak-willed enough to succumb to gigantic profiteroles. For a two-course meal you could pay around €15 (100FF), for three courses à la carte €26 (170FF) should suffice – but three courses require a healthier appetite than most visitors could muster. There is a simple but sensibly priced wine selection, a *familiale* atmosphere, good old-fashioned food and a genuinely happy welcome, all in a charming location.

Le Rendezvous des Quais 10 quai de Seine, 75019; tel: 01 40 37 02 81 [4 E3]
M̲ *Stalingrad;* Ē *Métro 5 to Stalingrad, exit quai de la Seine.*
In all the cinemas on all the canal banks in all the world, you have to walk into this one. The new 19th is seriously cultural, with the Cité de la Musique, the Cité des Sciences, the La Villette film and jazz festivals, so a cinema complex was inevitable. Less predictable, but equally welcome, is this restaurant terrace on the bankside, spilling out of a huge refurbished warehouse across the way from the Rendezvous de la Marine. In front of huge movie quotes – 'Tomorrow is another day', 'Phone home' and 'Rosebud' – one may sit and indulge in passable

terrines and veal standards as the barges, roller skaters and cyclists pass you by. Menus at €14 (90FF) and €22 (149FF) (including movie), à la carte nearer €30 (200FF). Service patchy.

Reveille du 10ème 35 rue du Château d'Eau, 75010; tel: 01 42 41 77 59

M̄ *Chateau-d'Eau;* Ē *Métro 4 to Château-d'Eau. Walk east on rue du Château-d'Eau to the rue fbg St-Martin.*

Amongst my favourite cheap and cheerful corners of Paris, with its *casbah* of shopping streets, is the area below Gare de l'Est. Just beside the local *mairie*, behind the barrels and Versailles tubs of greenery, is a modest bistro serving tripe and sweetmeats, sausages and genuine flavour-packed rustic *pâté*. Many basic specialities from the Auvergne because Monsieur et Madame Vidalenc, like all good bar owners of the quarter once-upon-a-time, hail from the green volcanic region. Daily specials cost around €9–11 (60–70FF) and are served in healthy-sized portions on plain cafétable tops. Eat for around €19 (120FF) and drink for less: a good selection of Beaujolais wines at under €15 (100FF).

Terminus Nord 23 rue de Dunkerque, 75010; tel: 01 42 85 05 15 [4 C4]

M̄ *Gare-du-Nord;* Ē *Opposite the station on the corner of rue de Dunkerque and bd de Denain.*

Now a part of the excellent Flo group (see page 62), the famous station brasserie still has the same mouth-watering display of seafood outside and the brass and aspidistra décor within known to generations of Channel hoppers. Irresistibly reminiscent of a golden age railway dining car, and also known as the Brasserie 1925, this was the first Parisian restaurant I ever visited, and it is still my choice for a farewell meal with chums before catching the Eurostar. Fresh food tastes even better accompanied by tearful farewells. For years I've imagined Noël Coward or Hercule Poirot stepping off the boat train and crossing the road to sit here with friends. A good choice for oysters and mussels and the *soupière d'homard à la Bretonne*. Recently I lunched here with a group of like-minded francophile British writers, and one colleague recalled a house dessert of three pots of *crème brulée*. He waxed lyrical over memories of rose and lavender flavours and was delighted to see the dish on that day's menu. This time he had vanilla, pistachio and caramel – but no complaints. Pay €18 (120–200FF) for a meal.

WHAT TO BUY

Marché St-Quentin 85bis bd Magenta, 75010. [4 C5]

Open Tue–Sat 08.00–13.00, Sun 08.00–13.00, also open some midweek afternoons from 16.00.

M̄ *Gare-du-Nord;* Ē *From the station follow rue de St-Quentin, cross bd Magenta to the market.*

An old-style covered market hall with stalls selling meat, fish, fruit and cheese. No cute packaging for the tourists, just fresh food for local shoppers. Pretty run-down these days, with a number of empty pitches, it still provides the scents and sounds of a French neighbourhood market. Buy patés, cheeses, salamis and fresh fruit for a picnic on the train.

Rue de Paradis [4 B–C5]

M̄ *Poissonière or Château-d'Eau;* Ē *Bus 26 direct to pl Franz Liszt stops outside number 28 rue du Paradis.*

The Baccarat museum (see page 171) may be the last of the original 19th-century factory-warehouses that once lined this street, but still the rue du Paradis remains heaven for tableware junkies. Since the Gare de l'Est provided a direct link with the great glass houses of Lorraine, the street has been the centre of the wholesale china and glass trade. This is where to pick up your dream dinner service at a fraction of the cost charged by the department stores. Some establishments, such as the **Centre International des Arts de la Table**, at number 32 (tel: 01 42 46 50 50), welcome browsers, others are wary of selling direct. Bluffers tend to get away with bargaining with wholesalers. As with the rag-trade dealers north of Les Halles, *chutzpah* can often pay off.

Beyond the Periphérique

It would take just a little over a lifetime to tire of all the diversions and treats that Paris has to offer. Yet beyond the Périphérique, a host of attractions vies for our attention. New RER express lines open each year, bringing the châteaux of the kings and the countryside of the Impressionists within easy reach of the city centre. In summer 2001, the TGV high-speed rail network was upgraded, and now the Mediterranean is only three hours from Paris. So if you are unable to get a table for lunch at your favourite Paris restaurant, you could pop down to Avignon, Aix-en-Provence or Marseille and be back in the capital in time to finish your shopping.

AUVERS-SUR-OISE

Tourist office Manoir des Colombières, rue de la Sansonne, 94430 Auvers-sur-Oise; tel: 01 30 36 10 06

€12.50 (80FF) combined rail ticket and château admission.

Ē *SNCF train from Gare-du-Nord to Pontoise and change for the Creil train to Auvers-sur-Oise.*

Thanks to Van Gogh's celebrated image of the church surrounded by slanting rooftops, and such easily identified sights as Cézanne's home *chez* Docteur Gachet, Auvers-sur-Oise is familiar to anyone who has visited an art gallery. Since Daubigny discovered the town in 1860, Auvers has played host to an impressive artists' colony. Corot and Pissarro were often to be found here and in 1890 Vincent Van Gogh spent his last weeks at the **Auberge Ravoux**, creating around 70 canvases in two months. He and his brother Théo are buried in the local cemetery.

Besides the conventional public transport options, a more evocative opportunity of stepping into these legendary images is offered each spring with special springtime Saturday excursions into the countryside. A chartered steam train leaves Paris' Gare St Lazare for the 35km journey to Auvers. Tickets cost under €60 (400FF) and include free admission to the entertaining *Voyage au Pays des Impressionistes* show at **Château d'Auvers**, which evokes the life and works of the great artists (tel: 01 34 48 48 50). Other attractions include the Auberge Ravoux, still a working café-restaurant, where Van Gogh's room has been preserved just as he left it, Daubigny's studio and the celebrated Maison de l'Absinthe, devoted to the illicit tipple of the talented.

Auberge Ravoux 52 rue du Gal de Gaulle, 94430; tel: 01 34 48 05 47
Open Tue–Sun 10.00–18.00.

Château d'Auvers Rue de Léry, 94430; tel: 01 34 48 48 48; web: www.impressionist-auvers.com
Open Apr–Sep 10.30–18.00, Oct.Mar 10.30–16.30.

DISNEYLAND PARIS

Marne-La-Vallé, 77700 Chessy; tel: 01 60 30 20 00 (France); tel: 0870 606 6800 (UK); www.disneylandparis.com
€26–351 (70–236FF) one-day ticket (also available from Gare du Nord métro station).
Ē *RER to Châtelet-Les-Halles then RER A to Marne-La-Vallée-Chessy. Check indicator board at Châtelet.*
Disneyland Paris is much more fun than EuroDisney, since the theme park made the decision to celebrate its European traditions alongside the Norman Rockwell American dream. In its opening year, the park had pretended Paris did not exist, and imposed stateside rules on local visitors. Now life is more laid back, with Dickensian Christmas shows, wine served in restaurants and staff that sometimes pout, sulk or smoke. Parisians come for the bars, diners, Cadillacs and clubs of the free-to-enter Disney Village outside the park gate, or buy cheap summer night-passes to visit Disneyland in the evenings when the kids have gone home. Fewer queues and a super atmosphere as adults ride the Thunder Mountain bone shaker after dark. The park has enjoyable floor shows, afternoon and evening parades and queue-buster tickets to eliminate time spent standing in line. The Honey I Shrunk the Audience experience suits those of us too nervous to risk the Space Mountain pitch-black roller coaster.

Everyone knows that Disneyland is around 40 minutes from central Paris on the RER, but Lille Europe is only 20 minutes further away by TGV, and a direct Thalys service from Brussels Gare du Midi takes just 90 minutes. RER, TGV and Thalys arrive at the same station, Marne-La-Vallée-Chessy, as does a regular direct Eurostar service from London. On-site accommodation is spread around a range of hotels. I have stayed at three of them. Best and priciest is the pink palace Disneyland Hôtel over the gates of the park itself. Low-budget options include the Hôtel Cheyenne, set out like a set from a Hollywood Western (good fun), and the Hôtel Santa Fe, with its remarkably slow, but relentlessly smiling, reception service and dreary décor.

MONT ST MICHEL

Formules Bretagne 203 bd St Germain, 75006; tel: 01 53 63 11 53; web: www.brittanytourism.com
See Mont St Michel from Paris. The famous abbey, Brittany's Emerald Coast, the medieval town of Dinan and the ramparts of the pirate port of St Malo now join the Eiffel Tower and the Louvre as must-see sights during a holiday in Paris. Dinan is a charming old walled town on the river Rance. Buy antiques along the 15th-century rue de Jerzual. In good weather walk the ramparts and take in the views from the Promenade de la Duchesse Anne. On rainy days step inside the St Sauveur church, which holds the heart of Bertrand de Guesclin who fought a duel with Thomas of Canterbury in Dinan's main square in 1357. Mont St Michel, with its monastery that appears to rise from the sea on misty mornings, has been the symbol of France since before the Eiffel Tower was a twinkle in an engineer's toolbox. A day-trip by TGV and minibus to Brittany and the Mont takes in these delights for €152 (995FF). Book before 15.00 on the eve of your departure to catch the 07.35 train from Gare Montparnasse and be back in the capital within 12 hours.

ST-DENIS

Tourist office tel: 01 55 87 08 70; web: www.ville-saint-denis.fr
M̄ *St-Denis, Basilique-St-Denis, St-Denis-Porte-de-Paris or Stade-de-France-St-Denis;*
Ē *RER D to St-Denis.*

PARK ASTÉRIX: MORE EURO THAN DISNEY

It's a big world after all. Just two thousand years and 30 miles from Disneyland is Paris' other theme park. Home-grown and far more Euro than Disney, Parc Astérix is officially based on an eponymous domestic comic book.

For the uninitiated, *Astérix* strips occupy the place in the hearts of France that would in other lands belong to Garfield or Doonesbury. The tales of the little Gaul fighting against the might of the Roman Empire weave a tapestry of Latin puns, satire and social observation that is closer to *The Simpsons'* Springfield than Uncle Walt's Main Street. The park's reputation could lead one to assume that this might be too much of an in joke for an outsider. Wrong! Just as one may happily spend a weekend in Disneyland without being forcibly comforted by a walking pyjama case with outsized ears, so there is much more to Parc Asterix than its eponymous hero. If you tune into history on the irony FM wavelength, you get the whole *schtick*. Ancient Gaul, Rome and Greece are represented with rides and sensations; the whitewater ride across the Styx is my favourite, others opt for the Ben-Hurly-burly of the Chariot Race.

Although much of the action is set around 50BC, there are plenty more centuries than centurions on the menu. Acrobats and tumblers play the big top; dolphins and sea-lions back-flip for sprats in the Seaworld tradition. As well as the obligatory 3D movie theatre, a high-tech magic-show seamlessly blends live legerdemain with state-of-the-art big-screen trickery.

Like its imported neighbour the place is divided into zones. But zoned by historical period. Pick your own epoch and pass under battlements to find d'Artagnan and the musketeers buckling swash against dastardly villains with appropriate Errol Flynnery. See classic marionettes retelling the fables of La Fontaine. A medieval village includes a musical cloister and craftsmen's hamlet where children can learn how to build cathedrals at stained-glass and stonemasonry workshops, where blacksmiths display their skills and their wares, and where souvenir shops sell replica panels from the Bayeux Tapestry rather than clip-on mouse ears.

Since for me it's the true flavour of France that supplies more tingles

Now all but swallowed by the capital, the neighbouring city of St Denis is home to the first landmark seen by arriving Eurostar passengers. The **Stade de France** was built for the soccer World Cup, and is one of many sights. France's football coronation as world champions was appropriate in the city of the kings. The **Cathedral-Basilica** of St Denis is the last resting place of 70 kings and other royals. Marie-Antoinette's body was moved here from the **Chapelle Expiatoire** (see page 42). The gothic church, built and restored by the men responsible for Notre Dame de Paris, has a spectacular collection of mediaeval and Renaissance sculpture. The city's **Museum of Art and History** is based in a Carmelite

than any white-knuckle ride, I could spend an entire afternoon in the reconstruction of 19th- and early 20th-century Paris. A gigantic dolls' house of Victorian automata featuring Offenbach, Lautrec, Degas and Gounod is a delightful tableau of Bohemian life. A cinema screens continuous film of the great singers and its floor-show recreates the world of the Guinguette and music hall with just one accordionist and a single gutsy Piaf-style chanteuse belting out classic *chansons*.

For larger-scale, bigger-budget drama, France's answer to Florida's studio tours offers a splendid live action re-enactment of a great chase movie with massive set-piece stunts including the full-scale destruction of an ocean liner, train, car, several motor bikes and the entire port of Le Havre!

Kids love it too. For purely avuncular and professional research purposes, my sister lent me one of her sons. At the time Ben was six (but his critical faculties should be calculated in dog-years which rates his opinions at around 40-something). We put Astérix to the Ben-test on a rainy day in October, and he gave thumbs up to the rides, the face-painting, the shows and the restaurants.

Best of all for Ben (apart from the stuntmen) was the family-friendly hotel Les Trois Hiboux, a cluster of 'tree-houses' in the woods with each room boasting a hideaway children's annexe cunningly separated from the parental sleeping area and a conveniently hewn log in the bathroom to let little people see over the basin at toothbrush time.

Do not expect to see all that Astérix has to offer, any more than you could cram Disneyland into the combined attention span of a child and budget of an adult. But there is nothing like knowing that, smaller than a certain Magic Kingdom in a land far far beyond the ringroad, it's a great big world after all.

Parc Astérix Tel: 08 36 68 30 10; www.parcasterix.fr
Open Apr–Aug 10.00–18.00 (09.30–19.00 school holidays and weekends).
Sep–mid-Oct, Wed, Sat, Sun, only. Including transport from Paris €34
(219FF), otherwise €28 (185FF) for 1 day or €60 (390FF) per year. Hôtel
packages from €97 (635FF) per person.
Ē RER B to Roissy Aéroport Charles-de-Gaulle 1. Then take Parc Astérix shuttle
bus service.

convent, once home to Louise de France, sister of Louis XVI. In spring, St-Denis hosts major jazz and film festivals. The St-Denis tourist office offers a package combining a visit to the basilica, a three-course lunch, and a tour of the stadium with its various exhibitions, all for under €45 (290FF). **Marques Avenue** (tel: 01 48 09 04 05) is a discount shopping mall with plenty of high-street branded clothing sold at factory outlet prices at 9 quai du Châtelier, on the Ile St-Denis (bus 166 from Porte de Clignancourt métro). St-Denis is served by three métro and RER lines and is just minutes from Gare du Nord. A modern tramway runs through the city, connecting most sights and attractions.

VERSAILLES

Tel: 01 30 83 78 00
Open summer 09.00–18.30, winter 09.00–17.30, closed Mon and holidays.
Average €7 (45FF), prices may vary according to date and scope of visit.
RER Versailles-Rive-Gauche; E̅ *RER B to St Michel-Notre-Dame then RER C to Versailles-Rive-Gauche. Check indicator board on the platform. Follow signposts to the château.*

Impossible to see everything in a day, so aim to visit the principal apartments and grounds. In the first-floor state apartments, the king's rooms line one wing and the queen's suite the other. They are linked by Mansart's magnificent Hall of Mirrors, with its unrivalled view over the great perspective of fountains and waterways. In 1919 the Treaty of Versailles was signed here. Incredibly, despite the grandeur, Louis XIV's 546-hectare estate and 740m palace manages to retain many human touches, such as the private passageways linking the royal bedrooms. In a daily ceremony, known as the *Levée*, the king would officially 'wake' in front of courtiers. Any upright citizen with the wherewithal to buy a smart hat from the hawkers at the gate could be granted the right to watch the royal wash and brush up. But that was nothing compared to the indignity faced by the queens who had to undergo the humiliation of childbirth as a spectator sport. The mantelpiece in Marie-Antoinette's bedroom still bears scars of a public scramble for the best view of the breaking of the waters royal. For a glimpse of life on the other side of the bedclothes, take a guided tour of Madame du Barry's rooms, daily at 14.00. Try to see the opera house, featured in the film *Dangerous Liaisons,* and the chapel. The best way to see the grounds is by hiring a bicycle or boat on site. Across the park are two smaller palaces, the Grand Trianon and Petit Trianon, and Marie-Antoinette's model farm, the Hamau. Few visitors discover the royal kitchen garden, with espaliered fruit trees and long-forgotten vegetable varieties. The Potager du Roi adjoining the estate is now the national agricultural college, and a charming contrast to the splendour of the fountains and *parterres* next door.

Entertainment

MUSIC

It is impossible to visit Paris without a musical soundtrack. The rumble of the drums in the métro, the soulful saxophone from a Left Bank doorway on a misty rainy night, the student cellist in front of a sunny summer café: the sounds of the city change with every mood swing.

The buskers on public transport are now part of folk legend. These days they have to compete with officially sanctioned professionals. The RATP stages concerts in its vast interchange halls: one month a tribute to Jacques Brel, the next a season of baroque chamber music.

Midsummer's Eve is *Fête de la Musique* – when the city eschews sleep on the weekend closest to June 21 and a party spirit takes over street corners and railway termini. Walk home from a free concert of rai, reggae or rock, then dance with a grandmother on the cobbles outside a backstreet café.

Throughout the summer, 20 parks present free jazz. The biggest names in the business play at the Gazebo of the Parc Floral in the Bois de Vincennes. Historic buildings become makeshift concert halls, with inexpensive classical recitals at the Sorbonne, and a constant stream of Chopin at the Parc de la Bagatelle's Orangerie and the Musée de la Vie Romantique. Once summer is over, Chopin makes way for winter-warming programmes of Bach and Vivaldi in the city's churches. Notre Dame and the **Cluny museum** host concerts all year round.

Opera and ballet are at home in the two opera houses. But operetta has made a comeback in recent years. The great theatrical showman Jérome Savary has revived the **Opéra Comique** on the Grands Boulevards and the **Opéra Péniche** presents chamber performances in a floating theatre on the canals.

The **Théâtre du Châtelet** has re-opened for business, with its stimulating and varied programmes of opera, dance, Broadway shows (with surtitles) and conventional concerts. The **auditoria of the Louvre** and **Bibliothèque Nationale** are the newest additions to the concert-hall circuit.

Jazz has been an essentially Parisian entertainment since the 1920s, and many of the old favourite clubs such as the **Duc des Lombards** still pack in the punters late into the night. The **Caveau de la Huchette** in the Latin Quarter celebrates with more of a swing style than before, and the mood continues at the legendary **Club Lionel Hampton**. If you arrive in town on a late Eurostar, and fancy chilling to mellower sounds, make your way from Gare du Nord to the rue des Pétites-Ecuries. **New Morning** has been home to the great blues singers and jazzmen for years, and is guaranteed to set the tone for a great weekend.

Rock stars tend to play stadia these days, and you can always buy tickets from FNAC for these 'events' (see page 54). But many still take to the hallowed stage of **Olympia**, the Carnegie Hall or London Palladium of Paris. If your name was Sinatra, Aznavour or Piaf, you played Olympia.

Since most of the golden-age performers are long gone, find their spirit in the smaller shrines to chanson. For years **Le Piano Zinc** in the Marais was the cellar bar that kept faith with the songs of the past. Now that the Bastille and Marais belong to *Génération Cool*, *La Java Bleu* is sung in the bars and dance halls of Belleville. At **Le Pataquès**, they take their nostalgia neat. Old songs, new songs, ethnic sounds and blue songs merge in the cellar of the **Sentier des Halles**.

To be honest, the best music refuses to be pigeonholed. In Paris, you hear a sound, you follow the sound: into a park, into a bar, down some stairs and into the night.

Classical venues

Auditorium du Louvre Pyramide, Cour Napoléon, 75001; tel: 01 40 20 51 86 Sep-Jun. [3 K7]
M̄ *Palais-Royal-Musée-du-Louvre;* Ē *RER to Châtelet-Les-Halles then métro 1 to Palais-Royal-Musée-du-Louvre.*

Bibliothèque Nationale de France quai François-Mauriac, 75013; tel: 01 53 79 40 45 [8 E5]
M̄ *Bibliothèque;* Ē *RER E to Haussmann-St-Lazare then métro 14 to Bibliothèque.*

Cluny Musée National du Moyen Age (see page 129) [8 A3]

Châtelet Théâtre Musical de Paris 2 rue Edouard Colonne 75001; tel: 01 40 28 28 40 [4 B8]
M̄ *Châtelet;* Ē *RER to Châtelet-Les-Halles. Exit av Victoria-Châtelet*

Cité de la Musique (see page 171) [5 G3]

Opéra Comique Salle Favart, pl Boïeldieu, 75002; tel: 01 42 44 45 40 [4 A6]
M̄ *Richelieu-Drouot;* Ē *Métro 4 to Strasbourg-St-Denis, then lines 8 or 9 to Richelieu-Drouot. Take rue Favart.*

Opéra Bastille (see page 95) [8 E2]

Opéra Garnier (see page 61) [3 K6]
Péniche Opéra opposite 42 quai de la Loire, 75019
M̄ *Jaurès;* Ē *Métro 5 to Jaurès.*

Jazz venues

Caveau de la Huchette 5 rue de la Huchette, 75005; tel: 01 43 26 65 05 [8 B2]
M̄ *St-Michel;* Ē *RER B to St Michel-Notre Dame.*

Duc des Lombards 42 rue des Lombards, 75001; tel: 01 42 33 22 88 [4 B7]
M̄ *Les-Halles.*

Lionel Hampton Jazz Club Le Méridien Etoile, 81 bd Gouvion-St-Cyr, 75017; tel: 01 40 68 30 42 [2 D4]
M̄ *Porte-Maillot;* Ē *RER to Châtelet-Les-Halles then métro 1 to Porte-Maillot.*

WHAT MAKES A PARISIAN MUSICAL?

The night that Ted Turner confided to the cameras of CNN, BBC, ABC, NBC and Rai Uno that getting into bed with *America-On-Line* was the biggest thrill of his life since losing his virginity, veteran burn-feeler Jane Fonda announced her return to Hollywood for a cameo role in the remake of *Barbarella*. I went to see a musical and found no problem in suspending disbelief in the tale of a media tycoon who marries the last great cinema sex symbol, who in turn bids farewell to the silver screen in order to help her husband become leader of the Western world. But then the classic rock musical *Starmania*, which first burst upon the stage in 1978 and has returned to Paris every couple of years since then, still manages to tingle all the right nerves.

Whereas *Les Misérables* was never as successful in its home town as abroad, the French adore Michel Berger and Luc Plamondon. Berger more or less invented crossover rock-theatre years before Elton John made the leap from the charts to the dress circle. Lyricist Plamondon is a folk poet – *Starmania*'s *Blues du Businessman* a shard of raw truth and simplicity that cuts to the soul of the listener.

Starmania is typical of successful French shows, less a sung-through drama than a concept album live on stage. No wonder that its songs have provided hits for Céline Dion, Cyndi Lauper and Tom Jones. Somehow, in true Paris fashion, shows like this manage to raise strong moral issues. The tycoon's presidential campaign and conflict with anarchists living in the underbelly of Monopolis City was in 1978 a bleak vision of the future.

Plamondon himself said, 'I have written today's sentiments projected on tomorrow's world.' It has not dated, as so much pop-political science-fiction crumbles to cringe, because audiences now recognise the world on stage. Rolling news is presented by a computer and face-to-face interviews conducted by a bland blonde shepherdess whose in-depth questioning of the leader of a terrorist movement includes probing as to his favourite pop song and star sign. We are not surprised when, urged on by the wide-screen glamour of a screen goddess, the world votes for a man named Zero, and we ache when we learn 'The World Is Stone'.

Away from the dumbing-down TV studios we are shown a world of lust, violence and street fighting in the Underground Café and society nightclub 'Naziland'. Despite the leather straps and shaven heads of the lost souls, these new age rebels seem strangely emasculated. At the dawn of a new century our future is castrated; sex is now a statement and a currency. Virility, potency, fecundity, fertility are in the world of *Starmania* mere lifestyle accessories and commodities, extraneous options available to the world on cable… or even 'Monopolis On Line'.

New Morning 7–9 rue des Pétites-Ecuries, 75010; tel: 01 45 23 51 41 [4 B5]
M̲ *Château-d'Eau;* E̲ *Métro 4 to Château-d'Eau. Go west on rue Château d'Eau to rue des Petites-Ecuries.*

Other venues
Olympia 28 bd des Capucines, 75009; tel: 01 55 27 10 00 [3 J6]
M̲ *Opéra;* E̲ *RER to Châtelet-Les-Halles then RER C to Auber.*

Le Pataquès 8 rue Jouye-Rouve, 75020; tel: 01 40 33 27 47 [5 F5]
Open Tue–Sun
M̲ *Pyrénées;* E̲ *Métro 5 to République, then line 11 to Pyrénées. West on rue Belleville then left to rue Jouye-Rouve.*

Sentier des Halles 50 rue d'Aboukir, 75002; tel: 01 42 61 89 96 [4 B6]
Open Mon–Sat; closed Aug.
M̲ *Sentier;* E̲ *Métro 4 to Réamur-Sébastopol, then line 3 to Sentier.*

THEATRE
Forget the floorshows and the feathers, and leave aside images of stuffed shirts and powdered wigs. Between the worlds of the cancan and the Comédie Française is one of the most vibrant and exciting theatre scenes in Europe. Molière, Feydeau and Marivaux can still be relied upon at the traditional playhouses, just as Shakespeare provides the staple entertainment at London's subsidised theatres. But the commercial scene has as many original takes on the classics as challenging new works.

Paris adores Shakespeare. Nowhere else have I even seen two rival commercial productions of *King John* in the same street. And French directors bring refreshingly original and daring interpretations to these classics. Audiences at a fabulously feminist *Taming of the Shrew* in the grounds of Versailles cheered, shrieked and stamped through the evening. Jérome Savary brought terrifyingly realistic storms at sea to his *Twelfth Night* at Chaillot (complete with live seagulls flying over the audience), and a cold war *Romeo and Juliet* sent thrills through a *café-théâtre* audience at Beaubourg.

The national theatres of **Odéon**, **la Colline** and **Chaillot** feature established writers from the classics to Beckett, and the **Comédie Française** has its new studio theatre in the **Carrousel du Louvre** (see page 39), with a Théâtrothèque video library of great performances. The grandfather of stage directors is Britain's Peter Brook whose **Bouffes du Nord** remains the benchmark of challenging work.

The inventive directors do not have to concentrate on theatre's back catalogue. World theatre matters here, with works by many leading international contemporary writers staged every week. If a performance in French seems a little daunting, then either choose a play you already know, or catch an English or bilingual production. Listing magazines usually detail up to six such presentations each week. Perhaps an English version of local hit comedies like *Art* or *Le Diner des Cons* ('The Dinner Game') or a classic by Miller, Pinter or Wilde. Broadway musicals are treated like opera with performances in English, surtitled in French, at Châtelet. Otherwise French versions of such shows as *Cats* or *Peter Pan* are staged at the **Mogador** or

Casino de Paris. New French musicals are always worth catching (see feature page 185).

Most boulevard theatres can be relied upon to provide rousing comedies for a traditional audience. Newer venues around town, such as the Cartoucherie, in the Bois de Vincennes, with five theatres within a former ammunition factory, pump new blood into the scene.

Small fringe shows can be fun (but you will need to be comfortable with the language to appreciate the in-your-face comedy), and revue still thrives here, with troupes such as Les Amuse Girls (a pun) serving musical wit in confined spaces. *Café-théâtre* in the Marais is a hit-and-miss affair, but never forget that Gerard Dépardieu was discovered at the Café de la Gare.

Most theatres close on Monday, but offer Sunday matinees. Prices are much cheaper than New York, and half-price same-day tickets are sold from midday at a booth in place Madeleine. Most seats (tickets) are available at FNAC (see page 187). As with the cinemas, usherettes and programme sellers receive no wages, so do tip 50 cents (2–5FF) when shown to your seats.

There are at least 50 theatres and *café-théâtres* in central Paris. Details and addresses may be found in the listing magazines, *Pariscope* and *l'Officiel des Spectacles*, on sale every Tuesday, or Wednesday's *Le Figaro*. *Pariscope* features an English-language digest, published by Britain's *Time Out* magazine.

Bouffes du Nord 37bis bd de la Chapelle, 75010; tel: 01 46 07 34 50 [4 C4]
M̄ *La-Chapelle;* Ē *Bus 65 to Cail-Demarquay, then walk east a few yards along the boulevard.*

Casino de Paris 16 rue Clichy, 75009; tel: 01 49 95 99 99 [3 K5]
M̄ *Trinité;* Ē *Métro 4 to Marcadet-Poissonniers, then line 12 to Trinité.*

Comédie Française (Salle Richelieu) 1 pl Colette, 75001; tel: 01 44 58 15 15; web: www.comedie-francaise.fr [3 K7] **Studio-Théâtre Carrousel du Louvre** Tel: 01 44 58 98 58
M̄ *Palais-Royal-Musée-du-Louvre;* Ē *RER to Châtelet-Les-Halles then métro 1 to Palais-Royal-Musée-du-Louvre.*

Guichet-Montparnasse 15 rue du Maine, 75014; tel: 01 43 27 88 61 [7 J4]
M̄ *Montparnasse-Bienvenüe;* Ē *Métro 4 to Montparnasse-Bienvenüe.*

Odéon-Théâtre de L'Europe 1 pl de l'Odéon, 75006; tel: 01 44 41 36 36 [8 A2]
M̄ *Odéon;* Ē *Métro 4 to Odéon. From carrefour de l'Odéon take rue de l'Odéon.*

Théâtre de la Huchette 23 rue de la Huchette, 75005; tel: 01 43 26 38 99 [8 B2]
M̄ *St-Michel;* Ē *RER B to St Michel-Notre Dame.*

Théâtre Mogador 25 rue Mogador, 75009; tel: 01 53 32 32 00 [3 K5]
M̄ *Trinité;* Ē *Métro 4 to Marcadet-Poissonniers, then line 12 to Trinité.*

Théâtre National de Chaillot Palais de Chaillot, 1 pl du Trocadéro, 75016; tel: 01 53 65 30 00 [2 E7]
M̄ *Trocadéro;* Ē *RER E to Haussmann-St-Lazare then métro 9 to Trocadéro.*

Théâtre National de la Colline 15 rue Malte-Brun, 75020; tel: 01 44 62 52 52 [5 G7]
M̄ *Gambetta;* Ē *Métro 5 to République, then line 3 to Gambetta. rue Malte-Brun crosses the rue Père Lachaise.*

Café-théâtre

Les Blancs Manteaux 15 rue des Blancs Manteaux, 75004; tel: 01 48 87 15 84; web: www.blancsmanteaux.claranet.fr [4 C8]
M̄ *Hôtel-de-Ville;* Ē *RER to Châtelet-Les-Halles then métro 1 to Hôtel-de-Ville. On rue de Rivoli turn left into rue des Archives then third right to rue des Blancs Manteaux.*

Café de la Gare 41 rue du Temple, 75004; tel: 01 42 78 52 51 [4 C8]
M̄ *Rambuteau;* Ē *RER to Châtelet-Les-Halles then métro 11 to Rambuteau. Walk south on rue du Renard taking any street left to rue du Temple.*

Le Point Virgule 7 rue Ste-Croix-de-la-Bretonnerie, 75004; tel: 01 42 78 67 03; web: www.point-virgule.fr [4 C8]
M̄ *Hôtel-de-Ville;* Ē *RER to Châtelet-Les-Halles then métro 1 to Hôtel-de-Ville. On rue de Rivoli turn left into rue des Archives then second right to rue Ste-Croix-de-la-Bretonnerie.*

CINEMA

France has a very special relationship with the cinema. Three hundred films are screened every week in this city where old stars never die and are never allowed to fade away.

Perhaps because France invented the movies, or maybe because the French do not insist on a dividing line between art and entertainment, whatever the reason, film is an essential part of life. Although traditionalists predicted the death of the art houses when the UGC chain launched its €15.50 (98FF) per month unlimited pass for its multiplexes, the truth is, people who love old movies, cult movies, art movies or long movies are not going to be satisfied with the latest Hollywood special effects blockbuster.

So wander through the Left Bank to the **Action** cinemas for Judy Garland, Fred Astaire, Monty Python and Woody Allen. *Rocky Horror* horror teenagers still swear in American and throw rice and water at midnight at the **Galande**. Squeeze into a fleapit miles from anywhere to watch all the Marx Brothers films in one night. Celebrate Marilyn Monroe in a small picture house behind the Etoile. The queues outside the multiplexes on the Champs Elysées and Grands Boulevards want to go to the flicks; everywhere else, they celebrate the *7ème art*.

Every screening is detailed in the weekly magazines, *Pariscope* and *l'Officiel des Spectacles*, on sale every Tuesday. Films on the Left Bank, Les Halles and Champs Elysées tend to be screened in the original language (listed as v.o.); elsewhere they are more likely to be dubbed (v.f.). On Mondays or Wednesdays many cinemas offer around 30% discount.

It is customary to tip the usherette around 50 cents (2–5FF) when she shows you to your seat. If you forget, she will remind you. Loudly.

The future of the cinemathèque and cinema museum is likely to be confirmed in early 2002, but attractions such as **Le Grand Rex** (see page 57) and screenings in museum auditoria continue to provide diversions for film buffs. Paris has a constant programme of film festivals. Spring sees the Paris Film Festival and the International Festival of Women's Cinema. Summer sees open-air screenings at La Villette (see pages 167 and 171).

Of course, Paris is a film star in its own right, with every quarter offering a view familiar from the silver screen, from the Musée d'Orsay's looming hulk, as featured in the films of Orson Welles, to the banks of the Seine seen in *Les*

Misérables and Woody Allen's *Everyone Says 'I Love You'*. The roads from Gare de l'Est to Montmartre featured in a car chase in Disney's *102 Dalmatians* and *Le Pont Neuf* has had more than its fair share of *amants*. To spend your time with like-minded *cinéastes* book into the Hôtel du 7ème Art in the Marais (see page 73).

Action Christine 4 rue Christine, 75006; tel: 01 43 29 11 30 [8 A2]
M̄ *Odéon;* Ē *RER B to St Michel-Notre-Dame. From quai des Grands Augustins turn left on rue des Grands Augustins and right to rue Christine.*

Action Ecoles 23 rue des Ecoles, 75005; tel: 01 43 29 79 89 [8 B3]
M̄ *Cardinal-Lemoine;* Ē *RER B to St Michel-Notre-Dame. Follow signs to Cluny-La-Sorbonne for métro 10 to Cardinal-Lemoine. Rue Monge to rue des Ecoles.*

Le Cinéma des Cinéastes 7 av d'Clichy, 75017; tel: 01 53 42 40 20 [3 J3–4]
M̄ *Place-de-Clichy;* Ē *Métro 4 to Barbès-Rochechouart, then line 2 to Place-de-Clichy.*

Gaumont Grand Ecran Italie 30 pl d'Italie, 75013; tel: 08 36 68 75 13
M̄ *Place-d'Italie;* Ē *Métro 5 to Place-d'Italie.*

La Géode (see La Villette page 171) [5 G2]

Grand Action 5 rue des Ecoles, 75005; tel: 01 43 29 44 40 [8 B3]
M̄ *Cardinal-Lemoine;* Ē *RER B to St Michel-Notre-Dame. Follow signs to Cluny-La-Sorbonne for métro 10 to Cardinal-Lemoine. From rue Cardinal Lemoine turn left into rue des Ecoles.*

Le Grand Rex (see page 57) [4 B6]

Studio Galande 42 rue Galande, 75005; tel: 01 43 26 94 08 [8 B2]
M̄ *St-Michel;* Ē *RER B to St-Michel-Notre-Dame. From rue de Petit Pont, bear left into rue Galande.*

FLOORSHOWS

Do not come to the big cabaret floorshows looking for the Paris of Lautrec, La Goulue or Nicole Kidman. Come instead for Vegas and glamour. Join the Japanese and German business guests enjoying the special effects at the **Lido** show: the set pieces always threaten to upstage the fabulous Bluebell Girls. Recent treats on stage have included volcanoes, waterfalls, helicopters and elephants. The new show *C'est Magique* features an aerial ballet, jazzier, showier routines and a dinner menu designed by the great chef Paul Bocuse. The headline attraction is, as ever, the girls. Whatever George Lucas-style miracle occurs on stage, the eyes, teeth and top-to-toe foundation listen patiently in a style that in the real world was long ago put into storage with Liberace's piano. Ritzy, glitzy and more.

If the Lido is slick, the **Moulin Rouge** is *schtick*. Even the name of the troupe, Les Doriss Girls, has a campy ring to it. And the tableaux are always outrageously, gloriously hackneyed. I love it. The last show, *Formidable*, reduced me to sobs of joy with its unintentionally hilarious neo-macho characters, a crocodile wrestler and the two creaking stalwarts from the corps de ballet of yesteryear who ricked their arthritic way through a *pas de deux*. We applauded on the grounds that anything that painful must have been art. I bought the cassette and the CD to make me smile when hoovering. Factored to the Max, the showgirls and boys of the new show *Féerie* now present brightly coloured routines set in the worlds of circus, pirates and the fabulous cancan.

Lido de Paris 116bis av des Champs Elysées, 75008; tel: 01 40 76 56 10; web: www.lido.fr [3 F5]
Dinner 20.00, show 22.00, 24.00 (occasional lower-priced lunch-matinées at 13.00). Dinner and show €124.50–155 (815–1,015FF), champagne and show €71–85.50 (460–560FF) lower-priced midweek late show only (including two drinks) €59 (385FF), matinée €70–109 (460–715FF).
M̄ *George-V;* Ē̄ *RER to Châtelet-Les-Halles then métro 1 to George-V.*

Moulin Rouge 82 bd de Clichy, 76018; tel: 01 53 09 82 82; web: www.moulin-rouge.com [3 K4]
Dinner 19.00, show 21.00 23.00. Dinner and show €120–150 (790–990FF), champagne and show €76–86 (500–560FF).
M̄ *Blanche;* Ē̄ *Métro 4 to Barbès-Rochechouart, then line 2 to Blanche.*

NIGHTLIFE

'Nighttime's the right time for just reminiscing'. So sung Peggy Lee, and if your idea of a night out in Paris involves two heads together in a candle-lit cellar, then stay in the blues and jazz clubs until the wee small hours. Should you fancy a dance without losing the *intime* mood, try the music barges on the Seine or the *guinguettes* on the Marne (see page 100). The **Batofar** floating lighthouse is the favourite mooring for the party crowd. Of course you could try a salsa or tango at **La Coupole** in Montparnasse (see page 112).

If you are in the mood for full-on nightclubbing, first spend a day doing some serious shopping, for in the truly fashionable venues image is everything. Start your night as you intend to live it. To mingle with supermodels and the very well-heeled, hang out at the **Hôtel Costes bar** (see page 31) or the **Buddha Bar** between the Madeleine and Concorde. Shining through the evocative shadow, the only thing more blinding than the famous golden Buddha is the combined heliographic dazzle of the platinum credit cards waved by the punters, dining, wining or just being. If table bopping is your thing, consider **Man Ray**, or perhaps the **Alcazar** (see page 131), with its mezzanine DJ zone open Wed–Sun, 22.00–02.00. To find yourself on the city's coolest, sharpest cutting edge, take to the trendiest streets where individual addresses are always too new and too transient to make it into print: follow the Bastille in-crowds to rue Oberkampf for the latest music sounds at **Underworld Café** or laid-back street poets at **Café Charbon**, or go with the flow along the banks of the Canal du Midi (see page 167). The gay rendezvous of the Marais are clustered around the rues des Archives, Vieille du Temple, St Croix de La Bretonnerie and their tributaries. Meanwhile, boys and girls for whom sexuality is not an issue tend to flirt along the rues des Lombards and la Verrerie between the lively **Banana Café** in Les Halles and the ultra-designed **Etoile Manquante** in rue Vieille du Temple (see page 67)

At **Les Bains**, a converted bathhouse that has lorded it over the scene for years, if you've not appeared on the cover of *Vogue*, you should at least carry signed witness statements that you've slept with someone who has appeared on the cover of *Vogue*. One way to get past the snooty door staff is to make a reservation at the club's pricey restaurant. Once inside, it is wall-to-wall supermodels and ear-to-ear House. Cool cats hang out at **L'Enfer.**

Fortunately, since it was the UK club scene that saved Paris venues from disappearing into revived sounds of the seventies long before it became retro-hip, a British accent is a passport into most happening venues. If you have to use French then imitate the vowels of Michael Caine. Speak English, dress right and you should make it past the bouncers. If you don't have the right wardrobe, play safe, wear black. And don't even think of arriving much before 02.00.

Since the heady days of Le Boy and Le Palace, the main club scene on dry land has moved to **Le Queen** on the Champs Elysées and **Rex Club** on the boulevards. The former was once just another gay club, but now is simply a place where everyone goes simply to be seen. The crew from Trade in London visit at least once each month, although on Monday and Thursday the place is more popular with kids from the suburbs bopping to seventies sounds. If you are truly accepted on the scene the barman at the **Rex Club** will not only know your name, he will also know your drink. The best techno night in Paris every Friday and one-nighters from Europe's hottest DJs.

Those who prefer partying to posing go to raves, known these days as *Teknivales*, or the more relaxed clubs around Pigalle and Clichy. Mainly one-off or one-night events, some, such as the **Bus Palladium**, even offer free admission for women. The **Locomotive** has been a stalwart of the scene for years. Everyone, gay or straight, turns up at the former strip club **Folies Pigalle** at some time over the weekend. Especially the legendary multi-ethnic BBB tea dance. BBB stands for 'Blancs, Blacks, Beurres'. A real sense of world music, representing the new cultures of Paris, emanates from the decks at **Le Gibus** and **Le Divan du Monde**. Serious clubbers make sure that they are seen at the afters clubs (see page 192) to prove their stamina.

If all this sounds a bit daunting, opt for a super-sophisticated bop at the **Man Ray** bar (midweek only), where the Champs Elysées set would never dream of dancing round their Gucci and Vuitton accessories.

Admission charges tend to float around €7 (45FF) at the less glamorous venues, upwards of €15 (100FF) at the hot spots. Sometimes admission prices include a first drink. Be warned: bars at French nightclubs charge a small fortune. Budget large sums if you are entertaining a guest. It is often cheaper to pay for a bottle of whisky or champagne than pay for two or three rounds of shorts.

Check out the club scene before you leave at the website www.novaplanet.com, and pick up flyers for clubs in clothes shops and bars around Bastille, Les Halles, rues Tiquetonne and Keller.

Les Bains 7 rue du Bourg-l'Abbé, 75003; tel: 01 48 87 01 80 [4 B7] M̄ *Etienne-Marcel.*

La Balajo (see page 95) [8 E2]

Banana Café 13 rue de la Ferronnerie, 75001; tel: 01 42 33 35 31 [4 B7] Open 16.30–dawn M̄ *Châtelet-Les-Halles*

Batofar 11 quai François-Mauriac, 75013; tel: 01 56 29 10 00 [8 E5] M̄ *Bibliothèque.*

Bus Palladium 6 rue Fontaine, 75009; tel: 01 53 21 07 33 [3 K4] M̄ *Pigalle.*

Buddha Bar 8 rue Boissy d'Anglas, 75008; tel: 01 53 05 90 00 [3 J6]
Open Mon–Sat 19.30–00.15. €42 (275FF)
M̄ *Madeleine.*

Cafe Charbon 109 rue Oberkampf, 75011; tel: 01 43 57 55 13 [4 DE7-F6]
M̄ *Oberkampf.*

Le Divan du Monde 75 rue des Martyrs, 75018; tel: 01 44 92 77 66 [4 A4]
M̄ *Pigalle.*

L'Enfer 34 Rue de Départ, 75014; tel: 01 42 79 94 94[7 J4]
Open Wed, Thu, Sun 23.30–dawn; Fri, Sat 23.30–12.00. Admission: 100F
M̄ *Montparnasse-Bienvenue;* Ē *Métro 4 to Montparnasse-Bienvenue, exit rue de Départ*

Folies Pigalle 11 pl Pigalle, 75009; tel: 01 48 78 25 26 [4 A4]
M̄ *Pigalle.*

Le Gibus 18 rue du Fbg-du-Temple, 75011; tel: 01 47 00 78 88 [4 D6]
M̄ *République.*

La Locomotive 90 bd de Clichy, 75018; tel: 08 36 69 69 28 [3 K4]
M̄ *Blanche.*

Man Ray 34 rue Marbeuf, 75008; tel: 01 56 88 36 36 [3 G6]
Open Mon–Thu 19.00–02.00.
M̄ *Franklin-D-Roosevelt.*

Le Queen 102 av des Champs-Elysées, 75008; tel: 01 53 89 08 90 [3 F6]
M̄ *George-V.*

Rex Club 5 bd Poissonnière, 75002; tel: 01 42 36 28 83 [4 B6]
M̄ *Bonne-Nouvelle.*

Underworld Café 25 rue Oberkampf, 75011; tel: 01 48 06 35 36 [4 DE7–F6]
M̄ *Oberkampf*

THE MORNING AFTER

At weekends, the nineties phenomenon of the 'Afters' club party is still going strong. New DJs and their teams take over the top venues around dawn for a full morning's chill-out music session. **Posh** at **Folies Pigalle** is a favourite with stars and the still-gorgeous tend to go to hell on Sunday mornings for the afters club at **l'Enfer**, underneath the Tour Montparnasse. Great music, lasers and atmosphere. The *Kwality* afters session on and below decks at the **Batofar** is the undisputed favourite with party people and music industry types, from 06.00 until 14.00 on a Sunday. Every fortnight the boat extends the chill-out zone well into the afternoon with a 'cakes and milk' party. **Underworld Café**, on rue Oberkampf, sees post-party-animals trading vinyl and other cool collectibles at the Sunday swap meet. Midweek, a more gentle nudge along your own evolutionary scale may be enjoyed on Tuesdays and summer Fridays. Visit the free catwalk shows at Printemps and Galeries Lafayette (see page 67) to let a constant parade of couture ease your vision from furred and blurred to normality. Let the incomparable blend of glamour and common sense lead you towards the light of the real world. I well remember the reaction of the Yorkshire mother and daughter at the next table, in town to choose the *trousseau*. As the final wedding dress took to the runway (slashed satin, slit skirt, *décolleté* to the navel and no visible signs of support), the verdict came with a snort, 'I give that marriage three months'!

Part Three

Lille

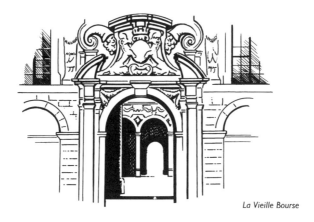

La Vieille Bourse

Introduction

When French mayors go to French Mayor School, they all learn several key buzzwords. By far the most popular is the phrase *'Carrefour de l'Europe'*. The crossroads of Europe. The crossroads of the silk route, the wine route, the tin route, even, I presume, the beetroot route. Almost every town in the country claims to have been, at some stage in its history, at the crossroads of Europe. A well-known resort on the Atlantic coast once seized the honour in a triumph of civic pride over orienteering. With so many mayors declaring crossroad status, the historic map of the continent must have resembled a particularly virulent tartan.

Pierre Mauroy, unique amongst his mayoral colleagues, claimed the status as a goal rather than mere heritage. City mayor for 29 years, until handing his flaming torch in 2001 to Martine Aubry, Mauroy was most famously President Mitterand's first Prime Minister. Like Mitterand, Thatcher and Reagan, his was an iron will, and so, when the Channel Tunnel rail link was agreed, Pierre Mauroy persuaded the world that the shortest distance between two points was a right angle. Thus the Eurostar route was swung in an arc to create a new European hub. With a flourish of the presidential and prime ministerial pens, Lille was transformed, Cinderella-like, from depressed centre of a mining district with 40% unemployment, to France's third most powerful financial, commercial and industrial centre.

Politically, Lille may be French, but it was most famously the old capital of Flanders. Perhaps the town's heritage as being variously successively Flemish, Burgundian, Spanish, Dutch, French, German, French, German and French again might have inspired Mayor Mauroy's ambitious vision to create the future of Europe in a town that had long been dismissed as a broken yesterday. Arguing that in an era of Eurostar, Thalys and TGV, geography could no longer be determined by distance but by time. These days, Paris, Brussels, Amsterdam and even London might be legitimately classed as the suburbs.

And so Lille, the best-kept secret in the world, with a population of 170,000, became one of the great capital cities of Europe. She may not be the capital of any nation state, but a morning, weekend or lifetime in her company proves without doubt that Lille is the capital city of life. With its high-flying business community and university campus, Lille is where Europe comes to party. The director of the Opéra de Lille told me how he nips between Germany and Britain to arrange meetings with soloists and musicians during the working day, and how he mixes and matches choruses, soloists and orchestras from around Europe. After all, he argued, the audiences pop over from Cologne, Brittany and Kent; why not the performers?

The opera is not the only lure in town: with the legendary Goyas, Impressionists and Dutch masters at the Palais des Beaux Arts; a national theatre, ballet company and orchestra; not to mention scores of smaller theatres and music venues, Lille can offer the Saturday night sensation seeker as much as any town ten times the size. Serious shopping, from Hermès and Chanel to the flea-market, pulls in bargain hunters and the money-no-object fraternity alike. Good food, great beers, cider and locally distilled *genièvre* are the recipe for a legendary good-natured northern welcome. The recent institution of city centre stewards (recognise them by their yellow sweaters, jackets and caps), whose sole function is to offer help and advice to visitors, is merely the official recognition of a long-time trait. I was not the first stranger to find himself lost in the old town, ask for advice in a bar and be personally escorted by the locals to my destination, with handshakes and good wishes all round.

Perhaps this attitude is born of Lille having discovered the secret of eternal youth. With 150,000 students living either in town and the dormitory suburbs of the campus of Villeneuve d'Asq, 42% of the local population is younger than 25. Every year brings a new influx of first-time residents to be wowed by the city, youngsters from all over France, and from Europe and beyond studying at the business, arts, journalism and engineering faculties. Lille hands over to these same *arrivistes* the responsibility of producing the annual *Ch'ti* guide. The *Ch'ti* (named for the local *patois*) is produced by the business school and is the most comprehensive local directory you will ever find anywhere. Each year a fresh editorial team spends 12 months visiting every establishment in town. Honest, often witty, reviews of every shop, photocopy bureau, bar, club and restaurant in Lille and the metropolitan area, the *Ch'ti* is a veritable bible. Until political correctness set in during the mid-1990s, the guide even rated local red-light streets with details of nearest cash and condom dispensers. Check out the number of 'C' symbols on the stickers in each restaurant window for an indication of the *Ch'ti* rating (C–CCCCC).

As such an international melting pot, it is sometimes easy to forget that Lille is also a real modern-day capital city. It is capital of a metropolitan area that embraces the former manufacturing towns of Roubaix and Tourcoing and urban areas touching the Belgian border. It is also capital of the Nord-Pas de Calais region, with Vimy Ridge, Montreuil, the floating market gardens of St-Omer, the Channel ports and the tunnel only an hour's drive away.

Although the heritage of the region is generously displayed on the tables of Lille, this is also a country of tomorrows, with wonderfully ambitious projects breathing new life into the old mining district. Perhaps no more so than in Lille, where the uncompromisingly modern Euralille stands comfortably next to the Flemish squares and deco shopping streets.

In other cities the grafting of a new high-tech glass and chrome futurescape on to a historical landscape will jar like UPVC double-glazing on a thatched cottage or ill-fitting dentures in a favourite smile. Lille's newest quarter, from the old railway station to the *périphérique* ring road, settles easily by its classical neighbour. Architect Rem Koolhaas was given free rein over the transformation of 173 acres of city centre wasteland reclaimed from the army. His brief, to create a city of the 21st century to greet the high-speed trains.

This new Lille Europe quarter is just one of the many welcomes that Lille showers on its visitors. If the Grand' Place is ever on the verge of a party, Vieux Lille is a portal of times past, the Citadelle and Bois de Boulogne a living legacy of the Sun King, and the marketplaces of Wazemmes and Solférino are the pulse of modern life.

Walk back towards your hotel in the late evening, tripping down the *pavé* of the old town towards the magnificent belfry, passing the illuminated ornate scrollwork and carvings over the shopfronts outside the Opéra. Look across the square to the crystal lights reflecting a hundred diners, families, friends and lovers. Then surrender to temptation and head across to the brasserie tables or jazz cellars to steal another hour or two of the perfect weekend.

Lille, capital of the past and beacon of the future, has found her time. As any self-respecting mayor would say, 'Welcome to the crossroads of Europe'.

BON WEEKEND – BON PRIX

Excellent value for weekend visitors to Lille is the *Bon Weekend en Ville* promotion. Guests staying on a Friday–Saturday or Saturday–Sunday short break may enjoy two nights' accommodation for the price of one at most of the city's hotels. This means that many hotels in the highest price range may yet work out at €38 (250 FF) per person per night for couples, and the budget hotels begin at €12–15 (75–100FF) per person per night. Visitors using the *Bon Weekend* deal also enjoy two-for-the-price-of-one offers on museum admission and the excellent one-hour minibus tour of the city. Stays have to be booked eight days in advance. Lille Tourist Office has details, as well as free copies of *Sortir* events listings magazine, street and transport maps, brochures and English-language advice.

Lille Tourist Office Place Rihour, 59002; tel: 03 20 21 94 21 [14 E4]
Open Mon–Sat 09.30–18.30, Sun, holidays 10.00–12.00, 14.00–17.00.

WHAT TO EAT

On the table, local specialities are a happy blend of the Flemish and northern French styles. Dishes may feature the cheeses of Mont des Cats and Maroilles, genièvre juniper gin, the famous Blanche de Lille white beer and other local brews: Ch'ti, La Goudale and Trois Monts. Waterzoi, on many a menu, is a stew usually of freshwater carp, tench and pike; rabbit may be prepared with prunes; winter warmers include the *hochepot* stew of meats and market garden vegetables, and the inevitable *carbonnade à la Flamande* stewed in beer, onions and brown sugar. And year-round favourite *potjevlesch* is a white meat *terrine*, usually of chicken and rabbit.

To round off the meal, modern chefs make ice-cream and *sorbet* with local flavourings *fleur-de-bière*, gin and the ubiquitous *chicorée*. Traditional desserts include *tarte au sucre* and a local variation of bread-and-butter pudding known as *pain perdu*.

GETTING AROUND

A superb automated métro system ties in with the tramways and buses. One ticket costs around ∈1.20 (7.5FF) and allows you to travel in one direction, changing from métro to tram to bus if necessary. Carnets of ten tickets are better value at ∈10 (65FF), and one-day tickets are available offering unlimited travel for around ∈3.50 (22FF). If you intend to stay around the Grand' Place and Vieux Lille the chances are you will not use much public transport, and may do better buying just the occasional ticket. Should your plans involve trips out to the outlet shopping malls of Roubaix, taking the tram to Tourcoing or Villeneuve d'Asq for the magnificent art collections, and using the métro when going to the Sunday market, a carnet or day card would be better value.

All trams, métro and bus services can be used with the new City pass, providing unlimited access to museums and attractions in Lille and the neighbouring towns, including the planetarium and distillery tour. It also offers discounts on concert, theatre, opera and ballet tickets. The pass costs ∈14.50 (95FF) for one day, ∈26 (165FF) for two days or ∈31 (205FF) for three days, and may be bought at any local tourist office.

The unmanned VAL métro is completely automated, and runs on two ever-expanding lines crossing central Lille and serving the suburbs and metropolitan area. Central métro platforms are sealed off from the tracks by sliding glass doors that open when the train comes to a standstill.

Twin tramways run out to Roubaix and Tourcoing, passing the pretty Parc Barbieux, and are a pleasant alternative to the underground on sunny days. Métro and tram services run from 05.15 to midnight (from 06.20 at weekends). The city bus network covers the areas of the old town that no métro could possibly reach, since so much of Lille is built on land reclaimed from canals and waterways. From the principal bus stops at place des Buisses, alongside Gare Flandres, services fan out to the outlying districts, even crossing the Belgian border. Buses generally run from around 05.30 until 20.30.

In the evening the Clair de Lune bus network meanders through the town centre, Vieux Lille and out to the satellite towns half hourly from approx 21.30 until 00.30. Four routes leave the place des Buisses and a further two depart from place de la République.

Buy tickets from the machine – not forgetting to frank them in the brightly coloured stamping machine at the entrance to the station, tram or bus.

Taxis may be found at clearly marked ranks, and hailed in the street. The main ranks are outside the two railway stations. An excellent way to see the sites in the shortest possible time is to take the one-hour minibus city tour. Buses leave every hour from outside the tourist office on place Rihour. The multilingual audio-visual commentary is first rate. Tickets ∈7 (45FF) from the tourist office.

Vieux Lille

Vieux Lille is a very special place. Looming gables, cobbled streets, intoxicatingly wonderful street names promising golden-lions, hunchbacked cats or freshly minted coins at every turn. Since the principal roads were laid out in sweeping arcs to protect the long forgotten castle on the old castrum, and many other streets were reclaimed from canals, no map will ever satisfactorily convey the geography of the place. The first, second or fifth-time visitor should be prepared to surrender to fate and banish any dreams of shortcuts. Wrong turnings are among the greatest pleasures that Lille has to offer its visitors, with so many entrancing little shops selling antiques, fragrant soaps and sumptuous linens, that every journey brings its own diversions.

From central Lille it seems that all roads lead to the old quarter. The Parc Matisse may be the shortcut from the station, and the Alcide archway on Grand' Place might seem an obvious entrance. However the most comfortable introduction is from the rue de la Bourse by the distinctive belfry on place du Théâtre. A few paces lead to rue de la Grande Chaussée. An iron arm above the corner shop will point you in the right direction. Charles, Comte d'Artagnan, lived at numbers 20 and 26; you can see the old walls from La Botte Chantilly, the shoe shop on the ground floor. Turn right along rue des Chats Bossus and admire the fabulous Breton art deco mosaic frontage of l'Huitrière restaurant. Continue across the place du Lion d'Or to the 17th-century rue de la Monnaie. Named after the royal mint, this is the oldest street and has many of the original traders' emblems above the regimented shopfronts. Like the rue Royale and rue Basse, it wraps around the cathedral, following the line of the moat. Houses of red Armentières brick and white Lezennes stone have doorways adorned with cherubs, cornucopia and wheatsheaves all painstakingly restored in the 1960s.

Rue de la Monnaie links the market square of place du Concert with the main hub of the old town, place du Lion d'Or and the adjacent place Louise de Bettignies. The latter was named for a local heroine, a spy who died at the hands of the Germans in 1915. Number 29 is *the* Demeure Gilles de la Boë, a handsome baroque house dating from 1636 that once overlooked the inland port. Lille's name derives from its original position as an island between the upper and lower Deûle rivers, and the wealth of Vieux Lille comes from the thriving trade between merchants plying the two routes between Paris and the Low Countries.

Furthest from the town centre is the quartier Royale, an elegant residential district, commissioned by King Louis XIV, who fell in love with the town when the Citadelle was built. These roads were built to link the marketplaces of the centre with the fortress in the woods of the Bois de Boulogne.

The quaint narrow streets of Vieux Lille today feel wonderfully safe, with cheery groups of students in animated discussion, well-dressed couples window shopping arm in arm on the narrow pavements, and traffic insinuating turns at a snail's pace, ensuring that the quarter's refined charm never slips into stuffiness. Mind you, the indiscreet working girls by the old Porte de Gand are a reminder that any town with a military presence can never become too prissy! Three decades ago, the kerbside trade was the only truly thriving *métier* of the old town, but as Lille reclaimed its streets, art dealers and restaurateurs moved into the renovated buildings to create the enchanting realm of refinement that we know today.

Carnality on the plate and the boudoir are not the only tastes catered for in this other world of 17th- and 18th-century houses and shops. No one should miss the pretty pleasures of saying 'I wish' to the latest fashions *chez* Michel Ruc on the rue des Chats Bossus, and 'I will, I do, I can't help myself' to the unrivalled confections of the Pâtisserie Meert on rue Esquermoise, just a whim and drop of the willpower away from the Grand' Place.

WHERE TO STAY

De la Treille 7/9 pl Louise de Bettignies, 59800; tel: 03 20 55 45 46 [15 G2]
E *Bus 3,6 or 9 from Flandres to Lion d'Or.*
Very popular, owing to its location, this modest hotel in the very heart of the old town bustle is a prime choice for many weekenders on an all-inclusive break. The famous cathedral, Notre Dame de la Treille, is just behind the hotel, and across the way, through a doorway by a craft shop is the unexpected treasure of the Hospice Comtesse. The hotel's entrance and reception area is very welcoming and fits in with some of the oldest buildings in the oldest quarter of town. The bedrooms, though clean, are by contrast lacking in style and imagination. Uniform eighties bland alas, with none of the centuries-old charm suggested by the view from the windows looking out towards the rue de Gand and down on the place du Lion d'Or. Rooms from €60 (400 FF). Breakfast €8 (50FF) extra. Staff are very helpful and patient with advice on how to negotiate the maze of Vieux Lille.

Chez Meaux 104 rue Royale, 59000; tel: 03 20 55 31 32
E *Bus 3 or 6 or 9 from Flandres to Magazin, walk along rue Royale.*
Bed and breakfast just ten minutes from the *estaminets* and flesh-pots of the Lion d'Or: the Meaux family are gently restoring their fabulous old town house on the rue Royale. Behind closed doors, a charming courtyard and impressive hallway with ivy-draped sweeping staircase greet the guests who spend the night or the week in one of the two especially adapted bedrooms on the first floor. The larger suite boasts a panelled double bedroom and a huge bathroom for around €53 (350FF) a night, and the other a pleasant sitting room beside the bedroom with its fitted modern shower unit at €30–40 (200–260FF). Breakfast may be taken in the charming morning room, or with the family beside the vast 19th-century range in the big working kitchen. Madame Meaux, who makes her visitors feel like house-

guests, is a fount of knowledge of Lille life, and the family's terrier flings himself at your feet in a reassuringly indiscriminate welcome. Home from home.

Alliance Golden Tulip Hôtel 17 quai de Wault, 59800; tel: 03 20 30 62 62 [14 D3]
Ē *Bus 12 from Gare Flandres to Foch. Walk through the park to the pond. The hotel is on the right bank.*
The highest profile hotel in the city may be found in a quiet street near the canal and citadel. The usual four-star perks of big buffet breakfasts in the morning, air-conditioning in the summer, and mini-bars and Muzak all year round. Service is courteous and efficient and all is as one would expect of an establishment of this quality. To be honest, if it had not once been a convent I'd enjoy the place a good deal more. But the fact that the old cloister of this listed 17th-century building has been smothered in glass and chrome and muzzled by an atrium and mezzanine piano bar gives what should have been a charming and tasteful conversion the air of an airport hotel. Thus the gentle strains of George Gershwin are usually muted by my murderous thoughts towards the architect or corporate philistines who conceived and executed the project. Perhaps I am being unfair or unduly sensitive. Most of the major hotel guides wax lyrical about the place. Some bedrooms are well equipped and comfortable, the live jazz evenings *tres décontracté*, and the restaurant in the glazed courtyard is well respected by business diners. The hotel room rate is around €152 (1,000 FF) and *demi-pension* rates are also available.

WHERE TO GO

L'Angle Saxo 36 rue d'Angleterre, 59800; tel: 03 20 51 88 89 [14 E2]
Open 21.00–02.00.
Ē *Bus 3 or 6 from Gare Flandres to Conservatoire.*
If you like your jazz hot and your scotch on the rocks, and you are old enough not to wince at the pun, you'll flop here for a mellow end to the day.

Blue Note Bar 8 pl St-André, 59000; tel: 03 20 55 28 62
Open Wed–Sat 20.30–02.00.
Ē *Bus 3 or 6 from Gare Flandres to Magazin. Rue Royale north to pl St-André.*
Exposed beams, bluesy music and great beers. Be guided by the barman and taste one of the lesser known brews of the region.

Bois de Boulogne av Mathias Delobel, 59000; tel: 03 20 57 38 08 (zoo) [14 A1–C2]
Open (zoo) Mon–Fri 10.00–18.00 Apr–Oct, 10.00–16.00 Nov–Mar, Sat–Sun and holidays 10.00–19.00 Apr–Oct, 10.00–17.00 Nov–Mar; closed 2nd Sun Dec, 2nd Sun Feb. Free.
Ē *Métro 2 to Gare Lille Flandres, then line 1 to République. Bus 14 to Jardin Vauban.*
The countryside comes to town where panthers prowl, joggers run and families take the air. Neatly tied up in a loop of the river Deûle's canals are 125 acres of greenery, picturesque towpaths and an island filled with monkeys. Home to the famous fortress (see *Citadelle*, page 203) the Bois de Boulogne is where the city loosens its tie on weekends and holidays. Children love the zoo, free to all, with its Ile des Singes and contented rhinos and zebras. There is also a playground for dodgems, side-shows and candyfloss moments. Outside the zoo is a cobbled pathway that forms part of the arduous Paris–Roubaix cycle race, known colloquially as 'The Hell of the North'. Fitness fanatics pace themselves running around the former moat, following the signposted route between the ramparts and the willow trees. You can

always tell the soldiers and foreign legionnaires by their blue tracksuits. Lovers wander into the woods, whilst more decorous strollers prefer the esplanade, landscaped in 1675 by Vauban himself, or the Champ de Mars where funfairs pitch their tents during school holidays. If all seems carefree and inconsequential, take a moment to pause by the Monument aux Fusillées on Square Daubenton at the edge of the Bois. Félix Desruelle's memorial pays tribute to those *Lillois* members of the French Resistance shot by the Nazis against the walls of the Citadelle.

Estaminet de la Royale 37 rue Royale, 59000; tel: 03 20 42 10 11 [14 E2] Closed evenings, Sun, holidays.
Ē *Métro 2 to Gare Lille Flandres then Line 1 to Rihour. Cross Grand' Place to rue Esquermoise into rue Royale.*
Despite the mode-rustic mirrors and milk-churn décor, this is the genuine article: a real *estaminet* neighbourhood bar in a centuries-old building in Vieux Lille, where a simple good, old-fashioned, home-cooked lunch is on offer at midday. *Rognons de veau* or a simple poultry dish might grace the €15 (100F) menu. Food is only served until 14.30, but you are welcome to drink with the chatty locals into the early evening.

Les Folies de Paris 52 av du Peuple Belge, 59000; tel: 03 20 06 62 64; www. lesfoliesdeparis.com [15 G1]
Ē *Bus 3,6 or 9 from Gare Flandres to Lion d'Or. Cross pl Louise de Bettignies and turn left.*
La Cage Aux Folles meets Hollywood on the avenue where the stars come out at night. The biggest floorshow north of Paris has showgirls galore – only which of the girls are really boys, which girls are truly girls and which boys are girls? These are the questions facing diners at the pancake-pasted flurry of feathers, sequins and star look-alikes that is Les Folies de Paris. Although the show is in French, many of the stars being sent up are easily recognisable: Marlene, Marilyn, Piaf, Céline, Gene Kelly, Madonna, Michael Jackson and their ilk brilliantly lip-synched by the talented team of waiters, dancers, magicians and long-legged drag artistes. Dinner is at 20.30, and in the two hours before show time, customers are entertained, mocked and teased by the revue's outrageous director Claude Thomas. Sit too near the front and run the risk of being hauled up on stage, but even in the shadows there is always the chance of being the butt of some affectionate leg pulling. The comedy is in French, and the banter throws in a smattering of local *argot*. This familiar frolicking is probably the key to the place's undeniable popularity. Where no self-respecting Parisian is likely to admit to visiting the Paris cabarets, you will always find locals here at the Folies. The party mood continues after the show with dancing, and the cast lines the aisles to kiss the evening's guests goodbye and wave them home at the door. Hard to believe that the show, in the plush velvet and glitzy gleaming chrome night-spot, started out as a simple back street café revue. Budget from €32 (235FF) for the basic midweek menu to the full treat at €93 (620FF) plus drinks. The food is not bad by cabaret standards.

Jardin Vauban bd Vauban, 59000 [14 A–B3]
Ē *Métro 2 to Gare Lille Flandres, then line 1 to République. Bus 14 to Jardin Vauban.*
A delightful 19th-century park, often overshadowed by the large lush expanses of the Bois de Boulogne across the Deûle, this is a pretty confection of dainty flowerbeds, waterfalls, lawns and grottoes, landscaped by Paris' chief gardener Barillet Deschamps in 1865. Poets' corner contains memorials to writers and

musicians, and a monument to Charles de Gaulle stands at the square Daubenton entrance. Locals visit the immaculate miniature orchard to meet the present-day gardeners who are always willing to give advice and tips on growing fruit and vegetables at home. The most famous corner of the park is the puppet theatre in Monsieur Rameau's Goat House, where every Sunday and Wednesday Jacques le Lillois performs for local children. This Chalet aux Chèvres was one of Charles Rameau's many eccentric legacies to the town. He was a noted horticulturist who gave Lille the splendid Palais Rameau at the junction of rue Solférino and bd Vauban, a vast horticultural hall that doubles as a circus and performing arts venue. These munificent bequests were given freely on the condition that his grave at the Cimetière du Sud is always marked by a bed of potatoes, a tomato plant, strawberries, a vine, rose bush and dahlias.

Meert 27 rue Esquermoise, 59800; tel: 03 20 57 07 44 [14 E3]
M̄ *Rihour;* Ē *Bus 12 from Gare Flandres to De Gaulle.*
Charles de Gaulle himself would never have dreamed of saying '*Non*' to the celebrated *gaufrettes* – or filled waffle – that has graced many a palace and presidential biscuit barrel since this shop started trading in the 1760s. At €1.5 (10FF) each, or 75 cents (5FF) for the mini version, this unassuming house speciality of the chocolate-box quaint *pâtisserie* is a tiny miracle, a light, feathery crispy wafer packed with a sugared explosion of flavour. The town's most famous son continued his regular order for the *gaufrettes* all his life, and ate them, so he wrote, 'with great pleasure'. The Belgian royal family gave their warrant to Monsieur Meert in 1849. The pretty cake shop, decorated in 1839 with mirrors, balconies and Arabian Nights exotica, is a feast for the eyes. The tea room behind the shop provides savoury lunchtime snacks and sumptuous afternoon teas, where a selection of cakes and a pot of tea should set you back around €6–12 (40–80FF). Lemon meringue tarts are creamy delights, the *Safari* a surprisingly heavy dose of fluffiness for hard-core chocolate addicts only.

WHAT TO SEE

Citadelle av du 42ème Régiment d'Infantrie, 59000; tel: 03 20 21 94 21 (tourist office) [14 A–B1]
Advance reservation essential; guided tours only Sun 15.00–17.00 May–Aug, and selected dates outside this period. €7 (45FF).
Ē *Métro 2 to Gare Lille Flandres, then line 1 to République. Bus 14 to Jardin Vauban.*
A town in its own right, France's Queen of Citadelles was the greatest fortress of the reign of Louis XIV. When the Sun King commissioned the great military architect Sébastien Le Prestre de Vauban to protect his kingdom with a ring of 100 fortified towns, this imposing and impenetrable pentagonal, star-shaped Citadelle was hailed as the masterpiece of the world's finest military engineer. Built by 400 men in just three years using 16 million newly baked bricks, the garrison opened in 1670 as home to 1,200 soldiers. Three hundred years on, it remains the nucleus of the modern army with 1,000 French soldiers and foreign legionnaires stationed here.

In April, 14 of the 28 northern fortresses hold an open day; otherwise the public are only permitted to tour the site on summer Sunday guided tours. Visitors are expected to behave themselves. When a couple of schoolchildren sat on the parade-ground rostrum, the young soldier of the *43ème régiment* accompanying our group was confined to barracks, a sharp reminder that this is no museum, but a working garrison. Its five-sided design is as effective a security measure today as it was in the 17th century – and is said to have inspired the US Pentagon. Soil banks the ramparts to absorb artillery shells, and the main walls are 4m thick. The principal entrance, the Porte Royale, was built at an angle to the drawbridge to avoid direct hits. This gateway, facing the old quarter of Lille, was a major strategic and symbolic feature with regal motifs and Latin mottoes representing the king himself. In the centre of the pentagonal parade ground is a ship's mast, a reminder that the fortress was built along the banks of a river, and was originally protected by the navy. The soldiers stationed here today still wear naval badges. Around the parade ground are the renovated barracks, an arsenal, the chapel officers' quarters.

The king, a regular visitor, appointed Vauban as the first governor of the Citadelle. His successor was Charles, Comte d'Artagnan and hero of Dumas' *Three Musketeers*, who died in 1673. The original governor's residence is no more, but traces may still be in the chapel of the gubernatorial doorway. Vauban's original models for the fortified towns of the north are displayed at the Palais des Beaux Arts (see page 229) and, for the rest of France, at Les Invalides (see *Paris*, page 128).

Maison Natale du Général de Gaulle (Général de Gaulle's birthplace) 9 rue Princesse, 59000; tel: 03 28 38 12 05
Open Wed–Sun 10.00–12.00, 14.00–17.00, closed holidays.
Ē *Bus 3 or 6 from Gare Flandres to Magasin. Take rue St-André to rue Princesse.*
War hero, statesman and Europe's most celebrated Britosceptic, Charles de Gaulle was born here, in his grandmother's house, on November 22 1890, opposite the Eglise St-André where the once and future president was baptised. See his christening robes at the refurbished museum devoted to the life of Lille's most famous son. The exhibition tells the story of the first president of the Fifth Republic with lesser-known tales from his early life, and documents his refusal to accept Marshall Pétain's 1940 truce with Nazi Germany, then rallying the Free French army with his historic broadcast from London that same year. Dramatic episodes are well illustrated, with the very Citroën DS in which the president was travelling outside Paris when he survived an assassin's bullet.

Musée des Canonniers Sédentaires de Lille 44 rue des Canonniers, 59000; tel: 03 20 55 58 90 [15 H2]
Open Wed, Fri, Sat, Sun, 14.00–17.00, closed holidays, first three weeks Aug, 15 Dec–15 Feb. ∈4.50 (30FF).
Gare Lille Flandres; Ē *Walk through the Parc Matisse and pass through the Porte de Roubaix to rue de Roubaix. Turn right into rue des Canonniers and second right into rue des Urbanistes.*
It's fitting that a garrison town should have a museum of military hardware, and over 3,000 weapons, documents and maps from 1777 to 1945 are on display in the former *Urbanistes* convent. The stars of the show are the magnificent cannons, most notably the *Gribeauval* – the Big Bertha of its day. Despite the postal address, the public entrance is in rue des Urbanistes.

Musée de l'Hospice Comtesse 32 rue de la Monnaie, 59000; tel: 03 28 36 84 00 [15 F2]
Open Mon 14.00–18.00, Wed, Thu, Sat, Sun 10.00–18.00, Fri 10.00–19.00; closed holidays. ∈2 (15FF). Joint tickets also available with Palais des Beaux Arts.
Ē *Bus 3, 6 or 9 from Gare Flandres to Lion d'Or.*
I love the stillness of the old hospital ward, with its boatbuilder-vaulted ceiling. This most tranquil of sanctuaries is a season apart, even from the rest of the historic quarter. Tucked away behind the shops and archways of the oldest street in town, the former 13th-century hospital captures the life and talents of another Lille in another time. The city's benefactress Jeanne de Constantinople, Countess of Flanders, built the hospice for the needy in 1237, a charitable gesture that has echoed down the centuries in a city that nurtures the ideals of civic responsibilities. After all, the

celebrated annual *braderie* (see page 226) was born of a sense of *noblesse oblige*, when servants were granted the right to sell their masters' clothes in these very streets. Once both a hospital and a convent, the site has been restored as a museum of local arts and crafts. Outside is a medicinal herb garden. Inside, find an eclectic collection of carved furniture and rare musical instruments, domestic tableaux and wooden panels adorned with paintings of local children. The art collection includes paintings by Flemish and northern French masters, among them Louis and François Watteau, as well as tapestries by Lille's famous weaver Guillaume Werniers. The kitchen is typically tiled with the traditional blue and white tiles of the Low Countries, and vestiges of the original murals can be seen in the 17th-century convent chapel. The chapel, the 15th-century ward and other buildings around the central courtyard are favourite locations for informal concerts and intimate musical recitals. Guided tours are available at no extra charge most afternoons.

Notre Dame de la Treille pl Gilleson; tel: 03 20 31 59 12 [15 F2]
Hours vary afternoons and services. Free.
Ē *Bus 3,6 or 9 from Gare Flandres to Lion d'Or. Take rue de la Monnaie then first left to pl Gilleson.*
For most of the last century, Lille was a city with three-quarters of a cathedral. Notre Dame de la Treille had not only a fine gothic chapel and apse, but also the largest expanse of corrugated iron in northern Europe. For, although the

foundation stone had been lain in 1854 and the bulk of the edifice completed by the turn of the 19th century, work during the 20th century finally ground to a halt when the money ran out in 1947. What should have been the great front entrance was hastily boarded up. By 1999 funding had finally been found and Lille was able to unveil its cathedral. From the outside, architect P L Carlier's designs are very much of the age of the out-of-town shopping mall. Nevertheless, the new rose window by Kijno produces fabulously spooky lighting effects inside, and the remarkable doors created by Holocaust survivor sculptor George Jeanclos, representing a barbed-wire vine of human suffering and dignity, are quite magnificent. The cathedral stands on the Îlot Comtesse, site of the former château of the Counts of Flanders, and the surrounding streets follow the line of the old fortifications, with traces of a moat still visible. A **Museum of Religious Art** in the crypt opens on Saturday afternoons from 16.00 to 17.00. Two hundred works of art and historic objects, including the original statue of Notre Dame de la Treille, dating from 1270.

Porte de Gand rue de Gand, 59000 [15 H1]
Ē *Bus 3,6 or 9 from Gare Flandres to Lion d'Or. Cross pl Louise de Bettignies to rue de Gand.*
The last remaining fortified entrance to Vieux Lille stands astride the rue de Gand looking down over the cobbles and menus of this fashionable dining area. From the old town, admire the coloured patterns in the brickwork above the archways. The windows at the top belong to a restaurant (see *Terrasse des Ramparts*, page 208). From the other side, the Porte de Gand can be seen as part

of some serious defensive walls. The original perimeter was strengthened twice in the 17th century, the *porte* and ramparts built in 1621 by the Spanish authorities against the French, and an extra line of defence added by Vauban against everybody else. Between the two walls are gardens that can be seen from the restaurant terrace in summer when diners may sit at tables on the ramparts. Since the winding road leading from the gate still serves working barracks, the rue de Gand has serviced the appetites of young soldiers since long before the restaurants arrived on the scene. Pools of lamplight under the trees beneath the city walls continue to offer late-night comforts *à la Lilli Marlène*.

Ste-Cathérine pl Jean-Jacques Louchard, 59000; tel: 03 20 55 45 92 [14 D2] Open only during Sunday masses and other services. Free.
Ē *Bus 3 from Gare Flandres to Conservatoire, walk west along rue d'Angleterre, left to rue Royale and right to rue de la Barre then sharp right to rue St-Jean.*
Out-of-towners rarely discover this 13th-century church. Yet until work started on Notre Dame de la Treille, this was home to the town's precious statue of the Virgin Mary (see page 205). Rubens' *Martyrdom of Ste* Cathérine, now in the Palais des Beaux Arts *(see page 229)* hung here for years, and many striking works by lesser-known artists may still be seen in the spacious and bright interior. The altar is graced by some excellent artworks including adoration of the shepherds and images inspired by Leonardo's *Last Supper*. Over the centuries the parish church of the rural suburb of faubourg de Weppes expanded to become a traditional Flemish *hallekerque*. Its three spacious naves were probably saved from demolition during the Revolution when the building was called into service as a barn, returning to the Catholic church in 1797. By then it had lost the ornate iron partition grilles and other elaborate furnishings. Other splendid items remain from the carved choir stalls to the beautifully painted pillars, and Ste-Cathérine has at last won historic monument listing status.

WHERE TO EAT
Le Jardin du Cloître 17 quai de Wault, 59800; tel: 03 20 30 62 62 [14 D3]
Ē *Bus 12 from Gare Flandres to Foch. Walk through the park to the pond. The restaurant is on the right bank.*
In the business-park perpendicular atrium of the Alliance Hotel is to be found a restaurant that boasts professional service, a fine *filet mignon* in the celebrated *Blanche de Lille* and the ubiquitous piano player. This is where business people from TGV business towns north, south and east of Lille meet up to discuss business policy over lunch. Menus from around ∈16 (100FF); otherwise budget around ∈33 (220FF) plus.

A l'Huîtrière 3 rue des Chats Bossus, 59000; tel: 03 20 55 43 41; web: www.a-l-huitiere.fr/ [15 F3]
Closed Sun evening.
Ē *Bus 3,6 or 9 from Gare Flandres to Lion d'Or.*
'Absolute perfection and faultless' was the verdict of my dinner guest. I just beamed in contentment. If I were a rich man, I'd spend the rest of my life introducing my friends to l'Huîtrière, if only to bask in the glow of unalloyed pleasure that this jewel-box of a fish shop presses upon even the sternest of gastronomes. The short walk past the fresh fish counters, the classic mosaics, baskets of shells and wondrous confections *en gelée* and in bottles is dappled in a maritime twilight. Once in the narrow vestibule twixt the domains of the fishmonger and the *maître cuisinier*, a warm welcome from the fabulously efficient and courteous staff instantly sets the standard for the evening.

In the restaurant itself all is calm, all is bright. Light wood panels adorned by lovely wool tapestry, table appointments charming, with the white and navy Limoges service atop crisp white linen. A sense of quality pervades exquisite and discreet service that is attentive without a hint of intimidation. François Foassier has been creating wonders in the kitchen here for a third of a century and never fails to stimulate nor enchant. An entrée of wild Scottish salmon *mi-cru mi-cuit* was lovingly prepared, briefly roasted, pan-fried and seared in spices on the outside, yet succulent and raw within and laced with a fine horseradish dressing. The *trois petites royales* revealed themselves as truffled-up seductions of leek, cabbage and petit pois, simply superb. Though this is a fish restaurant, honourable mention must go to the *escalope de foie gras de canard* in a *pot-au-feu de nouveaux legumes*. The main course varies with the catch and the season and according to the taste of the diner.

Our waiter regarded my companion's request for a variation on the menu suggestion as a challenge rather than an affront, and took a genuine delight in consulting with the kitchen to create the perfect dish to meet a customer's exacting tastes. John-Dory roasted in its skin with asparagus *meunière* with *vinaigrette au beurre* was proof, if such were ever needed, that the sea is no poor relation to the pasture. The *sorbet à la fleur de bière* is the northern answer to a *trou normand* and clears the appetite for game or *volaille*. Desserts are impeccable – do try the *mi-gratin, mi-soufflé* of wild woodland strawberries – and the pastries, chocolates and *petits fours* are simply heavenly. A wisely compiled wine list included our choice of a smooth and refined 1990 *Chateau Moulin Riche 2ème cru Bordeaux St-Julienne* decanted in time for the main course. Budget a good €68 (450FF) per head, or €92 (600FF) for the seven- course gastronomic menu. A very reasonable three-course lunch is served at €44 (290FF).

La Cave aux Fioles 39 rue de Gand, 59800; tel: 03 20 55 18 43; web: www.cave-aux-fioles.fr [15 G1]
Closed Sat lunch, Sun and holidays.
Ē *Bus 3,6 or 9 from Gare Flandres to Lion d'Or. Cross pl Louise de Bettignies to rue de Gand.*
Eccentric, eclectic and the warmest welcome in town. Happiness comes à la carte at the top of the dear old rue de Gand. When I close my eyes and think of eating out in Lille, it is La Cave aux Fioles that springs to mind. Follow the cobbles to the far end of the old town to the honey glow from the windows of a warm and friendly dining room. What looks like the front door to the restaurant remains resolutely locked, but enter the unmarked door to the side of the windows, and pass through a narrow and dark entrance hall lined with posters from legendary Lille Festivals past to reach the central covered courtyard between two houses. All around are the husks of 17th- and 18th-century homes, paneless casement windows open out to the brick, stone and cobbled court. Inside, tables are scattered through the various rooms, candlelight enhances the brickwork, and the trad jazz sounds mellow the scene even further. In winter a roaring fire concentrates the cosiness even more, but whatever the season, the true warmth comes from the welcoming and hospitable staff, from the barman who serve the house cocktail *Fiole d'Amour* (grapefruit, gin and grenadine), to the waitresses who patiently wait as you agonise over choices. The house *foie gras de canard* comes with a surprise tipple, but the fresh mushrooms stuffed with roquefort sound fabulous. Then again, what about a soup of mussels with leeks? Will tonight be the night for the local *waterzoi d' homard* or should we indulge in strips of goose *magret* dripping with a honey sauce? Whichever dish wins, the

garnish and vegetable accompaniment varies '*selon l'humour du chef*'! By dessert I have usually rediscovered decisiveness, and I forego such sirens as *gâteau au chocolat de la Tante Mazo* in favour of the remarkable *délicatesse du Nord* – the bitterest ice-cream I have ever tasted, blending chicory with *genièvre* gin. Although there are 20 tables here, such is the artful design that one never notices more than one's immediate neighbours and the sense of privacy is supreme. The full evening menu with cocktails and coffee comes to €31 (200FF); lunch options from €10 (65FF) are also available. If a day's shopping on the rickety paved streets has played havoc with your calf muscles, don't be daunted by the thought of the trek up the rue de Gand. The restaurant's private London taxi will collect you from your hotel.

La Terrasse des Remparts Logis de la Porte de Gand, rue de Gand, 59800; tel: 03 20 06 74 74 [15 H1]
Ē *Bus 3,6 or 9 from Gare Flandres to Lion d'Or. Cross pl Louise de Bettignies to rue de Gand.*
Easy to find your way to and from this the last restaurant on the rue de Gand gastronomic thoroughfare: it is a listed landmark and marked on all the maps. Housed in the original 1620 fortifications of the old town constructed during the Spanish invasion, there can be no more dramatic location for a restaurateur with a knack for the flamboyant and romantic gesture. My first experience of the restaurant had been pretty disappointing – a bland lunch served in a stuffy overheated function room on the day President Chirac opened the Palais des Beaux Arts. Even when chums began nagging me to give the restaurant a second chance, saying that the cuisine had enjoyed a thorough overhaul, I was not inclined to return. When, however, a sudden summer downpour found me stranded at the foot of the steps leading to the restaurant that straddles the main road, I decided to dry out and try out the new look Terrasse. The place was packed to capacity – the outside terrace on the fortification being *hors de combat* owing to the weather. Charming staff managed to find us a table amid the eccentric décor which resembles the private dream life of a hyperactive department-store window dresser. We made ourselves at home amongst wooden sunflowers beneath the huge polystyrene rabbits hibernating on mock grass and outsized daisies on the rafters overhead. The menus are bound in steel folders and offer a €15 (98FF) lunch and a €23 (153FF) evening *formule*. Thick fillet of steak served with stuffed jacket potato and a regional dish of cod in watercress sauce with crystallised potato were both succulent and filling. Desserts from the buffet are *à volonté*, but as disappointing as dessert buffets usually are. Each *flan* and *gâteau* seemed to share the same base, and though the mousses were a little better, my tip would be to take the two-course menu and enjoy a *pâté* starter and a main course. Service is hearty, clientele comfortably off but in birthday mood, and all plates are wiped clean. A memorable setting for a very pleasant meal, and a vast improvement on the bad old days.

Clair de Lune 50 rue de Gand, 59000; tel: 03 20 51 46 55 [15 G1–2]
Closed Sat lunch, Tue.
Ē *Bus 3,6 or 9 from Gare Flandres to Lion d'Or. Cross pl Louise de Bettignies to rue de Gand.*
A jolly good Sunday brunch for €13 (88FF) distinguishes this dining room from all its neighbours on the gastronomic street. From 11.00 to 16.00, omelettes, salmon, bacon and more augment the buffet of fruit, cereals and dairy. Midweek, the blue and yellow dining room specialises in twists on the norm. *Mignon* of pork in an *arabica* coffee sauce, halibut in cider, or a somewhat scrummy *oeuf*

cocotte with smoked trout and leeks. Though some claim the service to be brusque, I found nothing to complain about. Unpretentious staff did not bat an eyelid when I opted for a couple of starters one evening, having over indulged elsewhere at lunchtime, and paid me the same courtesies as those pigging out on the €19 (128FF) menu. Lunches from €14 (90FF).

Les Faits Divers 44 rue de Gand, 59000; tel: 03 20 21 03 63 [15 G2]
Closed Sat lunch, Sun.
Ē *Bus 3,6 or 9 from Gare Flandres to Lion d'Or. Cross pl Louise de Bettignies to rue de Gand.*
Young and buzzing, bright and lively. Wise regulars book early, because by mid-evening there is not a table to be had. Pretty good standard fish, farm and fowl fare served by staff who are on the ball and on the move. Not the choice for a romantic *diner à deux*, but the ideal venue for relaxing amongst friends. Menus around €16 (105FF), and à la carte probably double with a pleasant bottle of wine. If you have not booked at the weekend, then arrive before 20.30 to be in with a chance.

'T Rijsel 25 rue de Gand, 59800; tel: 03 20 15 01 59 [15 G1–2]
Closed Sun, Mon.
Ē *Bus 3,6 or 9 from Gare Flandres to Lion d'Or. Cross pl Louise de Bettignies to rue de Gand.*
Rijsel is the Flemish name for Lille, so no surprise to find a warm corner of old Flanders in this relative newcomer to the restaurant scene. Jean-Luc Lacante, whose *estaminet* T'Kasteel-Hof in nearby Cassel is a favourite with those who explore the countryside, brought his trademark combination of wit, style and homeliness to town at the turn of the Millennium. Expect all the regional specialities here, from *potlevlesch* to sugar flans, on menus printed in old school exercise books. Late one cold winter's morning, my parents and I stopped by for a hearty bowl of home-made soup, and very welcome we were made, even if the kitchen was not yet officially open. Budget well under €15 (100FF).

La Cour des Grands 61 rue de la Monnaie, 59000; tel: 03 20 06 83 61 [15 F2]
Closed Sat lunch, Mon lunch, Sun and holidays.
Ē *Bus 3,6 or 9 from Gare Flandres to Lion d'Or.*
Oh dear, perhaps it was just a bad day. Or perhaps the *plat du jour* was *oeuf du curé*. We had been so looking forward to visiting a local legend. Friends in town had urged us to venture away from the cobbled streets around the Musée de l'Hospice Comtesse into the sedate courtyard and through the elegant doors into the formal dining rooms of a well-respected restaurateur. Though the menu – strong on lobster and its cousins – looked promising, the elegant old-style rooms now seemed tired, and a grubby menu and a torn napkin told their own story. Service was accommodating, menus offered in daintily tied scrolls and the food beautifully presented: the speciality *gazpacho de homard* with *quenelles de mousse de courgette* proved appetising. However, whilst the *brandade de morue fraîche à la truffe* was beautiful on the plate, it proved remarkably bland on the palate. Thankfully desserts were excellent: we savoured a *croustillant à l'ananas glace au lait citronné* which tasted as lovely and pineapple-packed as it looked, and the *crème de yaourt glacé aux fraises chaudes* was similarly appreciated. Those same chums who had regaled me with stories of the restaurant's glory were surprised at our experience. However, we lunched here on a busy Friday when neighbouring establishments were packed and only one other table was occupied. Could be the A-team was on holiday. Updated comments from readers will be welcomed. Menus €29–48 (190–380FF), and à la carte nearer €50 (330FF) plus wine.

Le Chat Bossu 12 rue des Chats Bossus, 59000; tel: 03 20 74 57 96 [15 F3]
Closed evenings, Sun lunch.
Ē *Bus 3,6 or 9 from Gare Flandres to Lion d'Or.*
Another lunchtime favourite, slap bang in the middle of the cobbles and fantasy-shopping district, with swift service and standard sausage and sauerkraut dishes on the €10–14 (65–90FF) menus. A mix of visitors, shopkeepers, students and suits squeeze together to snatch half an hour away from the demands of the day.

Le Square 52 rue Basse, 59000; tel: 03 20 74 16 17 [15 F3]
Closed Mon evening, Sun and Aug.
Ē *Bus 3,6 or 9 from Gare Flandres to Lion d'Or. Rue des Chats Bossus into rue Basse.*
Big portions and no illusions of grandeur in a bustling, *bistrot*-style café that gets packed with families at lunchtimes and youngsters in the evenings. Value for money is the lure. Midday menus are priced at under €9 (60FF), but budget around €16 (110FF) for a free choice at night. Whatever you choose, the service is informal, €4 (30FF) starters big enough to eat as a main course, and local dishes full of flavour. The *salmon cru* marinated *in la bière de garde* is pretty damned yummy and *andouillette* with *frites* the most popular choice. Budget conscious tend to opt for the sizeable *salade lyonnaise* with *lardons* and a piquant mustard dressing or the pasta of the day from the small but wide-ranging menus.

La Petite Cour 17 rue du Curé St-Etienne, 59000; tel: 03 20 51 52 81 [15 F3]
Closed Sun, Mon.
Ē *Bus 12 from Gare Flandres to De Gaulle. Walk under the Alcide arch to the debris St-Etienne then left into the rue du Curé St-Etienne.*
Very busy café in a courtyard with basic seating and tables. If proof were ever needed that the average age in Lille is 25 then just look around. Popular with families during the day and with students at night. Food is fine – no classic moments – and generous. I could have re-enacted the forest scene from *Sleeping Beauty* just hacking my way through a never-ending *salade niçoise*. A smoked fish platter was a bit tough, but *steak haché* and *frites* proved more reliable. If your appetite is not up to the occasion, the staff will happily split a main course and offer two plates. The inner dining area is suitably eclectic, designed to look like a courtyard, but the real open-air court is a happy suntrap for a light lunch. The outside loo leaves little to the imagination by the way. Pay around €9 (60FF) for lunch, twice that in the evening.

L'Ardoise sur le Comptoir 4 rue des Bouchers, 59000; tel: 03 20 63 95 51 14 E3]
Closed Sun.
Ē *Métro 2 to Gare Lille Flandres then Line 1 to Rihour. Walk through Grand' Place to rue Esquermoise. At rue de la Barre turn left then left again into rue des Bouchers.*
It was a dark and stormy night when I last stepped across the threshold and into this tiny sanctuary. How they cram so many tables into such a tiny room is a mystery to me, but the place is always packed. All around the room the eponymous *ardoises* may be found – the blackboards that give the restaurant its name. Additions to the regular selections are posted in every nook and cranny of the room. The women who run the place have created a genuinely country feel in the heart of the old town. The food straddles farmyard and coast with a *cassoulet* of *confit de canard*, *chaud-froid* of lobster with saffron and a combination of the local Cambrai *andouillette* with that of Troyes served with a mustard sauce and fries. The rumble of thunder and reflected lightning from the weather-beaten cobbles outside proved the perfect background to an *assiette rustique* of potato, *raclette* and *charcuterie*. Meals are best washed down with a *pichet* of the house Chénas. Pay around €25 (160FF) unless you opt for the €11 (70FF) menu.

Les Compagnons de la Grappe 26 rue Lepelletier, 59800; tel: 03 20 21 02 79 [15 F3]
Closed Sun and Mon evenings (Oct–May only).
Ē *Bus 12 from Gare Flandres to De Gaulle. Walk under the Alcide arch to the debris St-Etienne into rue Lepelletier.*
I stumbled across this summer terrace quite by chance: there is a gap in an alleyway, which opens out to reveal a wine bar with a delightful courtyard. Families and friends sit and chat under sunshades, sipping wines from some of the lesser-known vineyards of France. Platters of *charcuterie* and farmhouse cheeses are colourful and plentiful. The place positively hums with contentment. It's worth popping in to check on any special theme evenings or culinary events. No reservations taken, service can be a hit and miss affair and the opening hours of noon 'til midnight vary with the weather. In winter enjoy a glass of wine in front of a roaring fire. Budget ∈8–16 (55–100FF) per person.
La Provinciale en Ville 8 rue des Urbanistes, 59800; tel: 03 20 06 50 79 [15 H2]
Closed Sat lunch, Sun.
M̄ *Gare Lille Flandres;* Ē *Walk through the Parc Matisse and pass through the Porte de Roubaix to rue de Roubaix. Turn right into rue des Canonniers to place aux Bluets.*
A charming rustic-style corner house, opposite the barracks in the undefined zone between the heart of the old town and the new Parc Matisse by the stations. Here, in small dining rooms, traditional dishes such as *potjevlesch*, and stews based on local beers, share the menu with poultry and fish variations on the theme. A world away from the stress of the working day, within the 200-year-old walls all that matters is good food and conversation. I jostled with perfect *rouget* served with good northern market-garden greens, as my lunch chums ploughed into the house *escargots* and we all marvelled at the tranquillity of the restaurant just yards from a ring road. By the time that we had made our choices from the extensive coffee selection – African and South American varieties ranged as on a wine list – we were suitably mellow. For main courses one could do worse than indulge the chef's eccentricities. Try the pan-fried salmon with *genièvre* or veal cooked with maroilles cheese as typical house twists. Lunch menu is ∈14 (90FF), evenings boast a selection of meals from ∈38–45(250–295FF).

WHAT TO BUY

Artisanat Monastique parvis Notre Dame de la Treille, pl Gilleson, 59000; tel: 03 20 55 22 19 [15 F2]
Open Mon 14.00–18.30, Tue–Sat 09.30–18.30.
Ē *Bus 3,6 or 9 from Gare Flandres to Lion d'Or then walk from rue de la Monnaie to the cathedral.*
Religious and liturgical gifts, from monastic-themed accessories to devotional items.
Artisans du Monde 42 rue Esquermoise, 59000; tel: 03 20 06 03 12 [14 E3]
Open Tue–Sat 10.00–19.00.
M̄ *Rihour;* Ē *Bus 12 from Gare Flandres to De Gaulle. Rue Esquermoise is north of Grand' Place.*
Assuage the guilt of a weekend's heavy consumerism by spending something at this shop built on the fair-trade principal. Whatever ethnic trinket or artefact catches your eye here, rest assured that your money goes directly to third-world community projects.
Atelier Un Vrai Semblance 3 rue au Peterink, 59800; tel: 03 20 15 08 99; email: contact@abcome.net [15 F2]
Ē *Bus 3,6 or 9 from Gare Flandres to Lion d'Or. From rue de la Monnaie turn left into rue au Peterink.*

The price of Rembrandts these days is really quite shocking. You will hardly see any change out of £20 million should you pop out for a Van Gogh landscape. No wonder people in the know pop into Guillaume Moisson's studio to see if he can run them up a quick Rubens or come up with a nice Cézanne for the spare bedroom. Moisson is a talented artist in his own right – well worth asking if you can see his private gallery – but he earns his living making copies of great artworks from the world's leading galleries. After a successful career recreating greatness as a scenic artist for the theatre, he set up this little studio, between the rue de la Monnaie and the cathedral,where he produces copies of Caravaggios on demand for €900 (6,000FF) and reproduction Monets from €750 (5,000FF). Commissions usually take three months.

Benoit 77 rue de la Monnaie, 59000; tel: 03 20 31 69 03 [15 F2]
Open Tue–Sat 09.30–19.30, Sun 09.00–13.30.
Ē *Bus 3,6 or 9 from Gare Flandres to Lion d'Or.*
Belgium's Neuhaus and Leonidas have high-profile counters in Lille, but forsake them in favour of a taste of the domestic product. The famous chocolate shop of Lille has over 50 varieties of chocolates and truffles to tempt the sweet tooth.

La Griffe 27 rue de la Barre, 59000; tel: 03 20 57 47 20 [14 D2]
Open Mon 14.30–18.30, Tue, Thu–Sat 12.00–19.00.
Ē *Bus 3 or 6 from Gare Flandres to Conservatoire. From rue Angleterre turn left into rue Royale and right into rue de la Barre.*
Second-hand clothes and shoes from the continent's leading fashion houses. Everything is in good condition and costs about a third of the original retail price.

Michel Ruc 23–25 rue des Chats Bossus, 59000; tel: 03 20 15 96 16 [15 F2]
Open Mon 14.00–19.00, Tue–Sat 10.00–19.00.
Ē *Bus 3,6 or 9 from Gare Flandres to Lion d'Or.*
The shopfront may be centuries old, but the window features the latest looks from Milan and Paris. Gaultier for the girls, Boss for the boys and Armani for everyone.

Par Hasard 44 rue des Trois Mollettes, 59000; tel: 03 20 06 34 13 [14 E2, 15 F2]
Open Tue–Sat 11.00–19.00, Sun 15.00–18.00.
Ē *Bus 3 or 6 from Gare Flandres to Conservatoir. From rue Angleterre turn left into rue des Trois Mollettes.*
Original gift shop specialising in tableware and home décor. Always worth a browse for that unusual finishing touch.

Pluriel 1 rue Jean Moulin, 59000; tel: 03 28 52 68 65 [14 E2]
Open Tue–Fri 10.00–14.00, 15.00–19.00, Sat 10.30–13.00, 14.00–19.00.
Ē *Bus 3 or 6 from Gare Flandres to Conservatoir. From rue Angleterre turn right into rue Jean Moulin.*
Accessorise with style at this outlet for Chanel and other designer labels.

RUK 14 bis pl du Lion d'Or, 59000; tel: 03 20 31 12 30 [15 G2]
Open Mon 14.00–19.00, Tue–Sat 10.00–19.00.
Ē *Bus 3,6 or 9 from Gare Flandres to Lion d'Or.*
Prada and other menswear for the lads with the wherewithal.

Grand' Place

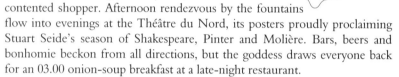

Find your way to the Grand' Place. After all, absolutely everything that matters in Lille begins here. The central column is a virtual sundial of life in the city. From sunrise over the Vieille Bourse's morning market selling cut flowers and uncut antiquarian books, to shirtsleeved lunchtimes on the terrace of the Coq Hardi. Carrier bags from FNAC and the Furet du Nord rest on tables during the 'anytime, coffee-time' of a contented shopper. Afternoon rendezvous by the fountains flow into evenings at the Théâtre du Nord, its posters proudly proclaiming Stuart Seide's season of Shakespeare, Pinter and Molière. Bars, beers and bonhomie beckon from all directions, but the goddess draws everyone back for an 03.00 onion-soup breakfast at a late-night restaurant.

The picture-book opera house around the corner is ever poised for its reopening after extensive renovation, and the circular Nouveau Siècle building is home to the Orchestre Nationale. Many weekends see displays or entertainment on the main square itself. Perhaps a bandstand will have been erected for a concert, or a marquee set up to house an exhibition sponsored by the local paper, *La Voix du Nord*, whose elegant building dominates the square.

The main commercial districts of Lille fan out from the Grand' Place, a giant compass, where all roads lead to shopping: chain stores, multiplex cinemas and boutiques line the rues de Béthune and Neuve. Since traffic was barred from these streets in 1973, visitors have been able to admire the art deco architecture above the shopfronts in the pedestrianised triangle between the stations, place République and the city squares. Along the rue Faidherbe are inexpensive shoe and clothes shops including the wonderful Tati (see Paris page 165); the wide rue Nationale has Printemps (see page 225) and the glitzier Parisian stores; and northwards, beyond the once-upon-a-time perpendicular-style belfry of the Chambre de Commerce are hidden the picture-perfect boutiques and galleries of Vieux Lille.

WHERE TO STAY

Brueghel 3–5 parvis St-Maurice, 59000; tel: 03 20 06 06 69 [15 G4]
Gare Lille Flandres; E̲ *av Le Corbusier to Gare Flandres, left into rue de Priez and walk round the church.*

PLACE GENERAL DE GAULLE [15 F3–4]

Named after Lille's most famous son, but known to everyone simply as the **Grand' Place**, the main square is the very heartbeat of the city. Almost pedestrianised, although a serpentine trail of traffic slithers safely along two sides, this is a veritable forum, where shoppers break their day, friends plot an evening, and revellers celebrate the night.

The essential rendezvous is the central fountain around the column of the *Déesse*, the goddess and symbol of the spirit of the city. The statue commemorates the bravery of the townsfolk, withstanding the siege of Lille by 35,000 Austrian soldiers in 1792. The original idea, mooted the day after the victory, was to build a monument by melting down all royal statues (the Revolution was at its height and Marie-Antoinette had not yet been executed). Enthusiasm waned, but eventually the *Déesse* was cast by Théophile Bra, with the intention of placing her atop his Arc de Triomphe in Paris. That plan too was abandoned, and the goddess returned to Lille, standing for three years in place Rihour before moving to Charles Benvignat's column on Grand' Place in 1845. Her crown represents Lille's ramparts, her right hand ever ready to fire another cannon, her left pointing to a plaque inscribed with the brave words of Mayor André's rebuttal of Austria's demands. Tongues soon began to wag, since from upper windows locals noted the goddess' uncanny resemblance to Mme Bigodanel, the then mayor's 54-year-old wife, whose fuller figure had not gone unnoticed by the artist.

The least-known and most charming of the central hotels, this little gem is very much a word-of-mouth favourite. Tucked away in a quiet pedestrianised street between the old Gare Flandres and the shops of the rue de Paris, the hotel faces the recently scrubbed and shining church of St-Maurice, which hosts some excellent classical concerts and organ recitals every summer Sunday afternoon. Overflowing window boxes announce the hospitality guaranteed within. Inside the cosy reception area, an authentic 1920s cage lift takes guests Noah-fashion two-by-two to the bedrooms. Each year another floor is carefully restored. With impeccable taste, the rooms have been styled to combine minimalism with elegance and comfort. Natural coir carpets, wrought-iron mirrors, picture frames from salvaged wood, classic bathrooms – all proof that a budget hotel need not lack artistic inspiration. Only the very smallest rooms miss the sophisticated touch, but with rates from €54–88 (360–560FF), comfort and a warm welcome will not break any bank and is genuine value for money.

Carlton 3 rue de Paris, 59026; tel: 03 20 13 33 13; toll free 0800 181 591 (UK), 800 888 4747 (USA and Canada); web: www.carlton.fr [15 F4]
M̲ *Gare Lille Flandres;* Ē̲ *Bus 12 from Gare Flandres to Théâtre. Or walk av le Corbusier and right into rue Faidherbe.*

Under her watchful gaze, students hold their protest rallies, bands play on Gay Pride Day and the city's tame giants parade during the Fêtes de Lille. Grand' Place has a habit of dressing for every occasion: most famously as a Christmas grotto in December and January, when a huge Ferris wheel swings sensation seekers into the skies to take in the panorama of gables and belfries from a swaying cradle high above the cobblestones. The wheel turns from mid-morning until well past midnight. Sometimes the cobbles are covered with plants, lawns and box hedges as the city gardeners decide to transform the square into a park. Perhaps the whole area will become a farmyard, with rows of market-garden cabbages in front of the theatre, and a herd of cows grazing contentedly outside McDonald's.

Around the square look out for carved and gilded images of the sun, symbol of King Louis XIV, whose royal bodyguard lived in the Grande Garde, a splendid galleried building that today houses the Théâtre du Nord. Alongside the theatre is the striking frontage of the home of *La Voix du Nord*, once a wartime Resistance news-sheet and now the regional daily newspaper. Dominating the square, its tiered roof is topped out by three golden Graces, symbolising the regional provinces of Artois, Flanders and Hainaut. Continental Europe's biggest bookshop, the Furet du Nord, boasts half a million volumes in stock, and is spread over eight storeys on different levels served by a complicated arrangement of lifts, staircases and walkways. Across the square, linking Grand' Place with place du Théâtre, is the stunning Vieille Bourse. The gateway to Vieux Lille is the archway bearing the name of the brasserie Alcide. Brasseries, bars and cafés abound, the square and its arteries liberally sprinkled with tables for al fresco dining and people-watching.

Ē *Bus 12 from Gare Flandres to De Gaulle. Or walk av Le Corbusier and right into rue Faidherbe then left to Grand' Place.*

A provincial grand hotel of the old school, with the usual four-star comforts liberally dispensed. Though the Alliance has the higher profile in the package tour brochures, the Carlton has an enviable location, one of the key corner sites in the very centre of town, a chime away from the belfry of the Chambre de Commerce. With rooms from €137–410 (900–2,700FF), it is always worth asking before booking for any weekend promotions that may easily halve the bill. An experience at any price is a stay in the panoramic rooftop cupola room actually inside a turret dome with the best view of any building in town, overlooking the squares, the Vieille Bourse, the opera house and the first cobbled alleys of Vieux Lille. A spa bath en suite adds to the feeling of luxury and romance. The public areas may seem slightly stuffy, but this is what the French consider British and therefore the height of sophistication. If breakfast at €12 (85FF) is not included in the deal, then the home-baked delights chez Paul are just yards away.

Grand Hôtel Bellevue 5 rue Jean Roisin, 59800; tel: 03 20 57 45 64 [14 E4]
M̄ *Rihour;* Ē *Métro 2 to Gare Lille Flandres then Line 1 to Rihour.*
Never mind the postal address, this hotel has double-glazed rooms on the Grand' Place itself, giving a thrilling goodnight view of a city at play. No mere onlooker however, this hotel has long played an active role in the city's party moments.

Since the evening that the young Mozart himself stayed in one of the building's original salons, the address has enjoyed much dabbling in the arts. A function room occasionally doubles as a theatre, and the hotel has just begun collaboration with chef Stéphane LePrince (see restaurant *Albert II*, page 231). The reception area adds a hint of a flourish to the décor, and the Windsor piano bar gives an air of weekend cocktails. The marbled en-suite facilities add a certain indulgence to prices that are comfortably lower three-star ∈122 (800FF).

De la Paix 46bis rue de Paris, 59800; tel: 03 20 54 63 93 [15 F4]
M̄ *Rihour;* Ē *av le Corbusier and right into rue Faidherbe, then left on rue des Ponts de Comines to rue de Paris, or bus 12 to Théâtre.*
Another family-run gem, this time just around the corner from the Grand' Place. Rooms here are devoted to great artists, and rather than merely hanging a few cheap prints in the bedrooms and lobbies, the walls are covered with neatly framed posters from great exhibitions around the world. You may share your room with Van Gogh, Lautrec or Magritte, or perhaps you might spend time getting to know a less vaunted talent. Of course the hotel provides great inspiration to visit the many museums and galleries in and around town. Don't forget that as well as the world famous Palais des Beaux Arts in Lille itself, Villeneuve d'Asq's modern art and Picasso collections are just a tram ride away, and Matisse's private collection is on show at his home town of le Cateau-Cambrésis, an easy drive from Lille. Larger rooms, at ∈72 (480FF), have a lounge area with soft furnishings for flopping after shopping, and each floor of the hotel boasts a residents' lounge by the lift, where one may admire the in-house exhibitions. Extremely helpful staff on duty day and night, and a room rate from ∈58 (380FF), make this a firm favourite. To be honest the only possible reason for the hotel remaining in the two-star category is the modest size of the bathrooms, with the teeniest tubs in town.

Le Royal 2 bd Carnot, 59800; tel: 03 20 14 71 47 [15 G3]
M̄ *Gare Lille Flandres;* Ē *Bus 12 from Gare Flandres to Théâtre, then walk behind the Opéra.*
An older, faded, slightly-worn chain hotel, with a friendly provincial welcome, just behind the opera house. With good-sized bedrooms and spacious en-suite bathrooms, this member of the Mercure chain is often the forgotten hotel of Lille. The long-promised renovations should be under way by the time you reach this page in the guide. Perfectly poised at the junction of the old and new towns. Rooms from ∈90 (600FF).

WHERE TO GO

FNAC Café 20 rue St-Nicolas, 59000; tel: 03 20 15 58 49 [15 F4]
Open Mon–Sat 10.00–15.00.
M̄ *Rihour;* Ē *Bus 12 from Gare Flandres to De Gaulle and walk through Voix du Nord building, or av le Corbusier, right into rue Faidherbe, left on rue des Ponts de Comines, right to rue de Paris, and left to rue St-Nicolas.*
Let the world know that you are techno-literate and nurse a trendy coffee or healthy salad in the land where DVD is king. The designer-sharp cafeteria of the smart hi-fi store has lighting that respects your body's commitment to an active nightlife, and staff that understand that you can't possibly eat at home in case you blind yourself on the morning glare from your i-mac.

Grand' Place pl Charles de Gaulle, 59000 [15 F3–4]
(see page 214)

Paul 8/12 rue de Paris, 59000; tel: 03 20 78 20 78 [15 F4]
M̲ *Rihour;* E̲ *Bus 12 from Gare Flandres to Théâtre. Or walk av le Corbusier and right into rue Faidherbe, then left to the Vieille Bourse.*
Don't bother with breakfast in your hotel. Come to Paul for the best breakfast in town. Not the biggest, nor the most varied, but certainly the best. This corner site bakery opposite the Vieille Bourse is the place to go for fresh croissants, just-baked bread and creamy, piping hot chocolate first thing in the morning. The €4.50 (30FF) breakfast tray served on solid wooden tables against the blue and white tiled walls and heavy tapestries of the bread and cake shop is the perfect way to start the day. Find inspiration in the words of wisdom painted on the old wooden beams, or concentrate on the scrumptious home-made jams and crunchy, crusty baguettes. Do not forget that food is served *chez* Paul until the witching hour, and it would be a pity to dismiss the pretty bakery as a mere breakfast and tea room. Up the curving wooden staircase is the bright and airy first-floor restaurant dining room. Here, elegance is the order of the day with echoes of a more leisurely era, from the tasteful tables by the windows to the marble-topped washstands, oak casks and mirrors in the washrooms. Huge, fabulous salads, tender and plentiful steaks, succulent fish, cheese and vegetable dishes, and the light and fresh *pâtisserie* one would expect from a century-old bakers and confectioners. Budget around €10–15 (65–170FF) for lunch or dinner. Paul has now spawned scores of satellite bakeries and *viennoiserie* counters across Lille, throughout Paris and beyond, but this old corner shop between the Opéra and the main square is something special.

Petit Marché de l'Art rue Leon Trulin, 59000 [15 G3]
Open 1st and 3rd Sat.
M̲ *Gare Flandres;* E̲ *Bus 12 from Gare Flandres to Théâtre.*
This twice-monthly Saturday morning art market alongside the opera house is a civilised alternative to the scrums fighting for discount clothing in the outlets and bazaars at the top of rue Faidherbe. You may find a little gem amongst the artworks on display, you might not. But the fun is in the atmosphere as local artists display their wares on the pavement.

Place Rihour [14 E4]
M̲ *Rihour;* E̲ *Métro 2 to Gare Lille Flandres then Line 1 to Rihour.*
Place de Gaulle trickles into place Rihour, home of the Palais Rihour (see page 218) and tourist office, by way of a row of restaurants, cafes and bars where late-night revellers adjourn for onion-soup breakfast in the small hours. A massive war memorial dominates the square, and is the scene of civic remembrance services on Armistice Day. Some rather disturbing coloured lighting illuminates the fountain that rinses the glass pyramid above the métro station. The result varies from fairground garish to an effect not unlike spilt hospital custard. In winter, a Christmas market of wooden chalets sells hot mulled wine and handmade gifts. The rue de la Vieille Comédie is named after Voltaire's visit to Lille in 1741 for the premiere of his play, *Mohamet.*

Place du Théâtre [15 F3–4]
E̲ *Bus 12 from Gare Flandres to Théâtre. Or walk av le Corbusier and right into rue Faidherbe.*
Behind the Vieille Bourse (see page 219), and looking down towards the old Flandres station, is the place du Théâtre. Only recently pedestrianised as part of the city's Millennium renovations, this is the junction of Lille ancient and modern. Spot the iron arm hanging above the junction of rue de la Bourse and rue de la Grande Chaussée pointing visitors to Vieux Lille. The two most striking buildings on the

square are surprisingly new, dating from the 1920s: the neo-classical opera house, with its monumental sculptures of Apollo and the Muses, and the splendid 76m neo-Flemish belfry of the imposing Chambre de Commerce et d'Industrie – both built by Louis Cordonnier. The Opéra has been closed for refurbishment and is scheduled to re-open in 2002 with its lavish interiors even more dazzling than ever. Inspired by the Palais Garnier in Paris, the Opéra de Lille has always been a place to be seen, and its programme usually features popular classics in productions from other European companies with an international cast of principals. Opposite is the Rang de Beauregard, an extraordinarily ornate terrace of 14 three-storey houses and shops constructed in 1687 to complement the Vieille Bourse. Look closely at the elegant shopfronts. Still embedded in the walls are cannonballs from the siege of 1792.

P'tit Quinquin sq Foch, rue Nationale, 59000 [14 D4]
M̄ Rihour; Ē Bus 12 from Gare Flandres to Foch.
How can you fail to fall in love with a town that erects a statue to a lullaby? If proof were ever needed that Lille has a generous and sweet nature, simply remember this: although the *Internationale* was composed in the bars of St-Sauveur, the song that the townsfolk took to their hearts was a sentimental *patois* melodrama of a poor lacemaker whose child would not stop crying. *Le P'tit Quinquin* was composed in 1852 by town hall clerk Alexandre Desrousseaux, and was soon adopted as a bedtime ballad by every mother in town. When the composer died in 1892 it was adapted as his funeral march, and the town commissioned Eugène Deplechin to build a memorial to the songwriter. The statue, ravaged by a million scrambled cuddles and kisses, shows Desrousseaux's working-class Madonna and child in a pose to melt the hardest of hearts. If you would like to hear the tune, make your way to the Place de Théâtre, where the bells of the clocktower chime the lullaby every day at noon.

WHAT TO SEE

Palais Rihour pl Rihour, 59000; tel: 03 20 21 94 21 [14 E4]
Tourist office hours Mon–Sat 09.30–18.30, Sun, holidays 10.00–12.00, 14.00–17.00. First floor by appointment. Free.
M̄ *Rihour;* Ē *Métro 2 to Gare Lille Flandres, then line 1 to Rihour.*
To most people this old building behind the monumental war memorial is merely a rather quaint tourist office. I've even heard some visitors dismiss the Gothic arches and mullioned windows as a Victorian folly. Heresy. Cross the threshold and you are standing in the remains of a ducal palace, seat of power in Lille for over 450 years, and boasting a guest list that has included England's Henry VIII and France's Louis XV. The original Palais Rihour was built by Philippe le Bon, Duke of Burgundy, when he moved the court to the city in 1453. His son Charles le Téméraire completed the palace 20 years later. It was through the Burgundian line that Lille passed to the Hapsburgs when Marie de Bourgogne married Maximillian of Austria in 1474. When Philip IV of Spain sold the palace to the city in the 17th century it began a new life as the town hall and continued to serve the community until ravaged by fire in 1916. The stairwell and chapels, among the finest surviving examples of flamboyant Gothic architecture in town, could hardly house a city's local government, so a new Hôtel de Ville was built in the St-Sauveur district (see page 237). The ground-floor guards' chapel is now the main tourist office, computer screens and brochure racks detracting from the original feel of the place. Climb the winding stairs to the upper chapel to admire the trefoil windows and vaulted ceiling. Burgundian coats of arms adorn the walls, and a real sense of the original palace remains. Exhibitions and concerts are sometimes held here.

St-Maurice parvis St-Maurice, rue de Paris, 59000; tel: 03 20 06 07 21 [15 G4]
Open daily. Free.
M̄ *Gare Lille Flandres;* Ē *av Le Corbusier to Gare Flandres, left into rue de Priez at the foot of rue Faidherbe.*

The first of the sudden surprises that make Lille so special. Unless you decide to take a shortcut from the station to the pedestrian shopping streets, you might never see this magnificent 15th-century church, its gleaming white stone façades restored to pristine condition. Built on marshland, it has five high naves to distribute its weight equally across a wide area, in a style known as *Hallekerque Flamande* – literally Flemish market church – after the airy market-hall style interior. Yet another unsung art collection may be viewed here, even if many original treasures have since found their way into the Palais des Beaux Arts. The dramatic stained-glass windows of *The Passion* were inspired by the heroic 19th-century style of Ingres. Summer Sunday organ recitals are worth catching, as are the occasional Saturday night concerts by local musicians.

Vieille Bourse pl de Général de Gaulle, 59000 [15 F4]
Open Tue–Sun 10.00–19.00. Free.
M̄ *Rihour;* Ē *Bus 12 from Gare Flandres to Théâtre. Or walk av le Corbusier and right into rue Faidherbe.*
Exquisite and unmissable, the most beautiful building in town has been restored to its original Flemish Renaissance brilliance. The greatest legacy of the Spanish occupation of the city was this jewel box of a *Bourse de Commerce* merchants' exchange between the two main squares. In fact the Bourse comprises 24 individual 17th-century houses ranged around a cloistered courtyard. Although at first glance the houses, with their ground-floor shops, may seem identical, the intricate carvings and mouldings on each façade are unique, thanks to the skills of builder Julien Destrez who worked on the project from 1652 to 1653. Destrez had already won a distinguished reputation as a carpenter and sculptor, and he dressed his masterpiece with ornate flourishes of masks and garlands on the outer walls. Lions of Flanders adorn the four doorways into the courtyard, which is itself decked with floral and fruit motifs. Today, above the symbols of the original guilds that once traded here, is a discreet row of contemporary logos representing the private enterprises sponsoring the restoration. As the sun rises over Lille, it catches the gilded bell-tower on the roof and radiates golden beams across the Grand' Place. Step inside the contemplative cloister to find a charming weekday market selling fresh flowers and antiquarian books under the gaze of busts of local pioneers of science and literature. A sanctuary from summer sun and winter winds alike, people come here to sit and read or play chess from mid-morning until early evening. Sundays bring impromptu tea dances with the old walls echoing to the sound of the waltzes and salsa.

WHERE TO EAT
Alcide 5 rue des Débris St-Etienne, 59800; tel: 03 20 12 06 95 [15 f3]
M̄ *Rihour;* Ē *Bus 12 from Gare Flandres to De Gaulle. Or walk av le Corbusier and right into rue Faidherbe then left to Grand' Place.*
Where better to indulge in a *carbonnade flamande* than in the most typical of brasseries? Alcide has been found under the arch at the main square since the

1870s, and it still retains its unmistakable Napoléon III style. Start with oysters or a *feuilleté* of asparagus or the ubiquitous *tarte aux maroilles* before succumbing to the main course. You may *moules-frites* your fill here, you may go for grilled fish, but the *carbonnade* is the house speciality; whether it be beef, fish or seafood, it will be cooked in good local beer and taste of tradition. Service is as solid and professional as you would expect from the white, starched table linen and polished mirrors of the light and bright dining room. A midweek beer and *carbonnade* menu for €19–25 (130–160FF) is value for money.

Brasserie André 71 rue de Béthune, 59800; tel: 03 20 54 75 51
M̄ *République;* Ē *Métro 2 to Gare Lille Flandres then Line 1 to République. Cross pl Richebé to rue de Béthune.*
This is where good *moules* go when they die. Sumptuous traditional brasserie décor, with wonderful wooden-panelled arches and dark wooden walls contrasting with white starched napkins, tablecloths and aprons. Not cheap by brasserie standards – your meal should set you back €38 (250FF), but your lunch companions will be businessmen, bankers and people who don't mind paying a tad over the odds for a classy setting for classic favourites. The pavement terrace spills out on to the main shopping area.

Brasserie de la Paix 25 pl Rihour, 59800; tel: 03 20 54 70 41 [14 E4]
Closed Sun.
M̄ *Rihour;* Ē *Métro 2 to Gare Lille Flandres then Line 1 to Rihour.*
Café society 1930s-style lives on here; the décor, the welcome and the food are from the heyday of the French brasserie. Great platters of seafood, roast *canette de Challans* cooked with fresh figs, and a chicory *crème brûlée* are amongst the attractions. The thirties feel is strictly for diners inside the restaurant. Sit outside on the pavement and you can enjoy the very modern spectacle of shoppers trekking from boutique to boutique and commuters emerging from beneath the queasy custard-coloured waters on the pyramid fountain at Rihour métro station. Menus from €15 (100FF) lunchtimes to €30 (200FF) in the evenings.

La Chicorée 15 pl Rihour, 59000; tel: 03 20 54 81 52 [14 E4]
M̄ *Rihour;* Ē *Métro 2 to Gare Lille Flandres then Line 1 to Rihour.*
Everyone has found himself here at some stage of some late-night session. Open from 10.00 until dawn, the old reliable brasserie on the corner is the perfect standby when an evening has just flown by at the bar, café or jazz-club and nobody is ready for bed yet. An all day menu of around €11 (70FF) is a bit limited, and the full-blown à la carte should run to around €25 (160FF). However a steaming bowl of onion soup topped with a gruyère-covered crouton should fill you up and leave the wallet relatively unscathed. Since prices rise by around 20% after midnight, the waiters are perfectly happy to serve just a starter or one-course refuelling option in the small hours. At sunrise the place is busy with night-shift workers, road sweepers and métro staff rounding off the night's work with a hefty steak and refreshing *bière*, as the rest of us follow our noses to the bakery for breakfast croissants and hot chocolate!

Clément Marot – Le Club 16 rue de Pas, 59000; tel: 03 20 57 01 10 [14 E3]
Closed Sun, Mon evening.
M̄ *Rihour;* Ē *Métro 2 to Gare Lille Flandres then Line 1 to Rihour. Rue Roisin into rue de Pas.*
It took me four years of eating and treating in Lille before I found myself crossing the threshold of Clement Marot's dining room near the up-front terraces of his louder neighbours. I could hardly wait four weeks before returning. Suffice to say,

this is the type of restaurant we all hope to stumble across in our journeys across France. The main dining room is somewhat post-war traditional in decorative style. Commemorative plates on a rack above panelled booths; heavy plate ice buckets and tureens on well-polished surfaces; certificates alongside framed paintings of favourite holiday spots; and a waitress in black skirt, white blouse and lace apron hovering by the champagne magnums and long-stemmed cut-flowers. The other room next door is more modern and presumably favoured by the business lunch brigade opting for the €15 (98FF) healthy-eating midday menu, which features prudently grilled offerings. In the older room, I settled down to wallow in the menu and wine list. The price of the carte-menu varies, depending on whether you choose a half bottle of wine or Tattinger on ice. I quickly discovered that recipes as described on the menu are not written on tablets of stone. A lively chat with the waiter, chef or (if you are lucky) *patron* brings plenty of alternative suggestions. The signature catch of *sandre* on the menu was intended to be prepared with sesame and a *coulis de poivrons*. I needed little persuasion to agree to an alternative version using Marot's hallmark flavour *chicorée*, a locally produced delicacy from the sandy soil of coastal Flanders that the chef uses in dishes from the main course to the *bavarois*. Inspiration! The smoky, coffee-like flavour of the sauce complemented the fish's crisp topping of sesame seed. I was equally glad to have been nudged away from my original thoughts of a *terrine* starter in favour of a *salade de poisson en escabèche*. This turned out to be a wonderfully old-fashioned and fabulously sharp presentation of sardines marinated in the house champagne vinegar (Marot eschews the balsamic), with a dash of lemon juice and thyme on local leaves to provide a truly kicking salad. Local produce is first choice wherever possible. Thus poultry comes from the town of Licques where free-range turkeys dine on corn and grain to become the north's answer to the legendary fowl of Bresse, and where, once a year – before Christmas – the mayor and corporation, and *confrères de la dinde*, march the town's flocks to one of the great gastronomic fairs of the region. Those birds that end up in these kitchens are presented with wild country mushrooms. I couldn't decide on a dessert and let the chef-patron choose for me. I may well never eat another *crème brûlée* as long as I live. It was pure cream, which still breathed the air of the dairy, and was quite simply the best I have tasted this side of childhood. The welcome from all the restaurant team was second to none, and hospitality seems to be the key to this place's discreet success. The 'be our guest' approach even extends to the wine list. Rather than compromise with a half-bottle of a lesser vintage, diners are encouraged to buy a full bottle with the assurance that, at the end of the meal, staff will wrap up the rest of the bottle to be enjoyed – as the wine list has it – at your own table in the comfort of your home. Lunch menus start at €15 (98FF). Other options €38–41 (250–280FF).

Le Compostelle 4 rue Saint-Etienne, 59800; tel: 03 28 38 08 30; web: www.chateauxhotels.com/compostelle [14 E3]
M̲ *Rihour;* E̲ *Métro 2 to Gare Lille Flandres then Line 1 to Rihour. Rue Roisin into rue de Pas then right into rue St-Etienne.*
'Make yourself at home' is the unspoken invitation at this great big popular restaurant just beside the main square of Lille. The building (a staging post on the pilgrims' route to Santiago de Compostela) may date from the 16th century, and boast the only Renaissance façade in Lille, but the refurbished décor is the very model of a modern appreciation of *temps perdus*. Alain Roussiez has glassed in the open courtyard and created a warren of colourful dining rooms on each floor. The bar and the Blue Room are my favourites, being packed with real bookcases – not stuffed with imposing leather-bound tomes, but well-thumbed

Le Compostelle

paperbacks stacked and piled at random. The urge to browse and dip when waiting for friends is irresistible. Other salons are *provençal* pink and theatrical yellow. The menu has a good blend of regional and national dishes for such a large restaurant, but no shocks when it comes to the bill. Good midweek menus from ∈14 (96FF) to ∈25 (168FF) (*vin compris*) or one may warn the waitress in advance and enjoy a free-range forage through three courses à la carte for a set '*Sans Surprise*' ∈23 (155FF). But what to choose? My advice would be to stick to the *cuisine du nord*: a cold North Sea *hochepot* of fish then the *noix de veau* prepared with melted maroilles cheese. A refreshing *sorbet* made from the *genièvre* gin from nearby Houlle makes for a sparky finale.

Le Coq Hardi 44 pl Général de Gaulle, 59800; tel: 03 20 55 21 08
M̄ *Rihour;* Ē *Bus 12 from Gare Flandres to De Gaulle. Or walk av le Corbusier and right into rue Faidherbe then left to Grand' Place.*
An institution on the central square of Lille for donkey's years, the tables spreading out across the pavement are better known than the small restaurant behind them. In fact it was only when the winter weather grumbled ominously that I ventured to check out the restaurant itself. Small but perfectly busy, with service on two floors, the Coq Hardi is unashamedly basic rustic. Untreated wooden ceilings, sacks of baguettes inside the front door and a constant flow of customers keen on value for money lunching. Huge portions are the order of the day, whether *andouillette de Cambrai* with *frites* or a *tartare des deux saumons*, served ready-mixed or with the additional ingredients on the side. Most *plats* between ∈7–12 (45–75FF). In the sunshine take a big bowl of *moules* or a huge summer salad and lunch outdoors for well under ∈15 (100FF), whilst people watching at this key corner between the old town and the main square.

La Coquille 60 rue St-Etienne, 59000; tel: 03 20 54 29 82 [14 E3]
Closed Sun.
M̄ *Rihour;* Ē *Métro 2 to Gare Lille Flandres then Line 1 to Rihour. Rue Roisin into rue de Pas and left along rue St-Etienne.*
Don't be misled by the name. La Coquille may be just across the way from l'Ecume des Mers, but it really belongs in the realm of the barnyard – very much the country of clucking and grain – as reflected by the décor of this tastefully refreshed old building with reds in the linens and dried flower baskets picking out the warm tones of the brickwork. It is a charming restaurant with the warmest of welcomes and a timelessly stress-free atmosphere despite its city centre location. Fish is not barred from the plate. Indeed the 85FF business lunch menu on the day of my visit featured a scrunchy salad of celeriac, beetroot and herring, and a crisp and tender salmon à *l'unilatérale*. However, it is the legendary house *foie gras*

with leeks and the almost *périgordine* duck dishes that are the hallmark of the house. A *caneton sauvageonne sur lie de vin* wrapped itself around the taste-buds with more than a hint of walnut oil, and the warm apricot tart is dressed with a cream that fills the mouth with a whirlpool of almond and lavender. Through a window one can peek into the compact and comfortingly un-hip kitchen next door. ∈30–36 (200–239FF) is a sensible budget for an unrestrained forage through the menus. A truly disarming welcome, good food and a real sense of place mark this find as one for the address book. The only bad news for travellers on a weekend break is that the opening hours are geared towards midweek dining.

L'Ecume des Mers 10 rue de Pas, 59800; tel: 03 20 54 95 40 [14 E3]
Closed Sun evening and most of August.
M̄ *Rihour;* Ē *Métro 2 to Gare Lille Flandres then Line 1 to Rihour. Rue Roisin into rue de Pas.*
Refurbished in pleasure-port seaside blues and framed Poseidonesque mosaic, the newest aspect of the restaurant is the menu, the entire *carte* printed daily to reflect the catch of the day. There are a few non-fishy items on the menu, but one comes here to taste the sea. This is the domain of a restaurateur who learnt his trade at l'Huitrière. However, you should not expect great works of art on the plate. At l'Ecume des Mers, they do what they do and they do it well and what they do is prepare freshly caught fish in the classic manner. Nothing too clever. Raw sardine in a tarragon marinade, a cold monkfish *bouillabaisse* perhaps, as a change to the standards, but traditional favourites follow the seasons. On a grey day go for an *aïoli* of *morue* or a warming and filling *choucroute* with halibut, smoked haddock and salmon. A mix of well-to-do couples and business foursomes choose to dine indoors; a younger element basks on the pavement terrace outside sharing platters of oysters. Eavesdroppers with a cultural bent might spot illustrious neighbour Jean-Claude Casadesus, director of the Orchestre National de Lille, in conversation with a world-renowned soloist. From every other table comes the reassuring clink-clank of *glaçons* in well-stocked ice buckets clinking against a crisp Chablis or a *demi* Pouilly-Fumé from the fairly priced wine list. Menus at the ∈15–22 (100–140FF) mark and à la carte around ∈38 (250FF).

Le Flam's 8 rue de Pas, 59000; tel: 03 20 54 18 38 [14 E3]
M̄ *Rihour;* Ē *Métro 2 to Gare Lille Flandres then Line 1 to Rihour. Rue Roisin into rue de Pas.*
Welcome to the home of the *flammekueche* – that not-quite-pizza, not-quite-*crêpe* speciality of the city. It's a large, thin, dough-base spread with either savoury or sweet toppings. The former based around cheeses, mushrooms and ham, the latter the blend of fruit, sweets and *eau de vie* toppings that one finds in any *crêperie*. Cut out a square of your *flam'*, roll it into a cigar shape and hold it with your fingers to munch over a chilled beer and a heated discussion about life, love and politics. Lunchtimes, the place is filled with office workers and shoppers taking advantage of the special deals (a savoury and a sweet *flammekueche* with a 25cl glass of *bière blonde* for ∈8 (50FF). Evenings, it's a regular student hang-out, 50m from the Grand' Place, with groups of friends sharing a selection of *flams*, picnic style. After dark, pay ∈11–15 (70–100FF) and feel replete. In good weather step across the road to the summer terrace; in winter stay cosy indoors amongst the warm brickwork.

Aux Moules 34 rue de Béthune, 59000; tel: 03 20 57 12 46
M̄ *Rihour;* Ē *Métro 2 to Gare Lille Flandres then Line 1 to Rihour. Rue de la Vieille Comédie leads to rue de Béthune.*

No surprises here – the menu pays lip service to other tastes, but the speciality of the house is *moules*, *marinières* or in beer, in big pots or small bowls, with or without *frites*. Mussels by name and mussels by the bucket load. When the establishment first opened its doors in 1930 the set menu was four francs; these days a moules meal will cost around ∈9 (58FF). Famous for boasting the highest pile of mussel shells stacked up on the pavement outside the restaurant during the *Braderie* festivities each September, the place is dominated by a huge mural of the heyday of the *plat du jour*. Waiters are either young and chirpy or lifers who can recall prices in old money! Great for late lunches on Sunday afternoon, or mid-afternoon *crêpes* during a shopping excursion through the pedestrianised streets south of the place de Gaulle. Leave room for the house rhubarb *tarte* at lunchtime or the massive *éclair* for self-indulgence at any hour.

Taverne de l'Ecu 9 rue Esquermoise, 59000; tel: 03 20 57 55 66 [14 E3]
M̲ *Rihour;* E̲ *Métro 2 to Gare Lille Flandres then line 1 to Rihour. Rue Roisin into rue de Pas.*
Once upon a time, 150 years ago, this was a dance hall, *café-concert*. Then the dancing girls extended a welcome that was a little too enthusiastic for the morals of the day. So the place became a brasserie. The affectionate nature of the personnel continued to enhance the reputation. It closed down for a while to reopen as an art cinema in the 1960s, then the programming nudged the frontiers of art, and it closed once again to reopen as the flamboyant brasserie of today. The old music-hall stage has been restored, and today it houses the vats for the home-brewed beers served on tap in house. Light pastel-painted plaster walls recall the theatrical past, and the lively crowd is as rumbustuous and enthusiastic as ever – quaffing home-brewed *blonde*, *blanche* and *ambrée* ales or more commercial beers. Menus show variations on *tartiflettes*, those oven-baked platters of potato, *crème fraiche*, cheese and ham or salmon. Main courses around ∈7 (50FF), *Chti'mi* dessert is rather like a fluffy chicory-themed mousse balanced on a cheesecake biscuit base. Pay ∈19 (120FF) plus, including drinks. One of only two brasseries in town to brew its own beer.

WHAT TO BUY

Benjamin 45 rue de Béthune, 59000; tel: 03 20 54 69 67 [14 E5, 15 F4–5]
Open Mon 13.45–19.00, Tue–Fri 09.30–19.00, Sat 09.30–12.30, 14.00–19.00.
M̲ *Rihour;* E̲ *Métro 2 to Gare Flandres then line 1 to Rihour. Rue de la Vieille Comédie leads to rue de Béthune.*
Hats, gloves, brollies and finishing touches for any outfit; Benjamin has been accessorising Lille's best-dressed set since 1926.

La Comtesse du Barry 21 rue Esquermoise, 59000; tel: 03 20 54 00 43 [14 E3]
Open Mon–Sat 09.30–19.30.
M̲ *Rihour;* E̲ *Bus 12 from Gare Flandres to De Gaulle.*
Pâtés in jars and tins of preserved delicacies from across France, but mostly from the farmyards of the southwest. *Foie gras*, smoked salmon, prepared *terrines* and cold platters for lunch, or gift-wrapped as savoury presents.

FNAC 20 rue St-Nicolas, 59000; tel: 03 20 15 58 15 [15 F4]
Open Mon–Sat 10.00–19.30.
M̲ *Rihour;* E̲ *Bus 12 from Gare Flandres to De Gaulle and walk through Voix du Nord building, or av le Corbusier, right into rue Faidherbe, left on rue des Ponts de Comines, right to rue de Paris, and left to rue St-Nicolas.*
Hi-fi, books, discs and videos at the nation's favourite chainstore and box office.

Le Furet du Nord pl Charles de Gaulle, 59000; tel: 03 20 78 43 43 [15 F4]
Open Mon–Sat 09.30–19.30.
M̄ *Rihour;* Ē *Bus 12 from Gare Flandres to De Gaulle. Or walk av le Corbusier and right into rue Faidherbe then left to Grand' Place.*
France's largest bookshop has a respectable international section and good ground-floor travel department.

Morel et Fils 33 pl du Théâtre, 59000; tel: 03 20 55 00 10 [15 F3]
Open Mon–Sat 10.00–18.30.
M̄ *Rihour;* Ē *Bus 12 from Gare Flandres to Théâtre.*
Buy lingerie, nightwear and lacy finery in the very prettiest of boutiques.

Le Page 6–10 rue de la Bourse, 59000; tel: 03 20 12 04 04 [15 F3]
Mon 14.00–19.00, Tue–Fri 10.00–13.00, 14.00–19, Sat 10.00–19.00; closed Mon in July and Aug.
M̄ *Rihour;* Ē *Bus 12 from Gare Flandres to Théâtre. Walk past the opera house to rue de la Bourse.*
A jewel box of a shop, the ornate façade is always one of the treats of the town when the Christmas light are switched on. Upstaging even the building are the watches and trinkets from Gucci and Cartier, Chanel and Rolex.

Pâtisserie Meert [14 E3] (see page 203)

Paul [15 F4] (see page 217)

Petit Marché de l'Art [14 E3] (see page 217)

Philippe Olivier 3 rue du Curé St-Etienne, 59000; tel: 03 20 74 96 99 [15 F3]
Open Mon–Sat 10.00–19.00.
M̄ *Rihour;* Ē *Bus 12 from Gare Flandres to De Gaulle. Walk under the Alcide arch then turn left.*
Maître Olivier is one of the country's grand masters of cheese. His main store in Boulogne supplies the Elysée Palace, Vatican and White House. Buy a camembert marinated in Calvados or try a local speciality.

Pomme Cannelle 5 rue du Curé St-Etienne, 59000; tel: 03 20 06 83 06 [15 F3]
Open Mon–Sat 10.00–20.00, Sun 10.00–13.00.
M̄ *Rihour;* Ē *Bus 12 from Gare Flandres to De Gaulle. Walk under the Alcide arch then turn left.*
I love this tiny little florist shop. Dinky and dainty terracotta pots of perfect miniature rosebushes from €4.50 (30FF), or unusual and exotic plants manicured to perfection.

Printemps 41–45 rue Nationale, 59000; tel: 03 20 63 62 00 [14 E4]
Open Tue–Thu, Sat 09.30–19.30, Fri 09.30–20.00.
M̄ *Rihour;* Ē *Métro 2 to Gare Flandres then Line 1 to Rihour. Behind the tourist office is the rear entrance to the store.*
A branch of the famous Parisian department store. See page 67.

Rouge 15 rue de la Clef, 59000; tel: 03 20 74 19 20 [15 F3]
Open Mon 14.00–19.00, Tue–Sat 10.30–13.00, 14.00–19.00.
Ē *av le Corbusier and right into rue Faidherbe; walk behind the opera house to rue de la Clef.*
Cool looks just outside Vieux Lille. This is where the younger designers showcase their outfits to a sympathetic, youthful market. Well-known names such as DKNY keep the place ticking over, whilst unknown labels get an early airing.

République and the Markets

The Palais des Beaux Arts is the magnet that pulls the world to the place République, providing an abundance of inspiration and fulfilment. How many visitors realise that the museum is but the gateway to the one time Latin Quarter of Lille, a 19th-century haven of culture and learning?. The boulevard de la Liberté was laid out when the original city walls came tumbling down in the mid-19th century. Originally named for the Empress Eugénie, this was the essential address for well to do families, enriched by the industrial revolution. Textile barons and their ilk competed to build grander and grander mansions with grand staircases for grand gestures and grander entertaining, many with their own private theatres – for after dinner opera at home.

The square itself is poised between the museum and the equally grand Préfecture, which was based on the design of the Paris Louvre. Notice the emblems on each wing, an eagle for the Second Empire, the letter N for Napoléon III. At the centre of the gardens is a stepped arena, providing a stage for musicians and a well of natural light for the métro station.

The Théâtre Sébastopol can be seen from here. An entertaining explosion of architectural styles – Renaissance, Moorish, Classical and sheer pantomime – this people's playhouse provides popular boulevard entertainment.

From populist entertainment to the arts: roads south lead to the former Faculté des Lettres, once a centre of study, reflection and tolerance. The Protestant Temple and Synagogue may be seen on rue Angellier. The secular university is now based outside the town centre. To the north, Boulevard Vauban is home to the Catholic University campus. Between the two sites, rue Solférino is the centre of Lille's student nightlife.

Lille is a market town, never more so than during the Braderie of the first weekend in September. For 48 hours non-stop the entire city sets out its stalls on doorsteps, pavements, trestles and pitches. Recycle your children's clothes for a few pence, rediscover stolen goods from that break-in in May and swap deco lampshades for sixties lavalamps in a tradition that dates back to the city fathers granting servants the right to earn money by selling their master's cast-off clothing once a year. A hundred kilometres of stalls appear every year, the métro runs all night long, and every hotel room for miles around is booked months in advance. The Braderie never sleeps and brasseries compete to sell the most *moules* and create the highest pile of shells on the pavement outside the front door. A special map-guide is published for the Braderie and may be picked up at the tourist office.

Since the event is held only once a year, a happy alternative takes place every week in the Wazemmes quarter, 15 minutes' walk or two métro stops from the town centre. This is the market of markets and a Sunday morning institution. A smaller market is held each Wednesday and Saturday at the place Sébastopol.

WHERE TO STAY

Chez B&B 78 rue Caumartin, 59000; tel: 03 20 13 76 57 [14 C8]

M̄ *République;* Ē *Métro 2 to Gare Lille Flandres, changing to line 1 to République. Take rue Nicolas Leblanc, cross pl Lebon to rue de Fleurus then left on to rue Caumartin.*

I am going to hate myself for including this special address in the book, since it is a secret I have previously only shared with family and friends. I have enjoyed the hospitality of B&B, Bernard and Béatrice Quillerou, since the days that they lived in a quiet street outside the city walls. After moving to their new home, a five-minute walk or ten-minute stroll from the Palais des Beaux Arts, they continued to offer bed and breakfast *en famille.* The welcome is heartfelt, Béatrice speaks flawless English and her two young sons are polite and charming. The guest accommodation is tastefully furnished and homely. Breakfast is taken with the family and might include home-made brioches and breads. Rooms are around the €50–60 (350–400FF) mark. The family can arrange to meet guests at the TGV station if necessary, and offers a *table d'hôte* dining option.

WHERE TO GO

Les Halles pl des Halles Centrales, rue Solférino, 59800 [14 B–C5]

M̄ *République;* Ē *Bus 12 from Gare Flandres to Eglise Sacré Coeur. Rue Solférino to pl des Halles Centrales.*

Wazemmes may be the daytime weekend capital, but another marketplace, the former Les Halles wholesale district straddling the rues Solférino and Masséna, is the centre of nightlife. Part student hangout, part city of singles and part party-animal safari park, the restaurants, bars and pavements are an electrifying life force on Friday and Saturday nights. The old covered market itself houses a run-down supermarket that still manages to catch some of the party buzz, cheery chaos as people stock up on last-minute supplies for rendezvous with friends in a student bedsit before hitting the bars. Like any city's party zone, a number of bars and restaurants open and close with the frequency of a revolving door, but firm favourites survive each new influx of undergraduate revellers. Those who care about looking cool hang out at the Café La Plage and Le 16. La Bucherie, an institution in the quarter since the social dark ages, is a veritable meat-rack – lively dance floor, cruisy cocktail bar and the benchmark of the social scene – and the first point of contact for making new friends. Restaurants like the Ducasse, on the other hand, are strictly for old acquaintance. The season's newest crop of dining rooms will provide a perfect hideaway for couples. Do not dismiss the area as merely the haunt of the green and trendy. There are more than a few bars and restaurants well worth a detour, both around the square and along the rues Gambetta and Puebla. As well as a local branch of Les Pêcheurs d'Etaples (owned by the fisherman of the Côte d'Opale), discover some excellent African, Asian and Greek restaurants. Never forget that the cosmopolitan community of Lille has gastronomic cultures with roots far from Flanders.

Café La Plage 122 rue Solférino, 59800

Le 16 42–44 rue Masséna, 59800; tel: 03 20 54 86 70

La Bucherie 32 rue Masséna, 59800; tel: 03 20 30 66 06

Aux Pêcheurs d'Etaples 150 rue Solférino, 59000; tel: 03 20 40 20 38

Closed Sun night. ∈40 (280FF).

La Petite Cave 2 pl Philippe de Girard, rue Nationale, 59000; tel: 03 20 57 13 34
Closed Sun, Mon and lunchtimes.
M̲ *Gambetta;* E̲ *Bus 12 from Gare Flandres to Colbert.*
Just far enough along the rue Nationale to discourage casual trippers, this
basement restaurant aims to recreate the Montmartre atmosphere of a *bouchon*
filled with *chanson*. Walls are lined with EP and LP sleeves of Montand,
Aznavour, long-forgotten Eurovision starlets and of course *La Môme* Piaf
herself. Though a high-tech pianola may be found on the ground floor in the
basement room, the singers perform to backing tapes or perhaps an accordion
or guitar. The musical menu is strictly *chanson*, those essentially French dance
hall and piano bar numbers that are our own private soundtrack to France.
Service is friendly and attentive, the three set four-course menus from ∈28–45
(198–298FF) including wine and *apéro* filled with standards, *châteaubriand*,
potlevlesch with *genièvre*, *escargot*, *tarte aux pommes* and a plate of local cheeses, all
reminiscent of the nutritious, generous portions of homely, robust fare served
by a preoccupied aunt.

Place Philippe Lebon [14 D7]
M̲ *République;* E̲ *Métro 2 to Gare Lille Flandres changing to Line 1 to République. Take
rue Nicolas Leblanc to place Lebon.*
This intersection of the rue Solférino boasts the kitschest statue in town. On the
edge of the original university district, this is a lavish homage to Louis Pasteur,
first dean of the science faculty. As the microbiologist who first discovered that
germs cause disease, and the pioneer of pasteurisation, the great man is shown
surrounded by grateful mothers offering their babies aloft. Fab. Across the square
is the Romanesque-Byzantine church of **St-Michel** surrounded by identikit
townhouses. The **Maison Coillot** is on the rue Fleurus. Walking south,
Solférino leads to an equestrian statue of Joan of Arc. To the north are the
Théâtre Sébastopol and Les Halles.

Wazemmes Market pl de la Nouvelle Aventure, 59000 [14 A7]
Sun morning.
M̲ *Gambetta;* E̲ *Métro 2 to Gare Lille Flandres, then line 1 to Gambetta.*
Emerge from Gambetta métro station and prepare all your senses to be ravaged.
Surrender to the pulse of the city and simply follow the crowds past puppies
and chickens, rabbits and budgerigars. Around the church of **St-Pierre and
St-Paul** swims the tide of humanity, past antiques, bric à brac and junk, past
piles of clothing. Into the place de la Nouvelle Aventure the adventure
continues, past mounds of gloriously plump fresh chicory, rose-red radishes
and tear-blushed artichokes from the market gardens of Artois and Flanders,
past puppets and playthings, smart coats and swimwear; shop doorways flung
open on a Sunday: past promises of 'Special prices just for you *Monsieur,
Madame*, only today from my cousin in Africa'. Into the red-brick market hall
itself: past fresh North Sea fish on the slab and crates of seafood; past cheeses
from the region and beyond; past exotic sausages and pristine plucked poultry.

Through the hall to the flower market, past carnations and lilies; past spring blooms or Christmas wreaths.

From café doorways hear the sound of the accordion playing. An old man on a bicycle offers bunches of herbs from his panniers to passers-by and a younger biker steps off his Harley to try on a new leather jacket for €68.5 (450FF in old money). Backs are slapped, hands are shaken, noses are tapped and deals are struck. As the church bells toll for mass, traders' cries mingle with the sound of a barrel organ. At the back of a lorry blocking the rue des Sarrazins, gleaming saucepans are offered at never to be repeated prices, and in the midst of the whirlpool of the market square a salesman demonstrates his miracle wonder-broom or incredible magical vegetable-slicing machine.

On street corners, enormous *rôtisseries* drip the juices from turning chickens on to trays of roast potatoes and vegetables, the scent of a traditional Sunday lunch competing with the more exotic aromas from the enormous drums of couscous and paella as a French market merges into the multi-ethnic north African *soukh*. Follow your nose and keep your hand on your wallet. All in all, Wazemmes on a Sunday morning is an unforgettable experience for bargain hunters and browsers alike.

WHAT TO SEE

Palais des Beaux Arts (Fine Arts Museum) pl de la République, 59000; tel: 03 20 06 78 00 [14 E6]
Open Mon 14.00–18.00, Wed–Thu, Sat–Sun 10.00–18.00, Fri 10.00–19.00; closed Tue, public holidays. €4.5 (30FF), free access to atrium.
M̲ *République;* E̲ *Métro 2 to Gare Lille Flandres, changing to line 1 to République.*
For six years, in a modest office tucked away behind the magnificent splendour of the museum, curator Arnaud Brejon de Lavergnée pondered over the Palais des Beaux Arts' many treasures. France's second museum after the Louvre has Goyas and Rubens, Picassos, Lautrecs and Monets, but the greatest treasure of them all is Arnaud Brejon de Lavergnée himself. The passions of this modest and unassuming art lover are as much a part of this fabulous palace as the rich red walls, the floppy chairs, and the catalogue of some of the world's greatest artworks. During the renovations, Monsieur Brejon de Lavergnée could be seen at the station platform, clutching bubble-wrapped masterpieces to his chest as he personally escorted the Palais' jewels to be restored at the National Gallery in London. Until the day in 1997 that President Chirac inaugurated the new museum, every picture, every frame and every detail came under his exacting scrutiny.

The breathtaking art collection was brought to Lille on the orders of Napoléon, who stripped the walls of palaces and private galleries throughout his European empire, from Italy to the Low Countries. The imposing palace was built from 1889 to 1892 by the Parisian architects Bérard et Delmas, and reinvented a century later by Jean-Marc Ibos and Myrto Vitart who, together with Monsieur Brejon de Lavergnée, were instructed by Mayor Mauroy to open up the museum to the town.

They redefined the ground floor as a light, airy atrium and terrace, open to the public as a meeting place or coffee stop – admission free. The plan paid off: what had been a pleasure for the cultured few is now a cherished symbol of civic pride, and was the triumph that awoke the world to the news that Lille had achieved greatness.

Today's visitors take one of the twin grand staircases adorned with leaded windows heralding the *arts et métiers* of Lille to the first floor, where room after room offers French, Flemish and European masterpieces from the 17th to the

19th centuries. Highlights include Rubens' *Descente de la Croix*, an entire room devoted to Jordaens, and a succession of high-ceilinged galleries housing the works of Van Dyck, Corot and Delacroix with Watteau, the collection's first curator. Best of all is the celebrated pair of Goyas, *Les Jeunes* and *Les Vieilles*, the former a timeless portrayal of a teenage crush and the latter a cruelly satirical dissection of old age: crones at one with their malevolence. So many riches, it is easy to overlook the corridor devoted to the Impressionists. Make time for Monet, Van Gogh, Renoir and Sisley, not to mention a Lautrec and Rodin's *Burghers of Calais*.

Back on the ground floor, the sculpture gallery includes the best of 19th-century classical statuary, some imperial, some disturbing. A good halfway refreshment point for your visit, the collection leads to the rear courtyard and the modern architects' remarkable prism comprising the glass-fronted administration block and a sheet of water that turns the grey skies of the north into pure natural light to illuminate the basement galleries.

The underground rooms should not be missed. The Renaissance room includes Donatello's bas relief *Festin d'Herod*, and many sketches by Raphaël. It also houses 19 of Vauban's detailed models of his fortified towns – among them Lille and Calais – frozen in time and space between sheets of glass in an otherwise blacked out exhibition of the landscape of 18th-century France and Flanders.

The catalogue of treasures on every floor could never leave anybody feeling short changed. Should you be lucky enough to come across Monsieur Brejon de Lavergnée himself escorting his guests around his gallery, his infectious enthusiasm drawing total strangers to his enlightening discourse on a favourite painting, that would be a bonus beyond price.

Maison Coillot 14 rue Fleurs, 59000 [14 D7]
M̄ *République;* Ē *Métro 2 to Gare Lille Flandres changing to Line 1 to République. Take rue Nicolas Leblanc to place Lebon, into rue Fleurs.*
An unexpected flourish of art nouveau in a quiet residential street off the place Lebon. All the houses around the church of St-Michel are identical. All but one that is. If 14 rue Fleurs looks more like a Paris métro station than a private home, then thanks are due to its original owner, Monsieur Coillot, a ceramics marker who commissioned Hector Guimard to redesign his house. Guimard's celebrated flourishes, dark green swirls and horticultural sweeps are the hallmark of the capital's subway system. His reinvention of the domestic townhouse is no less flamboyant, using Coillot's own ceramics alongside cast iron and volcanic rock. These remarkable windows, balconies, gables and even a suggestion of a pagoda on the roof are worth a modest detour when trekking between local museums, for although still a private address, the house was so designed that the interiors appear open to the street.

Musée d'Histoire Naturelle et de Géologie (Natural History Museum) 19
rue de Bruxelles, 59000; tel: 03 28 55 30 80 [14 E8]
Open Mon, Wed–Fri 9.00–12.00, 14.00–17.00, Sun 10.00–17.00; closed Tue, Sat.
Free midweek, €2.5 (15FF) Sun.
M̲ *République;* E̲ *Bus 13 from Gare Flandres to Jeanne d'Arc.*
A typical 19th-century museum, with its glass cases, iron walkways and spiral
staircases, this very old-fashioned throwback to the days of hands-off musty
scholarship is an oddity in a city that prides itself on cutting edge exhibitions.
There is something comfortingly nostalgic about the place, with its whale
skeletons suspended from the ceiling, tableaux of stuffed birds and animals and
studiously catalogued trays of geological specimens and fossils.

WHERE TO EAT

Albert II 38 rue de Puébla, 59800; tel: 03 20 57 91 51 [14 C5]
Closed Sat lunch, Sun night, Aug 1–15.
M̲ *République;* E̲ *Bus 12 from Gare Flandres to Eglise Sacré Coeur. Rue Solférino to pl des
Halles Centrales. Left to rue de Puébla.*
On a quiet street – if such a concept were possible around the eternal festival of
eating, drinking, flirting, cruising, schmoozing and double parking that hums in
neon and dark wood around the old market Halles – is Lille's quiet gastronomic
success story. This is Stéphane LePrince's baby, a modest restaurant serving
simple but imaginative fare with flair. Monsieur LePrince's catering empire has
flourished since the good and great discovered him, and he now spends much of
his time catering for outside events and establishing his second base at the
restaurant of the Hôtel Bellevue by the Grand' Place. Nonetheless he takes a
very much hands-on approach at this decidedly local dining room. Taking a cue
from the name given by the establishment's original Belgian owner, the rear
salon (its 18th-century woodwork restored to its original bourgeois splendour)
is something of a tongue-in-cheek shrine to the royal family of Belgium.
Portraits range from early 20th-century iconoclastic to the frankly suburban. But
the rigidised, l'Oréal-glazed heads of recent princesses and queens do not stare
down at diners in the main room. Here wrought-iron chandeliers and summer
poster-paint walls offer a more conducive atmosphere for comfortable dining
and experimenting with the range of menus, from €14 (98FF) at lunchtime, to
a fine range of brasserie-type meals from €19–30 (115–190FF) at night. Plenty
of local influences to choose from: violet, beer and juniper gin, with maroilles
and *mont des cats* cheeses, are amongst the dressings for traditional ingredients.
The marriage of surprising bedfellows is not confined exclusively to savours of
the north. *Tartare* of salmon with almonds had a pleasing and surprising texture;
a spiced *foie gras* was served on refreshing toasts of fruited brioche. *Dinde* stuffed
with that *foie gras* almost begs a new riddle (when is a turkey not a turkey? when
it's a duck). The *sandre Prince Philippe* has nothing to do with the Duke of
Edinburgh, but plenty with cognac and cream. Desserts include a scrumptiously
blended ice-cream of *specaloos* savoury biscuit, and a *rabote du nord,* an acquired
taste of butter croissant-like pastry, filled with warm apple, best tried in winter
months. An option for the adventurous with limited time is the €12.50 (81FF)
assiette gourmande, an *entrée* plate packed with a generous selection of house takes
on farmyard and maritime specialities. Service is just attentive enough to care
but discreet enough to relax with!

Le Bistroquet 44 rue de Puébla, 59000; tel: 03 20 42 03 47 [14 C5]
Closed Sun, Mon evening, Sat lunch.

$\overline{\text{M}}$ *République;* $\overline{\text{E}}$ *Bus 12 from Gare Flandres to Eglise Sacré Coeur. Rue Solférino to pl des Halles Centrales. Left to rue de Puébla.*
Don't let the rather strange green trellised ceiling or the tourist-taverna style mirror tiles put you off. Despite its garish décor, the Bistroquet is what it sounds like, a reliable source of bistro sustenance! The bistro style is less *flamand* than *montagnard* and *Savoie* flair, with dishes such as a much-appreciated *raclette* or *tartiflette*. The welcome is genuine and effusive, the ambience holiday happy – but not touristy – and the food just fine. €20 (125FF) per person.

La Ducasse 95 rue Solférino, 59800; tel: 03 20 57 34 10 [14 B5]
$\overline{\text{M}}$ *République;* $\overline{\text{E}}$ *Bus 12 from Gare Flandres to Eglise Sacré Coeur. Rue Solférino to pl des Halles Centrales.*
Just another corner bistro with an accordionist leading a singalong of Saturday-night standards. Perhaps, yet the atmosphere is second to none, the simple local stews and platters hit the spot, the beer and wine flow freely and the local crowd, the nicest people you could ever meet. The students who pass through Lille for two or three years may choose the newest addresses along the road, but those living in apartments in the streets between the boulevards drop in here to sup with friends and neighbours, rather than cook for themselves. After an arduous day recording our BBC feature *Allez Lille*, my colleagues and I chose this corner for an anonymous, off-duty collapse. Hearing our English conversation, a local birthday party at the next table sent us over a bottle of wine and invited us to join them for coffee. A coin or two in the ancient pianola, and the honky-tonk piano-roll music whirred into action. Thankfully producer Jerome Weatherald had a spare recorder in his pocket, and was able to capture a few moments of that magical mood on tape. We ended the programme with a hint of our wonderful evening at the Ducasse, and shared the true spirit of Lille in a way mere words might never have managed. Have a *hochepot* or *waterzoi*, a chunk of steak and a hefty slice of *tarte*, pour a large drink, sing along to a *chanson* from the golden age, and feel the glow for yourself. I returned a year later to celebrate the launch of the Beaujolais Nouveau. A bottle of wine was left on our table to tempt us to try it. Our meal came to €15 (98FF) per head.

Sébastapol 1 pl Sébastopol, 59000; tel: 03 20 57 05 05; web: www.lesebastopol.com [14 C6]
Closed Sat lunch, Sun evening, mid–Aug.
$\overline{\text{M}}$ *République;* $\overline{\text{E}}$ *Métro 2 to Gare Lille Flandres, then line 1 to République. Rue Inkermann to pl Sébastopol.*
When I first attempted to lunch at this distinguished ivy-covered building beside the wonderfully exaggerated Théâtre Sebastapol, a lone bastion of *toque* and napkin tradition in an area best known for excellent Asian restaurants, I had money in my pocket and an appetite to match. Alas, I had not booked and the dining rooms were packed. My second application proved more successful, but though the appetite was as sharp as ever, my wallet was showing signs of wear, so I opted for the *repas d'affaires*, the lowest priced meal on offer. Take it from me, bargain pricing on the menu does not mean corners cut in the kitchen. Dubbed the *Clin d'Oeil Flamande*, the €27 (165FF) selection promises flavours of the region from first 'til last. A recommended wine selection from the Loire – a Gamay this afternoon – is included in a €40 (265FF) option with the same meal. Chef Jean-Luc Germond concentrates on finding hidden flavours in fish and fowl, and the *clin d'oeil* voyeur need not worry about missing out on his celebrated techniques just because sea bass and St-Pierre swim in pricier streams on the bill of fare. After a piquant and lavish starter of strips of succulent salmon

cru marinated in *fleur de bière*, generously spiked with sea salt, the fisherman's friend turned his attention to *dos de cabillaud*, taking the humble cod from the chilly North Sea and throwing spells over it. So light is the delicious flaky fish and the feather bed of milky potatoes and *genièvre* gin that it all but defied the laws of physics, solid on the plate and melting like winter into spring on the tongue. What might have been sickly nursery-creamery sweet proved to have a stimulating bitter adult aftertaste. The same wit and talent for culinary paradox could be discerned in the dessert – which reflects the north of France's wonderful market gardens – a *feuilleté* of strawberries and rhubarb, the latter almost crisp to complement the softer fruit. The *pâtisserie* was excellent, as we had been led to expect from the three types of pastry offered with *apéritifs* and the *mis en bouche* revealed as a *croquillant des champignons* of the finest, crispest, lightest filo. The sweet berry *coulis* had tangy near jelly of sharper fruit. The gastronomic menu and à la carte could set you back nearer €46 (300FF) a head, and these, too, come with suggested wines from the impressive wine list. A nice touch is the menu note that '*nos hôtes*' under 12 can benefit from an especially created junior gastronomic menu – judicious variants on themes from the main adult selection. The old pre-war dining room is dressed in bright yellow with contemporary decorating techniques and art and sculptures from local galleries. Welcome is warm and genuine, with the chef keeping a close eye on the dining room whenever the swing doors afford a glance, rather than the uptight preening of certain other *maître cuisiniers*. Equally, the attentive and hospitable service does not come with the almost religious fervour one finds in many temples of cuisine. First-rate food, served well with good taste and no pretensions.

WHAT TO BUY

Rue Gambetta [14 A6–D5]
M̄ *République;* Ē *Métro 2 to Gare Lille Flandres, then line 1 to République. Rue Gambetta runs from here to Wazemmes market and beyond.*
Shops here open the same hours as the town centre, with the added bonus of Sunday trading. Mini-supermarkets for last-minute bottles of mineral water and hotel-room snacking. Kitschest of cheapo clothing from the **Kilo Shop** at number 25 and loads of bazaars selling everything under the sun. **Les Aubaines** is a Sunday-morning favourite at number 298. Here you will find saucepans, household goods, clothes, toys and games from last year's mail order catalogues. La Redoute use this Les Aubanes to offload surplus stock. Great for a budget Christmas list.

La 7ème Compagnie 11 rue Jean Sans Peur, 59000; tel: 03 20 54 39 63 [14 D5]
Open Mon 14.00–19.00, Tue–Sat 10.00–12.00, 14.00–19.00.
M̄ *République;* Ē *Métro 2 to Gare Lille Flandres, changing to line 1 to République. Walk north on bd de la Liberté to junction with rue Jean Sans Peur.*
Epaulettes, camouflage and good strong fabric. Outfits with a military look from practical combats and standard army surplus clubwear to costume items such as British Guardsman's uniforms.

Wazemmes Market pl de la Nouvelle Aventure, 59000 [14 A7]
M̄ *Gambetta;* Ē *Métro 2 to Gare Lille Flandres, then line 1 to Gambetta. Cross the rue du Marché and walk around the church to place de la Nouvelle Aventure.*
Besides the Sunday morning market event (see page 228), the covered produce market is open Tuesday to Saturday from 06.00 until late afternoon.

Les Gares

Not one station but two. The new Europe station welcomes the TGV and Eurostar and looks like the airports of tomorrow. Dominated by the boot-shaped Crédit Lyonnais building, this is the heartland of the new international business community. Constructed on land hived off by the military, there are hints of early fortifications scattered in the emerging Parc Matisse. The vast paved square of the place Mitterand is gradually being claimed by a generation of skateboarders, micro-scooter aces and mountain-bikers.

Across the square is the Euralille shopping centre, an indoor alternative to the rest of the city. A few yards along avenue le Corbusier is the public transport hive: underground are two métro stations, and the tramway to Roubaix and Tourcoing; at street level the bus station, taxi ranks and the original 19th-century station serving all points local and beyond, and all speeds under *très-grands*.

The older Gare Lille Flandres was Paris' original Gare du Nord. Moved brick by brick and stone by stone for the railway line's royal opening. The town elders, not wishing to appear satisfied with second-hand goods, insisted on building an extra storey on to the station façade to create an even more imposing frontage. The first train to arrive at the station was greeted by the Bishop of Douai, who blessed the locomotive, and by Hector Berlioz conducting the town band in a

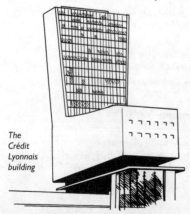

The Crédit Lyonnais building

specially composed concerto. Today, the place seems less grand, just the typical terminus hive of bars, cafes and eateries clustered around the fountains at the front of the station. Weekends see soldiers from the Citadelle flirting with students from the universities. After a while the incongruous sight of a young lad with a sub-machine-gun at his belt, composing text messages on his mobile phone, seems perfectly normal. At the side of the station, on rue de Tornai, eating is cheap with *frites* stands and burgers. Seamier services are available behind the line of brasseries facing the station, with flesh offered shrink-wrapped in cellophane in shops and in lycra on the pavements around the rues de Roubaix and Pont des Commines.

Close to the motorway intersections of the ring road, Lille Grand Palais is a huge exhibition arena. The Zenith auditorium hosts major rock concerts and lavish musicals, and is the place to see international superstars, such as David Bowie or Elton John.

Below the stations is the former St-Sauveur district, home to the new Hôtel de Ville. Further out to the east and across the railway lines is the district of Lille-Fives which grew up as a town in its own right. Fives has its own brass bands, festivals and customs, including a wine harvest festival every autumn, when the little local vineyards produce *vin de Fives*.

The walk along the av le Corbusier from Lille Europe past the old station, then along the rue Faidherbe to the Grand' Place and the old town is a gentle turning back of the clock as the architecture rewinds from Millennium ambitious, through 20th, 19th and 18th centuries to the 17th, 400 years of optimism, confidence and faith in the future, respecting the past.

WHERE TO STAY

Chagnot 24 pl de la Gare, 59800; tel: 03 20 74 11 87; web: www.chagnot.com [15 G4]
M̲ *Gare Lille Flandres;* E̲ *av le Corbusier to Gare Flandres and pl de la Gare.*
Helpful service and surprisingly comfortable and quiet (if bland and compact) rooms at the side of the Gare Flandres and above the fabulous Trois Brasseurs. The slowest lift in Christendom serves a remarkable 75 bedrooms. Reception and rooms are stocked with local entertainment guides for visitors and the location provides for a quick getaway if you have an early train in the morning. Rates at around ∈45 (300FF) not including the uninspiring breakfast. I prefer to have a quick coffee at the **Ralleye** bar next door then amble into town for hot chocolate and fresh bread by the Grand' Place.

Citadines Lille Centre av Willy Brandt, 59777; tel: 03 20 06 97 82; web: www.citadines.com [15 H4]
M̲ *Gare Lille Flandres;* E̲ *av le Corbusier to Euralille. Left into av Willy Brandt.*
In the Euralille building, this central self-catering option offers extremely competitively priced, modern studios and larger apartments with well-equipped kitchenettes with extra facilities from buffet breakfasts ∈7 (45FF) to an in-house laundrette – wash, dry, and detergent for ∈8 (50FF). Rooms begin at around ∈55 (350FF) a night. A slightly higher rate is charged for those requiring the full hotel package, with daily maid service. Otherwise pay the basic price and use the dishwasher, vacuum cleaner and ironing board provided. Security is pretty good, with the front doors locked, and guests given private entry codes whenever the main desk is unmanned. Very helpful staff at reception, and basement parking among the bonuses.

Flandres-Angleterre 13 pl de la Gare, 59800; tel: 03 20 06 37 76 [15 G4]
M̲ *Gare Lille Flandres;* E̲ *av le Corbusier to Gare Flandres and pl de la Gare.*
OK, so the hotel is hidden behind an infinite number of gaudy restaurant signs promising *frites* with everything! This is an unpretentious, old-fashioned railway station hotel. The current owners offer a family-style welcome to the simple yet

spotlessly clean rooms. Soundproofed against late-night revellers catching the last train to Brussels and all place names Flemish. Rooms from under €46–61 (310–410FF).

Lille Europe av le Corbusier, 59777; tel: 03 28 36 77 77 [15 H4]
M̲ *Lille Europe;* E̲ *av le Corbusier to Euralille.*
Suitably anonymous modern hotel in suitably anonymous modern building, the Hôtel de la Gare *de nos jours* has charming helpful staff, lots of identikit rooms and a buffet breakfast in a fully glazed first-floor salon. The hotel is part of the Euralille tower block shopping and business complex. The plus point for travellers with heavy luggage and plans to strip bare the shelves of the en-suite mall is its location, so close to the TGV Eurostar station for overnighters. But let's face it, with the Grand' Place and old town just five minutes away, this is unlikely to be a first choice for visitors seeking the charm of old Flanders. Rooms €55–62 (350–420FF). Run by the same management as the Citadines apartments around the corner.

WHERE TO GO

Euralille av Le Corbusier, 59000; tel: 03 20 14 52 20 (Euralille), 03 20 78 00 00 (Aeronef) [15 H4]
Open Mon–Thu, Sat 10.00–20.00, Fri 10.00–21.00.
M̲ *Gare Lille Europe, Gare Lille Flandres;* E̲ *cross the parvis François Mitterand.*
Between the two railway stations, Euralille is one of France's biggest shopping centres. Hard-core consumers may squeak with excitement at the massive Carrefour hypermarket and specialist shops such as the mug-shop Kitchenette and the arts and crafts wonderland of Loisirs et Création. Personally, I mourn the passing of the pet superstore which once advertised the special offer '15 caged birds for the price of 12', either the zenith or nadir of promotional hype. Exhibitions and displays in the centre have ranged from tableaux of zebra and rhino on loan from the natural history museum to a free circus with high wires and trapeze acts above the heads of bemused shoppers. The mall is more than merely 140 shops spread over two storeys of consumerism. Office units, hotel rooms and serviced short-stay apartments hide behind the smoked glass. Even the once underground nightclub l'Aeronef is now to be found several levels above ground in the Euralille complex, with its programme of cutting-edge rock music and bad-taste film festivals. Together with Christian de Portzampac's 'ski-boot' Tour Crédit Lyonnais balanced over Lille Europe station and Rem Koolhaas' own Grand Palais exhibition centre and concert venue, Euralille is testament to Koolhaas' concept of 21st-century living, Lille's remarkable civic optimism and Mayor Mauroy's belief in the Eurostar dream. Between Gare Europe and Euralille, the parvis François Mitterand has been colonised by the micro-scooter and rollerblade fraternity. A statue of President Mitterand waves passengers on their high-speed way, and the recently landscaped **Parc Matisse** offers a comfortable walk towards Vieux Lille.

Les Trois Brasseurs 22 pl de la Gare, 59800; tel: 03 20 06 46 25 [15 G4]
M̲ *Gare Lille Flandres;* E̲ *av le Corbusier to Gare Flandres and pl de la Gare.*
Flanders is famed for its beers – whatever you do you must try at least one of the region's distinctive flavours. Many local *artisanales* beers are made in the traditional method, and some larger breweries offer guided tours and tastings for the public. As for me, I stay in central Lille and always pay a visit to Les Trois Brasseurs opposite the old Lille Flandres station. The director of Pelforth – the commercial brewery behind the Pelican lagers favoured by Calais-trippers –

created this genuine brasserie. Monsieur Bonduel decided to get back to brewing basics, and we have all cause to be grateful to him. It was the welcome I found here that first drew me to Lille, and I will never cease to be thankful. The clientele ranges from solo business types at the bar to groups of friends, locals and visitors. The bar staff are rarely less than convivial, the waiters never less than harassed. In this always-packed bar-restaurant the only beers served are those brewed in copper vats on the premises. For around €4 (27FF) buy a *pallette* – a tasting tray of three or four small glasses of the various home brews, the *blonde, brune, ambrée* and *Blanche de Lille* – the refreshing bitter-sweet thirst quencher ideally served with a slice of lemon. This tasting tray is the best way to get to know the beers of Lille. March and Christmas see special seasonal beers added to the range. The menu is excellent northern home cooking: rabbit stews, roasts and the cholesterol-packed *Welsh*, a bowl of melted cheese and beer with a slice of bread and chips. Try the beer tart or beer *sorbet* – if you are feeling really adventurous! Set menu deals are the best value at around €10 (65FF), as are the house *flammekeuche*, and the daily special, such as marrow-bone or a *carbonnade*, is always reasonably priced. Otherwise budget €21 (130FF) à la carte. The house brews may be bought to take home by the bottle or *tonnelet* (mini-barrel), a useful souvenir on a Sunday when the Euralille shops are closed.

WHAT TO SEE

Hôtel de Ville (Town Hall) pl Roger Salengro, 59000; tel: 0 20 49 50 00
Open Mon–Fri 09.00–11.00, 14.00–16.00, Sun, holidays 09.30–12.00; closed Sat.
M̲ *Mairie de Lille;* Ē *Métro 2 to Mairie de Lille.*
Although the Christmas ferris wheel in Grand' Place offers the best view in town, there is a summer alternative. From April to September, take a detour from the main historic and shopping quarters and climb to the top of the 104m belfry of the town hall (a lift takes you most of the way). Completed in 1932, the tower crowned Emille Dubuisson's striking Hôtel de Ville which replaced the original gothic Palais Rihour building with a ferro-concrete tribute to the gabled houses of Flanders. More than merely a nice place to enjoy a pleasant view, in 1950 the top of the tower became the first regional television studio, Télé-Lille. The cost is approximately €1. Holding up the tower are the figures of giants Lydéric and Phinaert, the Romulus, Remus, Bambi and Voldemort of Lille. Lydéric was raised by wild deer and a hermit after his family was killed by the tyrant Phinaert. On June 15 605, the two fought, Lydéric was the victor and he founded the town. The history of Lille is told in a huge strip cartoon fresco inside the building, painted by the Icelandic artist Erro. The building was constructed over the ruins of the original working class quarter of St-Sauveur where, in the long demolished bar La Liberté, local wood-turner Pierre Degeyter composed and played the music for Eugène Pottier's socialist anthem *L'Internationale* for the very first time in 1888.

Porte de Paris pl Simon Volant, 59000 [15 F7]
M̲ *Lille Grand Palais;* Ē *Métro 2 to Lille Grand Palais. Take rue des Déportés past the Hôtel de Ville.*
On the traffic roundabout named after the Porte's architect stands the greatest of the three remaining city gates. Unlike the portes des Roubaix and Gand, this is an unashamed piece of monumental triumphalism, a lavish declaration of the might and majesty of Louis XIV and celebration of Lille's embrace into the Kingdom of France. Unveiled in 1692, this *arc de triomphe* has an image of the king himself surrounded by angels and cherubim. Columns frame niches holding classical

images of war and power, Hercules and Mars paying tribute to France's own Sun King. Originally the gateway rose above the towns fortifications. The walls were torn down in 1858 to make way for boulevards, and the rest of the district of St Sauveur was demolished in the slum clearance programmes of the 1920s. A small landscaped garden replaces the moat, once spanned by a drawbridge, and the baroque arch itself is as imposing as ever. Impress your new friends with the trivial nugget that the gateway was not dubbed the Porte de Paris until the Revolution. Despite its regal statuary, it was originally called the Porte des Malades ('sick people's gate') because it led to the hospital!

Porte de Roubaix Parc Matisse or rue de Roubaix, 59000 [15 H3]
M̄ *Gare Europe;* Ē *From the station enter the park and follow the footpath to the city walls.*
From the rue de Roubaix, this nearly neglected old gateway presents a rather sorry and run-down appearance, and most passers by simply pass it by. Yet this is the door that saved a city. The Parc Matisse offers a far more appropriate perspective from which to view this remnant of the old fortifications. Here the crenellations and drawbridge channels may be seen to best advantage, and you can imagine the moment in 1792 when the door was slammed in the face of the Austrian Duke of Saxe-Teschen and his army of 35,000 men. If the two smaller archways seem to give the gate an air of a triumphal arch, blame it on the commuters. The side-walls were opened up in the 19th century for a long-forgotten tramway to the suburbs.

WHERE TO EAT
Le Meunier 15–17 rue de Tournai, 59800; tel: 03 28 04 04 90 [15 H5]
M̄ *Gare Lille Flandres;* Ē *av le Corbusier, then left at Gare Flandres.*
Once upon a time every provincial French railway station had a stolid reliable railway restaurant serving basic meat, fish and chicken – standard fare to while away the two-hour delay between cross-country trains. At the side of the old Flandres station, amid the *friteries* and burger bars, is to be found one such old-fashioned *buffet de la gare*-style dining room. Canteen cutlery and heavy white plates and a respectable line in *pâtés* and *rillettes* to take away as well as eating in. *Tripes à la mode de Caen, tête de veau* or *tournedos rossini* rather than the pan-fried spring vegetables with steamed fruits in their *coulis* of pretention that one might find in more fashionable eateries. One eats here to remember railway holidays chugging through a less sophisticated France in less demanding times. Lots of choice on lots of set menus – from ∈11–25 (70–160FF). Friday and Saturday nights see a special three courses with wine, *apéritif* and coffee for ∈19 (125FF).

Les Trois Brasseurs [15 G4]
(see page 236)

WHAT TO BUY
Euralille [15 H4]
(See page 236)

Adéquat 2 rue des Ponts de Comines, 59000; tel: 03 20 78 14 60 [15 G4]
Open Mon 13.00–19.00, Tue–Sat 09.15–19.15.
M̄ *Gare Lille Flandres;* Ē *av le Corbusier and right into rue Faidherbe.*
The street corners of the rue Faidherbe are lined with racks of shiny new shoes at discount prices. This store has a good range from trainers, winter boots and walkwear to classy dress shoes.

Artès Euralille, 59777; tel: 03 20 78 06 51 [15 H4]
Open Mon–Sat 10.00–20.00.
M̄ *Lille Europe;* Ē *opposite the station.*
Interesting gifts inspired by the great art collections and museums of Europe.
Think bigger than the Mona Lisa T-shirt.

Carrefour Euralille, 59777; tel: 03 20 15 56 00 [15 H4]
Open Mon–Sat 10.00–22.00.
M̄ *Lille Europe;* Ē *Opposite the station.*
The massive hypermarket is the ideal place for stocking up before catching the
train home (except on Sundays). Look out for the logo of a belfry and a heart.
This denotes local products, and the store sells a good selection of ales and
prepared foods from the region.

Kitchenette Euralille, 59777; tel: 03 20 55 26 79 [15 H4]
Open Mon–Sat 10.00–20.00.
M̄ *Lille Europe;* Ē *Opposite the station.*
In a city where almost every other shop sells fine china and top-of-the-range
tableware to grace the most elegant of dining rooms, this shop sells everyday
mugs and plates for breakfast bars and morning rooms. Baskets of *demi-tasses* and
gift-wrapped *petit-déjeuner* sets of oversized cups and plates, all in the brightest
and cheeriest of colours.

Loisirs et Créations Euralille, 59777; tel: 03 20 51 39 01 [15 H4]
Open Mon–Sat 10.00–20.00.
M̄ *Lille Europe;* Ē *Opposite the station.*
Cross-stitch, watercolours or tie-dyeing; whatever your art or your craft, this
spacious store has everything for the creative hobbyist. Visit the studio for
workshops in new and different techniques.

Mad Man 6 rue Faidherbe, 59000; tel: 03 20 31 10 32 [15 G4]
Open Mon–Fri 10.00–19.00.
M̄ *Gare Lille Flandres;* Ē *av le Corbusier and right into rue Faidherbe.*
For a Cardin shirt or YSL suit at up to half the official price, rummage through
the rails and racks for the bargains of the day at this pile 'em high sell 'em cheap
outlet for high-profile menswear labels.

Maxi-Livres 54 rue Faidherbe; tel: 03 20 57 52 48 [15 F4]
Open Mon 14.00–19.00, Tue–Sat 10.00–19.00, Sun 10.00–13.00.
M̄ *Gare Lille Flandres;* Ē *av le Corbusier and right into rue Faidherbe then left into rue des
Ponts de Commines and right into rue de Paris.*
Discount book chain selling literary classics for under ∈2 (10FF) and coffee-table
books at silly prices.

Tati 12–14 rue Faidherbe, 59000; tel: 03 20 74 00 00; web: www.tati.fr [15 G4]
Open Mon–Sat 10.00–19.00.
M̄ *Gare Lille Flandres;* Ē *av le Corbusier and right into rue Faidherbe.*
See *Paris*, page 165 for the low-down on the store that sells wedding dresses at
∈75 (500FF) and kids' jeans from ∈2.50 (15FF).

Métropole
(just outside the city limits)

Pretty gardens of the Parc Barbieux and Disney-quaint houses line the roads on the half-hour tram route to the two major satellite towns of Tourcoing and Roubaix. These days the extended métro cuts journey times in half, blurring the boundaries between the city of Lille and the other towns that make up Lille Métropole. The metropolitan population is almost a million, and the artistic honours of the conurbation are now shared fairly around Lille's immediate neighbours. So the Ballet du Nord performs at the huge Colisée theatre in Roubaix, and the Atelier Lyrique at Tourcoing stages intimate productions of favourite operas from Mozart to Bernstein. Tourcoing has its annual Jazz Festival, whilst Roubaix holds an open-air art market. Villeneuve d'Asq may now be a university centre, but the area was once famous for its windmills and watermills. The mills and a museum of milling may be visited most afternoons (except Saturdays). Lille's tourist office has information on events in all the surrounding towns and offers plenty of seasonal alternatives to conventional public transport – canal boats and vintage trams amongst them.

ROUBAIX
Roubaix Tourist Office 10 rue de la Tuilerie, Roubaix 59100; tel: 03 20 65 31 90 Mon–Sat 09.00–18.00, closed Sun.

Where to go
Chez Rita 49 rue Daubenton, 59100 Roubaix; tel: 03 20 26 22 88 Open Mon–Fri 12.00–14.00.
M̄ *Gare Jean Lebas; Métro 2 to Gare Jean Lebas then bus 25 to Flandre.*
Is it a biscuit or is it art? When the Rita waffle factory closed down, the family who ran the business wanted to leave something to the local community that had served the company so well for so many years. So they handed over the factory building to a community of artists, who work, rest and play in the nooks and crannies, workshops and loading bays. Every corner has been converted into an individual's creative space, with easels, divans, installation art and canvases personalising each artist's studio. With superb art deco etched glass, wide industrial doorways and a romantic roof where invited guests might sit to watch a sunset, the building has a personality to rival any of the artworks on display and on sale. Each lunchtime, the artists open their *estaminet* bar and café, where modestly priced *pâté*, salads and locally brewed ale are always on the menu.

Le Parc Barbieux av Jean Jaurès, 59100 Roubaix; tel: 03 20 75 25 38
Ē *Tram (towards Roubaix) to Parc Barbieux.*
The Tourcoing and Roubaix trams run alongside this prettiest of gardens where,

for generations, middle-class families have pushed prams and strolled the hours of sunny Sunday afternoons. Delightful flowerbeds, some rare trees and hidden statuary punctuate the manicured lawns. You may be forgiven for imagining that these long narrow strips of colour might have been laid out to complement the tramway. In fact they were created in the 18th century by Georges Aumont, a Parisian landscape gardener, on a site earmarked for development as a canal.

What to see
Musée d'Art et d'Industrie (Art and Industry Museum) 23 rue de l'Espérance, 59100 Roubaix; tel: 03 20 69 23 60
€3.04–4.57 (20–30FF).
M̄ *Gare Jean Lebas;* Ē *Métro 2 to Gare Jean Lebas. On av Jean Lebas turn right to rue des Champs.*
The sun also rises at the former municipal swimming pool: a dramatic stained-glass window radiates stylised sunbeams over this most ambitious project. It has taken five years to convert the galleried art deco baths into a suitable home for a remarkable civic collection. Since Roubaix was home to northern France's textile manufacturing industry, the town fathers accumulated an incredible collection of sample books, fabrics, fashion designs and ephemera: a comprehensive catalogue of styles from the ancient Egyptians to the 20th century. This archive is now displayed to best effect, alongside the private art collections of the entrepreneurs who owned the original mills. The only Ingres in town (even Lille's Palais des Beaux Arts cannot claim that), Picassos and works of local artists Cogghe and Weerts are to be seen here. The exhibits' original home was destroyed in World War II and, in creating the new museum, architect Jean-Paul Philippon has incorporated as much of the original deco style as possible to give the collection the inter-war flair of its heyday. The designs can best be appreciated in the on-site restaurant. Local fashion designers often stage catwalk shows here.

What to buy
MacArthur Glen Mail de Lannoy, 59100 Roubaix; tel: 03 28 33 36 00
Open Mon–Sat 10.00–19.00.
M̄ *Eurotéléport;* Ē *Métro 2 to Eurotéléport, or tram to Roubaix.*
Confirming Roubaix's status as the home of bargain designer shopping, this open-air mall above the main métro station is an avenue of outlet stores. Mostly French high-street names, the international firms offering permanent discounts of between 30–70% on regular prices include Adidas, Reebok, Blanc Bleu, Cacherel and Gossard. Even Disney's upmarket label Donaldson may be found here: hacking jackets and tweeds with the most discreet Mickey Mouse buttons.

L'Usine 228 av Alfred Motte, 59100 Roubaix; tel: 03 20 83 16 20
Mon–Sat 10.00–19.00.
Ē *Métro 2 to Epeule Montesquieu then bus 25 to Les Hauts Champs.*
Not as neatly laid out as MacArthur Glenn, but this is where it all began. Three storeys of a former factory, stuffed with linens, clothes and shoes at ludicrously low prices. Since Roubaix is the capital of France's mail order industry, with Les Trois Suisses and La Redoute both based here, as new catalogues are published old stock has to be sold off as swiftly as possible. A children's playground and decent café-snack bar on the premises for those planning to make a day of it, walking from room to room to pick up Timberland, Wrangler and Levi products at well under half the shop price.

SECLIN
Where to stay and go
Domaine Mandarine Napoléon 204 rue de Burgault, 59113 Seclin; tel: 03 20 32 54 93
Ē *Métro 2 to Lille Porte des Postes, then bus 55 to Burgault.*
Something different for the weekend? Try self catering with an emperor, spending the night in a distillery and museum. If you are driving through the region, here's an imperial treat to consider. Ten minutes outside town at exit 19 of the A1 is the new home of the Mandarine Napoléon distillery. The liqueur, a firm favourite of the short man with big ideas, so we are told, is actually a Belgian tipple, but the distillery has now moved its operations across the border to this farm with arboretum and butterfly gardens. Visitors may tour the distillery and a superb private collection of memorabilia of the great military man himself. George Fourcroy, head of the drinks company, has created the Napoléon Bonaparte Museum with artefacts spanning 28 years from the legend's rise to political power to his death. From letters and uniforms to the bronze death mask, the collection is well displayed in a specially designed showroom. The complex also houses banqueting suites for weddings and conferences. An area is set aside for private games of *pétanque*, and a tasting lounge and gift shop cater to museum visitors. Not everyone gets to visit the old manor house at the centre of the farm. Exquisitely decorated and furnished, from the *trompe l'oeil* tent of the entrance hall to the elegant dining room, the beautifully and individually styled bedrooms and the honesty bar, where guests are trusted to pour their own drinks and settle their bills. Not a hotel as such, more a hugely upmarket *gîte* or *chambre d'hôte*; one may have the whole house to oneself or share with three strangers. Breakfast is laid out in the kitchen each morning and the huge fridge may be stocked with steaks, eggs and vegetables should guests wish to cook a late supper for themselves. The room rate is around €200 (1,300FF), breakfast €9 (60FF), with payment for any other food and drink settled privately on departure.

TOURCOING
Tourcoing Tourist Office 9 rue de Tournai, 59200 Tourcoing; tel: 03 20 26 89 03
Open Mon–Sat 10.00–12.00, 15.00–18.00; closed Sun.

Where to go
Le Fresnoy Studio National des Arts Contemporains 22 rue du Fresnoy, 59202 Tourcoing; tel: 03 20 28 38 00
Free admission to site, exhibition charges vary.

M̲ *Alsace;* E̲ *Métro 2 to Alsace. Walk south on bd d'Armentières then right to rue du Capitaine Aubert into rue du Fresnoy.*
The arts centre and college on the site of an old bowling alley, dance hall and fleapit cinema has a lively programme of exhibitions, but any event is easily upstaged by the building itself and the vision of architect Tschumi. Le Fresnoy is perhaps the only building ever to have been designed to pander to human nature. Its magic lies in the 'in-between', a magical hinterland between two roofs. Tschumi decided to retain the original shells of the 1905 movie theatre and hall, and create a footpath between the old tiles and the futuristic canopy of the modern centre. And so it is that students, locals and visitors alike can wander hand in hand around the chimney-stacks on a network of suspended metal gantries and steps. One path leads to a dead end behind a sloping roof. 'Why?', I asked. The answer was simple: 'The architect said that young people need somewhere to, you know, to kiss!'. On summer nights they may hold hands as well, since the design also incorporates a mini grandstand for watching old movies projected on to the tiles. Films are also screened in the art centre's two small cinemas.

What to see
Musée des Beaux Arts 2 rue Paul Doumer, 59200 Tourcoing; tel: 03 20 66 46 93
Open Wed–Mon 13.30–18.00; closed holidays. Free.
M̲ *Tourcoing Centre;* E̲ *Tram or métro to Tourcoing Centre. Rue Leclerc to rue Paul Doumer.*
Eclectic, imaginative and never less than stimulating. Tourcoing's art collection spans the artistic spectrum from Breughelesque Flemish works to the Cubists, and the archives are regularly ransacked by the curator to keep exhibitions fresh and nicely incongruous. So find a Rembrandt next to some local artist's portrait of a much-loved grandmother or discover a Picasso between a couple of mundane still lifes. My favourite painting is the deliciously grand portrait of *Mlle Croisette en Costume d'Amazon*, a prim and proper bourgeois equestrian pose with more than a hint of passion beneath the unseen corsetry. The pictures are housed in elegant galleries dating from the 1930s. If the pick-and-mix nature of the museum appeals to you, cast your eye over the front of the nearby **Maison du Collectionneur**, an architectural buffet of a house whose original owner wanted to combine as many styles as possible in one building, at 3 sq Winston Churchill.

VILLENEUVE D'ASQ
Office de Tourisme Château de Flers, Chemin du Chat Botte, 59650 Villeneuve d'Asq; tel: 03 20 43 55 75

What to see
Forum des Sciences Centre François Mitterand (Science Museum and Planetarium) 1 pl Hôtel de Ville, 59650 Villeneuve d'Asq; tel: 03 20 19 36 36
Tue, Thu, Fri 08.45–17.30, Wed 08.45–19.00, Sat, Sun, holidays 14.00–19.00 (term time), Tue–Fri 08.45–19.00, Sat, Sun, holidays 14.00–19.00 (school holidays), closed Jan 1, May 1, Dec 25. Tickets cost ∈4 (25FF) for the museum, ∈5.50 (35FF for the planetarium, and ∈7.50 (50FF) for both.
M̲ *Hôtel de Ville;* E̲ *Métro 2 to Gare Lille Flandres then line 1 to Hôtel de Ville*
See Lille's night sky by day at the planetarium. You will probably not want to take the trip to Villeneuve d'Asq simply to see the planetarium, but if you are

travelling with children, this science centre makes an enjoyable diversion and bargaining counter for buying your own time at the modern art museum. The entertaining and informative shows at the planetarium range from speculation as to life on Mars to the history of time itself. All presentations begin with a simulation of the Lille sky at dusk. A splashy, hands-on activity centre appeals to little ones, and adults will like the thought-provoking temporary exhibitions.

Musée d'Art Moderne 1 allée du Musée, 59650, Villeneuve d'Asq; tel: 03 20 19 68 68

Open Wed–Mon 10.00–18.00; closed Jan 1, May 1, Dec 25.

Ē *Métro 2 to Gare Lille Flandres then line 1 to Pont de Bois, then bus 41 to Parc Urbain-Musée, and follow the footpath into the park.*

The greatest artists of the 20th century can be found in the galleries and gardens of this unexpected cultural park in Villeneuve d'Asq, Lille's university campus suburb. A light and unassuming brick building makes no attempt to upstage the top-notch collection that it houses. A comprehensive tour through the most influential painters of each of the key artistic movements of the past 100 years includes a half dozen Picassos, Bracque's *Maison et Arbres*, works by Rouault, Miro and Masson, and some renowned canvases by Modigliani, including his *Nu Assis à la Chemise*. The bulk of the museum's wealth comes from generous bequests to the community from the private collections of Roger Dutilleul and Jean and Geneviève Masurel. The Fauvist and Cubist rooms are most popular, but post-war artists are equally well represented through more recent acquisitions. Temporary exhibitions vary in style and quality. If you are lucky you may spot an engaging new genius. Of course, you may have to wade through more than a few luminaries of the post-talent movement to find it. As you step between eras, huge plate-glass windows look out on the lawns where locals walk their dogs, ride their micro-scooters and kick footballs between installation sculptures, including Picasso's *Femme aux Bras Ecartés* and Alexander Calder's *Southern Cross*. Jewellery and other objects by local artists are sold in the museum shop, and the café and restaurant on site provide plenty of opportunity to continue the 'Yes, but is it Art?' debates.

WAMBRECHIES

Mairie 5 pl Général de Gaulle, 59118 Wambrechies; tel: 03 28 38 84 00

A vintage tram from 1906 runs along the canal bank between Wambrechies and Marquette on Sundays and public holidays every 15 minutes, 14.30–19.00. Passengers join the tram at Vent de Bise at Wambrechies or rue de la Deûle at Marquette. Pay €2.50 (15FF) return fare and sit on authentic wooden benches refurbished in 1926. Information tel: 03 28 42 44 58.

What to see

Distillerie Claeyssens 1 rue de la Distillerie, Wambrechies, 59118; tel: 03 20 14 91 91; web: www.wambrechies.net

Tours Mon–Fri 11.00–15.00, Sat 16.30, Sun 15.00, 16.00, 17.00. €4 (25FF).

Ē *Bus 9 from Gare Flandres to Wambrechies Château or Bus 3 from Gare Flandres to Wambrechies Mairie. From rue 11 Nov 1918 take rue Leclerc to rue de la Distillerie.*

There is nothing high-tech about this distillery that has been making *genièvre* gin from junipers for the past 200 years. The original wooden equipment still sifts seeds, mills flour, and heats, cools and distils the spirit, just as it did in Napoleonic times, when the waterways of the Deûle brought grain from Belgium after an edict banned the use of French crops. The hour-long tour is an anecdote-filled meander through a past that can hold its own in the present. An opportunity to taste the robust tipple follows the tour and a shop sells not only the *genièvre* itself, but two rather special by-products: beer made during the fermenting process, and a single malt of Highland quality.

Musée de la Poupée et de Jouet Ancien (Doll and Antique Toy Museum)
Château de Robersart, Wambrechies, 59118; tel: 03 20 92 69 28
Sun, holidays 14.00–18.00, closed Dec 25, Jan 1.
Ē *Bus 9 from Gare Flandres to Wambrechies Château.*
At last, they tie the knot. The wedding of Barbie and Ken is a glittering occasion, the guest list itself reads like a who's who of Barbie: there's Beach Barbie, and Beautician Barbie and Trolley Dolly Barbie and, for all I know, Management Consultant Barbie, in the biggest gathering of big hair since *Dynasty* slipped off the TV listings pages. The nuptial tableau featuring scores of versions of the doll from each year of her long career is set in a model of a Gothic cathedral, and typical of the imaginative displays at this charming museum of childhood. The setting of the museum itself is something of a happy ever after, housed in the family château of Juliette, the last countess of Robersart. Two galleries feature dolls and toys from every era. Victorian playthings and latter-day train sets provide plenty of 'ooh ahh' moments. Among the most interesting items in the permanent display are miniature fashion outfits made to patterns printed in the leading women's magazines of the last century.

Entertainment

Selected as European Cultural Capital for 2004, Lille city famously boasts that Saturday night always offers a choice of 100 alternative diversions – and it is no bragging exaggeration. Quite apart from the diversity of bars and restaurants, from the *intime* and quirky rue de Gand to the city of singles that is rue Solférino, the variety of performances would not disgrace a national capital city. *Sortir*, the listings magazine, is published every Wednesday. Pick up a free copy at your hotel or the tourist office. The local newspaper, *La Voix du Nord*, also carries comprehensive entertainment information.

THEATRE

The **Théâtre du Nord** on Grand' Place is a very good place to start. Stuart Seide's artistic direction really put this stage on the national cultural agenda. Challenging and fresh approaches to world classics have led to ground-breaking productions of Beckett, Molière and of course Shakespeare – a recent *Romeo and Juliet* turned round the central schism by 90 degrees, presenting the divide as less between Montague and Capulet than between the two generations. In a city where almost half the population is under the age of 25, that certainly created more than a murmur.

Young theatre has its own voice at **Le Grand Bleu**, where programmes are essentially geared to the hip-hop rather than hip-replacement set. Other fringe and new-wave venues include the **Théâtre de la Découverte à la Verrière** and the **Théâtre des Nuits Blanches**. Conventional and more comfortable family fare is served up at the **Théâtre Sébastapol**. Light comedies that would run on Shaftesbury Avenue, Broadway or the Grands Boulevards play here. The weekend bill may feature such old favourites as *Le Dîner des Cons* (*The Dinner Game*) or concerts by TV crooners. International visitors perform at the upfront **Le Prato** and Villeneuve d'Asq's **Rose des Vents**. During festivals, scores of other spaces, great and small, are called into service. The playhouses of other towns in the conurbation are also worth checking out. After all, public transport in the Métropole continues until midnight, since most venues are within half an hour from Grand' Place. Theatre culture and tipping rules are as for Paris (see page 183).

Le Grand Bleu 36 av Marx Dormoy, 59000; tel: 03 20 09 88 44; web: www.legrandbleu.com
Ⓜ *Bois Blancs;* Ⓔ *Métro 2 to Bois Blancs, then walk along the avenue.*

Le Prato 6 allée de la Filature, 59000; tel: 03 20 52 71 24
M̲ *Porte de Douai;* E̲ *Métro 2 to Porte de Douai. From rue de Douai turn left into allée de la Filature.*

La Rose des Vents – Scène Nationale bd Van-Gogh, 59650 Villeneuve d'Asq; tel: 03 20 61 96 90
M̲ *Pont de Bois;* E̲ *Métro 2 to Gare Lille Flandres then line 1 to Pont de Bois. Rue Vétérans to bd Van Gogh.*

Théâtre de la Découverte à la Verrière 28 rue Alphonse Mercier, 59800; tel: 03 20 54 96 75 [14 B5]
Closed Mon.
M̲ *République;* E̲ *Bus 12 from Gare Flandres to Eglise Sacré Coeur. Rue Solférino to pl des Halles Centrales, right on rue des Stations and right to rue Alphonse Mercier.*

Théâtre du Nord 4 pl du Général de Gaulle, 59000; tel: 03 20 14 24 24 [15 F4]
M̲ *Rihour;* E̲ *Bus 12 from Gare Flandres to Théâtre.*

Théâtre Sébastopol pl Sébastopol, 59000; tel: 03 20 54 44 50 [14 C6]
M̲ *République;* E̲ *Métro 2 to Gare Lille Flandres changing to line 1 to République. Rue Inkerman leads to the theatre.*

FLOOR SHOWS

Showbiz glamour and comedy are always served with a flourish and a flounce at **Les Folies de Paris** (see page 202). **La Petite Cave** (see page 247), whilst not a floor show, provides songs with your supper. More of a cross between the Lido and Crazy Horse topless revues is presented **Aux Rêves d'Adam**, an upmarket strip show with smart lighting, magicians, karaoke and dinner, in the old town. *Full Monty* style evenings are provided **Au Bonheur des Dames**, some way out of town, for those who like their hen nights scented with squeals and baby oil. A celebration of depilated masculinity, from the sunbed to the stage, it is proving a hit with office-party crowds who admire men who can still walk the walk after waxing the boxer line. More popular apparently than its predecessor in Lille itself, where the hunks lost a certain credibility by doubling as drag queens and dressing as Madonna before getting their more manly kit off for the girls. The most common complaint was that the boys' eyeliner used to detract from the full effect of the thongs.

Au Bonheur des Dames 61 rue Achille Pinteaux, 59136 Wavrin; tel: 03 20 58 55 53

Aux Rêves d'Adam 8 rue de Courtrai, 59000; tel: 03 20 06 04 14 [15 H2]

Les Folies de Paris [15 G1]
(See page 202)

CINEMA

Le 7ème art thrives in and around Lille. One out-of-town multiplex, Kinépolis at Lomme, boasts 23 screens. However, you will not need to leave the centre of Lille, unless you wish to catch a festival screening of an obscure classic at Le Fresnoy in Tourcoing (see page 242), since everything else will be available around the pedestrian shopping streets surrounding rue de Béthune. The main selection is that offered at the 14-screen **Ciné Cité UGC**. Just along the pavement, the six *salles* of the **Majestic** specialise in original-language versions of international flicks, with subtitles rather than the dubbed versions screened elsewhere. Artier yet are the preferences at the **Métropole** near the station. At the far end of the rue de Béthune, the Palais des Beaux Arts has its own art house **La Garance**. In addition to listings and reviews in *Sortir* magazine, a free guide is produced by the picture palaces of Lille, distributed in cinemas and tourist offices. Budget tip: midweek morning screenings, at 11.00, are half price.

Ciné Cité UGC 40 rue de Béthune, 59000; tel: 08 36 68 68 58; web: w.ugc.fr [14 E5]
M̲ *Rihour;* E̲ *Métro 2 to Gare Lille Flandres then line 1 to Rihour. Rue de la Vieille Comédie leads to rue de Béthune.*

La Garance Palais des Beaux Arts, pl République, 59000; tel: 03 20 15 92 20 [14 E6]
M̲ *République;* E̲ *Métro 2 to Gare Lille Flandres then line 1 to République.*

Le Majestic 54–56 rue de Béthune, 59000; tel: 03 28 52 40 40 [14 E5]
M̲ *Rihour;* E̲ *Métro 2 to Gare Lille Flandres then Line 1 to Rihour. Rue de la Vieille Comédie leads to rue de Béthune.*

Le Métropole 26 rue des Ponts de Comines, 59000; tel: 08 36 68 00 73; web: www.lemetropole.com [15 G4]
M̲ *Gare Flandres;* E̲ *av le Corbusier and right into rue Faidherbe left on rue des Ponts de Comines.*

MUSIC

The **Orchestre Nationale de Lille** is housed in the big round Nouveau Siècle building to the side of Grand' Place. Surrounded by restaurants, the building might easily be dismissed by diners as just another office block and underground car park. But nothing is ever quite what it seems in Lille, as I realised on my first visit to the car park when I noticed that signs for motorists were disconcertingly, albeit politically correctly, translated into Braille. Full orchestral programmes alternate with chamber concerts. The ONL's Sunday morning recitals are firm favourites with locals. The orchestra's director, Jean Claude Casadesus, woos international soloists to his concerts with lunch at local fish restaurants. Concerts are not limited to the Nouveau Siècle hall. They play at many other venues around the region, as well as many prestigious international events. Programme details are posted on the orchestra's website.

The other nationally acclaimed company is the **Ballet du Nord**. Performing all over Europe, its local base is the **Colisée** at Roubaix, a large theatre equally popular with the world of rock as of dance. Opera has abandoned the city centre during the refurbishment of the **Opéra de Lille's** elegant home at place du Théâtre. Inspired by the Paris opera house, the elegant bars and salons can match the stage for opulence and theatricality. With soloists and choirs mixed and matched from the leading companies of Europe, the season here is amongst the continent's best bargains. Just before the place closed for renovation, a production of *Eugène Onegin* boasted a chorus imported from St Petersburg and tickets from under €30 (200FF).

Fortunately, the district has a second opera venue: the **Atelier Lyrique** in Tourcoing produces studio versions of contemporary and classic works. A recent cycle of all the Mozart-Da Ponte comic operas shared the honours between the main house in Lille and this intimate space at Tourcoing.

Regular concerts and recitals are held at the various churches in central Lille and all venues are open during the year's many music festivals. The main event is the Mozart Festival running from November to April. Programmes are available at the tourist office.

Tourcoing hosts its own autumn jazz festival, with fringe events spilling over the Belgian border. Trad jazz may be enjoyed in central Lille every week of the year. Visit the **Anglo-Saxo**, in the old town (see page 201), or **Le 30**, by Grand' Place, for a fix of something mellow by night.

For a harder edge, rock is obviously at home in a district of 100,000 youngsters. Six thousand people a night can raise the roof at the **Zenith** Arena; smaller crowds pack the **Biplan**, **Le Splendid** and the **Blue Note**. Tickets for major events may be obtained through FNAC (see page 224). The **Aeronef** venue high above Euralille is a typical Lille curiosity. Originally an underground organisation for disaffected youth, the club moved to its new high rise home amongst the banks and financial institutions of the business district when it was offered the venue by the city. Multi-national corporations pitched in with generous grants, and the kids were left to organise their own fun. So much so that, when a band offended public morals with their antics on stage, organisers, expecting a mass withdrawal of funding or legal action, were merely sent a memo from the authorities.

Aeronef av Willy Brandt, Centre Commercial, Euralille, 59777; tel: 03 28 38 50 50; web: www.aeronef-spectacles.com [15 H4]
M̄ *Gare Lille Europe or Gare Lille Flandres;* Ē *av Le Corbusier to av Willy Brandt, look for the signs then scale the outside of the tower block.*

Anglo-Saxo
(see page 201)

Atelier Lyrique 82 bd Gambetta, 59200 Tourcoing; tel: 03 20 70 66 66
M̄ *Carliers;* Ē *Métro 2 to Carliers.*

Ballet du Nord Tel: 03 20 24 66 66

Le Biplan 19 rue Colbert, 59000; tel: 03 20 12 91 11
M̄ *Gambetta;* Ē *Bus 12 from Gare Flandres to Colbert.*

Blue Note
(see page 201)

Colisée Roubaix Culture rue de l'Epeule, 59100 Roubaix; tel: 03 20 24 50 51
M̄ *Gare Jean Lebas;* Ē *Métro 2 to Carliers. Walk down rue de l'Alouette.*

Opéra de Lille pl du Théâtre, 59000 [15 F3]
M̄ *Rihour;* Ē *Bus 12 from Gare Flandres to Théâtre.*

Orchestre Nationale Nouveau Siècle, 30 pl Mendès France, 59000; tel: 03 20 12 82 40; web: www.onlille.com [14 E3]
M̄ *Rihour;* Ē *Bus 12 from Gare Flandres to De Gaulle.*

Le Splendid 1 pl du Mont de Terre, 59000; tel: 03 20 33 17 34
M̄ *Hellemmes;* Ē *Métro 2 to Porte de Douai, then bus 7 to pl du Mont de Terre.*

Le 30 30 rue de Paris, 59800; tel: 03 20 30 15 54 [15 F4]
22.00–04.00, closed Sun.
M̄ *Rihour;* Ē *Bus 12 from Gare Flandres to Théâtre.*

Zenith Lille Grand Palais, 1 bd des Cités Unies, 59777; tel: 03 20 14 15 16 [15 J6]
M̄ *Lille Grand Palais;* Ē *Métro 2 to Lille Grand Palais then follow signs.*

NIGHTLIFE

Traditionally there have been only two rules to remember when setting out for a night's clubbing in Lille. Firstly, stay in the bars until late, since no one, but nobody, is seen in a club before well-past midnight, however early the doors officially swing open. Rule number two was that if you really want to party on down, you go to Belgium, move directly to Belgium, do not pass Go.

Although the hardened merry-maker continues to make the cross border trip to Brussels and other Belgian towns, and London's Ministry of Sound is on the main weekend agenda for the continental Eurostar set, the last tenet is perhaps a little unfair these days. Lille's smaller clubs are pretty cool and great for letting the evening spill into the night and flow towards the dawn. The night scene in Lille is pretty much an attitude-free zone of tolerance with fewer of the rigid barriers between crowds that one finds in Paris and London, yet manages to avoid the sorry air of piteous compromise found in many French provincial cities. Check out the *Ch'ti* guide at your hotel reception or online at www.lechti.com for the views of the student community as to which are the current clubs and bars to bless with your company. Listen to the word on the streets around Les Halles (see page 227) or find a stylish bar in Vieux Lille and pick up flyers for clubs.

Admission is often free midweek. Where door charges are made, this often includes the cost of a first drink. Drinks usually cost around double or treble the price charged in bars.

Le Duke's Club 6 rue Gosselet, 59000; tel: 03 20 52 97 98 [14 E8]
Open Thu–Sat 21.00–04.00.
M̄ *République;* Ē *Métro 2 to Gare Lille Flandres changing to Line 1 to République. Take rue Gaulthier de Châtillon to rue Jeanne d'Arc to rue Gosselet.*
An older crowd orders shorts from the bar and sips, smokes, talks and dances 'til late.

l'Opéra Night 84 rue de Trévise, 59800; tel: 03 20 88 37 25
Open Tue–Sat 21.00–04.00.
M̄ *Porte de Douai;* Ē *Métro 2 to Porte de Douai. Rue de Douai to rue de Trevise.*
For the past couple of years this venue has managed to stay ahead of the game, proving a favourite with 20-somethings. New Millenium cult attractions include the notorious sumo routines. Free admission.

La Scala 32 place Louise de Bettignies, 59800; tel: 03 20 42 10 60 [15 G2]
Open Mon–Sat 22.00–04.00.
Ē *Any Claire de Lune bus from Gare Flandres to Lion d'Or.*
Laid back yet lively, the Scala has a varied music policy and appeals to the discerning younger crowd without alienating veterans of the scene.

LEAVE THE COUNTRY

Just as Lille provides entertainment for the millions of people who live within an hour of the city, plenty of others exit aboard the high-speed trains which run in both directions. Once upon a time the weekend was an excuse for local teenagers to hop aboard the party trains to Amsterdam. These days, members of the speedily mobile social set use the fast trains to party in their capital city of choice. In fact, I have been known to base myself in Lille when researching Brussels by night. With Lille the least expensive and friendliest of the three continental Eurostar destinations, the combination of a comfortable hotel room in France, and lazy afternoons shopping and hanging around the town centre provides the ideal R&R for coping with the heady nightlife of the Belgian capital.

Brussels is the most popular cross-border break and most clubbing travellers aim for Fuse (see pages 316, 325–6), which is within walking distance of both the Eurostar terminal and countless other bars and clubs. Allow around 35 minutes by TGV, Thalys or Eurostar from Lille Europe. Cheap return tickets cost from just €12 (80f). The last Eurostar to London is a favourite for clubbers heading for the Ministry of Sound, Trade, Home and other cool clubs. Saturday sees Lillois day trippers heading to the West End for matinees of musicals and – since the British store announced it was closing its French outlets – shopping at Marks & Spencer.

France provides other lures. Paris of course is packed with clubbing, theatrical and gastronomic excuses for spending the evening away from home. In summer, the direct rail link from Lille to Disneyland (see page 179) is popular with the young, free and childless in search of the American dream during the late-night opening season. Since Marne-La-Vallée after midnight has little to offer, these superannuated *mousquetaires* tend to hit the night clubs of Pigalle and the Bastille then chill out at the Afters parties (page 192), before taking the return train home after lunch on Sunday.

Of course, good-time people armed with the Bradt guide should have no problem in finding plenty to do, wherever they find themselves in Paris, Brussels or Lille.

To be truly daring, take a TGV to Marseille, Lyon, Nice or Bordeaux. But you might not get home in time for breakfast!

La Touraille 40 rue Kuhlman, 59800; tel: 03 20 54 68 37
Open Wed–Sat 22.00–04.00.
M̄ *Porte des Postes;* Ē *Métro 2 to Porte des Postes.*
Cellar club underneath a brasserie boasting several dance floors and playing music from the 80s to chart sounds.

Le Tunnel 80 rue de Barthélémy Delespaul, 59800; tel: 03 20 14 37 50 [14 C8]
Open 21.00–04.00

M̄ *Wazemmes;* Ē *Métro 2 to Gare Lille Flandres changing to line 1 to Wazemmes. Rue des Postes leads to rue de Barthélémy Delespau.*

From House to good old-fashioned disco, a relative newcomer to the scene. Average age around 30, and a mixed gay and straight crowd.

THE MORNING AFTER

Fortified with a sturdy breakfast at Paul's, cross Grand' Place in time for a second cup of coffee at the Nouveau Siècle concert hall. The 11 o'clock Sunday morning chamber concerts offer an ideal programme of music to face the world by. The only tough challenge for those who have made the most of their Saturday night is finding the correct doorway in a 360° building when they are 2π-eyed!

Orchestre National Nouveau Siècle, 30 pl Mendès France, 59000; tel: 03 20 12 82 40; web: www.onlille.com [14 E3]

M̄ *Rihour;* Ē *Bus 12 from Gare Flandres to De Gaulle.*

Part Four

Brussels

Les Galeries St-Hubert

Introduction

Brussels is a capital city. It takes to government just as Imelda Marcos takes to shoes. Capital of the European Union, of NATO and of course Belgium, Brussels would no doubt bid to become the seat of the UN, Red Cross, Olympics and the Franklin Mint should any of these august institutions ever open for tender.

This passion for bureaucracy has lead to an undeserved reputation, among those who have never visited the city, for staid insipidity and greyness. An image that could not be further than the truth.

True, Brussels may have more civil servants to the metric memo than anywhere else in the free world. And, yes, vast tracts of the city are given over to administrative districts. And, hands up, I admit that even the city itself has 19 administrative districts of its own, never mind the national and international government quarters.

Despite all this serious grown-up stuff, Brussels is a city that is always teetering on the brink of a party. For, whilst the capital has a rich history, Belgium is a young nation. I might even call it adolescent, still testing and defining its own personality. With its two main cultural identities, the Dutch-speaking Flemish community and the French-speaking Walloons, and a third German culture, Brussels is the nation's one melting pot where any language may be spoken with impunity and no danger of tempers flaring.

With a reluctance to reject half its own heritage, Brussels has a genuine interest in internationalism and keenly welcomes its visitors, with none of the arrogance of older, more assured, cities. There could hardly be a more appropriate capital for Europe. Charles I of France governed here in the 10th century, the House of Burgundy took over from 1430 until 1515, then Spain ruled until 1706. The Austrian branch of the Hapsburgs then turned the city's royal quarter into a mini-Vienna. At the turn of the 19th century Napoléon reigned supreme, until Waterloo of course. Thereafter Brussels was Dutch, for 15 years at any rate. For in 1830 Belgium became the independent nation we know today, its royal house boasting six reigns and two regencies, and one 24-hour republic that nobody quite likes to mention.

This last situation came about towards the end of the reign of King Baudouin. When Parliament needed to pass abortion legislation, the king was unwilling to compromise his own beliefs by granting royal assent. So he abdicated in order that the bill could proceed. The monarchy, and Baudouin's reign, was reinstated the following morning.

Since each of the major international regimes stamped its mark on the city, Brussels is at turns a corner of France, a bastion of Flanders or a haven of the Hapsburgs. Although blighted, like every other first world city, by the great concrete pandemic of the sixties and seventies, the centre was mainly unscarred and remains a charming base for any weekend of the year.

As with the *arrondissements* of Paris, each of Brussels' 19 *communes* has its own neighbourhood personality and charms. The political, military and bureaucratic districts have the expense-account dining and appropriate hotel accommodation one would expect from any self-respecting international community.

Unlike Paris, the largely residential *communes* are spread across a wide area and the areas of most interest to visitors are concentrated in and around the central inner ring road. For Eurostar visitors, we have focused on this compact heart of town, dividing Brussels' core into five sectors:

- **Grand' Place** and the **Ilot Sacré**
- **West of Grand'Place** (Ste-Cathérine's fish market, St-Géry bars and the bd Anspach)
- **East of Grand' Place** (the Upper Town, Sablons antiques shops, royal palace and parks, fine arts museums)
- **North of Grand' Place** (downtown shopping, the regal estate of Laeken, the Atomium and the international hotel districts)
- **South of Grand' Place** (art nouveau houses in St-Gilles, markets, lesser known museums, and last minute diversions near the Eurostar station)

Whichever you decide as a base, don't confine yourself to one area. You will easily be able to reach neighbouring districts by métro, tram or bus or even on foot.

Brussels may be more expensive than its sister cities in France, but the Belgian capital has a style, and taste, all its own that make it a destination well worth a visit.

Those who come to Brussels and leave unmoved have sought the wrong city. Paris may have been described as lover or mistress, Lille as an affair to remember, but Brussels has to be visited as an eccentric uncle, a naughty nephew or the cousin that your mother never mentions. Don't look for passion, just good fun, and prepare yourself to be led ever so slightly astray.

PLACE NAMES AND ADDRESSES

Most streets have two names, one French and one Flemish. Where street signs and maps may read 'rue des Bouchers – Beenhouwersstraat' or 'Chaussé de Wavre – Waversesteenweg', we have chosen to use the French style. Similarly rail and métro stations that might bear two names (eg: Gare du Midi – Zuidstation) are listed under their French title.

TOURIST INFORMATION

Hôtel de Ville Grand' Place, 1000; tel: 02 513 89 40; email: tourism.brussels@tib.be; web: www.tib.be

Open Mon–Sat 09.00–18.00, Sun 10.00–14.00 (winter), 09.00–18.00 (summer); closed Jan 1, Dec 25, some winter Sundays.

With variable advice from the quite useful to the frankly dodgy, counter staff are always keen to sell their various specialist guidebooks, and sometimes have to be prodded into giving out free information. They will however hand visitors a complimentary street map. It often takes two or three telephone calls to obtain satisfactory answers to simple questions.

GETTING AROUND

The heart of Brussels is contained within a pentagon of dual carriageways and tunnels known to locals as the Ring – a belt of fast traffic boulevards looping the city from Gare du Midi to Gare du Nord, via Louise to the east and the canal to the west.

Public transport

Whilst central Brussels is easily conquered on foot, public transport is efficient, punctual and relatively inexpensive. Four services are interlinked and manage to cover most of the city: métro, underground trams (pré-métro), trams and buses. One ticket, or one franking of a multi-journey ticket, is valid for a full hour's hopping on and off various vehicles.

The STIB/MIVB transport authority claims to run five métro lines. In practice the visitor sees two main lines, with their various branches reaching out to the principal outlying districts. Recognise métro and pré-métro stations by the blue and white M signs on the streets.

Line 1 has two routes, A and B, that run mostly along the same track, bisecting the upper stretch of the Ring and extending up to the Heysel district. At Arts-Loi, Line 1 connects with Line 2 which follows the curve of the Ring from Gare du Midi to Simonis.

Platform indicators track the progress of each train arriving at the station, and timetables are clearly displayed. Services run from 05.30 to 00.30.

The phenomenon of the pré-métro was born of an understandable impatience to complete the métro network as soon as possible. Thus, once the tunnels were excavated for each section of the métro system, it was decided to run the city trams along the track instead of waiting for railway trains to be commissioned, constructed and delivered. Currently the main pré-métro line is an underground tramway beneath the boulevard between the south and north stations in what has long been pencilled in as métro Line 3. Since the 1970s, modest 15m and 30m trams have stopped at the huge 90m platforms of Bourse and De Brouckère, serving Grand' Place every couple of minutes. At the end of the underground section, the tramlines fan out across the city.

The other major tram interchange is place Louise, where lines depart for the royal palaces and avenues to the east, beyond the reach of the subway. Many bus services leave from Bourse, outside the Brasserie Falstaff in rue Henri Maus.

Trams and buses are painted bright yellow and blue and are easily spotted, unlike the red and white stops. Once you find a bus stop you will see a detailed and reliable timetable. Each stop has a name and is marked on free public transport maps available from station ticket offices. To stop a bus, put out your arm to attract the driver's attention. Principal bus and tram routes run from 05.30 to 00.30, although some services finish early in the evening. A free métro

THEY MAKE LACE AND POLICIES ... AND THEY CAN COOK TOO

Chocolates and mussels,
Beer, beef and chips,
That's eating in Brussels
The gastronome quips.

It seems a little unfair that a city credited with the most delicate and sophisticated confectionery skills should be the butt of so many cruel jibes from its neighbours. Fortunately, a weekend spent table-hopping in the market squares, wide boulevards and narrow cobbled side-streets of Brussels soon dispels the myths that have grown up around its menus.

After all, since Paris' most gregarious, blond and tanned celebrity chef, Yvan Zaplatilek, continues to wow even the picky French with the sophisticated delights of Belgian cuisine, at last the nation's longest-standing critics have been muted, if not exactly silenced.

As the kitchens of the world come of age, Brussels is no slower than any other city in encouraging its young chefs to experiment with new ingredients and new styles, and my prandial researches have turned up some highly original delights. Nevertheless, it would be a pity to travel to the Belgian capital and ignore the table traditions that have served its residents for centuries.

Obviously a plate of *moules-frites* is something of a national dish. There is probably no better city in the world to sample this relatively inexpensive and highly social lunchtime ritual of filling a side plate with mussel shells as you work your way through a mountain of freshly prepared seafood.

But just as typical as the counters piled high with crustaceans and shellfish is the sight of a wood-panelled brasserie steak-house. Autumn and winter, the house speciality in every other restaurant will be game, with wild boar and venison particular favourites. Stews and casseroles, such as *carbonnade flamande* of beef, onions and carrots in beer, or *lapin à la gueuze* (rabbit, prunes and the organically fermented local beer) are traditional choices. Other classic dishes are *waterzoi* (chicken stew), spicy meatballs and *steak tartare*, the latter often confusingly called *steak à l'Américaine* – bizarrely naming a dish of raw beef for a nation famed for chargrills.

Vegetables play their part on the bill of fare. A Belgian response to an Irish favourite is *stoemp* – mashed potatoes with various sidekicks from cabbage to carrot or even chopped meat. A popular snack meal served with sausages, *stoemp* is often found chalked on the blackboard as a budget bar-snack option. In all classes of restaurant, asparagus, chicory and wild Ardennes mushrooms In their seasons inspire entire menus.

Seasonal vegetables also provide a lifeline for the vegetarian visitor. If meat and seafood are both off your diet sheet, a great many traditional restaurants will offer little more than salads and an omelette for the visiting herbivore. Fortunately, in old-fashioned brasseries starters are often pretty huge, and two of these together will stave off hunger pangs. Trendier addresses are more likely to include a vegetarian option on the main menu.

When ordering one of the more traditional dishes in a brasserie, choose a beer rather than a wine to accompany the meal. Wine lists tend to concentrate on the riches of France, although a few restaurants are able to offer the rarely experienced native white wines of Belgium (see pages 276–7).

This is a city where beer may be taken with your main course. With around 500 domestic varieties to choose from, do not be afraid to ask advice from the waiter or barman. Restaurants and bars usually have two dozen beers on the menu, specialist bars may stock ten times that number. Most popular choices are lagers, but the real ales of Belgium are gaining international popularity. These usually have labels hinting at monastic origin, with images of be-cowled monks and ancient abbeys. Genuine Trappist beers are still brewed by monks – breweries to note are Chimay, Orval, Rochefort, Westmalle and Westvleteren; others are likely to be copies manufactured by large industrial breweries. All these ales come in different strengths, Chimay's red being slightly less heady than the blue variety. With so many Belgian beers to choose from, many travellers fail to taste the only truly Brussels beers. Lambic beers and Gueuze are the naturally fermented brews that use the city air to create distinctive bitter-sweet flavours. Once there were dozens of small family breweries around town. Today, the last of them still caters for the local demand, and welcomes visitors as a museum.

The range of glasses is almost as bewildering as the choice of beers. Order a Kwak, just to see the bizarre wooden contraption that holds the bizarre test-tube-shaped beaker that could never stand on its own round bottom. Apparently it is ideally formed for drinking on horseback.

Like Lille, Brussels makes *genièvre*, juniper gin, an ideal *digestif* or spirited accompaniment to a meal for clearing the system in preparation for yet another delicious dish.

With very few exceptions, you should be able to reach all the restaurants listed in the guide within a few minutes of any of the featured attractions, sights or museums. If you do decide to venture further afield, then the streets around the European Parliament tend to have a good range of Greek and Italian restaurants, fashionable with media types. You are as likely to bump into a BBC correspondent over the sun-dried tomatoes as you are to meet a genuine Belgian. Vietnamese restaurants east of the Ring and the north African cafés near the Eurostar terminus at Gare du Midi have the very cheapest food in town for a final meal – should you have seriously overtaxed your wallet at the Bradt choices.

Whether you choose to dine in an old-fashioned bistro, a typical seafood restaurant or a hip modern establishment, you will find that portions are usually more generous than in France, although the prices are around 40% higher too. Service is included, but a light tip (loose change or a euro or two) is always appreciated.

and bus map superimposes the routes on a street-plan: invaluable for planning itineraries. Michelin maps are best for more thorough investigation.

Rely on serendipity, or buy the €1.50 (50BEF) booklet from the tourist office, to discover the amazing variety of artworks at métro stations, ranging from the ubiquitous comic strip images to sculpture and installation pieces.

Tourist information Tel: 02 515 20 00
Open 08.00–19.00 Mon–Fri, 08.00–16.00 Sat.
Check bus, tram and métro routes on the website http://planitram.ibelgique.com

Tickets

Choose from four types of pass: single tickets (€1.50, 50BEF); five-journey tickets (€6, 240BEF); ten-journey tickets (€9, 360BEF); or the one-day card (€3.50, 140BEF).

Tickets may be purchased in advance from the main ticket desk at the Eurostar terminus at Waterloo, or 07.30–17.00 Monday to Friday at Gare du Midi. Ticket booths should not always be relied on, and new arrivals are frequently faced with only automatic machines to provide their tickets. These may only accept coins, so ensure that you carry enough loose change to get yourself moving.

Whether you use the bus, tram or métro, remember to validate the ticket in the machines on board or at the station. Check the time-stamp on your ticket. You may travel for one hour from the printed time on a single or multiple ticket, and until the last train on the date of a one-day card.

Taxis

As in most cities, taxi fares are calculated as a combination of time, distance and fixed-hire charges. They may be hailed at designated ranks, outside stations, or in the streets. Since the city centre area is relatively small, most journeys from Gare du Midi to your hotel should cost between €6–12.50 (250–500BEF). Service is included in the fare, but modest tips (loose change or a rounding up of the fare) are always appreciated.

Taxi companies:

Taxis Bleus Tel: 02 268 00 00
Taxis Oranges Tel: 02 349 43 43
Taxis Verts Tel: 02 349 49 49

Complaints about drivers should be made on 02 204 21 11. Make a note of the vehicle make, colour and registration number before calling.

Guided tours

Visit Brussels Line is an excellent hop-on hop-off bus line that leaves Gare Central every 30 minutes, 10.30–16.00, and takes in all the major sites around town, including the art nouveau district, Heysel and Laeken. The full trip lasts 90 minutes and is accompanied by a fascinating English-language commentary. The €12 (490BEF) ticket is valid for 24 hours, so should you break your afternoon's journey, you may return for the rest of the trip the following morning. Tickets are available from the driver or in advance from the tourist office.

Centre

GRAND' PLACE – ILOT SACRE

What becomes a legend most? To be honest it is usually the cliché, and Brussels is no exception to the rule. Everything is precisely as the brochures promised us – only somewhat smaller. The Grand' Place is the very heart of town, and is remarkably compact. The square of buildings straight out of a European fairy tale retains a remarkably unintimidating human scale. People pour in from each corner and every hidden alleyway to create the carnival atmosphere of a permanent opera finale.

There is always a sense of occasion on this city square. Perhaps a carpet of flowers, an evening concert or even a few clusters of tourists clicking their cameras obediently in the wake of their guide's finger. The finger usually prods towards the Hôtel de Ville and those houses belonging to the medieval guilds. Although much of the original square was destroyed in the 17th century, the rebuilt version, seen today, provided a healthy slap in the face of the architectural style of the day – which was for regal elegance – and followed the lines of the original oldest buildings. Below the *place* are the signs leading to the Manneken Pis, again far smaller than you had imagined, but always worth a visit if only to check out which of his hundreds of outfits the national incontinent has elected to wear today!

This central area is the perfect starting point for any voyage of discovery in search of any preconceived idea of Brussels. The museums of brewing, chocolate, lace and local history are just minutes from these cobbles, and even the comic strip museum to the north, and royal galleries eastward, are a manageable stroll away.

Between the tightly clustered guild houses of the Grand' Place may be found many a passageway to yet another quaint street. Most points north head to one address: the rue des Bouchers looks good in photographs, but most of the meals served in this serpentine *moules-frites* production line are tourist-trap-standard.

This area behind the classic façades of the big square is known as the Ilot Sacré and it is prime hunting ground for the hungry, as the restaurants around here never seem to close. Long-established international favourites, such as the genuine mussels from Brussels chez Léon, flaunt their menus and

tableware at almost every corner, and lesser-known chocolatiers sell cellophane-wrapped boxes of unfamiliar brand names at half the price of the famed *truffelmeisters*' emporia. Specialist shops deal in everything else from herbal teas to European Union branded brollies.

Most famously, the rue de la Colline leads to the Galeries St-Hubert. Europe's first commercial shopping arcade is today lined with boutiques, chocolate shops, tearooms, and even a cinema. The roads around this part of town are named after the markets and trades that once flourished in each street, so addresses conjure images of herbs, chickens, cheeses, furriers and butchers. To the west, they spill out on to the boulevard Anspach, one of the major thoroughfares of the city. Stores stud the pavements and an underground tram service complements the métro along the length of the boulevard, from the Gare du Midi up to the Gare du Nord.

Although the city's principal shopping zones are the rue Neuve to the north and avenue Louise to the east, this central area is perfect for browsing for that special gift. Lace shops abound, especially around the Costume and Lace Museum. There are also some splendid old-fashioned toyshops in the area for teddies, puppets and dolls houses.

Ignore the traditional Brussels souvenir merchants (remember the golden rule: quality of merchandise is usually in inverse ratio to the number of Manneken Pis statuettes in the window), and find the witty keepsake in one of the burgeoning EU gift shops. Alternatively, pick up a comic book, the national art form. Where the rue Marché aux Herbes disgorges at the fountain of Charles Buls, a Saturday craft market on place d'Espagne offers truly original and charming alternatives to artworks found in pricier galleries.

One pleasant surprise is the number of music shops around the quarter, especially in the roads fanning from place St-Jean. Best of a pretty classy bunch is **Azzato**, 42 rue de la Violette, its window crammed with bagpipes, bongos and banjos, stocking everything you could possibly pluck, strum, whistle or wallop from A to Zither.

Rue du Midi has long been an address for shops with an individual personality, from celebrity milliner Elvis Pompilio to the old honey store. Brussels is a city of party animals, and it dresses to the nines, and counting, whenever invitations drop on the mat. Women balking at buying the latest designer wear from the rue Dansaert across the boulevard Anspach, might visit Jonathan Bernard, 53 rue du Midi, for glamwear hire and advice on looking good enough to wear it. For the party with a costume theme, be it Hallowe'en or the whim of a host, fancy dress shops abound. Finest is Picard on rue du Lombard.

Picard is a perfect example of the subversive exuberance of rue du Lombard. If you blindly cross the road on the signposted route from Grand' Place to the Manneken Pis, all you would notice would be the lace and souvenir shops. Yet within yards of the crocodile tourists, Europe's lotus eaters are learning to tango and salsa in a chocolate shop.

You do not need an invitation to hop on the social whirligig. In the centre of town are found the traditional bars of old Brussels. North of the square are predominantly cosy little *estaminets* and beer cellars with exposed beams, bizarre-shaped beer glasses and an ambient glow from a roaring hearth. In the southern section, radiating from the rue du Lombard, there is a sharper, more contemporary feel to the bars and cafés. Here are hues of blues, minimalist décor and clinically tiled floors.

The rue du Marché aux Charbon is the main artery of Brussels' gay village, and therefore an indispensable address for the heterosexual 20-somethings who might otherwise hang out in the bars of St-Géry (see page 284). The gay fringe is an essential part of any boy-girl diary. It works something like this: straight girl fancies a no-strings, no-pressures night out with good-looking boys, so she heads for the gay bars. Straight lad on the pull wants to be seen as an accepting attitude-free new-man, comfortable with his own sexuality. So he follows her, secure in the lack of serious competition. Belgica has long been the gay bar for the straight party animal. Spot gay bars by the rainbow flags flying outside. In the same street, H2O and Au Soleil cater for a truly mixed clientele.

Whatever you seek, from nightlife to culture, the area around Grand' Place is an ideal base from which to take in the best of Brussels. Although the square has no métro station of its own, it is comfortably located between Bourse station on the north–south underground tram route and Gare Central métro on the slopes of the Upper Town, and is a starting point for excursions to the art galleries, palaces and parks of the east. Best of all, the spire of St-Michael on Grand' Place is a veritable Polaris, guiding safely homeward the happy and exhausted traveller after a night on the town.

WHERE TO STAY

Amigo 1–3 rue de l'Amigo, 1000; tel: 02 547 47 47; email: hotelamigo@hotelamigo.com; web: www.rfhotels.com [12 E2]
M̲ *Bourse;* E̲ *Underground tram to Bourse, then pass the Falstaff Brasserie at the side of the Bourse, right into rue du Midi then left to rue de l'Amigo.*
Go to jail, go directly to jail, do not pass Go – just call room service! With its certain style and the improbability of its story, the Amigo is more than a hotel – it's a five-star anecdote. Nowadays you may require a double-jointed credit card to stay in the bright and cheery suites, but 100 years ago, you would have needed but a drink too many and a personal hygiene problem. For the Amigo was not merely the only prison in 16th-century Brussels, it was where derelicts and drunks were

held on remand. If the name seems a little bizarre for a correctional institution, blame it on the Spanish who ruled the city at the time – even if they had not quite mastered the language, confusing the Flemish words for 'lock up' and 'friend'! The prison was razed to the ground at least twice during its chequered existence, but today's hotel uses the remaining brickwork, gates and smooth, worn flagstones to provide a unique welcome to the airy and spacious reception area. Classic Aubuisson tapestries and paintings from the Flemish and Italian schools are liberally displayed around the building. Higher-priced rooms, €818 (33,000BEF), are the considerate compromise between period furnishings and modern comfortable beds. Marbled bathrooms are well equipped – though the glass door to the toilet in one of the smaller suites gave me pause. Glass, even when frosted, is still glass, and we northern Europeans have our pruderies to maintain. More modest rooms, €195 (8,000BEF), are quite comfortable, although two twin beds pushed together rather than a queen sized or double are less than perfect for singles or couples. Breakfast is a choice of buffets, with a €10 (400BEF) supplement if you opt for the version with scrambled eggs and smoked salmon, rather than sticking to cold cuts and cereals. Posh choc shop Neuhaus is in-house, the Grand' Place is around the corner, and you could spend a happy hour just checking out the Amigo's art collection. Forget a room with a view, have a view in a room with a past – with historic Brussels en suite!

Le Dix-Septième 25 rue de la Madeleine, 1000; tel: 02 502 57 44; email: info@ledixseptieme.be; www.ledixseptieme.be [13 F2–3]
M̄ *Gare Centrale;* Ē *Underground tram to De Brouckère them métro to Gare Centrale. Take rue Putterie to rue de la Madeleine.*
The only word you need is 'wow'! This relatively recent conversion is recommended for elegance, comfort and charm. Less than two dozen rooms at €156–318 (6,300–12,800BEF) – each named after an artist, each originally styled – in the former residence of the Spanish ambassador. Several rooms overlooking the courtyard, such as Magritte on the third floor, have nice-sized kitchen and dining areas. Others, including Jardaens, are packed with antiques and 18th-century French furniture. Still others, Paulus for instance, are duplexes with private roof terraces for intimate coffee moments. A wonderful central staircase has been maintained beautifully and enhanced by lavish floral displays. Service is never short of genteel hospitality, and who would believe all this is but yards away from the tourist traps?

Les Eperonniers 1 rue des Eperonniers 1000; tel: 02 513 53 66 [13 F2]
M̄ *Gare Centrale;* Ē *Underground tram to De Brouckère them métro to Gare Centrale. Take rue Putterie to rue des Eperonniers.*
You might be tempted to dismiss this hotel out of hand, perched as it is above a busy snackery, attracting hordes of satchel-packing schoolkids and bescarved trippers. But climb the stairs and negotiate the warren of corridors, stairs and pathways. Rooms, at €50–65 (2,000–2,500BEF), may be a bit of a lottery, but draw the right straw as I did with number 20 – these bigger rooms at about €65 (2,500BEF) are the best – pass through double doors to a duplex garret with unvarnished wooden floors, clean linen and an irresistible sense of *La Bohème*.

La Légende 35 rue du Lombard, 1000; tel: 02 512 82 90; web: www.hotellalegende.com
M̄ *Bourse;* Ē *Underground tram to Bourse, then pass the Falstaff Brasserie at the side of the Bourse, right into rue de Midi then left into rue du Lombard.*
Don't be deterred by the pistachio-ice-cream green frontage of the hotel – you might miss out on a treat. Step along the cobbled path into the charming

courtyard and a warm welcome from the cheerful and helpful reception staff. Two classes of room: €42 (1,700BEF) and €96 (3,900BEF). The cheaper rooms are pretty much standard for the budget and the area, whilst modernised options have new wooden floors, a thrusting power shower and enough space to flop after buying too much lace in the gift shop next door, and before stepping out to take the second wind of the night air at the Grand' Place. The downside of the location is that it is on the main drag for bars, discos, bistros and hangouts for the young, gifted and Belgian – therefore light sleepers should ask for a room overlooking the courtyard. Breakfast, served in a pretty and bright panelled duplex, is toast, rolls and croissant, coffee and orange juice. On the plus side is a generous bowl of jam on each table; minus points for portion packs of cream for the fresh coffee. Charming translations in the rooms announce that 'complimentary' coffee and tea is available 24 hours at the reception – at a charge of 25BEF! Room phones may only be used for calls within Europe. Longer distance calls from a credit card phone in the hall.

Mozart 23 rue du Marché aux Fromages, 1000; tel: 02 502 66 61; email: hotel.mozart@skynet.be; web: www.hotel-mozart.be
M̲ *Gare Centrale;* E̲ *Underground tram to De Brouckère them métro to Gare Centrale. Take rue Putterie to rue des Eperonniers then right into the Marché aux Fromages.*
Absolutely fabulous, eccentric and delightful, a gem in the Little Athens quarter of central Brussels. Just an olive stone's throw from the Grand' Place, and skewered between kebab and hummus eateries in the road known locally as Pitta Street, the Hôtel Mozart has recently expanded to include a new street-level reception. Retaining the terracotta hues and exposed beams that have long been its hallmark, the hotel lobby is still packed with murals, portraits, reliefs and cameos of Mozart as a boy, as a man and as an icon. Dried herbs and *pot pourri* seduce you and classical music relaxes you as you take in the eccentric higgledy-piggledy array of antiques, art, drapes and staircases. Your room will, like as not, be up some steps across an upstairs terrace garden, then down another stairwell and around a corner. Expect the unexpected: desks and chairs tucked in nooks and crannies, beds on oak-beamed mezzanines, and dried flowers scattered on ledges; maybe a tiny window on to a secret basement garden or a nest under the eaves with twilight skylight views across the city. Friendly atmosphere in the breakfast room is yet another plus. If you prefer baths to showers, though, you are out of luck. Pay around €75 (3,000BEF). TV and minibars as standard. Favoured for the eccentric charm and professional welcome.

St-Michel 15 Grand' Place, 1000; tel: 02 511 09 56; email: hotelsaintmichel@hotmail.com [12 E2]
M̲ *Bourse or Gare Centrale;* E̲ *Underground tram to Bourse, then follow signs to Grand' Place.*
If you want to make an entrance on the Grand' Place, then the fabulous staircase from the front door of this hotel down to the cobbles offers the ideal opportunity. Remarkably, the most prestigious hotel address in Brussels boasts relatively modestly priced accommodation. Clean, slightly chintzy and compact, the rooms that matter overlook the bustling square – and give an enviable view – but then, what else would you expect from a wing of the 16th-century family home of the Duke of Brabant? Of course, the downside of taking one of the more expensive rooms with the imposing views is the noise level. Rooms at the rear of the hotel are €50 cheaper and quieter. However with *son et lumière*, concerts and even live opera staged in the square during summer months, would you quibble for a grandstand view? Furnishing and comfort is pot-luck, for

though some rooms boast antique furnishings to match the locale, others display more than a passing acquaintance with the worlds of the flat-pack and the car-boot sale. Budget €62–135 (2,500–5,500BEF).

Scandic Hôtel Grand' Place 18 rue d'Arenberg, 1000; tel: 02 548 18 11; email: grand.place@scandic-hotels.com [13 F1]
M̄ *Gare Centrale; Ē Underground tram to De Brouckère then métro to Gare Centrale. Rue de Loxum becomes rue d'Arenberg.*
If you recall the bluesy business-class hotel that used to occupy this site, be prepared for a shock. The original lobby and bar have been taken over by a coffee-shop restaurant, the big sauna lounges that doubled as reception rooms are now more traditional guest facilities and the clientele is more touristy than before. However, in place of pampering you can discover an entirely new feel-good factor, as the hotel has an impressive eco-friendly policy. Refurbishment comprises up to 97% recyclable products. Soap comes from wall-mounted dispensers and guests are encouraged to keep the same towels for the full weekend and save on detergents. Pay €186–236 (7,500–9,500BEF). Reception staff are overstretched and service can be a little slow, but any irritation is compensated for by the location, slap bang opposite the Galeries Hubert for a rain-free run down to the Grand' Place should the weather turn Brussels grey and wet.

SEMA 6–8 rue des Harengs, 1000; tel: 02 548 90 30 [12 E2]
M̄ *Bourse; Ē Underground tram to Bourse, then follow signs to Grand' Place; rue des Harengs is a side street to the north.*
Just steps from the Grand' Place is a little house tucked away in what is not so much a street as a blink between two buildings of the square. Double doors to the handful of bedrooms assist the soundproofing effort. Some rooms have exposed beams, adding to the romance of it all. One suite apparently has its own courtyard, but was occupied when I visited the hotel. Rates around €76–112 (3,000–4,500BEF).

WHERE TO GO
À la Becasse 11 rue Tabora, 1000 [12 E1]
M̄ *Bourse; Ē Underground tram to Bourse, rue de la Bourse then left. Look for neon arrow.*
If you enjoyed the *lambic* beers at the Chantillon brewery (see page 317) here is a rare opportunity near Grand' Place to savour the organic brew in this unprepossessing bar that is down-to-earth, rough-and-ready and any other euphemism you care to use for basic. Buy a jug of the unique tipple to share with friends, in the certain knowledge that most tourists will take one look at the place and pass on by to a prettier establishment.

Le Cercueil 10 rue des Harengs, 1000 [12 E2]
M̄ *Bourse or Gare Centrale; Ē Underground tram to Bourse, follow signs to Grand' Place. Tiny side street on the north of the square.*
Almost opposite the main tourist office, locals know this joint as a tourist trap. Ignore the raised eyebrows and pop in for one rather pricey drink, that is if Hallowe'en is your thing. The tables are coffins, the tankards are mock skulls, and the main entrance unsettlingly like a funeral chapel of rest. OK, so the crowd appears to be equal parts giggling office parties on a Eurostar shopping spree and gawking hicks from sticks far remote, shocked at the decadence of the big city. Nonetheless, despite the denials of the *Bruxellois*, this is an example of a very Belgian sense of humour.

Dalí's Bar 35 petite rue des Bouchers; http://home.freegates.be/dalisbar [12 E1]
M̄ *Bourse or Gare Centrale;* Ē *Underground tram to Bourse, rue Marché aux Poulets into Marché aux Herbes then left into petite rue des Bouchers.*
Posters line the passageway to the main entrance of this quite trendy venue for international party animals. They all show images of the great surrealist, a theme that is carried on in the interior design once you pass through the curtained doorway. Subdued lighting and the décor actually give the place a weirdly dated feel, but the Friday and Saturday night techno music is loud and insistent enough to remind you quite how contemporary is the target punter. No one arrives much before 11-ish but by midnight the dancing is under way and the place pounds with the sounds of generation party kicking its heels before embarking on the serious nightclubbing treks at around 02.00.

La Fleur en Papier Doré 53 rue Alexiens, 1000; tel: 02 511 16 59 [12 E4]
M̄ *Gare Centrale;* Ē *Bus 20 to pl de la Chapelle. Walk down rue de St-Esprit, cross bd de l'Empereur to rue Alexiens.*
Ignore the kitty at your peril. A cursory scratch behind the ear simply will not do. The house cat will nudge, nestle and try anything short of an out-and-out pounce to distract the visitor from the many other diversions of this atmospheric little tavern, once home to the surrealist painters, just far enough away from the usual visitor haunts. I allow my feline host to sit on the wooden tabletop next to my coffee cup as I drink in the details from the ancient cast-iron stove to the *papiers dorés* themselves. These golden papers from a time before post-it notes are scraps of *pensées*, paradoxes and pearls of wisdom, each framed and mounted alongside the other curios that cover the walls. The mellow mood is accentuated by the music from an easier age, Gainsbourg, Brel, the Beatles. Linger over a beer or fortify yourself with a light snack for around €7 (300BEF).

Galeries St-Hubert [13 F1–2]
M̄ *Gare Centrale;* Ē *Underground tram to De Brouckère, métro one stop to Gare Centrale. Follow rue de Loxum into rue d'Arenberg.*
These graceful covered walkways, leading down to the rue du Marché aux Herbes, are more than merely a beautiful sanctuary from the rain. The three grand arcades designed by Cluysenaer, blessed with their uniquely latticed dusting of natural light, have long been acclaimed as among the most beautiful shopping galleries in Europe, rating with those of Milan, Mayfair and Paris. Recently renovated, it is easy to see how, on the opening of the first arcade in 1847, this quickly became the home of the Low Countries' answer to the *passeggiata* of the Latin world. Well-to-do families would dress up in their Sunday finery to stroll past the shop windows and whisper sweet slanders about their neighbours as they compared window displays in the Galerie de la Reine, the Galerie du Roi and the Galerie des Princes. Intellectuals would take coffee and reassemble world order in the hushed, almost ecclesiastical nave of this temple to discreet consumerism. For Alexandre Dumas and Victor Hugo, the Galeries were almost a literary salon. Neuhaus opened the first praline shop here, and Belgium's answer to Gucci and Vuitton, the Delvaux handbag, with its trademark D, is sold at 31 Galerie de la Reine (02 512 71 98). Accessorise with Patrick Anciaux's fabulous period costume jewellery or antique brooches and chokers at 7–9 Galerie de la Reine (02 511 52 15). The Manufacture Belge de Dentelles, Galerie de la Reine 6-8, (02 511 44 77) is one of the best places to buy decent lace. The cafés and *crêperies* that seep across neighbouring shopfronts are ideal for giving your day the kindest of gentle nudges after a particularly heavy night on the town. The arcades also host an arthouse cinema in a rather attractive art deco theatre.

THEATRE ROYAL DE TOONE
At home with the Puppet Master of the rue des Bouchers

Not so much an alleyway as an intake of breath between the mussel-hustle, feeding-trough frenzy of this hair's-breadth tributary of the rue des Bouchers leads to the Théâtre Royale de Toone and an evening painted with the brushstrokes of a Breughel. Under 17th-century arches, guarded by a statue of the Madonna, step into the *estaminet*. Exposed beams and rustic charm cannot mask the green-room *bonhomie* of the place. A Mannekin Pis in stage costume, upstaged by marionettes hanging from every conceivable perch. Testament to the glories of each Harlequin and Musketeer are the ageing posters on the walls from past productions of *The Hunchback of Notre Dame*, passion plays and *Macbeth*.

At 20.30, climb the stairs to the second-floor theatre. Rows of benches and a patchwork of cushions await the always capacity audience who have come to hear Lorca, Dumas or Shakespeare liberally reinterpreted by a cast of some 60 puppets, seven manipulators and the voice of them all, the grand master, Toone himself. Perhaps tonight's show will be in French, or Dutch, English, German or the local *Brussels vloms* dialect. Maybe we will witness a re-enactment of Napoléon's defeat at Waterloo, or a cut-down, razor-sharp parody of *Carmen*. Whatever the language, whatever the production, however many characters, José Géal, officially known as Toone VII, will speak or sing every line, live and in person.

Géal was crowned as the current Toone puppet master in 1963, when the last of Brussels' 45 marionette troupes found itself homeless. In the 19th-century puppet shows for adults were the working-class alternatives to the bourgeoisie's opera and classical drama. One serial drama ran for over 70 nightly episodes. But Géal, inheriting over a hundred marionettes, had to find a home if the tradition was to continue. He discovered the present venue, then a ramshackle slum, and after inviting the queen and other VIPs to visit, he persuaded the state to fund the renovations.

Today, the company comprises 1,300 puppets, all made in the Toone workshops, many of which may be seen in the first-floor museum open during the interval of the play. Pride of place goes to the star of every show, Woltje, the Belgian teenager of folk legend who inspired Hergé to create

Goupil Le Fou 22 rue de la Violette, 1000; tel: 02 511 71 37 [12 E3]
M̲ *Gare Centrale or Bourse;* E̲ *Underground tram to De Brouckère them métro to Gare Centrale. Follow rue Putterie to rue Duquesnoy; turn right at the place St-Jean for rue de la Violette.*
If you are feeling mellow after visiting Avec Brel up the road (see page 271) or just cosily nostalgic, flop on a sofa and sip a beer in this comfy bar where Gainsbourg, Brel and vintage French pop plays in a *Gauloise*-fuelled haze.

H2O 27 rue du Marché au Charbon, 1000; tel: 02 512 38 42
M̲ *Bourse;* E̲ *Underground tram to Bourse then walk east along Plattesteen to rue Marché au Charbon.*

Tintin. He can be seen here as a newborn baby, still wearing his trademark cap, as a Musketeer, as a knight errant, Cyrano de Bergerac and in a dozen other guises.

Toone is now unique as a puppet theatre for adults, and has won new and devoted audiences. Apart from the good percentage of tourists in the house, a loyal following of locals queue for tickets, and the average age is 30. Ironically this anachronistic throwback to an allegedly redundant age of storytelling is probably the most successful example of the European ideal. Dumas' characters joke about the EU and dialogue can glide effortlessly between half a dozen languages.

Not surprisingly his country regards José Géal, with his dual cultural heritage and passion for his work, as a national institution. As he locked up the theatre one evening I noticed discreet slivers of ribbon on his lapel (symbols of state-awarded honours). 'What were they?' I asked. With typical modesty he replied, 'Every so often, the minister decides he will give me one of these. It is less expensive than offering us money!'

Théâtre de Toone 21 petite rue des Bouchers, 1000; tel: 02 511 71 37 [12 E1]
M̱ *Bourse or Gare Centrale;* Ē *Underground tram to Bourse then rue Marché aux Poulets into Marché aux Herbes, left into petite rue des Bouchers.*
Bar open from noon daily; shows at 20.30 except Sun, Mon. Show €10 (400BEF), concessions €6 (250BEF). Production puppets may be purchased from €618.50 (25,000BEF).

Quieter than most bars in the centre, this place does not open until 19.00 and so avoids the lingering late-shopping contingent. A refreshing music policy means that soothing classical music provides the background to a chat or rendezvous instead of the strident club sounds of neighbouring bars.

L'Image de Nostre Dame 6 rue du Marché aux Herbes, 1000; tel: 02 219 42 49 [12 E1]
M̱ *Bourse;* Ē *Underground tram to Bourse, then rue Marché aux Poulets becomes Marché aux Herbes*
Look out for the inn sign overhead or you will miss this tiny *estaminet* hidden among the shopping streets to the north of Grand' Place. Step under the sign and

follow a narrow alley to a tiny courtyard with one bench for summer couples too much in love to be disturbed by the steady procession of patrons seeking the outside loos. Inside, all is snug, cosy and grandmotherly. Dutch dressers and cabinets behind the bar hold the obligatory range of speciality glasses for the Bourgogne des Flandres and Maes beers. With lots of wooden tables with mismatched chairs, this favourite little bar, Toby jugs and all, remains a domestic parlour-cum-public bar. Very friendly, very Brussels and as other-worldly as anyone could desire.

À la Morte Subite 7 rue Montagne aux Herbes 1000; tel: 02 513 13 18 [13 F1]
M̲ *Gare Centrale;* Ē *Underground tram to De Brouckère, métro one stop to Gare Centrale Follow rue de Loxum into rue d'Arenberg. The bar is on the right, almost opposite the Galeries St-Hubert.*
Order a strong beer (the eponymous tipple *La Morte Subite* is French for 'sudden death' and the name of an obscure drinking game) and a plate of bar snacks to fully appreciate the evocative atmosphere of Jacques Brel's favourite hangout. The pre-war décor adds to the mood of the place, and the bar is always packed with good-natured 30–40-somethings in mellow humour.

Planète Chocolat 24 rue du Lombard, 1000; tel: 02 511 0755 [12 E1–2]
Closed Mon.
M̲ *Bourse;* Ē *Underground tram to Bourse, then turn east along Plattesteen which becomes rue du Lombard.*
This is the one that (almost) got away. I have been a fan of Frank Duval's strikingly individual chocolates ever since I first stumbled across his shop on the rue de Midi, opposite groovy hatter Pompilio. A much-loved hangout for art students and chocolate junkies alike, the shop sold light lunches as well as the obligatory pralines and *ganaches*. So imagine my distress on returning to Brussels to find the place boarded up. How could this be? Three visits later and I stumbled across the new-look, bigger and better Planète, a few yards around the corner in the rue du Lombard. Don't be misled by the conventional shop front. The Planète is still a haven for those needing a moment out of time. Behind the shop and the neat tea-room tables, the place opens out to a huge den with a definite end-of-term air. Banquettes with cover-throws for flopping, mix-and-match armchairs for hiding behind the stacks of old magazines and, best of all, the dance floor for the Sunday afternoon tea dance. Parisian pretty boys, Bohemian good-time girls, trim and lithesome 40-something-marrieds, hippie hedonists and free-spirits alike, all come to trip the light fantastic under the glitter-ball. Tango, salsa, waltz, twist, cha-cha-cha, the *palais* glide and rock-and-roll are the order of the day every Sunday afternoon from 15.00. On the first Sunday of the month, the hosts hold a two-hour dance class from 13.00 to introduce or refresh the memory of bygone steps. As the rhythm gets increasingly Latin, some seek the cooling air of the brick courtyard which, like the salon, is festooned with work of local artists. The talented young designers and artists of Brussels also design the unusual-shaped chocolates on sale at the counter and in the tea-room. Snacks are always interesting: try a salad of warm goat's cheese *au magret de canard* for €8 (325BEF), the breakfast at €5 (200BEF) or a *coupe planète*, scrumptious *specaloos* and chocolate ice-cream served with whipped cream and hot chocolate sauce, for around the same price (best enjoyed with a tall glass of mint tea). Or perhaps surrender to one of the many house platters of chocolates. A glass of red wine with a plate of home-made chocs costs €5 (200BEF). Decadence was never so sweet.

Au Soleil 86 rue du Marché au Charbon, 1000; tel: 02 513 34 30 [12 D2]
M̄ *Bourse;* Ē *Underground tram to Bourse then walk east along Plattesteen to rue Marché au Charbon.*
This particular place in the sun is a former gentlemen's outfitters and many of the original shopfittings remain in place to give this trendy bar its original style. A lively and talkative crowd stakes out favourite corners and scans the doors for networking opportunities.

Théâtre de Toone 21 petite rue des Bouchers, 1000; tel: 02 511 71 37 [12 E1]
M̄ *Bourse or Gare Centrale;* Ē *Underground tram to Bourse then rue Marché aux Poulets into Marché aux Herbes, left into petite rue des Bouchers.*
Estaminet bar and legendary puppet theatre (see feature, page 268).

WHAT TO SEE

Avec Brel Fondation Jacques Brel, 11 pl de la Vieille Halle aux Blés, 1000; tel: 02 511 10 20; web: www.jacquesbrel.org [12 E3]
Open Tue–Sat 11.00–18.00. €5 (200BEF), no credit cards accepted.
M̄ *Gare Centrale;* Ē *Underground tram to De Brouckère then métro to Gare Centrale. Follow rue Putterie to rue Duquesnoy, cross the place St-Jean to the place de la Vieille Halle aux Blés.*
Jacques Brel is alive, well and living in Brussels. If only. Alas he died in 1978, aged 49, leaving behind some of the most evocative songs ever written. If you were expecting the usual glass display cases of letters and personal effects, then step inside for a very pleasant surprise. Brussels' tribute to the nation's most famous singer-songwriter is a breath of fresh air. Avec Brel is a unique experience where visitors trail in the shadow of the great man one evening in his heyday, as he prepares for, performs and unwinds from a concert in the French town of Roubaix. From checking in at the same hotel, to dropping by his dressing room, to sitting at the local café-bar where the singer relaxes with friends, the visitor always feel as though Jacques Brel has simply popped out of the room for a second, and could return at any minute. The most magical experience is finding yourself in the wings during the performance. Clever sound- and light-play projects an animated spotlight silhouette on to a curtain. I could have sat, watched and listened to the seemingly live concert for hours. You'll need to understand French to enjoy the full experience. However, if you are a fan of *Ne me quitte pas* and *Jef*, or even know Brel's music from such English pop cover versions as *Seasons in the sun* and *Jacky*, this is just about as close as it gets. On the closest Saturdays to April 8 and October 9 (the dates of birth and death), admission is free.

Bruxella 1238 rue de la Bourse, 1000; tel: 02 279 43 55 [12 E1]
Wed guided tours only. €2.5 (100BEF).
M̄ *Bourse;* Ē *Underground tram to Bourse. Entrance on north side of the Bourse.*
This archaeological excavation under the rue de la Bourse has been preserved and glazed over so that visitors can walk through the old passageways by natural light. Four guided tours every Wednesday. English-language visit at 10.15. Information and reservations at the Musée de la Ville de Bruxelles on Grand' Place.

Hôtel de Ville (Brussels Town Hall) Grand' Place, 1000; tel: 02 279 4365
Tue, Wed, Sun morning guided visits; closed holidays. €2.50 (100BEF).
M̄ *Bourse or Gare Centrale;* Ē *Underground tram to Bourse then follow signs or take the rue au Beurre behind the Bourse building.*
Artworks from the city museum across the square, sumptuous Brussels tapestries and hangings from the 16th to the 18th centuries and rich wooden-panelled walls are among the ornate adornments of the civic reception rooms and aldermen's

offices in this most magnificent of the buildings on Grand' Place. Highlight of the visit is the gilded council chamber with its ebony and oak floor. Instantly recognisable due to the exquisitely proportioned spire dedicated to the archangel St-Michael, and the stunning statuary studding the outer walls, the Hôtel de Ville was originally constructed between 1402 and 1448. Bloodthirsty children, whose eyes glaze over as their parents wax lyrical over Renaissance beauty, should be reminded that the architect, Jan van Ruysbroek, is said to have been so unhappy with the symmetry of the finished building that he jumped off the top of the tower. Like most of its neighbours, the town hall was victim to the bombings of 1695. Despite this, the edifice was rebuilt, stone by stone, to the original designs. An ever-changing programme of exhibitions is usually well worth a visit. The main tourist information office is located on the ground floor.

Jeanneke-Pis impasse de la Fidélité, rue des Bouchers, 1000 [13 F1]
M̲ *Bourse or Gare Centrale;* Ē *Underground tram to Bourse, turn east to the rue de Marché aux Poulets, left into rue de la Fourche and right to rue des Bouchers. The impasse is on your left.*
Meet the Manneken Pis' younger, but no less incontinent, sister, who has squatted on this site since 1985. This statuette of a little girl relieving herself will furnish the snapshot your friends will not be expecting to see. PC or not PC? It is either very feminist or bizarrely voyeuristic. You decide.

Manneken Pis rue de l'Etuve, 1000 [12 E3]
M̲ *Bourse or Gare Centrale;* Ē *Underground tram to Bourse then pass behind the Bourse to turn right into rue de Midi, then left into rue du Lombard and right to rue de l'Etuve.*
Come early in the morning if you do not want to be seen checking out the nation's least sophisticated photo opportunity. Far smaller than you expected, the original statue was cast by Jérome Duquesnoy in the 17th century, supposedly in tribute to a child who extinguished a bomb with his own water supply. More probably the artist simply decided to succumb to his own sense of irony in an age when anatomical orifices provided the theme for so many civic fountains. If caught, bluff your way out of the corner with the following five items of trivia:

- His proper name is *Petit Julien*
- He has been kidnapped at least three times by taste-terrorists. By the English in 1745, then the French stole him in 1747. In 1817 an aggrieved French convict seized him and smashed the statue to smithereens.
- Undaunted by the Humpty-Dumpty nature of his injuries, a team of dedicated craftsmen re-used the remains of the original statue to build the replica that we see today.
- Despite his lack of modesty in the continence department, the *manneken* is often to be seen wearing donated costumes. The Elector of Bavaria presented Julien with his first outfit. The second, a gold-brocaded creation, given by Louis XV of France in reparation for the 1747 abduction. More recent donors include Maurice Chevalier and John Malkovich, minor heads of state and people who should have known better.
- At the last count, his costume collection ran to 654 outfits – these may be seen at the Museum of the City of Brussels.

Musée des Brasseurs (Brewing Museum) 10 Grand' Place, 1000; tel: 02 511 49 87; web: www.beerparadise.be [12 E2]
Open 10.00–17.00; closed Jan 1, Dec 25. ∈2.5 (100BEF).
M̲ *Bourse or Gare Centrale;* Ē *Underground tram to Bourse then follow signs or take the rue au Beurre behind the Bourse building. The building is on the far side of the square.*

A modest little exhibition with displays of historic brewing equipment and modern high-tech mass production. Far more interesting would be a visit to a real brewery. Without the smells and atmosphere this place offers little more than you could find on the internet. It does have a mini estaminet bar, however. For anyone seeking the true atmosphere of brewing I would recommend a trip to the Musée de la Gueuze (see page 317).

Musée du Chocolat (Cocoa and Chocolate Museum) 13 Grand' Place, 1000; tel: 02 514 20 48 [12 E2]
Open Tue–Sun 10.00–17.00. €5 (200BEF).
M̱ *Bourse or Gare Centrale;* Ē *Underground tram to Bourse then follow signs or take the rue au Beurre behind the Bourse building. The building is on the far side of the square.*
You actually get to taste the molten product at the end of this fascinating exhibition, which tells the story of the nation's favourite treat from the harvest to the box. Most interesting are the displays of cultural history and social accessories for drinking, serving and storing chocolates. All in all a mouth-watering history lesson, a stone's throw from many of the best choc shops in town.

Musée du Costume et de la Dentelle (Costume and Lace Museum) 6 rue de la Violette, 1000; tel: 02 512 77 09 [12 E2]
Open Mon, Tue, Thu, Fri 10.00–12.30, 13.30–17.00, Sat, Sun 14.00–16.30. €2.50 (100BEF).
M̱ *Bourse;* Ē *Underground tram to Bourse. Take rue Henri Maus, right into rue de Midi, first left into rue l'Amigo and into rue de la Violette.*
The second storey of this pretty 17th-century house has many examples of bobbin-lace, embroidery and handiwork from Belgium and around the world. Lower floors host fabulous temporary exhibitions ranging from the clothes of the suffragettes to drop-dead-gorgeous beaded gowns from the 1920s. Worth a visit in order to learn how to discern taste from tat at the many rip-off lace shops touting for the tourist trade. Forewarned is forearmed. Look for the plaque at Rose's Lace Shop at the rear of the building. It announces that on this site, once a hotel, Paul Verlaine shot Arthur Rimbaud on July 10 1873. If your history is hazy you'll be happy to deduce that it was not fatal since the sign was erected on the centenary of Rimbaud's death in 1891.

Musée de la Ville de Bruxelles (Brussels City Museum) Maison du Roi, Grand' Place, 1000; tel: 02 279 43 55 [12 E2]
Open Tue–Fri 10.00–17.00 (16.00 in winter), Sat–Sun 10.00–13.00; closed holidays. €2.50 (100BEF).
M̱ *Bourse or Gare Centrale;* Ē *Underground tram to Bourse then follow signs or take the rue au Beurre behind the Bourse building.*
Most people nip in and out of here merely to admire the Manneken Pis' ever-expanding wardrobe of donated finery. A pity to miss out on the other treats housed in this 19th-century copy of the 16th-century gothic Maison du Roi, itself built on the site of the original bread market. Whilst lace and chocolates are considered the main crafts of the city, the ground-floor display of other native arts reveals an awe-inspiring talent for tapestry, pottery and the skills of the silversmith. Climb the stairs to follow the physical, cultural and political growth of Brussels through the ages.

Puppet Museum Théâtre Royal de Toone, 21 petite rue des Bouchers, 1000; tel: 02 511 71 37 [12 E1]
M̱ *Bourse or Gare Centrale;* Ē *Underground tram to Bourse then rue Marché aux Poulets into Marché aux Herbes, left into petite rue des Bouchers.*
Open each evening during the interval of the play. See page 268.

GRAND' PLACE [12 E2]

In the morning you will be greeted by the flower sellers, in the evening by party-goers and revellers, for Grand' Place is the meeting place of Brussels. Summer sees the famous carpet of blooms covering the cobbles and *son et lumière* fills the square during July and August. On special sultry evenings, the gables and spires provide the backdrop to *al fresco* opera, and Christmas brings the huge Norwegian tree and living nativity crib. Whatever the townsfolk bring to fill this historic heart of Brussels, nothing will ever upstage the beauty and magnificence of Europe's most stunning baroque square. Impossible to believe that most of what you see was built in just five years. Yet, when the original 15th-century buildings were destroyed during the French bombardment of the city in 1695, the guilds of craftsmen, who had earlier overseen the foundation of a mayor and council, determined that the square would rise to its former glory for the turn of the 18th century.

Ornate swirls, carving, relief and gilding on each of the guild-houses would not disgrace a royal residence, but each of these buildings was raised to glorify commerce in a square whose Flemish name means 'market'. The symbols that adorn each house give it its common name. Thus the bakers' guild building at number 1, on the western terrace, is known as the Roi d'Espagne, after the bust of Charles II of Spain surrounded by slaves. The Wheelbarrow, La Brouette, marks out the grocers' guild-house at numbers 2 and 3. The Maison du Sac at number 4, home to coopers and carpenters, has upper storeys reminiscent of carved table legs. The archers' guild building, no 5, Maison de la Louve or she-wolf, is graced with classical allegories of peace and hunting, and is the only building to have survived the bombing. Number 6, Maison du Cornet, resembles a ship and is the watermen's building. The fox atop the front door of the Maison du Renard at number 7 guards the home of the city's haberdashers.

St-Nicholas' Church 1 rue au Beurre, 1000; tel: 02 513 80 22 [12 E2]
Open 07.45–18.30.
M̲ *Bourse;* E̲ *Underground tram to Bourse.*
What with poster hoardings to one side, visiting sports fans ogling the pictures from the transvestite cabaret opposite and the unrelenting surge of the Kodak classes pouring into the Grand' Place, you could be forgiven for failing to notice this quirky, misshapen, medieval church on the corner. A cannonball preserved in the wall is testament to its miraculous survival of the 17th-century bombing of the square. Pools of blue light from the stained-glass windows illuminate the elegantly carved altar and statuary, reflection of the spiritual calm of Brussels' oldest church, dating from the 13th century.

WHERE TO EAT
Armand & Ko 16 rue des Chapeliers, 1000; tel: 02 514 17 63 [12 E2]
M̲ *Gare Centrale;* E̲ *Underground tram to Bourse, follow signs to Grand' Place, leaving the square at the southeast corner.*

Along from the town hall on the south of the square by the rue Charles Buls is the smallest house, l'Etoile ('star'), demolished and rebuilt several times. The Maison du Cygne ('swan'), at number 9, still serves the interests of its original owners, the butchers' guild, since it is today a gastronomic restaurant. Likewise the brewers' guild, next door at the Maison de l'Arbre d'Or ('golden tree'), has its brewing museum (see page 273). The buildings along the east of the square are private houses; one even houses a modestly priced hotel. The city museum takes up most of the northern side of the square. A few doors along from the rue de la Colline, number 24, the Maison de la Chaloupe d'Or ('golden rowing boat') is protected by two saints. At the top of the building stands Brussels' own St-Boniface, whilst St Barbara, patron of tailors, whose guild constructed the house, is positioned above the entrance. An inscription reads, 'The house whose enemies fury destroyed by fire, we tailors have made rise anew and pay our dues to the magistrates'. Next door the Maison du Pigeon, once the painters' guild, was home to Victor Hugo during his exile to Brussels.

Other symbols to look out for are the rose at number 11, the deer above Godiva's chocolate shop, the angel at number 23, helmet at number 34, the peacock at number 35, a fox and an oak tree on the classical façade of numbers 36 and 37 and Ste Barbe and a donkey on numbers 38 and 39.

To take your mind off the inevitable crick in your neck, flop at a table at one of the brasseries and bars around the square to thumb through this book and your maps, for this is the perfect place for forays into nearby streets or sorties to neighbouring districts. When you return, enter the square by the splendid art nouveau memorial under the archway from rue Charles Buls, and rub the arm of the statue of Everard t'Serclaes, who freed the city from the rule of the Counts of Flanders. It is said to bring good luck.

M̲ *Bourse or Gare Centrale;* E̲ *Underground tram to Bourse then follow signs or take the rue au Beurre behind the Bourse building.*

In a Brussels where the newest restaurateurs tend to follow the European pack in creating themed and styled dining experiences, most of the restaurants that actually look like restaurants – around Grand' Place at any rate – turn out to be tourist traps. However. here is a bistro that not only looks like a bistro – it tastes like one too. Classic fare is served with *bonhomie* at the table and respect in the kitchen. Devoted carnivores are not sidelined here. House specialities such as beef stuffed with spinach vie with the daily blackboard specials including the perennial favourite, a mouth-watering *carbonnades flamandes à la gueuze* that tastes as good as it sounds. Such *plats de jour* won't break the bank, and we were delighted not to receive standard city-centre disapproval when we dropped in for an early evening one-course fuelling stop before an evening's musical entertainment, and spent just €25 (1,000BEF) between us on a main course and a bottle of water. The lunch menu is a modest €15 (600BEF). Budget €45 (1,800BEF) for a supper based on chicken *waterzoi* or *sole belle meunière* – cooked Ostende style – never forgetting that, in Belgium, Ostende has the continental claim to the flat fish assumed in Britain by Dover.

Aux Armes de Bruxelles 13 rue des Bouchers, 1000; tel: 02 511 21 18; web: www.armebrux.be [12 E1–2]
Closed Mon, early July.
M̱ *Bourse;* E̱ *Underground tram to Bourse, turn east to the rue de Marché aux Poulets to the rue de Marché aux Herbes then left into the petite rue des Bouchers.*
There are those Belgians who would rather starve than be seen dining anywhere near the rue des Bouchers. Having tried too many of the cloned *moules-friteries* along this narrow yet sprawling street, I have to admit that, by and large, I agree. Menus in a dozen languages, interchangeable gingham tablecloths, pavement seafood counters laden with ice and pretty shell displays, all guarded by wide-boy food pimps. These tourist traps are to be avoided at all costs. Yet at the heart of the *ici-on-parle-Thomas-Cook* labyrinth is an art deco jewel, polished for years by the Veulemans family. A century ago, Calixte Veulemans arrived in the city to work as a waiter, and in 1921 he bought the present restaurant. Here Veulemans came up with the idea of serving mussels in individual casseroles, now a national symbol. Gradually the family bought up the neighbouring houses as business expanded. The guestbook is awesome, witness scribbles, doodles and thank you notes from Danny de Vito to the pretender to the French throne, from Yehudi Menuhin to Charles Trenet. The restaurant continues to win fans thanks to fair service, starched white tablecloths and a million ways with *moules* and homage to *homard*. Aux Armes de Bruxelles gives tradition a good name. National classics, *waterzoi*, cauldrons stacked high with mussels served with the obligatory twin mountain of chips are the dishes of the day. But you could eat lobster here every night for a fortnight without having the same dish twice. And since the hustle and bustle of the rue des Bouchers has to be experienced at least once in a lifetime – why not eat well and feel smug watching the less well informed being ripped off just yards away from you. Lunch is good value: €23–45 (900–1,800BEF).

L'Eperon d'Or 8 rue des Eperonniers, 1000; tel: 02 512 52 39 [13 F2]
Closed Sat, Sun, and three weeks in summer. €19–50 (750–2,000BEF).
M̱ *Gare Centrale;* E̱ *Underground tram to De Brouckère then métro to Gare Centrale. Take rue Putterie to Carrefour de l'Europe and rue des Eperonniers.*
Michel Oostland gives Belgian favourites a decidedly Gallic flair in this listed 16th-century building on one of the main conduits of the historic town centre. Certificates from gastronomic *confreries* share the walls with an old master's view in moody oils of a heaving board of plenty. Don't however be duped by the comfortingly nostalgic décor. Though the food may be classic, it is anything but musty. It was rather late, and well past my suppertime, when I turned up on the doorstep one windswept, rain-soaked evening. Yet, despite the hour, and the fact that most other diners were well on their way towards coffee and *digestifs*, I was made more than welcome. I am sure that even had I decided to indulge myself with the full gastro-monty, the charming team would have indulged me with no hint of a hurry. Forsaking the ubiquitous *moules* (here in *bière blanche*), I opted for a *cassoulette* of wild mushrooms – positively popping with forest flavour, and baked cod in an orange and mint juice with a well-aimed kick of ginger to perk the late-night palate. Of course the wine list is rich with the Bordeaux and Burgundies one would expect. But I chose one of 20,000 bottles produced each year by Belgium's only château vineyard: a 1994 Château Schoonhoven. Since vine blight and the bully Bonaparte forcibly directed the nation's taste towards France, the low countries have rather neglected a wine that had a fine European reputation as far back as the 15th century. Made from Muller-Thurgen and

Sieger stock, the white wine is light, yet balanced, and a pleasant accompaniment to white fish. I was struck by the seasonal imagination on the menu. I dined at asparagus time, and was almost lured from my chosen dishes by the prospect of a four-course asparagus menu for €32 (1,300BEF), featuring the delicacy with scrambled eggs and smoked salmon, in *capuccino* with *crevettes*, and *en fricassée* with *suprème de poulet de grain*. Whatever you choose, don't expect much change from €50 (2,000BEF).

Le Falstaff 17–23 rue Henri Maus, 1000; tel: 02 511 98 77 [12 D–E2] €12–33 (500–1,300BEF).
M̲ *Bourse;* E̲ *Underground tram to Bourse.*
Something of a legend in its own mealtimes, the big bold brasserie at the side of the Bourse is probably the definitive Brussels refuelling stop, punctuating the days and evenings of busy city people, breaking from business, preparing to party, or simply doing the sights. Although it was closed for quite a chunk of 1999, I was pleased to note that on its re-opening there were no great visible signs of refurbishment. The scratched workhorse wooden stations and chipped marble tabletops that a lesser and more pretentious establishment would have replaced with brand new and expensively distressed copies remain in place, as does the stained glass. Enough heavy-leaded panes and scenes to create half a dozen cathedrals and still have enough left over to keep Britain's own dear Prince Albert occupied for years. The most notable images are scenes from the later life of Sir John Falstaff. Why Sir John? Why such an English character as a symbol of this most Flemish of dining rooms? After a couple of minutes staring at the Breughel scene on the place mat in front of me, and catching sight of the piled plates being served to my neighbours, I twigged the appeal of the man in the Low Countries. It is the debauchery of Verdi's Falstaff rather than the Bard's, and very fitting too. This is the realm of the trencherman, rather than the gourmet. I also sussed why there is no set menu on the bill of fare. A starter or a main course would satisfy most midday or early evening hungers. Three courses would be nigh on impossible! No pretension to gastronomy, just honest flavour and quantity: oysters (*Fines de Claires*) and mussels in white wine or *marinières* for around the €13 (500BEF) mark; the generous and savoury *carbonnade à la bière brune* is prepared '*comme grande-maman*' for €12 (450BEF); generous steaks with a choice of sauces for not much more; toasts and snacks from around €7 (250BEF). Even a modest starter salad at under €12 (450BEF) is something special. One glance at the piled plate of leaves, *chèvre* and toast proves that even if nouvelle cuisine passed this place by, there is nothing staid nor tired about the kitchen. The cheese is wrapped in smoked salmon then grilled, and served on a salad of walnut and pine kernels, laced with a knotted confusion of honeyed orange peel and redcurrants to taunt the jaded palate. The staff, more diner-tolerant than of yore, still have the hurried preoccupied air essential to brasserie work, and a bustling air pervades, from the chandeliered salons to the terrace. How could I have doubted that this place would return after being shuttered for so very long. As the man himself said, 'Banish plump Jack and banish all the world'.

Falstaff Gourmande 38 rue des Pierres, 1000; tel: 02 512 17 61 [12 D–E2]
M̲ *Bourse;* E̲ *Underground tram to Bourse. Walk past the other Falstaff on rue Henri Maus, turn right on rue du Midi and right again to the rue des Pierres.*
Do not confuse this address with the main Falstaff Brasserie around the corner – see above – with its own ebullience and deco panache. The more recent testament to Shakespearian *embonpoint* is rather like a restaurant from a Schnitzler play, or an operetta *ingenue's* first grown-up meal, or perhaps the place where a

family solicitor might encounter the ne'er-do-well younger son of a noble client entertaining an aspiring actress. So, we are talking candlelight reflected in polished wood, glass and cutlery. Panelled partitions with bevelled panes separate dining parties – my companion declared we sat at a four-poster table! Naturally the room is staffed exclusively by reproving uncles. A three-course meal with three wines reveals the Falstaff Gourmande to be a disciple of the 'big white plate' movement. Food is traditionally prepared, unsurprising and not too beholden to the realm of the crustacean. Reliable veg from sea-salty spinach to braised chicory accompany workaday *confits*, salmon and *bourgeois* standards, though I found the desserts to be a little heavy. Nonetheless this is deliciously old-fashioned stuff without the indigestion-inducing rush-hour feel of the tourist trap *mouletoria* of the rue des Bouchers. Pay €25–50 (1,000–2,000BEF).

Mystical Resto 57 rue des Eperonniers, 1000; tel: 02 512 11 11 [12 E2] €22–40 (850–1,600BEF).
M̲ *Gare Centrale;* E̲ *Underground tram to De Brouckère them métro to Gare Centrale. Take rue Putterie to Carrefour de l'Europe and rue des Eperonniers.*
Welcome to a cultural makeover: a Millennium take on religious flamboyance. With rough-hewn tables, mismatched wooden chairs, plaster saints, wrought-iron fixtures and candles in brick archways under canvas vaulting – all in celebration of young, hip, catholic chic. Yet it is not merely the *jeunesse dorée* that packs the modest-sized dining room. Tables of drop-dead-gorgeous-and-aware-of-it 20-something couples are seated cheek-by-cowl with empty-nesters on a ruby wedding binge. The religious theme continues with the menu (courses are listed as confirmations and communions) and the odd chalice amongst the table appointments. Not to everybody's taste, certainly; the room has a tendency to overshadow the plate. Nonetheless, a three-course set menu with coffee for around €22 (850BEF) features a respectable port-packed *fricassée* of *foies de volaille* and lamb *en croute* with creamed *flageolets*.

La Roue d'Or 26 rue des Chapaliers, 1000; tel: 02 514 25 54 [12 E2]
M̲ *Gare Centrale or Bourse;* E̲ *Underground tram to Bourse, follow signs to Grand' Place, leaving the square at the southeast corner.*
If the décor at the Roue d'Or should be described as '*après*' Magritte, then the great surrealist has only just left the building. This eccentric brasserie is sepia-tinted both by time and generations of carefree smokers, with its witty homage to the Master on murals above the dark wooden wall panels and polished glass. Yet one glimpse through the *faux-miroir* into the spotlessly clean kitchen tells you that the traditional food will be anything but fusty. The same mind that decided to adorn the dining room with potted trees and a silver-plated, light-bulb-studded cake-stand memorial to the triumph of ostentation over aesthetics, obviously determined that a sleeping taste-bud is a wasted taste-bud. Therefore feel free to choose anything from the lamb, pork and seafood-based menu, with no risk of boredom. Although oftentimes a full plate may not proclaim a thriving imagination, here *boeuf en brioche* will be packed with the flavours of the vineyards of Bordeaux. A salad of roasted goat cheese will boast assorted nuts, dried tropical fruits and a hint of honey in the warm vinaigrette. Vegetables are used to good effect, such as the enviable blend of paper, dry crispy leaves and succulent moist spinach above and below my turbot. Good value lunch at around €10 (400BEF), otherwise pay €35–45 (1,400–1,800BEF).

Brass plaques on seats proclaim the names of the restaurants *habitués* and sponsors. Most seats are already credited, but should you wish to record the magic of your romantic weekend for future generations, then a discreet passing of an indiscreet amount of money could leave a little piece of your happiness in the Roue d'Or for evermore. Whatever you decide, you will return. Same management as **T Kelderke,** 15 Grand' Place.

WHAT TO BUY

Azzato [12 E3] (see page 262)

La Boutique de Tintin 13 rue de la Colline, 1000; tel: 02 514 45 50 [12 E2] Open Mon 11.00–18.00, Tue–Sat 10.00–18.00.
M̄ *Gare Centrale;* Ē *Underground tram to De Brouckère them métro to Gare Centrale. Take rue Putterie to Carrefour de l'Europe then follow signs for Grand' Place. Rue de la Colline is the northeastern entrance to the square.*
From the books to the videos to the mugs to the leisurewear. Everything for the fan. Scores of other shops on the rue de Midi and bd Anspach sell *Hergébilia* and knick-knacks of other cartoon heroes, from Lucky Luke to Bart Simpson, but this place concentrates on the national hero.

Café-Tasse Store 15 rue Marché aux Herbes, 1000; tel: 02 502 49 07 [12 E1–2] Open Mon–Sat 10.00–18.30. [12 E1–2]
M̄ *Bourse;* Ē *Underground tram to Bourse then follow signs to Grand' Place, take north side streets to rue Marché aux Herbes.*
Those with a bittersweet tooth will like this alternative to the many traditional chocolatiers along this stretch of road. Coffee-flavour chocs and coated beans and rich cocoa powder, not to mention tea and coffee-flavoured jams, among the gift options.

Chocolate Shops (see feature, page 318)

Condomi 37 rue des Pierres, 1000; tel: 02 513 59 83 [12 D–E2] Open Mon–Sat 12.00–18.00.
M̄ *Bourse;* Ē *Underground tram to Bourse. Rue des Pierres is east of the boulevard.*
The condom boutique where responsibility in rubber comes in many flavours and sensitivity ranges from the ribbed to the hypoallergenic.

La Courte Echelle 12 rue des Eperonniers, 1000; tel: 02 512 47 59 [13 F2] Open 11.00–13.30 14.00–18.00, closed Wed, Sun.
M̄ *Gare Centrale;* Ē *Underground tram to De Brouckère them métro to Gare Centrale. Take rue Putterie to Carrefour de l'Europe and rue des Eperonniers.*
A delightful diversion just yards from Grand' Place, this quaint little shop selling exquisite dolls houses and dainty furnishings for the models. Even if you have to adopt or rent a daughter, it is well worth the visit.

Dandoy 31 rue au Beurre, 1000; tel: 02 511 03 26 [12 E2] Open Mon–Sat 08.30–18.30, Sun 10.00–18.30.
M̄ *Bourse;* Ē *Underground tram to Bourse then rue de Bourse to rue au Beurre.*
We say 'biscuits', the Americans say 'cookies' and the Belgians say *'speculoos'* and nobody calls the whole thing off. The best biscuit shop in town, this is where to go for almond confections, waffles, marzipan and dozens of other sweet treats, all nicely gift-wrapped as an alternative to *ballotins* of chocolate. This original branch has been serving fresh-baked nibbles since 1829. A new shop, with larger windows for hands-free salivating, may be found across the square on the rue Charles Buls.

Elvis Pompilio 60 rue du Midi, 1000; tel: 02 511 11 88 [12 D2–3] Open Mon–Sat 10.30–18.30.

M̄ *Bourse;* Ē *Underground tram to Bourse then any road east of the boulevard to rue de Midi. The shop is on the corner with rue des Lombards.*

With a name like that, her boy was going to be an accountant? Mrs Pompilio of Liège stood no chance of keeping her son out of the limelight. And so the world's extroverts come to Brussels to pay upwards of €125 (5,000BEF) for a hat from Elvis Pompilio. Men's hats, women's hats, hats with feathers and hats with veils, but always, always, hats that turn heads.

Euro Tempo 84 rue Marché aux Herbes, 1000; tel: 02 230 62 71 [12 E2]
Open Mon–Sat 10.00–18.30.
M̄ *Bourse or Gare Centrale;* Ē *Underground tram to Bourse then follow signs to Grand' Place, take north side streets to rue Marché aux Herbes.*

There are many gift shops in the streets around the square that put the stamp of the common market on the Grote Markt. Best merchandising is to be discovered at this smart boutique that sells quality watches and knitwear as well as the jigsaws, brollies and trinkets that make such good souvenirs. I chose a fun watch, which replaces numbers with the 12 national currencies overtaken by the euro in 2002, and I love the europhile teddies.

Galeries St-Hubert [13 F1–2]
Fashion accessories, jewellery, chocolate and trinkets in the covered arcades (see page 267)

Picard 71 rue du Lombard, 1000; tel: 02 513 07 90 [12 E3]
Open Mon–Sat 09.00–18.00.
M̄ *Bourse or Gare Centrale;* Ē *Underground tram to Bourse, then east along Plattesteen into rue du Lombard.*

Horror masks, whoopie cushions and fancy dress fill the window of Europe's best dressing-up party shop. More than just a huge costume and prank emporium, Picard has a nice sideline in catering to the sleight-of-hand brigade. Behind the counter are kept the impedimenta of illusion, for anyone wishing to develop a talent as a magician.

SOS Company 6 rue de la Bourse, 1000 [12 E1]
Open Mon–Sat 10.00–18.30.
M̄ *Bourse;* Ē *Underground tram to Bourse. Shop is to the left of the stock exchange.*

Bargain second-hand clothes for backpackers whose threads are getting too bare for comfort. Levis at €12 (500 BEF), jumpers at €2.50 (100BEF).

West of Grand' Place

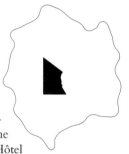

STE-CATHÉRINE AND ST-GÉRY

Once upon a time this was simply Chinatown. A reliable repository of Chinese, Thai or Vietnamese alternatives to the *moules-frites* menus on offer elsewhere. The boulevard Anspach in its various guises, running from the towers of the South and North stations, kept the two sides of Brussels from overlapping. Bookstores, popular *chocolatiers*, mini-malls and smart hotels ensured a buzz along the pavement, especially on the terrace outside the Hôtel Métropole. Nonetheless the smart money always remained on the eastern side of the street, and trickled away in the direction of the Grand' Place, so visitors never had to worry much about the unknown world across the boulevard to the west. Gradually, however, these streets have been reclaimed by the 21st century's answer to the guilds who laid out the old quarter of the Ilot Sacré: the foodies, the fashionable and the immortal young.

It was the smell of good food that first lured the open-minded across the road, just as the promise of a good hot meal had led hard-core carnivores south to sniff out a simple table on the abattoir side of the tracks, and the more cautious to seek the sanctuary of safe international cuisine in the international hotels of the international district.

Since the true taste of this city lies in its lobster pots rather than its melting pots and slaughterhouses, fish and seafood are the keys to the flavours of Brussels. The gaudy aquaria, vivaria and multifaria of the Ilot Sacré may pull in the unwary package punters doing the life-as-a-postcard tour around Grand' Place. However, locals quickly learned to cross the boulevard Anspach to the traffic-free streets around the Church of Ste-Cathérine.

Old images at the city museum show place Ste-Cathérine as a working port, with the river Senne flowing through the city and the morning-fresh catch sold on the quaysides. After a cholera outbreak in 1876 the river was paved over, and waterways diverted into canals by city planners inspired by the Haussmann Grands Boulevards of Paris. The port became a flourish of large squares, fanning out from the church, and retains the irresistible feel of a fishing community.

The area is *the* place to be for turbot, trout and all those shellfish delicacies that demand an R in your month. Although the row of restaurants facing the church may attract a lively crowd, fear not; the tourists who dine with the locals here certainly know their food. Just around the corner, quayside brasseries line the quais aux Briques and au Bois à Brûler – many of which have amazingly good-value lunch menus, offering an excellent meal at half the price you'd pay half a mile away. Just walk a little further from the Zeeland oyster and lobster specialists and you will find some excellent restaurants, whose imaginative *chef-patrons* have a real flair for preparing game or contemporary dishes, and at least two of the best lunches in all Brussels.

Not as brazenly hip as the rest of the rediscovered district, this understated quarter is a true find for the occasional weekender or the regular visitor. Even knowing of its existence sorts the insiders from the out-of-towners.

For those who live their lives with a style and dress sense so sharp that Elastoplast comes as standard, neighbouring rue Antoine Dansaert is the essential address for the personal organiser. Edouard Martin brings minimalism to floristry, while a branch of the classy bakery Pain Quotidien (see page 305) for food shopping and the speakeasy dash of the Archiduc bar would give the street more than enough cred. But catwalk fashion guarantees its place on the map. Nicole Kadine has eminently stylish outfits for the modern woman, but which allow comfort and movement for mere mortals whose bodies are not strictly geometrical. The talked-about designers from the city of Antwerp have several showcases on the street, and there is even a second-hand store for those who are not too proud to prowl the streets in finery with a past. Essentially, from couture to coffee, furnishings to flowers, this is where to wallow in consumerism without losing any avant garde credibility.

Halfway along the road is the place du Vieux Marché aux Grains, that graduated from being the original city cemetery to becoming the cattle market, the eponymous corn market (from 1650) and now a newly embraced residential address.

Keep going south for even more of a party atmosphere, on what was once an island in the river Senne. The Ile St-Géry, birthplace of Brussels, became, in the 19th century, a covered meat market, but in the 1980s deteriorated into a depressed backwater. The old market building was earmarked for demolition until, as suddenly as rue Dansaert was adopted by the arty set, St-Géry (see page 284) became the coolest spot on Planet Brussels, especially at cocktail hour and around midnight. The superficially grubby side streets that link Dansaert to St-Géry continue to spawn new bars and cafés to catch the overspill from the hipper joints or to challenge for the social crown. If the people who matter ever bother crossing the boulevard these days it would be to continue the small talk and flirting along the rue du Marché aux Charbon.

One of the nicer aspects of this western sector of the city centre is that its boundaries are comfortingly blurred, and there is a reassuring overlap between the *schlock* of the old and the chic of the new. Unlike many yuppie ghettos, the real world is never kept out of sight. Between two boutiques might be a condemned building wrapped in corrugated iron. A row of stylish bars and bistros can easily give way to a launderette and working man's bar.

A 15-minute early morning stroll took me from a voguish patisserie to a rat-infested wasteland by the railway tracks, returning to quiet squares of elegant renovated townhouses by way of a truckers' breakfast rendezvous.

The area may now be in everyone's address book, yet it manages somehow to remain refreshingly unmapped.

WHERE TO STAY
Métropole 31 pl de Brouckère, 1000; tel: 02 217 23 00; web: www.metropolehotel.com [10 E6]
M̄ *De Brouckère;* Ē *Underground tram to De Brouckère.*
The fabulous lift in the magnificent Renaissance-styled lobby whisks guests into the setting of romantic adventure. For the 100-year-old Hôtel Métropole is one of the world's most atmospheric hotels from the golden age – not so much of travelling, but of arriving! There is a buzz of occasion about the place, from the ultimate art nouveau café-bar to the terrace where *le tout Bruxelles* may be found sunning itself. Within the hotel itself, bell-boys, porters, clerks and even other guests are suffused with the glow of the heyday of European cinema. So much so that one is surprised to discover that this world exists in colour rather than monochrome! But colour there is, from the deep leather sofas to the greens of the stained glass.

You might be lucky enough to catch a recital in the Salon Artur Rubenstein, or dine at Dominique Michou's restaurant, l'Alban Chambon (see page 287). A modest alternative Métropole experience (say ∈20 or 800BEF) for those neither sleeping nor dining on site is to take a cold collation of *charcuterie* or smoked fish, a beer and the air at the pavement terrace of the café: people-watching and massaging your ears with the sounds of many, many accents as the city unwinds in the early evening. Rooms, of course, are precisely what you would expect of an hotel of this class, and priced ∈262–362 (10,560–14,700BEF). All the usual services may be called upon, with the additional bonus of free internet access for all guests.

Hôtel Welcome 23 quai au Bois à Brûler, 1000; tel: 02 219 95 46; web: www.hotelwelcome.com [10 D5]
∈55–90 (2,200–3,600).
M̄ *Ste-Cathérine.*
(see La Truite d'Argent, *Where to eat*, page 290)

Royal Embassy 159–163 bd Anspach, 1000; tel: 02 512 81 00; email: reservation@hotel-royal-embassy.be; web: www.hotel-royal-embassy.be [10 D7–8]
M̄ *Bourse;* Ē *Underground tram to Bourse.*
Right by the food, drink, business and pleasure districts, the location is excellent – even if the rooms are disappointingly standard comfortable-bland. Never mind ∈62–190 (2,500–7,500BEF), since the hotel finds its way into the guide for the reception's flexibility over weekend rates and the Dauphin Club Health Spa complex in the basement. The owner discovered the remains of a 16th-century bridge in the cellar and now part of the brick arch spans the pool and jacuzzi.

WHERE TO GO
Archiduc 6 rue Antoine Dansaert, 1000; tel: 02 512 06 52 [10 D7]
Open 16.00–06.00.
M̄ *Bourse;* Ē *Underground tram to Bourse; rue August Orts, left of McDonald's, becomes rue Antoine Dansaert.*
There is something of the buzz of the prohibition era about this bar. Perhaps it is the fact that you have to ring to enter, even in daylight. Maybe it is the live jazz

on Saturday afternoons. It might be the near-glamour of well-to-do types who regard shopping as a good reason to order cocktails at the art déco bar. Then again you could blame it on the fact that one may only pay in hard cash, since, surprisingly for such a smart watering hole, credit cards are not accepted.

Brabant Horse Market pl Duchesse de Brabant, 1080
Open Fri 06.30–12.00.
M̄ *Gare de l'Ouest;* Ē *Tram 82 to Triangle.*
Give yourself a timeless treat before breakfast, get up early and make your way from your hotel to Molenbeek-St-Jean horse and cattle market. Sights, sounds and smells from another era turn a European capital city into a provincial market town.

Fin du Siècle 9 rue des Chartreux, 1000 [10 D7]
M̄ *Bourse;* Ē *Underground tram to Bourse then rue August Orts, left of McDonalds, then left into rue des Chartreux.*
Far more expensive hairdressing to be seen in this bar than at the Greenwich next door. People here would rather discuss changing their colour scheme than the world. Slick, nearly chic, and a pleasant place in which to munch on a light snack before braving the seriously social venues of the quarter.

Le Greenwich 7 rue des Chartreux, 1000 [10 D7]
M̄ *Bourse;* Ē *Underground tram to Bourse then rue August Orts, left of McDonalds, then left into rue des Chartreux.*
If you'd rather chill than buzz, and prefer to choose a paperback than an outfit when heading out for a solitary drink, this is the place for you. If you'd rather talk face to face than text across a crowded room, head here rather than the corner bars of St-Géry. They play chess, smoke roll-ups, read second-hand paperbacks and meet up with old friends at Le Greenwich. Wood panels, mirrors and paintwork in that never-to-be-found-in-a-tin shade of 'nicotine with a hint of history'. Here naïve nice-girls who want to change the world fuel their intensity from the wisdom of mid-life-crisis professors who should know better; former lovers kiss welcome without rancour; foursomes bicker over listings magazines and loners are never out of place.

Place St-Géry pl St-Géry, 1000 [10 D7]
M̄ *Bourse;* Ē *Any underground tram to Bourse then take rue Jan Van Praet at the side of O'Reilly's Irish pub to pl St-Géry.*
At the heart of this suddenly hip and happening quarter, a Chinese whisper along the *dim-sum* and *sushi* drag of the Bourse's oriental refectory, is the red-brick, glass and steel market hall, dramatically saved from demolition. Les Halles, the market building itself, is a mixed exhibition, performance and information centre, but best loved as the cool **Café des Halles**, where drinks are served to busy people with busy lives taking time out to lounge in wicker chairs. Juices, beers and spirits on the menu, but the coffee of choice is a glass of *lait russe*. Wednesday evening sees live jazz, but anytime there is a strangely Latin feel to the place; when the rain lashes the pavement outside, the effect is almost tropical. Opposite the main entrances are clusters of well-cool street-corner hangouts, a must for people watching: **Mappa**, with its walls coated with louvre doors, and windows glazed in *retro-nouveau* style, somehow vacuum-packs its crowds into place. Opposite, **Zebra** is cosier, but no less effervescent with animated conversations played out against brick walls. Other smaller bars open and close with the changing of the winds, but whatever the name over the door, this is the place to meet friends, hang out or discover the newest R&B bands on their way to the top.

WHAT TO SEE
Album 25 rue des Chartreux, 1000; tel: 02 511 90 55; web:
http://home.tiscalinet.be/aalbum [10 D7]
Open Wed–Mon 13.00–18.00. €1.25–5 (50–200BEF).
M̲ *Bourse;* E̲ *Underground tram to Bourse then rue August Orts, left of McDonalds, then
left into rue des Chartreux.*
The least formal, most visitor-friendly museum in town. An open, fully glazed
frontage to this 17th-century house, the rear courtyard a stylish pond for koi
carp, where traditional institutions present an air of looming formality, this place
virtually cries 'Yo!'. The entire collection changes every few months, but of two
things you can be certain: you will be guaranteed a surprise around every corner,
and you will pay according to how much you enjoy yourself. Admission charges
range from €1.25 (50BEF) for up to 15 minutes to €5 (200BEF) for as long as
you like. Punch a time card when you arrive and pay when you leave. I caught a
fabulous expo explaining the European ideal – politics put into easy perspective –
on the ground floor; a multiple-choice quiz had optional answers printed on the
ebony keys of an old piano. All incorrectly labelled keys were mute; only the
right answer was rewarded by a note. Upstairs, I rummaged through a bedroom
cabinet representing the life and works of Leonardo da Vinci. His art was in the
top draw and his anatomical discoveries behind a cupboard door. Oh yes, and
proving that music has always united Europe, guests could watch Mozart opera
on video or spin original Beatles vinyl albums on an old Dansette. Cool or what?
The subsequent show took an off-beat look at the world of advertising, and who
knows what the theme will be when you next hit town. The place is seriously
addictive, and has won legions of regulars who drop in whenever they can.

Museum of Flemish Life in Brussels 13 rue des Poissonniers, 1000; tel: 02
512 42 81; email: amvb@medisoft.be [10 D7]
Open Mon, Wed–Sat 10.00–18.00; closed holidays, Dec 25–Jan 1. Free.
M̲ *Bourse;* E̲ *Underground tram to Bourse then rue August Orts, left of McDonalds, then
right into rue des Poissonniers.*
To understand better the twin identities of Belgium, with its twin tourist
authorities, separate national theatres and multilingual everything, it is worth
taking time to visit the museums and archives dedicated to a single identity. The
history of the Flemish community in Brussels, with the accent on its cultural
influences on the city, is told in photographs, maps and temporary exhibitions. If
you don't speak Dutch, speak English.

Ste-Cathérine's Church pl Ste-Cathérine, 1000; tel: 02 513 34 81 [10 D6]
Open 08.30–17.00.
M̲ *Ste-Cathérine;* E̲ *Underground tram to De Brouckère then métro to Ste* Cathérine.
There has been a chapel on this site since the year 1200, but the Black Tower of
the original ramparts and vestiges of the 17th-century church are all that remain
of early versions. These days the square is dominated by the 19th-century
replacement. From the outside, this church might not merit a second glance. Do
drop in to savour a unique collaboration between two very different architects,
who plundered the Romanesque, Gothic and Renaissance back catalogue of
church building to develop their own style of construction-sampling. Janssens,
responsible for many of the St-Gilles town houses, and Poelart, creator of the
looming Palais de Justice, between them produced an almost graceful, and
certainly tranquil, place of worship. Beneath white-vaulted ceilings, light filters
through blue and yellow windows, and a good collection of paintings are well
displayed. The main reason to visit is the rare 15th-century Black Madonna.

Guided tours of the church and its art treasures may be arranged by request on Sunday afternoons.

Scientastic Level –1, Bourse métro station, bd Anspach; tel: 02 732 13 36; web: www.scientastic.com [10 D7]
Open schooldays Mon–Fri 12.30–14.00, Sat, Sun and school holidays 14.00–17.30; closed Jan 1, Dec 25. ∈3.72 (150BEF).
M̄ *Bourse;* Ē *Underground tram to Bourse.*
The most low-tech science museum you will ever visit, and a glorious reminder, in the age of PlayStation and microchips, that natural technology can be pure magic, this engaging diversion within Bourse métro station is an unexpected simple pleasure. The brainchild of Baudouin Hubert who, after years in the grown-up world of international banking, commerce and business in the USA, decided to return to Brussels and reintroduce children to the tricks and treats of science. He discovered a cavernous hall under the boulevard Anspach that had been excavated during construction of the station. Here one may rediscover the joys of optical illusions, discover the magical effects of parabolas on sound waves, play tricks with mirrors and light and learn how to build one's very own rainbow. All is done on a realistically human scale so that children are inspired to recreate the same effects at home with a cardboard box and some string. Learn that a fakir's bed of nails is more comfortable than a bed of golf balls, discover how the mind plays tricks with perspective and scale, and rediscover all five senses. For kids the revelation is that mental stimulation does not require two AA batteries. Adults are wooed and won by the invitation to try the first attraction for free before deciding whether to pay the admission charge. Since the place is open every schoolday lunchtime, and every other afternoon of the year, except Christmas and New Year's Day, the noise level may be impressive. However, discreet logos on certain displays suggest which will be of more interest to the grown-ups. No IMAX screen, no computer-generated imagery, but Scientastic boasts the most special effect of all: turning this world-weary traveller with a wobbly cash flow and a creaky knee into a virtual 11-year-old.

WHERE TO EAT
L'Achepot 1 pl Ste-Cathérine, 1000; tel: 02 511 62 21 [10 D6]
Closed Sun.
M̄ *Ste-Cathérine;* Ē *Underground tram to De Brouckère then métro to pl Ste-Cathérine.*
Offal is as offal does, and kidney, tripe and other tavern staples of barnyard provenance do very well indeed to provide good honest fare on a relative budget. A simple bar with a decked terrace outside, sandwiched between the gastronomic and pizza alternatives in the centre of foodieland. Dining *al fresco* invites informal conversation between tables and is a great place to trade restaurant tips with *Bruxellois* in the know. Over the last couple of years, I could not help but notice that the Achepot seems to be becoming somewhat trendy with British Eurostar weekenders, who may threaten to outnumber the equally well bred but better-dressed locals some Saturday lunchtimes. So it will be interesting to see if it manages to retain its family feel into the 21st century. No credit cards accepted, by the way, but meals cost just ∈10–25 (400–1,000BEF).

Alban Chambon Hôtel Métropole, 31 pl de Brouckère, 1000; tel: 02 217 23 00; web: www.metropolehotel.com [10 E6]
Closed Sat, Sun and holidays, also mid-Jul–mid Aug. ∈39–80 (1,600–3,300BEF).
M̄ *De Brouckère;* Ē *Underground tram to De Brouckère.*

Dominique Michou's restaurant at the Hôtel Métropole. Michou is a *maitre cuisinier* in both Belgium and France, and is famed for his *tartare* of duck with truffles and a soufflé of turbot and lobster. I have known grown men whimper for his *crème des ravioles de crème brulée* on a bed of poached fresh fruit. Mind you, one pays ∈37–75 (1,500–3,000BEF) to eat here.

La Belle Maraîchère 11 pl Ste-Cathérine, 1000; tel: 02 512 97 59 [10 D6] Closed Wed and Thu.
M̲ *Ste-Cathérine;* E̲ *Underground tram to De Brouckère then métro to pl Ste-Cathérine.*
When your cooking is this good and your regulars travel 40km just for lunch, you don't need stuffy formality to prove your worth. So *toques* off to the Devreker brothers who are rightly members of the Belgian Brotherhood of *maître cuisiniers*, but don't make a song and dance about it. In the heart of the seafood quarter, a light, panelled, airy and delightfully unpretentious dining room has the unmistakable hum of quality and success. The core clientele is aged around 40-something-plus, gastronomically worldly and experienced enough not to be fobbed off with a fancy certificate, a *Gault Millau* listing and a pricey menu. So the brothers prepare a choice of lunches and dinners with no clever fireworks, just an appreciation of the sea's bounty, from the fish soup to the *plat de résistance*, be it sole, lobster or salmon. Talent is not strictly maritime. Even the house take on the *steak-frites* standard is an object lesson in meat texture, colour and flavour. *Habitués* are keen to offer advice and sing the praises of the chefs. The close-to-retirement couple from Antwerp at the next table ('My wife and I make love once a week, but we eat well six times a week') grew more and more flirtatous with each other as lunch progressed. They told me of the good and great who have discovered La Belle Maraîchère. Even as we chatted towards closing time there was a muted gasp as four of the country's most respected chefs arrived to lunch with Freddy Devreker (brother Eddy was still at work in the kitchen). If it's good enough for the best kitchen talent in the land to choose on their Mondays off, that is sufficient testimonial for *ambience*, service, food and value, not to mention combining the charms of a family table with the demands of a top-class restaurant. A rose amongst culinary thorns, it will cost you upwards of ∈25–45 (1,000–1,400BEF).

Bonsoir Clara 22–26 rue Antoine Dansaert, 1000; tel: 02 502 09 90 [10 D7] Closed weekend lunch. ∈13–40 (500–1,600BEF).
M̲ *Bourse;* E̲ *Underground tram to Bourse; rue August Orts, left of McDonald's, becomes rue Antoine Dansaert.*
Ratatouille of red mullet, *carpaccio* and the ubiquitous *tartare* mark out this fashionable eatery as modern, European/South Pacific stylish for the set that dresses to be informal. Once you take in the heat of the stained-glass patchwork walls, zinc-topped tables and velvet hangings, you know the food will be as hip as the punters. When busy, the waiting staff develop myopia, so not recommended for those on a tight schedule. Flavoursome food – if lighter than the Belgian norm. Lunch at under ∈13 (500BEF); à la carte is double and then some.

Cap Mange Tout 11 rue des Riches Claires, 1000; tel: 02 513 18 08 [10 D7]
M̲ *Bourse;* E̲ *Underground tram to Bourse. Rue des Riches Claires is a turning to the left of the bd Anspach.*
In a road that cannot quite decide if it's on the way up or down (the one-time sex shop at number 13 has now closed down, even if the rubber products in the window of number 9 suggest neither domestic plumbing nor bicycle repairs), a new restaurant has opened its doors on the wrong side of the bd Anspach. The

animal-print banquettes and deep red walls flaunting feathers and masks hint at a showgirl's dressing room. The stylish window display of ranged teacups promise a lighter bill of fare than the city standard. The menu tells its own story. Home made pastas with seafood and vegetarian sauces, imaginative salads and the more artery-friendly selection of specials are pleasing, simple, and tasty. Those who need their fix of trad grub should find the *côte de veau grandmère* and daily specials efficiently banish hunger for well under €20 (800BEF). Should you seek a break from the full ration then this little dining room off the boulevard makes a pleasant change.

François 2 quai aux Briques, 1000; tel: 02 511 60 89 [10 D5–6]
Closed Mon.
M̄ *Ste-Cathérine;* Ē *Underground tram to De Brouckère then métro to Ste-Cathérine.*
What started off as a modest local fish bar, was the inspiration for the restaurant frenzy that has now taken over the waterside sprawl as far as place Ste-Cathérine. Today, the children of the original François run the popular seafood restaurant and its fish shop and takeaway service next door. Eat well for €30–50 (1,300–2,000BEF).

The Gazebo 5 pl du Nouveau Marché au Grains, 1000; tel: 02 514 26 96; web: www.eurocom.be/gazebo [10 C6]
Closed lunch and Wed.
M̄ *Ste-Cathérine;* Ē *Underground tram to De Brouckère then métro to Ste-Cathérine. From rue du Vieux Marché aux Grains turn right into rue Dansaert to pl du Nouveau Marché-aux-Grains.*
In her other lives, Lee Better has worked in marketing, created Wrangler jeans, run a Michelin-noted restaurant with her chef husband, Argirios Carananos, and was a New York interior designer back in the days when 'designer' was *not* a dirty word. For her latest restaurant, on the ground floor of her 18th-century house in an up-and-coming corner of the city where rich girls shop for clothes and poor boys play ballgames, she has used all her life skills – except the denim! Straight out of *Interiors* magazine, the dining room is a symphony in light. Using the recently discovered, and lovingly restored, carved ceiling as the inspiration for the gazebo theme, tall swathes of fabric and taller windows create a sense of *al fresco* without the baroque *trompe l'oeil* effects that even the kiosks seem to favour in a city without understatement. As the sun goes down, the walls seem to disappear and one half expects Eleanor Powell to waft in from the shadows and fade away to dance beneath the moon. At the bar end of the room it is always the midnight ocean blue of Claude Rains and Paul Henried. Evening gets progressively darker and twilight lends magic to the décor. Outside the windows, old men walk their dogs and young men shoot basketball beneath the tall dusty trees of the square. I didn't even have to die to go to heaven for a broccoli soup cooked with a soul, the sort of recipe that can only be invented at two in the morning after a three-hour tearful heart-to-heart with a best friend. The Gazebo spring salad has endive in garlic and parmesan dressing, with thirst-quenching melon and wickedly spiced cashews. New, the week I first visited the restaurant, were lightly fried fillets of red mullet served with moreish *semoule* and lessish olives. Sauces are citrus rather than *crème*, the house white is a full fruity Gascogne and the desserts can wilt willpower at forty paces. Generally – in introducing genuine North American cuisine to the *bruxellois* – food is a mixture of classics, the very latest innovations from young chefs stateside, and Lee's grandfather's New York deli potato salad. Diners either make an evening of it starting early, or tumble in after the theatre to perch at the bar-crunching salads, sipping wine and dishing

with Lee. I was seduced by the warmth of my welcome, won over by the flavours on my plate and my wallet was scarcely bruised by a bill around €40 (1,600BEF). And I learnt something, as early evening chamber music segued into late-night Sarah Vaughan: comfort food may yet be cutting edge. This place has both a heart and a soul.

L'Huitrière 20 quai aux Briques, 1000; tel: 02 512 08 66 [10 D5–6]
M̲ *Ste-Cathérine;* E̲ *Underground tram to De Brouckère then métro to Ste-Cathérine.*
Classic décor, classic lobster, shellfish and *brasserie* fare. Goose liver with sauternes, champagne and oysters, the very menus that made hearty citizens toast the night 30, 40, 50 years ago in a setting that the grandparents of today's diners would comfortably recognise. Sit against oak walls under the brass chandelier in winter and, on balmy summer nights, dine *al fresco* on the waterside terrace. Budget €38 (1,500BEF(for dinner but it might be worth trying the €12 (500BEF) lunch.

Le Jardin de Cathérine 5–7 pl Ste-Cathérine, 1000; tel: 02 513 92 62 [10 D6]
Closed Sat lunch. €25–37 (1,000–1,500BEF).
M̲ *Ste-Cathérine;* E̲ *Underground tram to De Brouckère then métro to Ste-Cathérine.*
Van Gogh lived here, and nice bourgeois couples dine here. But then the starched napkins and safely spotless dining room has probably changed substantially over the years. Seafood, from the fisherman's *marmite* of autumn to the grilled oysters of a summer Sunday lunchtime, the house speciality, and all may be savoured on the eponymous terrace when the sun shines.

Le Loup Gallant 4 quai aux Barques, 1000; tel: 02 219 99 98 [10 C5]
Closed Sat lunch, Mon and holidays, Easter week, Christmas week and two weeks in Aug.
M̲ *Ste-Cathérine;* E̲ *Underground tram to De Brouckère then métro to Ste-Cathérine. Walk along the quai aux Briques to reach a second quayside.*
I just don't know on earth how they manage to create a fabulous €15 (600BEF) lunch without compromising the high house standard. *Terrine* of guinea fowl, *gigot*, then dessert. Amazing value. But even without the lunch deal, this little corner plot at the end of the paved-over port side of the lobster and seafood district is worth a visit. Evenings are dedicated to the main menu and especially to the fish dishes with the inventive sauces that have earned Daniel Mollemans serious respect. Pay €25–38 (1,000–1,400BEF) to discover the catch of the day tickled with blends of herb and wines, beers and fruits that one would never have imagined possible. The Mollemans magic is continually evolving. Every visit brings a new surprise, a new subtlety, a new approach to a traditional dish. It is generally accepted that no one in Brussels can top the house *bouillabaisse à la Marseillaise.* The only innovation that never crosses the threshold is the general practice of raising prices in line with popular success. This modest house at the corner remains excellent value. Dine in the little garden if the weather is good enough. Some Sundays sees a buffet menu rather than the main selection – so telephone to check. Recommended for its superb lunch menu and for imagination at all times.

La Marée 99 rue de Flandre, 1000; tel: 02 511 00 40 [10 C5]
Closed Sun evening, Mon, June, Christmas, Jan 1.
M̲ *Ste-Cathérine;* E̲ *Underground tram to De Brouckère then métro to Ste-Cathérine. From pl Ste-Cathérine turn right to the far end of rue de Flandre.*
Around the corner and up the road from the better-known addresses in the fish bar district of Ste-Cathérine and the Quays is an unpretentious local restaurant

with a sign in the doorway that, roughly translated, means 'To eat well, come in – you'll be back!' The welcome is warm and the place is full of locals who trust Thérèse in the kitchen to prepare *moules*, *escargots* and simple fish dishes. Simple does not mean boring. Subtle and succulent are two words rarely applied to fried cod and chips – but when the fish in question is a prime cutlet, moist and flaky and just lightly turned in oil, and the chips are those genuine Belgian *frites* of mayonnaise-dressed legend, simple comes into its own. Budget ∈25–38 (1,000–1,500BEF).

La Sirène d'Or 1a pl Ste-Cathérine, 1000; tel: 02 513 51 98 [10 D6] Closed Sun, Mon, three weeks in Sep. ∈31–50 (1,250–2,000BEF).
M̄ *Ste-Cathérine;* Ē *Underground tram to De Brouckère then métro to Ste-Cathérine.*
Seeming a little reserved, this Sirène sits on the corner of the sprawl of restaurants where locals pick and choose their weekend tables. A hundred yards from the brasher *brasseries* of the quais aux Briques and Bois à Brûler, this is altogether more formal. Muted yellows and creams in the dining room are the first clues that the master chef in the kitchen formerly worked in palace kitchens. There is a classic feel to Robert van Duuren's approach to seafood. *Gratin des coquilles St-Jacques* and *langoustines* with dry vermouth and a flourish of ginger sharpens grilled *St-Pierre*. Sumptuous desserts are good. Perhaps more business lunch than weekend grazing; you could leave with a sore wallet. There won't be much change from ∈50 (2,000BEF).

La Truite d'Argent/Hôtel Welcome 23 quai au Bois à Brûler, 1000; tel: 02 219 95 46; web: www.hotelwelcome.com [10 D5]
Closed Sat lunch and Sun.
M̄ *Ste-Cathérine;* Ē *Underground tram to De Brouckère then métro to Ste-Cathérine.*
A hundred years ago when this restaurant opened its doors by the old fish market it swiftly became known as the unofficial annexe to the Belgian Parliament. The quayside restaurant on the not-quite-fashionable side of town was an immediate hit with politicians and captains of industry. These pillars of the community found it an excellent location for dining with secretaries and other female companions – and the management thoughtfully provided six bedrooms upstairs to allow their diners either to sleep off the effects of the wine or otherwise burn off excess calories after dinner. Today's owners, Michel and Sophie Smeesters, are proprietors with propriety and the upper storeys of the building have been converted into what once claimed to be the smallest hotel in Brussels – now with ten bedrooms ranging from budget to first class standard, ∈55–90 (2,200–3,600BEF) the night. Downstairs, the restaurant, with its three dining rooms, turn-of-the-century style frescoed ceiling, and friendly waiting staff, is known for its lobster dishes, but specialises in its own take on *truite aux amandes*, popular with everyone from eurocrats to

honeymooners. Regulars opt for the jumbo *gambas* served on a bed of spinach with orange-flavoured butter, or the *foie gras* ravioli, to start with, then dive into my favourite pig-out selection – a rather lavish fish platter where bream meets pike, perch and a handful of local lake and river specialities. Spend €25–44 (1,080–1,800BEF). Regular diners in the restaurant in the 1960s included Jacques Brel. If you can get the staff talking when the salons are not too busy you will hear tales of the many other near-legendary, larger-than-life characters who have managed the restaurant, and sat at the tables, over the decades. The prettily tiled breakfast rooms, **Les Caprices de Sophie**, next door at 5 rue du Peuplier, double as a snack bar during the day.

WHAT TO BUY

Espace Bizarre – Modern Living 19 rue des Chartreux, 1000; tel: 02 514 52 56; email espace.bizarre@skynet.be [10 D7]
Open Mon–Sat 10.00–19.00.
M̄ *Bourse;* Ē *Underground tram to Bourse then rue August Orts, left of McDonald's, then left into rue des Chartreux.*
Modish wedding lists are left here, for this is the place for interiors if your future has no children, pets or jigsaws. Espace Bizarre makes Ikea seem like a sub-post office in the Cotswolds. Futons, glassware, foot mittens, even a chrome and glass cauldron designed to spew dry ice across your converted loft living space. Whatever you buy here is less a present than a statement.

Idiz Bogam 76 rue Antoine Dansaert, 1000; tel: 02 512 10 32 [10 C6–7]
Open Mon–Sat 10.30–18.30.
M̄ *Bourse or Ste-Cathérine;* Ē *Underground tram to De Brouckere then métro to Ste-Cathérine. Take rue du Vieux Marché aux Grains to rue Antoine Dansaert.*
This may be cast-off clothing, but don't dare to call it jumble. Posh frocks and showy gowns from to-die-for *marques*, or fabulously evocative salvage from grandmother's attic, are all given new life and waiting for a good home. Some of the offerings are straightforward second-hand treasures, others are patched and re-invented by in-house designers. A super place for unique accessories. Women can actually find a Fifth Avenue suit from around €120 (4,800BEF), but throw your budget to the wind and you might discover an outfit of the kind that Orry-Kelly designed for Joan Crawford and Bette Davis in 1940s Hollywood.

Johanne Riss 35 pl du Nouveau Marché aux Grains, 1000; tel: 02 513 09 00 [10 C6]
Open Mon–Sat 10.30–18.30.
M̄ *Ste-Cathérine;* Ē *Underground tram to De Brouckère then métro to Ste-Cathérine. From rue du Vieux Marché aux Grains turn right into rue Antoine Dansaert to pl du Nouveau Marché aux Grains.*
If the couture is so *haut* that you find yourself dizzy with vertigo, sit by the pool of the Japanese garden in this spacious warehouse-style womenswear emporium. Everything for the modern power-broker, be she the chairman of the board or mother of the bride.

Nicole Kadine 28 rue Antoine Dansaert, 1000; tel: 02 503 48 26 [10 D7]
Open Mon–Sat 10–18.30.
M̄ *Bourse;* Ē *Underground tram to Bourse. Rue August Orts, left of McDonalds, becomes rue Antoine Dansaert.*
A hint of the exotic, but the combination of generous swathes and classic tailoring are the true hallmark of the creations of a favourite Antwerp designer.

Women love the fact that Kadine's clothes are as practical for walking and sitting in as catching the eye.

Stijl 74 rue Antoine Dansaert, 1000; tel: 02 512 03 13 [10 C6–7]
Open Mon–Sat 10–18.30.
M̲ *Bourse or Ste Cathérine;* Ē̲ *Underground tram to De Brouckère then métro to Ste Cathérine. Take rue du Vieux Marché aux Grains to rue Antoine Dansaert.*
Designers of the moment from Paris and Belgium regard this address as their Brussels showroom. Ever since Sonia Noël opened this first of the Dansaert boutiques, career men and women have shopped here for the suits and partywear that serve as a passport for high fliers. This is the ideal place to get to know the Antwerp designers who have been giving Paris a run for its money over recent years. Labels to note: Ann Demeulemeester, Van Beirendock, Dries Van Noten and Dirk Bikkembergs.

North of Grand' Place

Platinum may be the preferred shade of the plastic bandied around the place Louise, but locals on a realistic budget go shopping along the rue Neuve, between De Brouckère and Rogier stations. Household names watch over every other doorway, including Inno, the Belgian department store, C&A, H&M and all those comforting initials familiar to every high street. In the midst of this very modern pedestrian quarter, a veritable pathway of Mammon, discover a reminder of less ephemeral values in the 18th-century church of Notre Dame de Finistère, halfway along the rue Neuve. Step inside during shopping hours for a sanity check, and don't miss the gothic statue of Notre Dame du Bon Succès. Nearby is the quaint old arcade of the Passage du Nord, linking the rue Neuve with the bd Adolphe Max. At the far end of the street, next to Rogier métro, is the main indoor shopping mall City 2, topped with a branch of FNAC.

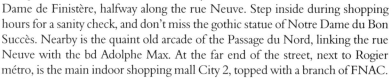

The place Rogier is home to the towering French-language National Theatre. Hard to believe that this cold and sterile area was once a bustling railway station. The original Gare du Nord saw the very first continental train journey in 1835. The present square was laid out when the station was transferred to the World Trade Centre district, and rebuilt in stern utility style to create a functional interchange and departure point for trams, métro and international trains. The Railway Museum inside the station was destroyed by fire in 2001, so check with tourist offices for news of its possible reopening.

Where the old station stood, just out of range of the click-and-tick tour groups doing Grand' Place, are now found geometric clusters of international business-class hotels, familiar names from airport shuttle-bus itineraries the world over. Huddled in convenient groups for executive comfort, the brand names of the frequent-flyer circuit – Sofitels, Sheratons and Golden Tulips – may be found at principal junctions on the bd d'Anvers, the northern section of the inner ring road surrounding the heart of Brussels. Fortunately, at key crossroads by the métro stations of Rogier and Botanique, these well-known chain hotels are not alone. Behind the 'international cuisine', shrink-wrapped in air-conditioned expense-account splendour, are real restaurants favoured by the locals, and several more modest hotels where personality reigns supreme. Of course the area is a prime base for culture infusions at the former botanical gardens and for trekking off to the royal residences.

Whilst the palaces and parks to the east testify to the glories of Belgium's regal past, travelling north (by tram or métro) to the Laeken district brings you to the residential area favoured by contemporary princes of the blood royal. Next to Laeken is the Heysel quarter. This name may strike chilly shudders through British and Italian visitors remembering the tragic aftermath of the Juventus v Liverpool match in 1985, when 39 people died at the eponymous football stadium. The centre was later rebuilt and renamed Roi Baudouin.

But for most visitors and locals alike, Heysel is the playground of Brussels. Placed on the pleasure map with the great exhibition of 1958, this is best known for the Atomium, the theme park pleasures around the Brupark and the exhibition and conference centre.

WHERE TO STAY

Art Hôtel Siru 1 pl Rogier, 1000; tel: 02 203 35 80; reservations 0800 44 44 44 (UK), 800 228 3323 (US and Canada); email: art.hotel.siru@skynet.be; web: www.comforthotelsiru.com [11 G4]

M̄ *Rogier;* Ē *Underground tram to Rogier.*

This is the ultimate crash pad for art lovers. If bland uniform production-line hotel décor makes you cringe, then check this out. One hundred and thirty 20th-century Flemish artists were commissioned to make over the bedrooms. Every one is different. Some merely exhibit paintings or sculpture, other rooms are works of art in themselves. Roger Raveel calls room 108's striking frieze *'Valium'.* He writes 'I hope that my mural will incite the temporary occupant of this room, instead of using artificial means for falling asleep, to explore my pictorial narrative of innocent sheep in order to reach the serenity he is seeking in a more natural way'. Upstairs Paul de Gobert's *trompe l'oeil* ceiling in room 208 is a patchwork of dreams, nightmare and desires, whilst along the corridor Jean-Marie Boompotte's hilarious vision of three lady travellers has his heroines tightrope-walking into the room above. If you have a particularly delicate constitution, then specify when booking your aversion to any art involving mummified animals or stylishly ranged axes in order to avoid any nasty surprises. Room bonuses include hairdryer and radio as well as TV. Car parking is also available. Glad to say that the hotel's  adoption by an international chain has not suppressed its artistic integrity. Near the métro, the posh international hotels, Gare du Nord and the red-light area – but hey that's artists for you! Rooms ∈137–190 (5,500–7,500BEF).

Astoria 103 rue Royale, 1000; tel: 02 227 05 05 [11 J5–6]

M̄ *Botanique;* Ē *Métro to Botanique then walk south along rue Royale.*

Part of the Sofitel chain, but still happily independent-minded, is the dear old Astoria. The old duck has seen better days, but I like staying here in the ∈170-plus rooms (7,500 in old money). The brass and crystal in the public rooms is still faithfully polished, the service more familiar than starched, and the corridor and lift permutations impractical, yet the rooms are nicely four-star, with facilities there when you need them, and the place does not scream 'breathe-and-you'll-have-to-tip' at every corner. The royal family may be seen performing public duties a stroll away, traffic is not too prevalent at weekends, and there is much inexpensive dining to be discovered in the back streets, if you cannot be bothered trekking down to the centre of town. Comfortably traditional the hotel may be, but there is nothing faded nor jaded about the hotel's own dining room Le Palais Royal (see page 300). Winston Churchill had a soft spot for the place, and it's nice to see that the old boy's judgement has not been superseded by the results of focus groups and marketing profiles.

Congrès 42–44 rue du Congrès, 1000; tel: 02 217 18 90; web: www.hotelducongres.com
M̄ *Madou;* Ē *Métro to Madou.*
Much less basic than its dowdier sister, the Madou across the road, the Congrès is a neatly renovated string of four townhouses. The Hôtel du Congrès has tasteful lighting, comfortable furniture and half-panelled walls in the smart breakfast room. Framed prints and smart uplighters give personality to the €62–105 (2,300–4,200BEF) bedrooms. Located an easy stroll from the palace and gardens, and a bracing downhill run to the old town centre. Buses 64 and 65 from central Brussels and the Eurostar station Gare du Midi stop by the two hotels.

Le Dôme 12–13 bd du Jardin Botanique, 1000; tel: 02 218 06 80 [11 G4]
M̄ *Rogier;* Ē *Underground tram to Rogier.*
Twin tower to the Siru across the place Rogier, the original Dôme is your actual 1902 art nouveau, though its annexe Dôme II is not even *art récent*. The hotel claims its rooms – in the older building – to be in the ubiquitous style. But unless art nouveau had a younger sister movement devoted to airport-hotel-style bucket seating, trouser presses and bedsteads with modern lamps and side tables attached, I remain sceptical. Nonetheless, it is smart enough, in an international hotel sort of way, and has wheelchair-friendly bedrooms and no-smoking accommodation option. Pay €180–225 (7,200–9,000BEF).

Madou 45 rue du Congrès, 1000; tel: 02 218 83 75; web: www.hotelmadou.com [11 J7]
M̄ *Madou;* Ē *Métro to Madou.*
Post-war basic at its most post-war basic. Sparsely furnished with no prizes for décor, this bargain-rate townhouse is the annexe to the Hôtel La Tasse d'Argent across the road. In fact, you have to check in at number 48 and brave the traffic before breakfast, which is served, in winter, around the roaring wood fire. Sizeable rooms, clean bathrooms and relative peace and quiet at one of the lowest hotel rates in the city. Handwritten notices abound, proclaiming 'Silence', and forbidding the washing of clothes and eating in the rooms, and all is reminiscent of austerity European city travel in the 1950s and 1960s. However, if cleanliness and a quiet night under candlewick are your priorities on a tight €65 (2,500BEF) budget, then you've all the more money to spend on other pleasures.

WHERE TO GO
Botanique Rue Royale, 1210; tel: 02 218 79 35 [11 J4–5]
M̄ *Botanique;* Ē *Métro to Botanique, walk north along rue Royale.*
These splendid greenhouses nurture the cultural identity of the French-speaking community. Once upon a time this neo-classical building, with its grand glass-houses, built in 1826, was home to the city's botanical gardens. Since the mid-1980s

Botanique has served as the francophone cultural centre, hosting big name music events, film shows, exhibitions and ad hoc recitals and performances. Although the central greenhouse corridor is filled with imposing tropical plants and trees, a notice on the door reminds casual visitors that this is no longer a horticultural centre. Best to check listing magazines or tourist office noticeboards for details of events.

Brupark 20 bd du Centenaire, 1020; tel: 02 474 83 77; web: www.brupark.com
M̲ *Heysel;* Ē *Métro 2 to Arts-Loi then line 1A to Heysel, or take tram 81 all the way. Follow station directions to Brupark.*
Home to mini Europe and the shriek 'n' splash flumatoria of the Océade swimming pool, waterslide and tropical beach complex, this is the playground of the Heysel district at the foot of the Atomium and in the shadow of the exhibition halls. Whilst the heated pools prove a draw whatever the weather, the main year-round crowd-puller here is Kinépolis, the world's largest movie complex with more than two dozen screens and an Imax theatre (see *Cinema* page 322). At Brupark's centre is The Village, a complex of 18 restaurants and bars, each privately owned, each offering an individual ethnic treat from Brussels mussels to tacos to pasta to cocktails served in a railway carriage. Despite a healthy portion of diners in suits from the nearby conference district, or maybe because of them, there was a sense of tourist trap in the attitude of the waiter who point blank refused to serve me a glass of water with my meal. Brupark is the focus of the New Year's Eve illuminations.

Le Corbeau 18 rue St-Michel, 1000; tel: 02 219 52 46 [11 F5]
M̲ *De Brouckère;* Ē *Underground tram to De Brouckère. Turn right past the Hôtel Métropole Hôtel into rue St-Michel.*
This is where young Brussels weekend whiz kids let their hair down on a Friday and Saturday night. A boisterous crowd drinks deep from glasses that are the euro-equivalent of the yard of ale.

WHAT TO SEE
Atomium bd du Centenaire, 1020; tel: 02 474 89 77; web: www.atomium.be
Open Sep–Mar 10.00–17.30, Apr–Aug 09.00–19.30. ∈5 (200BEF).
M̲ *Heysel;* Ē *Métro 2 to Arts-Loi then line 1A to Heysel, or take tram 81 all the way.*
The other symbol of Brussels besides the ubiquitous incontinent is the strangely sci-fi structure that provided the centrepiece of Expo '58. Nearly half a century later, the ooh-ah factor still provides a tingle, even if André Waterkeyn's futuristic design seems as quaintly old-fashioned as an episode of *Thunderbirds*. The Atomium is a steel and chrome recreation of an iron molecule magnified 165 billion times. The 102m-high structure was chosen as a national symbol because at the time of the exhibition its nine globes represented the then nine provinces of Belgium. Officially the Atomium is a science museum, but more fun is to be had riding the escalators through the tubes than traipsing round the exhibits. Go for the view, and the best one is to be had from the revolving restaurant at the very top (see page 299). A high-speed lift whooshes diners skyward in seconds.

Centre Belge de la Bande Dessinée (Comic Strip Centre) 20 rue des Sables, 1000; tel: 02 219 19 80 [11 G6]
Open Tue–Sun 10.00–18.00; closed Jan 1, Easter and Dec 25. ∈5 (200BEF).
M̲ *Rogier, Botanique or Gare Centrale;* Ē *Underground tram to Rogier. Walk east on bd du Jardin Botanique. Right along rue du Marais then left into rue des Sables.*
Comic strips are the great Belgian art form: two hundred million readers of the *Tintin* books cannot be wrong. Naturally Hergé's famous hero is the main draw,

with Tintin's red and white space rocket among the most popular exhibits. A useful introduction to the genre may be found on the mezzanine level with its exhibitions and cinema explaining the techniques and history of the *bande-dessinée* with a constantly changing selection from the museum's collection of storyboards. On the first floor, visitors are invited to discover the work of individual artists from the 1940s to today's Belgian, American and Japanese exponents. The ground floor houses the archive, a library and a reading room for browsing with a favourite comic. The building draws another breed of artistic pilgrim, since the comic strip collection is housed in the former Waucquez department store – one of the great art nouveau glass-and-steel creations of Baron Horta. The great staircase and plant-motif metalwork draw visitors in their own right, and there is an exhibition of Horta's industrial designs on the ground floor.

Congrès pl du Congrès, 1000 [11 H6]
The column commemorates the National Congress of 1831, which led to the Belgian constitution. At its base is the flame of the Unknown Soldier and a memorial to the dead of two World Wars. It is here that the king lays a wreath and leads the nation's tributes on the remembrance days for both conflicts. A statue of Léopold I stands atop the column looking out across the city.

Kinépolis Brupark, 20 bd du Centenaire, 1020; tel: 02 474 26 00
M̲ *Heysel;* E̲ *Métro 2 to Arts-Loi then line 1A to Heysel, or take tram 81 all the way. Follow station directions to Brupark.*

Mini-Europe 1 av du Football, Brupark, 1020; tel: 02 474 13 11; web: www.minieurope.com
Open late Mar–Jun 09.30–17.30, Jul, Aug 09.30–19.00 (until 23.00 certain weekends), Sep 09.30–17.00, Oct–early Jan 10.00–17.00. €10.50 (420BEF).
M̲ *Heysel,* E̲ *Métro 2 to Arts-Loi then line 1A to Heysel, or take tram 81 all the way. Follow station directions to Brupark.*
Bienvenue à Euroland. That may be the ironic moniker given by politics to the Brussels of strange directives and universal banknotes. However the nearest thing to a Euro-theme-park ride is the stroll through all the countries of the community in this miniature landscaped version of the politically united continent. Models of towns and monuments from all member states are created on a scale of 1/25. Eurostar runs under a mini English Channel from the white cliffs of Dover to the Eiffel Tower. The models are fine, but the perverse pleasure comes in musing as to which buildings were selected and which rejected for inclusion in this Eurotopia. I was surprised and delighted to see the royal saltworks of Arc-et-Senans in mini-France, probably the most beautiful and

certainly one of the least known examples of urban planning in the country. In such a PC environment, finding the Republic of Ireland in the middle of the UK section raises a wry smile, as does the fact that Scotland, the most pro-European member of the United Kingdom, is the one British country ignored by the continental landscape artists. Fun stuff includes the launch of the *Arianne* space rocket and the chance to make Vesuvius erupt at will, the Berlin Wall collapse at your command and to inspire a bullfight in Seville. Midsummer, the park opens at night for floodlit visits and firework shows.

Musée Renée Magritte (Magritte Museum) 135 rue Esseghem, 1080; tel: 02 428 26 26
Open Wed–Sun 10.00–18.00. ∈6 (250BEF).
M̄ *Bockstael;* Ē *Underground tram 18 to Cimietière de Jette. Rue Esseghem crosses rue Lahayes.*
With many original furnishings, Magritte's house has been restored and renovated to reflect its style during the artist's heyday. A library is open to serious students of the great surrealist's work. A little out of the way for most casual visitors, but a treat for admirers.

Notre Dame de Laeken parvis Notre Dame, 1020; tel: 02 479 23 62; email: cosijns.berman@skynet.be
Open Dec–Apr Sun 14.00–17.00, May–Nov Thu, Sat, Sun 14.00–17.00. Free.
Tram 81; Ē *Tram 81 to Royauté stop then turn right along rue Champs de l'Eglise.*
Suffer little children to go elsewhere, except on specified days and the anniversaries of royal deaths. There is nothing so desperate as a place of worship closed to casual visitors. On my first trip to the last resting place of kings, I found the place locked up with but a small notice announcing the very limited opening hours. Within the permitted hours, you will be able to admire the works of art adorning the tombs of the royal family in the crypt, and various 19th- and 20th-century Belgian celebrities within the church. The cemetery to the left of the church is the local cemetery and on the other side a tranquil memorial to Queen Astrid. Hers is the sad and eerily familiar story of beautiful European princesses fated to die in car crashes. Unlike the unofficial Diana shrine in Paris (see page 147) and the busy Princess Grace garden in Monaco, this is an elegant corner for quiet reflection in memory of the Swedish princess who married King Léopold III in 1926 and died aged just 29 in the summer of 1935.

Océade Brupark, 20 bd du Centenaire, 1020; tel: 02 478 00 90
Open school holidays 10.00–22.00, termtime Tue–Thu 10.00–18.00, Fri–Sun 10–22.00; closed Mon (Tue Sep–Mar). ∈12 (480BEF) valid for four hours. Those under 1.3m pay ∈9.50 (380BEF), under 1.15m get in free. Combined tickets available with Atomium or Mini-Europe.
M̄ *Heysel;* Ē *Métro 2 to Arts-Loi then line 1A to Heysel, or take tram 81 all the way. Follow station directions to Brupark.*
Waterslides, wave pools, jacuzzi, saunas and solariums in the ultimate swimming pool complex that is a regular school holiday bribe for Brussels families. Most daytimes, the place echoes to the shrieking euphoria of 100; evenings see the teenaged snogging brigade taking over. Lads strut nonchalantly at the poolside. Lasses test their Maybelline and Max Factor water-resistance promises to the limit, sliding down the chutes fully protected from the elements by armour-plated mascara and crimson pout-gloss. For a simple swim with style you might consider the art deco municipal baths in the St-Gilles area near the Gare du Midi.

Oriental Pavilions Tour Japonaise and Pavillon Chinois, av Jules van Praet-Iaan, 1020; tel: 02 268 16 08
Open Tue–Sun 10.00–16.30. €2 (80BEF) each, €3 (120BEF) both.
M̲ *Heysel;* E̲ *Métro 2 to Arts-Loi, then line 1A to Heysel, then bus 23 to de Wand.*
Visitors to the area may well expect to see replicas of the Brandenberg Gate and Big Ben, since Mini-Europe is well promoted across town. However, the sight of a Japanese pagoda and Chinese temple appearing between the trees of the royal park always raises an eyebrow. After seeing the 1900 Paris Exhibition, Belgium's Léopold II commissioned the French architect Alexandre Marcel to create an oriental zone in the park. Marcel bought the original Japanese pagoda from the Paris show to Brussels and hired artists from Yokohama to decorate the Tour Japonaise, which today hosts contemporary Japanese art displays. The Pavillon Chinois was actually made in Shanghai and contains a porcelain collection from the royal museums.

Serres Royales (Royal Greenhouses) av du Parc Royal, 1020
Open for a limited season in spring, Wed–Sun. Free daytimes; €2.50 (100BEF) evening sessions.
M̲ *Heysel;* E̲ *Métro 2 to Arts-Loi, then line 1A to Heysel, then bus 23 two stops to De Wand or walk through the park.*
As you drive on the city tour bus through the royal family's private estate at Laeken, over the walls you can see the shimmering roofs, rotundas, domes and atria of a crystal city, the grandest of the greenhouses topped with a gilded crown. For these are the *serres royales,* the king's own hothouses, a remarkable fairy-tale kingdom of glass and steel, each holding a tropical recreation of the natural glories of Europe's former empires. Never mind the bulb fields of Holland; here is northern Europe's real horticultural treasure. Originally built in 1870 by the architect Alphonse Balat to nurture, develop and display the prized collections of King Léopold II. I first heard about the place from keen gardeners who time their annual holiday around the opening. The exact dates of the public opening are announced at the end of January, and can be obtained from the tourist office.

WHERE TO EAT
Atomium bd du Centenaire, 1020; tel: 02 474 89 77; web: www.atomium.be
M̲ *Heysel;* E̲ *Métro 2 to Arts-Loi then line 1A to Heysel, or take tram 81 all the way.*
Hors d'oeuvre salad and cold cuts buffet and profiterole and gâteaux-style dessert buffet. These pick-and-pile-up options sandwich the €17.50–30 (700–1,500BEF) waiter-service main-course menu. Pleasant enough fare, but let's be honest, you take a lift 110m above the city for the view from the revolving restaurant.

Den Talurelekker 25 rue de l'Enseignement, 1000; tel: 02 478 30 00 [11 J7]
M̲ *Parc;* E̲ *Métro to Parc then walk north on rue Royale, turning right into rue de l'Enseignement.*
The rue de l'Enseignement is quietly becoming the place to dine at one's own expense in the shadow of business-account hotels. They are certainly not afraid of the spice rack in the kitchen of this rustic old-style dining room. With more than a whiff of the pre-war student hangout about the place, it is usually packed with neighbourhood flat-dwellers dining in couples or alone beneath the austere Victorian portraits on the dark walls. This is the true food of true Belgians. No 19th-century brewers' hangover, nor carbon-copy French cuisine, but family favourites. Sweetmeats, *Ballekes marolliennes* (savoury meatballs to the uninitiated), and a cinnamon and apple-punched *carbonnade flamande* are firm favourites with the regulars. Daily specials include white-meat standards with a fruit-flavoured

twist. Budget ∈15–20 (500–800BEF). Be warned: although the doors sport notices declaring that they remain open until 23.00, the kitchen staff will be tucked up at home in bed shortly after 22.00.

Da Rosella 27 rue de l'Enseignment, 1000; tel: 02 219 75 39 [11 J7]
Closed Sat, Sun. ∈9–15 (350–600BEF).
M̄ *Parc;* Ē *Métro to Parc then walk north on rue Royale, turning right into rue de l'Enseignement.*
'We don't go to Brussels for neighbourhood Italian restaurants,' I hear you mutter as you prepare to turn the page. But wait a while. If you are looking for honest family cooking, a homely atmosphere and a break from the gilt and crystal cuisine palaces up the road, then consider a poster-paint bright, simple, yet cheerful alternative in the up-and-coming eat street. Bearing in mind the cost of dining in the centre, reconsider a snack supper for around ∈9 (350BEF) with a glass of wine. All the pastas and breads are home-made, even the lesser-known treats such as *Orechietti Pugliese*. Sauces are simple but flavoursome and portions enormous. The waiter was near tears the night I was unable to finish my huge bowl of *tagliatelle*, and he begged me to try something else. I had eventually to go into the kitchen and apologise to the chef before I could leave with a clear conscience.

Chez Pierrot 21 rue Presse, 1000; tel: 02 217 38 31 [11 J7]
Closed Sun, Easter and summer holidays.
M̄ *Madou;* Ē *Métro to Madou. Walk towards the Congrès column, turn left into rue Presse.*
A halfway house between the unpretentious eateries for the locals, and the big hotel restaurants for the visitors. The ∈25 (1,000BEF) set menu with *escargot*, fish *tartares* and *brasserie* fare is served in a friendly dining room near the Enseignment drag. I have never known the staff to be less than courteous, and if dishes may seem unambitious, they are always efficiently prepared, and of reasonably good quality.

Le Palais Royal Hôtel Astoria, 103 rue Royale, 1000; tel: 02 227 05 05 [11 J5–6]
Closed Sat lunch, Sun evening.
M̄ *Botanique;* Ē *Métro to Botanique then walk south along rue Royale.*
Sunday lunch at the Hôtel Astoria promises plenty of courses, *amuse-bouches* and *mignardise* top and tails, and courteous service. Yet the glassware has the sparkle and the kitchen has the fizz to make sure that the meal is a highlight of any weekend. *Salade de caille et magret fumé* sets the tone. Classic food, but nothing too stodgy. *Potage Crècy* to follow. Dither between the *emincé de veau Claude Deligne* with braised chicory, a *gigot d'agneau* with traditional *gratin dauphinois*, or a freshwater fish alternative, then be virtuous with fresh fruit or wicked with creamy confections. Spend around ∈40–75 (1,600–3,000BEF). The whole event has the feel of grand hotel dining in the post-war years, but the taste and weight for today's constitution.

WHAT TO BUY

FNAC 123 rue Neuve, 1000; tel: 02 275 13 13 [11 G4]
Open Sat, Mon–Thu 10.00–19.00, Fri 10.00–20.00.
M̄ *Rogier;* Ē *Underground tram to Rogier. Enter the City2 mall.*
France's favourite music and bookstore fills the top floor of the City2 mall. Hi-fi equipment, disks, books, magazines and theatre tickets are all sold here. Before leaving, take advantage of the free self-serve gift-wrap table by the escalators. Envelopes, wrapping paper and sticky tape provided.

Inno 111 rue Neuve, 1000; tel: 02 211 21 11 [11 F5]
Open Mon–Sat 09.30–19.00.
M̄ *De Brouckère or Rogier;* Ē *Underground tram to Rogier and walk down rue Neuve.*
The last of the Belgian-owned department stores is the ideal compromise for
one-stop shopping if time is of the essence.

Sterling Books 38 rue du Fosse aux Loups, 1000; tel: 02 223 62 23 [11 F6]
Open Mon–Sat 10.00–19.00, Sun 12.00–18.30.
M̄ *De Brouckère;* Ē *Underground tram to De Brouckère then east into rue du Fosse aux
Loups.*
The 'Save the British Shilling' campaigners will love the name of this place and
approve of the pricing policy. British books are sold at the sterling cover price (at
daily exchange rate plus local tax). A good mix of holiday escapist blockbusters
and serious business tomes.

Waterstone's 71–75 bd Adolphe Max; tel: 02 219 27 08 [11 F5]
Open Mon, Wed–Sat 09.00–17.30, Tue 10.00–18.30.
M̄ *De Brouckère;* Ē *Underground tram to De Brouckère then walk north on the boulevard.*
Don't be confused, many locals still refer to this place as W H Smiths, although
it has long since changed hands. Continental branch of the UK bookstore chain,
also stocks British newspapers and magazines.

East of Grand' Place

ARTS AND PARKS AND PALACES

Only just outside the Brussels-in-a-morning circuit, yet still within the central area served by the métro and trams, are to be found the glitzy shopping district around place Louise and the sprawling palaces, museums and art galleries. The tower blocks and fast- track traffic tunnels of the Ring may trick the casual visitor into dismissing anything younger than the cobbled market streets as unworthy of attention. Truth to tell, much of the best of Brussels begins with the steep slopes from the Ilot Sacré towards the Beaux Arts museums and the Sablons.

Where else could you dine in Rodin's workshop or have a menu invented for you by an up-and-coming chef? Where might you spend an evening watching silent movies with live piano accompaniment? And what other district boasts the nation's finest *frites* and sauce?

Known today for the fabulous antiques market, and of course its wonderful and beautiful Gothic church of Notre Dame du Sablon, Grand Sablon is an oasis of civilisation, the arts and gastronomy, only minutes from the centre. Above Grand Sablon is the statuary garden of Petit Sablon, celebrating patronage, arts and *métiers* through the city's history.

The old royal quarter around the Parc du Bruxelles retains the classical elegance forsaken by those architects who rebuilt the city centre in neo-Gothic style. Wide avenues, clean and light refinement and a fine sense of proportion mark out the 18th-century Austrian-influenced Upper Town from the more obviously Flemish Lower Town.

Most of the main architectural movements of the end of the 19th and beginning of the 20th centuries had their moment in the residential streets beyond the Ring, once rival architects Victor Horta and Paul Hankar began building their show-homes in very unique modern styles (see *South of Grand' Place*, page 317). Alas, their more recent successors showed less imagination in working with concrete, glass and chrome in creating modern consumer units. Shopping here is for those who pay without flinching along the avenue de la Toison d'Or and the avenue Louise itself.

The path of least resistance for strolling visitors seeking the essential flavour of the area would be simply to follow the tramlines from the Sablons to the beginning of avenue Louise. This will take in the museums and royal estate, and guarantee the best view in town from the terrace below the Palais de Justice.

The city's métro system skirts rather than serves the area. However, it is a pleasant and easy enough climb up from the Central Station or down the Mont des Arts from the palace gardens. Plenty of buses and trams criss-cross the district. From avenue Louise, long *chaussées* stretch out to the dormitory districts where family homes sit comfortably amongst local shops, adventurous restaurants and plenty of parkland. If you follow the avenue to its natural conclusion (take tram 23 or 90; it's a long way on foot), you will find yourself at the Bois de la Cambre, a 124-hectare arm of the sprawling Forêt de Soignes, annexed by Brussels in the mid-19th century. The park's roads are closed to traffic at weekends. In summer, rowing boats may be hired on the park lake by the seriously sporting or incurably romantic. September is a good time for star spotting. Be the first to notice the next Jean-Claude Van Damme or Audrey Hepburn during the annual Premières Rencontres festival at the Théâtre de Poche, in the Bois, when drama schools showcase their new talent (tel: 02 649 17 27). Concerts are staged in many of the parks in the area during spring and summer months. A free programme of events is published each season by the tourist office.

The rond-point Schuman is the heart of the banking and political district with more suits and laptops to be seen than anywhere else in town. I cherish the comment by the guide on my first sightseeing tour of the district. Without a trace of irony, she announced, 'To your left are the European Parliament buildings and the Natural History Museum where you will find many old dinosaurs.'

WHERE TO STAY

Montgomery 134 av de Tervuren, 1150; tel: 02 741 85 11; toll free 0800 90 75 16 (UK), 800 525 48 00 (USA); web: www.montgomery.be
M̄ *Montgomery;* Ē *Métro 2 to Arts-Loi change to line 1B to Montgomery.*
The reassuring statue of Monty himself stands opposite this unassuming yet grand hotel, a ten-minute métro ride from the city centre, and a world away from the big international top-grade hotels that cluster around the Central Station and Botanic Gardens. True, at €300–480 (12,000–19,500BEF), 50% discount on Fridays and Saturdays, you'll find the luxuriously appointed rooms with king-sized beds, vast sofas and a list of extras, but it's the old-style homely touches that give this hotel the edge. I was won over by the stack of books on my bedside table – a favourite, if little-known, Enid Blyton melodrama from my childhood, a thriller, a James Baldwin and a heavyweight political commentary. So I did not find the time to play with the internet – provided via an infra-red keyboard link to the television in the bedroom. I wandered down to the well-stocked library downstairs in search of a copy of *Black Beauty*, which had eluded me in town earlier in the day. I found it! **La Duchesse** restaurant offers a fine menu at €32 (13,000BEF) midweek – although it is closed for service at weekends, when room rates are halved; but the kitchen still provides the popular dishes for room service. A well-equipped fitness centre with a large sauna has the full range of toiletries, towels and robes as found in the rooms. Suggested entertainment and a current arts guide is placed in all rooms. On the weekend that I visited, a free jazz concert in the nearby park was a Sunday morning tip-off

well appreciated. Staff are country-house friendly rather than city cool, an ideal welcome for a weekend away. The hotel has its own underground car park and is located next to Montgomery métro station, making it a good base for exploring.

Sofitel Toisson d'Or 40 av de la Toison d'Or, 1050; tel: 02 514 22 00; email: H1071@accor-hotels.com [13 F6]
M̄ *Louise;* Ē *Direct métro to Louise.*
No shortage of anonymous, international-standard deluxe chain hotels in Brussels, but this location at place Louise is perfect as a base for exploring Brussels by public transport. The major trams to far-flung points, as well as many bus services to hard-to-find places, interchange virtually outside the door. Taxis have an easy run from the Gare du Midi via the ring road and its tunnels, and the métro station is at your feet. You are within a Rolex-tick of the shops favoured by the nipped, tucked and liposucked, yet just a stroll away from a fantastic view of the old town. The staff here are extremely helpful, the rooms at €30 (12,000BEF), are comfortable, and an escalator from the first-floor reception area takes guests to the Espace Louise mall.

WHERE TO GO

Avenue Cyber Theatre 4/5 av de la Toison d'Or, 1050; tel: 02 500 78 78; web: www.cybertheatre.net [13 H6]
M̄ *Porte de Namur;* Ē *Métro to Porte de Namur.*
A new look for a new era. Closed at the time of going to press, but promising a major relaunch during 2001, this has always been more than a mere cyber café. Part bar, part meeting place, part nightclub, past treats have included free screenings of cult movies and celebrations of major international sporting events. Check the website for opening information.

Gourmet Gaillard 192 chaussée de Vleurgat, 1050; tel: 02 626 90 30
Christian Nihoul has been one of the city's most respected *chocolatiers* and *pâtissiers* for over 50 years. A bright new tearoom opposite St Andrew's Presbyterian Church, with its Sunday school and jumble sales, is clean and modern and a generation removed from Nihoul's former establishment with its eighties' chrome and crumb-covered carpet image. This new venue is spotlessly clean and serves sumptuous chocolate cakes, light lunches and super *orangettes* – chocolate-covered orange peel.

La Maison d'Antoine pl Jourdan, 1040; tel: 02 230 54 56
Open 11.30–23.30.
M̄ *Schuman;* Ē *Métro 2 to Arts-Loi change to line 1 for Schuman. Walk down rue Froissart to pl Jourdan.*
Not a *maison*, not even a *maisonette*, it's a chip stand in a square, behind the European Parliament and Natural History Museum. But those in the know declare Antoine to serve the best *frites* in Brussels, if not Belgium. And chips are, after all, the national dish. Cooked in beef fat and served with a unique variant on *sauce tartare*, as invented by the present owner's grandmother.

Musée du Cinéma 9 rue Baron Horta, 1000; tel: 02 507 83 70; email: info@museeducinema@ledoux.be
Open 17.30–22.30. €2 (90BEF).
M̄ *Gare Centrale;* Ē *Underground tram to De Brouckère, bus 71 to Beaux Arts. Walk past the Musée des Beaux Arts to the rue Horta.*
This unique cinema museum is no mere dusty archive of cans and posters; it is a great night out in its own right. Each evening two silent films are screened with

live piano accompaniment in a tiny, 30-seat cinema. Three classic talkies are shown in the adjacent 125-seat theatre. Tickets also allow visitors to tour the fascinating exhibitions, including some interactive displays of early projection equipment.

Nemrod 61 bd de Waterloo, 1000 [13 F6]
M̄ *Louise;* Ē *Métro to Louise.*
Pavement café at place Louise to hang out when waiting for a Sunday tram – some of which run up to 25 minutes apart. If it's raining, sit inside by the fireplace, though the décor is that excessive fake rustic favoured by Tudor pubs in international airport food courts. Cold collations and ice creams.

Pain Quotidien 11 pl du Grand Sablon, 1000; tel: 02 502 7073 [13 F4]
M̄ *Gare Centrale;* Ē *Bus 20 to Sablons.*
Breads, soups and delicious snacks are served in this huge and atmospheric baker's shop on the hallowed Grand Sablon itself, which gives us every day our daily bread and spreads. As you step inside from the famous antique furniture market in the street, you come face to face with a huge dresser of *Jack and the beanstalk* proportions, that positively creaks under the weight of bottles and vittels. The international language of aroma is represented by the smell of freshly baked bread, which lures you in further. Tread the well-worn wooden floors past the takeaway counter to the bright conservatory at the rear of a most reliable breakfast-elevenses-and-tea room. A crusty *tartine* served with a cup of proper hot chocolate – made with melted chocolate not the powdered stuff – staves off any unwanted pangs between meals. Budget €5–10 (200–400BEF).

Les Sablons [13 F4–5]
M̄ *Gare Centrale*; Ē *Bus 20 to Sablons.*
Almost every shop around the place du Grand Sablon is devoted to the best antique furniture or fine art, and the midweek market place is filled with plenty of 'if only' opportunities. The hilltop square was once a military training ground back in the days of crossbows. Now a more peaceful Saturday or Sunday morning diversion takes place, when the carvers and *escritoirs* of the midweek market are replaced by antiquarian books. Should an ancient volume take your fancy, you will be spoilt for choice in choosing a table at which to leaf through your prize. The fountain of Minerva, in the centre of the square, was commissioned in 1851 by Lord Bruce, the English peer, in gratitude for the hospitality of the people of Brussels. Dominating the square is the 15th-century church of Notre Dame du Sablon, the great Gothic church of the city. An earlier church on the site was built after a praying woman saw a vision commanding her to bring a statue of the Virgin Mary from Antwerp to Brussels. The choir, dating from 1435, and stained-glass windows are well worth a detour. Behind the church is the more tranquil square du Petit Sablon. Opened in 1890, this garden has 48 bronze statuettes representing the traditional arts and crafts of the city. Behind them is a row of statues of great 16th-century scholars. Less cerebral, in more ways than one, are the figures of Egmont and Hornes at the centre of the square. These statues, that originally graced the Grand' Place, were erected in honour of the two men who led the resistance against Spanish tyranny in the 16th century, and were beheaded by the Duke of Alba.

Wittamer 12 pl du Grand Sablon, 1000; tel: 02 512 2742
M̄ *Gare Centrale;* Ē *Bus 20 to Sablons.*
The pink and white chocolate shop next door sells the finest chocs in the world. Already established as one of the best *pâtisseries* in northern Europe, the family business ventured into the cutthroat world of truffles and *ganaches* about 15 years

ago. The result is breathtaking. The best taste in town is a sinful idyll made from the finest chocolate, filled with lightly whisked *crème fraîche* and fresh raspberries. Wittamer uses less sugar than most manufacturers and that means that the shelf life is the shortest, so, instead of risking buying a box of chocolates to take home from the shop, come and mingle with the beautiful people at the tea rooms. Rather than sit outside with those who know no better, climb the stairs to the stylish *salon du thé*. Two rooms are decorated in complimentary baroque and rustic styles, with Jean Cocteau *Beauty and the Beast* candelabra thrust through drapes by lifelike human hands. Around ∈15 (600BEF) will buy you coffee and a *haute de gamme* chocolate dessert such as the *Exotique*. The definitive pastry-chef cookbook based on family recipes is sold here.

WHAT TO SEE

Autoworld Brussels 11 parc de Cinquantenaire, 1000; tel: 02 736 41 65; web: www.autoworld.be
Open Oct–Mar 10.00–17.00, Apr–Sep 10.00–18.00. ∈5 (200BEF).
M̲ *Mérode;* E̲ *Tram 81 or 82*
The imperial wedding coach for the marriage of Napoléon III and the Empress Eugénie and a hansom cab are among the highlights of the horse-drawn vehicle collection. However, this museum pulls in the punters because of its excellent display of things that go vroom in the day. Cars, motorbikes and fire engines: this is a celebration of the horseless carriage from earliest Oldsmobile, through the model-T, to futuristic prototypes straight from the drawing board. Set out in

tableaux in the great hall setting of the Belgian Motor Show from 1902–34, each group of vehicles is shown to advantage. Even if coachwork and carburettors are not your bag, you will enjoy the glamour of seeing the cars of the famous, including JFK's presidential run-around and many royal motors. The most striking aspect of the exhibition is the realisation that, before the war, Belgium had a world-class manufacturing industry: Minerva, Nagant and Vinius amongst the *marques* on display.

Boyadjian Museum of the Heart 10 parc du Cinquantenaire, 1000; tel: 02 741 72 11
Hours as for Cinquantenaire Museum. Main arts collection ∈4 (150BEF).
M̲ *Mérode;* E̲ *Tram 81 or 82.*
From the votive to the valentine, hearts of all shapes and sizes fill a sweet and charming little gallery just off the tapestry wing of the main Cinquantenaire Museum. Flasks, love letters and statuary form the core of an unusual collection started by an eminent cardiologist who became obsessed by the romantic image of the organ which he had previously only considered as a medical challenge. From the mid-1950s until his death in 1994 he sought heart-shaped curios from around the world. Having been temporarily housed in museums across the city, the collection now has a home in the royal art and history museum.

Cathédrale des St-Michel et Ste-Gudule Parvis Ste-Gudule, 1000; tel: 02 277 83 45, 02 219 75 30 (to request a guided tour, phone four weeks in advance) [13 G2] Open 08.00–06.00.

M̲ *Gare Centrale;* E̲ *Underground tram to De Brouckère them métro to Gare Centrale.*

Two languages and two cultures; how appropriate that the city has a cathedral named after two saints. The archangel St-Michel has long been a symbol of Brussels, his statue dominating Grand' Place, and the city coat of arms. There has been a church dedicated to St-Michel on this hill for almost a thousand years, and the honours were soon shared with Flanders-born Ste-Gudule. Today's splendid cathedral is an invigorating culture shock to greet visitors emerging from the narrow streets around Grand' Place, a grand gesture of gleaming white stone perched atop a dramatic flight of steps. One almost expects a heavenly choir to herald the moment and would not be surprised to see the clouds part, revealing chubby Renaissance cherubim and seraphim blowing fanfares of glory. A fine confection of architectural styles, from reliable Romanesque to classical corners and Victorian trimmings, the museum's most memorable facet is the French Gothic-style frontage with its ranks of statuary and twin towers – a rare sight in Flanders. Most visitors are happy to gaze in wonder at the magi and apostles around the 15th-century entrance. Take time to step inside and discover your own favourite aspect. You might wish to bathe yourself in the sea-green light of the stained-glass 16th-century west windows' depiction of the Last Judgement. I never cease to marvel at the marvellous carved pulpit, decorated with a virtual biography of sin, from the expulsion from Eden to the Virgin Mary's promise of redemption. In every generation the artistic splendour of the past is eclipsed by contemporary glories as the cathedral becomes the background to royal weddings and coronations.

Musée du Cinquantenaire parc du Cinquantenaire, 1000; tel: 02 741 72 11 Open Tue–Fri 09.30–17.00, Sat–Sun 10.00–17.00; closed holidays and election days. ∈4 (150BEF).

M̲ *Mérode;* E̲ *Tram 81 or 82.*

With its theatrical Arc du Triomphe and colonnade linking the two exhibition wings, this is the splendid seat of the Royal Museums of Art and History, whose empire extends to the Japanese and Chinese pavilions at Laeken, the Porte de Hal and the musical instrument collection at old England. When it was decided to expand the city in 1875, architect Gédéon Bordiau created the Jubelpark, or Parc du Cinquantenaire, as a green space with exhibition halls to celebrate the 50th anniversary of the kingdom, along the lines of Britain's Great Exhibition. Such was the success of the event, it was decided to expand the project to house permanent cultural displays. Housed in the triumphant buildings of the Cinquantenaire Park are archaeological finds and trophies, treasures and acquisitions from long lost civilisations. Egyptian, Mesopotamian, Byzantine, Roman and Greek antiquities are on display as well as treasures from the cultures that occupied the Low Countries from the Palaeolithic era to the Middle Ages. A large wing is devoted to European decorative arts with stained-glass windows and tapestries, from the medieval to the dawn of art deco. A rather charming notice at the entrance assures visitors that, should a particular collection be closed to the public, it can always be re-opened on request.

Musée de la Dynastie Bellevue Hôtel, 7 pl des Palais, 1000; tel: 02 513 88 77 [13 G3] Open Tue–Sun 10.00–18.00; closed Dec 25, Jan 1. ∈6 (250). M̲ *Trône;* E̲ *Métro to Trône then walk around the palace.*

Although the royal palace opens to the public for a few weeks each year (ask at tourist office for dates), the Bellevue residence shows its sumptuous regal apartments every day. This museum, which includes a memorial to King Baudouin, tells the story of each of the reigns of this young dynasty, and explains the duties and political roles of a modern royal family.

Musée des Instruments de Musique (Musical Instrument Museum) Old England, 1 Montagne de la Cour, 1000; tel: 02 545 01 30; web: www.mim.be Open Tue, Wed, Fri 09.30–17.00, Thu 09.30–20.00, Sat, Sun 10.00–17.00; closed Mon, holidays. €4 (150BEF).
M̲ *Trône;* E̲ *Métro to Trône then tram two stops to Royale.*
For years the city dithered over what to do with the fabulous Old England department-store building, one of the architectural treasures of Brussels. There was talk of it being home to a national chocolate exhibition, and rumours of it falling into private hands. At last it has re-opened as the new home of the national musical instrument museum. Good fun, well laid out and very visitor friendly. Pick up the free headphones on your way in, and listen to the sound of whichever instrument on display takes your fancy. Just as kids might be on the point of whining and tugging, the basement provides a cool interactive diversion with computer programmes and hands-on displays explaining the theory and practice of music making, from how strings vibrate to analysing sound waves.

Musée Royal de l'Armée et d'Histoire Militaire 3 parc du Cinquantenaire, 1000; tel: 02 741 72 11; web: www.klm-mra.be
Open Tue–Sun 9.00–12.00, 13.00–16.30; closed holidays and election days. Free.
M̲ *Mérode;* E̲ *Tram 81 or 82.*
Within the Cinquantenaire Parc, appropriately enough on the site of the Civil Guard's parade ground from the mid-19th century, is the Royal Museum of the Army and Military History. One hundred and thirty aircraft, many armoured vehicles and terrifying weaponry, from 8th-century thug accessories to sub-machine guns, are among the boys' toys which make this a popular choice for divorced Belgian fathers on winter Sunday outings with their sons. Historians come to learn about Belgium's warring past from the Austrian period to the 19th-century revolution. Galleries devoted to World War I and II, the Resistance and deportations contain echoes of a more recent past. With over 100,000 items in the collection, this museum, founded in 1911, is one of the most comprehensive military archives in the world.

Musées Royaux des Beaux Arts (Fine Arts Museums) 3 rue de la Régence, 1000; tel: 02 508 32 11 [13 F–G4]
Open Tue–Sat 10.00–17.00, closed Jan 1, Nov 1 and 11, Dec 25. €4 (150).
M̲ *Parc or Gare Centrale;* E̲ *Underground tram to De Brouckère, bus 71 to Beaux Arts.*
Founded by Napoléon in 1801, this is Belgium's largest museum complex. The misleadingly entitled Museum of Ancient Art is home not to artefacts from long-lost civilisations, but to paintings and sculptures from the late 14th to the end of the 19th centuries. As you arrive, the full span of 19th-century creativity is laid out on the ground floor, from the idealism of the neo-classicists to the distinctive styles of the post-impressionists. This rich buffet of familiar styles includes David's *Marat Murdered in his Bath,* Ensor's *Scandalised Masks,* some suitably heroic Delacroix, and the individualism of Seurat, Gauguin and Bonnard. Arrive early to appreciate the most popular galleries on the first floor, since from 11.00 noisy groups tend to muster in the Breughel Room. Europe's second finest collection (after Vienna) of the works of Breughel *père et fils* includes *Census at Bethlehem,*

The Fall of Icarus and the much-copied *Winter Landscape with Ice Skaters*. Splendid works by Rubens, Jordaens and Van Dyke are also to be seen on this level. The 20th-century collection is housed in the subterranean Museum of Modern Art. These galleries are cunningly arranged over eight levels, around a well of natural light. Unsurprisingly, Delvaux and Magritte take pride of place, but this is a comprehensive account of a century of art, from Fauvism to more recent entries to the 'but is it art?' debate. Bacon, Chagall, Dalí, Ernst, Moore, Miró and Zadkine number among the treats on show.

Palais de Justice pl Poelaert, 1000; tel: 02 508 65 78 [12 E6]
M̄ *Louise;* Ē *Métro to Louise and follow tram lines down to the pl Poelaert.*
Justice has always been meted out on this site. Until the 19th century it was served by the Galgenberg gallows. The sheer scale of Joseph-Philippe Poelaert's vast domed palace, that dwarfs even St Peter's in Rome, wiped out that original modest, yet effective, edifice. Sprawling across a massive chunk of the Upper Town, and dominating the city's skyline, the Palais de Justice contains scores of courtrooms and auditoria. If there was any real justice in the world, this dramatically proportioned courthouse would be the symbol of Brussels. However, the city fathers prefer the images of urine and molecular structure to that of honour, fairness and moral rectitude. Guided tours (between 09.00 and 15.00) may be booked in advance. These are free, but it is customary to tip the guide. Outside, admire the imposing war memorial, and take advantage of sunny days by taking photographs of the city from the panoramic terrace.

Place Royal [13 G4]
M̄ *Trône;* Ē *métro to Trône then either take the tram 2 stops to Royale, or walk around the palace, rue Ducale, place des Palais then left into the square.*
The most elegant classical square in Brussels has as its centrepiece a statue of Godefroid de Bouillon, the first Christian ruler of Jerusalem. On all sides are elegant mansions, many now public offices. The perfectly symmetrical square was designed in the 18th century to honour Charles of Lorraine, governor of the Netherlands, and it was here that Albert I, the *Roi Chevalier*, was born. A good point for pigging out on museums, with the Dynasty Museum, Beaux Arts and Old England within metres of each other.

WHERE TO EAT

30 rue de la Paille 30 rue de la Paille, 1000; tel: 02 512 07 15 [13 F4]
Closed weekend lunches and Jul 15–Aug 15.
M̄ *Gare Centrale;* Ē *Bus 20 to Sablons.*
Modestly tucked away in an unassuming side street behind the more up-front galleries and antique shops of the Sablons is an unheralded mealtime event with no need of fanfare, red carpet nor stuffed shirt in the doorway. An effusion of fresh cut flowers and a theatrical sweep of heavy drapes temper any suggestion of formality from the polished silver-plated candles and the usual brick walls. Charming yet professional waiters shoehorn you to the table to rub elbows – if not shoulders – with fellow diners. Don't be fooled by the chumminess of the room; this is where one comes face-to-fork with hard-core gastronomy. Absolutely spot-on contemporary French dishes created by André Martiny are served here with none of the pretension that food of this quality so often inspires. We are talking salmon in the subtlest of lime marinades, satisfying yet leaving room for chocolate desserts that raise chocolate to an art form. Amongst the best food to be found in one of the classiest quarters of Brussels. Especially so at lunchtime, when a four-course lunch may be had for €30 (1,250BEF). Budget double à la carte and evenings. Free midday parking.

Amadeus 13 rue Veydt, 1050; tel: 02 538 34 27
Closed Mon.
M̄ *Louise;* Ē *Métro to Louise then tram 91 or 92 to Faider.*
Nearly five minutes too far along the chausée du Charleroi for most visitors, and just a step into a residential street, is an unlikely find. A turn-of-the-century garden, industrial glass doors and deep blue and dark green brickwork welcome you to this striking study in light and shadows. At Amadeus, you might be forgiven for thinking that you had stumbled on to the set of a Jonathan Miller staging of a favourite opera. Scores of candles flicker on every surface and tease your eyes towards subtle friezes, statuary and *trompe l'oeil* jests. The place has nothing whatsoever to do with classical composers, but the building was once the *atelier* of Rodin, whose statuary graces the city from the Bourse building to the church of Notre Dame de Laeken. Today's pensive expressions tend to be directed towards the menu. The food is geared towards any and every appetite. A selection marked *petit faim* features such treats as *profiteroles de caille au foie gras* with a Beaume de Venise sauce for around €25 (1,000BEF). Larger appetites are catered for on the *grand faim* menu, offering *millefeuille de riz de veau au pointes des asperges vertes* at a hundred or so francs more. A three-course lunch menu changes daily – and is published around three weeks in advance so that you may plan and budget your treats (a nice touch, this). Self-service brunch on Sunday costs around €18 (750BEF). Unpretentious service, strong wine list in a big-budget Bohemian setting.

Cap Sablon 5 rue Lebeau, 1000; tel: 02 512 01 70 [13 F4]
M̄ *Gare Centrale;* Ē *Bus 20 to Sablons.*
On sunny Sunday afternoons this pavement bar-restaurant with its cheesy-salads, smoky-sausages and *charcuterie*-based menu is the ideal place to people watch on the very corner of the Grand Sablon. Opt for coffee and a snack for around €12.50 (500BEF). It is also a comfortable and convenient option for taking the weight off your feet instead of waiting at the bus stop on the doorstep.

Le Grain de Sel 9 chaussée de Vleurgat, 1050; tel: 02 648 18 58
Closed Sat lunch, Sun, Mon.
M̄ *Trône;* Ē *Métro to Trône, then bus 38 or 71 to place Flagey.*
An easy walk from the smart avenue Louise along this run-down street takes you to a world apart. Perhaps the raucous market at place Flagey with its flowers, fountains and fairground attractions might not seem the ideal setting for a tiny little gem, but don't take Le Grain de Sel with a pinch of salt. And please, please don't be fooled by the friendly service – the welcome may lack the formality expected of this side of Brussels, but these are no mere amateurs at work in the kitchen nor in the dining room. The *choucroute* with *filet de bar* is as good as it sounds, and the pigeon and lentil risotto, prepared with white wine and parmesan, quite the exception to the norm. If your mouth is not watering by now you should see a doctor. The main fixed-price menu is excellent value, but the true bargain is the €12 (450BEF) lunch. The best place to sit – weather permitting – is the pretty little rose garden behind the dining room, where, with great food and super service, time stands still in deference to your tastebuds.

La Grignotière 2041 Chaussée de Wavre, 1160; tel: 02 672 82 85
Closed Sun, Mon and Aug. €45–75 (1,750–3,000BEF).
Ē *Taxi*
That happy meeting with the couple from Antwerp in the Belle Maraîchère (see page 287) provided lyrical outpourings about this seemingly modest dining room in the Auderghem district. 'Monsieur Chanson is simply the best chef in Belgium,'

my new friend told me. 'You must go, I will write down the phone number for you.' Advice from such a dedicated gastronome is not to be ignored – even if I could not find the place on any tourist maps, and several hotel concierges shrugged in apology when I asked for more information. A €18 (750BEF) taxi ride later, and I found for myself La Grignotière, a good distance from the town centre, next to a petrol station on the outer ring-road, by the motorway to Namur, and housed in a suburban domestic terrace. At the top of the stairs you come face to face with the kitchen before turning to a pleasant, inoffensive, pastel-painted dining room, with impressionist prints on the walls and double French windows leading to the mature, well-tended first-floor garden. Always completely booked up in advance, but never advertised; word of mouth brings the well-heeled and unpretentious lovers of good food to the house. The motorway location is explained when you realise that La Grignotière caters to guests from all over Belgium rather than relying on the *bruxellois*. The attraction is Monsieur Chanson's almost uncanny knack of discovering the perfect natural accompaniment to every sea and freshwater fish known to the market place. *Langoustines à la vapeur de verveine* with a *ragoût* of *girolles*, or the gravadlax infused with smoky-flavoured tea. Yet the aim is not to show off. Where traditional brasserie fare has created a classic, unsurpassable dish, brasserie fare will find its way on to a gastronomic menu. And should you dismiss *quenelles de brochet sauce écrevisses* as a glorified fish pattie, then you would probably regard *AAAAA andouillette* as a banger. The €45 (1,800BEF) set menu contains a few sops to hard-core carnivores: veal and pork, but fish is the guest of honour – the seven-course *dégustation* menu is exclusively piscatorial. Don't stint on an evening like this; expect to pay well for a special occasion. But remember to book in advance of your trip.

Les Salons de l'Atalaide 89 chaussée de Charleroi, 1060; tel: 02 537 21 54; web: www.lessalonsatalaide.be [13 F8]
M̄ *Louise;* Ē *Métro to Louise then tram 91 or 92 to Faider.*
A fantasia of baroque and droll, this vast auction house, a little more than a semi-precious stone's throw from the avenue Louise, is extraordinary, extravagant and an absolute hit with the well-heeled and well-turned-out. You won't be able to take your eyes away from the absolutely fabulous drapes and fireplaces, which is no bad thing because the seemingly relaxed waitresses are in fact rushed off their feet and you'll have to hang on for a while before anyone takes your order. The salons welcome a genuine cross-section of Brussels' hungry hordes. Classic fare with flair, served at Gothic tables in *faux-chinois* salons under convoluted *nouveau*-style chandeliers. The budget conscious may try to restrict themselves to the lunchtime specials – but the main €30–50 (1,250–2,000BEF) menus are just so tempting. *Poulet de Bresse* is served with raspberries and a sweet couscous of olive oil and almonds that, according to a trusted chum, is almost as delicious as it sounds. The wine list has good Loire whites and Bordeaux reds by the glass, jug or bottle at reasonable prices. Fair range of *tartes* and chocolate desserts too.

Les Temps Delire 175–177 chausée de Charleroi, 1050; tel: 02 538 12 10
Closed Sat lunch, Sun. €10–25 (400–1,000BEF).
M̄ *Louise;* Ē *Métro to Louise then tram 91 or 92 to Faider.*
Should you find yourself near the avenue Louise, the chances are your credit cards are suffering. Give the wallet a break and enjoy a good cheap meal a skip or three away from the more expensive shops. The trams run along the chausée de Charleroi every few minutes, and at midday carry more than a few economising lunchers to a rendezvous that has the air of well-to-do Brussels without the usual price tags. Most opt for the €10 (400BEF) bowl of *moules*, or the daily special

lunch menu for the same price, at this corner site with its serpentine lighting twisting over *tête à têtes* and office gossips. It is grill-type fare tweaked to the budget conscious and socially aware on the edge of an upmarket area. *Brochettes* of meat and seafood with dripping banana as a sweetener may be found amongst the variants on the brasserie norm.

Tour d'Y Voir 8–9 pl des Grand Sablons, 1000; tel: 02 511 40 43; web: www.tourdyvoir.com [13 F4]
Closed Mon.
M̲ *Gare Centrale;* E̲ *Bus 20 to Sablons.*
There has been a place of worship on this site for the best part of 600 years. Originally a modest chapel, later a Papal oratory – as the 18th-century windows bear testament. More recently, Brussels has fallen under the sway of a team of intelligent and skilful restaurateurs and their promising young chefs. In the kitchen, the team has a reputation for improvisation and, wisely, the restaurant owners Pascal and Tania Anciaux allow free reign. The house speciality is for meals devised on a whim and with an experienced market shopper's instinct. The price and number of courses offered on the *'surprise'* menu varies. Prices start at €25 (1,000BEF), with a half bottle of wine for just €7.50 (300BEF) extra. You could pay double that for a full gastronomic adventure with up to six courses. Menus are created on the spot for fully fledged carnivores, veggies or fish lovers. The fun really begins when the food arrives as the waiters are sworn to keep the details of the dish secret until you have finished eating. Forks and spoons cross the tables as dining partners play gastro-detectives to discover the clues to lunch or dinner. The choice of wine, too, is left to the restaurant team. A full bottle of a delightfully flavoursome Languedoc was left at my table – and I was trusted to sip no further than the halfway mark! Oranges and honey may trick a humble grey mullet into a state of near ecstasy; finely chopped apples might bring new style to a simple vinaigrette, drizzled over a dish of salmon roe and smoked trout. Whichever you choose, *surprise* menu or à la carte, you may be sure it will have the impact of the plaice urged on me by seasoned Brussels diners. This too-often-bland fish was revived with caramelised limes and subtly steamed broccoli and fennel. Tuesday to Saturday lunch special menus from €14 (600BEF) are previewed in advance on the website and there is no charge if the service is too slow. No slave to France, the innovative wine list has some gems from the New World and South America. Plain tables do not upstage the gentle and soothing atmosphere created by the ecclesiastical brickwork and the sighs of contented fellow diners in the tranquil first-floor dining room, hidden from Sablons shoppers and reached by a narrow staircase behind an antiques gallery. A 5% surcharge is added to credit card payments.

WHAT TO BUY
Avenue Louise [13 F7–8]
Versace, Mugler, Chanel and co may all be found around the Portes de Namur and Louise, avenue Louise, place Stéphanie and its tributaries. The notable exception is Armani, which is to be discovered on Grand Sablon.

Beermania 174–176 chaussée de Wavre; tel: 02 512 17 88; web: www.beermania.be
Open Mon–Sat 11.00–19.00.
M̲ *Porte de Namur;* E̲ *Métro to Porte de Namur, then 5 min walk along chaussée de Wavre.*
With an average of 400 different beers to choose from, this shop rivals the beer museums as an information point on the thousand or so individual brews created

by the monks, *brasseurs*, and industrial giants of Belgium. If you just want to quench your thirst, pick up the popular brands at the supermarket. For a nice box of beers with a couple of souvenir glasses, check out the gift emporia in the town centre. However, for those interested in the infinite variety of local ales, this is the Holy Grail. Brussels' answer to Beaujolais Nouveau is Gouden Carolus '*Cuvée* of the Emperor', a many-splendoured thing brewed on the birthday of Charles V, February 24. In stock from April onwards. This is also the place to ask about the strange and varied traditions surrounding beer glasses.

Delvaux 27 bd de Waterloo, 1000; tel: 02 513 05 02 [F–G6]
Open Mon–Sat 10.00–18.30.
M̄ *Louise;* Ē *Métro to Louise.*
Those Belgian handbags that shriek fine breeding and inherent class, Delvaux accessories are the mark of a good wife and perfect dinner guest, rather than career woman or shatterer of glass ceilings.

Francis Ferent 443–445 galeries de la Toison d'Or, 1050; tel: 02 513 12 49 [13 F7]
Open Mon–Sat 10.00–18.30.
M̄ *Louise or Porte de Namur;* Ē *Métro to Louise.*
One-stop label shop tending to the needs of the incurably wealthy.

Inno 12 av Louise, 1060; tel: 02 513 84 94 [13 F7]
Open Mon–Sat 10.00–18.30.
M̄ *Louise or Porte de Namur;* Ē *Métro to Louise.*
A branch of Belgium's famous and reliable department store, complete with scent-spraying sentinels guarding the perfume counters, and sensible gift options on all floors.

Royal Dog Shop 27 pl de la Justice, 1000; tel: 02 513 3261 [13 F3]
Open Mon–Sat 09.00–18.00.
M̄ *Gare Centrale;* Ē *Underground tram to De Brouckère, métro to Gare Centrale. Walk south along bd de l'Empereur.*
Dogs whose owners dress on the avenue Louise are themselves kitted out by the self-styled '*couturier pour chiens*'. Tailored outfits for pooch poseurs on the Grand Sablon, diamond-studded collars to inspire many a ransom note, and dry-clean-only coats for animals with the lamppost etiquette of the Manneken Pis. Enough said.

Senses Art Nouveau 31 rue Lebeau, 1000; tel: 02 502 15 30 [13 F4]
Open Mon–Sat 10.00–18.00.
M̄ *Gare Centrale;* Ē *Bus 20 to Sablons.*
Art nouveau mirrors, lamps and furnishings at a price. If your strolls around St Gilles and the centre have inspired you to take a little bit of Horta's Brussels home with you, this is where to find the real McCoy.

South of Grand' Place

GARE DU MIDI – ST-GILLES

Arriving at the Gare du Midi from London's revamped South Bank, Lille's futuristic Europe quarter or even the bustle of Paris, is certainly a culture shock.The streets around the station are certainly seedy, and the first reaction is always 'let's get out of here', as everyone shuts their eyes to the depressing local landscape and grabs a taxi, dives into the métro or hops on a tram to find the Brussels that the brochure promised. The honourable exception to the rule is the night-club crowd that rides the last Eurostar and Thalys services into Brussels in order to take to the dance floor of Fuse on a Saturday night.

Thus the average visitor averts his gaze from the peep shows and peeling paintwork of the run-down sex cinemas on bd Jamar, and turns away from the sight of boarded-up apartments alongside the railway lines. Alas, he may well be missing out on the most atmospheric and rewarding quarters of the capital.

Anderlecht, northwest of the station, is best known for Belgium's greatest soccer team. The Saturday afternoon match crowd trekking out to the stadium is generally good-natured. More pensive visitors take tram 56 from the station in search of the house and garden in which the humanist Erasmus spent several months of 1521 (**Maison Erasmus**, 31 rue de Chapitre, 1070; tel: 02 521 13 83. Open 10.00–12.00, 14.00–17.00, closed Tue and Thu. Admission €1.50. M̲ St-Guidon). The rich, dark, moody and evocative interior of the house became a museum in 1931. Over the years humanists and historians alike have come to leaf through the excellent archives of 16th-century writing, including *In Praise of Folly*, which Erasmus published after a visit to his good friend Sir Thomas More. Other visitors arrive to admire the brick building, its fine furnishings and an art collection, including a Holbein portrait of Erasmus himself. From the spiritual to the corporal, Anderlecht is the famous meatpacking district. At weekends the area around the 19th-century abattoir becomes a local market when the locals take to the streets for the weekly shop.

Markets are what southern Brussels is famous for. Sunday's North African bazaar around the station is an experience in itself. The flea market of **Marolles** every morning is my favourite. Whenever I arrive for the day on the early train, I walk along the rue Angleterre into the rue Blaes and can be sifting through the bargains on the cobbles within ten minutes of flashing my passport on the platform. Buses from rue Haute can drop me off near Grand' Place within another ten minutes and I usually arrive for my lunch date with yet another marionette, a 19th-century magazine or a carrier bag of paperbacks as the morning's trophies. Mooching around the Marolles, with its not-quite-junk-not-yet-antique shops and tired-looking small businesses clinging to existence, reflect on the spirit of the local community that 60 years ago formed the core of the Resistance movement and sheltered many Jewish families from the Nazis.

South of the flea market is the district of St-Gilles, an unmissable treat for lovers of art nouveau. Whilst uptown visitors generally approach St-Gilles from the avenue Louise, the area is easily accessible from the Gare du Midi. This is the residential neighbourhood adopted by the art-nouveau architects and designers of the turn of the last century. Principal Brussels tourist offices sell sightseeing maps of the architectural highlights, and even the hop-on hop-off bus tours suggest a comfortable strolling itinerary for the streets around the home of Victor Horta.

The other worthwhile themed route around Brussels is the comic strip trail of murals and frescos, many signed by the great artists themselves. The official illustrated 6km circuit within the Ring begins north of Grand' Place by the Comic Strip Centre (see page 297) and takes in each of the districts featured in this guide. Taking a taxi from Gare du Midi to Grand' Place, the first mural seen by most visitors is Philippe Geluck's surreal *Le Chat* in the guise of a bricklayer or architect assembling himself or bricking himself up on an exposed wall along boulevard du Midi. The route map, with illustrated cards featuring each of the frescos, costs just over €1 or 50BEF. Alternatively visit the website www.eurobd.com/planchedeville. Incidentally, on your way back to the station look out for the busts of Tintin and his dog Snowy (Milou in the original French) perched atop the Lombard building.

With several lesser-known museums, this area tends to attract fewer crowds than the centre of town, and provides plenty of last-minute treats for the hour or two before catching the train home.

WHERE TO STAY

Les Bluets 124 rue Berckmans, 1060; tel: 02 534 39 83 [12 E8]
M̲ *Porte des Monnaies;* Ē *Métro to Porte des Monnaies. From rue des Monnaies turn left on to rue Berkmans.*
Extraordinary value, this is one of those secret addresses that has delighted honeymooners and weekenders for years. On a residential street, the cascade of busy-lizzies and pansies from tubs and window boxes barely hint at the eclectic charms of the large, family-home townhouse built for his mother by a 19th-century architect and now run as a private hotel behind two substantial front doors. The public rooms are pretty splendid, with marble fireplaces and a grand piano holding the antiques, and countless kitsch collections accrued by the charming and hospitable owners. Bedrooms, at €37–75 (1,500–3,000BEF), are crammed with bric-à-brac, dolls, plants, pictures, magazines and scatter-cushions, and all is reminiscent of the guestrooms in the country house of a favourite, if somewhat dotty, aunt. There is always a selection of books in your own language placed by the bed – though not always the titles you might have chosen for yourself. I dithered between Georgette Heyer and a dictionary of diseases of the colon. The

breakfast room is the *pièce de résistance*: upstaging the pictures, vases, ashtrays, gnomes, teddies, clocks and mirrors, a *tableau vivant* is played out by the dog, the canaries and the mynah bird. Breakfast is taken at the big, round, family dining table where the morning's guests are introduced to each other. I met a Danish scientist, a London businesswoman, a brace of horticulturists from Bath (up for the royal greenhouse open days, see page 299) and a New York emergency-room doctor on her way to Bruges. The hotel has a garden for relaxing with the newspaper, a private phone line for each guest and kettles in the bedrooms. Bathrooms have no mini-freebies, but a decent-sized slab of soap. The very smallest bedrooms have en-suite shower but no loo. Be warned – hot water is only available mornings and evenings. No lift and no smoking.

Galia 15–16 pl du Jeu de Balle, 1000; tel: 02 502 42 43; email : hotelgalia@hotelgalia.com; web: www.hotelgalia.com [12 C6]
M̄ *Gare du Midi;* Ē *Bus 20 two stops to Jeu de Balle. Follow crowds down rue des Renards to flea market. Alternatively walk from the station (rue Angleterre–rue Blaes).*
Rooms are basic, though modernised, here at the best address in town for serious market punters. Forget the antiques quarter of Sablons – where even trade prices are sky high. Early birds hang out here. The Galia is in the heart of the flea-market that runs from 07.00 to 14.00, and guests can even get to the bargains before the local antique dealers who arrive at the crack of dawn. A decked terrace on the street doubles as a café bar for traders and shoppers alike. Colourful cartoon posters abound in the Brasserie Nicolas, reflecting the area's location on the comic fresco route. In the afternoons and early evening, views from hotel windows provide the biggest surprise: when the last trader packs away his bric-a-brac at 14.00, the pl Jeu de Balle is anything but shabby. Look out over a charming and attractive town square. The hotel is also popular with night-owls in town for serious clubbing at Fuse. Rooms €50–75 (2,000–3,000BEF).

WHERE TO GO

Les Marolles (Flea Market) pl de Jeu de Balle, 1000 [12 C6]
Open 06.00–14.00.
M̄ *Gare du Midi or Porte de Hal;* Ē *Bus 20 two stops to Jeu de Balle. Follow crowds down rue des Renards to flea market. Alternatively walk from the station (rue Angleterre–rue Blaes).*
Bargain hunters come in search of paradise on the cobbles at the Jeu de Balle flea market – an absolute must for hard-core junk junkies. A world away from the glossy sheen of the pavement traders at Sablons, the flea market is not the place for dithering over Chippendales nor discovering genuine Sheraton chairs. Nonetheless, in ten minutes over a 20m stretch of pavement, I have been offered a nearly complete set of human vertebrae, some stunning coffee-cups, a framed print of Hamlet scolding Gertrude, and a telex machine. Best times for bargain hunting are around daybreak on Tuesdays and Thursdays. Weekend prices tend to be higher.

Piscine Victor Boin 38 rue de la Perche, 1060; tel: 02 539 06 15
€1.50 (70BEF).
M̄ *Porte de Hal;* Ē *Tram 81 or 82 four stops to Barrière, walk down rue de la Perche.*
Allow 20 minutes for the usual traffic jams and escape from the pace of city life in the municipal baths of the St-Gilles district. Named after a local and national hero who was Queen Elizabeth's personal pilot in World War I and represented Belgium at fencing at every Olympic Games from 1908 to 1924. This fabulous art deco swimming pool with galleried changing cubicles is a world apart from the ultra-modern beach resort of Océade (see page 298) but a marvellous

opportunity to take the plunge before catching the train home. The centre's original Turkish and Russian steam baths are open to men (Mon, Thu, Sat) and women (Tue, Fri). Heath Robinsonian showers, plunge pools and crank-it-yourself steam jets (quite pricey).

WHAT TO SEE

Chantillon Brewery Musée Bruxellois de la Gueuze 56 rue Gheude, 1070; tel: 02 521 49 28 [12 A4]
Open Mon–Fri 08.30–17.00, Sat 10.00–17.00. €2.50 (100BEF).
M̄ *Gare du Midi;* Ē *Take av Paul-Henri Spaak (northwest exit of the station), cross into rue Limander, then into rue Gheude.*
A working brewery in Anderlecht, producing the city's distinctive Gueuze-Lambic beer, doubles as an informal museum of the ancient art of producing beer by natural spontaneous fermentation. Push open the door, pay your money, pick up the leaflet and guide yourself around the signposted trail through the nooks and crannies of this building that is still owned by the original brewing family that set up the company in 1900. End your tour with a tipple or two of the unusual brew itself and its fruit-flavoured variants, *kriek* (cherry) or *framboise* (raspberry). Pick up a bottle or case to take home with you.

Horta Museum 25 rue Américaine, 1060; tel: 02 543 04 90; email: musee.horta@horta.irisnet.be
Open Tue–Sun 14.00–17.30, closed holidays. €5 (200BEF).
Tram 81 82 91 92; Ē *Tram 81 or 82 to Janson. A museum flagpole marks the junction of rue Américaine with chaussée de Charleroi. A 20-minute journey.*
A century before yuppies reclaimed inner city lofts, Baron Victor Horta (1861–1947), the architect of Belgian art nouveau, experimented with the concept of indoor open spaces in his own home. The trademark swirls and floral flourishes of the movement are to be found here aplenty in Horta's house and workshop built between 1898 and 1901. Splendidly light and airy, these two town houses are blessed with vast windows, and the interior décor, mosaics, stained glass, graceful carved panels and striking murals – all designed by Horta himself – are lovingly preserved. Much of the original furniture and many charming items of *chinoiserie* have been returned to the house, and each room brings its own serendipity, from the practical (a cleverly concealed urinal in a wardrobe) to the indulgent (the extravagant door handles and breathtakingly beautiful staircase). Rear windows offer a glimpse of the garden where the sweep of the interior design's motif is subtly reflected in the slightly overgrown

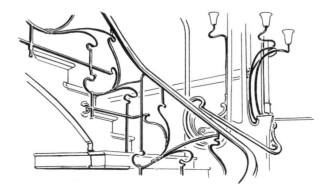

CHOCOLATE IN BRUSSELS

With dainty doilies, silken ribbons and pretty maids all in a row, nothing could be more genteel than a few minutes' delicious indecision in a Belgian chocolate shop. The etiquette of dithering over *ganaches* and *pralines* on silver trays, as patient shop-girls, with starched white aprons and elegant tongs, drop your choices one by one into cardboard *ballotins*, seems as timeless as an oriental tea-ceremony.

Yet when chocolate first arrived in Brussels, it was a commodity that could never be openly traded over the counter. What today is considered sinful, simply with regard to its effects on the waistline, was in the 17th century regarded as a class-A drug. Cocoa landed in Europe as part of the New World cult that gripped Europe's privileged class. It was taken as a drink and carried the risqué cachet of other imported pleasures, such as tobacco and opium.

A 1699 edict issued in Antwerp announced a fine of 500 florins and five years' exile for anyone found dealing in chocolate. Despite this, or perhaps because of this, a chic sub-culture developed in the salons of Brussels, complete with designer accessories such as copper *chocolatières* and tiny silver cups. Many of these may be seen at the Chocolate Museum on Grand' Place (see page 273).

By the 19th century, chocolate was decriminalised, and the Pharmacie Neuhaus was the first shop licensed to sell it as an aphrodisiac and a laxative (combination properties that almost certainly led to the first quips about Belgians not knowing if they are coming or going). By 1857, chocolate had overtaken the potions and pills side of the apothecary's business, and **Neuhaus** created an elegant boutique with crystal, mirrors and brightly polished counters to display his latest confections. The original branch in the Galerie de la Reine specialises in nougaty *caprices* and coffee-and-cream flavoured *tentations*. It was here, in 1912, that the shop sold the world's first ever *praline*.

As in all modern chocolate shops, the treats are sold in cartons or *ballotins* from 250g to a kilo, each box a personalised selection for each customer. Prices range from ∈12.50 (500BEF) a kilo at Leonidas to ∈40 (1,600BEF) at Wittamer.

Wittamer (see page 305) on Grand Sablon serves chocolates with more than a hint of privilege. The whiff of fortune around the smart counters almost overpowers the sugar-sweet temptations wafting from the kitchen. Pink pyramids and dark squares inscribed with real gold leaf wrap exotic fillings from cinnamon to Earl Grey tea. Tiny wild strawberries in season bathed in a lightly whisked *crème fraîche* create unimaginable sensations on the tongue. Wittamer may be the gastronomic

---

flowerbeds. In peak visitor season the house may get quite crowded, so head for the top-floor conservatory for moments of quiet contemplation. Do not leave the area without strolling the streets around rue Defacqz and rue Livourne to see

high spot of the city's cardio-vascular white-knuckle ride through quality cholesterol, but every *chocolatier* has a speciality quite unique.

At **Corné – Toison d'Or**, the *Manon* is created by rolling a pair of walnuts in sugar, coffee and butter cream. Not to be confused with rival confections simply dipped in white chocolate.

George Bush the Elder has a weakness for pralines created at **Mary**, the last of the original chocolate shops still run as a private business. **Godiva** is now one of the most successful international chains, long since sold to big business, and, alongside **Leonidas**, may be seen in most international cities. The granddaughter of the original founder decided to return to her roots and opened a shop of her own, **Les Délices de Mélanie**, on the site of the original shop.

Another relative newcomer is **Pierre Marcolini** who opened his shop on avenue Louise in 1996, after being crowned in Lyon as the world's finest *pâtissier*. Ginger and liquorice find their way into the soft centres of his slender *ganaches*. Worth a visit simply to see the amazing chocolate sculptures that Pierre creates for his favoured clients.

The next generation of artists working in cocoa find their work on the counters of **Planète Chocolat** (see page 270) and the **Maison du Chocolat Artisanal**.

Supermarkets sell boxes of mass-produced *pralines*, and there are always good selections of chocolates from all the major houses on sale at the station. But the opportunity to pick and choose your own selection box is a rare treat, and one not to be missed.

Corné – Toison d'Or Galerie de la Reine, 1000; tel: 02 512 23 60 [12 F1] M̄ *Gare Centrale*.

Les Délices de Mélanie 27 rue Grétry, 1000; tel: 02 217 90 31 [12 E1] M̄ *Bourse*.

Godiva 22 Grand' Place, 1000; tel: 02 511 25 37 [12 E2] M̄ *Gare Centrale*.

Leonidas 46 bd Anspach, 1000; tel: 02 218 03 63 [10 G6–7] M̄ *De Brouckère*.

Maison du Chocolat Artisanal 57 rue Marché aux Herbes, 1000; tel: 02 513 78 92 [10 E2] M̄ *Bourse*.

Mary 73 rue Royale, 1000; tel: 02 217 45 00 [13 H1–2] M̄ *Parc*.

Neuhaus Galerie de la Reine, 1000; tel: 02 512 63 59 [12 F1] M̄ *Gare Centrale*.

Pierre Marcolini Hotel Conrad, 77 av Louise, 1050; tel: 02 538 42 24 [13 G8] M̄ *Louise*.

Wittamer 12 pl du Grand Sablon, 1000; tel: 02 512 37 42 [13 F4] M̄ *Gare Centrale*.

houses designed by Horta's contemporaries, Janssens, Hankar and Van Rysselberghe. A dedicated Horta art nouveau route-map around the city and its fringes is available from the tourist office on Grand' Place.

Jewish Museum 74 av de Stalingrad, 1000; tel: 02 512 1963; web: www.mjb-jmb.org [12 C4]
Open Mon–Thu 13.00–17.00, Sun 10.00–13.00; closed Jewish and national holidays. €2.50 (100BEF).
M̄ *Lemonnier;* Ē *Underground tram one stop to Lemonnier. 200m walk along av Stalingrad.*
Americans seeking their European roots ring the discreet doorbell of this unassuming terraced townhouse, for here are housed the records of the 65,000 Jews who lived in the city at the outbreak of World War II. Although some managed to flee before the Nazi occupation, 40,000 died in concentration camps and only 1,207 survived. The first floor of the building is a small but moving museum displaying scenes from family life with mementos donated by both the local community and those displaced Europeans who sought sanctuary in Brussels after the war. During the next couple of years, the museum hopes to relocate to new premises in the Sablons area, where it plans a permanent exhibition, five times larger than the present display. Those who come in search of their families should also visit the National Monument to the Jewish Martyrs engraved with the names of 23,838 men, women and children deported from the Dossin Barracks in Malines between August 4 1942 and July 31 1944 (rue Emile Carpentier in the Anderlecht district; tram 56 from Gare du Midi).

Lift Museum 15 rue de la Source, 1060; tel: 02 535 82 11 [12 E8]
Open Tue, Thu 14.00–17.00, closed holidays, last week of the year. Free.
M̄ *Hôtel des Monnaies;* Ē *Métro Line 2 to Hotel des Monnaies, follow rue des Monnaies; rue de la Source is second left.*
American readers, please note: the Belgian Lift is not a technical move in Olympic ice-dancing. For 'Lift' read 'Elevator'. In a city that boasts a museum of birds' nests as well as the national chicory collection, foreign residents and long-term visitors compete to drop into conversation references to the least consequential gallery in town. A passing acquaintance in a bar off the Grand' Place told me, 'I went to the Door Museum, but it was shut.' Had it been open, or even slightly ajar, he might have won that round. However, I was able to trump his offering, having that very afternoon stumbled across this private exhibition of everything that you have ever wanted to know about getting from floor to floor in your hotel or apartment block without using the stairs. Perhaps a little too practical to be classed as eccentric, the Lift Museum is nonetheless a hit in engineering circles. Housed in the headquarters of the Schindler company are cables, parachutes, motors and call buttons. A laid-back guide, with piercing and combat trousers, guides architects, schoolchildren and refugees from the rainy streets around the display, offering off-beat anecdotes regarding Tom Cruise action movies and rare true-life disasters. Three early 20th-century lift cabins will be of most interest to technophobes, one a charming gazebo-style iron basket rescued from the Fine Arts Museum.

Porte de Hal bd du Midi, 1000 [12 C8]
M̄ *Porte de Hal;* Ē *Métro one stop or an easy 10-min stroll south along the bd du Midi.*
The Royal Museum of Art and History has long been promising to reopen the rooms inside the tower here, which has in the past served as an annexe to the Cinquantenaire collections (see page 307). Don't hold your breath. The last official opening date was October 2000, but the following spring saw the doors as resolutely locked as usual. Instead admire the building from the outside. This gateway is a rare remnant of the city walls that once enclosed old Brussels and protected it from attack from the armies of France, Spain and any other nation that fancied its chances.

WHERE TO EAT

Het Warm Water 19 rue des Renards, 1000; tel: 02 513 91 59,
08.00–17.00, closed evenings, Wed.
M̄ *Gare du Midi or Porte de Hal;* Ē *Bus 20 two stops to Jeu de Balle. Rue des Renards
links rue Haut and rue Blaes.*
What do you fancy for Sunday breakfast? Some bread? Cheese? Jam? *Tête de
veau?* Beer? Whatever you want, this little breakfast room on one of the spurs of
the Jeu de Balle flea market is sure to have it on the most eccentric *petit-déj* menu
I know. Food is served on large breadboards, and comprises any or all of the
suggested breakfast and brunch dishes. *Charcuterie*, omelettes, cheese, bars of dark
chocolate, *crudités*, muesli, bread, monastic beer, herbal tea, coffee or sherry. Yes,
sherry. Pay €2.5–10 (100–400BEF) according to your selection, but don't skip a
back-up breakfast at your hotel beforehand since the student-hangout service is
painfully slow. Whatever you choose, know that the bread is wholemeal, the
sugar cane, the jams home-made and the juice freshly squeezed. No one really
minds the wait because on Sunday morning a local singer and musicians offer
sounds from Trenet to jazz, folk songs to the swinging sixties. Have some loose
change at hand to tip into the ice bucket that does the rounds on behalf of the
music makers. Genuinely friendly, this outpost of Bohemia is eternally popular
with families, friends and shoppers alike. Children head upstairs to the
'Gingerbread House' playroom. The countless kettles on every downstairs
surface justify the name. On certain evenings the café stays open until 20.00 for
Flemish political cabaret performances.

WHAT TO BUY

Marché du Midi Gare du Midi [12 A6]
Open Sun, dawn–13.30.
M̄ *Gare du Midi.*
For one morning every week, Africa comes to northern Europe in a crazy bring-
and-buy bazaar. Barter for bargains, or wait until an hour before closing when
prices tumble of their own accord. Pick up colourful cheap clothing or just
wander around the stalls taking the pulse of St-Gilles at its busiest. A true
melting pot, all the immigrant communities of Brussels set out their stalls in
carnival mood. Popular with just about everybody in town, including the city's
hard-working pickpockets, so wear a money belt, keep your hand on your cash,
or leave your plastic in the hotel safe.

Les Marolles pl Jeu de Balle [12 C6]
Open 06.00–14.00.
M̄ *Gare du Midi or Porte de Hal;* Ē *Bus 20 two stops to Jeu de Balle.*
Flea market (see *Where to go*, page 314).

Entertainment

CINEMA

Belgium may have produced only two world-class Hollywood stars, yet Brussels loves the movies. Film going remains a social occasion here, with cinemas offering comfortable seats, licensed bars and weekly parties.

Both the French- and Dutch-speaking communities have developed their own distinct film industries, and it is always worth checking listings for domestic offerings. Invariably, home-grown projects end up in the world's art houses and in linguistically segregated cinemas in Brussels. The compromise appetite in the capital is for international films, usually shown in the original language with bilingual subtitles.

The best-known cinema is the **Kinépolis** multiplex at Heysel's Bruparck pleasure zone, with two dozen screens and an Imax theatre. However there are plenty of picture houses to choose from within the Ring. Sneak preview sessions in central Brussels are the most popular events and are held year round (except July and August): midnight on Saturdays at the **UGC De Brouckère**, and Tuesdays at 20.00 at Kinépolis are best for catching Hollywood blockbusters a few weeks before the official launch date. The true buzz for *cinéastes* is to be found on Thursday evening at the **Arenberg Galleries**, when film makers and distributors test unknown movies on a live audience for the first time. A truly pot-luck affair, you might find yourself seeing the most eagerly anticipated film of the decade or an obscure work of art destined for fleeting glory at the Cannes Film Festival.

The Arenberg Galleries cinema is a converted art deco theatre in the Galeries St-Hubert. It was in these arcades, if not on this actual site, that Brussels' first picture show took place in 1896. Silent movies are still screened daily, with live piano accompaniment, at the **Musée du Cinéma** (see page 304). Twice a month on Sunday afternoons, the cinema museum screens classic films and musicals for children.

A good number of independent cinemas may be discovered across Brussels. These are popular with students and are treasured stations on the classic and cult circuit. The Rocky Horror crowd may be seen at midnight sessions at the **Nova**, which also hosts alternative film nights, using old movies as the backdrop for newly mixed sounds by the hippest DJs. This trend for blending familiar images on the silver screens with the latest dance-floor culture has also been a huge success at the **Cyber Avenue** cybercafé (see page 304). French films are often screened at the **Botanique** cultural centre (see page 296). On summer weekends, locals park their convertibles at the Esplanade du Cinquantenaire for the July and August drive-in movie season. The rest of us take the métro to Mérode and hire a deckchair. Crowds arrive long before sunset, and the show starts at around 22.30. Ask at the tourist office for details of screenings, as well as Brussels' many international film festivals, which usually feature several bonus fringe events.

Cinema tickets cost around €6 (250BEF). Remember to tip the usher or usherette 50 cents or €1 (25–40BEF). Programmes change every Wednesday. Check out the English-language listings magazine *The Bulletin*, Wednesday's edition of *Le Soir* or the website www.cinebel.com for details. As in France, the abbreviation 'v.o.' after the title of a film means that the movie is being screened in its original language.

Arenberg Galeries 26 Galerie de la Reine, 1000; tel: 02 512 80 63 [13 F1] M̲ *Gare Centrale.*

Kinepolis Bruparck, 1 av du Centenaire, 1020; tel: 02 474 26 00 M̲ *Heysel.*

Musée du Cinéma Palais des Beaux Arts, 9 rue Baron Horta, 1000; tel: 02 507 83 70 [13 G3] M̲ *Gare Centrale or Parc.*

Nova 3 rue d'Arenberg, 1000; tel: 02 511 27 74 [13 F1] M̲ *Gare Centrale.*

UGC Acropole 17 Galerie de la Toison d'Or, 1050; tel: 0900 104 40 (recorded information in French) [13 F6] M̲ *Porte de Namur.*

UGC De Brouckère 38 pl de Brouckère, 1000; tel: 0900 104 40 (recorded information in French) [11 F6] M̲ *De Brouckère.*

THEATRE

The showcase theatre of Brussels is the **Théâtre Royal de la Monnaie**. Its place in history is assured, since it was here that the revolution of 1830 was born after the audience was stirred into anarchic insurrection by a poignant, patriotic love duet during a performance of Auber's *La Muette di Portici*. Although the original building was largely destroyed by fire in 1855, the theatre was rebuilt by Joseph Poelaert in neo-classical style, retaining the impressive façade that still dominates the place de la Monnaie. Home to the national opera company, the theatre has hosted performances by the world's leading singers and musicians, from Richard Wagner to Maria Callas. In 1968 Jacques Brel dreamed the impossible dream on this stage as the *Man of La Mancha*.

The other great theatre building, reliving the age of audiences being regarded as more important than mere actors, is the enchanting and beautiful **Théâtre Royal du Parc**. Once the Court paraded and peacocked in the theatre's boxes and on its staircases. Today's society hostesses continue the eternally smiling battle of couture and coiffure in the foyers during the intervals of classic Shakespeare and Molière, or lighter boulevard comedies from Feydeau to Ayckbourn.

Brussels has two national theatres. The architecturally uninspiring **Théâtre National** on place Rogier offers classical French fare in the main house and more experimental work in its smaller space. The Flemish community has rather more dramatic accommodation at the **Koninklijke Vlaamse Schouwburg**. A tribute to baroque flamboyance masks the building's humble origins as an 18th-century warehouse, until it was converted to a playhouse in 1882 by architect Jean Baes. British touring companies are regular guests here, whilst theatre companies from France generally collaborate with the rival Théâtre National. Just along the road, the great glass rotunda of the **Botanique** cultural centre also hosts contemporary and classic French works. Worth visiting are the **Toone puppet theatre** (see page 268) near Grand' Place and the **Théâtre de Poche** in the Bois de la Cambre.

Tip the usher or usherette around ∈1 per couple (40BEF). Theatre listings appear in Wednesday's *Le Soir*. Information in English may be found in the weekly magazine *The Bulletin* and at the main tourist office at Grand' Place.

Koninklijke Vlaamse Schouwburg 146 rue de Laeken, 1000; tel: 02 219 49 44 [10 E4]
M̄ *Rogier;* Ē *Underground tram to Rogier, then walk along bd d'Anvers to rue de Laeken.*

Théâtre National Centre Rogier, pl Rogier, 1210; tel: 02 203 53 03 [11 G4]
M̄ *Rogier;* Ē *Underground tram to Rogier.*

Théâtre de Poche chemin de Gymnase, Bois de la Cambre, 1000; tel: 02 649 17 27
Trams 23 90; Ē *Tram 90 to Legrand*

Théâtre Royal de la Monnaie pl de la Monnaie, 1000; tel: 02 229 12 11 [13 F6]
M̄ *De Brouckère;* Ē *Underground tram to De Brouckère then rue de l'Eveque to pl de la Monnaie.*

Théâtre Royal du Parc 3 rue de la Loi, 1000; tel: 02 512 23 39 [11 J8]
M̄ *Arts Loi;* Ē *Métro to Arts Loi then walk west on rue de la Loi.*

MUSIC

With concerts in the city parks from spring until late summer, jazz in bars and cellars all over town, and the thrill of dressing up for the opera, every day comes with the soundtrack of your choice.

The opera and ballet (see **Théâtre de la Monnaie**, page 323) are usually oversubscribed, but it is always worth checking for returns at the box office should you not have booked seats months in advance. Classical concerts are staged at the Salle Henri le Boeuf of the **Palais des Beaux Arts**, home to the national orchestra. The nearby **Conservatoire Royal de Musique** has an excellent programme of concerts.

Baroque music can also be appreciated at the **Cathedral** (see page 307), and **Notre Dame du Sablon** (see page 305) presents regular organ recitals.

Big-name singers and rock bands perform at the 11,000-seat **Forest National** and sometimes the Orangerie of the **Botanique** (see page 296). Less mainstream performers tend to play the AB – **Ancienne Belgique**, conveniently city central for evening gigs and lunchtime showcases. Local groups also play **Le Corbeau** bar close to the rue Neuve shopping area (see page 296).

Not surprisingly in a country that gave the world the saxophone, one is never too far from a jam session or jazz concert. Jazz may be heard in intimate venues from hotel lobbies in the business district to smoky dives in town. **L'Archiduc** (see page 283) has been welcoming small bands since the 1930s, and still offers some great Saturday afternoon entertainment.

Monday night jams are free and informal at the **Travers**, near Botanique, a great opportunity to catch future stars of the Brussels circuit on their first outing. The club posts programme details on its website. On Sunday in the Marolles flea market, light songs accompany breakfast at **Het Warm Water** (see page 321), and musicians play during brunch at **Phil's Jazz Kitchen Café**, which also hosts free live jazz in the evenings.

AB – Ancienne Belgique 114 bd Anspach, 1000; tel: 02 201 58 58 [10 D7]
M̄ *Bourse;* Ē *Underground tram to Bourse.*

Conservatoire Royal de la Musique 30 rue de la Régence, 1000; box office tel: 507 82 00 [13 F5]
M̄ *Parc;* Ē *Métro to Louise then tram 94 to Royale.*

Le Corbeau 18 rue St-Michel, 1000; tel: 02 219 52 46 [11 F4]
M̄ *De Brouckère;* Ē *Underground tram to De Brouckère. Walk north along the boulevard then right into rue St-Michel.*

Forest National 36 av du Globe; tel: 02 340 22 11
Tram 18; Ē *Tram 18 to St-Denis walk along rue Vampé to av Rousseau, right into av du Globe.*

Palais des Beaux Arts 23 rue Ravenstein, 1000; tel: 02 507 82 00 [13 G3]
M̄ *Parc;* Ē *Métro to Louise then tram 94 to Royale.*

Phil's Jazz Kitchen Café 189 rue Haute, 1000; tel: 02 513 95 88 [12 D6] Closed Mon.
M̄ *Porte de Hal;* Ē *Bus 20 to Jeu de Balle.*

Le Travers 5 rue Traversière, 1210; tel: 02 217 48 00; web: www.cyclone.be/travers [11 K4–5]
M̄ *Botanique;* Ē *Métro to Botanique then north on rue Royale to rue Traversière.*

NIGHTLIFE

Nightclubs slip in and out of fashion, and the hottest address in town will always be the newest. The website www.sortir.bxl.com is pretty reliable for checking on the current clubbing scene. In recent years a number of venues have established themselves as weekend favourites, and look to be around for some time.

Never arrive before 23.00 (some venues offer free admission or cheap drinks before midnight to kick off the evening, but serious party animals will not show their faces until well past the witching hour). Door charges vary depending on the event. In general, the price hike from bar drinks to club drinks is not as drastic as in France.

The main venues have their own websites, with details of forthcoming attractions and photographs of recent events. Go to www.fuse.be for the lowdown on the **Fuse**, in the Marolles district, where you are most likely to find the big-name international DJs on a Saturday night, serving techno and jungle for the city-hopping crowd. Fuse is also the venue for Benelux's major monthly, gay club night, La Démence, that pulls in the punters from Lille to Amsterdam. Post-Fuse, you will find clubbers sharing dawn breakfast tables with the bargain hunters in the cafés around the fleamarket.

Just north of the centre, by the freight warehouses of the city's port, **Tour & taxis** is less a club than a trendy venue for weekend club nights.

Smaller, friendly alternatives to the mega-club scene may be found nearer Grand' Place. Live saxophone players accompany House sounds from the decks on Friday night at **The House of Groove**, and a friendly crowd gathers at **Le Sonik**, cheek by jowl with the bars of rue Marché au Charbon.

Techno, House and Garage music tends to dominate the weekend party scene. An honourable exception is **The Sparrow**, where soul and Latin sounds regularly fill the floor. For a deliciously dated retro feel, with enough Abba, Claude François and Boney M to last a lifetime, try **Chez Johnny** for sheer kitsch escapism. A surprisingly mixed crowd, with as many youngsters as ageing swingers reliving their disco glory days.

Chez Johnny 24 chée de Louvain, 1030
Open Fri, Sat.
M̄ *Madou*.

Le Fuse 208 rue Blaes, 1000; web: www.fuse.be [12 D5–C7]
Open Sat.
M̄ *Porte de Hal*.

The House of Groove 1 rue St-Christophe, 1000
Open Fri.

Le Sonik 112 rue marché au Charbon, 1000; web: www.sonik.be [12 D2]
Open Fri, Sat.
M̄ *Bourse*.

The Sparrow 18 rue Duquesnoy, 1000; web: www.sparrowclub.com [13 F3]
Open Thu, Fri, Sat.
M̄ *Gare Centrale*.

Tour & Taxi 5 rue Picard, 1000
Open Fri, Sat.
M̄ *Ribeaucourt*.

THE MORNING AFTER

Familiar film fare is offered by city cinemas to the delicate and bleary-eyed who may wish to segue from the excess of Friday night into a state suitable for Saturday sightseeing without having to negotiate a full hotel breakfast and conversation. Free coffee and croissants are served with favourite flicks during **Les Petits Déjeuners du Cinéma** at the UGC Acropole at 10.00 on Saturday. Half an hour earlier, at 09.30, the big picture starts at the UGC De Brouckère, where free ice cream is handed out to fragile filmgoers.

Part Five

London

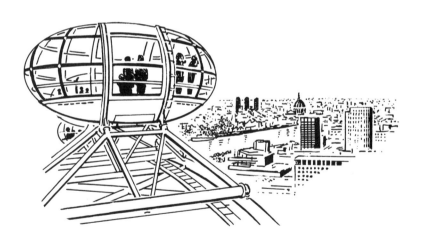

Around Waterloo

All good journeys begin on this side of the Thames. Chaucer's pilgrims set off from a local inn, and from Shakespeare's Globe Theatre audiences were transported to Agincourt, Verona and Illyria. Although one of Eurostar's main advantages is the short check-in time, anyone passing through London would be well advised to arrive early and see something of the real London on the opposite riverbank to the often overrated West End. Whether you decide to stay overnight in order to catch the early bird train in the morning, or opt for a day out before taking the afternoon journey, Southwark's Bankside rewards exploration.

Tate Modern (the gallery abolished its definite article) most recently pushed the riverbank into the mainstream, but the first revival of the South Bank came half a century ago with the Festival of Britain and opening of the Royal Festival Hall. The National (now Royal National) Theatre and the National Film Theatre further established the riverbank as a cultural centre. In front of the theatre and concert halls, along the footpath from Westminster to Tower Bridges, are many booksellers in the tradition of Paris' *bouquinistes*, and in summer the pavements and piazzas become impromptu stages for musicians, magicians and children's entertainers.

Scores of museums, large and small, may be found in the new market and trading estates within the former wharves, and many of London's most interesting new restaurants thrive along the river's Millennium Mile. Riverside pubs are rather too keen on the tourist pound, and some of their lunch menus are terribly over priced. Never pay £6 for a ploughman's lunch; instead wander along the smaller streets away from the water's edge to hunt for a far more rewarding treat.

If you are booked on a morning train, consider a different type of pub. London's market taverns are licensed to serve alcohol to night-shift workers at breakfast time. Pubs around Borough Market serve a hearty cooked breakfast at 07.00 or 08.00 in the morning, a perfect start to any voyage. Walk back along the river and watch the mudlarks, treasure hunters sifting through driftwood on the riverbed at low tide.

If you are travelling in the evening, consider a matinée at Shakespeare's Globe, the National Theatre, the Old Vic or Young Vic, or perhaps an afternoon recital at the Festival Hall.

You could of course cross the river. St Paul's Cathedral is reached via the notorious Millennium Footbridge. Unfinished on the day the Queen came to open it, the structure was closed to the public as soon as it was completed in order that its alarming 'wobble' might be treated. Cross Waterloo Bridge to explore the art galleries within Somerset House, pausing to examine the stainless steel plaques that detail the panoramic views from the bridge. Look closely at the illustration of the western skyline: one building has been erased from the official view. The Palace of Westminster does not feature on the plaque. Parliament had just abolished the Greater London Council, so the GLC decided to abolish the Houses of Parliament from the civic panorama.

The waterside attractions continue westward as far as Lambeth Palace (home of the Archbishop of Canterbury) and its gardens. Further east are *HMS Belfast*, Tower Bridge, and Butler's Wharf with its museums of tea and coffee, Design Centre and Terence Conran's gastrodome restaurants, where the Blairs and Clintons dined at Le Pont de la Tour (humidor available on request).

On the following pages you will find the pick of the best addresses within easy reach of Waterloo. Each location, although served by the new Jubilee Line tube stations (do admire the splendid architecture – reminiscent of the heyday of Metroland) is no more than 20 minutes' walk from the Eurostar check in, should traffic or public transport prove unreliable.

WHERE TO STAY

Southwark's Tourist Information Centre *[16 G3], in the shadow of the Southwark Needle, a 16-metre inclining obelisk on London Bridge, has a hotel reservation service, and can provide details of local bed & breakfast options for those on a limited budget. The office also offers advice on museums, sightseeing, dining and entertainment. Open (summer) Mon–Sat 10.00–18.00, Sun 11.00–18.00; (winter) Mon–Sat 10.00–16.00, Sun 11.00–16.00. Tel: 020 7403 8299.*

Bankside House Residence 24 Sumner St, SE1; tel: 020 7633 9877; fax: 020 7633 9877 [16 E3]
Open Jul–Sep only.
M̄ *Southwark;* Ē *Jubilee Line to Southwark then walk along Union St, turn left into Great Suffolk St leading to Sumner St.*
Best local value is a single room for under £30 in this student hall of residence next to Tate Modern. Twins and quad rooms also offered. There is even a launderette on site. Available during university vacations only. No double beds though, so ideal for the abstinent or resourceful.

London County Hall Travel Inn Belvedere Rd, SE1; tel: 020 7902 1600; web: www.travelinn.co.uk [16 A4]
M̄ *Waterloo;* Ē *Cross York Rd footbridge to Belvedere Rd.*
The poor cousin of the Marriott, this vast budget hotel in the old County Hall building has no river views, but each double bedroom can sleep up to four people – excellent value for around £75. Friendly staff and the option of checking out in the lift!

London Marriott County Hall Hotel The County Hall, Belvedere Rd, SE1; tel: 020 7928 5200; web: www.marriotthotels.com [16 A5]
M̄ *Waterloo;* Ē *Cross York Rd footbridge to Belvedere Rd then right to Westminster Bridge.*

If you thought that the only pool in the former County Hall was filled with sharks, then prepare for a pleasant surprise. True enough, the basement of the splendid council building may now be the London Aquarium, but the main wing is now a fabulous top-of-the-range hotel. The top-floor pool is open to guests, as is a well-equipped gym (with the option of joining the main County Hall health club at an extra charge). If you are more arty than sporty, then loiter in the public areas to savour the permanent exhibition of many of the Arts Council's Hayward Gallery treasures. Sickert and Hockney are among the British works in reception. County Hall was the home of London's government for over 60 years until Margaret Thatcher abolished the Greater London Council in the 1980s, and it is, quite rightly, a listed building. Many original features remain, from the lounge in the 'Nos' lobby of the council chamber to the members' library, with its busts of great writers atop the shelves, where today's guests may enjoy afternoon tea. The **County Hall Restaurant**, open to non-residents, has fabulous Thameside views. Many bedrooms offer the bonus of a permanent time-check facility: just look at the face of Big Ben outside the window, or plug your laptop into the fast-access internet socket (a full day's surfing for £12). My luxuries, after many months' hotel-hopping, are waking up to BBC Radio 4 in the bedroom and Marmite on the breakfast table. Rates begin at around £250.

Mercure London City Bankside 75–79 Southwark St, SE1; tel: 020 7902 0810; web: www.mercure.com [16 E3]
M̲ *Southwark;* E̲ *Jubilee Line to Southwark then walk north on Blackfriars Rd and turn into Southwark St.*
Good mid-range chain hotel with gym, bar and restaurant, close to Vinopolis, Tate Modern and Shakespeare's Globe. Budget around £150.

Holiday Inn Express 103–109 Southwark St, SE1; tel: 020 7401 2525
Around £95 for a double room. [16 D3]
M̲ *Southwark;* E̲ *Jubilee Line to Southwark then walk north on Blackfriars Rd and turn right into Southwark St.*

Uptown Reservations 41 Paradise Walk, SW3 4JL; tel: 020 7351 3445; web: www.uptownres.co.uk; email: inquiries@uptownres.co.uk
The elegant option. B&B with class. Stay in a top-drawer private residence in central London from £65 to £115 per night. Choice addresses include a smart townhouse just across the river from Eurostar. Deposits may be paid to the agency by credit card, but balances should be settled with your host in cash.

WHERE TO GO
Borough Market [16 G3]
M̲ *London Bridge;* E̲ *Jubilee Line to London Bridge, cross Borough High St and take the steps at the side of the cathedral to the market under the railway arches.*
One of London's hidden treats, the market was thrust into the world's consciousness by the film of *Bridget Jones' Diary*. The Globe pub served as Bridget's flat, and the hilarious street fight between Hugh Grant and Colin Firth took place in Bedale Street. Don't go looking for the Greek restaurant as it was mocked up for the movie in an empty archway. Market days are Friday and Saturday. But drink sarsparilla at the pie and mash stall, or blow the budget at Fish! restaurant at any time.

Gabriel's Wharf 56 Upper Ground, SE1; tel: 020 7401 2255; web: www.gabrielswharf.co.uk [16 C2–3]
M̲ *Waterloo or Southwark;* E̲ *From Waterloo Station, cross the York Rd footbridge to Belvedere Rd and walk east along the river.*

Waterside restaurants and craft stalls in this pleasant little artisans' quarter just along the river from the National Theatre and in the shadow of the Oxo Tower. Children love watching silversmiths create jewellery, and other artists at work.

George Inn 27 Borough High St, SE1; tel: 020 7407 2056 [16 G4]
M̲ *London Bridge.* E̲ *Jubilee Line to London Bridge, walk along Borough High St.*
The last of London's 17th-century galleried coaching inns with evocations of Dickens' Southwark is a great place to enjoy steak and kidney pie and fine ales.

Hays Galleria [16 H3] (see *What to buy*, page 329)

London Imax Tel: 020 7902 1234; web: www.bfi.org.uk [16 B3]
£7.
M̲ *Waterloo;* E̲ *Take the main exit from Waterloo Station and follow pedestrian subway signs for safest route under the roundabout to the cinema.*
Gasp with wonder at London's Imax showhouse and the UK's largest cinema screen. If you are lucky you might get a proper movie, such as Disney's *Fantasia*; otherwise expect the standard travelogue and wildlife documentaries. Part of the British Film Institute; check the BFI website for programme details and other nearby attractions.

London Eye Jubilee Gardens, SE1; tel: 0870 5000 600; web: www.british-airways.com/londoneye [16 A4]
Open Oct–Mar 10.00–19.00, Apr–May, Sep 10.00–20.00, Jun–Aug 10.00–22.00. £9.50.
M̲ *Waterloo;* E̲ *From Waterloo Station, cross the York Road footbridge to Belvedere Rd.*
The Millennium attraction that wiped the sky with the ill-fated Dome along the river. Not a ferris wheel but an entirely new concept inspired by the spokes of a bicycle; the pods carry sensation seekers to the best views in the capital. Journey time 30 minutes. Advance reservation recommended.

Old Vic Waterloo Rd, SE1; tel: 0207 928 2651; web: www.oldvictheatre.com [16 C4]
M̲ *Waterloo.* E̲ *Follow signs to Waterloo Rd from the main station concourse.*
Lillian Bayliss' pretty theatre was the first home of Britain's National Theatre. These days it tends to house transfers from the National and Royal Shakespeare companies, as well as visiting productions from respected regional theatres. Expect quality new writing, and reinterpretations of the classics.

Players Theatre The Arches, Villiers St, Strand, WC2; tel: 020 7839 1134; web: www.theplayerstheatre.co.uk
Open Tue–Sun 20.15, Thu 14.00. £15.00 (£7 Thu matinee).
M̲ *Charing Cross.* E̲ *Northern line to Charing Cross then walk down Villiers St to The Arches.*
A wonderfully eccentric British institution across Hungerford Bridge and under the railway arches of Charing Cross Station. In this Victorian music hall it is always 1899, the toast is 'Her Great and Glorious Majesty Queen Victoria', and the audience joins in with the jokes, never mind the choruses. Peter Ustinov and Maggie Smith are among the great talents to tread these boards and each evening's 'Late Joys' programme features a troupe of top-notch professionals spanning the generations who sing the lesser-known songs and ballads of a bygone age. A delightful conspiracy of entertainment that inspired the long-running *Good Old Days* BBC series. Dine at the theatre or enjoy a drink at the bar in the auditorium. At the end of the year, this is the home of Britain's last authentic Victorian pantomime.

Rose Theatre 56 Park St, SE1; tel: 020 7593 0026 [16 F3]
Open 10.00–17.00. £3
M̲ *London Bridge.* E̲ *Jubilee Line to London Bridge, cross Borough High St and take the steps at the side of the cathedral to Borough Market. Cathedral St to Clink St then left and right into Park St. Theatre site is just past Southwark Bridge Rd.*
Shakespeare's Globe may be a reconstruction of the original some yards from its original site, but this is the real McCoy. Here the young William Shakespeare acted in plays by his contemporaries. A high-profile campaign managed to save the archaeological finds, once threatened with destruction, and now an audiovisual show is presented over the remains of The Rose, the last Elizabethan playhouse. Nearby the site of the true Globe Theatre is marked on the housing estate constructed over the theatre's remains.

Royal Festival Hall Belvedere Rd, SE1; tel: 020 7960 4242; web: www.royalfestivalhall.org.uk [16 A3]
M̲ *Waterloo;* E̲ *Follow footpath signposts from station concourse.*
The South Bank Centre concert halls are worth a visit at any time – even if you cannot make the main event. Weekends see free performances in the foyers during the day and early evening. Regular exhibitions, good restaurants and arts shopping make for entertaining diversions. On certain Saturdays Richard Stilgoe hosts his wonderful concerts for children, when members of the orchestra mingle with the crowd and teach children about their instruments in the hour before the morning or afternoon performance. The Hayward Gallery stages world-class art exhibitions, from Hockney to Brassai.

Royal National Theatre South Bank, SE1; tel: 020 7452 3030; web: www.nationaltheatre.org.uk [16 B3]
M̲ *Waterloo;* E̲ *Follow footpath signposts from station concourse.*
Despite the Royal monicker, the institution is still known as 'the National' as in the days of its founder, Laurence Olivier. Three theatres with a repertoire of classic drama and new works. Recent years have also seen the regular revivals of Broadway musicals. Early evening platform performances often include readings by, or interviews with, famous actors or writers. Telephone for details.

Shakespeare's Globe New Globe Walk, SE1; tel: 020 7902 1500; web: www.shakespeares-globe.org [16 F2]
Exhibition May–Sep 09.30–12.30 Oct–Apr 10.00–17.00; closed Dec 24, 25. £7.50 (exhibition).
M̲ *London Bridge;* E̲ *Jubilee Line to London Bridge, cross Borough High St and take the steps at the side of the cathedral to Borough Market. Cathedral St to Clink St, then keep going until you reach the riverfront.*
The muse of fire of American actor Sam Wannamaker, this reconstruction of Shakespeare's 'wooden O' is far more than a museum (although it does offer a traditional visitor attraction tour). See plays by Shakespeare and his less well-known contemporaries in the style for which they were written. An excellent value £5 buys a 'groundling' ticket to stand in the open air in front of the stage of this beautifully recreated Elizabethan playhouse. Seats in the galleries cost much more. My main quibble is with the prices charged in the souvenir shop, where programmes cost half the price of a ticket for the play. The summer season sees two repertory teams (often with very well-known actors such as Vanessa Redgrave) offering a total of four main plays. Additional weekend performances, and out-of-season touring productions, are also worth catching. Every Saturday and Sunday at 10.00, an actor hosts a guided walk through Shakespeare's London.

Southwark Cathedral Montague Close, London SE1; tel: 020 7367 6700; web: www.dswark.org/cathedral [16 G3]

Free.

M̲ *London Bridge;* E̲ *Jubilee Line to London Bridge, cross Borough High St and take the steps to the cathedral.*

Scene of Nelson Mandela's London tribute to former curate Desmond Tutu, the cathedral has witnessed most of London's dramatic moments since Norman times. An early monastery became a Delftware factory, pig farm and bakery during the reign of Henry VIII. Later, local people purchased the church from James I, and it served as the parish church until attaining cathedral status in 1905. Come here to see the wonderful memorials and monuments. The Harvard Chapel remembers the founder of the university. Other greats to be recalled within these walls are John Fletcher and Augustus Pugin, who built the palace of Westminster. Pause by the memorial to the victims of the *Marchioness* pleasure-boat disaster, and give silent thanks at the tribute to Sam Wannamaker, the American actor who spent his life campaigning to rebuild the Globe Theatre (the only memorial to a Jew in a British cathedral). Shakespeare, his playhouses and his plays feature in a frieze and stained-glass window in the south aisle. If you are planning a row with your travelling companion in the cathedral grounds, avoid Nancy's Steps, where Bill Sykes killed the heroine of *Oliver Twist*. A new welcome centre is planned for the cathedral, which has proved a welcome diversion for visitors to the region for years: 'And so over the fields to Southwarke. I spent half an hour in St Mary Overy's church, where are fine monuments of great antiquity,' wrote Samuel Pepys on July 21 1663. If this place could appeal to one of the fussiest Londoners in history, it must be worth a detour.

Winchester Palace Clink St, SE1 [16 G3]

Free.

M̲ *London Bridge;* E̲ *Jubilee Line to London Bridge, cross Borough High St and take the steps at the side of the cathedral to Borough Market. Cathedral St into Clink St towards the junction with Storey St.*

The ruined west gable end, with its unusual round window, of the Great Hall of the 13th-century town house of the Bishops of Winchester, is all that survived the fire of 1814. Sympathetically blended into newer architecture, the site is often illuminated at night.

Young Vic Theatre 66, The Cut, SE1; tel: 020 7928 6363 [16 C4]

M̲ *Waterloo;* E̲ *Take Waterloo Rd exit, turning left at the Old Vic to walk along The Cut.*

Good repertory productions of the classics, from Pinter to Shakespeare.

WHAT TO SEE

Clink Prison Museum 1 Clink St, SE1; tel: 020 7378 1558; web: www.clink.co.uk [16 F3]

Open 10.00–18.00; closed Dec 25, Jan 1. £4.

M̲ *London Bridge;* E̲ *Jubilee Line to London Bridge, cross Borough High St and take the steps at the side of the cathedral to Borough Market. Cathedral St to Clink St.*

Despite the Hammer Horror feel of the dungeon-like entrance, this is quite a modest little museum of torture and retribution. Tableaux of ghastliness offer the kids a thrill on the site of the gaol that gave the dictionary a euphemism for prison. The anecdotal guided tour is worth the extra £1 charged. Otherwise, wander through punishments from Tudor to Victorian times. Clink is not named for the sound of chains, but taken from an old Dutch word for imprisonment.

Dalí Universe The County Hall, SE1; tel: 020 7620 2720; web: www.daliuniverse.com [16 A4]
Open 10.00–17.30; closed Dec 25. £8.50.
M̲ *Waterloo;* E̲ *Take York Rd footbridge from the station and walk towards the London Eye then turn left at the river by Jubilee Gardens towards Westminster Bridge.*
See the famous sofa modelled on Mae West's lips, and the original oil painting created for Hitchcock's 1945 classic *Spellbound*, at London's first permanent exhibition of the works of the surrealist master. A private museum like the Espace Montmartre (see *Paris*, page 159).

Golden Hinde St Mary Ovarie Dock, Cathedral St, SE1; tel: 020 7403 0123 [13 G3]
Open winter 10.00–17.00, summer 10.00–18.00; closed Dec 25. £2.50.
M̲ *London Bridge;* E̲ *Jubilee Line to London Bridge, cross Borough High St and take the steps at the side of the cathedral to Borough Market. Cathedral St to St Mary Ovarie Dock.*
An awfully big adventure on quite a small ship. A full-size replica of Sir Francis Drake's flagship is now a miniature museum devoted to the Elizabethan hero who sailed round the world and was knighted on the very deck. Since it is a copy, rather than an original, children can enjoy a very robust hands-on (and knees-on) experience involving the anchor, cannon and rigging. Lots of energetic school-holiday fun and games. Adults should read the tablet telling the delightfully melodramatic tale of how the dock got its name.

The London Aquarium The County Hall, SE1; tel: 020 7967 8000; web: www.londonaquarium.co.uk [16 A4]
Open 10.00–18.00. £8.
M̲ *Waterloo;* E̲ *Take York Rd footbridge from the station and walk towards the London Eye then turn left at the river by Jubilee Gardens towards Westminster Bridge.*
Piranhas, jellyfish, rays and most famously sharks are the stars of this entertaining glimpse of the undersea food chain, housed in the former home of London local government. Touch-tanks, coral reefs and rainforest zones are amongst the displays.

the.gallery@oxo Oxo Tower Wharf, SE1; tel: 020 7401 2255; web: www.oxotower.co.uk [16 C2]
Open 11.00–18.00.
M̲ *Waterloo or Southwark;* E̲ *From Waterloo Station, cross the York Rd footbridge to Belvedere Rd and walk east along the river.*
An art and design gallery on the ground floor of the tower that is perhaps more famous for its fashionable restaurants. Should the temporary exhibitions inspire you to rethink your domestic lifestyle, then the first and second floors host some excellent design shops. Next door is **The Museum of ...** which reinvents itself every season.

Old Operating Theatre & Herb Garret 9a St Thomas St, SE1; tel: 0207 955 4791 [16 G3]
Open 10.30–17.00; closed mid Dec–2nd week Jan. £3.25.
M̲ *London Bridge;* E̲ *Jubilee Line to London Bridge then follow signposts to St Thomas St.*
Life before laser treatment is revealed in England's last surviving 19th-century operating theatre. Original table, tools and furnishings to help the grisly imagination. A display of medicinal herbal remedies provides even more fascinating insights at this quaint museum that is the last remnant of the original St Thomas' Hospital, where Florence Nightingale once taught nursing.

Tate Modern Bankside, SE1; tel: 020 7887 8000 [16 E3]
Open Sun–Thu 10.00–18.00, Fri–Sat 10.00–22.00; closed Dec 24–26. Free.
M̄ *Southwark;* Ē *Jubilee Line to Southwark then walk along Blackfriars Rd, turning left at Blackfriars Bridge down to Queens Walk.*
The art gallery that awoke the world to London's best-kept secret, when the former Bankside power station was reborn as the city's home of contemporary art. Despite housing such a generous portion of the Emperor's New Wardrobe, that led one wag to comment that when pronouncing the word 'Tate', the E is silent, this is also the London address of Picasso's *Weeping Woman* and an example of Monet's *Waterlilies*. Matisse and Cézanne are also represented alongside Francis Bacon's *Momenta Mori* and Gilbert and George's photography. Work is displayed by theme rather than chronologically or by movement. Quibbles apart, remember that this place is free to enter, unlike many Continental European galleries. The main attraction is Giles Gilbert Scott's stunning building, as much a temple to the power harnessed by man, as the dome of St Paul's across the water is to divinity.

Vinopolis – City of Wine 1 Bank End, Bankside, SE1; tel: 0870 241 40 40; web: www.vinopolis.com [16 F3]
Open Sun, Tue–Fri 11.00–18.00, Sat 11.00–20.00, Mon 11.00–21.00, last admission two hours before closing. £11.50.
M̄ *London Bridge;* Ē *Jubilee Line to London Bridge, cross Borough High St and take the steps at the side of the cathedral to Borough Market. Cathedral St to Clink St to Bank End.*
Filling apparently endless brick-vaulted wine cellars under the railway arches, this is a theme park for adults. Walk through the entire world of wine. Inventive interactive displays teach visitors as much or as little as they wish to know about winemaking around the globe. In Italy we ride Vespa scooters through vineyards, in Australia we travel by plane with the flying doctors who planted the first vines.

At the end of the tour is a huge wine-tasting hall. Tickets allow visitors to sample up to six different wines, and extra tasting vouchers may be purchased. Membership of Vinopolis, at just £30 per year, allows unlimited admission and tastings for a year. Restaurants, wine bar and champagne bar on site should you wish to stay longer.

Winston Churchill's Britain at War Experience 64–66 Tooley St, SE1; tel: 0207 403 3171; web: www.britain-at-war.co.uk [16 H4]
Open Oct–Mar 10.00–16.30, Apr–Sep 10.00–17.30. £6.
M̄ *London Bridge;* Ē *Jubilee Line to London Bridge.*
If the very name Waterloo Bridge conjures images of Robert Taylor and Vivian Leigh in the classic movie, then you will relish the opportunity to experience life in 1940s Britain in the shadow of London Bridge. Not a gung-ho celebration of war, but an evocation of the home front during the war years. Wartime cinema newsreels and domestic ephemera are presented alongside the world of gas masks and air-raid shelters. Worth resisting the whines of children who would prefer you to have opted for the ghoulish horrors of the London Dungeon along the road.

WHERE TO EAT

The Cut and its side streets provide a good choice of international dining, from Turkish to Thai, Indian to Italian. Union Street and Southwark Street have some new cafés worth a visit. The principal museums and galleries boast their own cafés and snack bars, and Borough Market has food stands, restaurants, cafés and traditional market pubs. Here you will find something to eat from the small hours (the Borough Café in Park Street opens at 04.00, and the Market Porter in Stoney Street serves breakfast from 06.00 to 18.30). Belvedere Road has branches of popular cafés, *sushi* bars and mid-range restaurants. Walk past Tower Bridge to Butler's Wharf, home of Terence Conran's excellent flagship eateries: Pont de la Tour for pricey chic; Cantina de Ponte for young trendy Italian food; Blue Print Café for classy *dîner à deux*; and the Chop House for better-value British grub at the bar.

The Bridge 1 Paul's Walk, EC4; tel: 020 7236 0000 [16 E2]
M̄ *Blackfriars (When visiting Tate Modern, cross the Millennium Footbridge to the restaurant on the north bank.)*
The north bank offers the perfect perspective to appreciate the Bankside panorama. As darkness falls, a splendid kaleidoscope of colour dresses Tate Modern like a giant lava lamp. Cheery service, stylish contemporary decor (blue suede chairs at *faux*-butchers-block beech tables), and a world cuisine menu that is so hip it is certifiably pelvic bring a definite buzz to the post-meridian slumberland of the foothills of St Paul's. The food is generally pretty tasty: scrummy goat's cheese and roast tomato tartlets with a well-judged hollandaise, sizzle-cooked Mongolian lamb prepared to a good brasserie standard, or a spicy star anise and plum-packed sea bass on noodles. The best home made ice cream in Britain in fabulous flavours: pistachio hums, passion fruit puts *sorbet* to shame and coffee gives you double-jointed eyelids. But you pay. Brasserie food at £50 a head is not cheap. City traders may well be able to afford these prices; visitors to Tate might not. A terrace bar menu of *dim sum* and fries falls within the more reasonable 'under a tenner' budget.

Café One Seven One Jerwood Space, 171 Union St, SE1; tel: 020 7654 0100 [16 E4]
Open Mon–Sat 10.00–18.00, Sun 12.00–18.00.
M̄ *Southwark or Borough;* Ē *Jubilee Line to Southwark. Walk along Union St.*
An absolute gem, tucked away in a converted Victorian school. The freshest ingredients prepared with skill and imagination in what is, after all, a cafeteria in an art gallery. Succulent and savoury are the ideal adjectives to be applied to the chicken and tuna dishes. Salads to taunt the taste buds, and the lightest most delicious desserts ever. Pay around £9 per head for a meal that elsewhere would cost more than double.

Cantina Vinopolis 1 Bank End, SE1; tel: 020 7940 8333 [16 F3]
Closed Sun evening.
M̄ *London Bridge;* Ē *Jubilee Line to London Bridge, cross Borough High St and take the steps at the side of the cathedral to Borough Market. Cathedral St to Clink St to Bank End.*
Two hundred wines served by the glass. That is the promise that lures most of us into this cavernous restaurant area at the side of Vinopolis (see page 336) The wine bar by the main entrance and the refectory area are best value (pay around £20 a head excluding wine for a good, modernist meal). A brasserie serves more expensive fare to those wishing to impress their dining partners.

Chez Gerard The White House, 9 Belvedere Rd, SE1; tel: 0207 202 8470; web: www.santeonline.co.uk [16 A4]
M̄ *Waterloo;* Ē *Take York Rd footbridge from the station and walk towards the London Eye then turn right into Belvedere Rd.*
If France has a national dish, it is not *confit de canard*, nor *escargots*, nor *foie gras*, nor one of those *mille-feuilles* of something exotic in its *jus*. France's answer to roast beef and Yorkshire pud is the humble steak and chips. Boasting 'the best *steak-*

frites this side of Paris', Gerard is one of the few chain restaurants to live up to such a promise, judging from its popularity with the ex-pat French population in London. Good steak, chicken and fish cooked simply and well. Budget around £20, or go for the early bird £10 menu served until 19.00.

County Hall Restaurant (see page 331)

Fire Station 150 Waterloo Rd, SE1; tel: 020 7620 2226 [16 C4]
M̄ *Waterloo;* Ē *Take Waterloo Rd exit and walk towards the Old Vic.*
Once voted pub of the year, this is a lively, noisy and welcoming refuge a few yards from the station itself. Good value early evening menus; food is fashionable but not snooty. *Ciabatta* and chutney, Caesar and swordfish-style specials. Pay £6 for a bar snack or £18 for a sit down meal.

Fish! Cathedral St, Borough Market, SE1; tel: 020 7234 3333 [16 G3]
Closed Sat lunch, Sun.
M̄ *London Bridge;* Ē *Jubilee Line to London Bridge, cross Borough High St and take the steps at the side of the cathedral to Borough Market.*
Classy, trendy, designer eatery offers a choice of fish, a choice of cooking methods (steamed or grilled) and a choice of sauces. Good food, well prepared in sparkling company. Budget around £20 to dine in this gleaming modern conservatory under a railway bridge. City boys and businesswomen cross the bridge to lunch here and, unless you want to eat very early or very late, you book.

Globe Café Shakespeare's Globe, New Globe Walk, SE1; tel: 020 7902 1576 [16 F2]
Closed evenings.
M̄ *London Bridge;* Ē *Jubilee Line to London Bridge, cross Borough High St and take the steps at the side of the cathedral to Borough Market. Cathedral St to Clink St to the river.*
At once cosy yet bright, this pleasant dining room attached to the theatre offers splendid views across the river and acceptable traditional English fare of pies and crumbles, as well as lighter modern vegetarian dishes. Pay around £16.

Livebait 41–45 The Cut, SE1; tel: 020 7928 7211; web: www.santeonline.co.uk [16 C–D4]
Closed Sun.
M̄ *Waterloo or Southwark;* Ē *Follow Waterloo Rd towards the Old Vic and turn left into The Cut.*
Stylish retro fish-and-chips-tiling décor and delicious seafood and fish menu, this place has a very West End feel. Catch of the day may be chargrilled or pan-roasted and served with tapenade, lemon oil or salsa. Budget around £25 or opt for the lunchtime or early evening set menus from £12.50.

Oxo Tower 8th Floor, Oxo Tower Wharf, SE1; tel: 020 7803 3888 [16 C2]
M̄ *Southwark or Waterloo;* Ē *From Waterloo Station, cross the York Rd footbridge to Belvedere Rd and walk east along the river.*
A more modest restaurant may be found on the lower floors, but take the lift to the eighth floor for the full Oxo Tower experience. Fashionable foodic food with a strong modern Italian influence, stylishly served in the ultimate Thameside room with a view. Play spot the celebrity, as the place is a firm favourite with stars from the London TV studios and actors from the National Theatre. Pay £30 plus.

Porridge Clink St, SE1; tel: 020 7407 3400 [16 G3]
Open 09.30–18.00.
M̄ *London Bridge;* Ē *Jubilee Line to London Bridge, cross Borough High St and take the steps at the side of the cathedral to Borough Market. Follow Cathedral St to Clink St.*

When, as a birthday treat, I did not visit Tate Modern, I discovered this good value lunch café opposite the ruins of Winchester Palace. Generous pasta main courses for around £3 makes this the best bargain in Bankside. Friendly service and hearty portions served in a small bright room within a short stroll of all the attractions.

The Reef Waterloo Station Concourse [16 B4]
M̲ *Waterloo.*
Surprisingly stylish bar above the main concourse of Waterloo Station, with comfortable chairs and sofas, a balcony overlooking the bustle of the station and a menu of trendy snack meals, from Mexican dip-and-nibble side dishes to delicious salads. Snack for under £5; dine for around £9.

WHAT TO BUY

Bookcase 2 158 Waterloo Rd, SE1; tel: 020 7401 8528 [16 C4]
Open Mon–Fri 09.00–19.30, Sat 10.00–19.00.
M̲ *Waterloo;* E̲ *Take Waterloo Rd exit and walk towards the Old Vic.*
If you've the time, step outside the station to buy books for the journey at a fraction of the regular price. Hard-backed classics at around £2.50, paperbacks from £1. Lots of gift and coffee-table editions, and a fair selection of classical and jazz CDs.

Borough Market [16 G3] (see page 331)

Figs 2 Bedale St, SE1 [16 G3]
M̲ *London Bridge;* E̲ *Jubilee Line to London Bridge, cross Borough High St and take the steps at the side of the cathedral to Borough Market.*
Delicious delicatessen, with scrumptious sandwiches, and gift boxes of fine wines and *pâtés*. A great spot to stock up on food for the journey.

Green House 1 Bedale St, SE1; tel: 020 7403 6304 [16 G3]
M̲ *London Bridge;* E̲ *Jubilee Line to London Bridge, cross Borough High St and take the steps at the side of the cathedral to Borough Market.*
Beautiful plants, flowers, pots and arrangements at this most stylish of florists.

Hays Galleria Tooley St, SE1 [16 H3]
M̲ *London Bridge;* E̲ *Jubilee Line to London Bridge and follow the sign posts from Tooley St to Hays Galleria.*
A stunning conversion of an old wharf provides a charming riverside environment for browsing bookshops, art galleries, clothes rails and delis, and plenty of tables under the imposing barrel-vaulted roof for pondering your purchases and reading the paper over a coffee or light lunch.

Lower Marsh Market Lower Marsh, SE1 [16 B5–C4]
Open Mon–Fri 10.30–14.30.
M̲ *Waterloo;* E̲ *Take Waterloo Rd exit walk towards Old Vic and turn right on to Lower Marsh.*
Typical South London street market behind Waterloo Station. Pick up fruit and veg for the journey, plus cheap T-shirts and extra luggage.

Bradt Travel Guides

Bradt guides are available from bookshops or by mail order from:
Bradt Travel Guides, 19 High Street, Chalfont St Peter, Bucks SL9 9QE, England
Tel: 01753 893444   Fax: 01753 892333
Email: info@bradt-travelguides.com   www.bradt-travelguides.com

Appendix 1

DIARY

Check with national and city tourist offices for precise dates. Some events may spill over into the previous or subsequent month.

January
Paris	Postcard and phone-card fair
Lille	Mozart Festival (Nov–Apr)
Brussels	Film Festival
	Motor Show (even numbered years)

February
Paris	Book Fair
Lille	Tourissima holiday exhibition

March
Paris	Film Festival (until early April)
Brussels	Ars Musica (contemporary music festival)
	Book Fair

April
Paris	Marathon
	Foire du Trône in Bois de Vincennes
Lille	Short Film festival
	(4th weekend) 'Fortified Towns' open day at the Citadelle
	Paris-Roubaix cycle race
Brussels	Sablon Baroque Music Festival
	Royal Greenhouse open days (late Apr or early May)

May
Paris	Foire du Trône in Bois de Vincennes
Lille	Montgolfiades, hot-air balloon meeting
Brussels	Jazz Marathon

June
Paris	Jazz at La Villette
	French Tennis Open at Roland Garros stadium (from end May)
	Sorbonne Music Festival
Paris	Chopin Festival (to July)
Paris	Gay Pride
Paris	Paris Air Show at Le Bourget (odd-numbered years only)

Paris & **Lille** (weekend closest to 21st) Fête de la Musique
Lille Fêtes de Lille
Brussels Arts festival

July
Paris Jazz at La Villette
Tuileries Festival (to end Aug)
Tour de France finishes on the Champs Elysées
Paris & Lille (14th) Bastille Day celebrations in Grand' Place (Lille) and fire
stations (Paris) and city wide. Parade down Champs Elysées.
Fireworks.
Brussels Classical concerts in the Bois de la Cambre
Drive-in movies at Cinquantenaire Park
(21st) National day and fireworks

August
Paris Quartiers d'Eté summer music festival (from July 15)
Open-air movies at La Villette
Brussels Summer Concerts in the parks
Drive-in movies at Cinquantenaire Park
Kermesse (Fête around the Gare du Midi)
Grand' Place carpet of flowers (even numbered years)

September
Paris Antiques Fair
Ile de France Music Festival
Paris & Lille (3rd weekend) National Heritage Day. Open doors at historic
monuments and private buildings.
Lille Braderie
Half marathon
Brussels Marathon

October
Paris Contemporary Art Fair
Prix de l'Arc de Triomphe horse racing at Longchamps
Montmartre wine harvest
Lille Circus Festival
Brussels Jazz Festival (from mid-Sep)

November
Paris International Dance Festival (even years only)
Lille (until Apr) Mozart Festival
Jazz at Tourcoing

December
Paris Nativity crib outside Palais Royal, ice rink outside Hotel de Ville.
Special News Year's Eve parties at the Moulin Rouge, Lido,
Opéra Garnier, Château de Versailles and the Seine riverboats.
Lille Christmas Market in Place Rihour, and ferris wheel in Grand'
Place
Brussels Nativity crib, market and Christmas tree at Grand' Place

Appendix 2

FURTHER READING
Black
Paris' black culture took a long time in asserting itself, but is now an essential part of the city's social scene. The website www.cafedelasoul.com offers the best African American perspective on the capital.

Destination guides
www.franceguide.com
www.francetourism.com
www.paris-touristoffice.com
www.paris-ile-de-france.com
www.paris-france.org
www.lilletourism.com
www.brussels.org
www.trabel.com/brussels
www.tib.be
www.belgium-tourism.net
www.visitflanders.com
www.southwark-information.co.uk
www.disneylandparis.com
www.visiteurope.com

Of the major guidebook series, the bible for serious seekers of enlightenment is the Michelin Green Guide. Less flashy than many of its rivals, it is ever reliable. As well as the *Paris* and *Brussels* guides, Michelin also produces an English-language volume on *Northern France and the Paris Region*. If you like to travel to the cutting edge, consider the Time Out guides to both capitals.

Disabled
Disabled travellers will appreciate *Access in Paris*, published by Quiller Press, with its invaluable listings and reviews. The Lille VAL métro is wheelchair friendly, but visitors to Paris and Brussels should do some research on the public transport websites when planning their journeys. Another useful site is www.access-able.com.

Entertainment
In Brussels read *Le Bulletin* in English or *Le Soir* in French. In Lille pick up the free *Sortir* magazine from the tourist office or the local *La Voix du Nord* newspaper from news-stands or at www.lavoixdunord.fr. If you cannot get hold of a copy of the *Ch'ti* guide (see page 196), access the student perspective online at www.lechti.com. In Paris, pick up listings *magazines l'Officiel des Spectacles* or *Pariscope*, with its English supplement provided by *Time Out Magazine*

(www.pariscope.fr), or Wednesday's *Le Figaro* for local information on what's on and where to go. Other regularly updated on-line guides include:

www.whatsonwhen.com
www.timeout.com
www.theeuroguide.com
www.parisvoice.com
www.paris.org
www.brussels18-30.com
www.culture.fr

Gay

Gay travellers should consider the 1999-2000 *Paris Scene* guide, from Prowler Press, for its in-depth features on gay life in Paris, phrasebook and travel tips. Use it alongside updated listings from *Illico* magazine, free in bars or on line at www.e-llico.com . For on-line updated information on Lille, go to www.gaylille.free.fr, while Brussels' scene is listed at http://welcome.to/gaybelgium.

Hero worship

Literary and historical pilgrimages make excellent themed breaks. Besides the trails suggested in this guide, use the great pick-your-own-dead-Parisian search engine on the American site www.francetourism.com to plot your own tribute to a personal hero or heroine. Judi Culbertson and Tom Randall's *Permanent Parisians*, published by Robson Books, provides a superb tour of the great cemeteries.

Transport

www.eurostar.co.uk
www.eurostar.com
www.raileurope.co.uk
www.raileurope.com
www.sncf.com

Public transport maps fares and routefinders

Paris www.ratp.fr
Lille www.transpole.fr
Brussels http://ibelgique.ifrance.com/planitram/

Vegetarian

Vegetarians should arm themselves with a copy of *Vegetarian France* or *Vegetarian Europe* by Alex Bourke, available on line from www.focusguides.com, a fabulous travel website which has an unrivalled page of vegetarian links and resources, and is also one of the very few sources of Andrew Sanger's out-of-print *Vegetarian Traveller*. Travellers booking a Eurostar Paris holiday with Travelscene (see page 5) receive a free guide to meat-free dining in the city.

Cybercafés

Cybercafés open and close at an alarming rate, so check with tourist offices for latest information and addresses. Most four-star hotels, and many cheaper establishments, now offer email and internet facilities to guests. Waterloo station has internet telephones on the main concourse above the Eurostar booking office.

Le Smiley 2 rue Royale, 59000 Lille; tel: 03 20 21 12 19; www.le-smiley.fr
Ē *bus 12 to de Gaulle. Cross Grand' Place to rue Esquermoise to rue Royale.*

Easyeverything 31–37 bd de Sébastopol, 75001; tel: 01 40 41 09 10;
www.easyeverything.com
Open 24 hours
M̄ *Châtelet-Les-Halles;* Ē *RER to Châtelet-Les-Halles.*
New branches planned from 2002 at St Michel and the Champs Elysées.
Place de Brouckère, 1000 Bruxelles
M̄ *De Brouckère;* Ē *Underground tram direct to De Brouckère.*
Open 24 hours
Easy may not have the charm of the small, independent cybercafés around town, but it is
cheap, central and open all hours for swift emailing, thus freeing time to see the real city
instead of cyberspace. Around 350 terminals in the Paris branch and 450 in Brussels.

Index

*Page number in **bold** indicate major entries*

Key to Maps

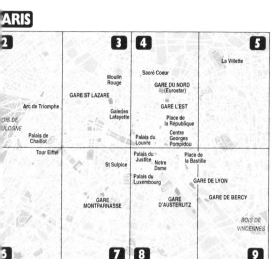

ARIS

2		3	4		5

La Villette

Moulin Rouge

Sacré Coeur

GARE DU NORD (Eurostar)

GARE ST LAZARE

GARE L'EST

Arc de Triomphe

Galeries Lafayette

Place de la République

OIS DE ULOGNE

Palais de Chaillot

Palais du Louvre

Centre Georges Pompidou

Tour Eiffel

Palais du Justice   Notre Dame

Place de la Bastille

St Sulpice

Palais du Luxembourg

GARE DE LYON

GARE MONTPARNASSE

GARE D'AUSTERLITZ

GARE DE BERCY

BOIS DE VINCENNES

6		7	8		9

BRUSSELS

10	11

GARE DU NORD

Bourse

Palais de la Nation

Mannekin Pis   CENTRALE

CHAPELLE

Palais Royal

GARE DU MIDI

12	13

LILLE

Citadelle

GARE LILLE EUROPE

GARE LILLE FLANDRES

Euralille

Hôtel de Ville   Lille Grand Palais

14	GARE MARCHANDISES	15

LONDON

LIVERPOOL ST

British Museum

West End   16   St Paul's   The City

Tower of London

South Bank   Tate Modern

Buckingham Palace

Westminster   WATERLOO

VICTORIA

LEGEND

- Tourist information
- Metro / Underground station
- Church
- Place of interest
- Railway station
- Open space or park
- Water
- Motorway
- Principal route
- Secondary road
- Minor road
- Pedestrian zone
- Rail line

STREET MAPS

The plans in this guide are ideal for orientation, but serious exploration demands a dedicated street map for each destination city. Our favourite maps and gazetteers may be picked up locally or in advance of your trip.

For **Paris**, choose any of the titles issued by Editions Indispensibles, with their clear colour maps of each *arrondissement* and excellent index. The inexpensive, pocket-sized *Paris Pratique* version is best for visitors. Residents or motorists should choose the heftier volumes.

Lille's tourist office produces a first-rate fold-out map with full street index. Collect it free from the tourist office.

The indexes to most free street maps of **Brussels** are incomplete. Our advice is to buy Michelin's *Brussels Plan* (#44). The comprehensive index even tracks down the tiniest alleys ignored by most rivals. Bulkier than most, it is best read at the table, since the map itself is a vast, fold-out affair.

London is most easily conquered with the famous A--Z street finder, available in countless formats and sizes from all news-stands and bookshops.

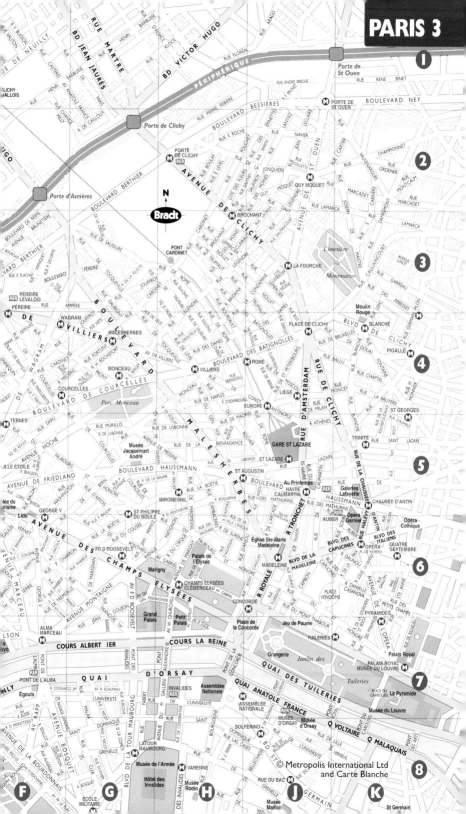

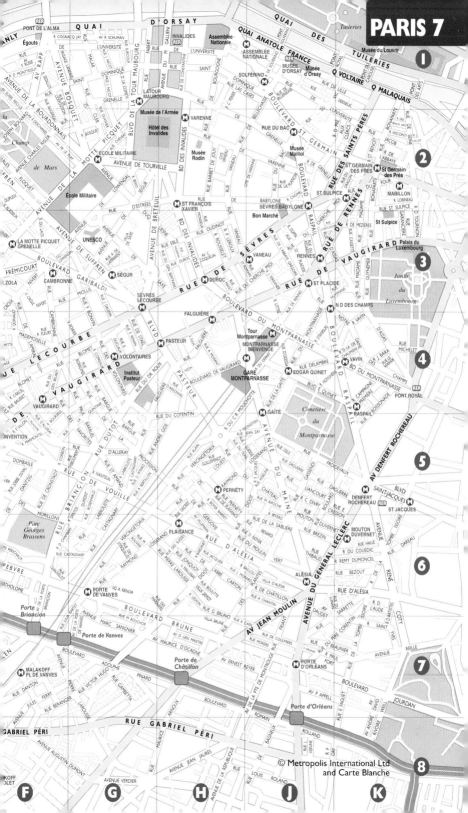

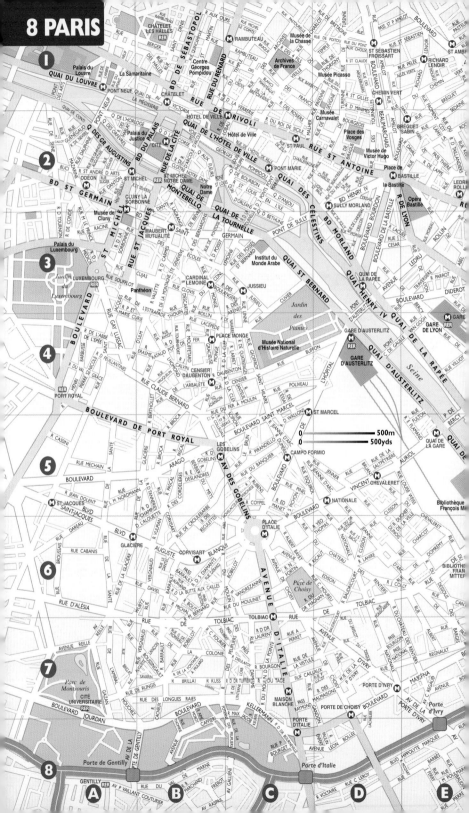

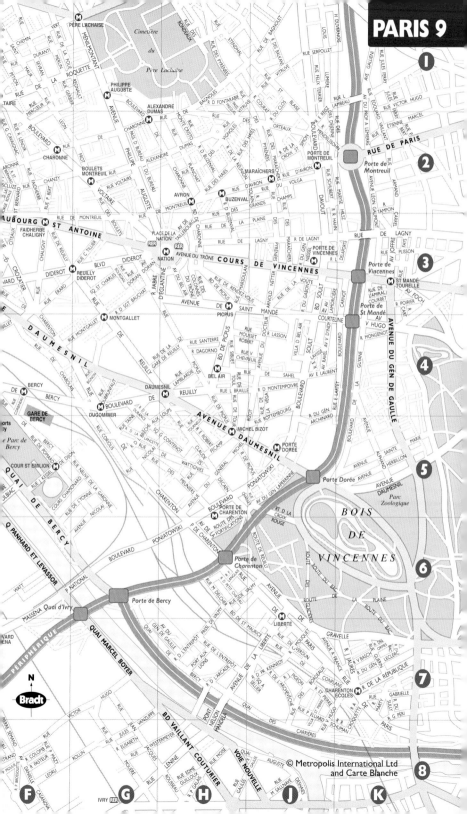

10 BRUSSELS

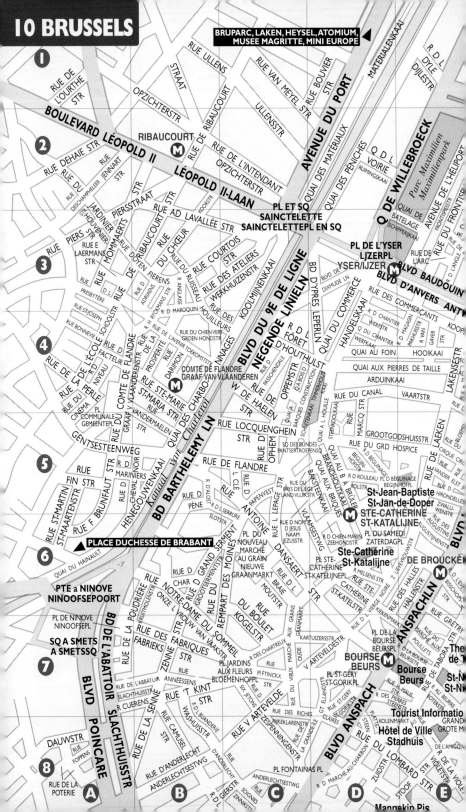

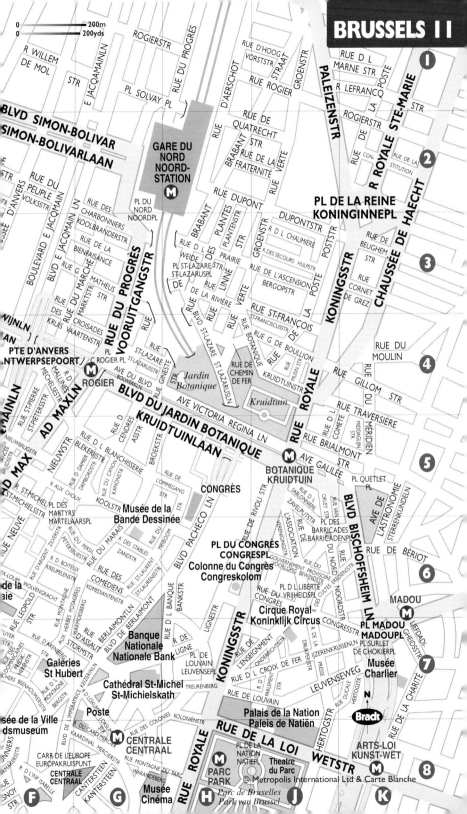

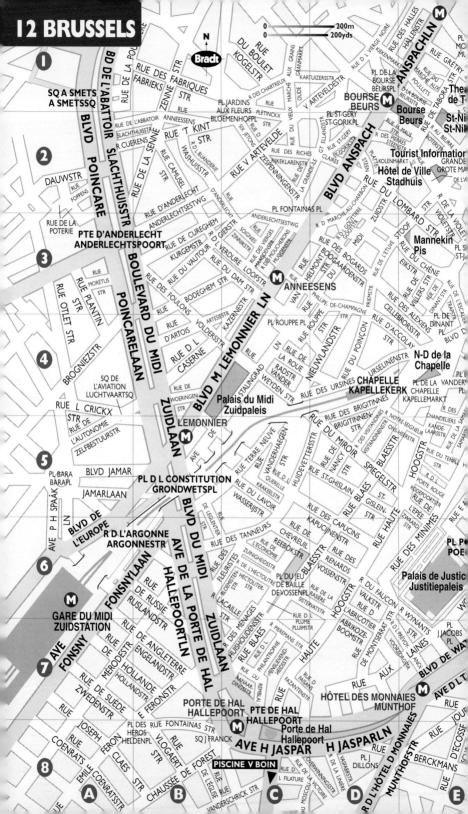

Théâtre de la Monnaie

RUE DU CONGRÈS

Cirque Royal
Koninklijk Circus

PL MADOU
MADOUPL

1

RUE DES HERBES POTAGÈRES
WARMOESBERG

CONGRESSTR

PL SURLET
DE CHOKIERPL

Musée
Charlier

Banque
Nationale
Nationale Bank

RUE DE L BANQUE
BANKSTR

RUE DE
LIGNE

PL DE
LOUVAIN
LEUVENSEPL

RUE DE
L'ENSEIGNEMENT
ONDERRICHTSTR

RUE D L CROIX DE FER

LEUVENSEWEG

RUE DE LA CHARITÉ

Galeries
St Hubert

Cathédral St-Michel
St-Michielskath

TREURENBERG

RUE DE LOUVAIN

2

RUE DUCALE
HERTOGSTR

Poste

RUE DES COLONIES KOLONIENSTR

Palais de la Nation
Paleis de Natiën

ée de la Ville
ismuseum

CENTRALE
CENTRAAL

RUE DE LA LOI

PL DE LA
NATION
NATIEPL

WETSTR

CARR DE L'EUROPE
EUROPAKRUISPUNT

KONINGSSTR

PARC
PARK

Theatre
du Parc

ARTS-LOI
KUNST-WET

3

CENTRALE
CENTRAAL

Musée
Cinéma

Parc de Bruxelles
Park van Brussel
(Warande)

RUE
ZINNER
STR

KUNSTLAAN

RUE STR
GUIMARD
STR

PL DE
L'ALBERTINE
ALBERTINAPL

RUE ROYALE

Palais des Beaux-Arts
Paleis voor Schone Kunsten

REGENTSLAAN

HANDELS

NIJVERHEIDSTR

Biblio Albert I
Albertina

Palais de Charles de Lorraine

RUE
LAMBERMONT
STR

RUE BELLIARD

4

Musée d'Art
Moderne

Musée de
la Dynestie

PL DES PALAIS
PALEIZENPL

CINQUANTENAIRE MUSEUMS ▶

RUE MONTOYER

RUE DE SCIENCE

Musée d'Art
Ancien

PL ROYALE
KONINGSPL

Palais Royal
Koninklijk
Paleis

RUE DE
COMMERCE

RUE DE
L'INDUSTRIE

SQ
DE MEEUS
SQ

RÉGENCESTR

St-Jacques
St-Jacob

PL DU TRÔNE
TROONPL

LUXEMBOURG

RUE DU LUXEMBOURG

5

du Sablon
avelkerk

RUE BRÉDERODE STR

REGENTSCHAPSSTR

RUE DES PETITS-CARMES

BLVD DU RÉGENT

AVE MARNIX LN

RUE DE PARIS

PL DU PETIT
SABLON
KLEINE ZAVEL

KERNSTR

RUE DE CHP DE MARS
MARSVELDSTR

RUE DU TRÔNE

6

Palais d'Egmont
Egmontpaleis

PORTE DE
NAMUR
NAAMESPOORT

RUE D'EDIMBOURG

RUE DE NAPLES
NAPELSSTR

RUE DU LONDRES

PL DE
LONDRES
LONDENPL

Jardin d'Egmont
Egmonttuin

PTE DE NAMUR
NAAMESPOORT

CHAUSSÉE DE WAVRE

WATERLOOLAAN

GULDEN VLEISLAAN

CHAUSSÉE D'IXELLES

WAVERSESTEENWEG

7

PL LOUISE
LOUIZAPL

RUE DES CHEVALIERS
RIDDERSTR

RUE STASSART

RUE DU BERGER
HERDERSTR

KONINKLIJKE
PRINSSTR

RUE DE LA PAIX
VREDESTR

RUE DE
L'ATHÉNÉE

RUE DU CONSEIL STR

SANS-SOUCI

AVENUE LOUISE

RUE DE WEVERSTR

PL
STÉPHANIE
STEPHANIEPL

RUE DE LA CONCORDE

ELSENESTEENWEG

PL
F COCQ

RUE DE COLLÈGE STR

8

CH DE CHARLEROI
CHARLEROISESTWEG

LOUIZA
LAAN

HORTA MUSEUM ▶

RUE MERCELIS STR

CH D'IXELLES

© Metropolis International Ltd
and Carte Blanche

F   **G**   **H**   **J**   **K**

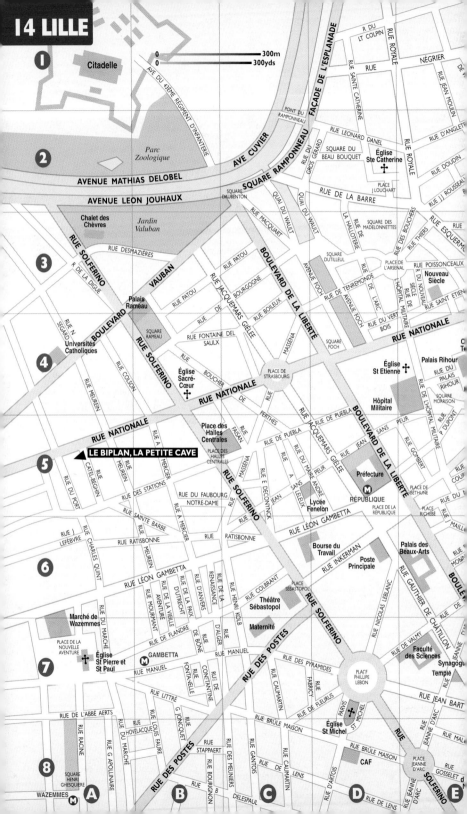

14 LILLE

Citadelle

Parc Zoologique

AVE CUVIER

SQUARE RAMPONNEAU

PONT DU RAMPONNEAU

FAÇADE DE L'ESPLANADE

R DU LT COLPIN

RUE ROYALE

RUE NÉGRIER

RUE JEAN MOULIN

RUE SAINTE CATHERINE

RUE LEONARD DANEL

Église Ste Catherine

SQUARE DU BEAU BOUQUET

RUE D'ANGLET

RUE ROYALE

RUE DOUDIN

PLACE J LOUCHART

RUE GROS GERARD

AVENUE MATHIAS DELOBEL

AVENUE LEON JOUHAUX

SQUARE D'AUBENTON

RUE DE LA BARRE

JJ ROUSSEAU

Chalet des Chèvres

Jardin Valuban

RUE DESMAZIÈRES

RUE MACQUART

QUAI DU WAULT

QUAI DU WAULT

RUE DE LA HALLOTERIE

SQUARE DES MADELONNETTES

RUE DES BOUCHERS

RUE THIERS

RUE ESQUERM

RUE SOLFERINO

R DE LA DIGUE

VAUBAN

Palais Rameau

RUE PATOU

RUE PATOU

RUE JACQUEMARS GIÉLÉE

RUE BOURGOGNE

RUE BOILEUX

BOULEVARD DE LA LIBERTÉ

AVENUE FOCH

SQUARE DUTILLEUL

RUE DE TENREMONDE

RUE DE L'ARC

AVENUE FOCH

RUE DU VERT BOIS

PLACE DE L'ARSENAL

PLACE DE L'HÔPITAL MILITAIRE

RUE DE SIÈCLE

RUE SAINT ETIEN

Nouveau Siècle

RUE POISSONCEAUX

R DU NOUVEAU

BOULEVARD

RUE N SEGARD

Universités Catholiques

SQUARE RAMEAU

RUE FONTAINE DEL SAULX

RUE COLSON

RUE SOLFERINO

RUE MEUREIN

RUE BOUCHER

RUE NATIONALE

Église Sacré-Cœur

RUE NATIONALE

DE

PLACE DE STRASBOURG

MASSÉNA

SQUARE FOCH

RUE NATIONALE

Église St Etienne

Palais Rihour

RUE DU PALAIS RIHOUR

SQUARE MORRISON

Hôpital Militaire

RUE DE L'HÔPITAL MILITAIRE

RUE DUPONT

RUE NATIONALE

RUE A

RUE MEUREIN

RUE MERCIER

Place des Halles Centrales

Place des Halles Centrales

RUE FAISAN

PERTHES

RUE DE PUEBLA

RUE DE PUEBLA

RUE JACQUEMARS GIÉLÉE

SANS PEUR

Préfecture

RÉPUBLIQUE

BOULEVARD DE LA LIBERTÉ

PLACE DE BÉTHUNE

RUE COURT

RUE DU

RUE MAILL

◄ **LE BIPLAN, LA PETITE CAVE**

RUE CATEL-BEGHIN

RUE DU PORT

RUE MEUREIN

RUE DES STATIONS

RUE A MERCIER

RUE DU FAUBOURG NOTRE-DAME

RUE E DECONYNCK

RUE SOLFERINO

MASSÉNA

RUE LELEUX

SANS PEUR

Lycée Fenelon

RUE JEAN

RUE A

RUE MARE PEUR

ANDRÉ

PLACE DE LA RÉPUBLIQUE

RUE GORBERT

RUE SAINTE BARBE

RUE RATISBONNE

RATISBONNE

RATISBONNE

RUE A MERCIER

RUE LÉON GAMBETTA

Bourse du Travail

RUE INKERMAN

Poste Principale

Palais des Beaux-Arts

RUE MONN

BOULE

RUE J LEFEBVRE

RUE CHARLES QUINT

RUE MEUREIN

RUE LÉON GAMBETTA

RUE DE LA RENAISSANCE

RUE HENRI KOLB

RUE COLBRANT

PLACE SÉBASTOPOL

RUE SOLFERINO

RUE NICOLAS LEBLANC

RUE GAUTHIER DE CHATILLON

Marché de Wazemmes

RUE DU MARCHE

RUE DE LA PAIX

RUE DE LA VIEILLE AVENTURE

RUE DUTRECHT

RUE D'ANVERS

Théâtre Sébastopol

RUE DE VALMY

Faculté des Sciences

PLACE DE LA NOUVELLE AVENTURE

Église St Pierre et St Paul

GAMBETTA

RUE MOURMANT

RUE DE BONE

RUE D'ALGER

Maternité

RUE DES POSTES

Synagogue Temple

RUE MANUEL

RUE DE FLANDRE

RUE MANUEL

RUE FONTA-NELLE

RUE CONSTANTINE

RUE MANUEL

RUE DES PYRAMIDES

RUE CAUMARTIN

PLACE PHILLIPE LEBON

RUE JEAN BART

RUE DE L'ABBÉ AERTS

RUE RACINE

RUE G MARCHE

RUE DU MARCHE

RUE HOVELACQUE

RUE LOUIS FAURE

RUE LITTRÉ

G JONCQUET

RUE STAPPAERT

RUE DES MEUNIERS

RUE GANTOIS

RUE CAUMARTIN

RUE FABRICY

RUE DE FLEURUS

PARVIS

ST MICHEL

Église St Michel

RUE BRÛLE MAISON

RUE JEANNE D'ARC

RUE MAL

SQUARE HENRI GHESQUIERE

WAZEMMES

RUE G APOLLINAIRE

RUE BOURIGNON

RUE DES POSTES

DELESPAUL

RUE DE LENS

RUE D'ARTOIS

RUE BRÛLE MAISON

CAF

RUE DE LENS

PLACE JEANNE D'ARC

RUE JEANNE D'ARC

SOLFERINO

GOSSELET

A **B** **C** **D** **E**

1 **2** **3** **4** **5** **6** **7** **8**

0 300m
0 300yds

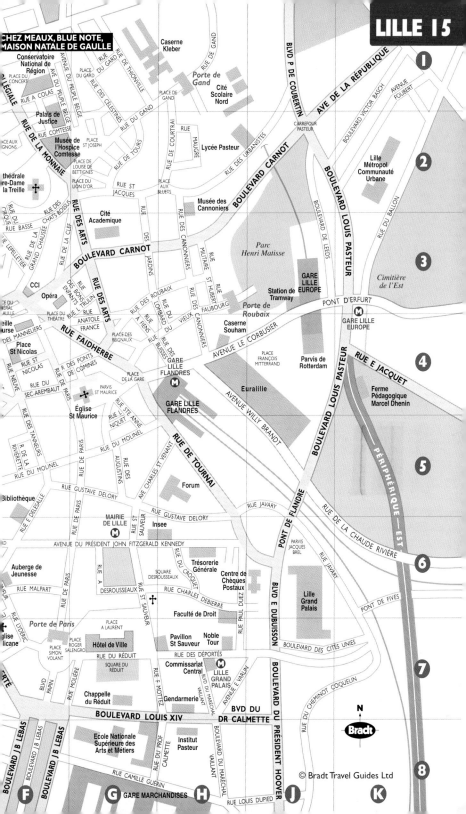

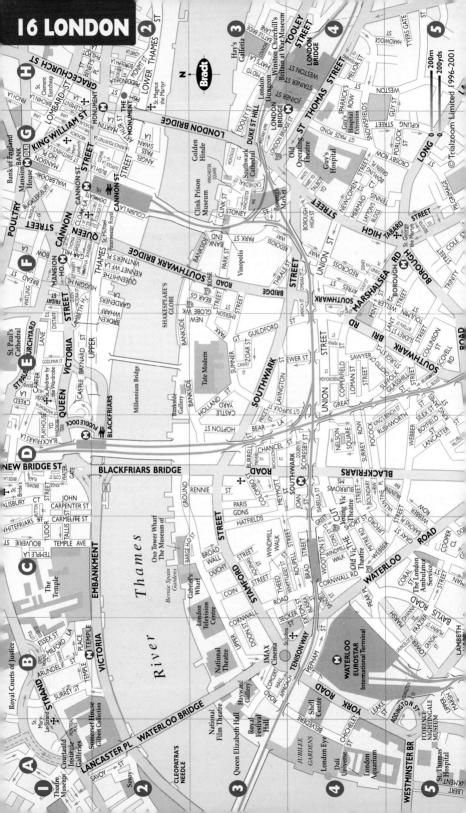